THE OFFICIAL® PR... W9-BPK-752

ANTIQUE AND MODERN
FIREARMS

Robert H. Balderson

EIGHTH EDITION

House of Collectibles • New York

Important Notice. All of the information, including valuations, in this book has been compiled from the most reliable sources, and every effort has been made to eliminate errors and questionable data. Nevertheless, the possibility of error, in a work of such immense scope, always exists. The publisher will not be held responsible for losses that may occur in the purchase, sale, or other transaction of items because of information contained herein. Readers who feel they have discovered errors are invited to *write* and inform us, so they may be corrected in subsequent editions. Those seeking further information on collectibles not covered in this book are advised to refer to the complete line of *Official Price Guides* published by the House of Collectibles.

 This is a registered trademark of Random House, Inc.

Published by: House of Collectibles
201 East 50th Street
New York, NY 10022

Distributed by Ballantine Books, a division of Random House, Inc., New York, and simultaneously in Canada by Random House of Canada Limited, Toronto.

http://www.randomhouse.com

Manufactured in the United States of America

ISSN: 0743-9776

ISBN: 0-876-37907-2

Text design by Holly Johnson
Cover design by Kristine V. Mills-Noble
Cover photo by George Kerrigan

Eighth Edition: September 1996
10 9 8 7 6 5 4 3 2 1

THE OFFICIAL® PRICE GUIDE TO

ANTIQUE AND MODERN
FIREARMS

CONTENTS

ACKNOWLEDGMENTS

The author expresses his profound appreciation to the associates and friends who so graciously gave their time and valued assistance. Without them this work would have been difficult; with them, it was a pleasure. Deep felt gratitude goes out to the following:

Kevin Cherry
Eric M. Larson
R. E. Magruder
Michael Krause
Mitchell Luksich
Victor Juskauskus
Peter Hischier
Bob Burton
Dave Soracco

Del Denny
Nick Todd
Stan Lukowicz
Curt Jones
Michael Grassia
Michael McHugh
Orvel L. Reichert
Frank Just
Ginny Simone

House of Collectibles would like to extend sincere gratitude to the following:

Iver Johnson
Raven Arms
R. G. Industries
Guy Lepeintre
Peter Potter
Col. Mel Pfankuche
Bill Drollinger
Ilan Shalev of I.M.I.
Marc Bauer of Action Arms Ltd.
Ira Trast of Auto Ordnance
George Numrich of Numrich Arms
Sig Himmelmann of United
  Sporting Arms

Bob Magee of Interarms
Ron Vogel of F.I.E.
Allen Fire Arms Co.
Boyd Davis of E.M.F.
V. Fresi and A. Seidel of
  Mauser-Werke
C. Ledoux of ManuFrance
Jennings Firearms
Beeman, Inc.
Rick Kenny of Stoeger Industries
J. P. Sauer and Sohn GmbH
John Hanson of Magnum
  Research, Inc.

Dynamit Nobel of America
Bill Clede and June Sears of
   Smith & Wesson
Sherry Rich of Browning
Bill Mrock and Chuck Lanham of
   the B.A.T.F.
Tim Pancurak of Thompson-Center
Nadine Ljutic of Ljutic Industries
Jim Casillo and Fred Paddock of
   Navy Arms
Vicky Barton of Universal
Fred Karp of Sears, Roebuck & Co.
Brian Herrick of Hi Standard
Charley Gara of Charter Arms
Nolen Jackson of Wichita Engineering
   & Supply
Sharon Cunningham of Dixie
   Gun Works
Pat Bogush of Colt
Judy Graziano of Ruger
Judy Schroepfer of Kreighoff
Jinny Sundius of Marlin
Bob Greenleaf of Savage
Fred Hill of Dan Wesson

Peter Hoffman of Carl Walther GmbH
Bob Saunders of American
   Derringer Corp.
Astra-Unceta y Cia.
Vincenzo Bernardelli
Dan Coonan of Coonan Arms, Inc.
Charles Meyers and Gary Rathman of
   the Florida Regional Crime Lab
Linda Lassotta of Heckler & Koch
Dot Ferreira of Remington
Jan Herriott of Detonics
Tol Cherry of Cherry's
Nancy Damone of Mossberg
Deanna McDermott of U.S.
   Repeating Arms
Frederich Hege of Hege Waffen
Bruce Hacker of Ventura Imports
Debbie Dean of Weatherby's
I. W. Walentiny of Tradewinds
Marian Partridge of Ithaca
Sy Wiley of Randall Firearms
John Hill of Webley & Scott
Tom Barness of Manurhin
John Leek of Sterling Arms Corp.

NOTE TO THE READER

The Official Price Guide to Antique and Modern Firearms is continually updated and revised with new factual material. Readers' comments and suggestions are respectfully solicited. The author is interested in previously unpublished information, articles, and photographs for future editions. Any individual or institution interested in having their collection or institution featured in a subsequent edition is also encouraged to contact the author.

Robert H. Balderson
P.O. Box 254886
Sacramento, CA 95865

MARKET REVIEW

The major developments on the demand side of the firearm market since the publication of our last edition are the changing demographics of the "collector," the level of consumer confidence, and the decline in buying power of the middle class. The prices in this edition, based on sales and input from collectors and dealers, reflect these changes.

The market for collector firearms is driven by collectors with a theme, passion and an ability to buy. In 1996 the largest group of potential collectors, the "baby boomers," began turning fifty years old, at a rate of 10,000 a day, entering the stage of life when their predecessors were financially free to spend on leisure activities and hobbies. For this group financial freedom may come much later, if at all. The massive change in the country's demographics, and economic realities, will affect every market in our economy, including alternative investments, such as collectibles.

No one needs collectibles—they are an optional item; their overall value is based on how many discretionary dollars are bid on them. The collectibles market has segmented into demand layers that mirror our economy's distribution of income and wealth. The top of the market, which includes firearms of grace, embellishment, and beauty on par with works of fine art and historically important pieces, is bringing astronomical prices, and seemingly with no end of the increase in sight. The bottom of the market, with items affordable to all, enjoys a constant demand. The vast middle of the market, which includes "representative samples," is lost in consternation and uncertainty; the buyers in this segment are saddled with a mortgage, children's college expenses, car payments, and health care costs, exhausting all of their income.

As to supply, collectors sell for four reasons (the four "Ds"); death, divorce, debt, and discretion. The most significant factor in our current economy and times is discretion. Discretion is the power of decision or choice; the substitution of one form of asset to another. An aging, uncertain population begins to look for more liquid and secure investments. If the supply of collector items increases because owners choose to sell, and demand decreases because buyers do not buy, prices will decline. In previous times a new generation came along, developed an interest in collectibles,

1

began purchasing, bolstered demand, and the market continued on—at this juncture, that may not be the case.

A few specific items are worthy of comment. First, "condition" is the most important factor in collecting today. The final few increments of condition, between excellent and perfect, are precious. The dollars chase the "best." Currently, it would only be a guess to estimate what premium a gun of rarity and demand in "new-in-the-box" condition would bring in an auction, but ten times the recent selling price of the same make and model in *only* excellent condition would not surprise me. Second, the bottom has dropped out of the price of the "high-capacity" semi-automatic handguns that many people ran out and purchased at inflated prices just prior to the federal ban. Those types of utility guns are not covered in this book because they do not possess the intrinsic value of a modern or antique "collector" firearm. Hoarding these shooters, as is demonstrated with the high-capacity pistols, is only speculation—not collecting or investing. Last, never forget there is power in knowledge; gun books are one of the few "tools" you can use to formulate better decisions that increase in value over time.

The market for collectibles, as with our national economy, is undergoing a period of adjustment. No one can predict, when or at what point, supply and demand will equalize, how consumers will spend, and whether market prices will establish a positive or negative trend. We may be moving toward (or back to) a period when a person buys a house for shelter, security, and pride of ownership; and collectors acquire items to fill their theme and satisfy their passion; with little thought toward short-term profit. That may be good!

FACTORS THAT DETERMINE VALUE

CONDITION

With the passage of time everything deteriorates and guns are no exception. Use, abuse, wear, and aging all adversely affect the price of guns to a varying degree, and in the case of collectible guns the difference in price can be quite significant. Because of the importance of describing the condition of a gun, the National Rifle Association (N.R.A.) devised a set of guidelines to standardize firearms grading. The prices listed in this guide are for guns in N.R.A. "very good" and N.R.A. "excellent" condition, and you can easily adjust those prices to determine the value of your gun if it does not fall into either of those categories. But strict grading of condition following N.R.A. guidelines is essential.

Antique firearms: In excellent to new condition add 50% to 200% to the "excellent" price depending on scarcity and demand. For antiques in good condition, deduct 30% to 35% from "very good."

Modern firearms: In good condition deduct 20% to 25% from "very good"; fair condition, deduct 45% to 55%. Arms in "perfect" to "new" add 30% to 75% depending on collectibility.

Any collectible firearm, no matter how poor the condition (so long as it hasn't been crushed or melted), should be worth 20% to 30% of the "very good" price.

N.R.A. CONDITION GUIDELINES

All of the N.R.A. Grading Standards in this section are reprinted with permission of the N.R.A.

New: Not previously sold at retail; the same as current factory production.
New-Discontinued: Same as new, but discontinued from factory production.

The following definitions will apply to all secondhand articles:

Perfect: In new condition in every respect.
Excellent: New condition, used but little, no noticeable marring of wood or metal, bluing perfect (except at muzzle or sharp edges).
Very Good: In perfect working condition, no appreciable wear on working surfaces, no corrosion or pitting, only minor surface dents or scratches.
Good: In safe working condition, minor wear on working surfaces, no broken parts, no corrosion or pitting that will interfere with proper functioning.
Fair: In safe working condition, but well worn, perhaps requiring replacement of minor parts or adjustments, which should be indicated in advertisement, no rust, but may have corrosion pits which do not render article unsafe or inoperable.

Another set of standards applies to "antique" arms as follows:

Factory New: 100% original finish and parts, everything perfect.
Excellent: All original parts and 80% to 100% finish original; all letters, numerals, designs sharp; unmarred wood, fine bore.
Fine: All original parts and over 30% finish original; all letters, numerals, designs sharp; only minor wood marks, good bore.
Very Good: Up to 30% original finish, all original parts; metal surfaces smooth, with all edges sharp; clear letters, numerals, designs, wood slightly scratched or bruised; bore on collector items disregarded.
Good: Only minor replacement parts; metal smoothly rusted or lightly pitted in places; cleaned or reblued; principal letters, numerals, designs legible; wood refinished, scratched, bruised, or with minor cracks repaired; mechanism in good working order.
Fair: Some major parts replaced; minor replacements; metal may be lightly pitted all over, vigorously cleaned or reblued, edges partly rounded; wood scratched, bruised, cracked or repaired; mechanism in working order.

To abbreviate the condition of a firearm to only the condition of its finish is an affront to the "gunsmith" and causes misunderstandings that can lead to costly litigation.

ORNAMENTATION

Engraving

It's hard to generalize about art, and that is what engraving is. You must examine a number of examples to learn to judge the quality of the work.

Crude engraving: Sparse, add about 25%; medium coverage, add 50% to 75%; full coverage, add 100% to 125%.

High quality engraving: Sparse, add 50% to 100%; medium coverage, add 150% to 200%; full coverage, add 300% up.

Ornate, high quality work with gold inlays, etc.: Add 400% and up.

Wood carving and marquetry (stock inlays)

This is also in the realm of art, and you should try to look at as many specimens as possible to compare craftsmanship.

Carvings: Simple, add $10 to $40 each depending on the quality of execution; complex, add $60 to $150. Full coverage, good quality, add $125 and up. Remember that a poor carving (such as crude initials) will detract from the value.

Inlays: Simple, add $10 to $25 each; ornate, add $50 and up. Exotic materials, such as ivory or mother-of-pearl, can double the value of the inlay. The value of wire inlays depends as much on the coverage as the execution. Simple wire inlays using brass or German silver should start at $40 each, tripling if silver is used, and multiplying by 10 if gold is used. Initial shields that are unmarked and not standard equipment on the gun add $15; $25 for sterling silver; $100 for 14k gold.

Heat carving, stampings, and woodburnings are becoming increasingly common and should not be confused with real carving. These should add about $25 if done well.

Custom checkering

As with carving, craftsmanship is paramount. A poorly done checkering job will lower the value of a gun. Nicely executed patterns on a long gun, add $35 to $50. Fine, complex patterns with wide coverage, add $60 and up.

Gold damascening

This is the art of applying gold leaf or gold plate in a fancy pattern, usually in conjunction with engraving, and should not be confused with gold inlay. Simple patterns, add $60 to $85; fancy patterns, add $265 to $395.

LOCATION OF SALE

As this guide lists average national prices, several regional factors must be considered.

Antiques: If a particular arm was made in your area, or saw wide service there, there should be more interest in it. This increased market demand will run prices 10% to 100% higher than listed.

Modern: Much depends on the type of area you live in. In wide-open places where long-range shooting is possible, high-powered rifles may bring 10% over value listed, whereas shotguns will be 15% less. In wooded areas the reverse will occur. In high crime areas, handguns for home protection will bring premiums. Trap and skeet generally stay constant. Wherever you are, judge the type of hobby shooting most prevalent, and the types of guns used for it will follow the above pattern.

SPECIAL MARKINGS

Standard firearms of most all companies have at some time been ordered or issued with special markings, special features, or as commemoratives. The important consideration in this section is that all deviations from the norm be factory original.

Governments, law enforcement agencies, and stores have ordered the factory to put special marks on guns, and the main requirement in adding value to a gun with these marks is that the gun itself be collectible. The percentage additions shown reflect "common" variations. Rare marks on already very scarce guns may run five to ten times that percentage; however, caution is advisable since this particular market is limited and highly specialized, and, as always with rare items, when you get out of your field it's best to consult an expert.

Special markings: Police or agency markings in lieu of regular marks (not over-stamps or extra stamps), add 25% to 50%; trademarks of stores in exotic locales (Nairobi, etc.), add 50% to 75%; foreign military marks, add 50% to 75%.

Mismarked guns: No stamps, upside-down stamps, wrong markings, etc., add 100% and up depending on the collectibility of the gun itself.

Special features: This section applies to custom modifications done by the factory and not listed under a particular manufacturer elsewhere in this guide. Special sights, add 10% to 15%; special metal finish (nickel, etc.), add 10% to 15%; extra-fancy wood on long guns, add 15% to 25%; special barrel lengths, add 20% to 30%.

HISTORIC RELICS

Provenance or documentation is the key concept in connecting an old gun with a historic event or famous person. Saying "it used to belong to grandpa and he was so and so" just isn't enough. To be absolutely certain of a weapon's ownership or use, records contemporary with its use must be available. They can be factory records showing the gun's disposition, wills, diaries, etc. Lacking that, if there is strong evidence of ownership such as a name engraved and some documentation showing that the person could have owned it, then it should be labeled "probably." "Grandpa" testimony without supporting evidence can be labeled "possibly." The value of a historic relic transcends the worth of the gun, and depends on the fame (or infamy) of the owner, the artistic value, the location of the sale, and the intangible "mood" of the public as to what period of history is in vogue at the time. An association with a person is often referred to as "autograph value."

LEGAL CLASSIFICATIONS OF FIREARMS

There are four classifications of firearms used by the Bureau of Alcohol, Tobacco, and Firearms (B.A.T.F.) of the Treasury Department:

Antique: Any firearm manufactured in or before 1898, and replicas that do not fire rim-fire or center-fire cartridges readily available in commercial trade. Antiques are exempt from federal regulation.
Modern: Firearms manufactured after 1898, excluding Replica Antiques, and with special regulations for Class III arms.
Curios and Relics: Certain modern firearms that can be sent interstate to licensed collectors.
Class III Arms: This includes machine guns, silencers, short (under 18″) shotguns, short (under 16″) rifles, modern smoothbore handguns, and modern arms with a rifled bore diameter greater than .50″.
Antiques: Many arms listed in this guide were produced between dates overlapping

the "antique" determination date. In cases where experts have given a recognized serial number cutoff for "antiques" I have tried to include it. In other instances where arms have no numbers, or where no number is generally recognized as the magic one, I have classified them as modern, or curio and relic, and leave it to a specialist to make an individual determination.

All of the above may be legally owned, notwithstanding federal regulations and local restrictions in a few areas. For further information, contact your local office of the Bureau of Alcohol, Tobacco, and Firearms.

Curios and relics

The Federal firearms classification of "curio and relic" is a very broad category. Under federal regulations, any gun that is at least fifty years old will automatically qualify as a curio and relic. Also, there are a number of guns that are specifically mentioned in the curio and relic list but are not fifty years old.

The B.A.T.F. looks at any prospective curio and relic on an individual basis. In regard to bonafide commemoratives, they look to see the production quality, whether it has a special and unique serial number, and the quality and pricing of the item, the latter to ascertain whether this gun will be purchased by a collector due to its unique features or will more likely be used by a shooter. A $50,000 highly engraved modern firearm would be a prime candidate for curio and relic status simply because of what it represents.

In order for a firearm manufactured less than fifty years ago to receive curio and relic status, it must be submitted to B.A.T.F. for review and approval. The process is not automatic.

Most commemorative firearms are submitted to B.A.T.F. requesting classification as curio and relic, approved, and released for original sale as such. According to Kevin Cherry of Cherry's Fine Guns, B.A.T.F. has been very willing and understanding when reviewing requests for curio and relic status. They have not turned down any of his proposals in the last six years.

The curio and relic license has become increasingly popular to the collector, who can bypass the normal 4473 form and, in most cases, not be burdened by the extra requirements many states impose on the purchase of modern firearms, since the B.A.T.F. does checks on applicants.

Collectors wishing to obtain a curio or relic determination from the B.A.T.F. on a specific firearm or round of ammunition should submit a letter to the Chief of the Firearms Technology Branch, Bureau of Alcohol, Tobacco, and Firearms, Washington, D.C. 20226. The letter should include a complete physical description of the firearm or ammunition, stating the reasons that the collector believes that the firearm or ammunition in question merits such classification, and supporting data concerning the history of the firearm or ammunition, including production figures, if available, and market value.

HOW TO BUY AND SELL FIREARMS

BUYING COLLECTOR GUNS

Where to buy

Reliable estimates place the number of guns in private hands in the U.S. at over 100 million! Quite a lot, but if you've picked out the special items you wish to collect and started looking you've probably noticed that you can generally find everything but what you want. So where do you go to find them? There are several sources.

MAIL ORDER

Even though the Gun Control Act of 1968 prohibited the mailing of firearms to individuals, the mail order gun business is alive and well. However, the method is a little different because of the laws and the nature of the business. According to U.S. law only federally licensed gun dealers may ship and receive modern firearms, but many dealers for a small fee will be happy to receive the gun you've ordered and transfer it to you. Another alternative for the collector is to apply for a collector's license from the Bureau of Alcohol, Tobacco, and Firearms. This license allows the collector to receive and send interstate shipments of modern firearms that are classified as curios to another licensee. For more information about licenses contact your local office of the B.A.T.F.

Mail order done properly is legal and fairly simple and, most importantly, an excellent way to build your collection and to take advantage of prices that may be more competitive than in your local area. Most specialist mail-order dealers are very reputable, and many offer an inspection period so that you may return the gun in the same condition as it arrived if you're not satisfied. Almost all of the dealers of collectible guns advertise, and many have regular lists of guns offered for sale that you can subscribe to for a nominal rate. Many gun magazines and collector newsletters have classified sections that provide good leads.

GUN SHOWS

There are a great many gun shows held in all parts of the United States with good frequency. They provide an opportunity to examine a large number of collectible guns at one place and a chance to bargain with the owners for a better price. Gun show listings can be found in many magazines.

GUN SHOPS

Gun stores and pawn shops offer an exciting chance to find a collector's item at a good price because they may not have a market to sell some of the more interesting items. As a result they sometimes buy low and sell low in order to turn their inventory.

PRIVATE INDIVIDUALS

This category includes nongun shops as well as individuals, and this is the area where real caution must be exercised. Although bargains may be found, many times people have an inflated idea of the value of their gun, and very often the article for sale is misidentified. Remember, knowledge is power!

Pitfalls

REFINISHED GUNS

A refinished gun can be beautiful. Unfortunately this also drastically reduces the value of a collector's item, so it's important to know how to spot refinishing. Most of the time when a gun is reblued or replated it must be heavily polished to remove small pits. A good craftsman will keep all of the edges sharp, will preserve the lettering, and will avoid "ripple" (waves polished into the gun in places where the metal should be flat). Poor craftsmen will remove lettering, round edges, and in general remove too much metal. The finish on a good job will be even and bright, on a poor job it will look splotchy and uneven. If you suspect that a gun has been refinished look for these signs: the lettering will have "drag-out marks" (one edge of the letter will be furrowed from polishing); the quality of finish doesn't match the original factory job; parts have been finished to a different color than original. Remember, most factories did an excellent job of finishing.

UPGRADES

Upgrading is taking a normal gun that is in decent condition and engraving or otherwise embellishing it so that it is more valuable. In many cases a good upgrade comes within 60% to 70% of the value of the factory original if the job is well done. But beware of guns that people try to pass off as original. The best defense is education. If you're interested in high grade guns try to examine as many known originals as you can to get a feel for that factory's style and quality, or enlist the aid of an expert to help you.

FAKES

Counterfeits, it seems, have always been with us, and as with any item of value, low-cost reproductions have been made and passed along as the real thing. There are all kinds of reproductions, from the crude kitchen table conversion with the uneven lettering stamps to the ultra-sophisticated copy made with some original parts. Fakes include complete reproductions of antique guns to adding police stamps on World War II German pistols. Once again knowledge is everything. Learn all you can before buying, and on valuable items buy from someone you can trust. Most dealers of collectible guns are honest, and it's uncommon to hear of a dealer intentionally trying to sell a fake.

CONDITION DESCRIPTIONS

The N.R.A. guidelines should always be used by dealers and collectors when describing their guns. Many times there will be descriptions such as "95% blue" or "near mint," which, while they sound good, sometimes mask a multitude of sins. Just because someone uses either vague descriptions or their own grading does not necessarily mean that they're trying to hide something. Sometimes people get entrenched in their ways and you have to learn their system. But it does pay to ask a few questions to make sure that everything is functioning as it should be, and that all of the parts are there. Accurate percentage descriptions are an acquired skill and when used in conjunction with the N.R.A. description can give an accurate picture. Always be sure that you have complete information.

SELLING COLLECTOR GUNS

As important as buying is the ability to sell what you have, and there are many ways to do this. The major factors to consider when you sell are how fast do you want to sell your guns and how much do you want for them. The two are not necessarily mutually exclusive, but usually if you want top price you have to compete with the dealer and it takes time. Always remember that guns are cashable items and the choice of what you are willing to take for them is yours and your return will be based on your salesmanship.

Where to sell

Gun Stores: The local gun dealer generally cannot pay you a top price on a collectible gun unless he has a good market for it. Even then he must make a profit. But this is a good source to sell your guns quickly.

Specialist and Mail-Order Dealers: Many times these dealers will pay somewhat higher prices and work on a slimmer margin because they have built up customer lists over the years and may have a guaranteed resale of your gun.

Your Own Ad: This may be the way to get the most for your guns, but it also takes the longest time and requires the cooperation of a firearms licensee for shipping. There is usually a four- to eight-week time lag between the time you place an ad and the time it is in print and the publication distributed. Additionally, you also have the cost of the ad to consider as well as the cost of packaging and shipping.

Gun Shows: This can provide not only a place to sell your guns but a great meeting ground for fellow collectors. Of course your salesmanship is of prime importance to get your best price, but you will meet people with similar interests who may be very interested in buying what you have.

Auctions: This can sometimes be a risky venture. In an unreserved auction the highest bid wins, and if there is a bad crowd your guns could go for very little, and to add insult to injury you will have to pay a commission. In a reserved auction you are allowed to set a reasonable bottom figure, and if the gun does not reach that amount you get it back. However, you will generally have to pay a small commission to have it returned on reserve. But the other side of the coin is that people sometimes get carried away at an auction, and many times guns fetch a much higher price than what is expected. Auctions are growing in popularity with collectors for both buying and selling.

Recordkeeping

U.S. law is very specific about a firearms licensee's recordkeeping responsibilities, but although the private individual is not required to, he should also keep records. Suggested information to keep for your own use would include the name and address of the person you acquired the gun from and the date, the make, model, caliber, type, and serial number of your gun, and when you sell it the name and address of the buyer and the date you sold it. It would also be handy to keep a record of the price you paid.

THE NATIONAL RIFLE ASSOCIATION OF AMERICA

The right to private ownership of firearms, a right so obviously vital to gun collectors as well as sportsmen, has been the primary cause championed by the National Rifle Association of Washington, D.C. This historic organization, now more than a century old and numbering well over 3 million members, has also made vast contributions toward the study, technology, history, and safe use of firearms. Nearly all U.S. gun dealers, and a large proportion of collectors, are members of the N.R.A., and have derived numerous benefits from membership.

Most readers of this book are, undoubtedly, already familiar with the N.R.A. But a work on forearms collecting could hardly be complete without a few words on the organization, and (at the end of this brief article) information on becoming a member.

While the firearms hobbyist has his choice of many organizations to join, membership in the nationwide N.R.A. seems almost basic for anyone interested in gun collecting. The N.R.A.'s strength, supplied by its ever-increasing roster of members, insures a strong voice for the hobby. Whether the collector cares to realize it or not, there are individuals—including some in government—who would strangle the hobby by outlawing the possession, sale, or trade of ALL firearms . . . or who would support such stringent restrictions on firearms ownership that gun collection would, for all practical purposes, come to an end. This is a battle that is never officially over. The tide can be kept in the collector's favor ONLY by interested parties making themselves known and counted. And the fact that the N.R.A. membership has increased more dramatically in recent years than ever in the past is solid evidence that the future will be bright for gun enthusiasts.

The National Rifle Association has many goals and serves multitudes of purposes. The public hears occasionally of its activities in lobbying against gun control legislation. Seldom does the news media report the numerous other N.R.A. functions. Among these are its continuing efforts to promote better understanding of the safe use and care of all types of firearms; in conjunction with this goal, the N.R.A. holds many seminars on gun-use instruction, as well as field meets and other training activities for firearms owners. It believes—and the belief is an historic one, a long tradition of the organization—that citizens well-trained in the use of firearms will be better citizens, and will be more capable of contributing to the defense of themselves, their community, and the nation. The N.R.A. is also very active in conservation programs to preserve endangered species and to encourage hunting only when and where the hunter presents no danger to the ecology.

HISTORY

The N.R.A. is now more than 125 years old, having been chartered (originally by the State of New York) in 1871. It was born as a direct outgrowth of the Civil War. Of the many lessons that came from the war's battlefields, one was imprinted indelibly on the minds of officers; the majority of infantry soldiers were simply unskilled in the use of firearms. Even the rudimentary rules of gun use were foreign to them. In part the military was to blame. It devoted more attention to parade marching and drills than to firearms instruction. If Uncle Sam could not be counted on to do the job, it was then the responsibility of concerned citizens to promote firearms training. In 1871, the New York National Guard comprised a number of such concerned citizens. They were all ex-Union veterans and had seen first-hand the severity of the problem in combat. So in September of that year an ambitious group of fifteen of them collected to establish an organization—the first of its kind in the country. It would strive to instill pride in proper gun handling, and marksmanship, to increase the level of firearms knowledge among U.S. citizens, and in this way, better prepare Americans for military service in the event of war. It was a lofty ideal, but history showed it was achievable. A hundred years earlier, the American colonists were highly skilled in firearms use because the necessity to hunt and protect one's property left little choice in the matter. There was no doubt that proper education could once again hone the shooting skills of the average citizen.

It was decided to model the organization after Britain's National Rifle Association, so the name National Rifle Association of America was chosen. A leader with military background and national recognition was a necessity; one was found in the person of General Ambrose Burnside who had served in the Civil War. On November 17, 1871, the charter was formally granted. But the new organization faced stiff challenges. The "media" of that time consisted almost wholly of newspapers, and newspaper accounts of the young N.R.A. brought no groundswell of membership. There were the inevitable difficulties with funding, which limited the number of tournaments and other activities, and the hazards faced by changes in the government's administration, since some presidents were more supportive of the N.R.A. than others.

Though times occasionally looked bleak, the organization pushed forward, spread its message, and succeeded in surviving. Finally, the country was awakened to the truth of the N.R.A.'s warnings about ill-prepared soldiers when the Spanish-American War broke out in the late 1890s. This conflict brought immediate attention to the

N.R.A., and when the war ended things began changing. In 1903 the government established its National Board for the Promotion of Rifle Practice, and N.R.A. training activities were greatly increased. Thanks to the N.R.A., which grew impressively in the years from 1903 to 1916, the country was far better prepared for entry into World War I than it could otherwise have been. Many of the enlisted men had received N.R.A. training. This was doubly so twenty-five years later when America went into World War II. In the meantime, the N.R.A. was also at work with law enforcement agencies, on federal and local levels, to promote more efficient firearms use by police officers. The firearms collector, if he takes an interest in memorabilia, has certainly seen and perhaps owned some of the N.R.A. award medals. These handsome medals took the place of large-size trophies of earlier years, and were eagerly competed for in N.R.A.-sanctioned events. A number of types exist, for competition among civilians and law enforcement agents.

After World War II, the N.R.A. inaugurated the first hunter safety program, designed to eliminate hunting accidents arising from ignorance of firearms use and/or poor marksmanship. Then in 1975 came the epochal establishment of the N.R.A. Institute for Legislative Action, to protect the right of law-abiding citizens to own firearms.

The three millionth member was added to the N.R.A. membership rolls in the mid-'80s—a striking record of growth for an organization that began with little more than guts, hope and 15 far-sighted members 125 years earlier.

N.R.A. INSTITUTE FOR LEGISLATIVE ACTION

The N.R.A.'s Institute for Legislative Action performs many functions. It monitors all gun-related bills put before Congress, to study their fairness and seek change when necessary. It likewise keeps careful watch on court rulings in all parts of the country, in cases involving the right to own and bear arms or similar questions. When rulings are made contrary to the N.R.A.'s position, it often assigns an attorney and allocates funds for the preparation of appeals, and to date has been very successful in this phase of its operations.

N.R.A. FIELD SERVICES

The N.R.A. Field Services was designed primarily for furthering the goals of the organization's founders and promoting a better understanding of firearms use among private citizens. Officers of the Field Services work closely with those of the Institute for Legislative Action in a number of interrelated areas. One of the primary arms of the N.R.A. Field Services is its Volunteer Resources Department, which recruits and trains volunteer members. The Range Development Department, also a branch of Field Services, is active in inspecting target-shooting ranges at various firearms clubs. One of the goals of the N.R.A., through its Field Services, is to arrive at a level of standardization in rifle and pistol tournaments so that each tournament is held under similar conditions and with corresponding rules and regulations. This, of course, is an aid to the shooter and a springboard to developing increased skill, rather than having to adapt to different rules and conditions at each tournament. Shooting tournaments are growing at such a rapid rate that the N.R.A. has had to greatly expand its staff to keep pace with the demand for skilled range and tournament supervision. The Field Services are also involved with selection of suitable sites for tournament and practice ranges; design of ranges for maximum efficiency and safety; and legal assistance on all aspects of range establishment and operation. This is vital because the laws of individual states sometimes differ and a range operator must be fully informed of the local applicable laws.

In 1981, the N.R.A. reached an all-time high in the number of its affiliated range clubs, with 12,560. Also, in 1981, the Field Services appointed separate State Association Coordinators for the range clubs in each State, thereby providing an individual with local knowledge to work directly with the clubs in his state and act as a kind of liaison between them and the N.R.A.

One of the chief aspects of Field Services is the N.R.A. Range Loan Program, which has so far supplied more than $400,000 to local clubs for the establishment or renovation of their range shooting facilities.

N.R.A. PUBLIC EDUCATION

The N.R.A. Public Education department is the link between the N.R.A. and the general public—"general public" meaning persons who are not members of the N.R.A. or are not even gun owners or hunting enthusiasts. Its purpose is to explain the position of N.R.A. members and sportsmen in general, on various affairs, to the public. This is, of course, of great significance because the general public elects the country's legislators and, in a roundabout way, makes its laws. Whenever an issue arises involving the ownership of firearms or anything to concern hunters and gun hobbyists, the Public Education branch of the N.R.A. prepares its view and disseminates it to the news media. Usually, the matters involved in legal questions or other complex subjects need to be put into plain language for the public to better understand. This is seldom done by the news media itself, which contains many elements opposed to the principles of the N.R.A. Unfortunately some segments of the public have formed very false conclusions about gun owners and hunters, and about the motives of the N.R.A. They assume that hunters are automatically bad for the ecology and that firearms ownership among private citizens breeds criminal activity. One project of the N.R.A. Public Education department has been an advertising campaign in various national magazines, picturing the hunter and gun hobbyist as he really is; just an average citizen like the "general public" and not someone to be feared or shunned.

But the Public Education activities go deeper than this. They involve the development of such tools as the Shooting Sports Library Kit, designed to be placed into public and school libraries and containing various publications on the positive aspects of hunting, shooting, and gun ownership. The N.R.A. strongly believes that gun education, like other forms of education, is most effective when begun early, and that the rudiments of gun knowledge should be taught to even very young children.

N.R.A.'S OTHER OPERATIONS

The other operations of the National Rifle Association comprise: Membership Services; Competitions; Hunter Services; Education and Training; Law Enforcement Services, and N.R.A. Publications. All of these interrelated activities bring the N.R.A.'s activities and purposes close to the public. Among the Membership Benefits are, of course, the well-known *American Rifleman* and *American Hunter* magazines which are sent automatically to N.R.A. members. The most widely read and authoritative publications of their kind, they carry articles on all aspects of hunting, shooting, gun care, and related topics, authored by experts in their fields. They also carry the latest reports on news of interest to hunters and gun hobbyists in the way of pending legislation, improvements in gun design, inauguration of new clubs, and so on.

The nation's leader in gun safety training for decades, the N.R.A. sponsors and underwrites safety training programs for all ages. More than 32,000 N.R.A.-certified instructors train 300,000 Americans in gun safety each year. The N.R.A. Eddie Eagle® child gun safety program teaches them not to play with guns with the simple message: *"If you find a gun: Stop! Don't touch. Leave the area. Tell an adult."* As of 1994, the program had reached more than 4.5 million preschool through sixth-grade children. And this safety training works: According to the National Safety Council, today's accidental firearm fatality rates are the lowest recorded in eighty-seven years.

The N.R.A. Hunter Services Division sponsors the Great American Hunters Tour, a coast-to-coast seminar series that gives American sportsmen and -women state-of-the-art techniques for safety and success in the field, with an emphasis on conservation and ethics.

Setting the standard for marksmanship excellence, N.R.A.'s Competitions Division sanctions more than 12,000 shooting tournaments annually, including the famous National Matches at Camp Perry, Ohio, which draw thousands of competitors each year.

For those who'd like to shoot but not necessarily compete, N.R.A.'s Recreational Shooting, Training, and Ranges Division sponsors a variety of programs and projects. Community Shooting Fairs, for example, give families a chance to experience and enjoy shooting in a safe, controlled setting that's fun for all ages.

Women concerned with their personal safety get the information and advice they want through the N.R.A. Refuse to Be a Victim program. It gives them the facts and techniques they need to plan their personal safety strategy—with or without a firearm.

Those who *do* choose to own a firearm are encouraged to get the proper training through an N.R.A. Women's Gun Safety and Personal Protection course.

A core objective of the Association, expressed in Article II of its bylaws, is "to promote public safety, law and order"—and that's evident in N.R.A.'s long-standing support for law enforcement. More than 9,000 N.R.A.-certified, law-enforcement marksmanship instructors train up to 400,000 law-enforcement and security personnel annually. N.R.A.-enrolled law officers get special insurance coverage, discounts on equipment, and scholarship opportunities for their children. CrimeStrike, a new N.R.A. effort, unites police, prosecutors, criminologists, victims, and volunteers to push for the tough, effective criminal justice reforms that can make America safer.

The N.R.A. National Firearms Museum, opened in the fall of 1994, has 16,000 square feet of exhibit space featuring approximately 3,000 antique, unique, and historical firearms, making it the nation's largest display of the American source and symbol of freedom.

At "Friends of the N.R.A." fundraising dinners in small towns across America, N.R.A. members and supporters get together to voice their concerns, find out about N.R.A. projects and priorities that affect them, and raise money for an important cause. Administered through a national network of N.R.A. field representatives and activists, this program is just one of the many ways the N.R.A. is moving out beyond Washington, D.C., and into the everyday lives of millions of Americans.

MEMBERSHIP

Membership in the N.R.A. is both inexpensive and rewarding for anyone interested in firearms. Membership places one in league with all the leading sportsmen and gun hobbyists of the country, and adds further weight to the N.R.A.'s ability to carry out its programs and objectives.

For further information on membership rates or for questions about the N.R.A., please call our customer service line, toll-free, at 1-800-NRA-3888.

HOW TO USE
THIS GUIDE

There are three price columns found next to each listing. The first two columns show the retail selling price for each piece in very good to excellent condition. The third column is last edition's value in excellent condition. It shows which items have decreased or increased in value over the previous period. The prices reflect the geographical differences in the market and were determined by averaging the prices of actual sales across the country. They should be used only as a guideline.

For the sake of simplicity the following organization has been adopted for this book:

1. Manufacturer, importer, or brand name
2. Type of gun
3. Type of action
4. Model
5. Caliber or gauge

To find your gun in this guide first look under the name of the manufacturer, importer, or brand name, then look under the subdivision "Type of Gun" (i.e., rifle, handgun, etc.). For instance, if you want to find a 6", .357 Magnum, Colt Python, look for:

COLT; HANDGUN, REVOLVER; Python, .357 Magnum, 6" barrel, blue, vent rib, 6 shot, adjustable sights, modern.

If nothing is known about the origin of a particular gun, an approximation of the value can be determined by checking the categories of "Type of Action" (wheel lock, percussion, cartridge weapon, etc.) and "Examples." To further aid in evaluating guns of unknown origin look under "Firearms, Custom Made," "Plains Rifles," "Scheutzen Rifles," and "Kentucky Rifles and Pistols."

In some cases there is a general listing for a manufacturer or a specific model of gun with instructions to "add" a given value. These additions should be made for all guns in the listed category that have the modification mentioned.

SCOPE OF THE BOOK

As implied by this book's imprint, House of Collectibles, the work covers antique and modern firearms demonstrated to be collectible. A "collectible" is an item that has attained significant collector interest to create a market and realized a value beyond its mere utility. Firearms that are simply "used," with their value a function of the price of a new comparable piece, may not be listed. Discontinuance of production, in and of itself, does not deem the existing items to be collectible. Generally, the items in highest demand by collectors were expensive and the "best" when new. For omissions the reader does feel exist, please write to the author with information for inclusion in future editions.

This book represents an analysis of prices for which collectible firearms have actually been selling during the preceding period. Although every reasonable effort has been made to compile an accurate and reliable guide, the prices of firearms vary significantly depending on such factors as the locality of the sale and changing economic conditions. Accordingly, no representation can be made that firearms listed may be bought or sold at the prices indicated, nor shall the author be responsible for any error made in compiling and recording the prices.

The reader is reminded to comply with all local, state, and federal firearm laws. The legality of ownership, transfer requirements, and firearms classifications change and vary from one jurisdiction to another. If in doubt, contact the Bureau of Alcohol, Tobacco, and Firearms or your local law enforcement agencies.

COMMEMORATIVES

BY KEVIN P. CHERRY

In the preface to the 1973 edition of *Colt Commemorative Firearms*, the late James E. Serven stated: "Nothing in material form has had a greater role than the gun in turning the frontier into a peaceful and productive land or in defending our national security." Commemorative firearms, with their many types, varied markings, different finishes, and interesting historical association, offer the collector items that are available and relatively inexpensive. Since 1961 the collecting of commemoratives has provided a promising field for capital gains, plus great dividends of pleasure along the way.

The commemorative marketplace is often confusing for the beginning commemorative collector. Bonafide commemoratives, which is what we will be discussing here, have very specific criteria. First, bonafide commemoratives must be limited in production. Second, they must bear their own unique serial number range. Third, they must be endorsed by the manufacturer, and, in most cases, be distributed through normal distribution channels. There are exceptions to the "normal" distribution channels when one entity may have an exclusive on the distribution process. Most commemoratives are classified as curios and relics under federal law.

There are numerous guns which appear to meet most of these requirements but are *not* bonafide commemoratives. For example, Ducks Unlimited guns and Friends of N.R.A. guns are considered "trade" guns. That is, they are produced for the specific purpose of auctions or raffles. They may or may not bear special serial numbers and will have a limited production. However, they are not endorsed by the manufacturer as a bonafide commemorative nor are they distributed through the normal channels.

Colt has made so many Special Editions and Private Editions that they are the most difficult to decipher. However, if the four-point criteria above are used, you should be able to tell which guns are true commemoratives and which are not.

The bonafide commemorative marketplace had its birth in 1961 in the small town of Geneseo, Illinois. At that time, Robert Cherry (my father), owner of Cherry's Sporting Goods, put out a Colt derringer to commemorate the 125th Anniversary of his hometown, Geneseo, in conjunction with Colt Firearms. A total of 104 pieces were produced and sold for a price of $27.50 each. Today they are worth $650 each.

This small beginning brought on a completely new type of gun collecting. In that same year, seven other commemoratives took place, six being done on Colt revolvers. By 1964, there had already been twenty-five separate commemorations made. That same year, Colt put together its first commemorative committee, made up of several well-known gun people all across the United States. That committee continued until late 1985, when bonafide commemorative production ceased at Colt.

Winchester also embarked upon bonafide commemoratives in 1964 with its Winchester Wyoming Diamond Jubilee Model 94. Winchester, which ultimately became known as the U.S. Repeating Arms Co., never had a "commemorative committee" but did seek the advice of many of the same people who assisted Colt.

The concept of the bonafide commemorative was to offer a higher quality product at an attractive price and limit the quantities available. The result was a very strong aftermarket and an ever-increasing interest in collecting commemorative firearms. This trend continued from 1961 until the very late 1970s and early 1980s. At that time, the two major manufacturers of commemoratives, Colt and U.S. Repeating Arms Co., made some detrimental mistakes. First, they began making too many guns in each commemoration, which left excess guns unsold, later to be dumped on the market. Second, they made too many separate commemorations in a year. Third, they no longer gave the collector an attractive price. The market collapsed; between the early 1980s and 1989 there was virtually no market for commemoratives.

By 1989, most of the excess commemoratives had been absorbed into the marketplace. As the price of standard product increased, the commemoratives had an attractive price and became desirable again. Since 1989, the market has gotten much stronger and the values on almost all of the bonafide commemoratives have rebounded. In particular, the larger caliber Colt commemoratives and almost all of the Winchester lever actions have been selling very well.

All of the commemoratives in this listing will be considered bonafide for collecting purposes. The values assume they are unfired, there are no marks or scratches on the guns, and there are no turn marks on the cylinders. If the gun came with a presentation case, the case must also be mint. Winchesters must be in the original factory box and, if they came with a decorative sleeve, the sleeve must be in fine condition. Some of the commemoratives came with medallions, scabbards, books, etc. It is preferable to have all of these but they are not absolutely essential in figuring the current market value. Any commemorative that has been shot or shows wear will have a value comparable to that of a standard gun.

Numerous books on commemoratives have been published, but, unfortunately, most of them are out of print. The following books are recommended: *Colt Commemorative Firearms* by R. L. Wilson, published by Charles Kidwell; *Colt Commemorative Firearms* by R. L. Wilson, published by Robert E. P. Cherry; *The Colt Commemoratives* by Ken Condry and Larry Jones, and *Winchester Commemoratives* by Tom Trolard, published by Commemorative Investments Press.

Note: The author wishes to thank Mr. Cherry for his contribution of the text and photographs in this section. For further information about commemorative firearms, Kevin Cherry may be contacted at Cherry's Fine Guns, 3402-A W. Wendover Avenue, Greensboro, NC 27407; (910) 854–4182.

	Production	Original Retail	Current Retail

1961 ISSUES

Colt Geneseo, Illinois, 125 Anniversary Derringer	104	$27.50	$650
Colt Sheriff's Model, Blue and Case Hardened	478	129.95	1995
Colt Sheriff's Model, Nickel	25	139.95	5000
Colt 125 Anniversary Model SAA	7390	150	995
Colt Kansas Statehood Scout	6197	75	350
Colt Pony Express Centennial Scout	1007	80	450
Colt Civil War Centennial Pistol	24,114	32.50	175
Marlin 90 Anniversary, 39A Rifle and Carbine	1000	100	795

1962 ISSUES

Colt Rock Island Arsenal Centennial Pistol	550	$38.50	$250
Colt Columbus, Ohio Sesquicentennial Scout	200	100	550
Colt Ft. Findlay, Ohio Sesquicentennial Scout	110	89.50	650
Colt Ft. Findlay, Ohio Cased Pair, 22LR/22 Magnum	20	185	2500
Colt New Mexico Golden Anniversary Scout	1000	79.95	375
Colt Ft. McPherson, Nebraska Centennial Derringer	300	28.95	395
Colt West Virginia Statehood Centennial Scout	3451	75	375

1963 ISSUES

Colt West Virginia Statehood, Centennial SAA .45	600	$150	$1095
Colt Arizona Territory Centennial Scout	5355	75	375
Colt Arizona Territory Centennial SAA .45	1264	150	1095
Colt Carolina Charter Tercentenary Scout	550	75	395
Colt Carolina Charter Tercentenary .22/.45 Combo	250	240	1495
Colt H. Cook "1 of 100" .22/.45 Combo	100	275	1695
Colt Ft. Stephenson, Ohio Sesquicentennial Scout	200	75	550
Colt Battle of Gettysburg Centennial Scout	1019	89.95	375
Colt Idaho Territory Centennial Scout	902	75	375
Colt General John Hunt Morgan, Indiana Raid Scout	100	74.50	650

1964 ISSUES

Colt Cherry's 35 Anniversary .22/.45 Combo	100	$275	$1695
Colt Nevada Statehood Centennial Scout	3981	75	375
Colt Nevada Statehood Centennial SAA .45	1684	150	1095
Colt Nevada Statehood Centennial .22/.45 Combo	189	240	1495
Colt Nevada State, Combo w/Extra English Cylinders	577	350	1595
Colt Nevada "Battle Born" Scout	981	85	375
Colt Nevada "Battle Born" SAA .45	80	175	1395
Colt Nevada "Battle Born" SAA .22/.45 Combo	20	265	2595
Colt Montana Territorial Centennial Scout	2296	75	375
Colt Montana Territorial Centennial SAA .45	850	150	1095
Colt Wyoming Diamond Jubilee Scout	2356	75	375
Winchester Wyoming Diamond Jubilee 94 Carbine	1500	99.95	1295
Remington Montana Territorial Centennial 600 Rifle	1005	124.95	495
Colt General Hood Centennial Scout	1502	75	375
Colt New Jersey Tercentenary Scout	1000	75	375
Colt New Jersey Tercentenary SAA .45	249	150	1095
Colt St. Louis Bicentennial Scout	801	75	375

	Production	Original Retail	Current Retail
Colt St. Louis Bicentennial SAA .45	199	$150	$1095
Colt St. Louis Bicentennial .22/.45 Combo	250	240	1495
Ithaca St. Louis Bicentennial Model 49 .22 Rifle	200	34.95	195
Colt California Gold Rush Scout	500	79.50	375
Colt Pony Express Presentation SAA .45	1004	250	1395
Colt Chamizal Treaty Scout	450	85	395
Colt Chamizal Treaty Single Action Army .45	50	170	1295
Colt Chamizal Treaty .22/.45 Combo	50	280	1995
Colt Col. Sam Colt Sesquicentennial Presidential SAA .45	4750	225	1095
Colt Col. Sam Colt Sesquicentennial Deluxe Presidential SAA .45	200	500	1950
Colt Col. Sam Colt Sesquicentennial Special Deluxe Presidential SAA .45	50	1000	2950
Colt Wyatt Earp Buntline SAA .45	150	250	1895

1965 ISSUES

	Production	Original Retail	Current Retail
Colt Oregon Trail Scout	1995	$75	$375
Colt Joaquin Murietta .22/.45 Combo	100	350	1695
Colt Forty-Niner Miner Scout	500	85	375
Colt Old Ft. Des Moines, Reconstruction Scout	700	89.95	375
Colt Old Ft. Des Moines, Reconstruction SAA .45	100	169.95	1095
Colt Old Ft. Des Moines, Reconstruction .22/.45 Combo	100	289.95	1695
Colt Appomattox Centennial Scout	1001	75	375
Colt Appomattox Centennial SAA .45	250	150	1095
Colt Appomattox Centennial .22/.45 Combo	250	240	1495
Colt General Meade Campaign Scout	1197	75	350
Colt St. Augustine Quadricentennial Scout	500	85	375
Colt Kansas Cowtown Series, Wichita Scout	500	85	350

1966 ISSUES

	Production	Original Retail	Current Retail
Colt Kansas Cowtown Series, Dodge City Scout	500	$85	$350
Colt Colorado Gold Rush Scout	1350	85	375
Colt Oklahoma Territory Scout	1343	85	375
Colt Dakota Territory Scout	1000	85	375
Winchester Centennial '66 Rifle	102,309	125	450
Winchester Centennial '66 Carbine	102,309	125	425
Colt General Meade SAA .45	197	165	1095
Colt Abercrombie & Fitch "Trailblazer" New York	200	275	1095
Colt Kansas Cowtown Series, Abilene Scout	500	95	350
Colt Indiana Sesquicentennial Scout	1745	85	375
Winchester Nebraska Centennial 94 Rifle	2500	125	1195
Colt Pony Express .45 SAA "4-Square"	----	1400	5500
Colt California Gold Rush SAA 45	130	175	1295
Colt Abercrombie & Fitch "Trailblazer" Chicago	100	275	1095
Colt Abercrombie & Fitch "Trailblazer" San Francisco	100	275	1095

1967 ISSUES

	Production	Original Retail	Current Retail
Remington Canadian Centennial 742 Rifle	1000	$199.95	$395
Ruger Canadian Centennial 10/22 Rifle	2000	99.95	250
Ruger Canadian Centennial, Matched #3 Set	1900	319	650
Ruger Canadian Centennial, Matched #2 Set	70	450	850

	Production	Original Retail	Current Retail
Ruger Canadian Centennial Matched #1 Special Deluxe Set	30	$600	$1050
Colt Lawman Series, Bat Masterson Scout	3000	90	375
Colt Lawman Series, Bat Masterson SAA .45	500	180	1295
Colt Alamo Scout	4239	85	350
Colt Alamo Single Action Army .45	750	165	1095
Colt Alamo .22/.45 Combo	250	265	1495
Colt Kansas Cowtown Series, Coffeyville Scout	500	95	350
Winchester Canadian '67 Centennial Rifle	90,301	125	450
Winchester Canadian '67 Centennial Carbine	90,301	125	425
Winchester Alaskan Purchase Centennial Carbine	1500	125	1495
Colt Kansas Trail Series, Chisholm Trail Scout	500	100	350
Colt WWI Series, Chateau Thierry .45 Auto	7400	200	695
Colt WWI Series, Chateau Thierry Deluxe .45	75	500	1350
Colt WWI Series, Chateau Thierry Special Deluxe .45	25	1000	2750
H&R "Abilene Anniversary" .22 Revolver	300	83.50	150

1968 ISSUES

	Production	Original Retail	Current Retail
Colt Nebraska Centennial Scout	6999	$100	$350
Colt Kansas Trail Series, Pawnee Trail Scout	500	110	350
Winchester Illinois Sesquicentennial, 94 Carbine	37,648	110	350
Winchester Buffalo Bill Rifle "1 of 300"	300	1000	2500
Winchester Buffalo Bill Rifle	112,923	129.95	450
Winchester Buffalo Bill Carbine	112,923	129.95	425
Colt WWI Series, Belleau Wood	7400	200	695
Colt WWI Series, Belleau Wood Deluxe	75	500	1350
Colt WWI Series, Belleau Wood Special Deluxe	25	1000	2750
Colt Lawman Series, Pat Garrett Scout	2966	110	375
Colt Lawman Series, Pat Garrett SAA .45	500	220	1095

1969 ISSUES

	Production	Original Retail	Current Retail
Colt General Nathan Bedford Forest Scout	2996	$110	$350
Colt Kansas Trail Series, Sante Fe Trail Scout	500	120	350
Colt WWI Series, Battle of 2nd Marne, .45 Auto	7400	220	695
Colt WWI Series, Battle of 2nd Marne, Deluxe	75	500	1350
Colt WWI Series, Battle of 2nd Marne, Special Deluxe	25	1000	2750
Colt Alabama Sesquicentennial Scout	2998	110	350
Colt Alabama Sesquicentennial SAA .45	1	- - - -	15,000
Winchester Golden Spike Carbine	69,996	119.95	350
Winchester Theodore Roosevelt Carbine	52,386	134.95	425
Winchester Theodore Roosevelt Rifle	52,386	134.95	450
Colt Golden Spike Scout	10,965	135	375
Colt Kansas Trail Series, Shawnee Trail Scout	500	120	350
Colt WWI Series, Meuse-Argonne .45 Auto	7400	220	695
Colt WWI Series, Meuse-Argonne .45 Auto Deluxe	75	550	1350
Colt WWI Series, Meuse-Argonne .45 Auto Special Deluxe	25	1000	2750
Colt Arkansas Territory Sesquicentennial Scout	3487	110	350
Colt Lawman Series, Wild Bill Hickock SAA	500	220	1095
Colt Lawman Series, Wild Bill Hickock Scout	2984	116	375
Colt California Bicentennial Scout	4997	135	350

	Production	Original Retail	Current Retail

1970 ISSUES

	Production	Original Retail	Current Retail
Colt Kansas Ft. Series, Ft. Larned Scout	500	$120	$350
Colt WWII Series, European Theater	9767	250	695
Colt WWII Series, Pacific Theater	9886	250	695
Winchester Northwest Territories	2500	149.95	850
Winchester Northwest Territories, Deluxe	500	249.95	1100
Winchester Northwest Territories, Donation	10	- - - -	- - - -
Winchester Cowboy Commemorative Carbine	27,549	125	450
Winchester Cowboy Commemorative Carbine "1 of 300"	300	1000	2500
Winchester Lone Star Carbine	38,385	140	425
Winchester Lone Star Rifle	38,385	140	450
Colt Texas Ranger Single Action Army .45	1000	650	1995
Colt Texas Ranger SAA, Grade II	- - - -	2250	4500
Colt Texas Ranger SAA, Grade III	- - - -	2950	5000
Savage 75 Anniversary Model 99 Rifle	9999	195	495
Colt Kansas Ft. Series, Ft. Hayes Scout	500	130	350
Colt Maine Sesquicentennial Scout	2987	120	350
Colt Missouri Sesquicentennial Scout	2975	125	350
Colt Missouri Sesquicentennial SAA .45	888	220	995
Colt Kansas Ft. Series, Ft. Riley	500	130	350
Colt Lawman Series, Wyatt Earp Scout	2968	125	450
Colt Lawman Series, Wyatt Earp SAA .45	500	395	1895

1971 ISSUES

	Production	Original Retail	Current Retail
Winchester NRA Centennial Musket	23,400	$149.95	$425
Winchester NRA Centennial Rifle	21,000	149.95	425
Winchester Yellow Boy	4903	149.95	1150
Winchester R.C.M.P.	9500	189.95	795
Winchester R.C.M.P. Members Issue	4850	189.95	795
Winchester R.C.M.P. Presentation	10	- - - -	9995
Winchester MPX	32	78	9995
Colt NRA Centennial Single Action Army .45	3475	250	1095
Colt NRA Centennial Single Action Army .357	3475	250	850
Colt NRA Centennial Gold Cup .45	2478	250	850
Colt 1851 Navy, U.S. Grant	4140	250	595
Colt 1851 Navy, Robert E. Lee	4645	250	595
Colt 1851 Navy, Lee-Grant Set	250	500	1350
Colt Kansas Series, Ft. Scott Scout	500	130	350
H&R Officer's Model .45-70	10,000	250	495
Marlin Zane Grey .30-30 Carbine	- - - -	150	350
Stevens Favorite '71 .22 Single Shot	1000	75	250
Marlin 336-39A Engraved Cased Pair	1000	750	995

1972 ISSUES

	Production	Original Retail	Current Retail
H&R Little Big Horn, .45-70	- - - -	$220	$495
Colt Florida Sesquicentennial Scout	1996	125	375
Colt Arizona Ranger Scout	3000	135	375
High Standard Olympic .22 Auto	- - - -	550	1500

	Production	Original Retail	Current Retail

1973 ISSUES

	Production	Original Retail	Current Retail
H&R 1873 Springfield	----	$250	$495
Smith & Wesson Texas Ranger w/Knife	10,000	250	595
Smith & Wesson Texas Ranger	----	195	475
H&R Custer Memorial, Officer's Model	25	3000	3995
H&R Custer Memorial, Enlisted Man's Model	243	2000	1995

1974 ISSUES

	Production	Original Retail	Current Retail
High Standard Griswold & Gunnison	500	$175	$250
High Standard Presidential Derringer	----	150	250
High Standard Leech & Rigdon	500	175	250
Winchester Texas Ranger Carbine	4850	129.95	695
Winchester Texas Ranger Presentation	150	1000	2500
Winchester Apache	8600	149.95	795
Winchester Klondike Gold Rush	10,200	229.95	795
Winchester Klondike Dawson City	25	----	8500
Winchester Comanche	11,511	229.95	795

1975 ISSUES

	Production	Original Retail	Current Retail
Colt Peacemaker Centennial .45	1500	$300	$1295
Colt Peacemaker Centennial .44-40	1500	300	1295
Colt Peacemaker Centennial Pair	500	625	2695
High Standard Schneider & Glassick	1000	325	325

1976 ISSUES

	Production	Original Retail	Current Retail
Ruger Colorado Centennial Single Six	----	$250	$325
Colt U.S. Bicentennial Set	1776	1695	1895
Winchester U.S. Bicentennial Carbine	19,999	325	595
Browning Bicentennial '78 .45-70 Rifle	1000	150	1850
Winchester Sioux	12,000	279.95	795
Winchester Little Big Horn	11,000	229.95	795

1977 ISSUES

	Production	Original Retail	Current Retail
Colt 2nd Amendment .22	3020	$194.95	$350
Winchester Wells Fargo	19,999	350	495
S&W 125 Anniversary Model 125	10,000	350	495
Winchester Cheyenne .44-40	11,225	300	795
Winchester Cheyenne .22	5000	319.95	695
Colt U.S. Calvary 200 Anniversary Set	2974	995	1250
Winchester "Limited Edition I"	1500	1500	1395
Winchester Cherokee .30-30	9000	384.95	795
Winchester Cherokee .22	3950	348.95	695
Winchester Legendary Lawman	19,999	375	495

1978 ISSUES

	Production	Original Retail	Current Retail
Browning Centennial Superposed Rifle-Shotgun	500	$7000	$5000
Browning Centennial M92 .44 Magnum	6000	219.95	425

	Production	Original Retail	Current Retail
Browning Centennial Hi-Power 9mm	3500	$495	$650
Jonathan Browning Mountain Rifle	1000	650	650
Winchester Antlered Game Carbine	19,999	375	495
Colt Statehood 3rd Model Dragoon	52	12,500	6995

1979 ISSUES

	Production	Original Retail	Current Retail
Winchester Legendary Frontiersman Rifle	19,999	$425	$495
Winchester Bat Masterson	8000	650	795
Winchester "Limited Edition II"	1500	1750	1395
Colt Ned Buntline Single Action Army .45	2973	895	795

1980 ISSUES

	Production	Original Retail	Current Retail
Colt Heritage-Walker .44 Percussion	1850	$1475	$950
Winchester Matched Set of 1000	1000	3000	2250
Winchester Alberta Diamond Jubilee	2700	650	795
Winchester Alberta Diamond Jubilee Deluxe	300	1900	1495
Winchester Saskatchewan Diamond Jubilee	2700	695	795
Winchester Saskatchewan Diamond Jubilee Deluxe	300	1695	1495
Winchester Calgary Stampede	1000	2200	1250
Winchester Canadian Pacific	2700	800	550
Winchester Canadian Pacific, Employee Edition	2000	800	550
Winchester Canadian Pacific, Presentation	300	2200	1100
Winchester "Oliver Winchester"	19,999	519.60	695

1981 ISSUES

	Production	Original Retail	Current Retail
Colt "John M. Browning" .45 Automatic	2986	$1099.95	$795
Winchester John Wayne	50,000	600	895
Winchester Canadian John Wayne	999	600	1095
Winchester "Duke"	1000	2250	2950
Browning "American Waterfowl" Superposed	500	7000	3500
Winchester U.S. Border Patrol, Members	800	950	595
Winchester U.S. Border Patrol	1000	950	595
Winchester John Wayne "1 of 300" Set	300	8500	6500
Winchester Great Western Artists I	999	2500	1195
Winchester Great Western Artists II	999	2500	1195

1982 ISSUES

	Production	Original Retail	Current Retail
Colt John Wayne, Standard	3100	$2995	$2250
Colt John Wayne, Deluxe	500	10,000	7500
Colt John Wayne, Presentation	100	20,000	12,000
Winchester Annie Oakley .22	6000	699	695
Winchester Oklahoma Diamond Jubilee	1000	2200	1395
Winchester Bald Eagle, Silver	2800	895	595
Winchester Bald Eagle, Gold	200	2950	2500

1983 ISSUES

	Production	Original Retail	Current Retail
Winchester Chief Crazy Horse	19,999	$600	$495
Colt Buffalo Bill Wild West Show Centennial SAA .45	283	1349.95	1250

	Original	Current
Production	Retail	Retail

1984 ISSUES

Winchester Colt	3250	$3995	$2250
Colt "USA Edition" SAA .44-40	100	4995	3500
Colt Kit Carson .22 New Frontier	951	549.95	395
Colt Theodore Roosevelt .44/40.	500	1695	1695
Winchester Boy Scout 75 Anniversary 9422	15,000	495	495
Winchester Eagle Scout 75 Anniversary 9422.	1000	1710	2500
Browning A-5 "Classic" Semi-Auto Shotgun	5000	1260	950
Browning Hi-Power "Classic" 9mm	5000	1000	850
Browning Hi-Power "Gold Classic" 9mm	500	2000	1800

1985 ISSUES

Colt Texas Sesquicentennial SAA .45, Standard	1000	$1836	$1095
Colt Texas Sesquicentennial SAA .45, Premier.	75	7995	5000
Winchester Texas Sesquicentennial, Carbine	15,000	695	695
Winchester Texas Sesquicentennial, Rifle and Bowie Knife	1500	2995	2400
Winchester Texas Sesquicentennial, Rifle, Carbine and Bowie	150	7995	6250

1986 ISSUES

Colt 150 Anniversary SAA .45	1000	$1595	$1595
Winchester 120 Anniversary .44-40.	1000	995	895
Browning A-5 "Gold Classic" Shotgun	500	6500	3500
Browning Superposed "Classic"	2500	2000	1750
Browning Superposed "Gold Classic" Shotgun	350	6000	4750

1987 ISSUES

Winchester U.S. Constitution 200 Anniversary .44-40	17	$12,000	$13,000

1990 ISSUES

Winchester Wyoming Centennial .30-30	500	$895	$995

1991 ISSUES

Winchester 125 Anniversary .30-30.	61	$4995	5250

1992 ISSUES

Winchester Arapaho .30-30	500	$895	$995
Winchester Ontario Conservation .30-30.	400	1195	1195
Winchester Kentucky Bicentennial .30-30.	500	995	995

1993 ISSUES

Winchester Nez Perce .30-30	600	$950	$950

1994 ISSUES

	Production	Original Retail	Current Retail
Uberti Nimschke 1866 Rifle, .44-40	150	$1495	$1495
Marlin "Century Limited" 94 Rifle .44-40	2500	1087.90	1100
Pedersoli Creedmoor Rifle, .45-70	250	1495	1495

Winchester Alaskan Purchase Centennial Carbine

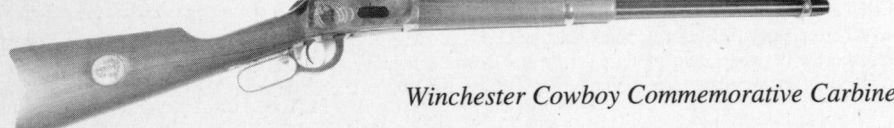

Winchester Cowboy Commemorative Carbine

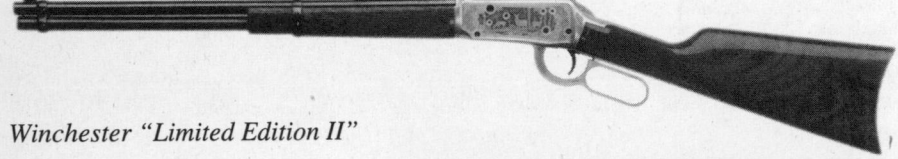

Winchester "Limited Edition II"

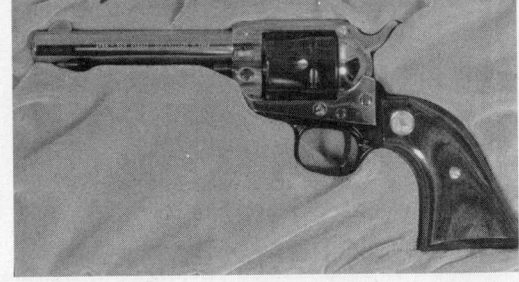

Colt New Jersey Tercentenary Scout

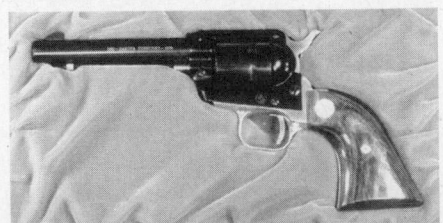

Colt Dakota Territory Scout

SMOOTHBORE PISTOLS THAT FIRE SHOTGUN SHELLS

BY ERIC M. LARSON

Smoothbore pistols designed to fire shotgun shells occupy a fascinating niche in U.S. firearms history—there's nothing else like them—and they are highly prized by collectors. Used mainly as relatively low-powered small-game and snake guns, a few models were marketed as defensive weapons. All were uncommon during the brief time (about 1920–34) that most of them were manufactured. In contrast to the production of conventional shotguns, which numbered in the tens of millions, total smoothbore pistol production was fewer than 100,000 guns. Today all models are rare, some are extremely rare, and all are undervalued in relation to their limited production.

Why were these guns made? Answer: The need for a specialized, compact, all-around gun for trappers, farmers, campers, and lumberjacks. One of the most successful of such firearms was Marble's Game Getter Gun, first introduced in 1908, whose entire production was sold by 1917. The Game Getter has 12″, 15″, or 18″ separated over/under rifled/smoothbore barrels in .22/.44 or .22/.410, a manually pivoted hammer striker to select the upper or lower barrel, an attached folding skeleton stock, and is intended to be fired from the shoulder. Continuing demand for the Game Getter caused Marble's to remanufacture it (in a different model) in 1921, shortly after World War I. While it is not a smoothbore pistol, the Game Getter is listed below because of its historical relevance—most smoothbore pistols were manufactured to obtain a share of the Game Getter market.

Rulings by the Treasury Department brought smoothbore pistols under the purview of the National Firearms Act (N.F.A.) of 1934, which is designed to control "gangster weapons" by requiring their registration, and uses prohibitive taxes to discourage their manufacture, distribution, and ownership. The then-$200 tax on each transfer of ownership vastly exceeded their monetary value, and no smoothbore pistol that was manufactured in 1934 was ever manufactured again. The transfer tax was changed to $5 in 1960. Today, smoothbore pistols cannot be legally possessed unless they are registered with the Bureau of Alcohol, Tobacco, and Firearms (B.A.T.F.). All of the smoothbore pistols listed below are *Class III* firearms; unless registered under the N.F.A., their sale, transfer, or possession is illegal. Modern rifled-barreled pistols that are designed to fire shotgun shells are exempt from the N.F.A.—no registration or tax payment is required.

Because smoothbore pistols are not frequently bought or sold, establishing reliable values can be difficult. The values listed here are approximate and may vary significantly according to local supply and demand. If these rare firearms were exempted from N.F.A. controls, as have been short-barreled Winchester and Marlin "trapper carbines" and various Luger, Mauser, and other shoulder-stocked pistols, their values would probably increase substantially.

	V.G.	*Exc.*	*Prior Edition Exc. Value*

California Arms Co., San Jose, California, 1926–30; 2½" shotgun or

tear gas shells only; variations exist; total production probably fewer than 400.

Defiance Anti-Bandit Gun, 20 gauge, 12¼" or 12½" double barrels,
Class III . . . . — *RARE* —

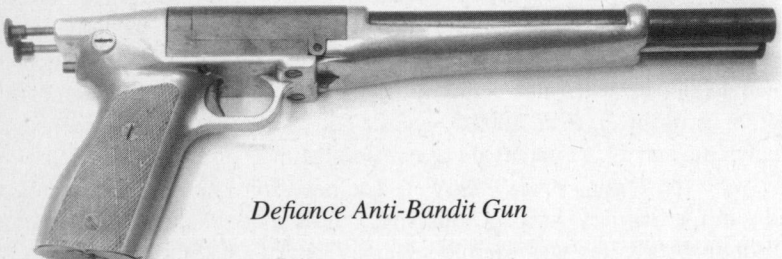

Defiance Anti-Bandit Gun

Crescent-Davis Arms Corp., Norwich, Connecticut, 1930–32; pro-

duction was probably fewer than 4000; receiver is blued, tiger-stripe or color case-hardened, and marked Crescent Certified Shotgun/Crescent-Davis Arms Corp./Norwich, Conn. U.S.A.

Crescent Certified Shotgun, .410 bore, 12¼" single barrel,
Class III, Curio (add $200 to $500 for original cardboard box) . . . . $650 $800   —

Crescent Fire Arms Co., Norwich, Connecticut, circa 1928–30; total

production unknown but probably fewer than 100; receiver is color case-hardened and marked NEW EMPIRE and Crescent Fire Arms Co./Norwich, Conn.

Crescent Auto and Burglar Gun, .410 bore, 12¼" double barrel,
Class III. . . . . — *RARE* —

Harrington & Richardson Arms Co., Worcester, Massachu-

setts, 1921–34; total production about 54,000; 8" or 12¼" barrel; more than fifty variations exist. Values below assume choked .410 or unchoked 28 gauge (and 12¼" barrel for 2½" shell), case-hardened receiver marked H.&R. HANDY-GUN, spur grip and plain trigger guard. The .410 H&R Handy-Gun is the most common of all pre-N.F.A. smoothbore pistols.

		Prior Edition Exc.
	V.G.	Exc.	Value
H&R Handy-Gun, .410 bore, *Class III, Curio* . . . . . . \. $375	$500	—
H&R Handy-Gun, 28 gauge, *Class III, Curio* 500	800	—

H&R Handy-Gun   Top: Model 3, Type II, .410 Bore, 12¼" Choked Barrel.
Two Middle: Model 2, Type III, .410 Bore, 12¼" Choked Barrel (most common type).
Bottom: Model 1, Type I, .410 Bore, 8" Unchoked Barrel.

Rare variations command premiums: 8" barrel, 25% to 50%; 18" barrel, 200% to 300%; unchoked .410, 20% to 40%; 28 gauge or Model 3 (only) with factory-equipped original detachable shoulder stock, 150% or more; holster, $75–$200; serial matching box, $100–$400; early boxes are extremely rare.

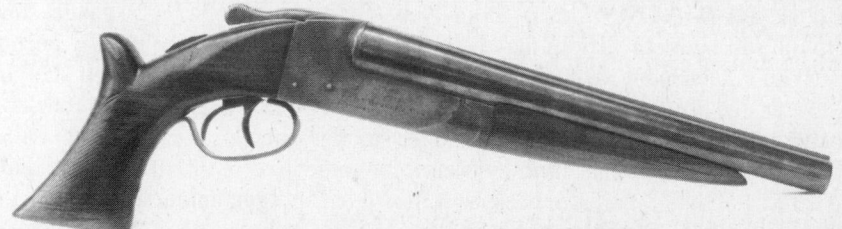

Ithaca Auto and Burglar Gun, Model A

Ithaca Gun Co.,   Ithaca, New York, 1922–34; Model A (grip spur), 2½" shells only, about 2500 manufactured; Model B (no spur), 2¾" shells, about 2000 manufactured; variations exist; values below assume 20 gauge, 10" side-by-side double barrels.

	V.G.	Exc.	Prior Edition Exc. Value
Ithaca Auto and Burglar Gun, Model A, *Class III, Curio* $1110		$1500	$850
Ithaca Auto and Burglar Gun, Model B, *Class III, Curio* 900		1200	850

Only eleven special order or nonstandard Auto and Burglar Guns have been documented. All are extremely rare and command premiums of 100% or more. Original holsters (marked Auto and Burglar Gun/MADE BY/ITHACA GUN CO./ITHACA, N.Y.) are rare and worth $300–$500.

J. Stevens Arms Co., Chicopee Falls, Massachusetts, Off-Hand from 1923–29, total production unknown, but probably fewer than 5000; Auto-Shot from 1929–34, about 2000 manufactured.

	V.G.	Exc.	Value
Off-Hand Shot Gun No. 35, .410 bore, 8″ or 12¼″ single barrel, *Class III, Curio*. 200		300	300
Auto-Shot No. 35, .410 bore, 8″ or 12¼″ single barrel, *Class III, Curio*. 250		350	300

Marble's Arms & Mfg. Co., Gladstone, Michigan, successor in 1911 to Marble Safety Axe Co. First model from 1908–14, second model from 1921–42 (total production was about 10,000 for each model). The 18″ barrel variations are exempt from the N.F.A. only if an original shoulder stock is attached.

	V.G.	Exc.	Value
Marble's Game Getter Gun, Model 1908			
12″ or 15″ barrels, *Class III, Curio*. 900		1500	—
18″ barrels, *Curio (exempt from N.F.A.)* 1000		1800	—
Marble's Game Getter Gun, Model 1921			
12″ or 15″ barrels, *Class III, Curio*. 650		850	—
18″ barrels, *Curio (exempt from N.F.A.)* 900		1000	—

Boxed guns with accessories, nonstandard calibers (.25–20, .32–20, .38–40, etc.) command premiums of 50% to 200% or more; add $75–$150 for original holster.

Remington Arms Co., Ilion, New York, circa 1867–75; 20 gauge, single shot with rolling block action; may be used as a pistol or shotgun; usually encountered with a detachable shoulder stock and classified as a "short-barreled shotgun" ($200 transfer tax) by A.T.F. in that configuration. Whether it qualifies for the $5 transfer tax if unaccompanied by a shoulder stock is unclear. It cannot be classified as a *Curio* because it is an *Antique* firearm manufactured in or before 1898, and is also a *Class III* N.F.A. firearm because it fires fixed shotgun ammunition that is currently available in ordinary commerce.

	V.G.	Exc.	Value
Remington Combination Pistol-Shotgun, 11¾″ single barrel, *Class III* . . . . . . —		RARE	—

Note: The author wishes to thank Mr. Larson for his contribution of the text and photographs in this section. For further information about smoothbore pistols, Mr. Larson may be contacted at P.O. Box 5497, Takoma Park, Maryland 20913; (301) 270–3450.

CARTRIDGES

BY R. E. MAGRUDER

Many cartridges have a more diverse and interesting historical and developmental background than the guns that fired them. Due to this fact the ranks of the cartridge collecting community continue to swell.

To a new collector the prices in this specialized field will seem quite volatile. Bear in mind that the average individual cartridge, relative to other collectibles, is inexpensive; thus one collector at an auction, attempting to complete a collection, can pay many times what the cartridge would normally bring, and distort the market. Unfortunately this is taking place continuously and with increasing frequency. The prices I have provided to you here are what collectors will pay in the open market, with discounts on large purchases common.

The prices shown are based on the average value of a single cartridge with (unless otherwise noted) a common headstamp ranging from very good to excellent condition. Rare headstamps, unusual bullets, and scarce case construction will add to the value of the item. On common cartridges, empty cases are worth about 20% to 25% of the value shown; with rare calibers the empties should bring about 75% to 80% of the price of the loaded round. Dummies and blanks are worth about the same as the value shown. Full boxes of ammunition of common types should earn a discount of 15% to 20% per cartridge, whereas full boxes of rare ammo will command a premium because of the collectibility of the box itself.

Listings with an "*" appearing in place of a price are valued at less than $1.

Note: The author wishes to thank Mr. Magruder for providing information on cartridges to our readers. For further information you may write to R.E. Magruder at 7613 Agustawood Place, Sacramento, CA 95828.

U.S. RIFLE—CURRENT MFG.

17 Remington	$1	220 Swift	$*
218 Bee	$1	22 Savage High Power (5.6 × 52 R)	$1
22 Hornet	$*	222 Remington	$*
22 PPC	$2	222 Remington Magnum	$*

223 Remington	$*	308 Winchester	$*
22-50 Remington	$*	30-06 Springfield (7.62 × 63 mm)	$*
224 Weatherby Magnum	$1	30-40 Krag	$*
225 Winchester	$1	300 H&H Magnum	$*
6mm PPC	$2	308 Norma Magnum	$2
6mm Bench Rest Remington	$1	300 Weatherby	$1
240 Remington	$1	303 Savage	$*
243 Winchester	$*	303 British	$*
6mm Remington (244 Rem)	$*	32-20 (Rifle and Revolver)	$*
25-20	$*	32 Winchester Special	$*
25-35	$*	8mm Mauser (7.92mm) (8 × 57 JS)	$*
250 Savage (250-3000)	$*	8mm Remington Magnum	$*
257 Roberts	$*	338 Winchester Magnum	$*
25-06 Remington	$*	340 Weatherby Magnum	$2
257 Weatherby Magnum	$1	348 Winchester	$1
6.5 × 55 mm Swedish Mauser	$*	35 Remington	$*
264 Winchester Magnum	$1	350 Remington	$1
270 Winchester	$*	356 Winchester	$1
7 × 64 mm	$*	358 Winchester	$1
270 Weatherby Magnum	$1	35 Whelen	$1
280 Remington (7mm Express)	$*	358 Norma Magnum	$2
7mm-08 Remington	$1	375 Holland & Holland Magnum	$*
7-30 Waters	$1	378 Weatherby Magnum	$2
7mm Mauser (7 × 57 mm)	$*	375 Winchester	$*
7 × 61 mm Sharpe Hart Super	$2	38-55 Winchester	$*
7mm Weatherby Magnum	$1	38-40 (Rifle and Revolver)	$*
7mm Remington Magnum	$*	416 Rigby	$5
284 Winchester	$1	416 Remington Magnum	$3
30 MI Carbine	$*	416 Weatherby Magnum	$5
7.62 × 39 mm Soviet	$*	44-40 Winchester (Rifle and Revolver)	$*
30 Remington	$*	444 Marlin	$1
30-30 Winchester (30 WCF)	$*	45-70 U.S. Government	$1
300 Savage	$*	460 Weatherby Magnum	$3
300 Winchester Magnum	$*	470 Nitro Express	$8
307 Winchester	$*		

U.S. RIFLE—NO LONGER MFG.

22 Winchester	$1	30 Newton	$10
22 Extra Long (Maynard)	$4	32 Long Rifle	$3
21-15-60 Stevens	$4	32 Self-Load Win.	$1
219 Zipper	$2	32 Ballard Extra Long	$3
6mm Lee Navy	$2	32 Ideal	$3
25-20 Singleshot	$2	32 Remington	$1
25-21 Stevens	$5	32 Winchester Self-Load	$*
25-25 Stevens	$5	32-30 Remington	$4
25 Remington	$1	32-35 Stevens	$4
25-36 Marlin	$2	32-40 Remington	$5
275 Holland & Holland	$5	32-40 Ballard	$8
256 Winchester	$1	32-40 Ballard	$25
256 Newton	$5	33 Winchester	$2
6.5 Remington	$2	351 Winchester SL.	$1
280 Ross	$3	35 Win SL	$1
28-30-120 Stevens	$8	35 Winchester	$1
30-30 Wesson	$55	35 Newton	$3

350 Griffin & Howe $5	44 XL Wesson $3
38 Long Center Fire . . . . $*	44-40 X Long $40
38 Ballard Extra Long $3	44-60 Sharps $5
38-35 Stevens $30	44-75 Ballard $15
38-40 Rem-Hepburn $7	44-77 Remington $10
38-45 Bullard $20	44-90 Remington $5
38-45 Stevens $50	44-90 Sharps $8
38-50 Ballard $5	44-90 Sharps 2⁷⁄₁₆ $35
38-50 Remington $3	44-95 What Cheer $125
38-56 Winchester $2	44-100 Remington $25
375 Weatherby $3	44-100 Ballard $20
38-70 Winchester $3	45-50 Peabody Sporting $8
38-72 Winchester $4	45-60 Winchester $5
38-90 Winchester Ex $12	45-70 Van Choate $150
40-50 Sharps $10	45-75 Winchester $4
40-50 Sharps (Necked) $12	45-75 Sharps Straight $35
40-60 Winchester $2	45-82 Winchester $15
40-60 Marlin $4	45-85 Winchester $10
40-60 Marlin Raised Headstamp $50	45-90 Winchester $5
40-63 Ballard $20	45-100 Ballard $25
40-65 Ballard $20	45-90 Sharps $15
40-65 Winchester $6	45-100 . . . . $20
40-70 What Cheer $85	45-100 Remington $35
40-70 Winchester $4	45-120, 125 Sharps $20
40-70 Sharps $8	45-125 Winchester $25
40-70 Sharps Bottle Neck $8	50-45 Carbine $5
40-70 Remington Brass and Steel Case $150	50-70 Government $3
40-72 Winchester $4	50-90 Sharps $20
40-82 Winchester $4	50-100 Sharps $20
40-90 Ballard $25	50-110 Sharps $30
40-90 Ballard $15	50-95 Winchester $8
40-90 Sharps (Necked) $12	50-100 Winchester $15
40-90 Sharps Straight $15	50-105 Winchester $25
40-90 What Cheer $200	50-110 Winchester $30
40-110 Winchester Ex $20	50-115 Bullard $40
401 Self-Load $2	50-140 Sharps $180
405 Winchester $2	50-140 Winchester $100
44 Henry Center Fire $75	58 Musket $5
44 Evans Short or Long $5	58 Carbine $25
44 Long, XL Ballard $4	70-150 Winchester $300

Note: Odd cartridges, having a raised headstamp, are worth many times more than values listed. Wildcats are valued from one to three times the basic case price unless headstamped.

PISTOL-REVOLVER

2.7 Kolibri $40	25 Auto . . . . $*
3 Kolibri $50	256 Winchester $1
4.25 Liliput $50	6.5 Bergmann $15
5 M/M Clement $10	7mm Nambu $15
5 M/M Bergmann $15	7mm BR . . . . $*
5.45 × 18 . . . . $5	7.62 × 25 . . . . $*
5.5 Velo Dog $1	7.62 Nagant $1
22 Jet . . . . $*	30 Mauser . . . . $*
221 Fire Ball . . . . $*	7.65 Borchardt $10

7.65 Mannlicher $1	9.8 Colt $10
30 Luger . . . . $*	40 SW . . . . $*
7.65 French . . . . $*	10mm . . . . $*
7.65 Roth Sauer $5	41 S., Long Colt $1
7.65-32 Auto . . . . $*	41 S.W. . . . . $*
32 SW S-L . . . . $*	41 Action Express $1
32 H. R. . . . . $*	10.4 Italian $2
320 Revolver . . . . $*	44 S-W American $1
32 S, L Colt . . . . $*	44 Webley $3
32-20 . . . . $*	44 S-W Russian $1
35 Smith Wesson $2	11mm French Ord. $2
7.5 Swiss $1	11mm German Ord. $15
7.5 Swedish $1	44 SPL . . . . $*
8mm Nambu $1	44 Colt $3
8mm Lebel $1	44 Magnum . . . . $*
8mm Roth Steyr $3	44 Bull Dog $3
8mm Rast Gasser $2	44 Auto Mag $2
9mm Ultra $1	11 Montenegrin $45
9mm Glisenti $1	45 Winchester . . . . $*
9mm Steyr $1	45 ACP. . . . . $*
9mm Luger. . . . . $*	45 Auto Rim. . . . . $*
9 × 21 . . . . $1	45 Colt . . . . $*
9mm Mauser $2	45 Scofield $2
9mm Federal, Rimmed. $2	454 Casull $2
9mm Browning Long. $1	45 Webley . . . . $*
9mm Bayard. $1	450 Long $2
9mm Makarov $1	455 Webley Auto $3
9mm Winchester $3	455 MKI-Colt. $3
357 Mag & Maximum . . . . $*	455 MKII . . . . $*
380 Revolver $1	476 Eley $10
38 Short, Long Colt and SPL. . . . . $*	50 Action Express $2
38 S.W. . . . . $*	50 Remington Army $8
38 Auto and Super . . . . $*	50 Remington Navy $20
380 Kurz 9 × 17 . . . . $*	

MILITARY CARTRIDGES

Bullet Diameter × case length, rim or rimless.

4.85 British. $5	7.35 Italian $1
5.45 × 39 . . . . $1	30 M-1 Carbine . . . . $*
5.56 × Nato . . . . $*	30-06 U.S. . . . . $*
5.7 × 28 . . . . $5	30-40 U.S. . . . . $*
6mm SAW $5	7.5 × 55 Swiss . . . . $*
6.5 × 53.5 . . . . $25	7.5 × 54 French . . . . $*
6.5 × 54 Greek $2	7.62 × 39 Soviet . . . . $*
6.5 × 53R Dutch $2	7.62 × 45 Czech $1
6.5 × 50 Japanese $1	7.62 × 51 Nato . . . . $*
6.5 × 55 Swedish. . . . . $*	7.62 × 53R Russian. . . . . $*
6.5 × 58 Portugese $2	303 British . . . . $*
6.5 × 52 Italian . . . . $*	7.7 × 58 Japanese $1
280 British $6	7.92 × 33 Kurz $2
7 × 57 Mauser . . . . $*	7.92 × 57 J-.318 . . . . $*
276 Enfield $10	7.92 × 57 S-.323 . . . . $*
276 Peterson. $2	7.65 × 53 Argentine . . . . $*

8 × 5OR French $1	11 × 53R Belgian $80
8 × 50R Austrian......................... $1	11 × 60 Japanese...................... $200
8 × 50R Siamese........................ $2	11.15 × 58R Spanish................... $2
8 × 52R Siamese....................... $2	11.15 × 60R Mauser $2
8 × 56R Maunlicher .... $*	11.15 × 58R Austrian $2
8 × 58R Danish......................... $1	11 × 59R French $2
8 × 60R Portugese....................... $1	577 × 450 English...................... $5
8 × 59 Breda $2	458 × 1½" Barnes $5
8 × 53R Japanese $150	11.43 × 55R Turkish................... $45
8 × 63 Swedish $3	11.4 × 50R Austrian $5
8.58 × 71 Magnum $8	11.43 × 50R Egyptian.................. $5
9.5 × 60R Turkish...................... $20	11.4 × 50R Brazilian.................. $50
10.15 × 61R Jarmann $8	11.4 × 51R Danish $10
10.15 × 63R Serbian $100	11.5 × 57R Spanish.................... $2
10.4 × 38R Swiss $3	11.3 × 50R Beaumont.................. $100
10.4 × 47 Italian $2	11 × 52R Netherlands................. $100
10.75 × 58R Russian.................... $2	50 Browning.......................... $3
11 × 50R Belgian $60	577 Snider $10

BRITISH SPORTING

Generally British cartidges give case size first, bullet size second.

297/230 Morris.......................... $1	360 Rook $2
240 Flanged $6	360 3"............................... $25
242 Rimless $10	360 2¼" $9
240 Belted $6	400/360 .... $10
244 Belted $15	360 No. 2 .... $25
246 Purdy............................. $250	400/375 .... $5
297/250 Rook........................... $1	369 Purdey........................... $20
255 Rook $3	375 Flanged 2½" $5
256 Gibbs $15	375 Flanged Magnum $8
26 Rimless BSA........................ $75	375 Rimless $4
275 Belted $5	380 Rifle............................. $2
275 Flanged $8	380 Rigby 2¼" $75
7mm Rimmed........................... $25	400 3"............................... $10
275 Rigby............................. $20	450/400 .... $10
7mm Rigby $30	450/400 3¼" $10
280 Flanged $3	450/400 3" $10
280 Rimless Jeffery (33/280)............... $5	404 Rimless $10
280 Ross.............................. $3	416 Rigby............................ $10
300 Rook $1	425 Westley Richards $10
300 Sherwood $2	500/450 3¼".......................... $15
30 H. H. Flanged $10	450 Needam........................... $150
30 Purdey............................. $65	450 No. 2 3½" $25
303 British .... $*	450 Rigby............................ $35
303 Magnum $50	500/450 No. 2 Musket $25
375/303 .... $15	500/450 No. 1 Express................. $15
310 Cadet............................. $1	577/450 .... $6
318 Rimless $2	450 Express 3¼"....................... $20
333 Flanged $25	500/465 .... $15
333 Rimless $5	470 Express $12
400/350 .... $5	475 Express $15
354 Ross $150	475 No. 2 .... $25
360 No. 3 .... $225	476 Express $20

577/500	$20	505 Gibbs	$15
500 No. 2	$15	577 Snider	$7
500 3″	$12	577 3″	$20
500 Nitro	$12	600 Nitro	$50
500 Jeffery	$100	700 Nitro	$150

METRIC RIFLE

Metric bore diameter × case length, rimmed or rimless. Many old, scarce cartridges have little interest, i.e., no value.

5.6 × 33	$2	8 × 58R	$3
5.6 × 35	$1	8 × 60R	$2
5.6 × 50	$1	8 × 54 Krag	$2
5.6 × 57	$1	8 × 56	$*
5.6 × 61	$3	8 × 57R	$1
6. × 29.5	$2	8 × 57J, JS, JRS	$1
6 × 57	$1	8 × 64	$1
6 × 58R	$30	8 × 68S	$2
244 Halger	$20	8 × 72R	$15
6 × 62	$3	8.15 × 46R	$2
6.5 × 53	$3	9 × 71	$15
6.5 × 40	$2	9 × 56	$*
6.5 × 27	$25	9 × 57R	$1
6.5 × 53.5	$25	9 × 63	$20
6.5 × 48R	$3	9 × 70	$15
6.5 × 52R	$1	9.1 × 40R	$2
6.5 × 54	$2	9.3 × 53	$1
6.5 × 57R	$1	9.3 × 72R Sauer	$20
6.5 × 58R	$3	9.3 × 57	$1
6.5 × 58	$2	9.3 × 62	$1
6.5 × 58R	$35	9.3 × 64	$2
6.5 × 61	$30	9.3 × 65R	$30
6.5 × 65R	$10	9.3 × 72R	$2
6.5 × 68	$3	9.3 × 74R	$2
7 × 33	$3	9.3 × 57	$1
7 × 57R	$1	9.3 × 73	$35
7 × 64	$3	10.25 × 69R	$5
7 × 65R	$5	10.3 × 60R Swiss	$5
7 × 66	$5	10.3 × 65R	$20
7.62 × 39	$*	10.5 × 47R	$5
7 × 75	$5	10.75 × 63	$5
7 × 72	$5	10.75 × 57	$3
7 × 73	$6	10.75 × 68	$2
30R Blaser	$5	10.75 × 65R	$15
7.7 × 60	$200	10.75 × 73	$4
8 × 48R	$2	10.8 × 47	$3
8 × 51	$2	11.2 × 60	$4
8 × 42	$2	11.2 × 72	$4
8 × 71	$10	12 × 44	$5
8 × 75R	$10	12.7 × 70	$50

RIMFIRE

Many old rimfires are of high value, but common .22 BB to Long Rifle manufactured since the turn of century are worth 10 cents to $1.

Some high-priced rimfires follow. If you question type or value, consult a collector.

14 A. J.	$15	32 Long L.	$40
177 High Std. Exper.	$50	32 Long Multiball	$40
22 Short No Headstamp S-W Mfg.	$10	32 Ex. Long Wesson	$300
22 Short Dish Base.	$10	38 Short LH	$100
22 Short Merwin's Pat	$500	38 Short R	$50
22 Short Raised AW	$20	38 Long Multiball	$40
22 Short Raised G	$60	41 Swiss Raised H	$50
22 Long Shot Wood Sabot.	$10	44 Henery Flat Raised C	$120
25-22 Win Experimental 1⅛″	$35	44 Henery Flat Raised H	$250
267 Rem U or P	$10	44 Henery Flat Raised P	$500
267 Rem Proof	$20	44 Howard Flat Raised U.	$450
267 Rem Dummy.	$35	45-45 Peaboady	$800
30 Short Raised W	$65	45-70 Peaboady	$600
30 Long Merwin's Pat.	$30	50-70 Peaboady	$1000
310 Eley Dished Base	$50	50 Ball Carbine	$100
31 Vase Base	$150	50 Naval Academy.	$150
32 Ex. Short Raised D	$75	56 46 Short Neck	$150
32 Ex. Short Raised U	$20	56-50 Spencer Raised U.	$200
32 Ex. Short Impressed D	$20	56-56 Spencer Raised U.	$150
32 Short Raised AW	$20	52-70 Sharps	$80
32 Short Raised G	$50	58 Musket CDL.	$250
32 Short Impressed C.	$25	58 Joslyn	$75
32 Short Explosive.	$175	58 Roberts Raised H	$750
32 Long Merwin's	$100	1″ Gatling.	$1500
32 Long CDL.	$40		

Some old cartridges available to the beginning collector:

36 Sharps Mule Ear	$250	54 Hunt & Jennings	$75
41 Roper Steel Case.	$150	54 Burnside	$15
50 Smith Rubber Case	$125	56 Billinghurst-Requa	$15

PAT IGNITION

31 Volcanic	$35	42 Eagle Cupfire	$10
41 Volcanic	$35	32 National Teat.	$5
50 Crispin.	$275	45 National Teat.	$125
44 Thures	$30	110 Needlefire	$15
25 Allen Lipfire	$10	90 Needlefire	$15
44 Allen Lipfire	$30	58 Schubarh	$3500
30 Eagle Cupfire	$10		

MAYNARDS

Common Maynards fall into three general types:

Model 1865—Thin rim tape primer	$*
Model 1873—Thick rim Berdan primer	$*
Model 1882—Thick rim normal primer	$*

	1965	1973	1982
35-30	$15	$20	$20
40-40	15	25	30
50-50	5	300	100
55 Shot	25	25	400
64 Shot	20	25	25

Note: There are many variations as to powder capacity and case construction that will double or triple price of case, size and type.

SHOTGUN GAUGES

The gauge of a shotgun or any smoothbore was standardized in the last half of the nineteenth century in England by the Gun Barrel Proof Act of 1868. Until that time the general rule of thumb among gunmakers was the formula that gauge was the number of round lead balls of a given bore diameter in a pound. This still holds true with the exception of the obsolete letter gauges, and .410 gauge which is the actual bore diameter.

Gauge	Diameter	Gauge	Diameter
A	2.000″	21	.605″
B	1.938″	22	.596″
C	1.875″	23	.587″
D	1.813″	24	.579″
E	1.750″	25	.571″
F	1.688″	26	.563″
1	1.669″	27	.556″
H	1.625″	28	.550″
J	1.563″	29	.543″
K	1.500″	30	.537″
L	1.438″	31	.531″
M	1.375″	32	.526″
2	1.325″	33	.520″
O	1.313″	34	.515″
P	1.250″	35	.510″
3	1.157″	36	.506″
4	1.052″	37	.501″
5	.976″	38	.497″
6	.919″	39	.492″
7	.873″	40	.488″
8	.835″	41	.484″
9	.803″	42	.480″
10	.775″	43	.476″
11	.751″	44	.473″
12	.729″	45	.469″
13	.710″	46	.466″
14	.693″	47	.463″
15	.677″	48	.459″
16	.662″	49	.456″
17	.649″	50	.453″
18	.637″		
19	.626″		
20	.615″	.410	.410″

A

A & R SALES South El Monte, Calif. Current.

HANDGUN, SEMI-AUTOMATIC

Government, .45 ACP, Lightweight, Patterned After Colt Govt.
Model, Modern.. $175 $225 $225

RIFLE, SEMI-AUTOMATIC

Mark IV Sporter, .308 Win., Clip Fed, Version of M-14, Adjustable
Sights, Modern... 225   295   295

ABBEY, GEORGE T. Chicago, Ill. 1858–1875.

RIFLE, PERCUSSION

.44, Double Barrel, Over-Under, Brass Furniture, Antique....................... 700   1,050   1,050
.44, Octagon Barrel, Brass Furniture, Antique.................................... 400   575   575

ABBEY, J.F. & CO. Chicago, Ill. 1858–1875. Also made by Abbey & Foster.

RIFLE, PERCUSSION

Various Calibers, Antique... 300   450   450

SHOTGUN, PERCUSSION

Various Gauges, Antique... 350   500   500

ABILENNE See Mossberg.

ACHA Domingo Acha y Cia., Ermua, Spain 1927–1937.

HANDGUN, SEMI-AUTOMATIC

Ruby M1916, 7.65mm, Clip Fed, Curio.................................... 150   200   150

ACME Made by Hopkins & Allen, Sold by Merwin & Hulbert, c. 1880.

HANDGUN, REVOLVER

.22 Short R.F., 7 Shot, Spur Trigger, Solid Frame, Single Action,
Antique.. 95   150   150
.32 Short R.F., 5 Shot, Spur Trigger, Solid Frame, Single Action,
Antique.. 95   165   165

	V.G.	Exc	Prior Edition

ACME ARMS Sold by J. Stevens Arms Co. and Cornwall Hardware Co., c. 1880.

HANDGUN, REVOLVER

	V.G.	Exc	Prior Edition
.22 Short R.F., 7 Shot, Spur Trigger, Solid Frame, Single Action, Antique	$200	$250	$160
.32 Short R.F., 5 Shot, Spur Trigger, Solid Frame, Single Action, Antique	225	275	175

SHOTGUN, DOUBLE BARREL, SIDE-BY-SIDE

	V.G.	Exc	Prior Edition
12 Gauge, Damascus Barrel, Antique	175	225	195

ACME HAMMERLESS Made by Hopkins & Allen for Hulbert Bros. 1893.

HANDGUN, REVOLVER

	V.G.	Exc	Prior Edition
.32 S & W, 5 Shot, Top Break, Hammerless, Double Action, 2½" Barrel, Antique	100	150	145
.38 S & W, 5 Shot, Top Break, Hammerless, Double Action, 3" Barrel, Antique	100	150	145

ACRA Tradename used by Reinhard Fajen of Warsaw, Mo., c. 1970.

RIFLE, BOLT ACTION

	V.G.	Exc	Prior Edition
M18, Various Calibers, Santa Barbara Barreled Action, Mannlicher Checkered Stock, Modern	175	275	275
RA, Various Calibers, Santa Barbara Barreled Action, Checkered Stock, Modern	125	200	200
S24, Various Calibers, Santa Barbara Barreled Action, Fancy Checkering, Modern	150	225	225

ACTION Modesto Santos; Eibar, Spain.

HANDGUN, SEMI-AUTOMATIC

	V.G.	Exc	Prior Edition
#2, 7.65mm, Clip Fed, Curio	125	225	225
Model 1920, .25 ACP, Clip Fed, Curio	75	150	150

ADAMS Made by Deane, Adams, & Deane, London, England.

HANDGUN, PERCUSSION

	V.G.	Exc	Prior Edition
12.4mm Beaumont–Adams, Revolver, Double Action, 7½" Barrel, Antique	1,200	1,500	850
12.4mm Beaumont–Adams, Revolver, Double Action, 7½" Barrel, Antique	1,500	1,750	1,200
12.4mm M1851, Revolver, Double Action, 7½" Barrel, Antique	800	1,200	775
12.4mm M1851, Revolver, Double Action, 7½" Barrel, Cased with Accessories, Antique	1,200	1,400	800
8.1mm Pocket, Revolver, Double Action, 4½" Barrel, Antique	750	1,000	1,000
8.1mm, Revolver, Double Action, 4½" Barrel, Cased with Accessories, Antique	850	1,200	1,200

	V.G.	Exc	Prior Edition

ADAMS, JOSEPH Birmingham, England 1767–1813.

RIFLE, FLINTLOCK

.65 Officers Model Brown Bess, Musket, Military, Antique..................	$1,750	$2,750	$1,750

ADAMY GEBRUDER Suhl, Germany 1921–1939.

SHOTGUN, DOUBLE BARREL, OVER-UNDER

12 and 16 Ga., Automatic Ejector, Double Trigger, Engraved, Cased, Curio....................	1,750	2,000	2,100

ADIRONDACK ARMS CO. Plattsburg, N.Y. 1870–1874. Purchased by Winchester 1874.

RIFLE, LEVER ACTION

Robinson 1875 Patent, First Model, Various Rimfires, Octagon Barrel, Open Rear Sight, Antique....................	2,000	2,500	1,250
Robinson Patent, Second Model, Various Calibers, Octagon Barrel, Antique....................	1,500	2,000	1,300

ADLER Engelbrecht & Wolff; Zella St. Blasii, Germany 1905–1906.

HANDGUN, SEMI-AUTOMATIC

7.25 Adler, Clip Fed, Curio....................	2,500	3,500	2,000

AERTS, JAN Maastricht, Holland, c. 1650.

HANDGUN, FLINTLOCK

Ornate Pair, Very Long Ebony Full Stock, Silver Inlay, High Quality, Antique....................	—	RARE	—

AETNA Made by Harrington & Richardson, c. 1870-1890.

HANDGUN, REVOLVER

.22 Short R.F., 7 Shot, Spur Trigger, Solid Frame, Single Action, Antique....................	200	250	100
Aetna 2, .32 Short R.F., 5 Shot, Spur Trigger, Solid Frame, Single Action, Antique....................	225	275	150
Aetna 2½, .32 Short R.F., 5 Shot, Spur Trigger, Solid Frame, Single Action, Antique....................	225	275	150

AETNA ARMS CO. N.Y.C., c. 1880.

HANDGUN, REVOLVER

.22 Short R.F., 7 Shot, Spur Trigger, Tip-Up Barrel, Antique..................	225	350	350
.32 Short R.F., 5 Shot, Spur Trigger, Tip-Up Barrel, Antique..................	250	375	375

	V.G.	Exc	Prior Edition

AFFERBACH, WILLIAM Philadelphia, Pa. 1860–1866.
HANDGUN, PERCUSSION
.41 Derringer, Full Stock, Antique.. $450 $650 $650

AGAWAM ARMS Agawam, Mass., c. 1970.
RIFLE, SINGLESHOT
Model M-68, .22 L.R.R.F., Lever Action, Open Sights, Modern.............. 35 65 65
Model M-68M, .22 W.M.R., Lever Action, Open Sights, Modern........... 45 75 75

AJAX ARMY Maker Unknown, Sold by E. C. Meacham Co., c. 1880.
HANDGUN, REVOLVER
.44 R.F., 5 Shot, 7" Barrel, Spur Trigger, Solid Frame, Single Action,
Antique... 400 500 250

AKRILL, E. Probably St. Etienne, France, c. 1810.
RIFLE, FLINTLOCK
.69, Smoothbore, Octagon Barrel, Damascus Barrel, Breech Loader,
Plain, Antique.. 1,000 2,500 2,500

ALAMO Tradename used by Stoeger Arms, c. 1958.
HANDGUN, REVOLVER
Alamo, .22 L.R.R.F., Double Action, Ribbed Barrel, Modern................. 50 125 50

ALASKA Made by Hood Firearms, Sold by E. C. Meacham Co. 1873–1882.
HANDGUN, REVOLVER
.22 Short R.F., 7 Shot, Spur Trigger, Solid Frame, Single Action,
Antique... 125 175 150

ALASKAN Skinner's Sportsman's Supply, Juneau, Alaska, C. 1970.
RIFLE, BOLT ACTION
Carbine, Various Calibers, Checkered Stock, Sling Swivels,
Modern.. 225 300 300
Magnum, Various Calibers, Checkered Stock, Recoil Pad, Sling
Swivels, Modern.. 225 300 300
Standard, Various Calibers, Checkered Stock, Sling Swivels,
Modern.. 195 295 295

ALBRECHT, ANDREW Lancaster, Pa. 1779–1782. See Kentucky
Rifles and Pistols.

ALBRIGHT, HENRY Lancaster, Pa. 1740–1745. See Kentucky Rifles and Pistols.

ALDENDERFER, M. Lancaster, Pa. 1763–1784. See Kentucky Rifles and Pistols.

ALERT Made by Hood Firearms Co., C. 1874.

HANDGUN, REVOLVER

.22 Short R.F., 7 Shot, Spur Trigger, Solid Frame, Single Action,
Antique.. $175 $200 $200

ALEXIA Made by Hopkins & Allen, c. 1880.

HANDGUN, REVOLVER

.22 Short R.F., 7 Shot, Spur Trigger, Solid Frame, Single Action,
Antique.. 150 175 175
.32 Short R.F., 5 Shot, Spur Trigger, Solid Frame, Single Action,
Antique.. 150 175 175
.38 Short R.F., 5 Shot, Spur Trigger, Solid Frame, Single Action,
Antique.. 150 175 175
.41 Short R.F., 5 Shot, Spur Trigger, Solid Frame, Single Action,
Antique.. 150 225 225

ALEXIS Made by Hood Firearms Co., Sold by Turner & Ross Co. Boston, Mass.

HANDGUN, REVOLVER

.22 Short R.F., 7 Shot, Spur Trigger, Solid Frame, Single Action,
Antique.. 125 175 150

ALFA Adolf Frank, Hamburg, Germany, c. 1900.

HANDGUN, MANUAL REPEATER

"Reform" Type, .230 C.F., Four-barreled Repeater, Engraved,
Curio... 150 250 250

HANDGUN, SEMI-AUTOMATIC

Pocket, 6.35mm, Clip Fed, Blue, Curio.. 100 150 150

RIFLE, PERCUSSION

Back-lock, Various Calibers, Carved, Inlaid Stock, Imitation
Damascus Barrel, Antique... 95 150 150
Back-lock, Various Calibers, Imitation Damascus Barrel,
Antique.. 75 100 100

	V.G.	Exc	Prior Edition

SHOTGUN, PERCUSSION

	V.G.	Exc	Prior Edition
Double Barrel, Various Gauges, Back-lock, Double Triggers, Damascus Barrels, Antique....................	$75	$125	$125
Double Barrel, Various Gauges, Back-lock, Double Triggers, Damascus Barrels, Carved Stock, Engraved, Antique............	125	175	175

SHOTGUN, DOUBLE BARREL, SIDE-BY-SIDE

Greener Boxlock, Various Gauges, Checkered Stock, Double Triggers, Curio............	150	200	200
Greener Boxlock, Various Gauges, Checkered Stock, Double Triggers, Engraved, Curio............	175	265	265

SHOTGUN, SINGLESHOT

Nuss Underlever, Various Gauges, Tip-Down Barrel, No Forestock, Curio............	50	65	65
Roux Underlever, Various Gauges, Tip-Down Barrel, No Forestock, Curio............	50	55	55
Sidebutton, Various Gauges, Tip-Down Barrel, No Forestock, Curio............	50	60	60

ALFA Armero Especialistas Reunidas, Eibar, Apain, c. 1920.

HANDGUN, REVOLVER

Colt Police Positive Type, .38, Double Action, Blue, Curio............	100	150	125
S. & W. #2 Type, Various Calibers, Double Action, Blue, BreakTop, Curio............	125	175	150
S. & W. M & P Type, .38, Double Action, 6 Shot, Blue, Curio............	100	150	125

ALKARTASUNA Spain. Made by Alkartasuna Fabrica De Armas 1910–1922

HANDGUN, SEMI-AUTOMATIC

Alkar 1924, 6.35mm, Cartridge Counter, Grips, Clip Fed, Curio............	225	350	350
Pocket, 7.65mm, Clip Fed, Long Grip, Curio............	125	175	175
Pocket, 7.65mm, Clip Fed, Short Grip, Curio............	125	175	175
Vest Pocket, 6.35mm, Clip Fed, Modern............	95	155	155
Vest Pocket, 6.35mm, Clip Fed, Cartridge Counter, Modern............	125	200	200

ALL RIGHT FIREARMS CO. Lawrence, Mass., c. 1876.

HANDGUN, REVOLVER

Little All Right Palm Pistol, .22 Short R.F., Squeeze Trigger, 5 Shot, Antique............	700	850	775

ALLEGHENY WORKS Allegheny, Pa. 1836–1875. See Kentucky Rifles and Pistols.

	V.G.	Exc	Prior Edition

ALLEN Made by Hopkins & Allen, c. 1880.

HANDGUN, REVOLVER

22 Short R.F., 7 Shot, Spur Trigger, Solid Frame, Single Action, Antique... $75 $165 $165

ALLEN Tradename used by McKeown's Guns of Pekin, Ill., c. 1970.

SHOTGUN, DOUBLE BARREL, OVER-UNDER

MCK 68, 12 Ga., Vent Rib, Double Triggers, Plain, Modern.................. 175 275 275
Olympic 68, 12 Ga., Vent Rib, Single Selective Trigger, Automatic Ejectors, Checkered Stock, Engraved, Modern........................ 250 425 425
S201, Various Gauges, Vent Rib, Double Triggers, Checkered Stock, Light Engraving, Modern... 225 375 375
S201 Deluxe, Various Gauges, Vent Rib, Single Trigger, Automatic Ejectors, Checkered Stock, Engraved, Modern......................... 300 450 450

ALLEN & THURBER Grafton, Mass. 1837–1842, Norwich, Conn. 1842-1847.

HANDGUN, PERCUSSION

.28, Singleshot, Bar Hammer, Various Barrel Lengths, Half-Octagon Barrel, Antique.. 600 650 285
.28 (Grafton) Pepperbox, 6 Shot, 3" Barrel, Antique..................... 1,750 2,000 1,700
.28 (Norwich) Pepperbox, 6 Shot, Bar Hammer, 3" Barrel, Antique... 600 675 600
.28 (Norwich) Pepperbox, 6 Shot, Hammerless, 3" Barrel, Antique... 1,250 1,500 675
.31, "In-Line" Singleshot, Center Hammer, Various Barrel Lengths, Half-Octagon Barrel, Antique........................... 450 400 325
.31, Singleshot, Tube Hammer, Various Barrel Lengths, Half-Octagon Barrel, Antique.. 1,000 1,250 1,000
.31, Singleshot, Under Hammer, Various Barrel Lengths, Half-Octagon Barrel, Antique.. 750 850 650
.31, Singleshot, Under Hammer, Various Barrel Lengths, Saw-Handle Grip, Half-Octagon Barrel, Antique.................... 800 900 475
.31 (Grafton) Pepperbox, 6 Shot, 3" Barrel, Antique..................... 1,000 1,250 1,000
.31 (Norwich) Pepperbox, 6 Shot, Bar Hammer, 3" Barrel, Antique... 295 650 650
.31 (Norwich) Pepperbox, 6 Shot, Hammerless, 3" Barrel, Antique... 600 675 775
.34, Singleshot, Side Hammer, Various Barrel Lengths, Half-Octagon Barrel, Antique.. 600 700 500
.36, Singleshot, Bar Hammer, Various Barrel Lengths, Half-Octagon Barrel, Antique.. 600 650 275
.36, Singleshot, Center Hammer, Various Barrel Lengths, Half-Octagon Barrel, Antique.. 150 300 300
.36 (Grafton) Pepperbox, 6" Barrel, Antique......................... 1,250 1,500 1,250
.36 (Norwich) Pepperbox, 6 Shot, Bar Hammer, 6" Barrel, Antique... 850 1,000 800
.36 (Norwich) Pepperbox, 6 Shot, Ring Trigger, 6" Barrel, Antique... 1,250 1,500 1,100

	V.G.	Exc	Prior Edition
.41, Singleshot, Side Hammer, Various Barrel Lengths, Half-Octagon Barrel, Antique.........	$625	$700	$450

ALLEN & THURBER Worcester, Mass. 1855–1856.

COMBINATION WEAPON, PERCUSSION

Over-Under, Various Calibers, Rifle and Shotgun Barrels, Antique.........	1,750	2,000	1,600

HANDGUN, PERCUSSION

.28, Pepperbox, Bar.Hammer, Various Barrel Lengths, 5 Shot, Antique.	450	500	475
.31, Pepperbox, Bar Hammer, 5 Shot, Various Barrel Lengths, Antique.........	400	450	400
.31, Pepperbox, Ring Hammerless, 6 Shot, Antique.........	1,000	1,250	600
.31, Pepperbox, Thumb Hammer, 5 Shot, Various Barrel Lengths, Antique.........	850	950	550
.34, Pepperbox, Bar Hammer, Various Barrel Lengths, 4 Shot, Antique.........	250	550	550
.36, Target Pistol, 12" Octagon Barrel, Adjustable Sights, Detachable Shoulder Stock, Antique.........	4,000	4,500	1,750

RIFLE, PERCUSSION

.43, Singleshot, Sporting Rifle, Antique.........	475	725	725

ALLEN & WHEELOCK Worcester, Mass. 1856–1865.

HANDGUN, PERCUSSION

.25, Pepperbox, 4" Barrel, 5 Shot, Antique.........	475	550	450
.28, Revolver, Side Hammer, Octagon Barrel, 3" Barrel, 5 Shot, Antique.........	150	600	375
.31, Revolver, Bar Hammer, Octagon Barrel, 2¼" Barrel, 5 Shot, Antique.........	150	400	300
.31, Revolver, Side Hammer, Octagon Barrel, 3" Barrel, 5 Shot, Antique.........	150	400	400
.34, Revolver, Bar Hammer, Octagon Barrel, 4" Barrel, 5 Shot, Antique.........	225	400	400
.34, Revolver, Bar Hammer, Octagon Barrel, 4" Barrel, 5 Shot, Antique.........	225	400	400
.36, Pepperbox, 6" Barrel, 6 Shot, Antique.........	1,000	1,250	750
.36, Revolver, Center Hammer, Octagon Barrel, 5" Barrel, 6 Shot, Spur Trigger, Antique.........	175	2,000	450
.36, Revolver, Center Hammer, Octagon Barrel, 7½" Barrel, 6 Shot, Antique.........	400	1,500	900
.36, Revolver, Side Hammer, Octagon Barrel, 6" Barrel, 6 Shot, Antique.........	400	1,750	800
.44, Revolver, Center Hammer, Half-Octagon Barrel, 7½" Barrel, 6 Shot, Antique.........	425	2,000	950

HANDGUN, REVOLVER

.22 Short R.F., 7 Shot, Side Hammer, Solid Frame, Antique.........	125	275	275
.25 L.F., 7 Shot, Side Hammer, Solid Frame, Antique.........	500	550	475
.32 L.F., 6 Shot, Side Hammer, Solid Frame, Antique.........	675	750	600
.32 Short R.F., 6 Shot, Side Hammer, Solid Frame, Antique.........	300	350	275
.36 L.F., 6 Shot, Side Hammer, Solid Frame, Antique.........	1,000	1,250	650

	V.G.	Exc	Prior Edition
.38 Short R.F., 6 Shot, Side Hammer, Solid Frame, Antique..................	$1,250	$1,500	$300
.44 L.F., 6 Shot, Side Hammer, Solid Frame, Antique............................	1,500	1,750	1,100
.44 Short R.F., 6 Shot, Side Hammer, Solid Frame, Antique.................	2,000	2,500	350

HANDGUN, SINGLESHOT

.22 Short R.F., Derringer, Spur Trigger, Antique.....................................	325	350	300
.22 Short R.F., Large Frame, Spur Trigger, Antique...............................	150	250	250
.32 Short R.F., Derringer, Spur Trigger, Antique.....................................	300	350	550
.32 Short R.F., Large Frame, Spur Trigger, Antique...............................	275	300	250
.41 Short R.F., Derringer, Spur Trigger, Antique.....................................	850	1,000	450

RIFLE, PERCUSSION

.36 Allen Patent, Carbine, Drop Breech Loader, Antique......................	750	850	850
.36 Allen Patent, Drop Breech Loader, Sporting Rifle, Antique..............	650	750	850
.38 Sidehammer, Plains Rifle, Iron Mounted, Walnut Stock, Antique........	1,250	1,500	525
.44 Center Hammer, Octagon Barrel, Iron Frame, Antique....................	750	850	600
.44 Revolver, Carbine, 6 Shot, Antique...	10,000	12,500	9,900

RIFLE, REVOLVING

.44 L.F., Walnut Stock, 6 Shot, Antique...	8,500	10,000	7,000

RIFLE, SINGLESHOT

.22 R.F., Falling Block, Sporting Rifle, Antique.......................................	300	500	500
.38 R.F., Falling Block, Sporting Rifle, Antique.......................................	285	400	400
.62 Allen R.F., Falling Block, Sporting Rifle, Antique............................	275	450	450
.64 Allen R.F., Falling Block, Sporting Rifle, Antique............................	275	450	450

SHOTGUN, PERCUSSION

12 Ga. Double, Hammers, Light Engraving, Antique...............................	525	600	425

SHOTGUN, DOUBLE BARREL, SIDE-BY-SIDE

12 Ga., Checkered Stock, Hammers, Double Triggers, Antique..............	525	600	425

ALLEN, C. B. Springfield, Mass. 1836–1841. See U.S. Military, Elgin.

HANDGUN, PERCUSSION

.36 Cochran Turret, 7 Shot, 4¾" Barrel, Antique....................................	7,500	10,000	8,500
.40 Cochran Turret, 7 Shot, 5" Barrel, Antique......................................	10,000	12,000	9,800

RIFLE, PERCUSSION

.40 Cochran Turret, 7 Shot, Octagon Barrel, Antique...........................	5,500	8,000	8,000
.40 Cochran Turret, 9 Shot, Octagon Barrel, Antique...........................	5,800	8,000	8,000

ALLEN, ETHAN Grafton, Mass. 1835–1837, E. Allen & Co. Worcester, Mass. 1865–1871. Became Forhand and Wadsworth Co.

HANDGUN, PERCUSSION

.31, Pepperbox, 6 Shot, 3" Barrel, Antique...	650	750	900
.36, Pepperbox, 6 Shot, 5" Barrel, Antique...	1,000	1,250	1,000
First Model Pocket "Rifle" Various Calibers, Various Barrel Lengths, Under Hammer, Singleshot, Saw Handle Grip, Antique............	650	750	450
Second Model Pocket "Rifle" .31, Singleshot, Under Hammer, Half–Octagon Barrel, Antique...	750	850	625

	V.G.	Exc	Prior Edition

HANDGUN, REVOLVER

.22 Short R.F., 7 Shot, Side Hammer, Sheath Trigger, Antique............... $300 $375 $250
.32 Short R.F., 6 Shot, Side Hammer, Sheath Trigger, Antique............... 275 325 250

HANDGUN, SINGLESHOT

Derringer, .32 Short R.F., Side-Swing Barrel, Half-Octagon Barrel,
Antique...................... 300 350 250
Derringer, .32 Short R.F., Side-Swing Barrel, Octagon Barrel,
Antique...................... 250 300 650
Derringer, .41 Short R.F., Side-Swing Barrel, Round Barrel,
Antique...................... 800 900 325
Derringer, .41 Short R.F., Side-Swing Barrel, Half-Octagon Barrel,
Antique...................... 750 850 475
Derringer, .41 Short R.F., Side-Swing Barrel, Octagon Barrel,
Antique...................... 850 950 325

RIFLE, SINGLESHOT

Sidehammer Muzzleloader, .38 Caliber, Sporting Rifle, Antique......... 1,000 1,250 1,200

ALLEN, SILAS Shrewsbury, Mass. 1796–1843. See Kentucky Rifles and Pistols.

ALLIES Berasaluze Areitio-Arutena y Cia., Eibar, Spain, c. 1920.

HANDGUN, SEMI-AUTOMATIC

Model 1924, .25 ACP, Clip Fed, Curio..................... 75 175 175
Pocket, .32 ACP, Clip Fed, Curio..................... 75 175 175
Vest Pocket, .25 ACP, Clip Fed, Curio..................... 75 150 150
Vest Pocket, .32 ACP, Clip Fed, Short Grip, Curio..................... 75 150 150

ALPINE INDUSTRIES Los Angeles, Calif. 1962–1965.

RIFLE, SEMI-AUTOMATIC

M-1 Carbine, .30 Carbine, Clip Fed, Military Style, Modern.................. 150 250 250

ALSOP, C.R. Middleton, Conn. 1858–1866

HANDGUN, PERCUSSION

.36 Navy, 5 Shot, Octagon Barrel, Spur Trigger, Top Hammer, Safety,
Antique...................... 1,500 2,000 1,750
.36 Navy, 5 Shot, Octagon Barrel, Spur Trigger, Top Hammer, No
Safety, Antique...................... 1,500 1,800 1,400
.36 Pocket, 5 Shot, Octagon Barrel, Spur Trigger, Antique..................... 575 750 750

AMERICA Made by Bliss & Goodyear, c. 1878.

HANDGUN, REVOLVER

.22 Short R.F., 7 Shot, Spur Trigger, Solid Frame, Single Action,
Antique...................... 95 175 175

	V.G.	Exc	Prior Edition

AMERICA Made by Norwich Falls Pistol Co., c. 1880.

HANDGUN, REVOLVER

.32 Long R.F., Double Action, Solid Frame, Antique.............................	$75	$125	$125

AMERICAN ARMS & AMMUNITION CO. Miami,

Florida, c. 1979. Successors to North Armament Corp. (Norarmco)

HANDGUN, SEMI-AUTOMATIC

TP-70, .22 L.R.R.F., Double Action, Stainless, Clip Fed, Modern...........	175	275	275
TP-70, .25 ACP, Double Action, Stainless, Clip Fed, Modern.................	150	250	250

AMERICAN ARMS CO. Boston, Mass. 1861–1897, Milwaukee,

Wisc. 1897–1901. Purchased by Marlin 1901.

HANDGUN, DOUBLE BARREL, OVER-UNDER

Wheeler Pat, .22 Short R.F., 32 Short R.F., Brass Frame, Spur Trigger, Antique......................	425	500	500
Wheeler Pat, .32 Short R.F., Brass Frame, Spur Trigger, Antique...........	450	500	500
Wheeler Pat, .41 Short R.F., Brass Frame, Spur Trigger, Antique...........	600	650	650

HANDGUN, REVOLVER

.32 S & W, 5 Shot, Double Action, Top Break, Antique...........................	125	175	125
.32 S & W, 5 Shot, Double Action, Top Break, Hammerless, Antique................	175	225	175
.32 S & W, 5 Shot, Single Action, Top Break, Spur Trigger, Antique................	150	200	150

SHOTGUN, DOUBLE BARREL, SIDE-BY-SIDE

12 Ga., Semi-Hammerless, Checkered Stock, Antique...........................	550	600	600
Whitmore Patent, 10 Ga., 27/8, Hammerless, Checkered Stock, Antique................	550	625	625
Whitmore Patent, 12 Ga., Hammerless, Checkered Stock, Antique................	450	675	675

SHOTGUN, SINGLESHOT

12 Ga., Semi-Hammerless, Checkered Stock, Antique...........................	200	250	250

AMERICAN ARMS INTERNATIONAL Salt Lake City,

Utah, Current.

RIFLE, SEMI-AUTOMATIC

American 180, .22 L.R.R.F., 177 Round Drum Magazine, Peep Sights, Modern........................	500	600	600
Extra Magazine, Add $50-$75			
Laser-Lok, Sight System, Add $350-$450			

	V.G.	Exc	Prior Edition

AMERICAN BARLOCK WONDER Made by Crescent for
Sears-Roebuck & Co.

SHOTGUN, DOUBLE BARREL, SIDE-BY-SIDE

	V.G.	Exc	Prior Edition
Various Gauges, Hammerless, Damascus Barrel, Modern........................	$150	$225	$225
Various Gauges, Hammerless, Steel Barrel, Modern..............................	240	275	275
Various Gauges, Outside Hammers, Damascus Barrel, Modern.............	150	225	225
Various Gauges, Outside Hammers, Steel Barrel, Modern......................	175	250	250

SHOTGUN, SINGLESHOT

	V.G.	Exc	Prior Edition
Various Gauges, Hammer, Steel Barrel, Modern.....................................	125	150	150

AMERICAN BOY Made by Bliss & Goodyear for Townley Hdw. Co.

HANDGUN, REVOLVER

	V.G.	Exc	Prior Edition
.32 Short R.F., Single Action, Solid Frame, Spur Trigger, 7 Shot, Antique...	100	125	125

AMERICAN BULLDOG Made by Johnson, Bye & Co., Worcester,
Mass. 1882–1900.

HANDGUN, REVOLVER

	V.G.	Exc	Prior Edition
.22 Short R.F., 7 Shot, Spur Trigger, Solid Frame, Single Action, Antique...	100	175	175
.32 S & W, 5 Shot, Spur Trigger, Solid Frame, Single Action, Curio...	100	150	150
.32 S & W, 5 Shot, Spur Trigger, Solid Frame, Single Action, Curio...	100	150	150
.32 Short R.F., 5 Shot, Spur Trigger, Solid Frame, Single Action, Antique...	100	175	175
.38 Short R.F., 5 Shot, Spur Trigger, Solid Frame, Single Action, Antique...	100	175	175
.41 Short C.F., 5 Shot, Spur Trigger, Solid Frame, Single Action, Antique...	100	200	200

AMERICAN CHAMPION

SHOTGUN, SINGLESHOT

	V.G.	Exc	Prior Edition
M1899, 12 Gauge, Plain, Modern...	75	100	100

AMERICAN DERRINGER CORP. Waco, Texas 1979 to
date.

HANDGUN, DOUBLE BARREL, OVER-UNDER

	V.G.	Exc	Prior Edition
Model AD, .32 S & W Long, Remington Style Derringer, Stainless Steel, Spur Trigger, Hammer, Modern......................................	150	175	175
Model AD, .357 Mag., Remington Style Derringer, Stainless Steel, Spur Trigger, Hammer, Modern..	150	175	175

	V.G.	Exc	Prior Edition
Model AD, .38 Spec., Remington Style Derringer, Stainless Steel, Spur Trigger, Hammer, Modern.....................	$150	$175	$175
Model AD, .41 Mag., Remington Style Derringer, Stainless Steel, Spur Trigger, Hammer, Modern.....................	175	275	275
Model AD, .44 Mag., Remington Style Derringer, Stainless Steel, Spur Trigger, Hammer, Modern.....................	200	275	275

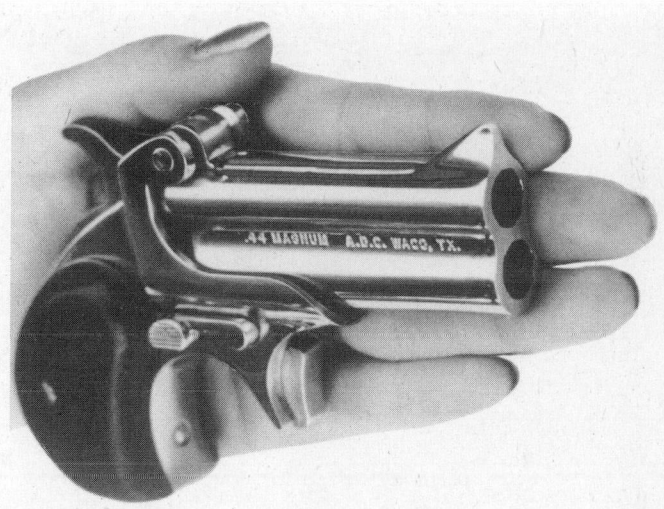

American Derringer AD, . 44 Magnum

Model AD, .45 ACP., Remington Style Derringer, Stainless Steel, Spur Trigger, Hammer, Modern.....................	150	200	200
Model AD, .45 Win Mag.., Remington Style Derringer, Stainless Steel, Spur Trigger, Hammer, Modern.....................	225	350	350
Model ADL, Various Calibers, Remington Style Derringer, Stainless Steel, Lightweight, Spur Trigger, Hammer, Modern.....................	125	150	150

HANDGUN, SEMI-AUTOMATIC

Model ADBS, .25 ACP, Clip Fed, Blue, Modern.....................	50	75	75
Model ADM, .250 Mag., Clip Fed, Stainless Steel, Modern.....................	75	125	125
Model ADMB, .250 Mag., Clip Fed, Blue, Modern.....................	50	75	75

	V.G.	Exc	Prior Edition
Model ADSS, .25 ACP, Clip Fed, Stainless Steel, Modern......	$50	$75	$75

American Derringer ADSS, .25 Auto

HANDGUN, SINGLESHOT

Model ADS, Various Calibers, Remington Style Derringer, Stainless Steel, Spur Trigger, Hammer, Modern......	125	150	150

AMERICAN EAGLE Made by Hopkins & Allen 1870–1898.

HANDGUN, REVOLVER

.22 Short R.F., 7 Shot, Spur Trigger, Solid Frame, Single Action, Antique......	125	175	175
.32 Short R.F., 5 Shot, Spur Trigger, Solid Frame, Single Action, Antique......	150	200	200

AMERICAN FIREARMS CO. San Antonio, Texas 1966–1974.

HANDGUN, SEMI-AUTOMATIC

.22 L.R.R.F., Clip Fed, Stainless Steel, Modern......	75	150	150
.25 ACP, Clip Fed, Blue, Modern......	125	150	150
.25 ACP, Clip Fed, Stainless Steel, Modern......	150	175	175
.380 ACP, Clip Fed, Stainless Steel, Modern......	500	600	300

	V.G.	Exc	Prior Edition

AMERICAN GUN CO. Made by Crescent Firearms Co. Sold By H. & D. Folsom Co.

HANDGUN, REVOLVER

.32 S & W, 5 Shot, Double Action, Top Break, Curio.............................	$150	$175	$175

SHOTGUN, DOUBLE BARREL, SIDE-BY-SIDE

Various Gauges, Hammerless, Damascus Barrel, Curio.........................	150	200	200
Various Gauges, Hammerless, Steel Barrel, Curio....................................	225	250	250
Various Gauges, Outside Hammers, Damascus Barrel, Curio.................	150	200	200
Various Gauges, Outside Hammers, Steel Barrel, Curio.........................	200	250	250

SHOTGUN, SINGLESHOT

Various Gauges, Hammer, Steel Barrel, Curio..	55	85	85

AMERICAN STANDARD TOOL CO. Newark, N.J. 1865–1870, Successor to Manhattan Firearms Co.

HANDGUN, PERCUSSION

Hero, .34, Screw Barrel, Center Hammer, Spur Trigger, Antique............	100	200	200

HANDGUN, REVOLVER

.22 Short R.F., 7 Shot, Spur Trigger, Tip-Up, Antique............................	250	375	375

AMERICUS Made by Hopkins & Allen 1870–1900.

HANDGUN, REVOLVER

.22 Short R.F., 7 Shot, Spur Trigger, Solid Frame, Single Action, Antique................	100	150	150
.32 Short R.F., 5 Shot, Spur Trigger, Solid Frame, Single Action, Antique................	100	175	175

AMSDEN, B.W. Saratoga Springs, N.Y. 1852.

COMBINATION WEAPON, PERCUSSION

.40-16 Ga., Double Barrel, Rifled, Antique..............................	650	900	900

RIFLE, PERCUSSION

.40, Octagon Barrel, Set Trigger, Rifled, Antique.....................................	400	600	600

A M T Arcadia Machine & Tool, since 1976 in Arcadia, Calif. See AutoMag.

HANDGUN, SEMI-AUTOMATIC

Back Up, .22 L.R.R.F., Stainless Steel, Clip Fed, Modern........................	225	250	250
Back Up, .380 ACP, AMT, Stainless Steel, Clip Fed, Modern.................	225	250	250
Back Up, .380 ACP, OMC, Stainless Steel, Clip Fed, Modern.................	150	175	175
Back Up, .380 ACP, TDE, Stainless Steel, Clip Fed, Modern..................	175	250	250

	V.G.	Exc	Prior Edition
Combat Skipper, .45 ACP, Stainless Steel, Clip Fed, Fixed Sights, Modern..........	$325	$375	$375
Government, .45 ACP, Stainless Steel, Clip Fed, Fixed Sights, Modern..........	300	400	310
Hardballer, .45 ACP, Stainless Steel, Clip Fed, Adjustable Sights, Modern..........	325	425	425
Lightning, .22 L.R., Stainless Steel, 5" Bull Barrel, Adjustable Sights, ...	200	275	280
As Above, Fixed Sights, ...	225	250	250
As Above, 6½" Bull Barrel, Adjustable Sights, ...	200	275	280
As Above, Fixed Sights, ...	225	250	250
Lightning, .22 L.R., Stainless Steel, 6½" Tapered Barrel, Adjustable Sights, ...	200	275	280
As Above, Fixed Sights, ...	200	250	250
Longslide, .45 ACP, Stainless Steel, Clip Fed, Adjustable Sights, Modern..........	400	500	450
Skipper, .45 ACP, Stainless Steel, Clip Fed, Adjustable Sights, Modern..........	300	400	350

AMT Skipper

ANDRUS & OSBORNE Canton, Conn. 1847–1850, moved to Southbridge, Mass. 1850–1851.

HANDGUN, PERCUSSION

.36 Underhammer, Boot Pistol, Half-Octagon Barrel, Antique..............	300	400	250

ANGSTADT, A. & J. Berks County, Pa. 1792–1808. See Kentucky Rifles and U.S. Military.

			Prior
	V.G.	Exc	Edition

ANGSTADT, PETER Lancaster County, Pa. 1770–1777. See Kentucky Rifles and Pistols.

ANGUSH, JAMES Lancaster Pa. 1771. See Kentucky Rifles and Pistols.

ANNELY, L. London, England 1650–1700.
HANDGUN, FLINTLOCK
.62, Holster Pistol, Brass Mounting, Antique.. $450 $950 $950

ANSCHUTZ Zella Mehlis, Germany 1922–1938, 1945 to date in Ulm, West Germany. Also see Savage Arms Co. for rifle listings.
HANDGUN, REVOLVER
J.G.A., 7mm C.F., Folding Trigger, Pocket Revolver, Curio.................... 125 200 200

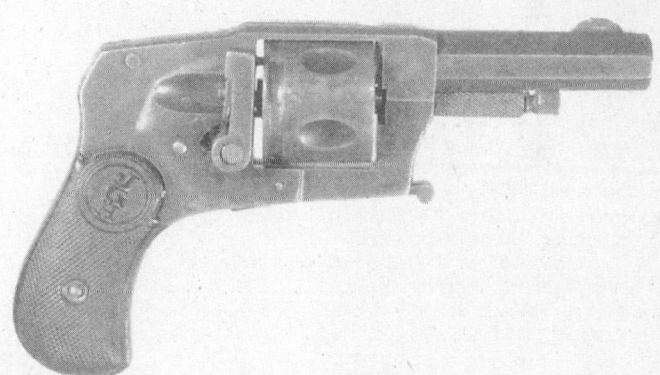

Anschutz J. G. Revolver

ANSCHUTZ, E. Philadelphia, Pa., c. 1860.
RIFLE, PERCUSSION
.36 Schutzen Rifle, Octagon Barrel, Target, Antique................................ 1,250 2,000 2,000

ANSCHUTZ, UDO Zella Mehlis, Germany 1927–1939.
HANDGUN, SINGLESHOT
Record-Match M1933, .22 L.R.R.F., Free Pistol, Martini Action,
Fancy Stocks, Target Sights, Curio.. 450 650 650

	V.G.	Exc	Prior Edition

Record-Match M210, .22 L.R.R.F., Free Pistol, Martini Action, Fancy Stocks, Target Sights, Light Engraving, Curio...................... $750 $850 $800

ANSTADT, JACOB Kutztown, Pa. 1815–1817. See Kentucky Rifles and Pistols.

APACHE Fab. de Armas Garantazadas, Spain, c. 1920.
HANDGUN, REVOLVER
Colt Police Positive Type, .38 Double Action, 6 Shots, Curio................. 75 125 100

APACHE Made by Ojanguren y Vidosa; Eibar, Spain.
HANDGUN, SEMI-AUTOMATIC
.25 ACP, Clip Fed, Modern.. 150 175 175

APAOLOZO HERMANOS Zumorraga, Spain, c. 1925.
HANDGUN, REVOLVER
Colt Police Positive Type, .38 Spec., Double Action, Curio................... 75 125 125

APEX RIFLE CO. Sun Valley, Calif., c. 1952.
RIFLE, BOLT ACTION
Apex Eight, Various Calibers, 8 Lbs., Monte Kennedy Stock, Standard Grade, No Sights, Modern..................... 200 350 350
Bantam Light Sporter, Various Calibers, 7 Lbs., Monte Kennedy Stock, Standard Grade, No Sights, Modern............................ 250 400 400
Bench Rester, Various Calibers, Monte Kennedy Laminated Stock with Rails, Bull Barrel, Canjar Trigger, Modern..................... 250 475 475
Reliable Nine, Various Calibers, 9 Lbs., Monte Kennedy Stock, Standard Grade, No Sights, Modern............................ 200 350 350
Varmint & Target, Various Calibers, Monte Kennedy Target Stock, Heavy Barrel, No Sights, Modern............................ 250 425 425

ARAMBERRI Spain
SHOTGUN, DOUBLE BARREL, SIDE-BY-SIDE
Boxlock, 12 Gauge, Single Trigger, Checkered Stock, Vent Rib, Modern.. 125 150 150

ARGENTINE MILITARY
HANDGUN, REVOLVER
Colt M 1892, Double Action Trigger, Solid Frame, Swing-Out Cylinder, Military, Curio.. 300 350 175
HANDGUN, SEMI-AUTOMATIC
Ballester–Molina, .45 ACP, Clip Fed, Curio............................. 350 400 295
Ballester–Rigaud, .45 ACP, Clip Fed, Curio............................. 400 450 325

	V.G.	Exc	Prior Edition
Modelo 1916 (Colt 1911), 11.25mm, Clip Fed, Curio	$550	$650	$375
Modelo 1927 (Colt 1911A1), .45 ACP, Clip Fed, Curio	650	750	400
Steyr M1905, 7.63 Mannlicher, Curio	275	325	250

RIFLE, BOLT ACTION

	V.G.	Exc	Prior Edition
M 1891, 7.65 Argentine, Carbine, Open Rear Sight, Full Stocked Military, Curio	250	300	100
M 1891, 7.65 Argentine, Rifle, Full Stocked Military, Curio	225	275	75
M 1909, 7.65 Argentine, Carbine, Open Rear Sight, Full-Stocked Military, Modern	225	275	150
M 1909, 7.65 Argentine, Rifle, Full Stocked Military, Curio	225	300	100

RIFLE, SINGLESHOT

	V.G.	Exc	Prior Edition
M 1879, .43 Mauser, Rolling Block, Antique	350	400	400

ARISTOCRAT Made by Hopkins & Allen for Suplee Biddle Hardware 1870–1900.

HANDGUN, REVOLVER

	V.G.	Exc	Prior Edition
.22 Short R.F., 7 Shot, Spur Trigger, Solid Frame, Single Action, Antique	75	150	150
.32 Short R.F., 5 Shot, Spur Trigger, Solid Frame, Single Action, Antique	75	175	175

ARISTOCRAT Made by Stevens Arms.

SHOTGUN, DOUBLE BARREL, SIDE-BY-SIDE

	V.G.	Exc	Prior Edition
M 315, Various Gauges, Hammerless, Steel Barrel, Modern	75	150	150

ARIZAGA, GASPAR Eibar, Spain.

HANDGUN, SEMI-AUTOMATIC

	V.G.	Exc	Prior Edition
.32 ACP, Clip Fed, Modern	100	150	125

ARMALITE Costa Mesa, Calif.

RIFLE, SEMI-AUTOMATIC

	V.G.	Exc	Prior Edition
AR-180 .223 Rem., Clip Fed, Folding Stock, Modern	750	875	875
AR-7 Explorer, .22 L.R.R.F., Clip Fed, Modern	75	100	100
AR-7 Explorer Custom, .22 L.R.R.F., Checkered Stock, Clip Fed, Modern	100	150	150

SHOTGUN, SEMI-AUTOMATIC

	V.G.	Exc	Prior Edition
AR-17, 12 Ga. Lightweight, Modern	475	575	575

ARMI JAGER Turin, Italy. Imported by E.M.F.

HANDGUN, REVOLVER

	V.G.	Exc	Prior Edition
Dakota Sheriff, Various Calibers, Single Action, Western Style, 3½" Barrel, Modern	125	200	200

	V.G.	Exc	Prior Edition
Dakota Target, Various Calibers, Single Action, Western Style, Adjustable Sights, Various Barrel Lengths, Modern.................................	$150	$200	$200
Dakota, .22 L.R.R.F. and .22 W.M.R., Single Action, Western Style, Various Barrel Lengths, Modern..	125	175	175
Dakota, .22 L.R.R.F., Single Action, Western Style, Various Barrel Lengths, Modern...	100	150	150
Dakota, Various Calibers, Single Action, Western Style, Various Barrel Lengths, Modern..	125	175	175
Dakota, Various Calibers, Single Action, Western Style, Buntline Barrel Lengths, Modern..	125	175	175
Dakota, Various Calibers, Single Action, Western Style, Engraved Barrel Lengths, Modern..	225	325	325

RIFLE, SEMI-AUTOMATIC

	V.G.	Exc	Prior Edition
AP-74, .22 L.R.R.F., Military Stock, Wood Stock, Modern......................	75	100	100
AP-74, .31 ACP, Military Style, Wood Stock, Modern...........................	75	125	125
AP-74 Commando, .22 L.R.R.F., Military Style, Wood Stock, Modern...	75	125	125
AP-74 Standard, .22 L.R.R.F., Military Style, Plastic Stock, Modern...	50	100	100
AP-74 Standard, .32 ACP, Military Style, Plastic Stock, Modern...	75	125	125

ARMINEX LTD. Scottsdale, Ariz. since 1982–1985

HANDGUN, SEMI-AUTOMATIC

	V.G.	Exc	Prior Edition
Trifire, .45 A.C.P., 9 mm Luger, or .38 Super, Blue or Nickel, Clip Fed, Hammer, Adjustable Sights, Modern...	350	450	400

Arminex Trifire Standard

	V.G.	Exc	Prior Edition
Trifire Presentation, .45 A.C.P., 9 mm Luger, or .38 Super, Cased, Blue or Nickel, Clip Fed, Hammer, Adjustable Sights, Modern...............	$400	$500	$450

Arminex Trifire Target

ARMINIUS Friedrich Pickert, Zella-Mehlis, Germany 1922–1939.

HANDGUN, REVOLVER

Model 1, .22 L.R.R.F., Hammerless, Curio..	200	250	250
Model 2, .22 L.R.R.F., Hammer, Curio..	250	300	300
Model 3, .25 ACP, Hammerless, Folding Trigger, Curio.........................	125	175	175
Model 4, 5.5 Vclo Dog, Hammerless, Folding Trigger, Curio............	75	150	150
Model 5/1, 7.5mm Swiss, Hammer, Curio..	100	175	175
Model 5/2, 7.62 Nagant, Hammer, Curio...	100	175	175
Model 7, .320 Revolver, Hammer, Curio...	75	125	125
Model 8, .320 Revolver, Hammerless, Folding Trigger, Curio................	125	150	150
Model 9, .32 ACP, Hammer, Curio..	125	175	175
Model 10, .32 ACP, Hammerless, Folding Trigger, Curio........................	100	150	150
Model 13, .380 Revolver, Hammer, Curio...	100	150	150
Model 14, .380 Revolver, Hammerless, Curio...	100	150	150

HANDGUN, SINGLESHOT

TP 1, .22 L.R.R.F., Target Pistol, Hammer, Modern..............................	200	250	300
TP 2, .22 L.R.R.F., Hammerless, Set Triggers, Modern..........................	225	275	300

ARMINIUS Herman Weihrauch Sportwaffenfabrik, Mellrichstadt/Bayern, West Germany before 1968; for Current Models, See F.I.E.

HANDGUN, REVOLVER

HW-3, .22 L.R.R.F., Modern...	50	75	50
HW-3, .32 S & W Long, Modern...	50	75	50
HW-5, .22 L.R.R.F., Modern...	50	75	25
HW-5, .32 S & W Long, Modern...	50	75	50
HW-7, .22 L.R.R.F., Modern...	50	75	50
HW-9, .22 L.R.R.F., Adjustable Sights, Modern........................	50	75	75

	V.G.	Exc	Prior Edition

ARMSPORT Importers Discontinued 1993, Miami, Fla.

HANDGUN, FLINTLOCK

	V.G.	Exc	Prior Edition
Kentucky, .45, Reproduction	$50	$85	$85

HANDGUN, PERCUSSION

	V.G.	Exc	Prior Edition
1847 Colt Walker, .44, Reproduction, Antique	75	125	120
1851 Colt Navy, .36, Brass Frame, Reproduction	50	75	75
1851 Colt Navy, .36, Steel Frame, Reproduction	50	100	100
1851 Colt Navy, .44, Brass Frame, Reproduction	50	75	75
1851 Colt Navy, .44, Steel Frame, Reproduction	50	100	100
1860 Colt Army, .44, Brass Frame, Reproduction	50	75	75
1860 Colt Army, .44, Steel Frame, Reproduction	50	100	100
Corsair, .44, Double Barrel, Reproduction	50	75	75
Kentucky, .45 or .50, Reproduction	50	75	75
New Hartford Police, .36, Reproduction	50	100	100
New Remington Army, .44, Blue, Brass Trigger Guard, Reproduction	75	100	100
New Remington Army, .44, Stainless Steel, Brass Trigger Guard, Reproduction	75	125	125
Patriot, .45, Target Sights, Set Triggers, Reproduction	75	100	100
Spiller & Burr, .36, Solid Frame, Brass Frame, Reproduction	50	75	75
Whitney, .36, Solid Frame, Brass Trigger Guard, Reproduction	75	100	100

RIFLE, BOLT ACTION

	V.G.	Exc	Prior Edition
Tikka, Various Calibers, Open Sights, Checkered Stock, Clip Fed, Modern	500	650	400

RIFLE, LEVER ACTION

	V.G.	Exc	Prior Edition
Premier 1873 Winchester, Various Calibers, Carbine, Engraved, Reproduction, Modern	650	850	850
Premier 1873 Winchester, Various Calibers, Rifle, Engraved, Reproduction, Modern	750	1,000	1,000

RIFLE, FLINTLOCK

	V.G.	Exc	Prior Edition
Deluxe Hawkin, .50, Reproduction	125	175	175
Deluxe Kentucky, .45, Reproduction	150	200	200
Hawkin, .45, Reproduction	125	175	175
Kentucky, .45, Reproduction	125	150	150

RIFLE, PERCUSSION

	V.G.	Exc	Prior Edition
Deluxe Hawkin, Various Calibers, Reproduction	150	175	175
Deluxe Kentucky, .45, Reproduction	150	200	200
Hawkin, Various Calibers, Reproduction	125	150	150
Kentucky, .45 or .50, Reproduction	100	150	150

COMBINATION WEAPON, OVER-UNDER

	V.G.	Exc	Prior Edition
Tikka Turkey Gun, 12 Ga. and .222 Rem., Vent Rib, Sling Swivels, Muzzle Break, Checkered Stock, Modern	450	625	625

	V.G.	Exc	Prior Edition

RIFLE, DOUBLE BARREL, SIDE-BY-SIDE

Emperor, Various Calibers, Holland and Holland Type Sidelock, Engraved, Checkered Stock, Extra Barrels, Cased, Modern......................$12,225 $16,250 $16,250

Emperor Deluxe, Various Calibers, Holland and Holland Sidelock, Fancy Engraving, Checkered Stock, Extra Barrels, Modern...................... 20,000 25,000 25,000

RIFLE, DOUBLE BARREL, OVER-UNDER

Emperor, Various Calibers, Checkered Stock, Engraved, Extra Barrels, Cased, Modern.. 12,000 15,000 15,000

Express, Various Calibers, Checkered Stock, Engraved, Modern............ 3,000 3,500 3,500

SHOTGUN, PERCUSSION

Hook Breech, Double Barrel, Side-by-Side, 10 and 12 Gauges, Reproduction 175 250 250

SHOTGUN, DOUBLE BARREL, OVER-UNDER

Model 2500, 12 and 20 Ga., Checkered Stock, Adjustable Choke, Single Selective Trigger, Modern.. 450 650 650

Premier, 12 Ga., Skeet Grade, Checkered Stock, Engraved, Modern.. 900 1,200 1,200

SHOTGUN, DOUBLE BARREL, SIDE-BY-SIDE

Express, 12 and 20 Gauges, Holland and Holland Type Sidelock, Engraved, Checkered Stock, Modern... 3,000 3,500 3,500

Goose Gun, 10 Ga. 3½" Mag., Checkered Stock, Modern..................... 375 475 475

Side-by-Side, 12 and 20 Gauges, Checkered Stock, Modern................... 325 425 425

Western Double, 12 Ga. Mag. 3", Outside Hammers Double Trigger, Modern.. 300 400 400

SHOTGUN, SINGLESHOT

Monotrap, 12 Ga., Checkered Stock, Modern............................. 1,200 1,550 1,550

Monotrap, 12 Ga., Two Barrel Set, Checkered Stock, Modern............... 1,600 2,300 2,300

ARMSTRONG, JOHN Gettysburg, Pa. 1813–1817. Also See Kentucky Rifles and Pistols.

ARRIOLA HERMANOS Eibar, Spain, c. 1930.

HANDGUN, REVOLVER

Colt Police Positive Copy, .38 Spec., Double Action, Curio.................. 50 100 100

ARRIZABALAGA, HILOS DE CALIXTO Eibar, Spain, c. 1915.

HANDGUN, SEMI-AUTOMATIC

Ruby Type, .32 ACP, Clip Fed, Blue, Curio... 125 150 150

ASCASO, FRANCISCO Tarassa, Spain, c. 1937.

HANDGUN, SEMI-AUTOMATIC

Astra 400 Copy, 9mm, Clip Fed, Military Type, Curio............................ 900 1,000 1,000

	V.G.	Exc	Prior Edition

ASHEVILLE ARMORY Asheville, N.C. 1861–1864.

RIFLE, PERCUSSION

.58 Enfield Type, Rifled, Brass Furniture, Military, Antique..................	$2,500	$3,500	$3,500

ASTRA Founded in 1908 as Unceta y Esperanza in Eibar, Spain. In 1913 moved to Guernica, Spain and the name was reversed to Esperanza y Unceta; name changed again in 1926 to Unceta y Cia.; named changed again in 1953 to Astra-Unceta y Cia.

HANDGUN, REVOLVER

250, .22 L.R.R.F., Double Action, Small Frame, Modern........................	100	150	150
250, .22 W.M.R., Double Action, Small Frame, Modern.........................	100	150	150
250, .32 S & W Long, Double Action, Small Frame, Modern...................	100	150	150
250, .38 Special, Double Action, Small Frame, Modern.........................	125	175	175
357 Magnum, .357 Magnum, Double Action, Adjustable Sights, Modern..	200	275	275
357 Magnum, .357 Magnum, Double Action, Adjustable Sights, Stainless Steel, Modern...	250	300	300
44 Magnum, .44 Magnum, Double Action, Adjustable Sights, Modern..	300	350	350

Astra 44 Magnum

960, .38 Special, Double Action, Adjustable Sights, Modern....................	100	175	175
Cadix, .22 L.R.R.F., Double Action, Adjustable Sights, Modern.............	75	150	150
Cadix, .22 W.M.R., Double Action, Adjustable Sights, Modern..............	100	150	150
Cadix, .32 S & W Long, Double Action, Adjustable Sights, Modern..	100	150	150
Cadix, .38 Special, Double Action, Adjustable Sights, Modern...............	150	175	175
Inox, .38 Special, Stainless Steel, Double Action, Small Frame, Modern..	150	200	200
Match, .38 Special, Double Action, Adjustable Sights, Modern..............	100	175	175
Model 41, .41 Magnum, Blue, Modern...	250	275	275

	V.G.	Exc	Prior Edition
Model 45, .45 Colt, Blue, Modern..	$300	$350	$350

HANDGUN, SEMI-AUTOMATIC

Chrome Plating, Add $25.00-$45.00
Light Engraving, Add $60.00-$110.00

	V.G.	Exc	Prior Edition
A-50, Various Calibers, Blue, Single Action, Modern.............................	150	225	225
A-80, Various Calibers, Double Action, Blue, Large Magazine, Modern........................	300	375	375
A-80, Various Calibers, Double Action, Chrome, Large Magazine, Modern........................	300	400	400
Constable, Various Calibers, Blue, Modern...	250	300	300

Astra Constable

	V.G.	Exc	Prior Edition
Constable Pocket, Various Calibers, Blue, Modern................................	250	300	300
Constable Sport, Various Calibers, Blue, Modern.................................	250	300	300
Constable Target, .22 L.R.R.F., Blue, Modern......................................	300	350	350
Model 100, .32 ACP, Curio..	225	275	275
Model 100 Special, .32 ACP, 9 Shot, Curio..	250	300	300
Model 1000, .23 ACP, 12 Shot, Modern...	400	500	500

	V.G.	Exc	Prior Edition
Model 1911, .32 ACP, Curio.....	$250	$300	$300

Astra M1911 .32

	V.G.	Exc	Prior Edition
Model 1915, .32 ACP, Curio.....	200	275	275
Model 1916, .32 ACP, Curio.....	200	300	300
Model 1924, .25 ACP, Curio.....	175	225	225
Model 200 Firecat, .25 ACP, Early Model, Concave Indicator Cut, Modern.....	200	250	250

	V.G.	Exc	Prior Edition
Model 200 Firecat, .25 ACP, Late Model, Long Clip, Modern...............	$125	$175	$175

Astra Model 200 with Long Clip

	V.G.	Exc	Prior Edition
Model 200 Firecat, .25 ACP, Late Model, Rear Indicator, Modern.........	100	150	150
Model 2000 Camper or Cub, Conversion Kit Only	75	100	100
Model 2000 Camper, .22 Short R.F., Modern...	250	300	300

	V.G.	Exc	Prior Edition
Model 2000 Cub, .22 Short R.F., Modern	$150	$175	$175

Astra Cub

	V.G.	Exc	Prior Edition
Model 2000 Cub, .25 ACP, Modern	150	175	175
Model 300, .32 ACP, Clip Fed, Modern	200	300	300
Model 300, .32 ACP, Nazi-Proofed, Clip Fed, Curio	375	475	475
Model 300, .380 ACP, Clip Fed, Modern	225	325	325
Model 300, .380 ACP, Nazi-Proofed, Clip Fed, Curio	400	500	500
Model 3000 (Late), .380 ACP, Clip Fed, Modern	200	250	250
Model 400, .32 ACP, Modern	500	600	600
Model 400, 9mm Bayard Long, Modern	300	375	375
Model 400, 9mm Bayard Long, Nazi-Proofed, Clip Fed, Curio	700	750	750
Model 4000 Falcon, .22 L.R.R.F., Clip Fed, Modern	400	500	500
Model 4000 Falcon, .32 ACP, Clip Fed, Modern	250	300	300
Model 4000 Falcon, .380 ACP, Clip Fed, Modern	250	300	300
Model 4000 Falcon, Conversion Kit Only,	75	100	100
Model 5000 Sport (Constable), .22 L.R.R.F., Target Pistol, Clip Fed, Modern	250	300	300
Model 600, .32 ACP, Clip Fed, Modern	200	300	300
Model 600, 9mm Luger, Clip Fed, Modern	200	300	300
Model 600, 9mm Luger, Nazi-Proofed, Clip Fed, Curio	400	500	500
Model 700 Special, .32 ACP, 12 Shots, Clip Fed, Modern	500	600	600
Model 700, .32 ACP, Clip Fed, Curio	450	500	500
Model 7000, .22 L.R.R.F., Clip Fed, Modern	125	175	175
Model 800 Condor, .380 ACP, Clip Fed, Modern	850	1,000	1,000

	V.G.	Exc	Prior Edition
Model 900, 7.63 Mauser, Holster Stock, Modern....................................	$1,750	$2,000	$2,000

Astra Model 900

Model TS-22, .22 L.R.R.F., Target Pistol, Single Action, Clip Fed, Modern..	225	325	325

AstraTS-22

RIFLE, SEMI-AUTOMATIC

Model 1000, .32 ACP, Clip Fed, Modern..	325	450	450
Model 3000 (Early), .32 ACP, Modern..	125	175	175
Model 3000 (Late), .22 L.R.R.F., Modern..	100	150	150
Model 3000 (Late), .32 ACP, Modern..	100	175	175
Model 800 Condor, 9mm Luger, Curio...	450	650	650
Model 902, 7.63 Mauser, Modern...	1,000	1,600	1,600

SHOTGUN, DOUBLE BARREL, OVER-UNDER

Model 650, 12 Gauge, Checkered Stock, Double Triggers, Vent Rib, Modern..	200	275	275

	V.G.	Exc	Prior Edition
Model 650E, 12 Gauge, Checkered Stock, Double Triggers, Vent Rib, Selective Ejectors, Modern......................	$225	$375	$375
Model 750 Skeet, 12 Gauge, Checkered Stock, Single Trigger, Vent Rib, Selective Ejectors, Modern......................	350	500	500
Model 750 Trap, 12 Gauge, Checkered Stock, Single Trigger, Vent Rib, Selective Ejectors, Modern......................	350	500	500
Model 750, 12 Gauge, Checkered Stock, Double Trigger, Vent Rib, Modern......................	225	375	375
Model 750E, 12 Gauge, Checkered Stock, Single Trigger, Vent Rib, Selective Ejectors, Modern......................	350	525	525
Model ID-13, 12 Gauge, Checkered Stock, Single Trigger, Selective Ejectors, Vent Rib, Modern......................	325	475	475

SHOTGUN, DOUBLE BARREL, SIDE-BY-SIDE

	V.G.	Exc	Prior Edition
Model 805, Various Gauges, Checkered Stock, Double Triggers, Modern......................	150	250	250
Model 811, 10 Gauge Magnum, Checkered Stock, Double Triggers, Modern......................	195	275	275

SHOTGUN, SINGLESHOT

	V.G.	Exc	Prior Edition
Cyclops, Various Gauges, Checkered Stock, Modern......................	75	100	100

ATIS Ponte S. Marco, Italy.

SHOTGUN, SEMI-AUTOMATIC

	V.G.	Exc	Prior Edition
12 Ga., Lightweight, Vent Rib, Modern......................	150	225	225
12 Ga., Lightweight, Vent Rib, Left-Hand, Modern......................	200	275	275

ATKIN, HENRY E. & CO. London, England 1874–1900.

SHOTGUN, DOUBLE BARREL, SIDE-BY-SIDE

	V.G.	Exc	Prior Edition
Raleigh, 12 Gauge, Sidelock, Double Triggers, Checkered Stock, Engraved, Automatic Ejectors, "Purdey" Barrels, Curio......................	7,000	8,500	8,750

ATLAS Domingo Acha y Cia., Ermua, Spain, c. 1920.

HANDGUN, SEMI-AUTOMATIC

	V.G.	Exc	Prior Edition
Vest Pocket, .25 ACP, Clip Fed, Curio......................	100	125	125

ATLAS ARMS Chicago, Ill. from about 1962 to 1972.

HANDGUN, DOUBLE BARREL, OVER-UNDER

	V.G.	Exc	Prior Edition
Derringer, .22 L.R.R.F., Remington Style, Modern......................	50	75	75
Derringer, .38 Spec., Remington Style, Modern......................	50	75	75

SHOTGUN, DOUBLE BARREL, OVER-UNDER

	V.G.	Exc	Prior Edition
Grand Prix, 12 or 20 Gauge, Merkel Type Sidelock, Single Selective Trigger, Fancy Engraving, Automatic Ejectors, Modern......................	850	1,200	1,200
Model 65, Various Gauges, Boxlock, Double Trigger, Vent Rib, Modern......................	250	350	350
Model 65-ST, Various Gauges, Boxlock, Single Trigger, Vent Rib, Modern......................	250	400	400

	V.G.	Exc	Prior Edition
Model 87, Various Gauges, Merkel Type Sidelock, Single Trigger, Vent Rib, Engraved, Modern	$350	$450	$450
Model 150, Various Gauges, Boxlock, Single Trigger, Vent Rib, Modern	250	400	400
Model 150, Various Gauges, Boxlock, Single Trigger, Vent Rib, Automatic Ejectors, Modern	300	425	425
Model 160, Various Gauges, Boxlock, Single Trigger, Vent Rib, Automatic Ejectors, Modern	350	450	450
Model 180, Various Gauges, Boxlock, Single Trigger, Vent Rib, Automatic Ejectors, Light Engraving, Modern	375	500	500
Model 750, Various Gauges, Merkel Type Sidelock, Single Trigger, Vent Rib, Engraved, Modern	350	450	450
Model 750, Various Gauges, Merkel Type Sidelock, Single Trigger, Vent Rib, Engraved, Automatic Ejectors, Modern	375	550	550

SHOTGUN, DOUBLE BARREL, SIDE-BY-SIDE

	V.G.	Exc	Prior Edition
Model 145, Various Gauges, Boxlock, Vent Rib, Engraved, Hammerless, Checkered Stock, Modern	300	425	425
Model 200, Various Gauges, Boxlock, Double Triggers, Hammerless, Checkered Stock, Modern	175	275	275
Model 204, Various Gauges, Boxlock, Single Trigger, Hammerless, Checkered Stock, Modern	225	275	275
Model 206, Various Gauges, Boxlock, Single Trigger, Automatic Ejector, Hammerless, Checkered Stock, Modern	275	350	350
Model 208, Various Gauges, Boxlock, Double Triggers, Vent Rib, Recoil Pad, Modern	250	325	325
Model 500, Various Gauges, Boxlock, Double Triggers, Vent Rib, Recoil Pad, Modern	250	325	325

SHOTGUN, SINGLESHOT

	V.G.	Exc	Prior Edition
Insuperable 101, Various Gauges, Vent Rib, Engraved, Checkered Stock, Modern	75	100	100
Trap Gun, 12 Gauge, Automatic Ejector, Engraved, Checkered Stock, Modern	425	525	525

AUBREY Made by Meridan Arms Co., sold by Sears-Roebuck 1900–1930.

HANDGUN, REVOLVER

	V.G.	Exc	Prior Edition
.32 S & W, 5 Shot, Double Action, Top Break, Modern	75	95	95
.38 S & W, 5 Shot, Double Action, Top Break, Modern	75	95	95

AUDAX Trade name of Manufacture D'Armes Des Pyrenees, Hendaye, France, marketed by La Cartoucherie Francaise, Paris 1931–1939.

HANDGUN, SEMI-AUTOMATIC

	V.G.	Exc	Prior Edition
.25 ACP, Clip Fed, Magazine Disconnect, Grip Safety, Curio	75	95	95
.32 ACP, Clip Fed, Magazine Disconnect, Blue, Curio	75	95	95

AUSTRALIAN MILITARY

RIFLE, BOLT ACTION

	V.G.	Exc	Prior Edition
Mk. III, .303 British, Clip Fed, WW I Issue, Curio	225	275	175
Mk. III, .303 British, Clip Fed, WW II Issue, Curio	200	250	150

	V.G.	Exc	Prior Edition
RIFLE, SINGLESHOT			
Martini, .310 Greener, Small Action, Curio	$275	$325	$225

AUSTRIAN MILITARY

HANDGUN, PERCUSSION

	V.G.	Exc	Prior Edition
.54 Dragoon, with Shoulder Stock, Singleshot, Antique	350	550	550

HANDGUN, REVOLVER

M1898 Rast & Gasser, 8mm Rast & Gasser, Curio	250	275	250

HANDGUN, SEMI-AUTOMATIC

M1907 Roth Steyr, 8mm Roth-Steyr, Curio	400	450	275

Austrian Military M1907 Roth Steyr

M1908 Steyr, 8mm Roth-Steyr, Curio	350	400	250
M1911 Steyr Hahn, 9mm Steyr, Curio	325	375	275
M1912 Steyr Hahn, 9mm Steyr, Curio	250	300	225
Mannlicher 1901, 7.63 Mannlicher, Curio	2,000	2,500	250
Mannlicher 1905, 7.63 Mannlicher, Curio	350	400	250

HANDGUN, SINGLESHOT

Werder Lightning, 11mm, Antique	650	750	575

HANDGUN, TUBELOCK

.69 Dragoon, with Shoulder Stock, Singleshot, Antique	350	400	375

RIFLE, BOLT ACTION

M1883 Schulhof, 11.15 X 58R Werndl, 8 Shot, Antique	375	575	575
M1885 Steyr, 11.15 X 58R Werndl, Straight-Pull, Antique	375	450	450
M1886 Steyr, 11.15 X 58R Werndl, Straight-Pull Bolt, Antique	150	175	150
M1888, 8 X 50R Mannlicher, Antique	150	175	150
M1888/90, 8 X 50R Mannlicher, Antique	150	175	150
M1890, 8 X 50R Mannlicher, Carbine, Antique	150	175	150
M1895, 8 X 50R Mannlicher, Curio	100	125	100

	V.G.	Exc	Prior Edition
M1895, 8 X 50R Mannlicher, Carbine, Modern..	$100	$125	$100
M1895 Stutzen, 8 X 50R Mannlicher, Curio..	125	150	125

AUTO MAG Started at Pasadena, Calif. in 1968, and moved to North Hollywood, Calif. when purchased by TDE in 1971. Marketed by TDE, JurrasAssociates, and High Standard. See A M T.

HANDGUN, SEMI-AUTOMATIC

Alaskan Model, .44 AMP, Clip Fed, Stainless Steel, Hammer, Adjustable Sights, Cased, Modern..	1,600	1,950	1,950
First Model (Pasadena), .44 AMP, Clip Fed, Stainless Steel, Hammer, Adjustable Sights, Cased, Modern..	1,750	2,000	2,000
High Standard, .44 AMP, Clip Fed, Stainless Steel, Hammer, Adjustable Sights, Cased, Modern...	1,500	1,800	1,800
Jurras Custom Model 200, .44 AMP, Clip Fed, Stainless Steel, Hammer, Adjustable Sights, Cased, Modern................................	2,350	2,500	2,500
Model 160, .357 AMP, Clip Fed, Stainless Steel, Hammer, Adjustable Sights, Cased, Modern..	1,700	1,800	1,800
Model 170, .41 JMP, Clip Fed, Stainless Steel, Hammer, Adjustable Sights, Cased, Modern..	1,400	1,500	1,500
Model 180, .44 AMP, Clip Fed, Stainless Steel, Hammer, Adjustable Sights, Cased, Modern..	1,750	1,850	1,850

Auto Mag Model 180

Model 260, .357 AMP, Clip Fed, Stainless Steel, Hammer, Adjustable Sights, Cased, Modern...	1,250	1,350	1,350
Model 280, .44 AMP, Clip Fed, Stainless Steel, Hammer, Adjustable Sights, Cased, Modern...	1,100	1,200	1,200

AUTOMATIC Made by Hopkins & Allen, c. 1900.

HANDGUN, REVOLVER

.32 S & W, 5 Shot, Top Break, Hammerless, Double Action, Curio..	75	100	100

	V.G.	Exc	Prior Edition
.38 S & W, 5 Shot, Top Break, Hammerless, Double Action, Curio............	$75	$100	$100

AUTOMATIC HAMMERLESS Made by Iver Johnson, c. 1900.

HANDGUN, REVOLVER

.22 L.R.R.F., 7 Shot, Double Action, Top Break, Hammerless, Curio............	75	100	100
.32 S & W, 5 Shot, Top Break, Hammerless, Double Action, Curio............	50	75	75
.38 S & W, 5 Shot, Top Break, Hammerless, Double Action, Curio............	50	75	75

AUTOMATIC PISTOL Spain.

HANDGUN, SEMI-AUTOMATIC

Pocket, .32 ACP, Clip Fed, Modern............	50	75	75

AUTOMATIC POLICE See Forehand & Wadsworth.

AUTO-ORDNANCE CORP. West Hurley, NY. Also see Thompson and Numrich Arms Co.

HANDGUN, SEMI-AUTOMATIC

1991 A1 Various Calibers, Based on the Colt Pistol, Modern............	300	350	325
ZG–51 "Pit Bull," Compact Model of the 1911 A1, 3.5" Barrel, Modern............	325	375	350

CARBINE SEMI-AUTOMATIC (THOMPSON REPLICAS)

1927 A1 "Submachine Gun," .45 ACP, 16" Barrel, Modern............	450	500	475
1927 A1 Deluxe "Submachine Gun," .45 ACP, Finned Barrel, Adjustable Sights, Pistol–Grip Forearm, Modern............	600	700	650
1927 A1C "Submachine Gun," .45 ACP, Aluminum Alloy Receiver, Modern............	525	600	575
1927 A3 "Submachine Gun," .22 LR, 16" Barrel, Aluminum Alloy Receiver, Modern............	475	550	575
1927 A5 "Submachine Gun/Pistol," .45 ACP, Compact Variation, 13" Finned Barrel, Aluminum Alloy Receiver, No Shoulder Stock, Modern............	525	600	600

AUTO-POINTER Made by Yamamoto Mfg. Co., Imported by Sloans.

SHOTGUN, SEMI-AUTOMATIC

12 and 20 Gauges, Tube Feed, Checkered Stock, Modern............	200	300	275

AUTOSTAND Made for ManuFrance by Mre. d'Armes des Pyrenees.

HANDGUN, SINGLESHOT

E-1 (Unique), .22 L.R.R.F., Target Pistol, Adjustable Sights, Curio............	50	75	75

	Prior
V.G.	Exc	Edition

AVENGER

HANDGUN, REVOLVER

.32 Long R.F., 5 Shot, Single Action, Spur Triggers, Antique................. $75 $125 $125

AVION   Azpiri y. Cia., Eibar, Spain, c. 1915.

HANDGUN, SEMI-AUTOMATIC

Vest Pocket, .25 ACP, Clip Fed, Curio... 75   125   125

A Y A   Aguirre y Aranzabal, Spain. Now Imported by Ventura.

SHOTGUN, DOUBLE BARREL, OVER-UNDER

Model 37 Super, Various Gauges, Single Selective Trigger,
Automatic Ejectors, Fancy Engraving, Sidelock, Modern........................ 1,450   2,100   2,100

SHOTGUN, DOUBLE BARREL, SIDE-BY-SIDE

Bolero, Various Gauges, Single Trigger, Checkered Stock,
Modern.. 325   350   350

Matador, Various Gauges, Single Selective Trigger, Checkered
Stock, Selective Ejector, Modern... 325   375   375

Matador II, Various Gauges, Single Selective Trigger, Checkered
Stock, Selective Ejector, Vent Rib, Modern... 350   425   425

Model 1, Various Gauges, Automatic Ejectors, Sidelock, Fancy
Checkering, Engraved, Lightweight, Modern.. 2,250   2,750   2,750

Model 117, 12 Gauge, Sidelock, Single Selective Trigger, Engraved,
Checkered Stock, Modern... 650   725   725

Model 2, Various Gauges, Automatic Ejector, Sidelock, Engraved,
Checkered Stock, Double Trigger, Modern.. 950   1,250   1,250

Model 53E, 12 and 20 Gauges, Sidelock, Single Selective Trigger,
Fancy Checkering, Fancy Engraving, Modern.. 1,500   1,950   1,950

Model 56, 12 and 20 Gauges, Sidelock, Raised Matted Rib, Fancy
Checkering, Fancy Engraving, Modern... 2,500   3,000   3,000

Model 76, 12 and 20 Gauges, Automatic Ejectors, Single Selective
Trigger, Engraved, Checkered Stock, Modern.. 375   650   650

Model 76, .410 Gauge, Double Triggers, Engraved,
Checkered Stock, Modern.. 375   550   550

Model 400, Various Gauges, Single Trigger, Checkered Stock,
Modern... 325   575   575

Model 400E, Various Gauges, Single Selective Trigger, Checkered
Stock, Selective Ejector, Modern.. 375   450   450

Model XXV/SL, 12 Ga., Sidelock, Automatic Ejector, Engraved
Checkered Stock, Modern.. 1,250   1,600   1,600

AZANZA Y ARRIZABALAGA   Eibar, Spain, c. 1916.

HANDGUN, SEMI-AUTOMATIC

M1916, .32 ACP, Clip Fed, Long Grip, Curio.. 100   150   150

	V.G.	Exc	Prior Edition

AZUL Eulegio Aristegui, Eibar, Spain, c. 1930.

HANDGUN, SEMI-AUTOMATIC

	V.G.	Exc	Prior Edition
Azul, .25 ACP, Clip Fed, Hammerless, Curio...	$75	$125	$125
Azul, .32 ACP, Clip Fed, Hammer, Curio...	100	150	150
Azul, .32 ACP, Clip Fed, Hammerless, Curio...	75	125	125
Azul, 7.63mm Mauser, Copy of Broomhandle Mauser, Curio..................	550	950	950

B

BABCOCK c. 1880.

HANDGUN, REVOLVER

.32 Short R.F., 5 Shot, Spur Trigger, Solid Frame, Single Action,
Antique... $75 $150 $150

BABY BULLDOG

HANDGUN, REVOLVER

.22 L.R.R.F., Double Action, Hammerless, Folding Trigger,
Modern... 75   150   150
.32 Short R.F., Double Action, Hammerless, Folding Trigger,
Modern... 75   125   125

BABY RUSSIAN Made by American Arms Co. c. 1890.

HANDGUN, REVOLVER

.38 S & W, 5 Shot, Single Action, Spur Trigger, Top Break,
Curio... 125   225   225

BACKHOUSE, RICHARD Easton, Pa. 1774–1781. See Kentucky Rifles.

BACKUP See TDE, and AMT.

BACON ARMS CO. Norwich, Conn. 1858–1891. Also known as Bacon & Co. and Bacon Mfg. Co.

HANDGUN, PERCUSSION

.34, Boot Gun, Underhammer, Half-Octagon Barrel, Antique.................. 200   350   350
6 Shot, Fluted Barrel, Pepperbox, Underhammer, Pocket Pistol,
Antique... 625   850   850

HANDGUN, REVOLVER

.22 Short R.F., 7 Shot, Spur Trigger, Solid Frame, Single Action,
Antique... 125   175   175
.32 Short R.F, 6 Shot, Solid Frame, Single Action with Trigger
Guard, Antique.. 150   300   300

	V.G.	Exc	Prior Edition
.32 Short R.F., 5 Shot, Spur Trigger, Solid Frame, Single Action, Antique....................	$125	$175	$175
.32 Short R.F., 6 Shot, Solid Frame, Spur Trigger, Single Action, Antique....................	175	300	300
"Navy," .38 Long R.F., 6 Shot, 7½" Barrel, Solid Frame, Spur Trigger, Single Action, Antique....................	175	375	375

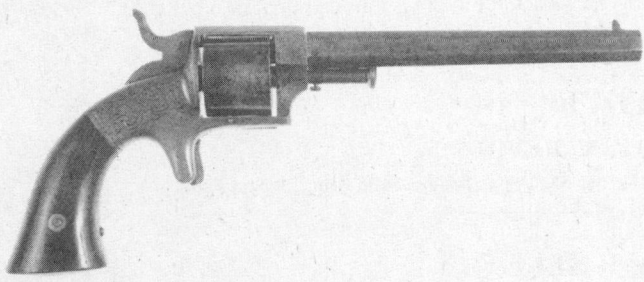

Bacon Navy Six Shot, .38 Caliber

HANDGUN, SINGLESHOT

Derringer, .32 R.F., Spur Trigger, Side–Swing Barrel, Antique..............	175	350	350
SS Percussion, .31 Cal., Ring Trigger, Antique..	175	275	275

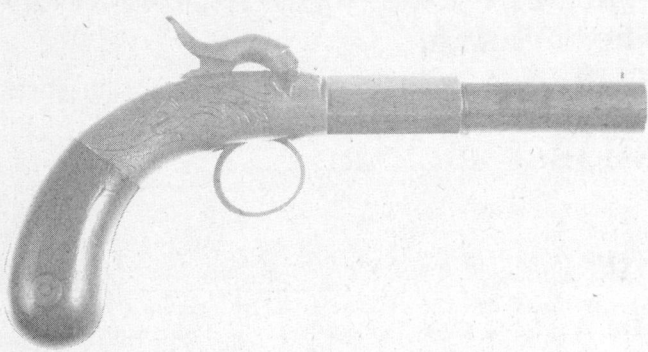

Bacon Ring Trigger, Single Shot .31 Caliber

BAIKAL Made in U.S.S.R., imported by Commercial Trading Imports.

SHOTGUN, DOUBLE BARREL, OVER-UNDER

IJ-27E1C, 12 or 20 Gauge, Boxlock, Engraved, Checkered Stock, Single Selective Trigger, Selective Ejectors, Vent Rib, Modern..............	225	375	375
IJ-27E1C Silver, 12 or 20 Gauge, Boxlock, Engraved, Checkered Stock, Single Selective Trigger, Selective Ejectors, Vent Rib, Modern....................	200	300	300

	V.G.	Exc	Prior Edition
IJ-27E1C Super, 12 or 20 Gauge, Boxlock, Engraved, Checkered Stock, Single Selective Trigger, Selective Ejectors, Vent Rib, Modern.............	$350	$550	$550
MC-109, 12 Gauge, Sidelock, Engraved, Checkered Stock, Single Selective Trigger, Selective Ejectors, Vent Rib, Modern..........................	2,500	3,000	3,000
MC-5-105 , 20 Gauge, Boxlock, Engraved, Checkered Stock, Double Triggers, Solid Rib, Cased, Modern..	875	950	950
MC-6-105, 12 Gauge, Boxlock, Engraved, Checkered Stock, Double Triggers, Solid Rib, Cased, Modern..	950	1,500	1,500
MC-7-105, 12 or 20 Gauge, Boxlock, Engraved, Checkered Stock, Single Triggers, Selective Ejectors, Solid Rib, Cased, Modern................	1,700	2,300	2,300
MC-8-105, 12 Gauge, Trap or Skeet, Boxlock, Engraved, Checkered Stock, Single Trigger, Solid Rib, Cased, Modern............................	1,400	1,900	1,900
TOZ-34E, 12 or 28 Gauge, Boxlock, Engraved, Checkered Stock, Double Triggers, Vent Rib, Modern.........................	325	450	450

SHOTGUN, DOUBLE BARREL, SIDE-BY-SIDE

	V.G.	Exc	Prior Edition
IJ-58MAE, 12 or 20 Gauge, Boxlock, Engraved, Checkered Stock, Double Triggers, Modern......................	100	200	200
MC-110, 12 or 20 Gauge, Boxlock, Engraved, Checkered Stock, Double Triggers, Solid Rib, Cased, Modern........................	1,500	2,000	2,000
MC-111, 12 Gauge, Sidelock, Engraved, Checkered Stock, Single Selective Trigger, Selective Ejectors, Cased, Modern..............................	2,500	3,000	3,000

SHOTGUN, SINGLESHOT

	V.G.	Exc	Prior Edition
IJ-18E, 12 or 20 Gauge, Checkered Stock, Modern.............................	50	75	75

BAKER GUN & FORGING CO. Batavia, N.Y. 1886–1919,

RIFLE, SEMI-AUTOMATIC

	V.G.	Exc	Prior Edition
Batavia, .22 Short, Clip Fed, Curio...	275	450	450

Single Trigger, Add $90.00-165.00
Deduct 50% for Damascus Barrels
Automatic Ejectors, Add $110.00-225.00

SHOTGUN, DOUBLE BARREL, SIDE-BY-SIDE

	V.G.	Exc	Prior Edition
Batavia Leader, Various Gauges, Sidelock, Double Trigger, Checkered Stock, Curio..	425	500	500
Batavia Special, Various Gauges, Sidelock, Double Trigger, Checkered Stock, Automatic Ejectors, Curio..	300	400	625
Black Beauty, Various Gauges, Sidelock, Double Trigger, Checkered Stock, Curio...	450	675	675
Black Beauty Special, Various Gauges, Sidelock, Double Trigger, Checkered Stock, Automatic Ejectors, Curio...................................	750	850	850
Deluxe ($1,000 Grade), Various Gauges, Sidelock, Fancy Wood, Fancy Engraving, Fancy Checkering, Automatic Ejector, Curio.............	3,500	5,000	4,500
Deluxe ($300 Grade), Various Gauges, Sidelock, Fancy Wood, Fancy Engraving, Fancy Checkering, Automatic Ejectors, Curio.............	2,950	3,250	3,250
Expert, Various Gauges, Sidelock, Fancy Wood, Fancy Engraving, Fancy Checkering, Automatic Ejectors, Curio.................................	1,850	2,100	2,100
Grade A, Various Gauges, Sidelock, Hammerless, Engraved, Damascus Barrel, Curio...	200	350	350
Grade B, Various Gauges, Sidelock, Hammerless, Engraved, Damascus Barrels, Curio..	175	310	310

	V.G.	Exc	Prior Edition
Grade C Batavia, Various Gauges, Boxlock, Hammerless, Engraved, Damascus Barrels, Curio............	$175	$250	$250
Grade H Deluxe, Various Gauges, Sidelock, Fancy Engraving, Curio............	2,850	3,650	3,650
Grade L Pigeon, Various Gauges, Sidelock, Fancy Engraving, Curio............	1,550	2,150	2,150
Grade N Krupp Trap, 12 Ga., Sidelock, Engraved, Curio............	950	1,400	1,400
Grade R, Various Gauges, Sidelock, Light Engraving, Curio............	1,000	1,500	675
Grade S, Various Gauges, Sidelock, Light Engraving, Curio............	850	1,000	575
Model 1896, 10 and 12 Gauges, Hammers, Curio............	225	275	275
Model 1897, Various Gauges, Hammers, Curio............	225	275	275
New Baker Model, 10 and 12 Gauges, Hammers, Curio............	260	300	300
Paragon, Various Gauges, Sidelock, Double Trigger, Engraved, Fancy Checkering, Curio............	1,350	1,450	1,450
Paragon, Various Gauges, Sidelock, Double Trigger, Engraved, Fancy Checkering, Automatic Ejectors, Curio............	1,475	1,575	1,575
Paragon Special, 12 Ga., Sidelock, Fancy Wood, Fancy Engraving, Curio............	1,250	1,950	1,950

SHOTGUN, SINGLESHOT

	V.G.	Exc	Prior Edition
Elite, 12 Ga., Vent Rib, Fancy Engraving, Curio............	775	1,250	1,250
Sterling, 12 Ga., Vent Rib, Light Engraving, Curio............	550	775	775
Superba 12 Ga., Trap Grade, Fancy Wood, Fancy Engraving, Fancy Checkering, Automatic Ejectors, Antique............	1,950	2,775	2,775

BAKER GUN CO. Made in Belgium for H & D Folsom Arms Co.

SHOTGUN, DOUBLE BARREL, SIDE-BY-SIDE

	V.G.	Exc	Prior Edition
Various Gauges, Hammerless, Damascus Barrel, Antique............	100	175	175
Various Gauges, Hammerless, Steel Barrel, Antique............	125	200	200
Various Gauges, Outside Hammers, Damascus Barrel, Antique............	75	175	175
Various Gauges, Outside Hammers, Steel Barrel, Antique............	100	200	200

SHOTGUN, SINGLESHOT

	V.G.	Exc	Prior Edition
Various Gauges, Hammer, Steel Barrel, Antique............	50	75	75

BAKER, EZEKIEL London, England 1784–1825.

HANDGUN, PERCUSSION

	V.G.	Exc	Prior Edition
.58, Holster Pistol, Round Barrel, Light Ornamentation, Antique............	550	750	750

BAKER, JOHN Providence, Pa. 1768–1775. See Kentucky Rifles.

BAKER, W. H. & CO. Marathon, N.Y. 1870, Syracuse, N.Y. 1878–1886.

COMBINATION WEAPON, DRILLING

	V.G.	Exc	Prior Edition
Hammer Drilling, Various Gauges, Damascus Barrels. Front Trigger Break, Antique............	450	725	725

	V.G.	Exc	Prior Edition

RIFLE, PERCUSSION

.60, Brass Furniture, Scope Mounted, Target, Octagon Barrel, Antique... $2,000 $2,750 $2,750

SHOTGUN, DOUBLE BARREL, SIDE-BY-SIDE

Hammer Double, 10 and 12 Gauges, Damascus Barrels, Front Trigger Break, Antique.. 275 375 375

BALL & WILLIAMS Worcester, Mass. 1861–1866.

RIFLE, SINGLESHOT

Ballard, .44 Long R.F., Milliary, Carbine, Falling Block, Antique.......... 600 700 700
Ballard, .46 Long R.F., Kentucky Rifle, Falling Block, Antique............. 750 875 875
Ballard, Various Rimfires, Falling Block, Sporting Rifle, Antique.......... 425 525 525
Ballard, Various Rimfires, Military, Falling Block, Antique.................... 675 950 950
Merwin & Bray, .54 Ballard R.F., Military, Carbine, Falling Block, Antique.. 625 825 825
Merwin & Bray, Various Rimfires, Falling Block, Sporting Rifle, Antique.. 525 650 650

BALLARD & CO. Worcester, Mass 1861–1971. Also See U.S. Military.

RIFLE, SINGLESHOT

#2 (Marlin), Various Calibers, Falling Block, Sporting Rifle, Antique.. 700 750 750
#3 Gallery (Marlin), Various Calibers, Falling Block, Target Rifle, Antique.. 700 750 750
#3 Gallery (Marlin), Various Rimfires, Falling Block, Target Rifle, Antique.. 400 600 600
#3–F Gallery (Marlin), .22 Long R.F., Falling Block, Target Rifle, Fancy Wood, Antique.. 700 800 800
#4 Perfection (Marlin), Various Calibers, Falling Block, Target Rifle, Target Sights, Set Triggers, Octagon Barrel., Antique.................... 750 650 650

BALLARD RIFLE Made by Ball & Williams 1861–1866, Merrimack Arms & Mfg. Co. 1866–1869, Brown Mfg. Co. 1869–1873, J. M. Marlin from 1875.

RIFLE, SINGLESHOT

#1 Hunter (Marlin), .44 Long R F/C F, Falling Block, Sporting Rifle, Recoil Pad, Antique.. 500 900 900
#1½ Hunter (Marlin), .40-65 Ballard Everlasting, Falling Block, Sporting Rifle, Open Rear Sight, Antique................................. 600 1,250 1,250
#2 (Marlin), .44-40 WCF, Falling Block, Sporting Rifle, Open Rear Sight, Antique.. 500 800 800
#2 (Marlin), Various Calibers, Falling Block, Sporting Rifle, Recoil Pad, Early Model, Antique.. 400 750 750
#3 Gallery (Marlin), .22 Short R.F., Falling Block, Target Rifle, Early Model, Antique.. 400 800 800
#3½ (Marlin), .40–65 Ballard Everlasting, Falling Block, Target Rifle, Target Sights, Octagon Barrel, Antique............................. 700 1,100 1,100

	V.G.	Exc	Prior Edition
#4 Perfection (Marlin), Various Calibers, Falling Block, Target Rifle, Target Sights, Set Trigger, Early Model, Antique............................	$600	$950	$950
#4½ (Marlin), .40–65 Ballard Everlasting, Falling Block, Mid-Range Target Rifle, Checkered Stock, Antique..	1,050	1,700	1,700
#4½ (Marlin), .45–70 Government, Falling Block, Sporting Rifle, Antique........................	875	1,250	1,250
#4½ (Marlin), Various Calibers, Falling Block, Mid–Range Target Rifle, Target Sights, Fancy Wood, Antique..	1,500	2,500	2,500
#4½ (Marlin), Various Calibers, Falling Block, Sporting Rifle, Antique..	950	1,150	1,150
#5 Pacific (Marlin), .45–70 Government, Falling Block, Target Rifle, Open Rear Sight, Set Trigger, Octagon Barrel, Antique..................	700	1,500	1,500
#5 Pacific (Marlin), Various Calibers, Falling Block, Target Rifle, Open Rear Sight, Set Trigger, Octagon Barrel, Antique............................	650	1,250	1,250
#6 Pacific (Marlin), Various Calibers, Falling Block, Schutzen Rifle, Target Sights, Fancy Wood, Set Triggers, Antique........................	1,700	3,000	3,000
#6½ (Marlin), .40–65 Ballard Everlasting, Falling Block, Off-Hand Target Rifle, Target Sights, Set Trigger, Antique...	900	2,000	2,000
#6½ (Marlin), Various Calibers, Falling Block, Mid–Range Target Rifle, Antique.......................	1,200	3,000	3,000
#7 A (Marlin), .44–100 Ballard Everlasting, Falling Block, Long Range Target Rifle, Target Sights, Set Trigger, Antique............................	2,200	3,200	3,200
#7 A-1 (Marlin), .44–100 Ballard Everlasting, Falling Block, Long Range Target Rifle, Target Sights, Set Trigger, Fancy Wood, Antique....	2,000	4,000	4,000
#7 A-1 (Marlin), .44–75 Ballard Everlasting, Falling Block, Creedmore Long Range, Target Sights, Fancy Wood, Set Trigger, Antique.....................	2,500	3,500	3,500
#7 A-1 Extra Deluxe, .44–100 Ballard Everlasting, Falling Block, Long Range Target Rifle, Target Sights, Set Trigger, Fancy Wood, Antique........................	2,500	5,000	5,000
#8 (Marlin), .44–75 Ballard Everlasting, Falling Block, Creedmore Long Range, Target Sights, Pistol–Grip Stock, Set Trigger, Antique..........................	800	1,500	1,500
#9 (Marlin), .44–75 Ballard Everlasting, Falling Block, Creedmore Long Range, Target Sights, Set Trigger, Antique.........................	700	1,200	1,200
(Ball & Williams), .54 Ballard R.F., Military, Carbine, Falling Block, Antique..........................	675	950	950
(Ball & Williams), .44 Long R.F., Military, Carbine, Falling Block, Antique..........................	675	850	850
(Ball & Williams), .46 Long R.F., Kentucky Rifle, Falling Block, Antique..........................	850	1,025	1,025
(Ball & Williams), Various Rimfires, Falling Block, Sporting Rifle, Antique..........................	475	675	675
(Ball & Williams), Various Rimfires, Military, Falling Block, Antique..........................	750	1,050	1,050
1½ Hunter (Marlin), .45–70 Government, Falling Block, Sporting Rifle, Open Rear Sight, Set Trigger, Antique............................	700	1,200	1,200
1¾ Far West (Marlin), .40–65 Ballard Everlasting, Falling Block, Sporting Rifle, Open Rear Sight, Set Trigger, Antique.......................	625	1,200	1,200
1¾ Far West (Marlin), .45–70 Government, Falling Block, Sporting Rifle, Open Rear Sight, Set Trigger, Antique........................	675	1,250	1,250
5½ Montana (Marlin), .45–100 Sharps, Falling Block, Sporting Rifle, Octagon Barrel, Antique.........................	1,500	3,000	3,000
Brown Mfg. Co., .44 Long R.F., Falling Block, Mid–Range Target Rfile, Antique.........................	875	1,175	1,175

	V.G.	Exc	Prior Edition
Hunter, .44 Long R F/C F, Falling Block, Sporting Rifle, Recoil Pad, Antique...............	$675	$750	$750
Merrimack Arms, .44 Long R.F., Falling Block, Carbine, Antique...............	675	950	950
Merrimack Arms, .46 Long R.F., Falling Block, Military, Antique...............	775	1,025	1,025
Merrimack Arms, .56–52 Spencer R.F., Falling Block, Military, Antique...............	675	925	925
Merrimack Arms, Various Rimfires, Falling Block, Sporting Rifle, Antique...............	675	950	950
Merwin & Bray, Various Rimfires, Falling Block, Sporting Rifle, Antique...............	575	775	775

BANG-UP Made by Hopkins & Allen, c. 1880.

HANDGUN, REVOLVER

	V.G.	Exc	Prior Edition
.22 Short R.F., 7 Shot, Spur Trigger, Solid Frame, Single Action, Antique...............	100	150	150

BARKER, F.A. Fayetteville, N.C. 1860–1864. See Confederate Military.

BARKER, T. Made by Crescent; Also Made in Belgium.

SHOTGUN, DOUBLE BARREL, SIDE-BY-SIDE

Various Gauges, Hammerless, Damascus Barrel, Modern............	75	150	150
Various Gauges, Hammerless, Steel Barrel, Modern............	100	175	175
Various Gauges, Outside Hammers, Damascus Barrel, Modern............	100	125	125
Various Gauges, Outside Hammers, Steel Barrel, Modern............	75	175	175

SHOTGUN, SINGLESHOT

Various Gauges, Hammer, Steel Barrel, Modern............	50	75	75

BARLOW, J. Moscow, Ind. 1836–1840. See Kentucky Rifles.

BARNETT & SON London, England 1750–1832.

RIFLE, FLINTLOCK

.75, 3rd. Model Brown Bess, Musket, Military, Antique............	1,250	1,850	1,850

BARNETT, J. & SONS London, England 1835–1875.

RIFLE, PERCUSSION

.577, C.W. Enfield, Rifled, Musket, Military, Antique............	500	750	750

BARRETT, J. Wythesville, Va. 1857–1865. See Confederate Military.

	V.G.	Exc	Prior Edition

BAUER FIREARMS (FRASER ARMS CO.) Fraser, Mich.

HANDGUN, SEMI-AUTOMATIC

25-Bicentennial, .25 ACP, Clip Fed, Pocket Pistol, Stainless Steel, Hammerless, Engraved, Modern..	$150	$225	$225
25-SS, .25 ACP, Clip Fed, Pocket Pistol, Stainless Steel, Hammerless, Modern..	125	200	125

COMBINATION WEAPON, OVER-UNDER

Rabbit, .22/.410, Metal Frame, Survival Gun, Modern............................	100	125	75

BAUER, GEORGE Lancaster, Pa. 1770–1781. See Kentucky Rifles.

BAY STATE ARMS CO. Uxbridge & Worcester, Mass. 1873–1874.

RIFLE, SINGLESHOT

.32 Long R.F., Dropping Block, Antique...	125	175	175
Various Calibers, Target Rifle, Antique..	600	875	875

SHOTGUN, SINGLESHOT

Davenport Patent, 12 Ga., Antique..	200	275	275

BAYARD Belgium. Made by Anciens Etablissments Pieper, c. 1900. Also see Bergmann and Danish Military.

HANDGUN, REVOLVER

S & W Style, .32 S&W Long, Double Action, Curio................................	50	100	100
S & W Style, .38 S&W, Double Action, Curio...	50	100	100

HANDGUN, SEMI-AUTOMATIC

Bergmann/Bayard 1910, 9mm Bayard, Clip Fed, Blue, Commercial, Curio..	1,000	1,500	675
Bergmann/Bayard 1910, 9mm Bayard, Clip Fed, Blue, Commercial, with Holster/Stock, Curio..	1,500	1,750	850

	V.G.	Exc	Prior Edition
Model 1908 (1910) Pocket, .32 ACP, Blue, Clip Fed, Curio.................	$275	$350	$225

Bayard Model 1908 (1910) .32 ACP

	V.G.	Exc	Prior Edition
Model 1908 (1910) Pocket, .32 ACP, Blue, Clip Fed, German Military, Curio......................	300	375	225
Model 1908 (1910) Pocket, .32 ACP, Nickel, Clip Fed, Curio...............	300	375	225
Model 1908 (1911) Pocket, .380 ACP, Blue, Clip Fed, Curio................	300	375	300
Model 1908 (1911) Pocket, .380 ACP, Nickel, Clip Fed, Curio.............	325	400	300
Model 1908 (1912) Pocket, .25 ACP, Blue, Clip Fed, Curio..................	300	350	195
Model 1908 (1912) Pocket, .25 ACP, Nickel, Clip Fed, Curio..............	325	400	225
Model 1923 Pocket, Early, .25 ACP, Blue, Clip Fed, With Magazine Safety, Curio......................	200	275	200
Model 1923 Pocket, Early, .32 ACP, Blue, Clip Fed, With Magazine Safety, Curio......................	225	275	200
Model 1923 Pocket, Early, .380 ACP, Blue, Clip Fed, With Magazine Safety, Curio......................	375	450	325
Model 1923 Pocket, Standard, .25 ACP, Blue, Clip Fed, No Magazine Safety, Curio......................	200	250	195
Model 1923 Pocket, Standard, .32 ACP, Blue, Clip Fed, No Magazine Safety, Curio......................	250	300	225
Model 1923 Pocket, Standard, .380 ACP, Blue, Clip Fed, No Magazine Safety, Curio......................	275	350	225

	V.G.	Exc	Prior Edition
Model 1930 Pocket, .25 ACP, Blue, Clip Fed, Curio.............................	$200	$275	$200

Bayard Model 1930

	V.G.	Exc	Prior Edition
Model 1930 Pocket, .32 ACP, Blue, Clip Fed, Curio..............................	200	275	200
Model 1930 Pocket, .380 ACP, Blue, Clip Fed, Curio.............................	300	375	325

RIFLE, SINGLESHOT

Boy's Rifle, .22 L.R.R.F., Plain, Takedown, Curio....................................	50	75	75
Half-Auto Carbine, .22 Short, Checkered Stock, Curio..........................	50	75	75
Half-Auto Carbine, .22 Short, Plain, Curio...	50	75	75

SHOTGUN, DOUBLE BARREL, SIDE-BY-SIDE

Hammer, 12 Gauge, Double Triggers, Fancy Engraving, Boxlock, Steel Barrels, Curio....................	125	225	225
Hammer, 12 Gauge, Double Triggers, Light Engraving, Boxlock, Damascus Barrels, Curio....................	75	150	150
Hammer, 12 Gauge, Double Triggers, Light Engraving, Boxlock, Steel Barrels, Curio....................	75	150	150
Hammerless, 12 Gauge, Double Triggers, Light Engraving, Boxlock, Steel Barrels, Curio....................	125	200	200

BECK, GIDEON Lancaster, Pa. 1780–1788. See Kentucky Rifles and Pistols.

BECK, ISAAC Miffinberg, Pa. 1830–1840.

RIFLE, PERCUSSION

.47, Octagon Barrel, Brass Furniture, Antique...	1,200	1,500	1,500

BECK, JOHN Lancaster, Pa. 1772–1777. See Kentucky Rifles and Pistols.

	V.G.	Exc	Prior Edition

BEEMAN PRECISION FIREARMS San Raphael, Calif., Importers.

HANDGUN, PERCUSSION

Hege-Siber, English, .33, Checkered Stock, Light Engraving, Cased, Reproduction, Antique.. $500 $750 $600

Hege-Siber, French, .33, Checkered Stock, Engraved, Gold Inlays, Cased, Reproduction, Antique.. 750 1,250 1,100

PB Aristocrat, .36 or .44, Single Set Trigger, Fluted Stock, Reproduction, Antique.. 175 250 225

HANDGUN, SEMI-AUTOMATIC

Agner M80, .22 L.R.R.F., Clip Fed, Stainless Steel, Adjustable Target Grips, Adjustable Trigger, Modern... 925 1,000 800

Beeman Agner M80

	V.G.	Exc	Prior Edition
FAS Model 601, .22 Short R.F., Clip Fed, Target Grip, Rapid Fire, Target Pistol, Modern..	$650	$750	$600

Beeman FAS Model 601

FAS Model 602, .22 L.R.R.F., Clip Fed, Target Grip, Match Pistol, Modern..	750	850	775

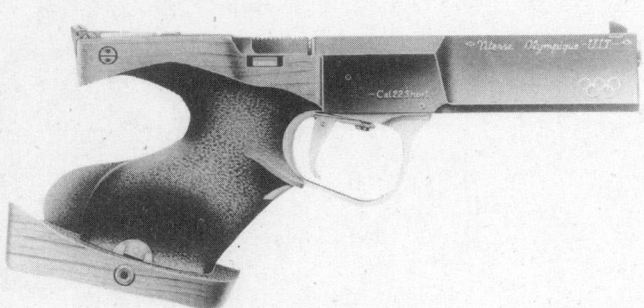

Beeman Unique Model 823-U

FAS Model 603, .32 S&W Wadcutter, Clip Fed, Target Grips, Match Pistol, Modern..	775	850	725

	V.G.	Exc	Prior Edition
Unique Model 69, .22 L.R.R.F., Clip Fed, Adjustable Target Grips, Match Pistol, Modern..............	$700	$800	$550

Beeman Unique Model 69

Unique Model 823-U, .22 Short R.F., Clip Fed, Adjustable Target Grips, Rapid Fire Match Pistol, Modern.....................................	700	800	600

RIFLE, BOLT ACTION

Feinwerkbau 2000 Match, .22 L.R.R.F., Single Shot, Adjustable Trigger, Adjustable Target Stock, Modern..................................	750	850	575

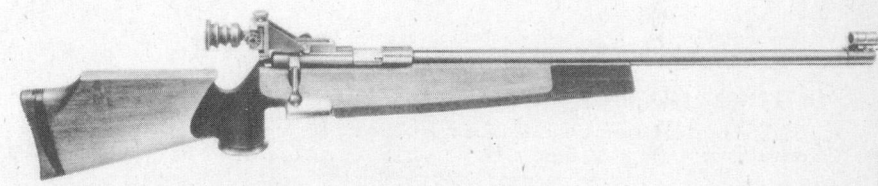

Beeman Feinwerkbau 2000 Match

Feinwerkbau 2000 Mini, .22 L.R.R.F., Single Shot, Adjustable Trigger, Adjustable Target Stock, Modern....................................	700	800	550
Feinwerkbau 2000 Running Target, .22 L.R.R.F., Single Shot, Adjustable Trigger, Adjustable Target Stock, Modern............................	750	850	650
Feinwerkbau 2000 Universal, .22 L.R.R.F., Single Shot, Adjustable Trigger, Adjustable Target Stock, Modern................................	750	850	600
Feinwerkbau Free Rifle, .22 L.R.R.F., Single Shot, Adjustable Electric Trigger, Adjustable Target Stock, Counterweights, Hook Buttplate, Modern...	1,000	1,250	1,100
Krico Model 302, .22 L.R.R.F., Clip Fed, Checkered Stock, Open Sights, Modern..	400	450	300
Krico Model 304, .22 L.R.R.F., Clip Fed, Checkered Stock, Mannlicher Stock, Set Triggers, Open Sights, Modern............................	450	500	375
Krico Model 340, .22 L.R.R.F., Metallic Silhouette Match Rifle, Clip Fed, Checkered Stock, Target Stock, Modern....................................	625	700	450

	V.G.	Exc	Prior Edition
Krico Model 340, .22 L.R.R.F., Mini-Sniper Match Rifle, Clip Fed, Checkered Stock, Target Stock, Modern.....................	$650	$725	$475
Krico Model 400, .22 Hornet, Clip Fed, Checkered Stock, Open Sights, Modern...........................	650	675	425
Krico Model 420, .22 Hornet, Clip Fed, Checkered Stock, Set Triggers, Mannlicher Stock, Open Sights, Sling Swivels, Modern...........	650	725	475
Krico Model 600, Various Calibers, Clip Fed, Checkered Stock, Open Sights, Sling Swivels, Recoil Pads, Modern......................	800	900	650
Krico Model 620, Various Calibers, Clip Fed, Checkered Stock, Set Triggers, Mannlicher Stock, Open Sights, Sling Swivels, Modern..............	775	875	650
Krico Model 640, Various Calibers, Deluxe Varmint Rifle, Clip Fed, Checkered Stock, Target Stock, Modern......................	625	700	650
Krico Model 650, Various Calibers, Sniper/Match Rifle, Clip Fed, Checkered Stock, Target Stock, Modern.....................	850	1,000	800

Beeman Krico Model 650

	V.G.	Exc	Prior Edition
Krico Model 700, Various Calibers, Clip Fed, Checkered Stock, Open Sights, Sling Swivels, Recoil Pad, Modern.....................	850	1,000	650
Krico Model 720, Various Calibers, Clip Fed, Checkered Stock, Set Triggers, Mannlicher Stock, Open Sights, Sling Swivels, Modern..............	800	900	650
Weihrauch HW60, .22 L.R.R.F., Singleshot Target Rifle, Target Sights, Target Stock, Heavy Barrel, Modern...........................	525	500	400

SHOTGUN, DOUBLE BARREL, OVER-UNDER

	V.G.	Exc	Prior Edition
Fabarm Gamma, 12 Gauge, Field Model, Single Selective Trigger, Checkered Stock, Vent Rib, Modern.........................	700	775	450

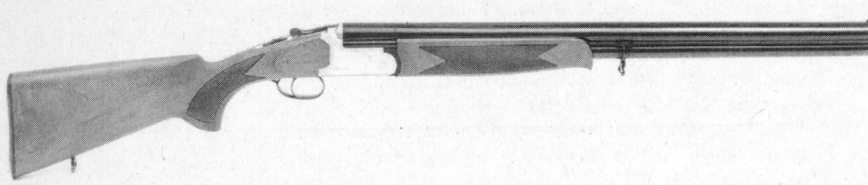

Beeman Fabarm Gamma

	V.G.	Exc	Prior Edition
Fabarm Gamma, 12 Gauge, Skeet Model, Single Selective Trigger, Checkered Stock, Vent Rib, Modern........................	775	800	450
Fabarm Gamma, 12 Gauge, Trap/Skeet Combo, 2 Barrels, Single Selective Trigger, Checkered Stock, Vent Rib, Modern...........................	800	875	700

BEERSTECHER, FREDERICK Lewisburg, Pa. 1849–1860.

HANDGUN, PERCUSSION

.40, Double Shot, Superimposed Loading, Derringer Style,
Antique.. $4,000 $4,750 $4,750

BEHOLLA Made by Becker & Hollander, Suhl, Germany c. 1910. Also made under this patent were the Stenda, Leonhardt, and Menta.

HANDGUN, SEMI-AUTOMATIC

		V.G.	Exc	Prior Edition
.32 ACP,	Clip Fed, Commercial, Blue, Hard Rubber Grips, Curio	250	300	200
.32 ACP,	Clip Fed, Commercial, Blue, Wood Grips, Curio	200	250	150
.32 ACP,	Clip Fed, Military, Blue, Hard Rubber Grips, Curio	200	250	150
.32 ACP,	Clip Fed, Military, Blue, Wood Grips, Curio	200	250	150

BELGIAN MILITARY Also see Browning, FN.

RIFLE, BOLT ACTION

M 1889 Mauser,	Carbine, Military, Curio	325	350	125
M 1889 Mauser,	Military, Curio	300	325	100
M 1924,	Various Calibers, Military, Curio	225	250	150
M 1930,	Various Calibers, Military, Curio	225	250	150
M 1934/30,	Various Calibers, Military, Curio	200	225	125
M 1935 Mauser,	Military, Curio	275	300	125
M 1936 Mauser,	Military, Curio	150	175	100
M 1950,	.30–06 Springfield, Military, Curio	250	275	175

RIFLE, SEMI-AUTOMATIC

M 1949,	.30–06 Springfield, Military, Curio	300	450	450
M 1949,	Various Calibers, Military, Curio	250	375	375

BELL, JOHN Carlisle, Pa. c. 1800. See Kentucky Rifles and Pistols.

BELLMORE GUN CO. Made by Crescent, c. 1900.

SHOTGUN, DOUBLE BARREL, SIDE-BY-SIDE

Various Gauges,	Hammerless, Damascus Barrel, Curio	75	175	175
Various Gauges,	Hammerless, Stel Barrel, Curio	100	175	175
Various Gauges,	Outside Hammers, Damascus Barrel, Curio	75	150	150
Various Gauges,	Outside Hammers, Steel Barrel, Curio	100	200	200

SHOTGUN, SINGLESHOT

Various Gauges,	Hammer, Steel Barrel, Modern	50	100	100

BENELLI Made in Italy, imported by H & K Inc. and Sile.

HANDGUN, SEMI-AUTOMATIC

B 76,	9mm Luger, Clip Fed, Blue, Modern	375	450	350

	V.G.	Exc	Prior Edition

RIFLE, SEMI-AUTOMATIC

Model 940, .30–06 Springfield, Clip Fed, Open Sights, Recoil Pad, Sling Swivels, Modern.. $400 $475 $425

SHOTGUN, SEMI-AUTOMATIC

	V.G.	Exc	Prior Edition
Model 123V Deluxe, 12 Gauge, Engraved Model, Checkered Stock, Vent Rib, Modern..........................	350	425	425
Model 123V, 12 Gauge, Standard Model, Checkered Stock, Vent Rib, Modern..........................	325	400	325
Model SL 121MI, 12 Gauge, Police, Open Sights, Checkered Stock, Recoil Pad, Modern..........................	300	375	325
Model SL 121V, 12 Gauge, Slug Gun, Open Sights, Checkered Stock, Recoil Pad, Modern..........................	300	375	275
Model SL 201, 20 Gauge, Checkered Stock, Plain Barrel, Modern.........	275	350	300
Special Skeet, 12 Gauge, White Receiver, Checkered Stock, Vent Rib, Modern..........................	400	475	475
Special Trap, 12 Gauge, White Receiver, Checkered Stock, Vent Rib, Modern..........................	375	450	450

BENFER, AMOS Beaverstown, Pa. c. 1810. See Kentucky Rifles and Pistols.

BERETTA Pietro Beretta; Gardone V.T., Italy. Company history extends back to 1680. Beretta U.S.A. Corp. formed in 1977.

HANDGUN, SEMI-AUTOMATIC

	V.G.	Exc	Prior Edition
1910, .25 ACP, Clip Fed, Curio.....................	250	300	275
1915, .32 ACP, Clip Fed, Military, Curio.....................	300	350	275
1915, 9mm Glisenti, Clip Fed, Military, Curio.....................	375	425	350
1915/1919, .32 ACP, Clip Fed, Military, Curio.....................	250	300	275
1919 V P, .25 ACP, Clip Fed, Curio.....................	250	300	275
Cougar, .380 ACP, Clip Fed, Modern.....................	175	225	225
Jaguar, .22 L.R.R.F., Clip Fed, Modern.....................	150	200	200
Jetfire, .25 ACP, Clip Fed, Blue, Modern.....................	100	150	150
Jetfire, .25 ACP, Clip Fed, Nickel, Modern.....................	100	150	150
Minx, .22 Short, Clip Fed, Blue, Modern.....................	100	125	150
Minx, .22 Short, Clip Fed, Nickel, Modern.....................	100	125	150
Model 100, .32 ACP, Clip Fed, Modern.....................	175	200	175
Model 101, .22 L.R.R.F., Clip Fed, Adjustable Sights, Modern.............	175	200	175
Model 1923, 9mm Luger, Clip Fed, Military, Curio.....................	375	425	225
Model 1923, 9mm Luger, Clip Fed, Military, with Detachable Shoulder Stock, Curio.....................	575	650	550
Model 1931 Navy, .32 ACP, Clip Fed, Military, Curio.....................	300	350	175
Model 1934, .380 ACP, Clip Fed, Commercial, Curio.....................	325	375	250
Model 1934, .380 ACP, Clip Fed, Military, Curio.....................	250	300	125

	V.G.	Exc	Prior Edition
Model 1935, .32 ACP, Clip Fed, Commercial, Curio........................	$275	$325	$200

Beretta Model 1935 .32 ACP

	V.G.	Exc	Prior Edition
Model 1935, .32 ACP, Clip Fed, Military, Curio.......................................	225	275	100
Model 318, .25 ACP, Clip Fed, Modern..	250	275	200
Model 418, .25 ACP, Clip Fed, Modern..	200	225	175
Model 420, .25 ACP, Clip Fed, Chrome, Light Engraving, Modern..	250	300	300
Model 421, .25 ACP, Clip Fed, Gold Plated, Fancy Engraving, Modern..	450	500	400
Model 70S, .380 ACP, Clip Fed, Modern...	225	250	225
Model 70T, .32 ACP, Clip Fed, Adjustable Sights, Modern.....................	200	225	200
Model 76, .22 L.R.R.F., Clip Fed, Adjustable Sights, Modern.................	250	300	275
Model 81, .32 ACP, Clip Fed, Double Action, Modern.............................	300	350	325
Model 82, .32 ACP, Clip Fed, Double Action, Modern.............................	275	325	300
Model 84, .380 ACP, Clip Fed, Double Action, Modern...........................	375	425	300
Model 84 Tercentennial, .380 ACP, Clip Fed, Double Action, Engraved, Cased, Modern...	750	1,000	1,250
Model 85, .380 ACP, Clip Fed, Double Action, Modern...........................	350	400	325
Model 90, .32 ACP, Clip Fed, Double Trigger, Modern............................	200	225	275
Model 92, 9mm Luger, 14 Shot Clip Fed, Double Action, Modern..	375	425	450
Model 92, 9mm Luger, 16 Shot Clip Fed, Double Action, Modern..	450	500	450
Model 948, .22 L.R.R.F., Clip Fed, Lightweight, Modern........................	150	175	150
Model 949 Olympic, .22 L.R.R.F., Clip Fed, Target Pistol, Modern..	550	650	350
Model 949 Olympic, .22 Short R.F., Clip Fed, Target Pistol, Modern..	550	650	350
Model 950 Minx, .22 Short R.F., Clip Fed, 2" Barrel, Modern...............	100	150	150
Model 950B Minx, .22 Short R.F., Clip Fed, 4" Barrel, Modern.............	100	150	150
Model 951 Brigadier, 9mm Luger, Clip Fed, Commercial, Modern..	275	325	325
Model 951 Egyptian, 9mm Luger, Clip Fed, Military, Curio...................	250	375	375
Model 951 Israeli, 9mm Luger, Clip Fed, Military, Curio.......................	250	375	375
Puma, .32 ACP, Clip Fed, Modern..	175	200	200

	V.G.	Exc	Prior Edition

RIFLE, SEMI-AUTOMATIC

	V.G.	Exc	Prior Edition
Olympia, .22 L.R.R.F., Clip Fed, Tangent Sights, Checkered Stock, Modern	$150	$200	$200
Silver Gyrfalcon, .22 L.R.R.F., Checkerd Stock, Modern	150	225	225
Super Sport, .22 L.R.R.F., Fancy Checkering, Clip Fed, Modern	150	225	225

SHOTGUN, DOUBLE BARREL, OVER-UNDER

	V.G.	Exc	Prior Edition
Golden Snipe Deluxe, 12 and 20 Gauges, Single Selective Trigger, Automatic Ejector, Fancy Engraving, Fancy Checkering, Modern	625	750	750
Golden Snipe, 12 and 20 Gauges, Single Selective Trigger, Automatic Ejector, Engraved, Fancy Checkering, Modern	600	675	675
Golden Snipe, 12 and 20 Gauges, Single Trigger, Automatic Ejector, Engraved, Fancy Checkering, Modern	550	600	600
Model 680, 12 Gauge, Mono Trap Grade, Automatic Ejector, Single Trigger, Checkered Stock, Light Engraving, Modern	950	1,100	950
Model 680, 12 Gauge, Skeet Grade, Automatic Ejector, Single Selective Trigger, Engraved, Checkered Stock, Light Engraving Modern	875	950	875
Model 680, 12 Gauge, Trap Grade, Automatic Ejector, Single Selective Trigger, Checkered Stock, Light Engraving, Modern	850	1,000	925
Model 686, 12 Gauge, Field Grade, Automatic Ejector, Single Selective Trigger, Checkered Stock, Light Engraving, Modern	800	900	675
Model 687EL, 12 Gauge, Skeet Grade, Automatic Ejector, Single Selective Trigger, Checkered Stock, Fancy Engraving, Modern	1,750	2,000	1,275
Model ASEL, 12 Gauge, Single Trigger, Checkered Stock, Modern	1,000	1,250	950
Model BL 1, 12 Ga., Field Grade, Double Trigger, Checkered Stock, Modern	275	350	350
Model BL 2, 12 Ga., Field Grade, Single Selective Trigger, Checkered Stock, Modern	325	375	375
Model BL 3, 12 Ga., Trap Grade, Single Selective Trigger, Checkered Stock, Light Engraving, Vent Rib, Modern	475	550	550
Model BL 3, Various Gauges, Field Grade, Single Selective Trigger, Checkered Stock, Light Engraving, Vent Rib, Modern	500	550	550
Model BL 3, Various Gauges, Skeet Grade, Single Selective Trigger, Checkered Stock, Light Engraving, Vent Rib, Modern	550	600	550
Model BL 4, 12 Ga., Trap Grade, Single Selective Trigger, Selective Ejector, Engraved, Vent Rib, Modern	600	650	650
Model BL 4, Various Gauges, Field Grade, Single Selective Trigger, Selective Ejector, Engraved, Vent Rib, Modern	600	675	625
Model BL 4, Various Gauges, Skeet Grade, Single Selective Trigger, Selective Ejector, Engraved, Vent Rib, Modern	625	700	700
Model BL 5, 12 Ga., Trap Grade, Single Selective Trigger, Selective Ejector, Fancy Engraving, Vent Rib, Modern	700	800	850
Model BL 5, Various Gauges, Field Grade, Single Selective Trigger, Selective Ejector, Fancy Engraving, Vent Rib, Modern	750	825	825
Model BL 5, Various Gauges, Skeet Grade, Single Selective Trigger, Selective Ejector, Fancy Engraving, Vent Rib, Modern	725	875	875
Model BL 6, 12 Ga., Trap Grade, Single Selective Trigger, Selective Ejector, Fancy Engraving, Vent Rib, Modern	925	1,000	1,000
Model BL 6, Various Gauges, Field Grade, Single Selective Trigger, Selective Ejector, Fancy Engraving, Vent Rib, Modern	1,000	1,100	1,100
Model BL 6, Various Gauges, Skeet Grade, Single Selective Trigger, Selective Ejector, Fancy Engraving, Vent Rib, Modern	1,050	1,125	1,125

	V.G.	Exc	Prior Edition
Model S55B, 12 and 20 Gauges, Single Selective Trigger, Automatic Ejector, Vent Rib, Checkered Stock, Modern.........................	$425	$475	$625
Model S56E, 12 and 20 Gauges, Single Selective Trigger, Automatic Ejector, Engraved, Checkered Stock, Modern.......................	475	525	625
Model S58, 12 and 20 Gauges, Skeet Grade, Automatic Ejector, Single Selective Trigger, Engraved, Checkered Stock, Light Engraving, Modern......................	600	650	775
Model S58, 12 Ga., Trap Grade, Automatic Ejector, Single Selective Trigger, Engraved, Checkered Stock, Modern...........................	550	600	750
Model SO2, 12 Ga., Sidelock, Selective Ejector, Single Trigger, Checkered Stock, Engraved, Modern........................	3,000	3,500	2,375
Model SO3 EELL, 12 Ga., Sidelock, Automatic Ejector, Single Selective Trigger, Fancy Engraving, Fancy Wood, Modern.....................	6,500	7,500	6,175
Model SO3 EL, 12 Ga., Sidelock, Automatic Ejector, Single Selective Trigger, Fancy Engraving, Fancy Wood, Modern.....................	5,500	6,500	4,150
Model SO3, 12 Ga., Sidelock, Automatic Ejector, Single Selective Trigger, Fancy Engraving, Fancy Wood, Modern....................	5,000	6,000	3,650
Model SO4, 12 Ga., Sidelock, Automatic Ejector, Single Trigger, Fancy Engraving, Fancy Wood, Modern.....................	5,000	6,000	3,950
Model SO5, 12 Ga., Sidelock, Selective Ejector, Single Trigger, Fancy Engraving, Fancy Checkering, Modern.........................	6,500	8,000	5,475
Silver Snipe, 12 and 20 Gauges, Single Selective Trigger, Checkered Stock, Light Engraving, Modern............................	400	450	400
Silver Snipe, 12 and 20 Gauges, Single Selective Trigger, Light Engraving, Vent Rib, Modern	450	500	650
Silver Snipe, 12 and 20 Gauges, Single Trigger, Checkered Stock, Light Engraving, Modern................................	375	400	500
Silver Snipe, 12 and 20 Gauges, Single Trigger, Checkered Stock, Light Engraving, Vent Rib, Modern......................	400	450	425

SHOTGUN, DOUBLE BARREL, SIDE-BY-SIDE

	V.G.	Exc	Prior Edition
Model 409PB, Various Gauges, Double Trigger, Light Engraving, Checkered Stock, Modern.................................	600	675	675
Model 410 E, 10 Ga. 3½", Double Trigger, Engraved, Checkered Stock, Modern.................................	675	750	550
Model 410, 10 Ga. 3½", Modern....................	875	975	975
Model 411E, Various Gauges, Double Trigger, Engraved, Fancy Checkering, Automatic Ejector, Modern........................	1,050	1,125	1,125
Model 424, 12 and 20 Gauges, Double Trigger, Light Engraving, Checkered Stock, Modern....................	625	700	700
Model 426E, 12 and 20 Gauges, Single Selective Trigger, Automatic Ejector, Engraved, Checkered Stock, Modern......................	775	875	875
Model GR 2, 12 and 20 Gauges, Double Trigger, Checkered Stock, Light Engraving, Modern......................	475	600	600
Model GR 3, 12 and 20 Gauges, Single Selective Trigger, Checkered Stock, Light Engraving, Modern....................	575	675	675
Model GR 4, 12 Ga., Single Selective Trigger, Selective Ejector, Checkered Stock, Engraved, Modern......................	650	725	725
Silver Hawk, 10 Ga. 3½", Double Trigger, Magnum, Modern..................	425	475	475
Silver Hawk, 12 Ga. Mag. 3", Magnum, Modern....................	350	400	400
Silver Hawk, 12 Ga., Mag. 3", Double Trigger, Magnum, Modern........	325	375	375
Silver Hawk, Various Gauges, Double Trigger, Lightweight, Modern..................	375	450	450
Silver Hawk, Various Gauges, Single Trigger, Lightweight, Modern..................	450	500	500

	V.G.	Exc	Prior Edition

SHOTGUN, SEMI-AUTOMATIC

	V.G.	Exc	Prior Edition
Gold Lark, 12 Ga., Vent Rib, Light Engraving, Checkered Stock, Modern	$350	$425	$425
Model A301, 12 and 20 Gauges, Field Grade, Vent Rib, Modern	300	350	375
Model A301, 12 and 20 Gauges, Skeet Grade, Vent Rib, Modern	300	350	400
Model A301, 12 Ga., Mag. 3", Field Grade, Vent Rib, Modern	325	375	450
Model A301, 12 Ga., Slug, Open Rear Sight, Modern	300	350	400
Model A301, 12 Ga., Trap Grade, Vent Rib, Modern	275	325	425
Model A302, 12 and 20 Gauges, Field Grade, Vent Rib, Modern	300	350	375
Model A302, 12 and 20 Gauges, Skeet Grade, Vent Rib, Modern	300	350	375
Model A302, 12 Ga., Mag. 3", Field Grade, Vent Rib, Modern	325	375	400
Model A302, 12 Ga., Slug, Open Rear Sight, Modern	325	375	425
Model A302, 12 Ga., Trap Grade, Vent Rib, Modern	300	350	375
Model AL 1, 12 and 20 Gauges, Checkred Sock, Modern	300	350	350
Model AL 2, 12 and 20 Gauges, Vent Rib, Checkered Stock, Modern	275	300	300
Model AL 2, 12 and 20 Gauges, Vent Rib, Skeet Grade, Checkered Stock, Modern	325	350	350
Model AL 2, 12 Ga., Vent Rib, Trap Grade, Checkered Stock, Modern	275	325	350
Model AL 3, 12 and 20 Gauges, Vent Rib, Checkered Stock, Light Engraving, Modern	300	350	375
Model AL 3, 12 and 20 Gauges, Vent Rib, Checkered Stock, Light Engraving, Skeet Grade, Modern	300	350	375
Model AL 3, 12 Ga. Mag. 3", Vent Rib, Checkered Stock, Light Engraving, Modern	325	375	400
Model AL 3, 12 Ga., Vent Rib, Checkered Stock, Light Engraving, Trap Grade, Modern	275	325	350
Ruby Lark, 12 Ga., Vent Rib, Fancy Engraving, Fancy Checkering, Modern	450	525	525
Silver Lark, 12 Ga., Checkered Stock, Modern	200	250	275

SHOTGUN, SINGLESHOT

	V.G.	Exc	Prior Edition
Companion FS 1, Various Gauges, Folding Gun, Modern	125	150	150
Model Mark II, 12 Ga., Trap Grade, Vent Rib, Light Engraving, Checkered Stock, Monte Carlo Stock, Modern	375	450	450
Model TR 1, 12 Ga., Trap Grade, Vent Rib, Light Engraving, Checkered Stock, Monte Carlo Stock, Modern	200	250	250

SHOTGUN, SLIDE ACTION

	V.G.	Exc	Prior Edition
Gold Pigeon, 12 Ga., Vent Rib, Checkered Stock, Engraved, Modern	300	350	375
Gold Pigeon, 12 Ga., Vent Rib, Fancy Engraving, Fancy Checkering, Modern	375	425	475
Model SL 2, 12 Ga., Vent Rib, Checkered Stock, Modern	250	275	275
Ruby Pigeon, 12 Ga., Vent Rib, Fancy Engraving, Fancy Checkering, Modern	425	475	475
Silver Pigeon, 12 Ga., Light Engraving, Checkered Stock, Modern	150	200	200

BERETTA, GIOVANNI Brescia, Italy, c. 1700.

HANDGUN, SNAPHAUNCE

	V.G.	Exc	Prior Edition
Belt Pistol, Engraved, Carved, Light Ornamentation, Antique	3,000	4,250	4,250

	V.G.	Exc	Prior Edition

BERGMANN Gaggenau, Germany 1892–1944: Company renamed Bergmann Erben 1931. Also see Bayard.

HANDGUN, SEMI-AUTOMATIC

	V.G.	Exc	Prior Edition
Bergmann Mars, 9mmB, Clip Fed, Curio	$3,250	$3,500	$3,250
Bergmann/Bayard, Model 1908, 9mmB, Clip Fed, Curio	1,500	1,750	1,200
Bergmann/Bayard, Model 1910, 9mmB, Clip Fed, Curio	1,000	1,500	950
Bergmann/Bayard, Model 1910/21, 9mmB, Clip Fed, Curio	1,600	1,850	1,250
Erben Model I, .25 ACP, Clip Fed, Modern	275	325	275
Erben Model II, .25 ACP, Clip Fed, Modern	300	350	300
Erben Special, .32 ACP, Clip Fed, Modern	325	375	325
Model 1894, 5mm, Blow Back, Clip Fed, Antique	5,000	6,500	6,500
Model 1894, 8mm, Blow Back, Clip Fed, Antique	3,500	4,000	4,000
Model 1896 #2, 5mm, Small Frame, Clip Fed, Curio	2,200	2,700	1,800
Model 1896 #3, 6.5mm, Clip Fed, Curio	2,000	2,500	2,000

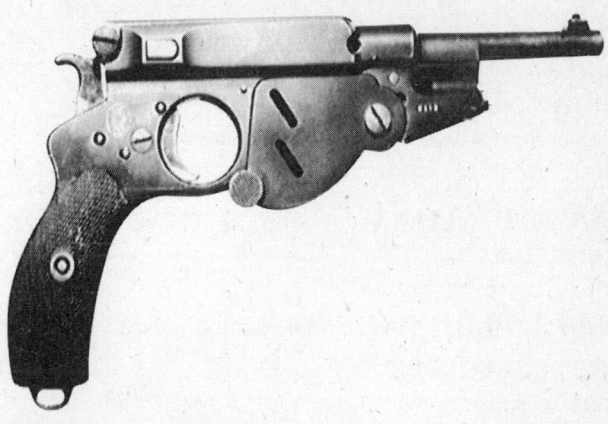

Bergmann Model 1896 #3

	V.G.	Exc	Prior Edition
Model 1896 #4, 8mm, Military, Clip Fed, Curio	2,100	2,600	2,150
Model 1897 #5, 7.8mm, Clip Fed, Curio	2,200	2,700	2,400
Model 1899 #6, 8mm, Clip Fed, Curio	1,750	2,000	975

	V.G.	Exc	Prior Edition
Model 2, .25 ACP, Clip Fed, Modern...	$250	$350	$350

Bergmann Model 2

Model 2A, .25 ACP, Einhand, Clip Fed, Modern......................................	300	400	400
Model 3, .25 ACP, Long Grip, Clip Fed, Modern......................................	250	300	300
Model 3A, .25 ACP, Einhand, Long Grip, Clip Fed, Modern...................	250	350	350

RIFLE, SEMI-AUTOMATIC

Model 1897, Karabiner, 7.8mm, Long Barrel, Detachable Stock, Modern...	4,400	5,250	5,250

BERLIN, ABRAHAM Caston, Pa. 1773–1786. See Kentucky Rifles and Pistols.

BERNARDELLI Vincenzo Bernardelli, Gardon V.T., Italy.

HANDGUN, REVOLVER

Standard, .22 L.R.R.F., or .32 S & W Long, Double Action, Blue, Modern..	200	275	275
Target, .22 L.R.R.F., Double Action, Blue, Target Sights, Modern..	200	275	275
Target, .22 L.R.R.F., Double Action, Engraved, Chrome Plated, Target Sights, Modern..	350	425	425

HANDGUN, SEMI-AUTOMATIC

M1956, 9mm Luger, Clip Fed, Curio......................................	975	1,250	1,250
Model 100, .22 L.R.R.F., Clip Fed, Blue, Target Pistol, Modern.............	250	300	300
Model 60, .22 L.R.R.F., Clip Fed, Blue, Modern.................................	125	175	175
Model 60, .22 L.R.R.F., Clip Fed, Blue, 8" Barrel, Detachable Front Sight, Adjustable Sights, Modern.....................................	275	350	350
Model 60, .32 ACP, Clip Fed, Blue, Modern.................................	150	200	200
Model 60, .380 ACP, Clip Fed, Blue, Modern.............................	150	200	200
Model 80, .22 L.R.R.F., Clip Fed, Blue, Modern.................................	125	175	175
Model 80, .22 LR.R.F., Clip Fed, Blue, 6" Barrel, Modern......................	125	200	200
Model 80, .32 ACP, Clip Fed, Blue, Modern.................................	125	175	175
Model 80, .380 ACP, Clip Fed, Blue, Modern.............................	125	200	200
Model V P, .22 L.R.R.F., Clip Fed, Blue, Modern................................	150	200	200

	V.G.	Exc	Prior Edition
Model V P, .25 ACP, Clip Fed, Blue, Modern..	$100	$175	$175
Standard, .22 L.R.R.F., Clip Fed, Blue, Modern....................................	100	175	175
Standard, .22 L.R.R.F., Clip Fed, Blue, 6" Barrel, Detachable Front Sight, Modern...	150	225	225
Standard, .22 L.R.R.F., Clip Fed, Blue, 10" Barrel, Detachable Front Sight, Modern...	225	350	350
Standard, .22 L.R.R.F., Clip Fed, Blue, 8" Barrel, Detachable Front Sight, Modern...	150	275	275
Standard, .32 ACP, Clip Fed, Blue, Modern....................................	150	200	200
Standard, .32 ACP, Clip Fed, Blue, 10" Barerl, Detachable Front Sight, Modern...	350	425	425
Standard, .32 ACP, Clip Fed, Blue, 6" Barrel, Detachable Front Sight, Modern...	225	300	300
Standard, .32 ACP, Clip Fed, Blue, 8" Barrel, Detachable Front Sight, Modern...	325	400	400

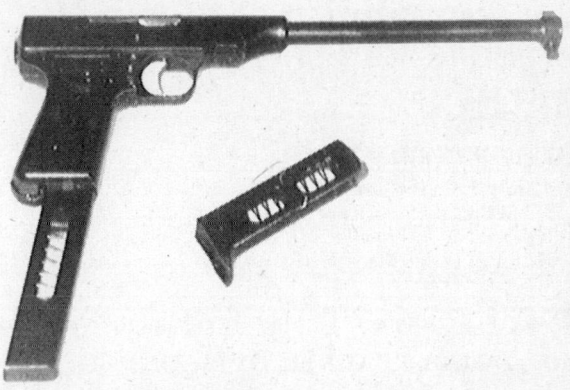

Bernardelli Standard .32, 8" Barrel

Standard, .380 ACP, Clip Fed, Blue, Modern..	150	250	250
Standard, 9mm Luger, Clip Fed, Blue, Modern....................................	325	450	450

RIFLE, DOUBLE BARREL, OVER-UNDER

Various Calibers, Checkered Stock, Engraved, Modern.........................	975	1,150	1,150

SHOTGUN, DOUBLE BARREL, SIDE-BY-SIDE

Brescia, 12 and 20 Gauges, Checkered Stock, Hammer, Modern...........	1,200	1,650	1,650
Elio, 12 Ga., Checkered Stock, Light Engraving, Lightweight Selective Ejector, Modern..	775	950	950
Game Cock Premier, 12 and 20 Gauges, Checkered Stock, Single Trigger, Selective Ejector, Modern...	700	850	850
Game Cock, 12 and 20 Gauges, Checkered Stock, Double Trigger, Modern..	575	675	675
Holland Deluxe, Various Gauges, Sidelock, Fancy Engraving, Fancy Checkering, Automatic Ejector, Modern......................................	3,850	4,250	4,250
Holland Presentation, Various Gauges, Sidelock, Fancy Engraving, Fancy Checkering, Automatic Ejector, Modern......................................	5,250	6,150	6,150
Holland, Various Gauges, Sidelock, Engraved, Checkered Stock, Automatic Ejector, Modern...	3,350	3,950	3,950

	V.G.	Exc	Prior Edition
Italia, 12 and 20 Gauges, Checkered Stock, Hammer, Light Engraving, Modern	$725	$875	$875
Roma #3, Various Gauges, Engraved, Checkered Stock, Automatic Ejector, Modern	750	825	825
Roma #4, Various Gauges, Fancy Engraving, Fancy Checkering, Automatic Ejector, Modern	650	875	875
Roma #6, Various Gauges, Fancy Engraving, Fancy Checkering, Automatic Ejector, Modern	825	950	950
St. Uberto F.S., 12 and 16 Gauges, Checkered Stock, Double Trigger, Automatic Ejector, Modern	750	875	875
Wesley Richards, Various Gauges, Checkered Stock, Light Engraving, Double Trigger, Modern	1,650	2,150	2,150
Wesley Richards, Various Gauges, Fancy Checkering, Fancy Engraving, Single Trigger, Selective Ejector, Vent Rib, Modern	2,875	3,650	3,650

BERNARDON–MARTIN St. Etienne, France 1906–1912.

HANDGUN, SEMI-AUTOMATIC

	V.G.	Exc	Prior Edition
Automatique Francais, .32 ACP, Clip Fed, Curio	225	275	275

BERSA Baraldo S.A.C.I. Argentina.

HANDGUN, SEMI-AUTOMATIC

	V.G.	Exc	Prior Edition
Model 62, .22 L.R.R.F., Clip Fed, Blue, Modern	100	125	125
Model 622, .22 L.R.R.F., Clip Fed, Blue, Modern	100	150	150
Model 644, .22 L.R.R.F., Clip Fed, Blue, Modern	100	150	150
Model 97, .380 ACP, Clip Fed, Blue, Modern	125	175	175

BERTUZZI Gardone V.T., Italy; Imported by Ventura.

SHOTGUN, DOUBLE BARREL, OVER-UNDER

	V.G.	Exc	Prior Edition
Zeus, 12 Ga., Sidelock, Automatic Ejector, Single Selective Trigger, Fancy Checkering, Fancy Engraving, Modern	6,500	7,500	7,500
Zeus Extra Lusso, 12 Ga., Sidelock, Automatic Ejector, Single Selective Trigger, Fancy Checkering, Fancy Engraving, Modern	8,500	10,500	10,500

BICYCLE Bicycle by Harrington & Richardson c. 1895.

HANDGUN, REVOLVER

	V.G.	Exc	Prior Edition
.22 L.R.R.F., Top Break, Double Action, Curio	100	125	125
.32 S & W, 5 Shot, Double Action, Top Break, Curio	75	100	100

BICYCLE French.

HANDGUN, SINGLESHOT

	V.G.	Exc	Prior Edition
.22 L.R.R.F., Auto Styling, Modern	275	350	350

BIG BONANZA Made by Bacon Arms Co. c. 1880.

HANDGUN, REVOLVER

.22 Short R.F., 7 Shot, Spur Trigger, Solid Frame, Single Action, Antique.. $125 $175 $175

BIG HORN ARMS CO. Watertown, S.D.

HANDGUN, SINGLESHOT

Target Pistol, .22 Short, Plastic Stock, Vent Rib, Modern...................... 100   150   150

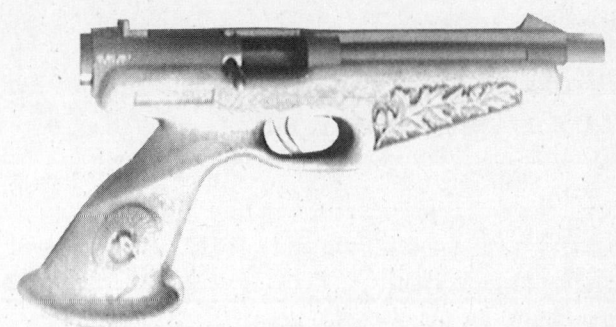

Big Horn .22 Pistol

SHOTGUN, SINGLESHOT

12 Ga. Short, Plastic Stock, Modern.. 75   100   100

BILLINGHURST, WILLIAM Rochester, N.Y. 1843–80.

HANDGUN, PERCUSSION

Buggy Pistol, Various Calibers, Detachable Stock, Heavy Barrel, Antique.. 750 1,500 1,500

RIFLE, PERCUSSION

.36, Revolver, 7 Shot, Octagon Barrel, Antique... 2,150 2,750 2,750
.40, Revolver, 7 Shot, Octagon Barrel, Antique... 1,875 2,400 2,400

RIFLE, PILL LOCK

.40, 7 Shot, Octagon Barrel, Antique... 2,425 2,775 2,775
.40, Carbine, 7 Shot, Octagon Barrel, Antique... 2,275 2,775 2,775

BISBEE, D. H. Norway, Me. 1835–1860.

RIFLE, PERCUSSION

.44, Octagon Barrel, Silver Inlay, Antique... 1,750 2,175 2,175

	V.G.	Exc	Prior Edition

BISON Imported from Germany by Jana International c. 1971.

HANDGUN, REVOLVER

	V.G.	Exc	Prior Edition
.22 L.R.R.F., Adjustable Sights, Western Style, Single Action, Modern	$50	$75	$50
.22 LR/.22 WMR Combo, Adjustable Sights, Western Style, Single Action, Modern	50	75	50

BITTERLICH, FRANK J. Nashville, Tenn. from about 1855 until about 1867.

HANDGUN, PERCUSSION

Derringer, .40, Plain, Antique	1,200	1,350	1,350

BITTNER, GUSTAV Vejprty, Bohemia, Austria–Hungary c. 1893.

HANDGUN, MANUAL REPEATER

Model 1893, 7.7mm Bittner, Box Magazine, Checkered Stocks, Antique	2,500	2,800	2,800

BLAKE, ANN London, England c. 1812.

HANDGUN, FLINTLOCK

Holster Pistol, .62, Walnut Stock, Antique	575	725	725

BLANCH, JOHN A. London, England 1809–1835.

HANDGUN, PERCUSSION

.68 Pair, Double Barrel, Side by Side, Officer's Belt Pistol, Engraved, Silver Inlay, Steel Furniture, Cased with Accessories, Antique	3,500	4,250	4,250
Pair, Pocket Pistol, Converted from Flintlock, High Quality, Cased with Accessories, Antique	2,500	3,000	3,000

BLAND, T & SONS London & Birmingham, England from 1876.

SHOTGUN, DOUBLE BARREL, SIDE-BY-SIDE

12 Ga., Boxlock, Adjustable Choke, Color Case Hardened Frame, Engraved, Antique	1,875	2,250	2,250

BLANGLE, JOSEPH Gratz, Styria, Austria, c. 1670.

RIFLE, WHEEL-LOCK

Brass Furniture, Engraved, Silver Inlay, Light Ornamentation, Full–Stocked, Antique	5,800	6,500	6,500

	V.G.	Exc	Prior Edition

BLEIBERG London, England c. 1690.

HANDGUN, FLINTLOCK

	V.G.	Exc	Prior Edition
Holster Pistol, Engraved, Silver Inlay, High Quality, Antique	$7,900	$9,500	$9,500

BLICKENSDOERFER & SCHILLING St. Louis, Mo. 1871–1875.

RIFLE, PERCUSSION

.48, Octagon Barrel, Fancy Wood, Brass Furniture, Antique	950	1,325	1,325

BLOODHOUND Made by Hopkins & Allen c. 1880.

HANDGUN, REVOLVER

.22 Short R.F., 7 Shot, Spur Trigger, Solid Frame, Single Action, Antique	75	150	150

BLUE JACKET Made by Hopkins & Allen c. 1880.

HANDGUN, REVOLVER

Model 1 , .22 Short R.F., 7 Shot, Spur Trigger, Solid Frame, Single Action, Antique	100	150	150
Model 2, .32 Short R.F., 5 Shot, Spur Trigger, Solid Frame, Single Action, Antique	100	175	175

BLUE WHISTLER Made by Hopkins & Allen c. 1880.

HANDGUN, REVOLVER

.32 Short R.F., 5 Shot, Spur Trigger, Solid Frame, Single Action, Antique	100	175	175

BLUMENFELD Memphis, Tenn. c. 1970

SHOTGUN, DOUBLE BARREL, SIDE-BY-SIDE

Arizaga, 20 Gauge, Double Triggers, Checkered Stock, Modern	125	200	200

SHOTGUN, SEMI-AUTOMATIC

Volunteer Pointer, 12 Gauge, Checkered Stock, Modern	125	225	225

BLUNT, ORISON, & SIMS N.Y.C. 1837–1865.

HANDGUN, PERCUSSION

Belt Pepperbox, Various Calibers, Ring Trigger, Antique	375	425	350
Boot Pistol, Various Calibers, Bar Hammer, Antique	325	375	250
Boot Pistol, Various Calibers, Ring Trigger, Antique	375	425	275
Boot Pistol, Various Calibers, Side Hammer, Antique	350	400	300
Boot Pistol, Various Calibers, Side Hammer, Ramrod, Antique	350	400	300
Boot Pistol, Various Calibers, Underhammer, Antique	325	375	250
Dragoon Pepperbox, Various Calibers, Ring Trigger, Antique	575	650	550

	V.G.	Exc	Prior Edition
Pocket Pepperbox, Various Calibers, Ring Trigger, Antique..................	$400	$450	$350

RIFLE, PERCUSSION
.37, Octagon Barrel, Brass Furniture, Antique..	525	625	625

BOITO Brazil.
HANDGUN, SINGLESHOT
.44 C.F., Break–Open, Hammer, Blue, Modern......................	75	100	100

SHOTGUN, DOUBLE BARREL, OVER-UNDER
O/U, 12or 20 Gauge, Checkered Stock, Modern......................................	100	175	175

SHOTGUN, DOUBLE BARREL, SIDE-BY-SIDE
S/S, 12 or 20 Gauge, Checkered Stock, Modern...........................	75	150	150

SHOTGUN, SINGLESHOT
SS, 12 or 20 Gauge, Checkered Stock, Modern............................	25	50	50

BONANZA Made by Bacon Arms Co.
HANDGUN, REVOLVER
Model 1½, .22 Short R.F., 7 Shot, Spur Trigger, Solid Frame, Single Action, Antique..	100	175	175

BOND, EDWARD London, England 1800–1830.
HANDGUN, FLINTLOCK
.68, Pair Officers' Type, Holster Pistol, Brass Furniture, Plain, Antique...	2,450	2,950	2,950

BOND, WM. London, England 1798–1812.
HANDGUN, FLINTLOCK
Pair, Folding Bayonet, Belt Pistol, Box Lock, Cannon Barrel. Brass Frame and Barrel, Cased with Accessories, Antique......................	5,225	5,850	5,850

BONEHILL, C.G. Birmingham, England c. 1880.
SHOTGUN, DOUBLE BARREL, OVER-UNDER
.450 N.E. 3¼", Under-Lever, Recoil Pad, Plain, Modern........................	1,250	1,500	1,500

BONIWITZ, JAMES Lebanon, Pa. c. 1775. See Kentucky Rifles.

BOOWLES, R. London, England c. 1690.
HANDGUN, FLINTLOCK
Holster Pistol, Engraved, Iron Mounts, Medium Quality, Antique..........	975	1,425	1,425

	V.G.	Exc	Prior Edition

BORCHARDT Made by Ludwig Lowe, Berlin, Germany 1893–1897. In 1897 acquired by D.W.M., superseded by the Luger in 1900.

HANDGUN, SEMI-AUTOMATIC

DWM, 7.65mm, Borchardt, 8 Shot Magazine, Blue, with
6½" Barrel and Walnut Grips, Cased with Accessories, Curio.................$15,000 $17,500 $9,500
Lowe, 7.65mm, Borchardt, 8 Shot Magazine, Blue, with
6½" Barrel and Walnut Grips, Cased with Accessories, Antique.............. 17,500 20,000 10,500
Deduct 40% without Case and Accessories

BOSS & CO. LTD. London, England 1832 to Date.

SHOTGUN, DOUBLE BARREL, OVER-UNDER

12 Ga., Single Selective Trigger, Straight Grip, Vent Rib, Trap
Grade, Cased, Curio.. 18,750 24,225 24,225
16 Ga., Double Trigger, Plain, Curio.. 8,275 7,950 7,950
20 Ga., Single Selective Trigger, Vent Rib, High Quality,
Curio.. 22,500 27,500 27,500

SHOTGUN, DOUBLE BARREL, SIDE-BY-SIDE

12 Ga., Vent Rib, Fancy Wood, Fancy Checkering, Fancy
Engraving, Curio.. 6,500 7,750 7,750
Pair, 12 Ga., Straight Grip, Plain, Cased, Curio...................... 18,750 22,500 22,500

BOSTON BULLDOG Made by Iver Johnson, sold by J. P. Lovell & Sons, Boston, Mass.

HANDGUN, REVOLVER

.22 Short R.F., 7 Shot, Double Action, Solid Frame, Curio..................... 75 100 100
.32 S & W, 5 Shot, Double Action, Solid Frame, Curio........................... 75 100 100
.32 Short R.F., 5 Shot, Double Action, Solid Frame, Curio................... 75 100 100
.38 S & W, 5 Shot, Double Action, Solid Frame, Curio........................... 75 100 100
.38 Short R.F., 5 Shot, Double Action, Solid Frame, Curio................... 50 100 100

BOSWORTH Lancaster Pa. 1760–1775. See Kentucky Rifles.

BOY'S CHOICE Made by Hood Firearms Co. c. 1875.

HANDGUN, REVOLVER

.22 Short R.F., 7 Shot, Spur Trigger, Solid Frame, Single Action,
Antique.. 100 175 175

BOYINGTON, JOHN S. Coventry, Conn. 1841–1847.

RIFLE, PERCUSSION

.50, Octagon Barrel, Brass Furniture, Antique............................. 775 · 925 925

	V.G.	Exc	Prior Edition

BREDA Brescia, Italy, Diana Import Co., Current.

SHOTGUN, DOUBLE BARREL, OVER-UNDER

.410 Ga., Light Engraving, Checkered Stock, Modern............................ $425 $475 $475

SHOTGUN, SEMI-AUTOMATIC

"Magnum," 12 Ga., Mag. 3", Checkered Stock, Vent Rib,
Lightweight, Modern... 400 475 475

Grade 1, 12 Ga., Checkered Stock, Vent Rib, Lightweight,
Engraved, Modern.. 425 500 500

Grade 2, 12 Ga., Fancy Checkering, Vent Rib, Lightweight,
Fancy Engraving, Modern.. 575 650 650

Grade 3, 12 Ga., Fancy Checkering, Vent Rib, Lightweight, Fancy
Engraving, Modern.. 750 825 825

Standard, 12 Ga., Checkered Stock, Plain Barrel, Lightweight,
Modern.. 300 375 375

Standard, 12 Ga., Checkered Stock, Vent Rib, Lightweight,
Modern.. 250 325 325

BRETTON St. Etienne, France.

SHOTGUN, DOUBLE BARREL, OVER-UNDER

Deluxe, 12 Gauge, Engraved, Dural Frame, Double Triggers,
Barrels Can Be Unscrewed, Modern... 600 750 750

Standard, 12 gauge, Dural Frame, Double Triggers, Barrels Can
Be Unscrewed, Modern... 500 625 625

B.R.F. Successor to Pretoria Arms Factory, South Africa, 1950's.

SHOTGUN, SEMI-AUTOMATIC

"Junior," .25 ACP, Clip Fed, Blue, Modern... 225 300 300
"Junior," .25 ACP, Clip Fed, Blue, Low Slide, Modern........................... 175 225 225
"Junior," .25 ACP, Clip Fed, Blue, PAF Logo on Slide, Modern........... 200 300 300
"Junior," .25 ACP, Clip Fed, Blue, Raised Sight Rib, Modern............... 225 275 275
"Junior," .25 ACP, Clip Fed, Blue, Rough Ground Slide, Modern......... 175 200 200
"Junior," .25 ACP, Clip Fed, Factory Chrome Plated, Modern.............. 325 400 400
"Junior," for Cocking Indicator, Add $75-$125

BRIGGS, WILLIAM Norristown, Pa. 1848–1875.

SHOTGUN, PERCUSSION

12 Ga., Underhammer, Antique... 275 350 350

BRITARMS Aylesbury, England.

HANDGUN, SEMI-AUTOMATIC

M2000 Mk.II, .22 L.R.R.F., Clip Fed, Target Pistol, Modern.................. 650 775 775

	V.G.	Exc	Prior Edition

BRITISH BULLDOG Made by Forehand & Wadsworth.

HANDGUN, REVOLVER

.32 S & W, 5 Shot, Double Action, Solid Frame, Modern.........................	$75	$100	$100
.38 S & W, 5 Shot, Double Action, Solid Frame, Modern.........................	75	100	100
.44 S & W, 5 Shot, Double Action, Solid Frame, Modern.........................	100	125	125

BRITISH MILITARY

HANDGUN, FLINTLOCK

.58, New Land M1796 Tower, Long Tapered Round Barrel, Belt Hook, Brass Furniture, Antique..	1,750	2,250	2,250
.67, George III Tower, Calvary Pistol, Military, Tapered Round Barrel, Brass Furniture, Antique..	1,250	1,550	1,550
.80, Modified M1796 Spooner, Holster Pistol, Plain Brass Furniture, Antique..	1,450	1,950	1,950

HANDGUN, REVOLVER

#2 Mk I R.A.F., .38 S & W, Military, Top Break, Curio..........................	250	300	125
#2 Mk I, .38 S & W, Military, Top Break, Curio.....................................	250	300	125

British Military Webley MK 1 No. 2 .455

S & W M38/200, .38 S & W, Solid Frame, Swing-Out Cylinder, Double Action, Military, Curio..	150	175	125
Webley Mk I, .455 Revolver Mk I, Top Break, Round Butt, Military, Antique...	225	350	350
Webley Mk I*, .455 Revolver Mk I, Top Break, Round Butt, Military, Antique...	225	300	300
Webley Mk I,** .455 Revolver Mk I, Top Break, Round Butt, Military, Curio...	225	250	150
Webley Mk II, .455 Revolver Mk I, Top Break, Round Butt, Military, Curio...	275	325	200

	V.G.	Exc	Prior Edition
Webley Mk II*, .455 Revolver Mk I, Top Break, Round Butt, Military, Curio..............	$250	$275	$175
Webley Mk II**, .455 Revolver Mk I, Top Break, Round Butt, Military, Curio..............	200	225	150
Webley Mk III, .455 Revolver Mk I, Top Break, Round Butt, Military, Curio..............	250	300	225
Webley Mk IV, .455 Revolver Mk I, Top Break, Round Butt, Military, Curio..............	225	275	175
Webley Mk V, .455 Revolver Mk I, Top Break, Round Butt, Military, Curio..............	250	300	200
Webley Mk VI, .455 Revolver Mk I, Top Break, Square Butt, Military, Curio..............	350	400	175

HANDGUN, SEMI-AUTOMATIC

	V.G.	Exc	Prior Edition
M1911A1 Colt, .455 Webley Auto, Clip Fed, Military, Curio................	1,250	1,500	1,250
Webley Mk.I, .455 Webley Auto, Clip Fed, Curio............	850	1,000	650
Webley Mk.I No. 2 R.A.F., .455 Webley Auto, Clip Fed, Cut for Shoulder Stock, Curio..............	4,000	4,500	4,250

RIFLE, BOLT ACTION

	V.G.	Exc	Prior Edition
Lee Metford Mk I, .303 British, Clip Fed, Curio...............	175	200	150
Lee Metford Mk I, .303 British, Clip Fed, Carbine, Curio............	200	225	175
Lee Metford Mk I*, .303 British, Clip Fed, Carbine, Curio............	125	175	175
Lee Metford Mk II, .303 British, Clip Fed, Curio...............	150	175	150
Lee Metford Mk II*, .303 British, Clip Fed, Curio...............	175	200	175
M1896 Lee Metford, .303 British, Clip Fed, Military, Carbine, Curio............	175	200	150
Pattern 14 (U.S.), .303 British, Curio........	250	300	175
Santa Fe Jungle Carbine Mk.I MD12011, .303 British, Peep Sights, No Flash Hider, Commercial, Modern............	125	175	125
SMLE #1 MK I, .303 British, Military, Curio............	225	250	150
SMLE #1 MK III, .303 British, Military, Curio........	200	225	150

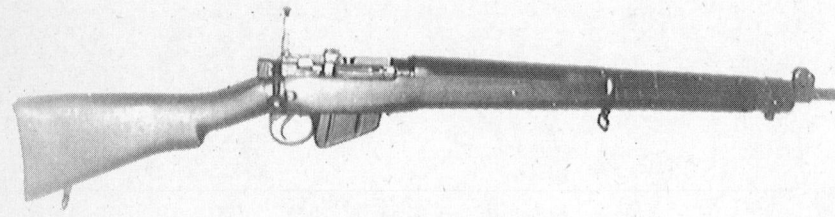

British Military #1 MK III

	V.G.	Exc	Prior Edition
SMLE #1 MK III*, .303 British, Military, Curio............	225	250	125
SMLE #1 MK III*, .303 British, Tangent Sights, Military, Ishapore, Curio............	175	200	125
SMLE #2 MK IV, .22 L.R.R.F., Singleshot, Training Rifle, Curio........	175	200	150
SMLE #3 MK I* (1914 Enfield), .303 British, Military, Curio............	175	200	125
SMLE #4 MK I*, .303 British, Military, Curio........	175	200	100
SMLE #4 MK I*, .303 British, Military, Canadian, Lightweight, Curio............	125	150	125
SMLE #4 MK I*, .303 British, Military, Lightweight, Curio........	175	200	150

	V.G.	Exc	Prior Edition
SMLE #4 MK I*, .303 British, Military, New Zealand, Lightweight, Curio	$175	$200	$175
SMLE #4 Sniper, .303 British, Military, Scope Mounted, Curio	475	550	550
SMLE #7, .22 L.R.R.F., Singleshot, Training Rifle, Curio	75	150	150
SMLE #8, .22 L.R.R.F., Singleshot, Training Rifle, Curio	100	150	150
SMLE #9, .22 L.R.R.F., Singleshot, Training Rifle, Curio	100	150	150
SMLE #MK V Jungle Carbine, .303 British, Peep Sights, Military, Curio	250	300	175

RIFLE, FLINTLOCK

.75, 1st Model Brown Bess, Musket, Brass Furniture, Antique	4,200	4,800	4,800
.75, 2nd Model Brown Bess, Musket, Military, Antique	2,800	3,300	3,300
.75, 3rd Model Brown Bess, Musket, Military, Antique	2,350	2,475	2,475

RIFLE, PERCUSSION

.58 Snider-Enfield, Military, Musket, Antique	525	675	675
.60 M1856 Tower, Military, Musket, Antique	350	550	550
.60 M1869 Enfield, Military, Musket, Antique	350	475	475

RIFLE, SINGLESHOT

Martini-Henry, .303 British, Antique	275	325	325
Martini-Henry, .303 British, Carbine, Antique	175	275	275
Martini-Henry, .577/.450 Martini-Henry, Antique	225	275	275
Martini-Henry, .577/.450 Martini-Henry, Carbine, Antique	175	250	250
Martini-Henry, .577/.450 Martini-Henry, Long Lever, Antique	200	250	250

SHOTGUN, SINGLESHOT

Martini-Henry, .12 Gauge Special, Long Lever, Antique	125	175	175

BRNO Ceska Zbrojovka, Brno, Czechoslovakia since 1922.

RIFLE, BOLT ACTION

21 H, Various Calibers, Sporting Rifle, Express Sights, Cheekpiece Checkered Stock, Set Trigger, Modern	675	750	750
22 F, Various Calibers, Sporting Rifle, Express Sights, Mannlicher Checkered Stock, Set Trigger, Modern	650	825	825
Model I, .22 L.R.R.F., Sporting Rifle, Express Sights, 5 Shot Clip, Checkered Stock, Set Trigger, Modern	350	400	400
Model II, .22 L.R.R.F., Sporting Rifle, Express Sights, 5 Shot Clip, Fancy Wood, Set Trigger, Modern	275	375	375
Z-B Mauser, .22 Hornet, Sporting Rifle, Express Sights, 5 Shot Clip, Checkered Stock, Set Trigger, Modern	575	800	800
ZKB 680 Fox, .222 Rem., Clip Fed, Checkered Stock, Sling Swivels, Modern	350	475	475
ZKM 452, .22 L.R.R.F., Clip Fed, Checkered Stock, Tangent Sights, Modern	100	150	150

RIFLE, SEMI-AUTOMATIC

ZKM 581, .22 L.R.R.F., Clip Fed, Checkered Stock, Tangent Sights, Modern	300	375	375

RIFLE, DOUBLE BARREL, OVER-UNDER

Super Express, Various Calibers, Fancy Checkering, Sidelock, Engraved, Double Triggers, Modern	1,600	2,250	2,250

	V.G.	Exc	Prior Edition
Super Express Grade III, Various Calibers, Fancy Checkering, Sidelock, Fancy Engraving, Double Triggers, Modern	$3,250	$3,750	$3,750
Super Express Grade IV, Various Calibers, Fancy Checkering, Sidelock, Fancy Engraving, Double Triggers, Modern	2,650	3,250	3,250

SHOTGUN, DOUBLE BARREL, OVER-UNDER

	V.G.	Exc	Prior Edition
Super, 12 Gauge, Fancy Checkering Sidelock, Plain, Ejectors, Double Triggers, Modern	475	725	725
Super Grade I, 12 Gauge, Fancy Checkering, Sidelock, Fancy Engraving, Ejectors, Double Triggers, Modern	1,275	1,850	1,850
Super Grade IV, 12 Gauge, Fancy Checkering, Sidelock, Engraved, Ejectors, Double Triggers, Modern	625	875	875
ZH 303 Field, 12 Gauge, Boxlock, Checkered Stock, Modern	400	500	500

SHOTGUN, DOUBLE BARREL, SIDE-BY-SIDE

	V.G.	Exc	Prior Edition
ZP 47, 12 Gauge, Sidelock, Double Triggers, Extractors, Checkered Stock, Modern	275	350	350
ZP 49, 12 Gauge, Sidelock, Double Triggers, Ejectors, Checkered Stock, Modern	450	525	525

BROCKWAY, NORMAN S. West Brookfield, Mass. 1861–1867, Bellows Falls, Vt. 1867–1900.

RIFLE, PERCUSSION

	V.G.	Exc	Prior Edition
Various Calibers, Target Rifles, Antique	1,750	2,450	2,450

BRONCO Echave y Arizmendi, Eibar, Spain 1911–1974.

HANDGUN, SEMI-AUTOMATIC

	V.G.	Exc	Prior Edition
1918 Vest Pocket, .32 ACP, Clip Fed, Curio	100	150	150
Vest Pocket, .25 ACP, Clip Fed, Modern	100	150	150
Vest Pocket, .25 ACP, Clip Fed, Light Engraving, Modern	125	200	200

BRONCO Imported by Garcia, c. 1970.

COMBINATION WEAPON, OVER-UNDER

	V.G.	Exc	Prior Edition
.22/.410, Skeleton Stock, Modern	75	100	100

RIFLE, SINGLESHOT

	V.G.	Exc	Prior Edition
Skeleton Stock, Modern	50	75	75

SHOTGUN, SINGLESHOT

	V.G.	Exc	Prior Edition
.410 Ga., Skeleton Stock, Modern	50	75	75

	V.G.	Exc	Prior Edition

BROOKLYN ARMS Brooklyn, N.Y. 1863–1867.

HANDGUN, REVOLVER

Slocum Patent, .32 R.F., 5 Shot Cylinder with Sliding Chambers,
Spur Trigger, Single Action, Engraved, Antique.. $275 $395 $395

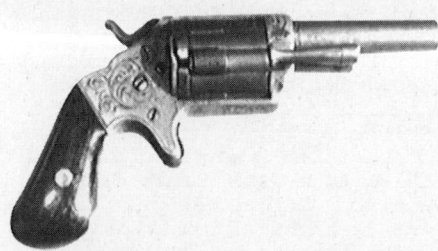

Brooklyn Arms Co. Slocum Revolver

BROWN MFG. CO. Newburyport, Mass. 1869–73. Also see Ballard Rifles.

HANDGUN, SINGLESHOT

Southerner Derringer, .41 R.F., Side-Swing Barrel, Spur Trigger,
Brass Frame, Antique.. 250   325   325

RIFLE, BOLT ACTION

1853 Long Enfield, .58 U.S. Musket, Converted from Percussion,
Brass Furniture, Antique.. 325   500   500
U.S. M1861 Musket, .58 U.S. Musket, Converted form Percussion,
Brass Furniture, Antique.. 350   525   525

BROWN PRECISION CO. San Jose, Calif. since 1975.

RIFLE, BOLT ACTION

Sporter, Various Calibers, Fiberglass Stock, Rem. 700 ACtion,
Sling Swivels, Modern.. 750   850   750

BROWN, JOHN & SONS Fremont, N.J. 1840–1871.

RIFLE, PERCUSSION

.50, Target Rifle, Scope Mounted, Set Trigger, Antique............................ 1,650   2,250   2,250
Various Calibers, Sporting Rifle, Antique... 850   1,275   1,275

	V.G.	Exc	Prior Edition

BROWNING Established 1870 in St. Louis, Mo., 1880 to Date
Ogden/Morgan, Utah. (See F.N.) Primary Manufacturer Fabrique National in Herstal and Liege, Belgium. Also see Commemoratives.

HANDGUN, SEMI-AUTOMATIC

	V.G.	Exc	Prior Edition
Baby Standard, .25 ACP, Clip Fed, Modern	$225	$275	$275
Baby, .25 ACP, Clip Fed, Lightweight, Nickel Plated, Modern	300	350	395
Baby, .25 ACP, Clip Fed, Renaissance, Nickel Plated, Engraved, Modern	600	800	875
BDA 38 Super, .38 Super, Clip Fed, Double Action, Fixed Sights, Modern	475	550	650
BDA 380, .380 ACP, Clip Fed, Double Action, Fixed Sights, Modern	300	350	375
BDA 380, .380 ACP, Clip Fed, Double Action, Fixed Sights, Nickel, Modern	300	375	400
BDA 45, .45 ACP, Clip Fed, Double Action, 7 Shot, Modern	325	400	500
BDA 9, 9mm Luger, Clip Fed, Double Action, 9 Shot, Modern	300	350	450
Challenger II, .22 L.R.R.F., Clip Fed, Adjustable Sights, Modern	175	225	225
Challenger III, .22 L.R.R.F., Clip Fed, Adjustable Sights, Modern	150	200	200

Browning Challenger III

	V.G.	Exc	Prior Edition
Challenger, .22 L.R.R.F., Clip Fed, Checkered Wood Grips, Adjustable Sights, Modern	250	300	375
Challenger, .22 L.R.R.F., Clip Fed, Gold Line, Checkered Wood Grips Gold Inlays, Engraved, Modern	850	1,200	1,400
Challenger, .22 L.R.R.F., Clip Fed, Renaissance, Checkered Wood Grips, Fancy Engraving, Nickel Plated, Modern	650	1,000	1,100
Classic Hi Power Pistol, 9mm, Engraved with Lynx and Bald Eagle, Modern	750	950	950

	V.G.	Exc	Prior Edition
Gold Classic Hi Power Pistol, 9mm, Engraved with Lynx and Bald Eagle, Modern	$1,250	$1,750	$1,500

Browning - Gold Classic Hi Power Pistol

	V.G.	Exc	Prior Edition
Hi Power "FM" Argentine, 9mm, Clip Fed, Made under License, Military, Modern	425	475	475
Hi Power Estonian, 9mm, Clip Fed, Military, Curio	775	1,250	1,250
Hi Power Inglis #1 Mk I*, 9mm, Tangent Stocks, Slotted for Shoulder Stock, Military, Curio	550	750	750
Hi Power Inglis #1 Mk I*, 9mm, Tangent Stocks, with Shoulder, Stock, Military, Curio	825	1,050	1,050
Hi Power Inglis #1 Mk I, 9mm, Tangent Stocks, Slotted for Shoulder Stock, Military, Curio	675	950	950
Hi Power Inglis #2 Mk I*, 9mm, Fixed Sights, Slotted for Shoulder Stock, Military, Curio	750	900	475
Hi Power Inglis #2 Mk I, 9mm, Fixed Sights, Military, Curio	550	650	450
Hi Power Louis XVI, Fancy Engraving, Nickel Plated, Adjustable Sights, Cased, Modern	875	1,050	1,200
Hi Power Louis XVI, Fancy Engraving, Nickel Plated, Fixed Sights, Cased, Modern	850	1,000	1,100
Hi Power Renaissance, 9mm, Clip Fed, Nickel Plated, Engraved, Modern	725	1,100	1,100
Hi Power Renaissance, 9mm, Clip Fed, Nickel Plated, Engraved, Adjustable Sights, Modern	850	1,200	1,200
Hi Power Renaissance, 9mm, Clip Fed, with Ring Hammer, Nickel Plated, Engraved, Modern	875	1,250	1,250
Hi Power Standard, 9mm, Clip Fed, with Ring Hammer, Modern	400	450	450
Hi Power Standard, 9mm, Clip Fed, with Spur Hammer, Modern	375	400	400
Hi Power Standard, 9mm, Clip Fed, with Spur Hammer, Adjustable Sights, Modern	375	450	450
Hi Power Standard, 9mm, Clip Fed, with Spur Hammer, with Tangent Sights, Modern	575	650	650

	V.G.	Exc	Prior Edition

Hi Power Standard, 9mm, Clip Fed, with Spur Tangent Sights,
Slotted for Shoulder Stock, Modern.. $850 $950 $950
Hi Power Standard, 9mm, Nickel Plating, Add 5%
Hi Power, 9mm, Clip Fed, Military, Curio... 375 450 450

Browning Hi Power 9mm Military

Hi Power, 9mm, Clip Fed, Military, Tangent Sights, Curio...................... 650 750 650
Hi Power, 9mm, Clip Fed, Military, Tangent Sights, with
Detachable Shoulder Stock, Curio.. 575 750 775
Hi Power, 9mm, Clip Fed, Nazi-Marked Military, Curio.......................... 500 550 525
Hi Power, 9mm, Clip Fed, Nazi-Marked Military,
Tangent Sights Curio... 850 1,000 675
Hi Power, 9mm, Clip Fed, Nazi-Marked Military, Tangent Sights,
Curio... 850 1,000 600
Hi Power, 9mm, Clip Fed, Nazi-Marked Military, Tangent Sights,
with Detachable Shoulder Stock, Curio.. 2,250 2,500 975
Hi Power, 9mm, Clip Fed, Pre-War Military, Tangent Sights, Curio....... 750 1,000 750
Hi Power, 9mm, Clip Fed, Pre-War Military, Tangent Sights,
with Detachable Shoulder Stock, Curio.. 1,250 1,500 1,050
Medalist Goldline, .22 L.R.R.F., Clip Fed, Checkered Wood Target
Grips, Wood Forestock, Gold Inlays, Engraved, Modern......................... 750 1,250 2,200
Medalist International Early Model, .22 L.R.R.F., Clip Fed,
Checkered Wood Target Grips, Target Sights, Modern............................ 600 650 600
Medalist International Second Model, .22 L.R.R.F., Clip Fed,
Checkered Wood Target Grips, Gold Inlays, Engraved,
Target Sights, Modern.. 550 600 550
Medalist Renaissance, .22 L.R.R.F., Clip Fed, Checkered Wood
Target Grips, Fancy Engraving, Target Sights, Modern............................ 1,000 1,500 2,500
Medalist, .22 L.R.R.F., Clip Fed, Checkered Wood Target Grips,
Wood Forestock, Target Sights, Modern.. 575 700 700

	V.G.	Exc	Prior Edition
Model 1900, .32 ACP, Clip Fed, Curio...	$200	$275	$275

Browning Model 1900

	V.G.	Exc	Prior Edition
Model 1900, .32 ACP, Clip Fed, Military, Curio......................................	275	325	325
Model 1900, .32 ACP, Clip Fed, Early Type, No Lanyard Ring, Curio...	325	425	425
Model 1903, 9mm Browning Long, Clip Fed, Curio...............................	350	450	30

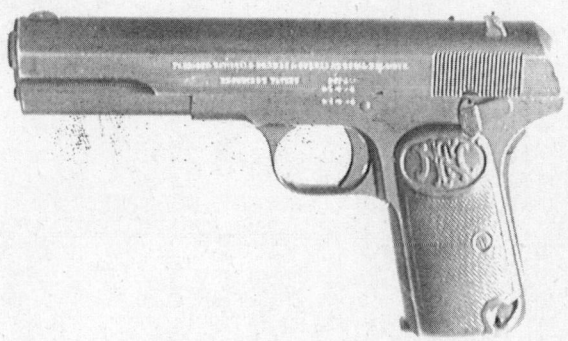

Browning M1903 9mm

	V.G.	Exc	Prior Edition
Model 1903, 9mm Browning Long, Clip Fed, Cut for Shoulder Stock, Military, Curio..	750	850	450
Model 1903, 9mm Browning Long, Clip Fed, Cut for Shoulder Stock, with Holster Stock, Military, Curio...			
Model 1903, 9mm Browning Long, Clip Fed, Light Engraving, Curio...	450	650	650
Model 1903, 9mm Browning Long, Clip Fed, Military, Curio.................	450	500	325
Model 1903, 9mm Browning Long, Swedish Contract, Clip Fed, Curio...	250	275	200

	V.G.	Exc	Prior Edition
Model 1905, First Variation, .25 ACP, Clip Fed, Grip Safety, Nickel, Modern...............	$250	$325	$325
Model 1905, First Variation, .25 ACP, Clip Fed, Grip Safety, Modern....	225	275	275
Model 1905, Second Variation, .25 ACP, Clip Fed, Grip Safety, Nickel, Modern...............	200	250	450
Model 1910, .32 ACP, Clip Fed, Curio...............	225	300	300
Model 1910, .32 ACP, Clip Fed, Military, Curio...............	325	400	400
Model 1910, .32 ACP, Clip Fed, German Police, Modern...............	275	325	275
Model 1910, .32 ACP, Clip Fed, Japanese Military, Curio...............	225	325	325
Model 1910, .32 ACP, Clip Fed, Peruvian Military, Curio...............	275	325	325
Model 1910, .32 ACP, Clip Fed, Syrian Police, Curio...............	300	350	350
Model 1910, .380 ACP, Clip Fed, Curio...............	300	350	350
Model 1922, .32 ACP, Clip Fed, Curio...............	200	250	250

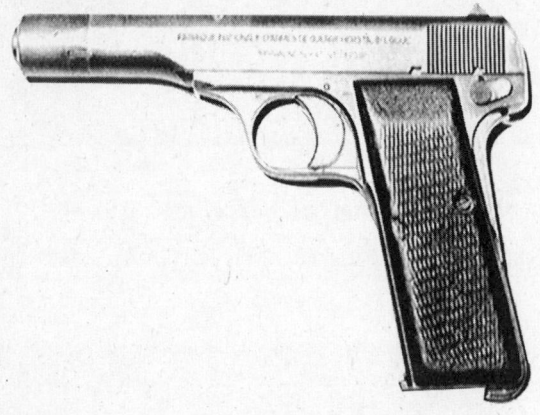

Browning M1922

Model 1922, .32 ACP, Clip Fed, Nazi–Marked Military, Curio...............	250	300	275
Model 1922, .32 and .380 ACP, Clip Fed, Curio...............	175	225	225
Model 1922, .32 and .380 ACP, Clip Fed, Renaissance, Nickel Plated, Engraved, Curio...............	750	950	1,050
Model 1922, .380 ACP, Clip Fed, Curio...............	225	275	225
Model 1922, .380 ACP, Clip Fed, Dutch Military, Curio...............	250	300	275
Model 1922, .380 ACP, Clip Fed, Nazi–Marked, Military, Curio............	300	350	350
Model 1922, .380 ACP, Clip Fed, Turkish Military, Curio...............	225	300	300
Model 1922, .380 ACP, Clip Fed, Waffenampt Proofed, Curio...............	250	300	300
Model 1922, .380 ACP, Clip Fed, Yugoslavian Military, Curio...............	225	300	300
Nomad, .22 L.R.R.F., Clip Fed, Plastic Grips, Adjustable Sights, Modern...............	250	300	300
Renaissance Set, Baby-.389 Hi Power, Nickel Plated, Engraved, Modern...............	2,500	3,500	3,500

	V.G.	Exc	Prior Edition

RIFLE, BOLT ACTION

Model BBR, Various Calibers, Checkered Stock, Modern...................... $350 / $400 / $450

Browning BBR

	V.G.	Exc	Prior Edition
Exhibition Olympian Grade, Various Calibers, Gold Inlays, Fancy Wood, Fancy Checkering, Engraved, Modern..	8,500	9,500	8,700
Medallion Grade, .458 Win. Mag., Long Action, Fancy Wood, Fancy Checkering, Engraved, Open Rear Sight, Modern.........................	1,250	1,500	1,500
Medallion Grade, Various Calibers, Long Action, Magnum, Fancy Wood, Fancy Checkering, Engraved, Modern...	1,250	1,600	1,600
Medallion Grade, Various Calibers, Short Action, Fancy Wood, Fancy Checkering, Engraved, Modern...	1,150	1,400	1,400
Olympian Grade, .458 Win. Mag., Long Action, Fancy Wood, Fancy Checkering, Engraved, Modern...	2,750	3,000	2,825
Olympian Grade, Various Calibers, Long Action, Fancy Wood, Fancy Checkering, Fancy Engraving, Modern...	2,500	2,750	2,250
Olympian Grade, Various Calibers, Long Action, Magnum, Fancy Wood, Fancy Checkering, Fancy Engraving, Modern...	2,750	3,000	2,850
Olympian Grade, Various Calibers, Medium Action, Fancy Wood, Fancy Checkering, Fancy Engraving, Modern...	2,500	2,750	2,250
Olympian Grade, Various Calibers, Short Action, Fancy Wood, Fancy Checkering, Engraved, Modern...	2,250	2,500	2,250
Safari Grade, Various Calibers, Long Action, Checkered Stock, Modern...	725	850	850
Safari Grade, Various Calibers, Long Action, Magnum, Checkered Stock, Modern...	800	1,000	1,000
Safari Grade, Various Calibers, Medium Action, Checkered Stock, Modern...	700	825	825
Safari Grade, Various Calibers, Short Action, Checkered Stock, Modern...	675	800	800
T-Bolt T-1, .22 L.R.R.F., 5 Shot Clip, Plain, Open Rear Sight, Modern...	250	300	250
T-Bolt T-1, .22 L.R.R.F., 5 Shot Clip, Plain, Open Rear Sight, Left-Hand, Modern...	275	325	300
T-Bolt T-2, .22 L.R.R.F., 5 Shot Clip, Checkered Stock, Fancy Wood, Open Rear Sight, Modern..	325	400	400

RIFLE, LEVER ACTION

	V.G.	Exc	Prior Edition
BL-22 Grade 1, .22 L.R.R.F., Tube Feed, Checkered Stock, Modern...	200	250	285
BL-22 Grade 2, .22 L.R.R.F., Tube Feed, Checkered Stock, Light Engraving, Modern..	225	275	325
BL-22, Belgian Manufacture, Add 15%–25%			
Model 81 BLR, Various Calibers, Center–Fire, Plain, Clip Fed, Checkered Stock, Modern..	300	350	325
Model 92 Centennial, Tube Feed, Open Sights, Modern.....................	325	375	400

	V.G.	Exc	Prior Edition
Model 92, .357 Mag., Tube Feed, Open Sights, Modern............................	$275	$325	$275

Browning B-92

Model 92, .44 Mag., Tube Feed, Open Sights, Modern............................	300	350	300

RIFLE, PERCUSSION

J. Browning Mountain Rifle, Various Calibers, Singleshot, Octagon Barrel, Open Rear Sight, Single Set Trigger, Brass Finish, Reproduction, Antique.................................	350	600	375
Mountain Rifle, Various Calibers, Singleshot, Octagon Barrel, Open Rear Sight, Single Set Trigger, Browned Finish, Reproduction, Antique.................................	250	400	375

RIFLE, SEMI-AUTOMATIC

Auto–Rifle, Belgian Mfg., Add 20%–30%			
Auto–Rifle Grade I, .22 L.R.R.F., Tube Feed, Takedown, Open Rear Sight, Checkered Stock, Modern......................................	300	375	225

Browning Auto-Rifle Grade I

Auto–Rifle Grade I, .22 Short, Tube Feed, Takedown, Open Rear Sight, Checkered Stock, Modern..............................	350	450	225
Auto–Rifle Grade II, .22 L.R.R.F., Tube Feed, Takedown, Open Rear Sight, Satin Chrome Receiver, Engraved, Modern............................	550	650	350
Auto–Rifle Grade III, .22 L.R.R.F., Takedown, Satin Chrome Receiver, Fancy Wood, Fancy Checkering, Fancy Engraving, Cased, Modern..................................	1,000	1,250	650

	V.G.	Exc	Prior Edition
BAR–22 Grade I, .22 L.R.R.F., Checkered Stock, Modern.....................	$200	$225	$225

Browning BAR

BAR–22 Grade II, .22 L.R.R.F., Checkered Stock, Modern..................	275	325	275
BAR, Various Calibers, Center–Fire, Belgian Mfg., Add 15%-25%			
BAR, Various Calibers, Center–Fire, Magnum Calibers, Add 10%			
BAR Grade 1, Various Calibers, Center–Fire, Checkered Stock, Plain, Modern..................	400	450	450

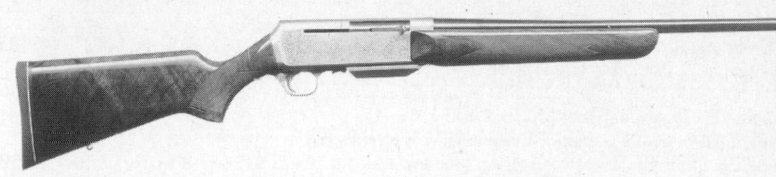

Browning BAR 22

BAR Grade 2, Various Calibers, Center–Fire, Checkered Stock, Light Engraving, Modern..................	500	575	500
BAR Grade 3, Various Calibers, Center–Fire, Fancy Wood, Fancy Checkering, Engraved, Modern..................	650	800	800
BAR Grade 4, Various Calibers, Center–Fire, Fancy Wood, Fancy Checkering, Fancy Engraving, Modern..................	1,125	1,300	1,300
BAR Grade 5, Various Calibers, Center–Fire, Fancy Wood, Fancy Checkering, Fancy Engraving, Gold Inlays, Modern..................	2,250	2,500	2,750
Classic Light, 12 Gauge, Engraved With Mallard Ducks, Labrador Retriever and Portrait of John M. Browning, Modern..................	1,250	1,500	1,450
Gold Classic Light, 12 Gauge, Engraved With Mallard Ducks, Labrador Retriever and Portrait of John M. Browning, Modern..................	3,750	4,500	4,275

RIFLE, SINGLESHOT

Model 78, .30–06, 1 of 50 Bicentennial Rifle, .30–06 Caliber, Commemorative, Curio..................	3,000	5,000	4,500
Model 78, Various Calibers, Various Barrel Styles, Checkered Stock, Modern..................	15,000	17,500	15,000

RIFLE, DOUBLE BARREL, OVER-UNDER

Express Rifle, 30/06 or .270 Win., Engraved, Fancy Wood, Fancy Checkering, Cased, Modern..................	1,850	1,750	2,575

RIFLE, SLIDE ACTION

BPR, .22 L.R.R.F., Grade I, Checkered Stock, Modern..................	150	200	200
BPR, .22 Mag., Grade I, Checkered Stock, Modern..................	175	225	225

	V.G.	Exc	Prior Edition
BPR, .22 Mag., Grade II, Checkered Stock, Engraved Modern...............	$350	$375	$350

SHOTGUN, DOUBLE BARREL, OVER-UNDER

Citori, 12 and 20 Gauges, Standard Grade, Vent Rib, Checkered Stock, Modern..	725	850	850
Citori, 12 Ga., Early Model, Vent Rib, Checkered Stock, Modern..........	700	750	850

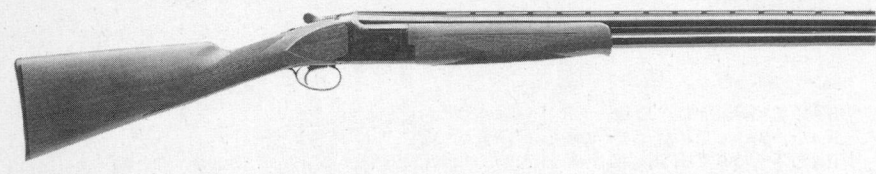

Browning Citori Superlight

Citori, 12 Gauge, Magnum, Vent Rib, Checkered Stock, Modern..	850	1,000	925
Citori Grade I, 12 Ga., Skeet Grade, Vent Rib, Checkered Stock, Modern...	750	850	925
Citori Grade I, 12 Ga., Trap Grade, Vent Rib, Checkered Stock, Modern...	850	1,000	950
Citori Grade II, Trap and Skeet Models, Add 10%			
Citori Grade II, Various Gauges, Hunting Model, Engraved, Checkered Stock, Single Selective Trigger, Modern...............................	800	950	950
Citori Grade V, Trap and Skeet Models, Add 10%			
Citori Grade V, Various Gauges, Fancy Engraving, Checkered Stock, Single Selective Trigger, Modern.....................................	1,250	1,400	1,400
Classic, 20 Gauge, 26" Barrel, Engraved with Bird Dogs, Pheasant, and Quail, Modern..	1,500	1,750	2,250
Gold Classic, 20 Gauge, 26" Barrel, Engraved with Bird Dogs, Pheasant, and Quail, Modern..	4,500	5,000	7,500

Browning Gold Classic Light

Grand Liege, 12 Ga., Engraved, Single Trigger, Checkered Stock, Modern..	700	800	625

	V.G.	Exc	Prior Edition
Liege, 12 Ga., Engraved, Single Trigger, Checkered Stock, Modern	$525	$600	$350
ST-100, 12 Ga., Trap Special, Engraved, Checkered Stock, Modern	1,750	2,000	1,725

Superposed, Various Gauges, Presentation Grade 1, Extra Sets of Barrels, Add for each: $725.00–$1100.00

Superposed, Various Gauges, Presentation Grade 2, Extra Sets of Barrels, Add for each: $825.00–$1250.00

Superposed, Various Gauges, Presentation Grade 3, Extra Sets of Barrels, Add for each: $900.00–$1500.00

Superposed, Various Gauges, Presentation Grade 4, Extra Sets of Barrels, Add for each: $1200.00–$1700.00

Superposed, For .410 or 28 Gauge, Add 15%–25%

Superposed, For 20 Gauge, Add 10%–15%

Superposed, Pre–1977, Lightning Skeet, Add 5%–10%

Superposed, Pre–1977, 4–Barrel, Skeet Set,, Add 275%–300%

Superposed, Pre–1977, Broadway Trap Model, Add 8%–13%

Superposed, Pre–1977, Extra Barrel, Add 35%–40%

Superposed, Pre–1977, Lightning Trap Model, Add 5%–10%

Superposed, Pre–1977, Super–Light Lightning, Add 15%–20%

Superposed, Pre–1977, Vent Rib, Pre–War, Add 10%–15%

Superposed, Pre–War, Raised Solid Rib, Add $60.00–$90.00

	V.G.	Exc	Prior Edition
Superposed Bicentennial, Fancy Engraving, Gold Inlays, Fancy Wood, Fancy Checkering, Cased, Commemorative, Modern	7,500	8,500	7,800
Superposed, 12 and 20 Gauges, Lightning Hunting Model, Presentation Grade 4, Fancy Engraving, with Sideplates, Gold Inlays, Fancy Checkering, Fancy Wood, Extra Barrels, Modern	5,750	6,750	6,725
Superposed, 12 and 20 Gauges, Lightning Hunting Model, Presentation Grade 4, Fancy Engraving, with Sideplates, Fancy Checkering, Fancy Wood, Extra Barrels, Modern	5,250	6,000	5,500
Superposed, 12 and 20 Gauges, Lightning Hunting Model, Presentation Grade 2, Fancy Engraving, Fancy Checkering, Fancy Wood, Extra Barrels, Modern	3,500	3,750	3,575
Superposed, 12 and 20 Gauges, Lightning Hunting Model, Presentation Grade 2, Fancy Engraving, Gold Inlays, Fancy Checkering, Fancy Wood, Extra Barrels, Modern	2,750	3,750	4,150
Superposed, 12 and 20 Gauges, Lightning Hunting Model, Presentation Grade 1, Engraved, Gold Inlays, Fancy Checkering, Fancy Wood, Modern	2,250	2,500	2,450
Superposed, 12 and 20 Gauges, Lightning Hunting Model, Presentation Grade 1, Engraved, Fancy Checkering, Fancy Wood, Modern	2,000	2,250	2,000
Superposed, 12 and 20 Gauges, Lightning Skeet Model, Presentation Grade 4, Fancy Engraving, with Sideplates, Gold Inlays, Fancy Checkering, Fancy Wood, Modern	5,500	6,500	5,675
Superposed, 12 and 20 Gauges, Lightning Skeet Model, Presentation Grade 4, Fancy Engraving, with Sideplates, Fancy Checkering, Fancy Wood, Extra Barrels, Modern	5,500	6,500	6,475
Superposed, 12 and 20 Gauges, Lightning Skeet Model, Presentation Grade 3, Fancy Engraving, Gold Inlays, Fancy Checkering, Fancy Wood, Modern	4,750	5,500	3,250
Superposed, 12 and 20 Gauges, Lightning Skeet Model, Presentation Grade 2, Fancy Engraving, Gold Inlays, Fancy Checkering, Fancy Wood, Modern	3,000	3,500	2,575

	V.G.	Exc	Prior Edition
Superposed, 12 and 20 Gauges, Lightning Skeet Model, Presentation Grade 1, Engraved, Gold Inlays, Fancy Checkering, Fancy Wood, Modern..	$2,500	$2,750	$2,325
Superposed, 12 and 20 Gauges, Lightning Skeet Model, Presentation Grade 1, Engraved, Fancy Checkering, Fancy Wood, Modern........................	2,250	2,500	2,350
Superposed, 12 and 20 Gauges, Super–Light Hunting Model, Presentation Grade 4, Extra Barrels, Fancy Engraving, with Sideplates, Gold Inlays, Fancy Checkering, Fancy Wood, Modern.........	5,750	6,750	5,825
Superposed, 12 and 20 Gauges, Super–Light Hunting Model, Presentation Grade 4, Fancy Engraving, with Sideplates, Fancy Checkering, Fancy Wood, Extra Barrels, Modern.........................	5,750	6,250	5,000
Superposed, 12 and 20 Gauges, Super–Light Hunting Model, Presentation Grade 2, Fancy Engraving, Fancy Checkering, Fancy Wood, Extra Barrels, Modern......................	3,500	4,000	3,625
Superposed, 12 and 20 Gauges, Super–Light Hunting Model, Presentation Grade 2, Fancy Engraving, Gold Inlays, Fancy Checkering, Fancy Wood, Extra Barrels, Modern....................	2,750	3,750	3,650
Superposed, 12 and 20 Gauges, Super–Light Hunting Model, Presentation Grade 1, Engraved, Gold Inlays, Fancy Checkering, Fancy Wood, Modern..	2,500	2,750	2,350
Superposed, 12 and 20 Gauges, Super–Light Hunting Model, Presentation Grade 1, Engraved, Fancy Checkering, Fancy Wood, Modern..	2,250	2,500	2,225
Superposed, 12 Ga., Broadway Trap Model, Presentation Grade 4, Fancy Engraving, with Sideplates, Gold Inlays, Fancy Checkering, Fancy Wood, Modern..	5,500	6,500	5,000
Superposed, 12 Ga., Broadway Trap Model, Presentation Grade 4, Fancy Engraving, with Sideplates, Fancy Checkering, Fancy Wood, Modern..	5,000	6,000	5,500
Superposed, 12 Ga., Broadway Trap Model, Presentation Grade 3, Fancy Engraving, Gold Inlays, Fancy Checkering, Fancy Wood, Modern..	4,500	5,000	4,675
Superposed, 12 Ga., Broadway Trap Model, Presentation Grade 2, Fancy Engraving, Fancy Checkering, Fancy Wood, Modern...................	3,500	4,000	2,675
Superposed, 12 Ga., Broadway Trap Model, Presentation Grade 2, Fancy Engraving, Gold Inlays, Fancy Checkering, Fancy Wood, Modern..	3,000	3,500	3,250
Superposed, 12 Ga., Broadway Trap Model, Presentation Grade 1, Engraved, Gold Inlays, Fancy Checkering, Fancy Wood, Modern..........	2,500	3,000	2,650
Superposed, 12 Ga., Broadway Trap Model, Presentation Grade 1, Engraved, Fancy Checkering, Fancy Wood, Modern..............................	2,250	2,750	2,475
Superposed, 12 Ga., Lightning Trap Model, Presentation Grade 4, Fancy Engraving, with Sideplates, Gold Inlays, Fancy Checkering, Fancy Wood, Modern..	5,000	6,000	5,750
Superposed, 12 Ga., Lightning Trap Model, Presentation Grade 4, Fancy Engraving, with Sideplates, Fancy Checkering, Fancy Wood, Modern..	4,750	5,500	5,250
Superposed, 12 Ga., Lightning Trap Model, Presentation Grade 3, Fancy Engraving, Gold Inlays, Fancy Checkering, Fancy Wood, Modern..	3,750	4,500	4,225
Superposed, 12 Ga., Lightning Trap Model, Presentation Grade 2, Fancy Engraving, Fancy Checkering, Fancy Wood, Modern...................	3,250	3,750	2,750

	V.G.	Exc	Prior Edition
Superposed, 12 Ga., Lightning Trap Model, Presentation Grade 2, Fancy Engraving, Gold Inlays, Fancy Checkering, Fancy Wood, Modern..............	$2,750	$3,250	$3,750
Superposed, 12 Ga., Lightning Trap Model, Presentation Grade 1, Engraved, Gold Inlays, Fancy Checkering, Fancy Wood, Modern..........	2,250	2,750	2,500
Superposed, 12 Ga., Lightning Trap Model, Presentation Grade 1, Engraved, Fancy Checkering, Fancy Wood, Modern...............................	2,000	2,500	2,225
Superposed, 28 Ga. or .410 Ga., Lightning Hunting Model, Presentation Grade 4, Fancy Engraving, with Sideplates, Gold Inlays, Fancy Checkering, Fancy Wood, Modern.......................................	4,750	5,500	5,250
Superposed, 28 Ga. or .410 Ga., Lightning Hunting Model, Presentation Grade 4, Fancy Engraving, with Sideplates, Gold Inlays, Fancy Checkering, Fancy Wood, Modern.......................................	4,500	5,250	4,800
Superposed, 28 Ga. or .410 Ga., Lightning Hunting Model, Presentation Grade 4, Fancy Engraving, with Sideplates, Fancy Checkering, Fancy Wood, Modern.......................................	4,250	5,000	3,950
Superposed, 28 Ga. or .410 Ga., Lightning Hunting Model, Presentation Grade 3, Fancy Engraving, Gold Inlays, Fancy Checkering, Fancy Wood, Modern...............................	4,000	4,500	3,575
Superposed, 28 Ga. or .410 Ga., Lightning Hunting Model, Presentation Grade 2, Fancy Engraving, Fancy Checkering, Fancy Wood, Modern..	3,250	3,500	2,850
Superposed, 28 Ga. or .410 Ga., Lightning Hunting Model, Presentation Grade 2, Fancy Engraving, Gold Inlays, Fancy Checkering, Fancy Wood, Modern............................	3,500	4,000	2,875
Superposed, 28 Ga. or .410 Ga., Lightning Hunting Model, Presentation Grade 1, Engraved, Gold Inlays, Fancy Checkering, Fancy Wood, Modern....................................	2,500	3,000	2,250
Superposed, 28 Ga. or .410 Ga., Lightning Hunting Model, Presentation Grade 1, Engraved, Fancy Checkering, Fancy Wood, Modern..	2,250	2,500	1,975
Superposed, 28 Ga. or .410 Ga., Lightning Skeet Model, Presentation Grade 4, Fancy Engraving, with Sideplates, Gold Inlays, Fancy Checkering, Fancy Wood, Modern.....................................	4,750	5,500	5,475
Superposed, 28 Ga. or .410 Ga., Lightning Skeet Model, Presentation Grade 4, Fancy Engraving, with Sideplates, Gold Inlays, Fancy Checkering, Fancy Wood, Modern.....................................	4,500	5,250	5,125
Superposed, 28 Ga. or .410 Ga., Lightning Skeet Model, Presentation Grade 4, Fancy Engraving, with Sideplates, Fancy Checkering, Fancy Wood, Modern................................	4,250	5,000	3,750
Superposed, 28 Ga. or .410 Ga., Lightning Skeet Model, Presentation Grade 3, Fancy Engraving, Gold Inlays, Fancy Checkering, Fancy Wood, Modern............................	4,000	4,500	3,125
Superposed, 28 Ga. or .410 Ga., Lightning Skeet Model, Presentation Grade 2, Fancy Engraving, Fancy Checkering, Fancy Wood, Modern....................................	3,250	3,500	2,550
Superposed, 28 Ga. or .410 Ga., Lightning Skeet Model, Presentation Grade 2, Fancy Engraving, Gold Inlays, Fancy Checkering, Fancy Wood, Modern............................	3,500	4,000	3,100
Superposed, 28 Ga. or .410 Ga., Lightning Skeet Model, Presentation Grade 1, Engraved, Gold Inlays, Fancy Checkering, Fancy Wood, Modern............................	2,750	3,250	2,250
Superposed, 28 Ga. or .410 Ga., Lightning Skeet Model, Presentation Grade 1, Engraved, Fancy Checkering, Fancy Wood, Modern..	2,500	2,750	2,250

	V.G.	Exc	Prior Edition
Superposed, Various Gauges, Pre–1977, Diana Grade Hunting Model, Satin Nickel–Plated Frame, Fancy Engraving, Fancy Checkering, Fancy Wood, Modern	$1,825	$3,500	$2,350
Superposed, Various Gauges, Pre–1977, Exhibition Grade, Fancy Engraving, Fancy Checkering, Fancy Wood, Gold Inlays, Modern		7,500	
Superposed, Various Gauges, Pre–1977, Grade 1, Engraved, Checkered Stock, Vent Rib, Single Selective Trigger, Modern	700	1,000	950
Superposed, Various Gauges, Pre–1977, Midas Grade Hunting Model, Fancy Engraving, Fancy Checkering, Fancy Wood, Gold Inlays, Modern	2,575	5,000	3,250
Superposed, Various Gauges, Pre–1977, Pigeon Grade Hunting Model, Satin Nickel–Plated Frame, Fancy Engraving, Fancy Checkering, Fancy Wood, Modern	1,625	2,250	1,950
Superposed, Various Gauges, Pre–1977, Pointer Grade, Fancy Engraving, Fancy Checkering, Single Selective Trigger, Modern	1,625	3,000	2,150
Superposed, Various Gauges, Pre–1977, Super Exhibition Grade, Fancy Wood, Fancy Checkering, Fancy Engraving, Gold Inlays, Modern	20,000	25,000	21,750

SHOTGUN, DOUBLE BARREL, SIDE-BY-SIDE

	V.G.	Exc	Prior Edition
B–SS, 12 and 20 Gauges, Checkered Stock, Field Grade, Modern	450	500	500
B–SS, 12 and 20 Gauges, Checkered Stock, Grade II, Engraved, Modern	775	975	975
B–SS, 12 and 20 Gauges, Checkered Stock, Sporter Grade, Modern	550	600	600

SHOTGUN, SEMI-AUTOMATIC

	V.G.	Exc	Prior Edition
Auto–5, For Belgian Make Add 15%–25%			
Auto–5 , Various Gauges, Vent Rib, Add $50.00–$75.00			
Auto–5, 12 and 20 Gauges, Magnum, Checkered Stock, Light Engraving, Plain Barrel, Modern	400	450	450
Auto–5, 12 and 20 Gauges, Skeet Grade, Checkered Stock, Light Engraving, Vent Rib, Modern	500	550	550
Auto–5, 12 Ga., Trap Grade, Vent Rib, Checkered Stock, Modern	400	475	475
Auto–5, 16 Ga., 29/16", Pre–WW2, Checkered Stock, Light Engraving, Plain Barrel, Modern	250	275	525
Auto–5, 16 Gauge, Sweet Sixteen, Lightweight, Checkered Stock, Light Engraving, Plain Barrel, Modern	350	400	500
Auto–5, Various Gauges, Buck Special, Checkered Stock, Light Engraving, Plain Barrel, Modern	475	525	525
Auto–5, Various Gauges, Grade 2, Pre–WW2, Plain Barrel, Fancy Engraving, Modern	850	1,000	1,200
Auto–5, Various Gauges, Grade 2, Pre–WW2, Plain Barrel Fancy Engraving, Gold Inlays, Modern	2,000	2,250	1,450
Auto–5, Various Gauges, Grade IV, Plain Barrel, Fancy Engraving, Modern	3,250	3,750	2,650
Auto–5, Various Gauges, Lightweight, Checkered Stock, Light Engraving, Plain Barrel, Modern	450	525	525
Auto–5, Various Gauges, Raised Solid Rib, Add $50.00–$75.00			

	V.G.	Exc	Prior Edition
B–80, 12 Gauge, Lightweight, Checkered Stock, Vent Rib, Modern...	$300	$375	$375

Browning B-80

	V.G.	Exc	Prior Edition
Double–Auto, 12 and 20 Gauges, Checkered Stock, Engraved, Plain Barrel, Modern....................................	325	375	325
Double–Auto, 12 Ga., Trap Model, Add 10%–15%			
Double–Auto, 12 Gauge, Checkered Stock, Engraved, Vent Rib, Barrel Modern..	425	475	275
Double–Auto, Skeet Model, Add 10%-15%			
Double–Auto, Vent Rib, Add $50.00–$75.00			
Model 2000 Montreal Olympic, 12 Ga., Trap Grade, Vent Rib, Engraved, Gold Inlays, Commemorative, Tube Feed, Checkered Stock, Modern..........................	700	1,000	1,550
Model 2000, 12 and 20 Gauges, Buck Special, Open Rear Sight, Tube Feed, Checkered Stock, Modern...................	250	325	325
Model 2000, 12 and 20 Gauges, Skeet Grade, Vent Rib, Tube Feed, Checkered Stock, Modern.............................	275	350	350
Model 2000, 12 and 20 Gauges, Vent Rib, Tube Feed, Checkered Stock, Modern..	250	325	325
Model 2000, 12 Ga., Trap Grade, Vent Rib, Tube Feed, Checkered Stock, Modern..	275	325	375

SHOTGUN, SINGLESHOT

	V.G.	Exc	Prior Edition
BT–99, 12 Ga., Pigeon Grade, Checkered Stock, Engraved, Vent Rib, Modern...................................	850	1,000	1,250
BT–99, 12 Ga., Trap Grade, Vent Rib, Checkered Stock, Engraved, Modern...................................	650	750	450
BT–99, 12 Ga., Trap Grade, Vent Rib, with extra Single Trap Barrel, Checkered Stock, Engraved, Modern............	675	850	850

SHOTGUN, SLIDE ACTION

	V.G.	Exc	Prior Edition
BPS, 12 Ga., Buck Special, Rifle Sights, Modern............	300	375	375
BPS, 12 Ga., Checkered Stock, Vent Rib, Modern..........	300	375	375
BPS, 12 Ga., Invector Trap, Checkered Stock, Vent Rib, Modern...........	275	300	300

BRUTUS Made by Hood Firearms Co. c. 1875–76.

HANDGUN, REVOLVER

	V.G.	Exc	Prior Edition
.22 Short R.F., 7 Shot, Spur Trigger, Solid Frame, Single Action, Antique..	100	175	175

	V.G.	Exc	Prior Edition

BSA Birmingham Small Arms, Ltd., Birmingham, England, From 1885.

RIFLE, BOLT ACTION

	V.G.	Exc	Prior Edition
Imperial, Various Calibers, Sporting Rifle, Muzzle Brake, Checkered Stock, Open Rear Sight, Modern...	$175	$275	$275
Imperial, Various Calibers, Sporting Rifle, Muzzle Brake, Checkered Stock, Open Rear Sight, Lightweight, Modern........................	300	275	275
Majestic Deluxe, .458 Win. Mag., Sporting Rifle, Muzzle Brake, Lightweight, Checkered Stock, Open Rear Sight, Modern........................	225	325	325
Majestic Deluxe, Various Calibers, Sporting Rifle, Checkered, Stock, Open Rear Sight, Modern.....	175	275	275
Majestic Deluxe, Various Calibers, Sporting Rifle, Muzzle Brake, Lightweight, Checkered Stock, Open Rear Sight, Modern........................	175	275	275
Model CF–2, Various Calibers, Sporting Rifle, Checkered Stock, Open Rear Sights, Modern........................	225	375	375
Model CF–2, Various Calibers, Sporting Rifle, Checkered Stock, Double Set Triggers, Open Rear Sights, Modern.....	275	400	400
Monarch Deluxe, Various Calibers, Sporting Rifle, Checkered, Stock, Open Rear Sight, Modern........................	200	300	300
Monarch Deluxe, Various Claibers, Varmint, Heavy Barrel, Checkered Stock, Open Rear Sight, Modern............................	225	300	300

RIFLE, SINGLESHOT

	V.G.	Exc	Prior Edition
#12 Martini, .22 L.R.R.F., Target, Target Sights, Checkered Stock, Modern............	200	300	300
#12/15 Martini, .22 L.R.R.F., Target, Target Sights, Target Stock, Modern............	250	350	350
#12/15 Martini, .22 L.R.R.F., Target, Target Sights, Target Stock, Heavy Barrel, Modern............	250	375	375
#13 Martini, .22 Hornet, Sporting Rifle, Checkered Stock, Modern............	275	375	375
#13 Martini, .22 L.R.R.F., Target, Target Sights, Checkered Stock, Modern............	200	275	275
#15 Martini, .22 L.R.R.F., Target, Target Sights, Target Stock, Modern............	350	450	450
Centurian Martini, .22 L.R.R.F., Target, Target Sights, Target Stock, Target Barrel, Modern............	250	375	375
International Martini, .22 L.R.R.F., Target, Target Sights, Heavy Barrel, Target Stock, Modern............	250	400	400
International MK 2 Martini, .22 L.R.R.F., Target, Target Sights, Target Stock, Modern............	275	400	400
International MK 2 Martini, .22 L.R.R.F., Target, Target Sights, Target Stock, Heavy Barrel, Modern............	250	375	375
International MK 3 Martini, .22 L.R.R.F., Target, Target Sights, Target Stock, Heavy Barrel, Modern............	325	400	400
Mark V, .22 L.R.R.F., Heavy Barrel, Target Rifle, Target Sights, Target Stock, Modern............	350	475	475
Martini I S U, .22 L.R.R.F., Target Rifle, Target Sights, Target Stock, Modern............	250	475	475

RIFLE, SLIDE ACTION

	V.G.	Exc	Prior Edition
.22 L.R.R.F., Clip Fed, Takedown, Modern............................	75	150	150
.22 L.R.R.F., Tube Feed, Takedown, Modern............................	100	150	150

BUCHEL, ERNST FRIEDRICH   Zella Mehlis, Germany, 1919–1926.

HANDGUN, SINGLESHOT

	V.G.	Exc	Prior Edition
Luna, .22 L.R.R.F., Rotary Breech, Free Pistol, Set Triggers, Light Engraving, Curio............	$650	$750	$750
Model W.B., .22 L.R.R.F., Roux Action, Target Pistol, Hammerless, Tip–Down Barrel, Curio............	350	475	475
Practice, .22 Short R.F., Warnant Action, Hammer, Target Pistol, Curio............	225	300	300
Tell I, .22 L.R.R.F., Rotary Breech, Free Pistol, Set Triggers, Light Engraving, Curio............	700	850	850
Tell II, .22 L.R.R.F., Rotary Breech, Free Pistol, Set Triggers, Light Engraving, Curio............	700	850	850

BUDDY ARMS   Fort Worth, Tex. during the early 1960's.

HANDGUN, DOUBLE BARREL, OVER-UNDER

	V.G.	Exc	Prior Edition
Double Deuce, .22 L.R.R.F., Remington Derringer Copy, Modern............	50	75	75

BUDISCHOWSKY   Made by Norton Armament (Norarmco), Mt. Clemens, mich. 1973–1977.

HANDGUN, SEMI-AUTOMATIC

	V.G.	Exc	Prior Edition
TP-70, .22 L.R.R.F., Clip Fed, Double Action, Pocket Pistol, Stainless Steel, Steel Hammer, Modern............	350	425	425
TP-70, .25 ACP, Clip Fed, Double Action, Pocket Pistol, Stainless Steel, Hammer, Presentation, Custom Serial Number, Curio............	750	950	950

	V.G.	Exc	Prior Edition
TP-70, .25 ACP, Clip Fed, Double Action, Pocket Pistol, Stainless Steel, Hammer, Modern......	$250	$325	$325

Budischowsky TP-70

BUFALO Gabilondo y Cia., Elgobar, Spain.

HANDGUN, SEMI-AUTOMATIC

Model 1920, .25 ACP, Clip Fed, Modern............	100	150	150
Pocket, .32 ACP, Clip Fed, Modern............	100	150	150

BUFFALO ARMS Tonawanda, N.Y.

HANDGUN, DOUBLE BARREL, OVER-UNDER

Model 1, .357 Mag., Hammer, Blue or Nickel, Modern...........	75	100	100

BUFFALO BILL Sold by Homer Fisher Co.

HANDGUN, REVOLVER

.22 Short R.F., 7 Shot, Spur Trigger, Solid Frame, Single Action, Antique........	100	150	150

BUFFALO STAND Tradename used by ManuFrance.

HANDGUN, SINGLESHOT

Bolt Action, .22 L.R.R.F., Target Pistol, Modern..........	50	100	100

	V.G.	Exc	Prior Edition

BUHAG Buchsenmacher-Handwerkgenossenschaft M.B.H. of Suhl, East Germany.

HANDGUN, SEMI-AUTOMATIC

Olympia, .22 Short R.F., Clip Fed, Target Pistol, Modern.........................	$375	$550	$550

BULL DOZER Made by Norwich Pistol Co., Sold by J. McBride & Co. c. 1875–1883.

HANDGUN, REVOLVER

.22 Short R.F., 7 Shot, Spur Trigger, Solid Frame, Single Action, Antique...................	100	175	175
.38 Short R.F, 5 Shot, Spur Trigger, Solid Frame, Single Action, Antique...................	100	200	200
.41 Short R.F., 5 Shot, Spur Trigger, Solid Frame, Single Action, Antique...................	125	200	200
.44 Short R.F., 5 Shot, Spur Trigger, Solid Frame, Single Action, Antique...................	175	275	275

BULLARD REPEATING ARMS CO. Springfield, Mass. 1887–1889.

RIFLE, LEVER ACTION

Various Calibers, Light Engraving, Add $55.00–$160.00
Various Calibers, Medium Engraving, Add $220.00–$435.00
Various Calibers, Octagon Barrel, Add $75.00–$110.00
Various Calibers, Ornate Engraving, Add $775.00–$1150.00
Various Calibers, Target Sights, Add $125.00–$185.00
Various Calibers, Fancy Checkering, Add $75.00–$110.00
Various Calibers, for Express Sights, Add $110.00–$160.00
Various Calibers, for Fancy Wood, Add $30.00–$50.00
Various Calibers, for Lyman Sights, Add $45.00–$75.00
Various Calibers, for Standard Checkering, Add $35.00–$50.00
Various Calibers, Full Nickel Plating, Add $55.00–$80.00
Various Calibers, Half-Octagon Barrel, Add $35.00–$65.00

Carbine, Various Calibers, Open Rear Sight, Carbine, Antique.................	3,750	4,250	1,500
Military, Musket, with Bayonet, Open Rear Sight, Antique....................	3,250	3,750	3,800
Various Calibers, Large Frame, Tube Feed, Round Barrel, Plain, Open Rear Sight, Sporting Rifle, Antique.........................	2,000	2,500	1,050
Various Calibers, Small Frame, Tube Feed, Round Barrel, Plain, Open Rear Sights, Sporting Rifle, Antique.................................	1,750	2,000	900

RIFLE, SINGLESHOT

Military, Full–Stocked, with Bayonet, Open Rear Sight, Antique..........	1,450	3,250	2,500
Military, Full–Stocked, with Bayonet, Open Rear Sight, Carbine, Antique....................	1,500	2,750	2,750
Various Calibers, Schuetzen Target Rifle, Octagon Barrel, Target Sights, Swiss Buttplate, Checkered Stock, Antique....................	1,150	2,750	2,500
Various Calibers, Target Gallery/Hunting, Lightweight, Open Rear Sights, Antique....................	450	1,500	950

	V.G.	Exc	Prior Edition
Various Rimfires, Target Gallery/Hunting, .22 Caliber, Open Rear Sights, Antique..	$575	$1,250	$975
Various Rimfires, Target Rifle, Octagon Barrel, Target Sights, Swiss Buttplate, Checkered Stock, Antique................................	750	2,500	1,750

BULLDOG Made by Forehand & Wadsworth.

HANDGUN, REVOLVER

.32 S & W, 7 Shot, Double Action, Solid Frame, Curio............................	75	100	100
.38 S & W, 6 Shot, Double Action, Solid Frame, Curio............................	75	100	100
.44 S & W, 5 Shot, Double Action, Solid Frame, Curio............................	75	125	125

BULLS EYE c. 1875.

HANDGUN, REVOLVER

.22 Short R.F., 7 Shot, Spur Trigger, Solid Frame, Single Action, Antique..	100	150	150

BULWARK Beistegui Hermanos, Eibar, Spain.

HANDGUN, SEMI-AUTOMATIC

.25 ACP, External Hammer, Clip Fed, Blue, Curio....................................	225	325	325
.25 ACP, Hammerless, Clip Fed, Blue, Curio..	100	150	150
.32 ACP, External Hammer, Clip Fed, Blue, Curio....................................	175	300	300
.32 ACP, Hammerless, Clip Fed, Blue, Curio..	100	150	150

BUMFORD London, England 1730–1760.

HANDGUN, FLINTLOCK

.38, Pocket Pistol, Boxlock, Queen Anne Style, Screw Barrel, Silver Inlay, Antique..	550	775	775

BURGESS, ANDREW Oswego, N.Y. 1874–1887.

RIFLE, LEVER ACTION

Model 1876, .45-70 Government, Tube Feed, Octagon Barrel, Antique..	950	1,750	1,750

RIFLE, SLIDE ACTION

Various Calibers, Folding Gun, With Case, Antique................................	850	1,475	1,475

SHOTGUN, SLIDE ACTION

12 Ga., Folding Gun, With Case, Antique..	475	750	750
12 Ga., Takedown, Solid Rib, Light Engraving, Antique.........................	325	475	475

BUSHMASTER Gwinn Arms Co., Winston-Salem, N.C.

HANDGUN, SEMI-AUTOMATIC

Bushmaster, .223 Rem., Clip Fed, Modern..	250	325	325

	V.G.	Exc	Prior Edition

RIFLE, SEMI-AUTOMATIC
.223 Rem., Clip Fed, Folding Stock, Modern... $275 $350 $350
.223 Rem., Clip Fed, Wood Stock, Modern...................................... 250   300   300

BUSOMS   Spain c. 1780.
HANDGUN, MIQUELET-LOCK
.70 Pair, Belt Pistol, Belt Hook, Engraved, Brass Furniture,
Antique... 2,150   2,475   2,475

BUSTINDIU, AUGUSTIN   Toledo, Spain c. 1765.
HANDGUN, MIQUELET-LOCK
Pari, Locks by Guisasola, Half–Octagon Barrel, Antique........................ 4,175   5,275   5,275

BUSTINDIU, JUAN ESTEBAN   Eibar, Spain c. 1775.
HANDGUN, MIQUELET-LOCK
Pair, Half–Octagon Barrel, Silver Inlay, Light Decoration,
Antique... 2,950   4,000   4,000

C

		Prior
V.G.	Exc.	Edition

C.A.C. Made by A.I.G. Corp., North Haven, Conn. Distributed by Mossberg.
HANDGUN, SEMI-AUTOMATIC
Combat, .45 ACP, Clip Fed, Stainless Steel, Modern............................... $375 · $450 $450

CADET Sold by Maltby–Curtis Co.
HANDGUN, REVOLVER
.22 Long R.F., 7 Shot, Single Action, Solid Frame, Spur Trigger,
Antique... 100 150 150

CALDERWOOD, WILLIAM Phila., Pa. 1808–1816. See Kentucky Rifles and Pistols and U.S. Military.

CANADIAN MILITARY
HANDGUN, SEMI-AUTOMATIC
Hi Power Inglis #1 Mk I, 9mm, Tangent Sights, Slotted for
Shoulder Stock, Military, Curio..................... 850 1,000 950
Hi Power Inglis #1 Mk I*, 9mm, Tangent Sights, Slotted for
Shoulder Stock, Military, Curio..................... 550 750 750
Hi Power Inglis #2 Mk I, 9mm, Fixed Sights, Military, Curio............... 500 550 450
Hi Power Inglis #2 Mk I*, 9mm, Tangent Sights, Slotted for
Shoulder Stock, Military, Curio..................... 400 450 475

RIFLE, BOLT ACTION
1907 MK 2 Ross, .303 British, Full–Stocked, Military, Curio................. 250 300 175
1910 MK 3 Ross, .303 British, Full–Stocked, Military, Curio................. 275 325 175
SMLE #4 Mk.1*, .303 British, Clip Fed, Curio....................................... 150 175 150

CAPT. JACK Made by Hopkins & Allen 1871–1875.
HANDGUN, REVOLVER
.22 Short R.F., 7 Shot, Spur Trigger, Solid Frame, Single Action,
Antique.. 75 · 150 150

	V.G.	Exc	Prior Edition

CAROLINE ARMS Made by Crescent Firearms Co. 1892–1900.

SHOTGUN, DOUBLE BARREL, SIDE-BY-SIDE

	V.G.	Exc	Prior Edition
Various Gauges, Hammerless, Damascus Barrel, Modern......................	$75	$175	$175
Various Gauges, Hammerless, Steel Barrel, Modern.............................	100	175	175
Various Gauges, Outside Hammers, Damascus Barrel, Modern............	75	150	150
Various Gauges, Outside Hammers, Steel Barrel, Modern.....................	75	175	175

SHOTGUN, SINGLESHOT

	V.G.	Exc	Prior Edition
Various Gauges, Hammer, Steel Barrel, Modern....................................	50	75	75

CARPENTER, JOHN Lancaster, Pa. 1771–1790. See Kentucky Rifles.

CARROLL, LAWRENCE Philadelphia, Pa. 1786–1790. See Kentucky Rifles.

CARTRIDGE FIREARMS

COMBINATION WEAPON, DRILLING

	V.G.	Exc	Prior Edition
German, Various Calibers, Light Engraving, Modern.............................	500	850	850

HANDGUN, REVOLVER

	V.G.	Exc	Prior Edition
.22 Short, Small Pocket Pistol, Double Action, Modern..........................	50	75	90
.22 Short, Small Pocket Pistol, Folding Trigger, Modern........................	50	125	125
.25 ACP, Small Pocket Pistol, Double Action, Modern...........................	25	75	75
.25 ACP, Small Pocket Pistol, Folding Trigger, Modern..........................	50	100	100
11mm Pinfire, Lefaucheux Military Style, Antique................................	150	225	225
11mm Pinfire, Lefaucheux Military Style, Engraved, Antique................	225	375	375
7.62mm Nagent, Nagent Style Gas Seal, Solid Frame, Double Action, Modern......	75	150	150
7mm Pinfire, Pocket Pistol, Folding Trigger, Engraved, Antique...........	75	125	125
Belgian Proofs, Various Calibers, Top Break, Double Action, Medium Quality, Modern......................	50	75	75
Belgian Proofs, Various Calibers, Top Break, Double Action, Engraved, Medium Quality, Modern........................	75	125	125
Belgian Proofs, Various Calibers, Top Break, Double Action, Folding Trigger, Medium Quality, Modern.....................	75	100	100
Chinese Copy of Colt Police Positive, .38 Special, Double Action, Solid Frame, Swing–Out Cylinder, Low Quality, Modern.....................	50	75	75
Chinese Copy of Police Positive, 9mm Luger, Double Action, Solid Frame, Swing–Out Cylinder, Low Quality, Modern.....................	50	75	75
Chinese Copy of S&W M-10, .38 Special, Double Action, Solid Frame, Swing–Out Cylinder, Low Quality, Modern................................	50	75	75
Copy of Colt SAA, Various Calibers, Western Style, Single Action, Low Quality, Modern................................	50	100	100
Copy of Colt SAA, Various Calibers, Western Style, Single Action, Medium Quality, Modern.,.....................	75	125	125
Copy of S&W Russian Model, Various Calibers, Break, Single Action, Low Quality, Antique........................	75	150	150

	V.G.	Exc	Prior Edition
Copy of S&W Russian Model, Various Calibers, Top Break, Single Action, Medium Quality, Antique.....................	$150	$250	$250
Copy of S&W Russian Model, Various Calibers, Top Break, Single Action, High Quality, Antique.....................	350	500	500
Spanish Copy of S&W M–10, .38 Special, Double Action, Solid Frame, Swing–Out Cylinder, Low Quality, Modern.................	50	75	75
Spanish Copy of S&W M–10, .32–20 WCF, Double Action, Solid Frame, Swing–Out Cylinder, Low Quality, Modern.................	50	75	75
Spanish Copy of S&W M–10, .38 Special, Double Action, Solid Frame, Swing–Out Cylinder, Low Quality, Modern.................	50	75	75
Various Centerfire Calibers, Bulldog Style, Double Action, Solid Frame, Modern.............................	50	75	75
Various Centerfire Calibers, European Military Style, Double Action, Solid Frame, Modern.................	75	150	150
Various Centerfire Calibers, Folding Trigger, Open Top Frame, Modern.................	75	100	100
Various Centerfire Calibers, Gasser Style, Solid Frame, Double Action, Modern.................	75	150	150
Various Centerfire Calibers, Small Pocket Pistol, Hammerless, Folding Trigger, with Safety, Modern.................	75	100	100
Various Centerfire Calibers, Warnant Style, Top Break, Double Action, Modern.................	75	150	150

HANDGUN, SEMI-AUTOMATIC

Chinese Broomhandle, 7.63 Mauser, Low Quality, Modern.................	100	175	175
Chinese Copy of FN 1900, Various Calibers, Clip Fed, Low Quality, Modern.................	75	100	100
Chinese Pocket Pistols, Various Calibers, Clip Fed, Low Quality, Modern.................	75	100	100
Copy of Colt M1911, .45 ACP, Clip Fed, Military, High Quality, Modern.................	175	250	250
Spanish Pocket Pistols, .25 ACP, Clip Fed, Low Quality, Modern.........	75	100	100
Spanish Pocket Pistols, .32 ACP, Clip Fed, Low Quality, Modern.........	75	125	125
Spanish Pocket Pistols, .32 ACP, Clip Fed, Low Quality, Ruby Style, Modern.................	75	125	125

HANDGUN, SINGLESHOT

Flobert Style, Various Configurations, Modern.................	50	100	100
.22 R.F, Fancy Target Pistol, Hammerless, Set Triggers, Modern............	275	425	425
.22 Short, Fancy German Target Pistol, Tip–Up Barrel, Engraved, Set Triggers, Modern.................	350	450	450
.22 Short, Target Pistol, Tip–Up Barrel, Plain, Modern.................	75	125	125

RIFLE, BOLT ACTION

Various Centerfire Calibers, Commercial Sporting Rifle, Low Quality, Modern.................	75	125	125
Various Rimfire Calibers, Singleshot, Checkered Stock, European, Modern.................	25	50	50
Arabian Copies, Various Calibers, Military, Reproduction, Low Quality, Modern.................	50	75	75

RIFLE, SINGLESHOT

Various Calibers, Flobert Style, Checkered Stock, Modern.................	75	100	100
Various Calibers, Warnant Style, Checkered Stock, Modern.................	75	125	125
Belgian Proofs, .22 Long R.F., Tip–Up, Octagon Barrel, Medium Quality, Antique.................	75	100	100

	V.G.	Exc	Prior Edition

SHOTGUN, DOUBLE BARREL, SIDE-BY-SIDE

	V.G.	Exc	Prior Edition
Belgian Proofs, Various Gauges, Damascus Barrel, Low Quality, Outside Hammers, Modern......	$75	$100	$100
English Proofs, Various Gauges, Damascus Barrel, Low Quality, Outside Hammers, Modern.........	75	125	125
No Proofs, Various Gauges, Damascus Barrel, Low Quality, Outside Hammers, Modern......	50	100	100
Various Gauges, American, Hammerless, Damascus Barrel, Modern......	75	150	150
Various Gauges, American, Hammerless, Steel Barrel, Modern......	100	175	175
Various Gauges, American, Outside Hammers, Damascus Barrel, Modern......	75	150	150
Various Gauges, American, Outside Hammers, Steel Barrel, Modern......	75	175	175

SHOTGUN, SINGLESHOT

	V.G.	Exc	Prior Edition
"Zulu," 12 Ga., Converted from Perc. Musket, Trap Door Action, Antique......	75	125	125
Various Gauges, American, Hammer, Steel Barrel, Modern......	50	75	75
Various Gauges, Warnant Style, Checkered Stock, Modern......	50	75	75

CEBRA Arizmendi, Zulaika y Cia., Eibar, Spain.

HANDGUN, SEMI-AUTOMATIC

	V.G.	Exc	Prior Edition
Pocket, .25 ACP, Clip Fed, Curio......	75	125	125

CELTA Tomas de Urizar y Cia., Eibar, Spain c. 1935.

HANDGUN, SEMI-AUTOMATIC

	V.G.	Exc	Prior Edition
Pocket, .25 ACP, Clip Fed, Curio......	75	125	125

CENTENNIAL Made by Derringer Rifle & Pistol Works 1876.

HANDGUN, REVOLVER

	V.G.	Exc	Prior Edition
.22 Short R.F., 7 Shot, Spur Trigger, Tip–Up, Antique......	250	350	350
.32 Short R.F., 5 Shot, Spur Trigger, Solid Frame, Single Action, Antique......	100	175	175
.38 Short R.F., 5 Shot, Spur Trigger, Solid Frame, Single Action, Antique......	100	175	175
Centennial '76, .38 Long R.F., 5 Shot, Single Action, Spur Trigger, Tip–Up, Antique......	250	350	350
Model 2, .32 R.F., 5 Shot, Single Action, Spur Trigger, Tip–Up, Antique......	250	350	350

CENTRAL Made by Stevens Arms.

SHOTGUN, DOUBLE BARREL, SIDE-BY-SIDE

	V.G.	Exc	Prior Edition
Model 215, 12 and 16 Gauges, Outside Hammers, Steel Barrel, Modern......	100	175	175
Model 311, Various Gauges, Hammerless, Steel Barrel, Modern......	100	175	175
Model 315, Various Gauges, Hammerless, Steel Barrel, Modern......	100	175	175

	V.G.	Exc	Prior Edition

SHOTGUN, SINGLESHOT

Model 94, Various Gauges, Takedown, Automatic Ejector, Plain
Hammer, Modern.. $50 $75 $75

CENTRAL ARMS CO. Made by Crescent, For Shapleigh Hardware Co., c. 1900.

SHOTGUN, DOUBLE BARREL, SIDE-BY-SIDE

Various Gauges, Hammerless, Damascus Barrel, Modern...................... 75 150 150
Various Gauges, Hammerless, Steel Barrel, Modern............................. 100 175 175
Various Gauges, Outside Hammers, Damascus Barrel, Modern............. 75 150 150
Various Gauges, Outside Hammers, Steel Barrel, Modern...................... 100 175 175

SHOTGUN, SINGLESHOT

Various Gauges, Hammer, Steel Barrel, Modern.................................... 50 75 75

CHALLENGE Made by Bliss & Goodyear, c. 1878.

HANDGUN, REVOLVER

.32 Short R.F., 5 Shot, Spur Trigger, Solid Frame, Single Action,
Antique.. 100 150 150

CHAMPION c. 1870.

HANDGUN, REVOLVER

.22 Short R.F., 7 Shot, Spur Trigger, Solid Frame, Single Action,
Antique.. 100 150 150

CHAMPLIN FIREARMS Enid, Oklahoma.

RIFLE, BOLT ACTION

Basic Rifle, with Quarter Rib, Express Sights,
Add $185.00–$270.00
Basic Rifle, Fancy Checkering, Add $30.00-$45.00
Basic Rifle, Fancy Wood, Add $55.00-$90.00
Basic Rifle, Various Calibers, Adjustable Trigger, Round or
Octagon Tapered Barrel, Checkered Stock, Modern................................. 2,750 3,500 3,500

SHOTGUN, DOUBLE BARREL, OVER-UNDER

12 Ga., Extra Barrels, Add $175.00–$250.00
Model 100, 12 Ga., Field Grade, Checkered Stock, Vent Rib,
Single Selective Trigger, Engraved, Modern................................. 525 850 850
Model 100, 12 Ga., Skeet Grade, Checkered Stock, Vent Rib,
Single Selective Trigger, Engraved, Modern................................. 575 925 925
Model 100, 12 Ga., Trap Grade, Checkered Stock, Vent Rib,
Single Selective Trigger, Engraved, Modern................................. 575 925 925
Model 500, 12 Ga., Field Grade, Checkered Stock, Vent Rib,
Single Selective Trigger, Engraved, Modern................................. 850 1,375 1,375
Model 500, 12 Ga., Skeet Grade, Checkered Stock, Vent Rib,
Single Selective Trigger, Engraved, Modern................................. 900 1,500 1,500

	V.G.	Exc	Prior Edition
Model 500, 12 Ga., Trap Grade, Checkered Stock, Vent Rib, Single Selective Trigger, Engraved, Modern	$975	$1,600	$1,600

SHOTGUN, SINGLESHOT

	V.G.	Exc	Prior Edition
Model SB 100, 12 Ga., Trap Grade, Checkered Stock, Vent Rib, Single Selective Trigger, Engraved, Modern	575	875	875
Model SB 500, 12 Ga., Trap Grade, Checkered Stock, Vent Rib, Single Selective Trigger, Engraved, Modern	875	1,350	1,350

CHAPUIS St. Bonnet–le–Chateau, France.

SHOTGUN, DOUBLE BARREL, SIDE-BY-SIDE

	V.G.	Exc	Prior Edition
Progress RBV, R20, 12 or 20 Gauge, Automatic Ejectors, Sideplates, Double Triggers, Checkered Stock, Modern	1,275	1,450	1,450
Progress RG, 12 or 20 Gauge, Automatic Ejectors, Double Triggers, Checkered Stock, Modern	1,800	2,000	2,000
Progress Slug, 12 or 20 Gauge, Automatic Ejectors, Slug Barrel, Double Triggers, Checkered Stock, Modern	1,975	2,200	2,200

CHARLES DALY Tradename on guns made in Suhl, Germany prior to WWII, and by Miroku and Breda after WWII.

COMBINATION WEAPON, DRILLING

	V.G.	Exc	Prior Edition
Diamond, Various Calibers, Fancy Engraving, Fancy Checkering, Modern	6,000	6,700	6,700
Regent Diamond, Various Calibers, Fancy Engraving, Fancy Checkering, Fancy Wood, Modern	4,400	4,800	4,800
Superior, Various Calibers, Engraved, Modern	2,300	2,600	2,600

RIFLE, BOLT ACTION

	V.G.	Exc	Prior Edition
.22 Hornet, 5 Shot Clip, Checkered Stock, Modern	550	625	625

SHOTGUN, DOUBLE BARREL, OVER-UNDER

For 28 Ga., Add 10%–15%
12 Ga., For Wide Vent Rib, Add $25.00–$45.00

	V.G.	Exc	Prior Edition
Various Gauges, Field Grade, Light Engraving, Single Selective Trigger, Automatic Ejector, Post–War, Modern	300	425	425
Commander 100, Various Gauges, Automatic Ejector, Checkered Stock, Single Trigger, Modern	375	500	500
Commander 100, Various Gauges, Automatic Ejector, Checkered Stock, Double Trigger, Modern	325	450	450
Commander 200, Various Gauges, Automatic Ejector, Checkered Stock, Engraved, Single Trigger, Modern	550	725	725
Commander 200, Various Gauges, Double Trigger, Modern	475	650	650
Diamond, 12 Ga., Trap Grade, Selective Ejector, Single Selective Trigger, Post–War, Modern	500	700	700
Diamond, 12 or 20 Gauges, Field Grade, Trap Grade, Selective Ejector, Single Selective Trigger, Post–War, Modern	500	750	750
Diamond, 12 or 20 Gauges, Skeet Grade, Trap Grade, Selective Ejector, Single Selective Trigger, Post–War, Modern	500	750	750
Diamond, Various Gauges, Double Trigger, Automatic Ejector, Fancy Engraving, Fancy Checkering, Modern	2,500	4,575	4,575
Empire, Various Gauges, Double Trigger, Automatic Ejector, Checkered Stock, Engraved, Modern	1,875	3,650	3,650

	V.G.	Exc	Prior Edition
Superior, 12 Ga., Trap Grade, Automatic Ejector, Single Selective Trigger, Post–War, Modern................	$350	$475	$475
Superior, Various Gauges, Field Grade, Trap Grade, Automatic Ejector, Single Selective Trigger, Post–War, Modern...............	350	475	475
Superior, Various Gauges, Skeet Grade, Trap Grade, Automatic Ejector, Single Selective Trigger, Post–War, Modern............	350	475	475
Venture, 12 Ga., Trap Grade, Single Trigger, Monte Carlo Stock, Post–War, Modern.................	250	375	375
Venture, 12 or 20 Gauges, Field Grade, Single Trigger, Trap Grade, Post–War, Modern................	250	375	375
Venture, 12 or 20 Gauges, Skeet Grade, Single Trigger, Trap Grade, Post–War, Modern................	275	375	375

SHOTGUN, DOUBLE BARREL, SIDE-BY-SIDE

	V.G.	Exc	Prior Edition
Diamond, Various Gauges, Double Trigger, Fancy Engraving, Fancy Checkering, Fancy Wood, Automatic Ejector, Modern............	3,275	3,950	3,950
Empire, Various Gauges, Double Trigger, Engraved, Checkered Stock, Automatic Ejector, Modern.............	1,825	2,525	2,525
Empire, Various Gauges, Vent Rib, Single Trigger, Checkered Stock, Engraved, Post–War, Modern.............	250	350	350
Regent Diamond, Various Gauges, Double Trigger, Fancy Engraving, Fancy Checkering, Fancy Wood, Automatic Ejector, Modern.............	2,875	5,250	5,250
Superior, Various Gauges, Double Trigger, Light Engraving, Checkered Stock, Modern.............	850	1,275	1,275

SHOTGUN, SEMI-AUTOMATIC

	V.G.	Exc	Prior Edition
Novamatic, 12 Ga., Mag. 3", Takedown, Vent Rib, Checkered Stock, Magnum, Modern..............	275	300	300
Novamatic, 12 Ga., Takedown, Trap Grade, Vent Rib, Checkered Stock, Monte Carlo Stock, Modern.............	275	325	325
Novamatic, 12 or 20 Gauges, Takedown, Plain Barrel, Checkered Stock, Lightweight, Modern..............	225	275	275
Novamatic, 12 or 20 Gauges, Takedown, Plain Barrel, Checkered Stock, Lightweight, Interchangable Choke Tubes, Modern............	250	275	275
Novamatic, 12 or 20 Gauges, Takedown, Vent Rib, Checkered Stock, Lightweight, Modern..............	200	250	250
Novamatic, 12 or 20 Gauges, Takedown, Vent Rib, Checkered Stock, Lightweight, Interchangable Choke Tubes, Modern............	250	275	275
Novamatic, 20 Ga., Takedown, Checkered Stock, Magnum, Lightweight, Modern..............	250	300	300
Novamatic Super Light, 12 and 20 Gauges, Takedown, Plain Barrel, Checkered Stock, Modern..............	200	275	275
Novamatic Super Light, 12 and 20 Gauges, Takedown, Plain Barrel, Checkered Stock, Interchangable Choke Tubes, Modern............	175	250	250
Novamatic Super Light, 12 and 20 Gauges, Takedown, Vent Rib, Checkered Stock, Modern..............	150	325	325

SHOTGUN, SINGLESHOT

	V.G.	Exc	Prior Edition
Empire, 12 Ga., Trap Grade, Fancy Engraving, Fancy Wood, Automatic Ejector, Modern..............	3,450	4,750	4,750
Sextuple Empire, 12 Ga., Trap Grade, Fancy Checkering, Fancy Engraving, Fancy Wood, Automatic Ejector, Modern..............	3,675	4,975	4,975
Sextuple Regent Diamond, 12 Ga., Trap Grade, Fancy Checkering, Fancy Engraving, Fancy Wood, Automatic Ejector, Modern..............	4,625	6,675	6,675

	V.G.	Exc	Prior Edition
Superior, 12 Ga., Trap Grade, Monte Carlo Stock, Selective Ejector, Engraved, Post–War, Modern..	$275	$375	$375

CHAROLA Y ANITUA Garate, Anitua y Cia., Eibar, Spain, c. 1898.

HANDGUN, SEMI-AUTOMATIC

	V.G.	Exc	Prior Edition
Charola, 5mm Clement, Locked Breech, Box Magazine, Belgian Made, Curio...	450	625	625
Charola, 5mm Clement, Locked Breech, Box Magazine, Spanish Made, Curio...	575	875	875

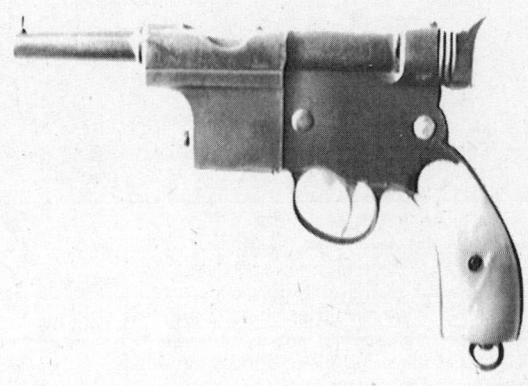

Charola y Anitua, Spanish

CHARTER ARMS Stratford, Conn. since 1965.

HANDGUN, REVOLVER

	V.G.	Exc	Prior Edition
Milestone Limited Edition, .44 Special, Bulldog, Engraved, Silver Plated, Cased with Accessories, Modern..	775	995	995

	V.G.	Exc	Prior Edition
Bulldog Tracker, .357 Magnum, Double Action, Blue, Adjustable Sights, Modern..	$200	$225	$225

Charter Arms Bulldog Tracker .357 Magnum, 6" Barrel

Bulldog, .44 Special, Double Action, Blue, Modern................................	175	200	200
Bulldog, .44 Special, Double Action, Nickel Plated, Modern.................	200	225	225
Bulldog, .44 Special, Double Action, Stainless, Modern..........................	225	250	250
Off–Duty, .38 SPL, 5 Shot, 2" Barrel, Stainless, Modern......................	225	275	275
Off–Duty, .38 SPL, 5 Shot, 2" Barrel, Steel Frame, Modern..................	150	175	175
Pathfinder, .22 L.R.R.F., Adjustable Sights, Bulldog Grips, Double Action, Modern...	175	200	200
Pathfinder, .22 L.R.R.F., Adjustable Sights, Bulldog Grips, Double Action, Stainless Steel, Modern...	225	275	275
Pathfinder, .22 L.R.R.F., Adjustable Sights, Square–Butt, Double Action, Modern...	125	175	175
Pathfinder, .22 WMR, Adjustable Sights, Double Action, Bulldog Grips, Modern...	125	175	175
Pathfinder, .22 WMR, Adjustable Sights, Double Action, Square– Butt, Modern...	125	175	175
Police Bulldog, .32 H&R Magnum, 4" Bull Barrel, Checkered Grips, Blue, Modern..	175	225	225
Police Bulldog, .38 Special, 1" Bull Barrel, Stainless, Modern..............	250	275	275
Police Bulldog, .38 Special, 4" Tapered Barrel, Square Grips, Stainless, Modern..	175	250	250

	V.G.	Exc	Prior Edition
Police Bulldog, .38 Special, Double Action, Blue, Adjustable Sights, Modern..........................	$125	$200	$200

Charter Arms Police Bulldog

Police Bulldog Tracker, .357 Magnum, 2½" Barrel, Blue, Modern..........................	200	250	250
Police Bulldog Tracker, .357 Magnum, 4" Barrel, Bulldog Grips, Blue, Modern..........................	200	250	250
Police Undercover, .32 H&R Magnum, 2" Barrel, Checkered Panel Grips, Blue, Modern..........................	175	200	200
Police Undercover, .38 Special, 2" Barrel, Blue, Pocket Hammer, Modern..........................	175	200	200
Police Undercover, Law Enforcement Version, .38 Special, Five Shot, Neoprene Grips, Modern..........................	250	275	275
Target Bulldog, .357 Magnum, Double Action, Blue, Adjustable Sights, Modern..........................	150	175	175
Target Bulldog, .44 Special, Double Action, Blue, Adjustable Sights, Modern..........................	150	200	200
Undercover, .38 Special, Double Action, Blue, Bulldog Grips, Modern..........................	125	175	175
Undercover, .38 Special, Double Action, Blue, Modern..........................	125	175	175
Undercover, .38 Special, Double Action, Nickel Plated, Modern..........................	125	175	175
Undercover, .38 Special, Double Action, Stainless Steel, Modern..........	175	225	225
Undercoverette, .32 S & W Long, Double Action, Blue, Bulldog Grips, Modern..........................	100	150	150

HANDGUN, SEMI-AUTOMATIC

Explorer II, .22 L.R.R.F., Clip Fed, Takedown, Modern..........................	75	100	100
Explorer SII, .22 L.R.R.F., Clip Fed, Takedown, 6" and 10" Optional Barrels, Modern..........................	100	125	125

	V.G.	Exc	Prior Edition

Model 40, .22 L.R., 8 Shot Mag, Checkered Walnut Gripstock,
Stainless, Modern.. $200 $225 $225

Charter Arms M40 Double Action Pistol

Model 79K, .380 Autoloader, 7 Shot Mag, Checkered Gripstock,
Stainless, Modern.. 250   300   300

Charter Arms M79K, .380 Caliber

	V.G.	Exc	Prior Edition
Model 79K32, .32 Caliber Autoloader, 7 Shot Mag, Stainless, Modern	$350	$400	$400

RIFLE, SEMI-AUTOMATIC

AR–7 Explorer, .22 L.R.R.F., Clip Fed, Takedown, Modern	100	125	125

CHASE, WILLIAM Pandora, Ohio 1854–1860.

COMBINATION WEAPON, PERCUSSION

Various Calibers, Double Barrel, Antique	850	1,250	1,250

CHEROKEE ARMS CO. Made by Crescent, C. M. McClung & Co. Tennessee, c. 1900.

RIFLE, SINGLESHOT

Various Gauges, Hammer, Steel Barrel, Modern	50	75	75

SHOTGUN, DOUBLE BARREL, SIDE-BY-SIDE

Various Gauges, Hammerless, Damascus Barrel, Modern	75	150	150
Various Gauges, Hammerless, Steel Barrel, Modern	100	175	175
Various Gauges, Outside Hammers, Damascus Barrel, Modern	75	150	150
Various Gauges, Outside Hammers, Steel Barrel, Modern	75	175	175

CHERRINGTON, THOMAS P. Cattawissa, Pa. 1847–1858.

RIFLE, PILL LOCK

.40, Revolver, Octagon Barrel, Antique	2,000	2,500	2,500

CHESAPEAKE GUN CO. Made by Crescent c. 1900.

SHOTGUN, DOUBLE BARREL, SIDE-BY-SIDE

Various Gauges, Hammerless, Damascus Barrel, Modern	75	150	150
Various Gauges, Hammerless, Steel Barrel, Modern	100	175	175
Various Gauges, Outside Hammers, Damascus Barrel, Modern	75	150	150
Various Gauges, Outside Hammers, Steel Barrel, Modern	100	175	175

SHOTGUN, SINGLESHOT

Various Gauges, Hammer, Steel Barrel, Modern	50	75	75

CHICAGO ARMS CO. Sold by Fred Bifflar Co. Made by Meriden Firearms Co. 1870–1890.

HANDGUN, REVOLVER

.32 S & W, 5 Shot, Double Action, Top Break, Antique	50	100	100
.38 S & W, 5 Shot, Double Action, Top Break, Antique	50	100	100
.38 S & W, Top Break, Hammerless, Double Action, Grip Safety, Antique	75	125	125

	V.G.	Exc	Prior Edition

CHICAGO FIRE ARMS CO. Chicago, Ill. 1883–1894.

HANDGUN, PALM PISTOL

.32 Extra Short R.F., Blued, Antique.. $1,000 $1,200 $1,000

Chicago Fire Arms Palm Pistol

.32 Extra Short R.F., Nickel, Antique.. 650 850 850

CHICNESTER Made by Hopkins & Allen, c. 1880.

HANDGUN, REVOLVER

.38 Short R.F., 5 Shot, Spur Trigger, Solid Frame, Single Action,
Antique.. 100 175 175

CHIEFTAIN Made by Norwich Pistol Co., c. 1880.

HANDGUN, REVOLVER

.32 Short R.F., 5 Shot, Spur Trigger, Solid Frame, Single Action,
Antique.. 100 150 150

CHILEAN MILITARY

RIFLE, BOLT ACTION

M1895 Carbine, 7mm Mauser, Military, Curio.. 275 300 100
M1895 Rifle, 7mm Mauser, Military, Curio... 225 250 100
M1895 Short Rifle, 7mm Mauser, Military, Curio.................................. 250 275 100

CHINESE MILITARY

HANDGUN, SEMI-AUTOMATIC

Makarov, 9mm Mak., Clip Fed, Modern.. 650 750 775

	Prior
	V.G.	Exc	Edition

Tokarev, 7.62mm Tokarev, Clip Fed, Modern... $300 $350 $275

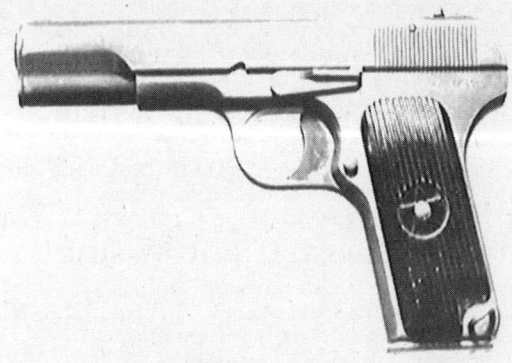

Chinese Military Tokarev

Walther PPK Type, .32 A.C.P., Double Action, Blue, Clip Fed,
Military, Modern.. 650 750 950

RIFLE, BOLT ACTION

Type 53 (Nagent), 7.62 x 54R Russian, Modern...................................... 75 175 175

RIFLE, SEMI-AUTOMATIC

SKS, 7.62 x 39 Russian, Folding Bayonet, Military, Modern.................... 250 375 375

CHINESE NATIONALIST MILITARY

HANDGUN, SEMI-AUTOMATIC

Hi Power, 9mm Luger, Clip Fed, Military, Tangent Sights, Curio.......... 650 750 575
Hi Power, 9mm Luger, Clip Fed, Military, Tangent Sights, with
Detachable Shoulder Stock, Curio.. 1,000 1,250 675

RIFLE, BOLT ACTION

Kar 98k Type 79, 8mm Mauser, Modern.. 275 300 150
M1871 Mauser, .43 Mauser, Carbine, Antique.. 325 350 175
M1888, Hanyang, 8mm Mauser, 5 Shot, Curio.. 250 275 125
M98 Mukden, 8mm Mauser, Modern.. 350 375 175

CHIPMUNK Medford, Ore. since 1982.

RIFLE, BOLT ACTION

.22 L.R.R.F. , Single Shot, Manual Cocking, Modern............................. 75 100 100

	V.G.	Exc	Prior Edition

CHURCHILL, E. J. LTD. London, England 1892 to date.

RIFLE, BOLT ACTION

One of 1,000, Various Calibers, Checkered Stock, Recoil Pad,
Express Sights, Cartridge Trap, Modern.................... $100 $1,250 $1,250
One of 1,000, Various Calibers, Fancy Checkering, Engraved
Expressed Sights, Cartridge Trap, Cased with Accessories, Modern........ 1,850 2,575 2,575

SHOTGUN, DOUBLE BARREL, OVER-UNDER

Premeir Quality, for Raised Vent Rib, Add $350.00–$520.00
Premier Quality, for Single Selective Trigger, Add $400.00–$535.00
Premier Quality, Various Gauges, Hammerless Sidelock, Fancy
Checkering, Automatic Ejectors, Engraved, Modern.............................. 12,000 15,000 15,000

SHOTGUN, DOUBLE BARREL, SIDE-BY-SIDE

Field Model, Various Gauges, Hammerless Sidelock, Fancy
Checkering, Automatic Ejectors, Engraved, Modern............... 6,000 7,000 7,000
Hercules Model XXV, Various Gauges, Hammerless Sidelock,
Engraved, Fancy Checkering, Fancy Wood, Cased, Modern.................... 6,000 7,000 7,000
Imperial Model XXV, Various Gauges, Hammerless Sidelock,
Fancy Checkering, Automatic Ejectors, Engraved, Modern.................... 7,500 9,500 9,500
Premier Quality, Various Gauges, Hammerless Sidelock, Fancy
Checkering, Automatic Ejectors, Engraved, Modern.............................. 10,000 12,000 12,000
Regal Model XXV, Various Gauges, Hammerless Sidelock, Fancy
Checkering, Automatic Ejectors, Engraved, Modern.............................. 3,750 4,300 4,300
Utility Model, Various Gauges, Boxlock, Double Triggers, Color
Case with Hardened Frame, Engraved, Modern... 3,500 4,500 4,500
For Single Selective Trigger, Add $375.00–$535.00

CHYLEWSKI, WITOLD Austria, 1910–1918. Pistols made by S.I.G.

HANDGUN, SEMI-AUTOMATIC

Einhand, .25 A.C.P., Clip Fed, Blue, No Locking Screw, Curio............. 650 875 875
Einhand, .25 A.C.P., Clip Fed, Blue, With Locking Screw, Curio.......... 675 750 750

Chylewski .25 With Locking Screw

	V.G.	Exc	Prior Edition

CLARK, F. H. Memphis, Tenn., c. 1860.

HANDGUN, PERCUSSION

Deringer, .41, German Silver Mountings, Antique...................................... $750 $1,100 $1,100

CLARKSON, J. London, England 1680–1740.

HANDGUN, FLINTLOCK

.32, Pocket Pistol, Queen Anne Style, Box Lock, Screw Barrel,
Silver Furniture, Antique.. 475 700 700

CLASSIC ARMS Palmer, Mass.

HANDGUN, PERCUSSION

.36 Duckfoot, 3 Shot, Brass Frame, Reproduction, Antique...................... 25 50 50
.36 Ethan Allen, Pepperbox, 4 Shot, Brass Frame, Reproduction,
Antique.. 25 50 50
.36 Snake–Eyes, Double Barrel, Side by Side, Brass Frame,
Reproduction, Antique.. 25 50 50
.36 Twister, 2 Shot, Brass Frame, Reproduction, Antique........................ 25 50 50
.44 Ace, Rifled, Brass Frame, Reproduction, Antique.............................. 25 25 25

CLEMENT, CHARLES Liege, Belgium 1886–1914.

HANDGUN, SEMI-AUTOMATIC

M1903, 5.5mm Clement, Clip Fed, Blue, Curio.. 375 500 500

Clement M1903 5mm

M1907, .25 ACP, Clip Fed, Blue, Curio.. 250 325 325
M1907, .32 ACP, Clip Fed, Blue, Curio.. 275 375 375
M1908, .25 ACP, Clip Fed, Blue, Curio.. 325 400 400
M1910, .25 ACP, Clip Fed, Blue, Curio.. 225 325 325

	V.G.	Exc	Prior Edition
M1910, .32 ACP, Clip Fed, Blue, Curio..	$275	$375	$375
M1912 Fulgor, .32 ACP, Clip Fed, Blue, Curio......................................	450	650	650

RIFLE, SEMI-AUTOMATIC

	V.G.	Exc	Prior Edition
Clement–Neumann, .401 Win., Clip Fed, Checkered Stock, Matted Rib, Curio..	450	650	650

SHOTGUN, DOUBLE BARREL, SIDE-BY-SIDE

	V.G.	Exc	Prior Edition
Various Gauges, Hammerless, Damascus Barrel, Curio.........................	125	200	200
Various Gauges, Hammerless, Steel Barrel, Curio.................................	150	225	225
Various Gauges, Outside Hammers, Damascus Barrel, Curio................	125	200	200

CLEMENT, J. B. Belgium.

SHOTGUN, DOUBLE BARREL, SIDE-BY-SIDE

	V.G.	Exc	Prior Edition
Various Gauges, Hammerless, Steel Barrel, Modern..............................	150	225	225
Various Gauges, Outside Hammers, Steel Barrel, Modern.....................	150	200	200

CLERKE Santa Monica, Calif.

HANDGUN, REVOLVER

	V.G.	Exc	Prior Edition
32–200, .32 S & W, Nickel Plated, Modern...	25	50	50
CF200, .22 L.R.R.F., Nickel Plated, Modern..	25	50	50

RIFLE, SINGLESHOT

	V.G.	Exc	Prior Edition
Hi–Wall, Various Calibers, Fancy Wood, Modern....................................	200	250	250
Hi–Wall Deluxe, Various Calibers, Octagon Barrel, Fancy Wood, Modern...	250	300	300
Hi–Wall Deluxe, Various Calibers, Octagon Barrel, Set Trigger, Fancy Wood, Modern...	275	325	325

CLIMAS Made by Stevens Arms.

SHOTGUN, SINGLESHOT

	V.G.	Exc	Prior Edition
Model 90, Various Gauges, Takedown, Automatic Ejector, Plain Hammer, Modern...	50	75	75

CLIPPER Maker unknown, c. 1880.

HANDGUN, REVOLVER

	V.G.	Exc	Prior Edition
.22 Short R.F., 7 Shot, Spur Trigger, Solid Frame, Single Action, Antique...	100	150	150

CODY MANUFACTURING CO. Chicopee, Mass. 1957–1959.

HANDGUN, REVOLVER

	V.G.	Exc	Prior Edition
Thunderbird, .22 R.F., 6 Shot, Double Action, Aluminum with Steel Liners, Modern...	125	175	175

	V.G.	Exc	Prior Edition

COGSWELL & HARRISON London, England 1770 to Date;
Branch in Paris 1924–1938.

HANDGUN, REVOLVER

S & W Victory, .38 Special, Double Action, Swing–Out Cylinder, Refinished and Customized, Rebored from .38 S & W and may be unsafe with .38 Spec., Modern.. $75 $150 $150

RIFLE, BOLT ACTION

BSA–Lee Speed, .303 British, Sporting Rifle, Express Sights, Engraved, Checkered Stock, Commercial, Modern................................... 550 825 825

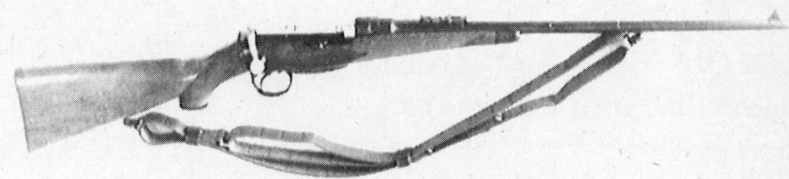

Cogswell & Harrison Lee Speed

SHOTGUN, DOUBLE BARREL, SIDE-BY-SIDE

Avant Tout (Konor), Various Gauges, Box Lock, Automatic Ejector, Fancy Checkering, Fancy Engraving, Double Trigger, Modern... 2,025 2,375 2,375

Avant Tout (Konor), Various Gauges, Box Lock, Automatic Ejector, Fancy Checkering, Fancy Engraving, Single Trigger, Modern ... 2,350 2,750 2,750

Avant Tout (Konor), Various Gauges, Box Lock, Automatic Ejector, Fancy Checkering, Fancy Engraving, Single Selective Trigger, Modern.. 2,775 2,925 2,925

Avant Tout (Rex), Various Gauges, Box Lock, Automatic Ejector, Checkered Stock, Light Engraving, Double Trigger, Modern................... 1,450 1,750 1,750

Avant Tout (Rex), Various Gauges, Box Lock, Automatic Ejector, Checkered Stock, Light Engraving, Single Trigger, Modern.................... 1,275 1,750 1,750

Avant Tout (Rex), Various Gauges, Box Lock, Automatic Ejector, Checkered Stock, Light Engraving, Single Selective Trigger, Modern.. 1,700 1,925 1,925

Avant Tout (Sandhurst), Various Gauges, Box Lock, Automatic Ejector, Fancy Checkering, Engraved, Double Trigger, Modern.............. 1,875 2,450 2,450

Avant Tout (Sandhurst), Various Gauges, Box Lock, Automatic Ejector, Fancy Checkering, Engraved, Single Trigger, Modern............... 1,850 2,675 2,675

Avant Tout (Sandhurst), Various Gauges, Box Lock, Automatic Ejector, Fancy Checkering, Engraved, Single Selective Trigger, Modern.. 2,275 2,850 2,850

Huntic, Various Gauges, Sidelock, Automatic Ejector, Checkered Stock, Double Trigger, Modern... 3,000 3,200 3,200

Huntic, Various Gauges, Sidelock, Automatic Ejector, Checkered Stock, Single Trigger, Modern... 2,675 3,350 3,350

Huntic, Various Gauges, Sidelock, Automatic Ejector, Checkered Stock, Single Selective Trigger, Modern... 2,875 3,325 3,325

	V.G.	Exc	Prior Edition
Markor, Various Gauges, Box Lock, Automatic Ejector, Checkered Stock, Double Trigger, Modern	$1,350	$1,500	$1,500
Markor, Various Gauges, Box Lock, Checkered Stock, Double Trigger, Modern	1,200	1,350	1,350
Primic, Various Gauges, Sidelock, Automatic Ejector, Fancy Engraving, Fancy Checkering, Double Trigger, Modern	2,750	3,850	3,850
Primic, Various Gauges, Sidelock, Automatic Ejector, Fancy Engraving, Fancy Checkering, Single Trigger, Modern	3,375	4,150	4,150
Primic, Various Gauges, Sidelock, Automatic Ejector, Fancy Engraving, Fancy Checkering, Single Selective Trigger, Modern	3,150	4,275	4,275
Victor, Various Gauges, Sidelock, Automatic Ejector, Engraved, Checkered Stock, Double Trigger, Modern	4,450	5,125	5,125
Victor, Various Gauges, Sidelock, Automatic Ejector, Engraved, Checkered Stock, Single Trigger, Modern	5,225	5,875	5,875
Victor, Various Gauges, Sidelock, Automatic Ejector, Engraved, Checkered Stock, Single Selective Trigger, Modern	4,675	6,150	6,150

COLON Antonio Azpiri y Cia. Eibar, Spain 1914–1918.

HANDGUN, SEMI-AUTOMATIC

Pocket, .25 ACP, Clip Fed, Curio	100	125	125

COLON Made by Orbea Hermanos Eibar, Spain c. 1925.

HANDGUN, REVOLVER

Colt Police Positive Copy, .32/20 Double Action, Blue, Curio	100	125	125

COLONIAL Fabrique d' Armes de Guerre de Grand Precision, Eibar, Spain.

HANDGUN, SEMI-AUTOMATIC

.25 ACP, Clip Fed, Blue, Modern	75	125	125
.32 ACP, Clip Fed, Blue, Modern	100	150	150

COLT Patterson, N.J. 1836–1841. Whitneyville, Conn. 1847–1848. Hartford, Conn. 1848 to Date; London, England 1853–1864. Also see U.S. Military. Also see Commemorative Section.

HANDGUN, PERCUSSION

.28 Model 1848 Patterson (Baby), 5 Shot, Various Barrel Lengths, Octagon Barrel, no Loading Lever, Antique	25,000	27,500	24,000
.28 Model 1848 Patterson (Baby), 5 Shot, Various Barrel Lengths, Octagon Barrel, with Factory Loading Lever, Antique	26,000	28,500	26,000

	V.G.	Exc	Prior Edition

.28 Model 1855 (Root), Full Fluted Cylinder, Side Hammer, Spur Trigger, Revolver, Octagon Barrel, Antique... $3,000 $3,500 $1,000

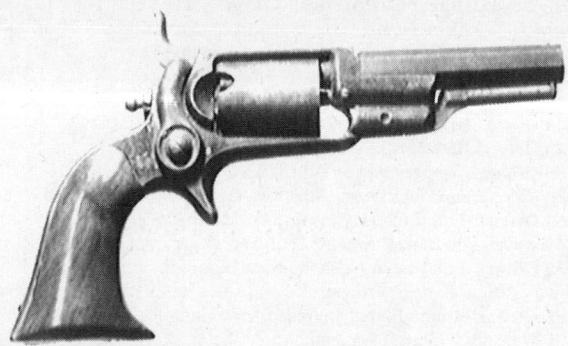

Colt Model 1855 Root Fluted Cylinder

.28 Model 1855 (Root), Full Fluted Cylinder, Side Hammer, Spur Trigger, Revolver, Round Barrel, Antique.. 2,000 2,500 1,250

.28 Model 1855 (Root), Round Cylinder, Side Hammer, Spur Trigger, Revolver, Octagon Barrel, Antique... 2,000 2,500 850

.28 Model 1855 (Root), Round Cylinder, Side Hammer, Spur Trigger, Revolver, Round Barrel, Antique.. 2,500 3,000 2,000

.31 Model 1848 Patterson (Baby), 5 Shot, Octagon Barrel, Various Barrel Lengths, no Loading Lever, no Capping Groove, Antique............. 26,000 27,500 7,000

.31 Model 1848 Patterson (Baby), 5 Shot, Octagon Barrel, Various Barrel Lengths, with Factory Loading Lever, Antique............................... 26,000 28,500 7,500

.31 Model 1848 Revolver, Baby Dragoon, 5 Shot, Various Barrel Lengths, no Loading Lever, no Capping Groove, Antique....................... 10,000 12,000 9,225

.31 Model 1848 Revolver, Baby Dragoon, 5 Shot, Various Barrel Lengths, no Loading Lever, Stagecoach Cylinder, Antique...................... 8,200 10,500 8,250

.31 Model 1848 Revolver, Baby Dragoon, 5 Shot, Various Barrel Lengths, no Loading Lever, Antique... 8,250 11,000 8,450

.31 Model 1848 Revolver, Baby Dragoon, 5 Shot, Various Barrel Lengths, with Loading Lever, Antique.. 9,000 11,500 8,675

.31 Model 1849 Revolver, Pocket Pistol, with Loading Lever, 5 Shot, Round–Backed Trigger Guard, Large, 1–Line N.Y. Address, Brass Frame, Antique.. 2,200 2,800 2,800

.31 Model 1849 Revolver, Pocket Pistol, with Loading Lever, 5 Shot, Large Round–Backed Trigger Guard, 1–Line Hartford Address, Brass Frame, Antique.. 2,400 3,000 3,000

.31 Model 1849 Revolver, Pocket Pistol, with Loading Lever, 5 Shot, Round–Backed Trigger Guard, Large, 1–Line Hartford Address, Iron Frame, Antique.. 2,200 3,200 3,200

.31 Model 1849 Revolver, Pocket Pistol, with Loading Lever, 5 Shot, Large Round–Backed Trigger Guard, 1–Line London Address, Iron Frame, Antique.. 1,500 2,000 1,250

.31 Model 1849 Revolver, Pocket Pistol, with Loading Lever, 5 Shot, Round–Backed Trigger Guard, Small, 2–Line N.Y. Address, Iron Frame, Antique.. 1,600 1,750 850

	V.G.	Exc	Prior Edition
.31 Model 1849 Revolver, Pocket Pistol, with Loading Lever, 5 Shot, Round–Backed Trigger Guard, Small, 2–Line N.Y. Address, Brass Frame, Antique..	$1,550	$1,750	$850
.31 Model 1849 Revolver, Pocket Pistol, with Loading Lever, 5 Shot, Round–Backed Trigger Guard, Small, 2–Line N.Y. Address, Antique.....................	2,000	2,500	1,850
.31 Model 1849 Revolver, Wells Fargo, 5 Shot, no Loading Lever, Pocket Pistol, Antique.........................	7,500	8,500	5,500
.31 Model 1849, 6 Shot (Model 1850), Add 15%–25%			
.31 Model 1849, For 5" Barrel, Add 10%–15%			
.31 Model 1849, For 6" Barrel, Add 15%–25%			
.31 Model 1855 (Root), For 4½" Barrel, Add 10%–15%			
.31, .28 Model 1855, London Markings, Add 50%–75%			
.31 Model 1855 (Root), Full Fluted Cylinder, Side Hammer, Spur Trigger, Revolver, Octagon Barrel, Antique.....................	2,000	2,500	1,350
.31 Model 1855 (Root), Full Fluted Cylinder, Side Hammer, Spur Trigger, Revolver, Round Barrel, Antique.....................	2,000	2,500	2,100
.31 Model 1855 (Root), Round Fluted Cylinder, Side Hammer, Spur Trigger, Revolver, Octagon Barrel, Antique.....................	2,000	2,500	1,350
.31 Model 1855 (Root), Round Fluted Cylinder, Side Hammer, Spur Trigger, Revolver, Round Barrel, Antique.....................	2,500	3,000	1,450
.31 Model Patterson (Belt), 5 Shot, Octagon Barrel, Various Barrel Lengths, no Loading Lever, no Capping Groove, Straight Grip, Antique.....................	22,500	25,000	8,500
.31 Model Patterson (Belt), 5 Shot, Octagon Barrel, Various Barrel Lengths, no Loading Lever, no Capping Groove, Flared Grip, Antique.....................	20,000	23,000	9,500
.31 Model Patterson (Pocket), 5 Shot, Octagon Barrel, Various Barrel Lengths, with Factory Loading Lever, Antique.....................	26,000	28,500	9,000
.31, Model Patterson (Pocket), 5 Shot, Octagon Barrel, Various Barrel Lengths, no Loading Lever, no Capping Groove, Antique.....................	26,000	27,500	8,000
.36 Model 1851 Navy, Revolver, with Loading Lever, 6 Shot, Small Round–Backed Guard, Small Loading Cut, Antique.....................	3,500	4,500	2,400
.36 Model 1851 Navy, Revolver, with Loading Lever, 6 Shot, Round–Backed Trigger Guard, Large Loading Cut, London Address, Iron Frame, Antique.....................	3,000	3,500	3,000
.36 Model 1851 Navy, Revolver, with Loading Lever, 6 Shot, Round–Backed Guard, Small Loading Cut, London Address, Iron Frame, Antique.....................	3,000	3,500	3,500
.36 Model 1851 Navy, Revolver, with Loading Lever, 6 Shot, Small Round–Backed Guard, Large Loading Cut, Antique.....................	3,250	4,000	2,250
.36 Model 1851 Navy, Revolver, with Loading Lever, 6 Shot, Large Round–Backed Guard, Large Loading Cut, N.Y. Address, Antique.....................	3,000	3,500	1,650
.36 Model 1851 Navy, Revolver, with Loading Lever, 6 Shot, Large Round–Backed Guard, Large Loading Cut, Hartford Address, Antique.....................	5,000	6,500	2,000
.36 Model 1851 Navy, Revolver, with Loading Lever, 6 Shot, Large Round–Backed Guard, Cut for Shoulder Stock, Iron Backstrap, Antique.....................	7,500	10,000	3,500
.36 Model 1851 Navy, Revolver, with Loading Lever, 6 Shot, Large Round–Backed Guard, with Detachable Shoulder Stock, Iron Backstrap, Antique.....................	12,500	15,000	7,500

	V.G.	Exc	Prior Edition
.36 Model 1851 Navy, Revolver, with Loading Lever, Square–Backed Trigger Guard, 1st Type, Under #1250, 6 Shot, Antique	$8,000	$9,500	$6,500
.36 Model 1851 Navy, Revolver, with Loading Lever, Square–Backed Trigger Guard, 2nd Type, #1250 to #3500, 6 Shot, Antique	5,000	6,500	4,500
.36 Model 1851, Half–Fluted, Rebated Cylinder, Add 25%–40%			
.36 Model 1861 Navy, Revolver, Round Barrel, Civilian Model, no Cuts for Shoulder Stock, Antique	8,000	9,000	3,250
.36 Model 1861 Navy, Revolver, Round Barrel, Military Model, no Cuts for Shoulder Stock, Antique	8,500	10,000	4,500
.36 Model 1861 Navy, Revolver, Round Barrel, Military, Cut for Shoulder Stock, Antique	9,500	11,000	5,500
.36 Model 1861 Navy, Revolver, Round Barrel, Military, With Shoulder Stock, Antique	12,500	15,000	8,500
.36 Model 1862 Navy, Revolver, New Navy Pocket Pistol 4½" Barrel, Rebated Cylinder, Antique	7,000	5,000	1,250
.36 Model 1862 Navy, Revolver, New Navy Pocket Pistol 5½" Barrel, Rebated Cylinder, Antique	5,000	6,500	1,650
.36 Model 1862 Navy, Revolver, New Navy Pocket Pistol 1861, 6½" Barrel, Rebated Cylinder, Antique	5,000	6,000	1,475
.36 Model 1862 Police, for Hartford Marks, Add 10%–20%			
.36 Model 1862 Police, for London Marks, Add 10%–20%			
.36 Model 1862 Police, Revolver, Half–Fluted Rebated Cylinder, Antique	5,500	6,500	1,000
.36 Model Patterson (Texas), 5 Shot Octagon Barrel, Various Barrel Lengths, no Loading Lever, no Capping Groove, Antique	75,000	85,000	12,500
.36 Model Patterson (Texas), 5 Shot Octagon Barrel, Various Barrel Lengths, with Factor Loading Lever, Antique	85,000	95,000	15,000
.44 Dragoon 1st Model, Revolver, 6 Shot, Civilian, Antique	25,000	30,000	10,000
.44 Dragoon 1st Model, Revolver, 6 Shot, Fluck Variation, Antique	30,000	35,000	8,500
.44 Dragoon 1st Model, Revolver, 6 Shot, Military, Antique	30,000	35,000	12,000
.44 Dragoon 2nd Model, Revolver, 6 Shot, Civilian, Antique	20,000	25,000	7,500
.44 Dragoon 2nd Model, Revolver, 6 Shot, Military, Antique	22,500	28,000	8,500
.44 Dragoon 2nd Model, Revolver, 6 Shot, Militia, Antique	32,500	36,000	12,000
.44 Dragoon 3rd Model, Revolver, 6 Shot, Civilian, Antique	7,500	9,000	6,000
.44 Dragoon 3rd Model, Revolver, 6 Shot, Military, Antique	8,500	10,000	8,000
.44 Dragoon 3rd Model, Revolver, 6 Shot, Military, Cut for Shoulder Stock, Antique	15,000	18,000	10,000
.44 Dragoon 3rd Model, Revolver, 6 Shot, Military, With Shoulder Stock, Antique	19,000	22,000	14,000
.44 Model 1847 Revolver, Whitneyville, (Hartford) Horizontal Loading Lever Latch, 6 Shot, Antique	60,000	75,000	20,000
.44 Model 1847, Revolver, Whitneyville Walker (U.S.M.R.), Square–Backed Trigger Guard, 6 Shot, Antique	25,000	35,000	28,500
.44 Model 1860 Army, Revolver, Cut for Shoulder Stock, Antique	5,000	6,000	2,500
.44 Model 1860 Army, Revolver, Cut for Shoulder Stock, Four–Screw Frame, Antique	5,500	6,500	2,800
.44 Model 1860 Army, Revolver, Cut for Shoulder Stock, Four–Screw Frame, with Shoulder Stock, Antique	9,000	10,500	5,000
.44 Model 1860 Army, Revolver, Cut for Shoulder Stock, Four–Screw Frame, Fluted Cylinder, Antique	5,500	6,500	4,500
.44 Model 1860 Army, Revolver, Cut for Shoulder Stock, Four–Screw Frame, Fluted Cylinder, Hartford Address, Antique	6,000	7,000	4,800

	V.G.	Exc	Prior Edition
.44 Model 1860 Army, Revolver, Cut for Shoulder Stock, Four–Screw Frame, Fluted Cylinder, Hartford Address, with Shoulder Stock, Antique	$10,500	$12,000	$5,500
.44 Model 1860 Army, Revolver, Cut for Shoulder Stock, Civilian Model, Antique	6,500	7,500	3,000
.44 Model 1860 Army, Revolver, Cut for Shoulder Stock, London Markings, Add 50%–75%			

HANDGUN, CARTRIDGE CONVERSIONS

	V.G.	Exc	Prior Edition
Model 1851 Navy, .36 Thuer, Thuer Style, Antique	5,500	6,500	4,500
Model 1851 Navy, .38 R.F., or C.F., Richards–Mason, Antique	3,500	6,500	4,500
Model 1860 Army, .44 Colt, Richards, Antique	2,750	3,250	2,000
Model 1860 Army, .44 Colt, Richards–Mason, Antique	4,000	5,000	6,000
Model 1860 Army, .44 Thuer, Thuer Style, Antique	6,000	7,000	4,500
Model 1861 Navy, .36 Thuer, Thuer Style, Antique	6,500	8,000	5,500
Model 1862 Pocket Navy, .36 Thuer, Thuer Style, Antique	5,500	6,500	5,500
Model 1862 Pocket Navy, .38 R.F., no Ejector, Octagon Barrel, Antique	1,750	2,000	1,250
Model 1862 Pocket Navy, .38 R.F., no Ejector, Round Barrel, Antique	1,500	1,800	1,000
Model 1862 Pocket Navy, .38 R.F., with Ejector, Round Barrel, Antique	1,450	1,600	1,500

HANDGUN, REVOLVER

	V.G.	Exc	Prior Edition
".357 Magnum," .357 Magnum, 6 Shot, Various Barrel Lengths, Adjustable Sights, Target Hammer, Target Grips, Modern	325	475	475
".357 Magnum," .357 Magnum, 6 Shot, Various Barrel Lengths, Adjustable Sights, Modern	275	400	400
"Old Line" Pocket, .22 Short R.F., Open Top, First Model with Ejector, 7 Shot, Spur Trigger, Antique	775	875	875

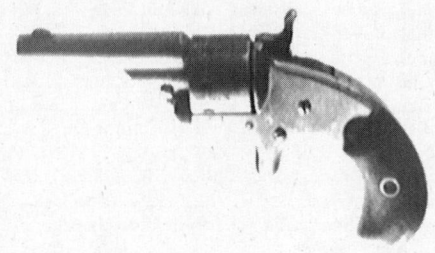

Colt Old Line .22

	V.G.	Exc	Prior Edition
"Old Line" Pocket, .22 Short R.F., Open Top, Second Model, No Ejector, 7 Shot, Spur Trigger, Antique	275	425	425
Agent Early, .38 Special, 6 Shot, 2" Barrel, Lightweight, Modern	275	325	250

	V.G.	Exc	Prior Edition
Agent, .38 Special, 6 Shot, Blue, 2" Barrel, Lightweight, Modern...........	$150	$225	$225

Colt Agent

	V.G.	Exc	Prior Edition
Agent, .38 Special, 6 Shot, Nickel Plated, 2" Barrel, Lightweight, Modern........................	150	250	250
Agent, .38 Special, 6 Shot, Parkerized, 2" Barrel, Lightweight, Modern........................	150	250	250
Argentine M1895, .38, Double Action, Solid Frame, Swing–Out Cylinder, Military, Curio........................	300	375	175
Banker's Special, .38 Special, 6 Shot, 2' Barrel, Modern........................	500	600	850
Banker's Special, Fitzgerald Trigger Guard, Add $150.00–$250.00			
Cobra Early, .38 Special, 6 Shot, 2" Barrel, Lightweight, Hammer Shroud, Modern........................	275	375	375
Cobra Early, .38 Special, 6 Shot, 4" Barrel, Lightweight, Hammer Shroud, Modern........................	250	350	350
Cobra, .38 Special, 6 Shot, 2" Barrel, Military, Lightweight, Modern........................	200	275	275
Cobra, .38 Special, 6 Shot, 4" Barrel, Military, Lightweight, Modern........................	200	300	300
Cobra, .38 Special, 6 Shot, 5" Barrel, Military, Lightweight, Modern........................	150	225	225
Cobra, .38 Special, Blue, 2" Barrel, 6 Shot, Lightweight, Modern...........	175	250	250
Cobra, .38 Special, Nickel Plated, 2" Barrel, 6 Shot, Lightweight, Modern........................	175	275	275

	V.G.	Exc	Prior Edition
Commando Special, .38 Caliber, Snub Nose, Similar to Banker's Special, Matt Finish, Modern.....................	$200	$250	$250

Colt Commando Special

Commando, .38 Special, 6 Shot, Military, Curio.....................	200	250	250

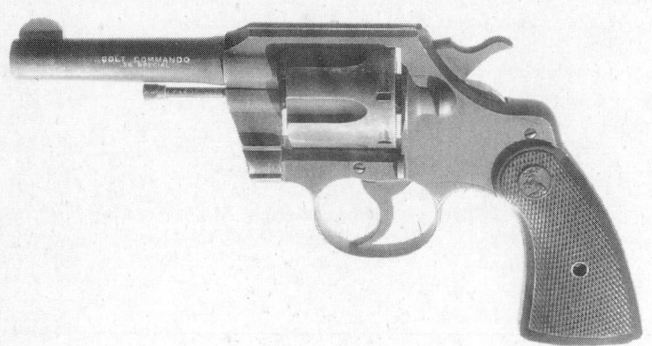

Colt Commando

Courier, .22 L.R.R.F., 6 Shot, 3" Barrel, Lightweight, Modern..............	400	500	675
Courier, .32 S & W Long, 6 Shot, 3" Barrel, Lightweight, Modern....................	550	650	725
Detective Special Early, .32 S & W, 6 Shot, 2" Barrel, Modern............	175	325	325
Detective Special Early, .38 S & W, 6 Shot, 2" Barrel, Modern............	175	350	350
Detective Special Early, .38 Special, 6 Shot, 2" Barrel, Modern............	200	400	400
Detective Special Late, .38 Special, 6 Shot, 2" Barrel, Blue, Modern....................	175	250	250
Detective Special Late, .38 Special, 6 Shot, 2" Barrel, Nickel Plated, Modern....................	225	400	400

	V.G.	Exc	Prior Edition
Detective Special Late, .38 Special, 6 Shot, 2" Barrel, Electroless Nickel Plated, Modern.............	$225	$425	$425
Detective Special, .38 Special, 6 Shot, 4" Barrel, Heavy Barrel, Modern..............	275	425	425

Colt Detective Special

Diamondback, .22 L.R.R.F., Blue, Vent Rib, 6 Shot, Modern..............	225	300	300
Diamondback, .22 L.R.R.F., Electroless Nickel Plated, Vent Rib, 6 Shot, Modern..............	250	350	350

Colt Diamondback

Diamondback, .38 Special, Blue, Vent Rib, 6 Shot, Modern..............	200	275	275
Diamondback, .38 Special, Electroless Nickel Plated, Vent Rib, 6 Shot, Modern..............	250	375	375
Diamondback, .38 Special, Nickel Plated, Vent Rib, 6 Shot, Modern..............	250	325	325
For Nickel Plating, Add $20.00-$30.00			
Frontier Model 1878 , Serial #'s under 39,000 are Antique			
Frontier Model 1878 Double Action, Phillipine Model, .45 Colt, 6" Barrel, Large Trigger Guard, Curio..............	1,500	1,850	1,250

	V.G.	Exc	Prior Edition
Frontier Model 1878 Double Action, Sherrif's Model, Various Calibers, Various Barrel Lengths, no Ejector, Curio	$1,000	$1,250	$975
Frontier Model 1878 Double Action, Various Calibers, Various Barrel Lengths, with Ejector, Curio	1,250	1,500	950
House Pistol, .41 Short R.F., Cloverleaf–Cylinder Model 1871, 4 Shot, 3" Barrel, Round Barrel, Spur Trigger, Antique	700	950	650
House Pistol, .41 Short R.F., Cloverleaf–Cylinder Model 1871, 4 Shot, 1½" Barrel, Round Barrel, Spur Trigger, Antique	1,500	1,750	950
House Pistol, .41 Short R.F., Standard Cylinder Model of 1871, 5 Shot, 2 5/8" Barrel, Round Barrel, Spur Trigger, Antique	450	650	550
House Pistol, .41 Short R.F., Standard–Cylinder Model 1871, 4 Shot, 1½" Barrel, Round Barrel, Spur Trigger, Antique	500	750	1,500
Lawman MK III, .357 Magnum, Various Barrel Lengths, Blue, 6 Shot, Modern	200	275	200
Lawman MK III, .357 Magnum, Various Barrel Lengths, Nickel Plated, 6 Shot, Modern	250	325	225
Lawman MK V, .357 Magnum, Various Barrel Lengths, Blue, 6 Shot, Modern	225	300	200

Colt Lawman MK V

	V.G.	Exc	Prior Edition
Lawman MK V, .357 Magnum, Various Barrel Lengths, Nickel Plated, 6 Shot, Modern	275	350	225
Lightning Model 1877, .38 Colt, 6 Shot, Double Action, Standard Model, Curio	950	1,200	550
Lightning Model 1877, .38 Colt, 6 Shot, Double Action, Sheriff's Model, without Ejector, Curio	700	850	650
Lightning Model 1877, Serial Numbers under 105, 123 are Antique			
Maine Sesquicentennial, .22 L.R.R.F., Frontier Scout S.A., Commemorative, Gold Plated, with Nickel Plating, 4¾" Barrel, Cased, Curio	225	350	350
Marshal, .38 Special, 6 Shot, Round Butt, Modern	500	600	425
Metropolitan MK II, .38 Special, 4" Barrel, 6 Shot, Modern	300	350	225
Model 1872 Army, .44 Henry R.F., Open–Top Frontier Single Action, Army Style Gripframe, Antique	5,000	6,500	4,500
Model 1872 Army, .44 Henry R.F., Open–Top Frontier Single Action, Navy Style Gripframe, Antique	6,000	7,500	5,000

	V.G.	Exc	Prior Edition
Model 1889 Navy, .38 Long Colt, 6 Shot, Military, 6" Barrel, Double Action, Swing–Out Cylinder, Antique..........	$1,000	$1,250	$775
Model 1889, .38 Long Colt, 6 Shot, Commercial, Various Barrel Lengths, Double Action, Swing–Out Cylinder, Antique..........	600	700	550
Model 1889, .41 Long Colt, 6 Shot, Commercial, Various Barrel Lengths, Double Action, Swing–Out Cylinder, Antique..........	650	750	575
Model 1892 New Army, .38 Long Colt, 6 Shot, Military, 6" Barrel, Double Action, Swing–Out Cylinder, Antique..........	550	700	500
Model 1892 New Navy, .38 Long Colt, 6 Shot, Commercial, 6" Barrel,			

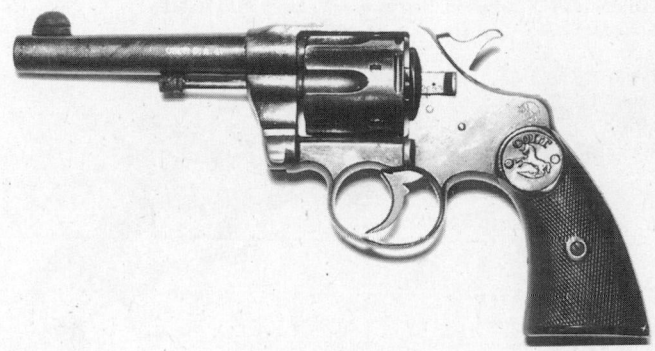

Colt Model 1892 New Navy

	V.G.	Exc	Prior Edition
Various Barrel Lengths, Double Action, Swing–Out Cylinder, Antique..........	300	350	275
Model 1892 New Navy, .38 Long Colt, 6 Shot, Military, 6" Barrel, Double Action, Swing–Out Cylinder, Antique..........	650	800	600
Model 1892 New Navy, .41 Long Colt, 6 Shot, Commercial, Various Barrel Lengths, Double Action, Swing–Out Cylinder, Antique..........	325	375	275
Model 1894 New Army, .38 Long Colt, 6 Shot, Military, 6" Barrel, Double Action, Swing–Out Cylinder, Antique..........	600	675	325
Model 1894 New Navy, .38 Long Colt, 6 Shot, Military, 6" Barrel, Double Action, Swing–Out Cylinder, Antique..........	700	775	350
Model 1895 New Army, .38 Long Colt, 6 Shot, Military, 6" Barrel, Double Action, Swing–Out Cylinder, Antique..........	575	650	300
Model 1895 New Navy, .38 Long Colt, 6 Shot, Military, 6" Barrel, Double Action, Swing–Out Cylinder, Antique..........	675	750	375
Model 1896 New Army, .38 Long Colt, 6 Shot, Military, 6" Barrel, Double Action, Swing–Out Cylinder, Curio..........	275	625	325
Model 1896 New Navy, .38 Long Colt, 6 Shot, Military, 6" Barrel, Double Action, Swing–Out Cylinder, Curio..........	175	725	325
Model 1901 New Army, .38 Long Colt, 6 Shot, Military, 6" Barrel, Double Action, Swing–Out Cylinder, Curio..........	200	600	250
Model 1903 New Army, .38 Long Colt, 6 Shot, Military, 6" Barrel, Double Action, Swing–Out Cylinder, Curio..........	200	575	275
Model 1903 New Navy, .32–20 WCF, 6 Shot, Commercial, Various Barrel Lengths, Double Action, Swing–Out Cylinder, Curio..........	275	350	350

	V.G.	Exc	Prior Edition
Model 1903 New Navy, .38 Long Colt, 6 Shot, Commercial, Various Barrel Lengths, Double Action, Swing–Out Cylinder, Curio.	$275	$350	$350
Model 1905 U.S.M.C., .38 Long Colt, 6 Shot, Military, 6" Barrel, Swing–Out Cylinder, Curio.	2,500	2,750	2,250
Model 1909 Army, .45 Colt, 6 Shot, Military, 5½" Barrel, Curio.	725	950	950
Model 1909 U.S.M.C., .45 Colt, 6 Shot, 5½" Barrel, Modern.	2,000	2,500	1,450
Model 1909 U.S.N., .45 Colt, 6 Shot, Military, 5½" Barrel, Modern.	1,000	1,250	1,750
Model 1917 Army, .45 Auto–Rim, 6 Shot, Military, 5½" Barrel, Modern.	500	650	650
New Frontier, .22 L.R.R.F., 7½" Barrel, Blue, 6 Shot, Adjustable Sights, Modern.	150	225	200

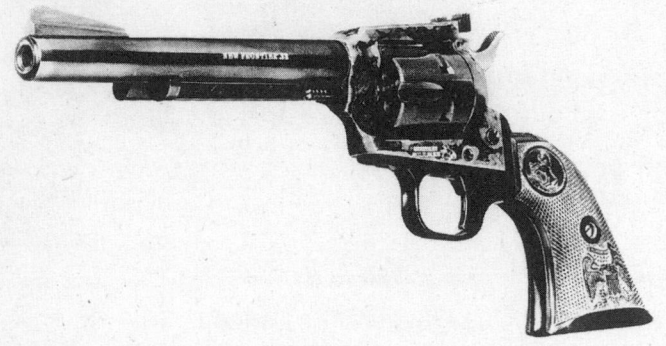

Colt New Frontier

	V.G.	Exc	Prior Edition
New Frontier, .22 L.R.R.F., Various Barrel Lengths, Blue, 6 Shot, Adjustable Sights, Modern.	150	200	225
New Frontier, .22 LR/.22WMR Combo, 7½" Barrel, Blue, 6 Shot, Adjustable Sights, Modern.	200	275	275
New Frontier, .22 LR/.22WMR Combo, Various Barrel Lengths, Blue, 6 Shot, Adjustable Sights, Modern.	175	250	250
New Line Pocket, .22 Long R.F., "the Little Colt," 7 Shot, Spur Trigger, Antique.	250	375	375
New Line Pocket, .30 Long R.F., "the Pony Colt," 5 Shot, Spur Trigger, Antique.	275	375	375
New Line Pocket, .32 Long Colt, "the Ladies Colt," 5 Shot, Spur Trigger, Antique.	275	350	350
New Line Pocket, .32 Long R.F. or .32 Long Colt, for 4" Barrel, Add 100%–150%			
New Line Pocket, .32 Long R.F., "the Ladies Colt," 5 Shot, Spur Trigger, Antique.	225	325	325
New Line Pocket, .38 Long Colt, "the Pet Colt," 5 Shot, Spur Trigger, Antique.	300	375	375
New Line Pocket, .38 Long R.F., "the Pet Colt," 5 Shot, Spur Trigger, Antique.	275	325	325
New Line Pocket, .41 Long R.F., "the Big Colt," 5 Shot, Spur Trigger, Antique.	350	425	425

	V.G.	Exc	Prior Edition
New Line Pocket, .41 Short C.F., "the Big Colt," 5 Shot, Spur Trigger, Antique	$350	$425	$425
New Line Pocket, Locking Notches on Cylinder Periphery, Add 20%–30%			
New Line, .38 Long Colt, "Police and Cop" Model, with Ejector, 5 Shot, Spur Trigger, Standard, Antique	1,650	1,850	1,200

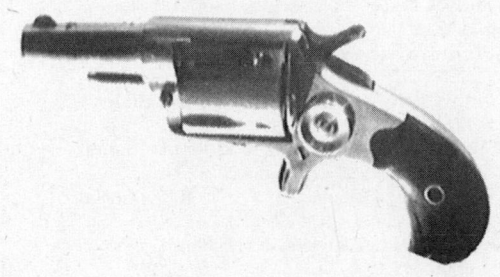

Colt New Line

	V.G.	Exc	Prior Edition
New Line, .38 Long Colt, House Civilian Model, No Ejector, 5 Shot, Spur Trigger, Antique	350	425	425
New Line, .38 Long Colt, House Civilian Model, with Ejector, 5 Shot, Spur Trigger, Antique	350	425	425
New Line, .41 Short C.F., House Civilian Model, No Ejector, 5 Shot, Spur Trigger, Antique	375	450	450
New Line, .41 Short C.F., House Civilian Model, with Ejector, 5 Shot, Spur Trigger, Antique	375	475	475
New Pocket, .32 Long Colt, 6 Shot, Various Barrel Lengths, Curio	250	325	325
New Pocket, .32 S & W Long, 6 Shot, Various Barrel Lengths, Curio	275	350	350
New Police Target, .32 Long Colt, 6 Shot, 6" Barrel, Adjustable, Curio	400	500	500
New Police Target, .32 S & W Long, 6 Shot, 6" Barrel, Adjustable Sights, Curio	500	525	525
New Police, .32 Long Colt, 6 Shot, Various Barrel Lengths, Curio	350	425	425
New Police, .32 or .41 C.F., "Cop and Thug" Model, with Ejector, 5 Shot, Spur Trigger, Antique	950	1,400	1,400
New Police, .32 S & W Long, 6 Shot, Various Barrel Lengths, Curio	300	375	375
New Police, Serial Numbers under 7,300 are Antique			
New Service Target, .44 Special, 6 Shot, Commercial, 7½" Barrel, Adjustable Sights, Curio	1,000	1,375	1,375
New Service Target, .45 Auto–Rim, 6 Shot, Commercial, 7½" Barrel, Adjustable Sights, Curio	1,200	1,400	1,400
New Service Target, .45 Colt, 6 Shot, Commercial, 7½" Barrel, Adjustable Sights, Curio	1,350	1,425	1,425
New Service, .357 Magnum, 6 Shot, Commercial, Various Barrel Lengths, Curio	1,000	1,225	1,225
New Service, .38 Special, 6 Shot, Commercial, Various Barrel Lengths, Curio	950	1,075	1,075

	V.G.	Exc	Prior Edition
New Service, .38 Special, 6 Shot, Various Barrel Lengths, Curio	$450	$550	$350
New Service, .38–40 WCF, 6 Shot, Commercial, Various Barrel Lengths, Curio	1,025	1,150	1,150
New Service, .38–40, 6 Shot, Various Barrel Lengths, Curio	450	550	350
New Service, .38–44, 6 Shot, Commercial, Various Barrel Lengths, Curio	975	1,200	1,200
New Service, .44 Special, 6 Shot, Commercial, Various Barrel Lengths, Curio	1,000	1,250	1,250
New Service, .44 Special, 6 Shot, Various Barrel Lengths, Curio	450	550	350
New Service, .44–40 WCF, 6 Shot, Commercial, Various Barrel Lengths, Curio	1,025	1,225	1,225
New Service, .45 Auto–Rim, 6 Shot, Commercial, Various Barrel Lengths, Curio	800	1,100	1,100
New Service, .45 Colt, 6 Shot, Commercial, Various Barrel Lengths, Curio	975	1,175	1,175
New Service, .455 Colt, 6 Shot, Commercial, 7½" Barrel, Adjustable Sights, Curio	1,375	1,450	1,450
New Service, .455 Colt, 6 Shot, Commercial, Various Barrel Lengths, Curio	900	1,125	1,125
Officer's Model Match, .22 L.R.R.F., 6 Shot, Adjustable Sights, 6" Barrel, Target Grips, Target Hammer, Curio	350	475	475
Officer's Model Match, .22 W.M.R., 6 Shot, Adjustable Sights, 6" Barrel, Target Grips, Target Hammer, Curio	675	775	775
Officer's Model Match, .32 S&W Long, 6 Shot, Adjustable Sights, 6" Barrel, Target Grips, Target Hammer, Curio	650	750	750
Officer's Model Match, .38 Special, 6 Shot, Adjustable Sights, 6" Barrel, Target Grips, Target Hammer, Curio	300	375	375
Officer's Model Special, .22 L.R.R.F., 6 Shot, Adjustable Sights, 6" Barrel, Heavy Barrel, Curio	250	350	350
Officer's Model Special, .38 Special, 6 Shot, Adjustable Sights, 6" Barrel, Heavy Barrel, Curio	275	375	375
Officer's Model Target, .22 L.R.R.F., 6 Shot, Adjustable Sights, 6" Barrel, Second Issue, Curio	400	475	475
Officer's Model Target, .32 S & W Long, 6 Shot, Adjustable Sights, 6" Barrel, Second Issue, Curio	425	500	500
Officer's Model Target, .38 Special, 6 Shot, Adjustable Sights, 6" Barrel, Curio	375	450	450
Officer's Model Target, .38 Special, 6 Shot, Adjustable Sights, 6" Barrel, Second Issue, Curio	425	500	500

	V.G.	Exc	Prior Edition
Officer's Model, .38 Special, 6 Shot, Adjustable Sights, with Detachable Shoulder Stock, Curio..	$750	$1,650	$1,650

Colt Officer's Model .38

Official Police MK III, .38 Special, 6 Shot, Curio....................................	175	225	225
Official Police, .22 L.R.R.F., 6 Shot, Various Barrel Lengths, Curio..	275	325	325
Official Police, .32–30 WCF, 6 Shot, Curio..	275	325	325
Official Police, .38 Special, 6 Shot, Curio..	250	300	300
Official Police, .41 Long Colt, 6 Shot, Curio..	200	250	250
Pocket Positive, .32 Long Colt, 6 Shot, Various Barrel Lengths, Modern..	300	375	375
Pocket Positive, .32 S & W Long, 6 Shot, Various Barrel Lengths, Modern..	325	400	400
Police Positive Late, .38 Special, Blue, 4" Barrel, Modern.....................	175	225	225

Colt Police Positive, Late

Police Positive Late, .38 Special, Nickel Plated, 4" Barrel, 6 Shot, Modern..	200	250	250
Police Positive Special, .32 S & W Long, 6 Shot, Various Barrel Lengths, Modern...	200	250	250

	V.G.	Exc	Prior Edition
Police Positive Special, .32–20 WCF, 6 Shot, Various Barrel Lengths, Modern....................	$250	$300	$300
Police Positive Special, .38 S & W Long, 6 Shot, Various Barrel Lengths, Modern..................	175	225	225
Police Positive Special, .38 Special, Shot, Various Barrel, Lengths, Modern.......................	225	275	275
Police Positive Target, .22 L.R.R.F., 6 Shot, 6" Barrel, Adjustable Sights, Modern...............	475	525	525
Police Positive Target, .22 WRF, 6 Shot, 6" Barrel, Adjustable Sights, Modern....................	500	550	550
Police Positive Target, .32 Long Colt, 6 Shot, 6" Barrel, Adjustable Sights, Modern.............	450	500	500
Police Positive Target, .32 S & W Long, 6 Shot, 6" Barrel, Adjustable Sights, Modern............	450	500	500
Police Positive Target, .38 S & W Long, 6 Shot, 6" Barrel, Adjustable Sights, Modern............	425	475	475
Police Positive, .22 L.R.R.F., 6 Shot, Various Barrel Lengths, Modern............................	275	325	325

Colt Police Positive

	V.G.	Exc	Prior Edition
Police Positive, .22 WRF, 6 Shot, Various Barrel Lengths, Modern................................	300	350	350
Police Positive, .32 Long Colt, 6 Shot, Various Barrel Lengths, Modern..........................	200	250	250
Police Positive, .32 S & W Long, 6 Shot, Various Barrel Lengths, Modern.........................	225	275	275
Police Positive, .38 S & W Long, 6 Shot, Various Barrel Lengths, Modern.........................	250	300	300
Python, .357 Magnum, 2½" Barrel, Blue, Vent Rib, Adjustable Sights, 6 Shots, Modern...........	450	550	500
Python, .357 Magnum, 4" Barrel, Blue, Vent Rib, 6 Shot, Adjustable Sights, Modern.............	425	500	500

	V.G.	Exc	Prior Edition
Python, .357 Magnum, 4" Barrel, Nickel, Vent Rib, 6 Shot, Adjustable Sights, Modern..	$450	$525	$525

Colt Python .357 Magnum

	V.G.	Exc	Prior Edition
Python, .357 Magnum, 6" Barrel, Blue, Vent Rib, 6 Shot, Adjustable Sights, Modern...	475	550	550
Python, .357 Magnum, 6" Barrel, Nickel, Vent Rib, 6 Shot, Adjustable Sights, Modern...	500	575	575
Python, .357 Magnum, 8" Barrel, Blue, Vent Rib, 6 Shot, Adjustable Sights, Modern...	525	600	600
Python, .357 Magnum, 8" Barrel, Nickel, Vent Rib, 6 Shot, Adjustable Sights, Modern...	575	650	650
Shooting Master, .357 Magnum, 6 Shot, Commercial, 6" Barrel, Adjustable Sights, Modern...	825	900	900
Shooting Master, .38 Special, 6 Shot, Commercial, 6" Barrel, Adjustable Sights, Modern...	750	825	825
Shooting Master, .44 Special, 6 Shot, Commercial, 6" Barrel, Adjustable Sights, Modern...	800	875	875
Shooting Master, .45 Auto–Rim, 6 Shot, Commercial, 6" Barrel, Adjustable Sights, Modern...	725	800	800
Shooting Master, .45 Colt, 6 Shot, Commercial, 6" Barrel, Adjustable Sights, Modern...	775	850	850

HANDGUN, SEMI-AUTOMATIC

	V.G.	Exc	Prior Edition
Ace 45–22 Conversion Unit, .45 ACP, Clip Fed, Adjustable Sights, Target Pistol, Curio...	350	450	300
Ace Service Model, .22 L.R.R.F., Clip Fed, Adjustable Sights, Target Pistol, Curio...	1,750	2,000	1,350
Ace Signature, .22 L.R.R.F., Clip Fed, Adjustable Sights, Target Pistol, Etched and Gold Plated, Modern...	500	750	750
Ace, .22 L.R.R.F., Clip Fed, Adjustable Sights, Target Pistol, Blue, Curio..	1,500	1,750	1,250
Ace, Mk. IV, .22 L.R.R.F., Clip Fed, Adjustable Sights, Target Pistol, Blue, Modern..	425	500	500
Ace, Mk. IV, .22 L.R.R.F., Clip Fed, Adjustable Sights, Target Pistol, Nickel Plated, Modern..	450	550	550

	V.G.	Exc	Prior Edition
Challenger, .22 L.R.R.F., Clip Fed, Modern...	$300	$350	$275
Combat Commander, .38 Super, Clip Fed, Blue, Modern......................	450	550	425

Colt Mark IV/80 Combat Commander

	V.G.	Exc	Prior Edition
Combat Commander, .45 ACP, Clip Fed, Blue, Modern.........................	450	550	375
Combat Commander, .45 ACP, Clip Fed, Satin Nickel, Modern............	500	600	400
Combat Commander, 9mm Luger, Clip Fed, Blue, Modern...................	400	450	400
Commander, .45 ACP, Clip Fed, Blue, Lifghtweight, Modern...............	400	500	425
Conversion Unit, .22 L.R.R.F., Clip Fed, Blue, Adjustable Sights, Modern...	225	250	195
Conversion Unit, Service Ace, .22 L.R.R.F., Clip Fed, Blue, Adjustable Sights, Modern...	750	950	950
GM Mark IV/80 380 Auto, ...	275	325	325
GM Mark IV/80 380 Auto, .380 Caliber ACP, 7 Round Mag, Composition Gripstock, Blue, Modern..	225	275	275

	V.G.	Exc	Prior Edition
GM Mark IV/80 380 Auto, As Above, Nickel	$300	$350	$350

Colt GM Mark IV/80 380 Auto

	V.G.	Exc	Prior Edition
GM Mark IV/Series 80 Combat, As Above, Light Weight	425	500	500
GM Mark IV/Series 80 Combat, As Above, Satin Nickel	425	500	500
GM Mark IV/Series 80 Combat, As Above, Stainless Steel	475	550	550
GM Mark IV/Series 80 Combat, Various Calibers, Checkered Walnut Gripstock, Blue, Modern..............	400	475	475
GM Mark IV/Series 80, Various Calibers, Checkered Walnut Gripstock, Blue, Modern.............	375	450	450

Colt GM Mark IV/Series 80

	V.G.	Exc	Prior Edition
Gold Cup MK III, .38 Special, Clip Fed, Adjustable Sights, Target Pistol, Military Style Stock, Modern..	$600	$675	$675
Gold Cup MK IV, .45 ACP, Clip Fed, Blue, Target Trigger, Modern..	550	650	525
Gold Cup, .45 ACP, Clip Fed, Adjustable Sights, Target Pistol, Military Style Stock, Modern..	550	650	550
Government 1911 English, .455 Webley Auto., Clip Fed, Military, Curio..	1,200	1,500	1,075
Government 1911 English, .455 Webley Auto., Clip Fed, Military, R.A.F. Markings, Curio..	850	950	875
Government BB 1911A1, .45 ACP, Clip Fed, Curio............................	550	650	550
Government M1911, .45 ACP, Clip Fed, Commercial, Curio................	1,500	1,750	1,400
Government M1911, .45 ACP, Clip Fed, Military, Curio.......................	1,250	1,500	975
Government M1911, M1911A1, Also See U.S. Military.			
Government M1911A1, .45 ACP, Clip Fed, Military, Modern..............	650	800	625
Government MK IV, .38 Super, Clip Fed, Blue, Modern.......................	275	500	500
Government MK IV, .45 ACP, Clip Fed, Blue, Modern.......................	350	475	425
Government MK IV, .45 ACP, Clip Fed, Nickel Plated, Modern..........	425	525	450
Government MK IV, 9mm Luger, Clip Fed, Blue, Modern..................	400	475	400
Government, .45 ACP, Clip Fed, Commercial, Modern..........................	1,250	1,500	750
Junior, .22 Short R.F., Clip Fed, Modern.......................................	250	300	250

Colt Junior

Junior, .25 ACP, Clip Fed, Modern..	225	275	225
M 1911A1 (British), .455 Webley Auto., Clip Fed, Military, Curio...	500	725	725
Mark IV/80 Combat Commander, Various Calibers, O Frame, Checkered Walnut Gripstock, Blue, Modern...............................	450	525	525

	V.G.	Exc	Prior Edition
Mark IV/80 Gold Cup National Match, .45 ACP, 7 Round Mag, 5" Barrel, Blue, Modern..	$600	$675	$675

Colt Mark IV/80 Gold Cup National Match

	V.G.	Exc	Prior Edition
Model 1900 U.S. Army, .38 ACP, Clip Fed, 6" Barrel, Military, Curio..	7,500	9,000	6,000
Model 1900 U.S. Navy, .38 ACP, Clip Fed, 6" Barrel, Military, Curio..	8,500	10,000	6,500
Model 1900, .38 ACP, Clip Fed, 6" Barrel, Commercial, Sight Safety, Curio..	3,500	5,000	5,000
Model 1900, .38 ACP, Clip Fed, 6" Barrel, Commercial, Forward Slide Serrations, Curio...	3,000	3,800	3,800
Model 1900, .38 ACP, Clip Fed, 6" Barrel, Commercial, Altered Rear Sight, Curio..	2,700	3,500	3,500
Model 1902 Military U.S. Army, .38 ACP, Clip Fed, 6" Barrel, Curio..	4,500	5,500	5,000

	V.G.	Exc	Prior Edition
Model 1902 Military, .38 ACP, Clip Fed, 6" Barrel, Curio......................	$1,000	$1,250	$1,650

Colt Model 1902 Military

	V.G.	Exc	Prior Edition
Model 1902 Military, .38 ACP, Clip Fed, 6" Barrel, Forward Slide Serrations, Curio..	1,250	1,750	1,750
Model 1902 Sporting, .38 ACP, Clip Fed, 6" Barrel, Commercial, Curio..	1,500	2,000	1,950
Model 1902 Sporting, .38 ACP, Clip Fed, 6" Barrel, Forward Slide Serrations, Sporting, Curio...	2,000	2,500	2,000
Model 1903 Hammerless 1st Type, .38 ACP, Clip Fed, Barrel Bushing, Commercial, Curio...	400	525	525
Model 1903 Hammerless 2nd Type, .38 ACP, Clip Fed, Commercial, Curio..	375	500	500
Model 1903 Hammerless Pocket 3rd Type, .38 ACP, Clip Fed, Commercial, Magazine Disconnect, Modern...	375	450	500
Model 1903 Hammerless U.S., .32 ACP, Clip Fed, Military, Magazine Disconnect, Parkerized Curio...	650	750	650

Colt Model 1903 Pocket Military

Model 1903 Pocket, Round Hammer, .38 ACP, Clip Fed, Curio.............	1,000	1,200	775

	V.G.	Exc	Prior Edition
Model 1903 Pocket, Spur Hammer, .38 ACP, Clip Fed, Curio................	$900	$1,050	$750
Model 1905, .45 ACP, Clip Fed, Curio..	1,500	2,500	2,500
Model 1905, .45 ACP, Clip Fed, Adjustable Sights, with Detachable Shoulder Stock, Curio....................	8,500	10,000	5,000
Model 1905/07, .45 ACP, Clip Fed, Blue, Military, Curio......................	4,500	7,500	7,500
Model 1908 Hammerless Pocket 1st Type, .380 ACP, Clip Fed, Barrel Bushing, Commercial, Curio..........................	575	625	625
Model 1908 Hammerless Pocket 2nd Type, .380 ACP, Clip Fed, Commercial, Curio..............	525	600	600
Model 1908 Hammerless Pocket 3rd Type, .380 ACP, Clip Fed, Commercial, Magazine Disconnect, Modern............	525	600	600
Model 1908 Hammerless U.S., .380 ACP, Clip Fed, Military, Magazine Disconnect, Curio....................	1,250	1,500	850
Model 1908 Pocket, .25 ACP, Clip Fed, Hammerless, Curio..................	275	350	350
Model 1908 Pocket, .25 ACP, Clip Fed, Hammerless, Magazine Disconnect, Modern....................	250	325	325
Model 1908 Pocket, .25 ACP, Clip Fed, Hammerless, Magazine Disconnect, Military, Curio....................	2,250	2,500	750
National Match, .45 ACP, Clip Fed, Target Pistol, Modern....................	2,250	2,500	1,850
National Match, .45 ACP, Clip Fed, Target Pistol, Adjustable Sights, Modern....................	2,500	3,000	1,450

Colt National Match with Adjustable Sights

	V.G.	Exc	Prior Edition
Officer's ACP MK IV/80, .45 ACP, 6 Round Clip, Checkered Walnut Gripstock, Matt Finish, Modern......................	450	525	525
Officer's ACP MK IV/80, As Above, Satin Nickel	350	500	500
Super Match, .38 Super, Clip Fed, Adjustable Sights, Target Pistol, Modern....................	3,750	4,250	3,500
Super Match, .38 Super, Clip Fed, Target Pistol, Modern......................	3,500	4,000	3,750
Super Mexican Police, .38 Super, Clip Fed, Military, Modern................	600	750	750
Super, .38 Super, Clip Fed, Commercial, Modern....................................	2,000	2,500	1,500

	V.G.	Exc	Prior Edition
Woodsman Huntsman, .22 L.R.R.F., Clip Fed, Blue, Adjustable Sights, Modern..	$250	$300	$300

Colt Woodsman Huntsman

	V.G.	Exc	Prior Edition
Woodsman Match Target 1st Type, .22 L.R.R.F., Clip Fed, Extended Target Grips, Modern..	700	1,500	950
Woodsman Match Target 2nd Type, .22 L.R.R.F., Clip Fed, Blue, Adjustable Sights, Modern..	425	800	475
Woodsman Sport 1st. Type, .22 L.R.R.F., Clip Fed, Adjustable Sights, Modern...	500	550	550
Woodsman Sport, .22 L.R.R.F., Clip Fed, Blue, Adjustable Sights, Modern..	375	450	450
Woodsman Target 1st Type, .22 L.R.R.F., Clip Fed, Adjustable Sights, Modern...	400	475	475
Woodsman Target 1st Type, .22 L.R.R.F., Clip Fed, Adjustable Sights, with Extra Mainspring Housing, Modern......................................	325	500	500
Woodsman Target 2nd Type, .22 L.R.R.F., Clip Fed, Adjustable Sights, Modern...	325	400	400
Woodsman Target 3rd Type, .22 L.R.R.F., Clip Fed, Blue, Adjustable Sights, Modern..	275	350	350
Woodsman Targetsman, .22 L.R.R.F., Clip Fed, Blue, Adjustable Sights, Modern...	300	375	300

HANDGUN, SINGLE ACTION

	V.G.	Exc	Prior Edition
Second Amendment, .22 L.R.R.F., Frontier Scout, Cased, Curio...........	200	325	325
Single Action Army, 8" or 9" Barrel, Add $375.00–$600.00			
Single Action Army, Folding Rear Sight, Long Barrel, Add $1975.00–$3000.00			
Single Action Army, for 12" Barrel, Add $445.00–$700.00			
Single Action Army, for 16" Barrel, Add $580.00–$995.00			
Single Action Army, for Rare Calibers, Add 50%–200%			
Single Action Army, Long–Fluted Cylinder #'s 330,000 to 331,379, Commercial, Curio...	3,000	3,500	2,500

	V.G.	Exc	Prior Edition
Single Action Army, Nickel Plating, Add 15%–25%			
Single Action Army, Rimfire Calibers, Add 100%–125%			
Single Action Army, Shoulder Stock, Add $995.00–$1850.00			
Single Action Army, Target Model (Flat–Top), Add $975.00–$1900.00			
Single Action Army Buntline Late, .45 Colt, 12" Barrel, Blue, 6 Shot, Modern	$550	$625	$625
Single Action Army Buntline New Frontier, .45 Colt, 12" Barrel, Blue, 6 Shot, Adjustable Sights, Modern	600	675	675
Single Action Army Late, .357 Magnum, 7½" Barrel, Blue, 6 Shot, Modern	600	675	625
Single Action Army Late, .357 Magnum, Various Barrel Lengths, Blue, 6 Shot, Modern	575	650	650
Single Action Army Late, .44 Special, 7½" Barrel, Blue, 6 Shot, Modern	600	675	625
Single Action Army Late, .45 Colt, 7½" Barrel, Blue, 6 Shot, Modern	625	700	700
Single Action Army Late, .45 Colt, 7½" Barrel, Nickel Plated, 6 Shot, Modern	650	725	725
Single Action Army Late, .45 Colt, Various Barrel Lengths, Blue, 6 Shot, Modern	675	750	750
Single Action Army New Frontier, .357 Magnum, Various Barrel Lengths, Blue, 6 Shot, Adjustable Sights, Modern	400	475	475
Single Action Army New Frontier, .44 Special, 7½" Barrel, Blue, 6 Shot, Adjustable Sights, Modern	425	500	500
Single Action Army New Frontier, .45 Colt, Various Barrel Lengths, Blue, 6 Shot, Adjustable Sights, Modern	425	500	500
Single Action Army, #'s over 182,000 are Modern, #'s under 165,000 are Black Powder Only			
Single Action Army, .45 Colt, Artillery Model, Screw–Retained Cylinder Pin, Military, 5½" Barrel, Antique	5,000	6,500	3,000
Single Action Army, .45 Colt, Standard Cavalry Model # Under 15,000, Screw–Related Cylinder Pin, Blue, Military, 7½" Barrel, Antique	12,500	15,000	8,500
Single Action Army, Various Calibers, Standard Peacemaker, Calibers: .45 Colt, .44–40, .38–40, .41, .32–20, Commercial, Antique	9,000	10,500	7,500
Single Action Army, Various Calibers, Storekeeper's Model, No Ejector, Short Barrel, Commercial, Antique	10,000	12,000	12,000
Single Action Bisley, No Ejector Housing, Add 25%–35%			
Single Action Bisley, Non–Standard Barrel Lengths, Add 20%–35%			
Single Action Bisley, other than Standard Calibers, Add 50%–100%			
Single Action Bisley, Various Calibers, Standard Model, Calibers: 32–20, 38–40, 41, 41–40, 45, Target Trigger, Modern	4,500	5,500	6,500
Single Action Bisley, Various Calibers, Target Model, (Flat–Top), Modern	8,000	9,500	7,500
"Thunderer" Model 1877, .41 Colt, 6 Shots, Double Action, Standard Model, Modern	900	1,500	1,500
"Thunderer" Model 1877, .41 Colt, 6 Shots, Double Action, Sheriff's Model, Modern	1,200	1,700	1,700
Trooper, .22 L.R.R.F., 6 Shot, Adjustable Sights, Target Grips, Target Hammer, Modern	275	325	325
Trooper, .357 Magnum, 6 Shot, 4" Barrel, Adjustable Sights, Modern	250	300	300

	V.G.	Exc	Prior Edition
Trooper, .357 Magnum, 6 Shot, Adjustable Sights, Target Grips, Target Hammer, Modern...........	$275	$325	$325
Trooper, .38 Special, 6 Shot, 4" Barrel, Adjustable Sights, Modern...........	250	300	300
Trooper, .38 Special, 6 Shot, Adjustable Sights, Target Grips, Target Hammer, Modern...........	250	300	300
Trooper MK III, .22 L.R.R.F., 4" Barrel, Blue, 6 Shot, Adjustable Sights, Modern...........	175	225	225
Trooper MK III, .22 L.R.R.F., 6" Barrel, Blue, 6 Shot, Adjustable Sights, Modern...........	175	225	225
Trooper MK III, .22 L.R.R.F., 8" Barrel, Blue, 6 Shot, Adjustable Sights, Modern...........	225	275	275
Trooper MK III, .357 Magnum, 4" Barrel, Blue, 6 Shot, Adjustable Sights, Modern...........	175	225	225
Trooper MK III, .357 Magnum, 4" Barrel, Nickel Plated, 6 Shot, Adjustable Sights, Modern...........	175	225	225
Trooper MK III, .357 Magnum, 6" Barrel, 6 Shot, Adjustable Sights, Modern...........	175	225	225
Trooper MK III, .357 Magnum, 6" Barrel, Nickel Plated, 6 Shot, Adjustable Sights, Modern...........	200	250	250
Trooper MK III, .357 Magnum, 8" Barrel, 6 Shot, Adjustable Sights, Modern...........	200	250	250
Trooper MK III, .357 Magnum, 8" Barrel, Nickel Plated, 6 Shot, Adjustable Sights, Modern...........	175	225	225
Trooper MK V, .357 Magnum, 4" Barrel, Blue, 6 Shot, Adjustable Sights, Modern...........	225	275	275
Trooper MK V, .357 Magnum, 4" Barrel, Nickel, 6 Shot, Adjustable Sights, Modern...........	250	300	300
Trooper MK V, .357 Magnum, 6" Barrel, Blue, 6 Shot, Adjustable Sights, Modern...........	225	275	275
Trooper MK V, .357 Magnum, 6" Barrel, Nickel, 6 Shot, Adjustable Sights, Modern...........	250	300	300
Viper, .38 Special, Blue, 4" Barrel, 6 Shot, Lightweight, Modern...........	225	275	230

HANDGUN, SINGLESHOT

	V.G.	Exc	Prior Edition
#1 Deringer, .41 Short R.F., all Metal, Sput Trigger, Light Engraving, Antique...........	1,000	1,250	950
#2 Deringer, .41 Short R.F., Wood Grips, Spur Trigger, Light Engraving, Antique...........	700	850	750
#2 Deringer, .41 Short R.F., "Address Col. Colt," Wood Grips, Spur Trigger, Light Engraving, Antique...........	1,250	1,500	1,250
#3 Deringer Thuer, .41 Short R.F., Wood Grips, Spur Trigger, 1st Issue, Contoured Swell at Pivot, High–Angled Hammer, Antique......	2,000	2,500	1,850
#3 Deringer Thuer, .41 Short R.F., Wood Grips, Spur Trigger, 2nd Issue, Angled Frame, no Swell, High Angled Hammer, Antique...........	1,500	1,750	1,250
#3 Deringer Thuer, .41 Short R.F., Wood Grips, Spur Trigger, 3rd Issue, Straight Thick Frame, High–Angled Hammer, Antique...........	400	550	550
#3 Deringer Thuer, .41 Short R.F., Wood Grips, Spur Trigger, London Marked, Antique...........	500	650	650
#4 Deringer, .22 Short R.F., Spur Trigger, Modern...........	75	100	100
#4 Deringer, .22 Short R.F., Spur Trigger, Cased Pair, Modern...........	150	225	225
#4 Lady Deringer, .22 Short R.F., Spur Trigger, Cased Pair, Modern...........	100	150	150

	V.G.	Exc	Prior Edition
#4 Lord and Lady Deringer, .22 Short R.F., Spur Trigger, Cased Pair, Modern	$150	$275	$275
#4 Lord Deringer, .22 Short R.F., Spur Trigger, Cased Pair, Modern	100	150	150
Camp Perry 1st Issue, .22 L.R.R.F., Adjustable Sights, Target Pistol, Modern	750	975	975
Camp Perry 2nd Issue, .22 L.R.R.F., Adjustable Sights, Target Pistol, Modern	850	1,250	1,250

RIFLE, BOLT ACTION

	V.G.	Exc	Prior Edition
Colteer 1–22, .22 L.R.R.F., Singleshot, Plain, Modern	150	200	150
Colteer 1–22, .22 WMR, Singleshot, Plain, Modern	175	225	175
Coltsman Custom (FN), Various Calibers, Sporting Rifle, Fancy Wood, Light Engraving, Checkered Stock, Monte Carlo Stock, Modern	425	550	550
Coltsman Custom (Sako), Various Calibers, Sporting Rifle, Fancy Wood, Light Engraving, Checkered Stock, Monte Carlo Stock, Modern	400	500	600
Coltsman Deluxe (FN), Various Calibers, Sporting Rifle, Checkered Stock, Monte Carlo Stock, Modern	500	600	425
Coltsman Deluxe (Sako), Various Calibers, Sporting Rifle, Checkered Stock, Monte Carlo Stock, Modern	475	550	475
Coltsman Deluxe (Sako), Various Calibers, Sporting Rifle, Checkered Stock, Modern	300	375	375
Coltsman Standard (FN), Various Calibers, Sporting Rifle, Checkered Stock, Modern	275	350	350
Sauer Grand African, .458 Win. Mag., Clip Fed, Fancy Wood, Modern	775	1,075	1,075
Sauer Grand Alaskan, .375 H & H Mag., Clip Fed, Checkered Stock, Magnum, Modern	725	1,025	1,025
Sauer, Various Calibers, Clip Fed, Checkered Stock, Magnum, Modern	675	975	975
Sauer, Various Calibers, Clip Fed, Checkered Stock, Short Action, Modern	575	875	875

RIFLE, PERCUSSION

	V.G.	Exc	Prior Edition
1st Model Ring Lever, Various Calibers, 8 or 10 Shot Revolving Cylinder, with Topstrap, Antique	12,500	15,000	10,500
2nd Model Ring Lever, .44, 8 or 10 Shot Revolving Cylinder, no Topstrap, Antique	10,000	12,500	8,500
Model 1839, 6 Shot Cylinder, with Hammer, Antique	12,000	14,000	7,300
Model 1855 Carbine, Various Calibers, 6 Shot Revolving Cylinder, Sidehammer, no Forestock, Antique	4,250	7,500	7,500
Model 1855 Military Rifle, Various Calibers, 6 Shot Revolving Cylinder, Sidehammer, Fullstock, U.S. Military, Antique	8,500	12,000	12,000
Model 1855 Sporting Rifle, .36, 6 Shot Revolving Cylinder, Sidehammer, no Forestock, Spur Triggerguard, Antique	6,500	8,000	5,200
Model 1855 Sporting Rifle, Various Calibers, 6 Shot Revolving Cylinder, Sidehammer, Halfstock, Scroll Triggerguard, Antique	4,000	5,000	4,400
Model 1855 Sporting Rifle, Various Calibers, 6 Shot Revolving Cylinder, Sidehammer, Fullstock, Scroll Triggerguard, Antique	4,500	5,500	4,200
Model 1861 Musket, .58, Military Contract Musket, Antique	1,750	2,000	1,750

	V.G.	Exc	Prior Edition

RIFLE, SEMI-AUTOMATIC

AR–15, .223 Rem., Clip Fed, Modern.. $750 $1,000 $850

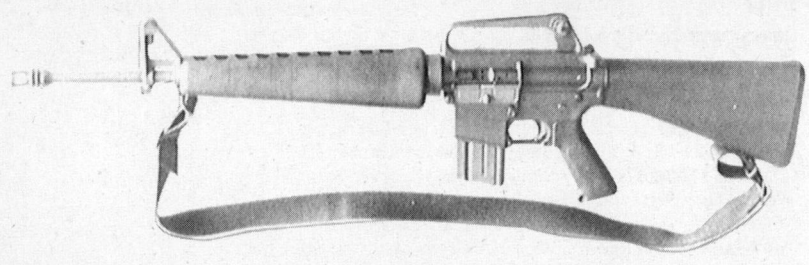

Colt AR- 15

AR–15, .223 Rem., Clip Fed, Collapsible Stock, Modern........................	800	950	950
AR–15 A2 Sporter II, .223 Rem., Pistol Grip, 20" Barrel, Modern...	725	850	850
Colteer 22 Autoloader, .22 L.R.R.F., Tube Feed, Plain, Modern...	200	250	175
Colteer Stagecoach, .22 L.R.R.F., Tube Feed, Light Engraving, Modern...	250	300	225

RIFLE, SINGLESHOT

Sharps, Various Calibers, Fancy Wod, Fancy Checkering, Cased with Accessories, Modern...	1,750	2,000	1,850

RIFLE, SLIDE ACTION

Lightning, .22 R.F., Small Frame (Numbers over 35,300 are Modern), Antique...	850	950	1,050

Colt Lightning Rifle, Small Frame

Lightning, Various Calibers, Large Frame, Antique................................	3,500	4,250	4,250
Lightning, Various Calibers, Medium Frame (Numbers over 84,000 are Modern), Antique...	1,500	2,000	2,000
Lightning Baby Carbine, Various Calibers, Large Frame, Antique........	7,500	9,000	9,000
Lightning Baby Carbine, Various Calibers, Medium Frame (Numbers over 84,000 are Modern), Antique.........................	2,750	5,000	5,000
Lightning Carbine, Various Calibers, Large Frame, Antique.................	4,500	6,500	6,500
Lightning Carbine, Various Calibers, Medium Frame (Numbers over 84,000 are Modern), Antique.........................	2,000	3,500	3,500

	V.G.	Exc	Prior Edition

SHOTGUN, DOUBLE BARREL, SIDE-BY-SIDE

	V.G.	Exc	Prior Edition
Model 1878 Standard, Various Gauges, Outside Hammers, Damascus Barrel, Antique	$2,500	$3,000	$2,750
Model 1883 Standard, Various Gauges, Hammerless, Damascus Barrel, Antique	3,000	3,500	3,250

SHOTGUN, SEMI-AUTOMATIC

	V.G.	Exc	Prior Edition
Various Gauges, for Solid Rib, Add $15.00–$25.00			
Various Gauges, for Vent Rib, Add $25.00–$35.00			
Ultra–Light, 12 and 20 Gauges, Checkered Stock, Takedown, Modern	275	350	350
Ultra–Light Custom, 12 and 20 Gauges, Checkered Stock, Light Engraving, Takedown, Modern	300	375	375
Ultra–Light Magnum, 12 and 20 Gauges 3", Checkered Stock, Takedown, Modern	300	375	375
Ultra–Light Magnum Custom, 12 and 20 Gauges 3", Checkered Stock, Light Engraving, Takedown, Modern	325	400	400

SHOTGUN, SLIDE ACTION

	V.G.	Exc	Prior Edition
Coltsman Custom, Various Gauges, Takedown, Checkered Stock, Vent Rib, Modern	275	350	350
Coltsman Standard, Various Gauges, Takedown, Plain, Modern	225	300	300

COLUMBIA ARMORY Tenn., Maltby & Henley Distributors c. 1890.

HANDGUN, REVOLVER

	V.G.	Exc	Prior Edition
New Safety, .22 L.R.R.F., 7 Shot, Double Action, Solid Frame, Grip Safety, Modern	100	125	125
New Safety, .32 S & W, 5 Shot, Double Action, Solid Frame, Grip Safety, Modern	100	125	125
New Safety, .38 S & W, 5 Shot, Double Action, Solid Frame, Grip Safety, Modern	125	150	150

COLUMBIAN Made by Foehl & Weeks, Philadelphia, Pa. c. 1890.

HANDGUN, REVOLVER

	V.G.	Exc	Prior Edition
.32 S & W, 5 Shot, Double Action, Solid Frame, Curio	75	100	100
.38 S & W, 5 Shot, Double Action, Solid Frame, Curio	75	100	100

COMET

HANDGUN, REVOLVER

	V.G.	Exc	Prior Edition
.32 Long R.F., 7 Shot, Single Action, Spur Trigger, Solid Frame, Antique	75	150	150

COMINAZZO OR COMINAZZI Family of Armorers in Brescia, Italy from about 1593 to about 1875.

HANDGUN, FLINTLOCK

	V.G.	Exc	Prior Edition
.54, Mid–1600's, Belt Pistol, Brass Furniture, Ornate Antique	4,150	5,750	5,750

	V.G.	Exc	Prior Edition

HANDGUN, WHEEL-LOCK

Ebony Full Stock, Ivory Pom, Holster Pistol, German Style,
Military, Engraved, Antique... $4,250 $5,950 $5,950

COMMANDER

HANDGUN, REVOLVER

.32 Long R.F., 7 Shot, Single Action, Spur Trigger, Solid Frame,
Antique... 100 150 150

COMMANDO ARMS Made by Volunteer Enterprises in Knoxville, Tenn. since 1969. Company name changed to Commando Arms in 1978.

RIFLE, SEMI-AUTOMATIC

Commando MK III, .45 ACP, Clip Fed, Horizontal Forend, with
Compensator, Carbine, Modern.. 225 275 250
Commando MK III, .45 ACP, Clip Fed, Vertical Forend, with
Compensator, Carbine, Modern.. 250 300 275
Commando MK 9, 9mm Luger, Clip Fed, Horizontal Forend, with
Compensator, Carbine, Modern.. 225 275 250
Commando MK 9, 9mm Luger, Clip Fed, Vertical Forend, with
Compensator, Carbine, Modern.. 250 300 275
Commando MK 45, .45 ACP, Clip Fed, Horizontal Forend, with
Compensator, Carbine, Modern.. 225 275 250
Commando MK 45, .45 ACP, Clip Fed, Vertical Forend, with
Compensator, Carbine, Modern.. 250 300 275

COMMERCIAL See Smith, Otis A.

COMPEER Made by Crescent for Van Camp Hardware c. 1900.

SHOTGUN, DOUBLE BARREL, SIDE-BY-SIDE

Various Gauges, Hammerless, Damascus Barrel, Modern...................... 150 175 175
Various Gauges, Hammerless, Steel Barrel, Modern.............................. 150 175 175
Various Gauges, Outside Hammers, Damascus Barrel, Modern............. 150 175 175
Various Gauges, Outside Hammers, Steel Barrel, Modern...................... 125 200 200

SHOTGUN, SINGLESHOT

Various Gauges, Hammer, Steel Barrel, Modern.................................... 75 100 100

CONE, D.D. Washington, D.C. c. 1865.

HANDGUN, REVOLVER

.22 Long R.F., 7 Shot, Single Action, Spur Trigger, Solid Frame,
Antique... 125 200 200
.32 Long R.F., 6 Shot, Single Action, Spur Trigger, Solid Frame,
Antique... 150 225 225

	V.G.	Exc	Prior Edition

CONFEDERATE MILITARY

HANDGUN, PERCUSSION

	V.G.	Exc	Prior Edition
.36 Columbus, Revolver, Brass Trigger Guard, 6 Shot, Antique..............	—	RARE	—
.36 Dance Box, Revolver, Iron Frame, 6 Shot, Antique...........................	—	RARE	—
.36 Griswald & Gunnison, Revolver, Brass Frame, 6 Shot, Serial No. is the Only Marking, Antique..	—	RARE	—
.36 Leech & Co., Revolver, Brass Grip Frame, 6 Shot, Antique..............	—	RARE	—
.36 Leech & Rigdon, Revolver, Brass Grip Frame, 6 Shot, Antique..	—	RARE	—
.36 Rigdon & Ansley, Revolver, Brass Grip Frame, 6 Shot, Antique..	—	RARE	—
.36 Shawk & McLanahan, Revolver, Brass Frame, 6 Shot, Antique..	—	RARE	—
.36 Spiller & Burr, Revolver, Brass Frame, 6 Shot, Antique..	—	RARE	—
.36 T.W. Cofer, Revolver, Brass Frame, 6 Shot, Antique........................	—	RARE	—
.44 Dance Bros., Revolver, Brass Grip Frame, 6 Shot, Antique.............	—	RARE	—
.44 Tucker & Sherrod, Revolver, Copy of Colt Dragoon, Serial Number is the Only Marking, Antique.....................................	—	RARE	—
.54 J. And F. Garrett, Singleshot, Brass Barrel, Converted from Flintlock, Antique..	$1,450	$2,500	$2,500
.54 Palmetto, Singleshot, Brass Furniture, Antique.............................	—	RARE	—
.58 Fayetteville, Singleshot, Rifled, Antique......................................	—	RARE	—
.58 Fayetteville, Singleshot, Rifled, with Shoulder Stock, Antique.........	—	RARE	—

RIFLE, PERCUSSION

	V.G.	Exc	Prior Edition
.52, "P," Tallahassee, Breech Loader, Carbine, Antique...........................	—	RARE	—
.52, Tarpley, Breech Loader, Carbine, Brass Breech, Antique.................	50,000	RARE	—
.54, L.G. Sturdivant, Brass Furniture, Rifled, Serial No. is the Only Marking, Antique..	2,500	RARE	—
.54, Wytheville–Hall, Muzzle Loader, Rifled, Brass Frame, Antique.......	7,500	RARE	—
.57, Tyler, Texas Enfield, Brass Furniture, Antique................................	18,500	RARE	—
.58, Cook & Brother, Artillery Carbine, Brass Furniture, Military, Antique..	14,000	RARE	—
.58, Cook & Brother, Infantry Type, Brass Furniture, Military, Antique..	15,000	RARE	—
.58, Cook & Brother, Musketoon, Brass Furniture, Military, Antique.....	12,500	RARE	—
.58, D.C., Hodgkins & Co., Iron Mounts, Rifled, Carbine, Antique.........	8,500	RARE	—
.58, Dickson, Nelson & Co., Military, Carbine, Antique.......................	12,000	RARE	—
.58, Dickson, Nelson & Co., Military, Rifle, Antique............................	15,000	RARE	—
.58, Fayetteville, Brass Furniture, 2 Bands, Rifled, Antique....................	8,500	RARE	—
.58, Georgia, Brass Furniture, Rifled, Antique....................................	3,500	RARE	—
.58, H.C. Lamb & Co., Brass Furniture, 2 Bands, Rifled, Antique............	15,000	RARE	—
.58, Palmetto, "Mississippi" Rifle, Antique..	17,500	RARE	—
.58, Richmond, Carbine, Antique..	7,500	RARE	—
.58, Richmond, Musket, Rifled, Antique...	8,500	RARE	—
.58, Tallahassee, Carbine, Brass Furniture, 2 Bands, Antique..................	35,000	RARE	—
.58, Whitney, U.S. Contract 1861, Rifle, Musket, Antique......................	2,500	RARE	—
.62, Richmond Navy, Musketoon, Smoothbore, Antique........................	7,500	RARE	—
.69, Prussian Musket, Brass Furniture, Military, Antique.......................	750	RARE	—
.69, Whitney, Model 1861, Rifled, Brass Furniture, Antique....................	3,000	RARE	—

RIFLE, SINGLESHOT

	V.G.	Exc	Prior Edition
.50, Morse, Musket, Breech Loader, Antique...	4,750	RARE	—

	V.G.	Exc	Prior Edition
.58, S.C. Robinson, Model 1861, Brass Furniture, Breech Loader, Carbine, Imitation Sharps, Antique	3,500	RARE	—
.71, Morse, Carbine, Breech Loader, Antique	4,500	RARE	—

CONN. ARMS & MFG. CO. Naubuc, Conn. 1863–1869.

HANDGUN, SINGLESHOT

	V.G.	Exc	Prior Edition
Hammond Patent Bull–Dozer, .44 R.F., Pivoting Breechblock, Hammer, Spur Trigger, Antique	$225	$325	$325
Hammond Patent Bulldog, .44 R.F., Pivoting Breechblock, Hammer, Spur Trigger, Antique	200	325	325
Hammond Patent Bulldog, .44 R.F., Pivoting Breechblock, Hammer, Spur Trigger, Very Long Barrel, Antique	300	450	450

CONN. ARMS CO. Norfolk, Conn. 1862–1869.

HANDGUN, REVOLVER

	V.G.	Exc	Prior Edition
Wood's Patent, .28 T.F., Tip–Up Barrel, 6 Shot, Spur Trigger, Antique	175	325	325

CONQUERER Made by Bacon Arms Co., c. 1880.

HANDGUN, REVOLVER

	V.G.	Exc	Prior Edition
.22 Short R.F., 7 Shot, Spur Trigger, Solid Frame, Single Action, Antique	100	175	175
.32 Short R.F., 5 Shot, Spur Trigger, Solid Frame, Single Action, Antique	100	175	175

CONSTABLE, RICHARD Philadelphia, Pa. 1817–1851.

HANDGUN, PERCUSSION

	V.G.	Exc	Prior Edition
Dueling Pistols, Cased Pair, with Accessories, Antique	1,800	3,500	3,500

RIFLE, PERCUSSION

	V.G.	Exc	Prior Edition
.44, Octagon Barrel, Brass Furniture, Antique	950	1,800	1,800

CONTENTO See Ventura Imports.

CONTINENTAL Made by Hood Firearms Co., Successors to Continental Arms Co.; Sold by Marshall Wells Co., Duluth, Minn., c. 1870.

HANDGUN, REVOLVER

	V.G.	Exc	Prior Edition
.22 Short R.F., 7 Shot, Spur Trigger, Solid Frame, Single Action, Antique	100	175	175
.32 Short R.F., 5 Shot, Spur Trigger, Solid Frame, Single Action, Antique	100	175	175

	V.G.	Exc	Prior Edition

CONTINENTAL Made by Jules Bertrand, Liege, Belgium c. 1910.

HANDGUN, SEMI-AUTOMATIC

	V.G.	Exc	Prior Edition
Pocket, .25 ACP, Clip Fed, Curio...	$175	$250	$250

CONTINENTAL Made by Stevens Arms.

RIFLE, BOLT ACTION

Model 52, .22 L.R.R.F., Singleshot, Takedown, Modern..........................	50	75	75

SHOTGUN, DOUBLE BARREL, SIDE-BY-SIDE

Model 215, 12 and 16 Gauges, Outside Hammers, Steel Barrel, Modern.........	100	175	175
Model 311, Various Gauges, Hammerless, Steel Barrel, Modern.........	125	200	200
Model 315, Various Gauges, Hammerless, Steel Barrel, Modern............	125	175	175

SHOTGUN, SINGLESHOT

Model 90, Various Gauges, Takedown, Automatic Ejector, Plain Hammer, Modern.....................	50	75	75

CONTINENTAL Rheinische Waffen u. Munitionsfabrik. Cologne, Germany.

HANDGUN, SEMI-AUTOMATIC

.25 ACP, Clip Fed, Blue, Curio.................	150	225	150
.32 ACP, Clip Fed, Webley Copy, Blue, Curio..	200	275	200

CONTINENTAL ARMS CO. Norwich, Conn. 1866–1867.

HANDGUN, PEPPERBOX

Continental 1, .22 R.F., 7 Shot, Spur Trigger, Solid Frame, Antique......	450	575	575

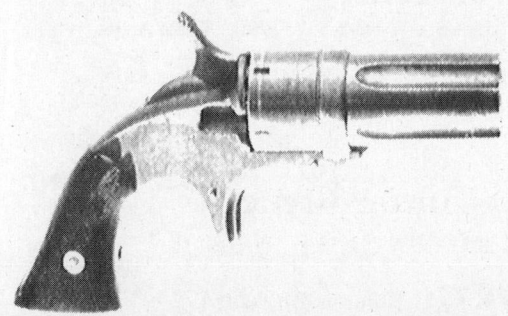

Continental Arms Co. Pepperbox

Continental 2, .32 R.F., 5 Shot, Spur Trigger, Solid Frame, Antique.......	525	600	600

	V.G.	Exc	Prior Edition

COONAN ARMS, INC. St. Paul, Minn. since 1982.

HANDGUN, SEMI-AUTOMATIC

Comp. 1, .357 Magnum, Standard Production Model, Stainless
Steel, Clip Fed, Adjustable Sights, Modern.. $900 $1,050 $650
Model A, .357 Magnum, Single Action, Stainless, Modern...................... 550 650 600
Model B, .357 Magnum, Pre–Production Model, Serial Numbers
under 1000, Stainless Steel, Clip Fed, Adjustable Sights, Modern............ 350 675 675

COOPER FIREARMS MFG. CO. Philadelphia, Pa. 1851–1869.

HANDGUN, PERCUSSION

Navy, .31, 5 Shots, Double Action, Antique... 475 550 550
Pocket, .31, 5 or 6 Shots, Double Action, Antique................................... 425 500 500

C.O.P. M & N Distributers, Torrance, Calif.

HANDGUN, REPEATER

Model Mini, .22 L.R.R.F., Four Barrels, Aluminum Frame,
Hammerless, Double Action, Modern.. 250
Model Mini, .22 W.M.R., Four Barrels, Stainless Steel, Hammerless,
Double Action, Modern.. — RARE —
Model SS–1, .357 Mag., Four Barrels, Stainless Steel, Hammerless,
Double Action, Modern.. 250 300 275

HANDGUN, SEMI-AUTOMATIC

TP–70 AAI, .22 L.R.R.F., Double Action, Clip Fed, Stainless Steel,
Hammer, Modern.. 125 175 170
TP–70 AAI, .25 A.C.P., Double Action, Clip Fed, Stainless Steel,
Hammer, Modern.. 125 175 165

COPELAND, F. Made by Frank Copeland, Worcester, Mass.

1868–1874.

HANDGUN, REVOLVER

.22 Short R.F., 7 Shot, Spur Trigger, Solid Frame, Single Action,
Antique.. 200 250 200
.32 Short R.F., 5 Shot, Spur Trigger, Solid Frame, Single Action,
Antique.. 175 225 225

COQ Spain, c. 1900.

HANDGUN, SEMI-AUTOMATIC

K-25, .25 ACP, Clip Fed, Modern.. 75 125 125

CORNFORTH London, England 1725–1760.

HANDGUN, FLINTLOCK

Pair, Belt Pistol, Brass Barrel, Brass Furniture, Plain, Antique.............. 2,700 4,000 4,000

COSENS, JAMES Gunmaker in Ordinary to Charles II England, Late 1600's.

HANDGUN, FLINTLOCK

Pair, Holster Pistol, Silver Furniture, Engraved Silver Inlay,
High Quality, Antique.. $9,350 $16,000 $16,000

COSMI Made for Abercrombie & Fitch c. 1960.

SHOTGUN, SEMI-AUTOMATIC

12 or 20 Gauge, Top Break, Engraved, Checkered Stock, Vent Rib,
Modern.. 3,000 3,500 2,850

COSMOPOLITAN ARMS CO. Hamilton, Ohio 1860–1865.

Also see U.S. Military.

RIFLE, PERCUSSION

.45, Sporting Rifle, Antique.. 1,200 1,500 1,400
.50, Carbine, Antique.. 850 1,200 1,200

COWELS & SMITH Chicopee Falls, Mass. 1863–1876. Became Cowels & Son in 1871.

HANDGUN, SINGLESHOT

.22 R.F., Side–Swing Barrel, Hammer, Spur Trigger, Antique................ 150 225 225
.30 R.F., Side–Swing Barrel, Hammer, Spur Trigger, Antique................ 150 250 250

COWLES & SON Cowles & Smith, 1866–1871, Cowles & Son 1871–1876 in Chicopee Falls, Mass.

HANDGUN, SINGLESHOT

.22 Short R.F., Brass Frame, Side Swing Barrel, Antique...................... 175 250 250

CRAFT PRODUCTS

HANDGUN, SEMI-AUTOMATIC

.25 ACP, Clip Fed, Modern.. 75 125 125

CREEDMORE Made by Hopkins & Allen, c. 1870.

HANDGUN, REVOLVER

#1, .22 Short R.F., 7 Shot, Spur Trigger, Solid Frame, Single
Action, Antique... 100 175 175

	V.G.	Exc	Prior Edition

CRESCENT Made by Norwich Falls Pistol Co., c. 1880.

HANDGUN, REVOLVER

.32 Short R.F, 5 Shot, Spur Trigger, Solid Frame, Single Action, Antique.. $100 $175 $175

CRESCENT FIRE ARMS CO. Norwich, Conn., 1892; Purchased by H & D Folsom in 1893, and Absorbed by Stevens Arms & Tool 1926.

SHOTGUN, DOUBLE BARREL, SIDE-BY-SIDE

Various Gauges, Hammerless, Damascus Barrel, Modern...................... 175 225 225
Various Gauges, Hammerless, Steel Barrel, Modern............................. 225 300 300
Various Gauges, Outside Hammers, Damascus Barrel, Modern............. 175 225 225
Various Gauges, Outside Hammers, Steel Barrel, Modern..................... 200 275 275

SHOTGUN, SINGLESHOT

Various Gauges, Hammer, Steel Barrel, Modern.................................... 75 100 100

CRIOLLA Hispano Argentine Automoviles, Buenos Aires, Argentina, c. 1935.

HANDGUN, SEMI-AUTOMATIC

La Criolla, .22 L.R.R.F., Colt M1911, Ace Copy, Clip Fed, Blue, Modern.. 250 325 325

CROWN JEWEL Made by Norwich Falls Pistol Co., c. 1880.

HANDGUN, REVOLVER

.32 Short R.F., 5 Shot, Spur Trigger, Solid Frame, Single Action, Antique.. 100 175 175

CRUCELEGUI Spain, Imported by Mandall Shooting Supplies, Scotsdale, Ariz.

SHOTGUN, DOUBLE BARREL, SIDE-BY-SIDE

Model 150, 12 or 20 Gauges, Outside Hammers, Double Trigger, Modern.. 150 200 200

CRUSO Made by Stevens Arms.

RIFLE, BOLT ACTION

Model 53, .22 L.R.R.F., Singleshot, Takedown, Modern........................ 50 75 75

SHOTGUN, SINGLESHOT

Model 90, Various Gauges, Takedown, Automatic Ejector, Plain Hammer, Modern.. 50 75 75

CUMBERLAND ARMS CO. Made by Crescent for Hibbard–

Spencer Bartlett Co., c. 1900.

SHOTGUN, DOUBLE BARREL, SIDE-BY-SIDE

	V.G.	Exc	Prior Edition
Various Gauges, Hammerless, Damascus Barrel, Modern......................	$125	$200	$200
Various Gauges, Hammerless, Steel Barrel, Modern..............................	150	225	225
Various Gauges, Outside Hammers, Damascus Barrel, Modern.............	125	200	200
Various Gauges, Outside Hammers, Steel Barrel, Modern.....................	150	200	200

SHOTGUN, SINGLESHOT

Various Gauges, Hammer, Steel Hammer, Modern................................	50	100	100

C.V.A. (Connecticut Valley Arms), Norcross, Ga.

HANDGUN, FLINTLOCK

.45 Kentucky, Brass Furniture, Reproduction	50	75	75
.50 Hawken, Brass Furniture, Reproduction	75	125	125

HANDGUN, PERCUSSION

.45 Kentucky, Brass Furniture, Reproduction	50	75	75

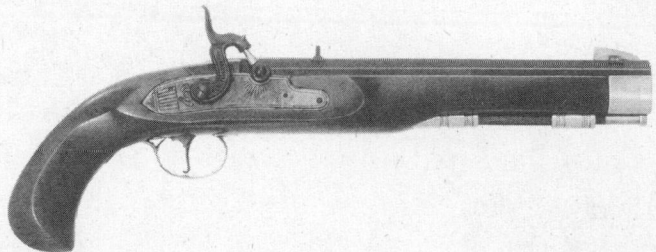

CVA Kentucky Pistol

	V.G.	Exc	Prior Edition
.45 or .50 Mountain Pistol, Brass Furniture, Reproduction	$50	$100	$100

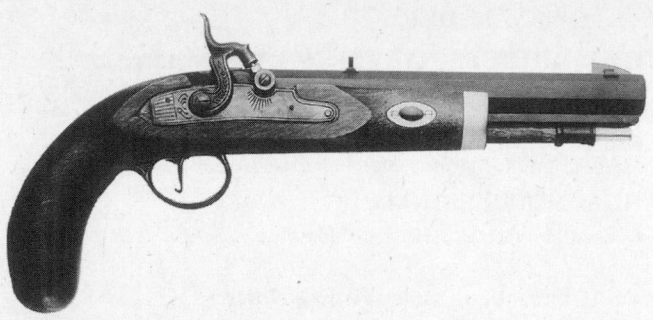

CVA Mountain Pistol

| **.45 Philadelphia Derringer,** Reproduction .... | 25 | 75 | 75 |

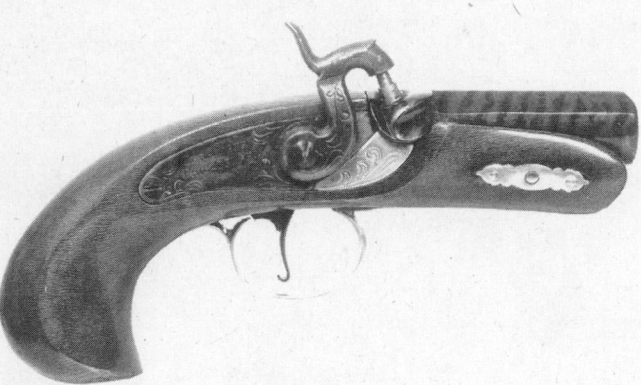

CVA Philadelphia Derringer

	V.G.	Exc	Prior Edition
.45 Tower Pistol, Brass Furniture, Reproduction	$25	$75	$75

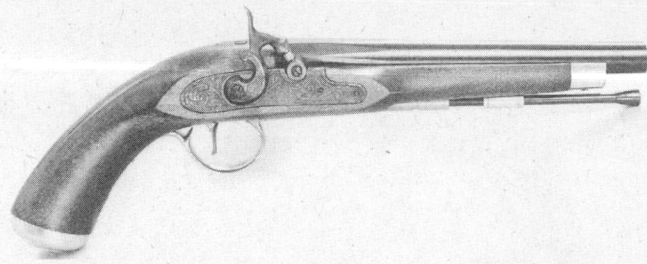

CVA Tower Pistol

.50 Hawken, Brass Furniture, Set Triggers, Reproduction	50	100	100

CVA Hawken Pistol

45 Colonial Pistol, Brass Furniture, Reproduction	25	50	50

CVA Colonial Pistol

	V.G.	Exc	Prior Edition
PP258, Pioneer, .32 Caliber, Octagonal Barrel, Reproduction	$75	$100	$100

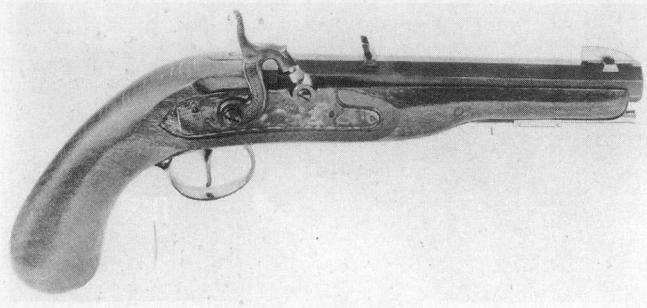

CVA Pioneer Pistol

PP640, Prospector, .44 Caliber, Single Shot, Reproduction	75	100	100

CVA Prospector Pistol

HANDGUN, REVOLVER

	V.G.	Exc	Prior Edition
RV 630, 1858 Remington Army, .44 Caliber, One Piece Frame, Reproduction	150	200	200
RV 632, 1858 Remington Army, .44 Caliber, Brass Frame, Reproduction	125	150	150

	V.G.	Exc	Prior Edition
RV600, 1851 Colt Navy, .36 Caliber, Six Shot, Brass Frame, Reproduction	$75	$125	$125

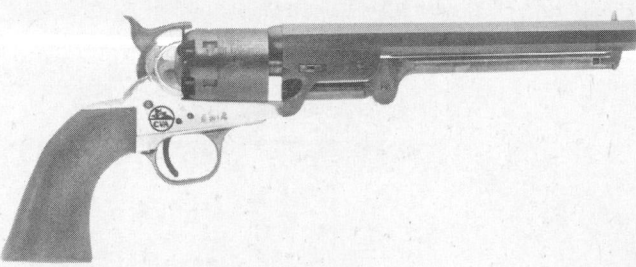

CVA 1851 Colt Navy

RV610, 1860 Colt Army, .44 Cailber, Six Shot, Reproduction	150	200	200
RV650, New Model Pocket Remington, .31 Caliber, Spur Trigger, Reproduction	75	100	100

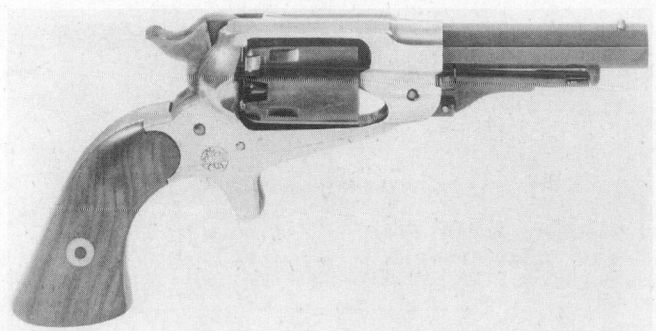

CVA New Pocket Remington

RVF620, 1861 Colt Navy, .44 Caliber, Steel Frame, Reproduction	125	175	175
RVF622, 1861 Colt Navy, .44 Caliber, Steel Frame, Reproduction	75	125	125

RIFLE, FLINTLOCK

.45 Kentucky Rifle, Brass Furniture, Reproduction	100	150	150
.45 or .50 Mountain Rifle, German Silver Furniture, Reproduction	125	200	200
.50 Frontier Rifle, Brass Furniture, Reproduction	100	150	150
.50 or .54 Hawken Rifle, Brass Furniture, Reproduction	125	175	175
FR503, Squirrel Rifle, .32 Caliber, Double Set Triggers, Reproduction	200	250	250
FR504, Pennsylvania Long Rifle, .50 Caliber, Brass Butt Plate, Reproduction	300	375	375

RIFLE, PERCUSSION

.45 Kentucky Rifle, Brass Furniture, Reproduction	75	125	125
.45 or .50 Frontier Rifle, Brass Furniture, Reproduction	100	150	150

	V.G.	Exc	Prior Edition
.45, .50, .54, or .58 Mountain Rifle, German Silver Furniture, Reproduction	$125	$175	$175
.50 .54 Hawken Rifle, Brass Furniture, Reproduction	125	175	175
.58 Zouave, Brass Furniture, Reproduction	100	150	150
PR403, Squirrel Rifle, .32 Caliber, Right Handed Model, Reproduction	175	225	225

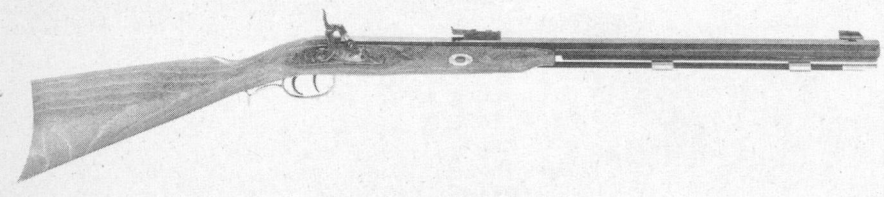

CVA Squirrel Rifle

PR404, Pennsylvania Long Rifle, .50 Caliber, Brass Butt Plate, Reproduction	300	375	375

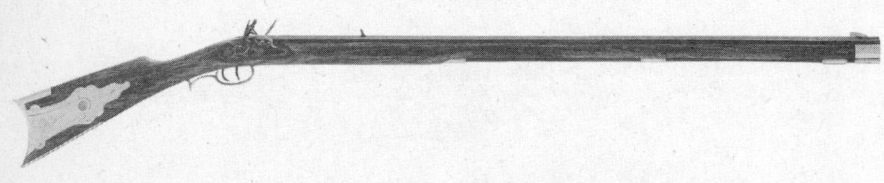

CVA Pennsylvania Long Rifle

PR407, Big Bore Mountain Rifle, .54 Cailiber, Undecorated Stock, Beavertail Cheekpiece, Reproduction	300	350	350
PR456, Squirrel Rifle, .32 Caliber, Left Handed Model, Reproduction	175	225	225

SHOTGUN, DOUBLE BARREL, SIDE-BY-SIDE

PS409, .12 Gauge, Percussion, Muzzleloading, Reproduction	225	275	275

	V.G.	Exc	Prior Edition

SHOTGUN, SINGLE BARREL

FB557, Blunderbuss, .69 Caliber, Flintlock, Brass Trigger,
Reproduction $225 $275 $275

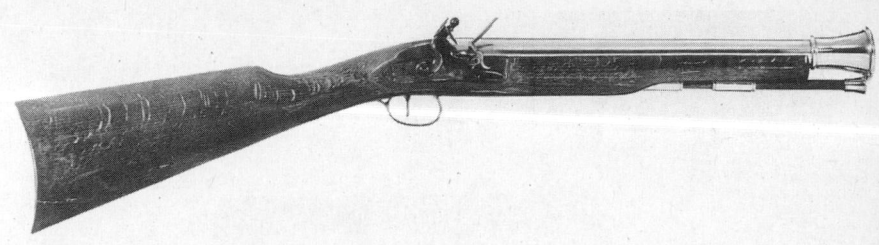

CVA Blunderbuss

CZ Czechoslovakia from 1918 to date. This listing includes both Ceska
Zbrojovka Brno and Ceskslovenska Zbrojovka. Also see BRNO.

HANDGUN, REVOLVER

Grand, .357 Mag., Double Action, Swing–Out Cylinder, Modern...........	125	175	175
Grand, .38 Spec., Double Action, Swing–Out Cylinder, Modern...........	125	175	175
ZKR 551, .38 Spec., Single Action, Swing–Out Cylinder, Target Pistol, Modern...	175	250	250

HANDGUN, SEMI-AUTOMATIC

"Vest Pocket" CZ 1945, .25 ACP, Clip Fed, Modern.............................	150	175	175
CZ 1924 Navy, .380 ACP, Clip Fed, Nazi–Proofed, Curio.....................	950	1,200	375
CZ 1938, .380 ACP, Clip Fed, Double Action, Curio.............................	250	300	300

CZ VZ 38

CZ 1938, .380 ACP, Clip Fed, Double Action, Nazi–Proofed,
Curio.. 1,300 1,350 1,350

	V.G.	Exc	Prior Edition
CZ 1938, .380 ACP, Clip Fed, Double Action, With Safety, Curio..........	$750	$950	$950
CZ 70, .32 ACP, Clip Fed, Blue, Double Action, Modern........................	150	175	300
CZ 75, 9mm P. Clip Fed, Double Action, Blue, Modern...........................	300	350	350
CZ NB 50 Police, .32 ACP, Clip Fed, Double Action, Curio...................	275	350	350
CZ1922, .380 ACP, Clip Fed, Curio..	300	375	375
CZ1922, .380 ACP, Clip Fed, Curio..	250	325	325
CZ1924, .380 ACP, 10 Shot, Long Grip, Clip Fed, Curio........................	550	650	600
CZ1924, .380 ACP, Clip Fed, Curio..	300	350	350
CZ1924, .380 ACP, Clip Fed, Curio..	250	325	325
CZ1936, .25 ACP, Clip Fed, Curio..	225	250	250
CZ27 Communist, .32 ACP, Clip Fed, Curio..	150	175	300

CZ VZ 27

CZ27 Early Luftwaffe, .32 ACP, Clip Fed, Nazi–Proofed, Curio...........	350	425	300
CZ27 Late Luftwaffe, .32 ACP, Clip Fed, Nazi–Proofed, Curio.............	300	375	275
CZ27 Navy, .32 ACP, Clip Fed, Nazi–Proofed, Curio..............................	400	500	350
CZ27 Police, .32 ACP, Clip Fed, Nazi–Proofed, Curio............................	350	450	375
CZ27 Postwar, .32 ACP, Clip Fed, Commercial, Curio............................	175	200	200
CZ27 Pre–War, .32 ACP, Clip Fed, Commercial, Curio........................	300	400	250
CZ50, .32 ACP, Clip Fed, Double Action, Military, Modern...................	125	150	150
CZ52, 7.62mm Tokarev, Clip Fed, Single Action, Curio........................	100	135	135
Duo, .25 ACP, Clip Fed, Modern..	125	175	175
Fox, .25 ACP, Clip Fed, Curio..	275	325	325
Niva, .25 ACP, Clip Fed, Curio...	275	325	325
PAV, .22 ACP, Clip Fed, Modern...	75	85	75

HANDGUN, SINGLESHOT

Drulov 75, .22 L.R.R.F., Top Break, Target Pistol, Target Sights, Modern...	200	250	200
Model P, .22 L.R.R.F., Top Break, Target Pistol, Modern.....................	175	250	250
Model P, 6mm Flobert, Top Break, Target Pistol, Modern......................	150	225	225

RIFLE, BOLT ACTION

ZKK 600, Various Calibers, Checkered Stock, Express Sights, Modern...	400	500	350

	V.G.	Exc	Prior Edition
ZKK 602, Various Magnum Calibers, Checkered Stock, Express Sights, Modern..	$500	$600	$450

SHOTGUN, DOUBLE BARREL, OVER-UNDER

Model 581, 12 Gauge, Checkered Stock with Cheekpiece, Modern...	450	550	400

CZAR Made by Hood Firearms, c. 1876.

HANDGUN, REVOLVER

.22 Short R.F., 7 Shot, Spur Trigger, Solid Frame, Single Action, Antique...	100	175	175

CZAR Made by Hopkins & Allen, c. 1880.

HANDGUN, REVOLVER

.22 Short R.F., 7 Shot, Spur Trigger, Solid Frame, Single Action, Antique...	100	150	150
.32 Short R.F., 5 Shot, Spur Trigger, Solid Frame, Single Action, Antique...	125	175	175

CZECHOSLAVAKIAN MILITARY Also see German Military, CZ.

RIFLE, BOLT ACTION

GEW 33/40, 8mm Mauser, Military, Nazi-Proofed, Carbine, Curio...	225	300	250
Gewehr 24 T, 8mm Mauser, Military, Nazi-Proofed, Curio....................	150	250	200
VZ 24, 8mm Mauser, Military, Curio...	125	200	175
VZ 33, 8mm Mauser, Military, Carbine, Curio...	125	175	150

D

| | V.G. | Exc. | Prior Edition |

DAISY Made By Bacon Arms Co., c. 1880.

HANDGUN, REVOLVER

.22 Short R.F., 7 Shot, Spur Trigger, Solid Frame, Single Action,
Antique.. $75 $150 $150

DAKIN GUN CO. San Francisco, Ca., c. 1960.

SHOTGUN, DOUBLE BARREL, OVER-UNDER

Model 170, Various Gauges, Light Engraving, Checkered Stock,
Double Triggers, Vent Rib, Modern... 450 550 650

SHOTGUN, DOUBLE BARREL, SIDE-BY-SIDE

Model 100, 12 or 20 Gauges, Boxlock, Light Engraving, Double
Triggers, Modern.. 300 350 350
Model 147, Various Magnum Gauges, Boxlock, Light Engraving,
Double Triggers, Vent Rib, Modern... 350 400 400
Model 215, 12 or 20 Gauges, Sidelock, Fancy Engraving, Fancy
Wood, Ejectors, Single Selective Trigger, Vent Rib, Modern.................. 800 975 950

DALBY, DAVID Lincolnshire, England, c. 1835.

HANDGUN, FLINTLOCK

.50, Pocket Pistol, Box Lock, Screw Barrel, Folding Trigger,
Silver Inlay, Antique.. 350 400 850

DALY ARMS CO. N.Y.C., c. 1890.

HANDGUN, REVOLVER

.22 Long R.F., 6 Shot, Double Action, Ring Trigger, Solid Frame,
Antique.. 175 250 250
Peacemaker, .32 Short R.F., 5 Shot, Spur Trigger, Solid Frame,
Single Action, Antique... 100 175 175

DAN WESSON ARMS Monson, Mass. since 1970.

HANDGUN, REVOLVER

Extra Barrel Assemblies, Add:

	V.G.	Exc	Prior Edition

15", 15–2 $75.00–$110.00; 15–2H $95.00–$135.00; 15-2V $95.00–$135.00; 15–2VH $120.00–$160.00; 715 $80.00–120.00; 715V $95.00–$140.00; 715VH $100.00–$155.00

12", 15-2 $50.00–$80.00; 15-2VH $75.00–$110.00; 715 $75.00–$110.00; 715V $80.00–$120.00; 715VH $95.00–$140.00

10", 15-2 $20.00–$40.00; 15–2H $35.00–$55.00; 15–2V $35.00–$55.00; 15-2VH $40.00–$70.00; 44-V $55.00–$85.00; 44–VH; 715 $35.00–$55.00; 715V $45.00–$65.00; 715VH $50.00–$80.00; 744–V $60.00–$100.00; 44–VH $70.00–$110.00

Others: 15-2 $20.00–$40.00; 15-2H $35.00–$55.00; 15-2V $35.00–$55.00; 15-2VH $40.00–$70.00; 44-V $55.00–$85.00; 44-VH; 715 $35.00–$55.00; 715V $45.00–$65.00; 715VH $50.00–$80.00; 744-V $60.00–$100.00; 44-VH $70.00–$110.00

	V.G.	Exc	Prior Edition
Model 11, .357 Magnum, Double Action, 3–Barrel Set, Nickel Plated, Modern	$200	$250	$225
Model 11, .357 Magnum, Double Action, 3–Barrel Set, Satin Blue, Modern	45	50	50
Model 11, .357 Magnum, Various Barrel Lengths, Nickel Plated, Double Action, Modern	150	225	175
Model 11, .357 Magnum, Various Barrel Lengths, Satin Blue, Double Action, Modern	150	200	150
Model 11, .38 Special, Various Barrel Lengths, Nickel Plated, Double Action, Modern	125	200	125
Model 11, .38 Special, Various Barrel Lengths, Satin Blue, Double Action, Modern	150	175	125
Model 12, .357 Magnum, 3–Barrel Set, Satin Blue, Adjustable Sights, Modern	225	300	250
Model 12, .357 Magnum, Various Barrel Lengths, Double Action, Blue, Adjustable Sights, Modern	200	250	275
Model 12, .357 Magnum, Various Barrel Lengths, Double Action, Nickel Plated, Adjustable Sights, Modern	175	300	175
Model 12, .38 Special, Various Barrel Lengths, Double Action, Blue, Adjustable Sights, Modern	100	150	125
Model 12, .38 Special, Various Barrel Lengths, Double Action, Nickel Plated, Adjustable Sights, Modern	100	175	150
Model 14, .357 Magnum, Double Action, 3–Barrel Set, Nickel Plated, Modern	225	300	300
Model 14, .357 Magnum, Double Action, 3–Barrel Set, Satin Blue, Modern	225	275	275
Model 14, .357 Magnum, Various Barrel Lengths, Double Action, Satin Blue, Modern	175	225	150
Model 14, .357 Magnum, Various Barrel Lengths, Double Action, Nickel Plated, Modern	125	175	175
Model 14, .38 Special, Various Barrel Lengths, Double Action, Satin Blue, Modern	100	150	150
Model 14, .38 Special, Various Barrel Lengths, Double Action, Nickel Plated, Modern	100	150	150
Model 14–2, .357 Magnum, Double Action, 4–Barrel Set, Blue, Modern	250	325	325
Model 14–2, .357 Magnum, Various Barrel Lengths, Double Action, Satin Blue, Modern	125	150	150
Model 14–2B, .357 Magnum, Double Action, 4–Barrel Set, Brite Blue, Modern	275	350	350

	V.G.	Exc	Prior Edition
Model 14–2B, .357 Magnum, Various Barrel Lengths, Double Action, Brite Blue, Modern	$100	$150	$150
Model 15, .357 Magnum, Double Action, 3–Barrel Set, Satin Blue, Adjustable Sights, Modern	250	325	325
Model 15, .357 Magnum, Double Action, 3–Barrel Set, Blue, Adjustable Sights, Modern	250	350	350
Model 15, .357 Magnum, Various Barrel Lengths, Double Action, Nickel Plated, Adjustable Sights, Modern	175	275	175
Model 15, .357 Magnum, Various Barrel Lengths, Double Action, Satin Blue, Adjustable Sights, Modern	175	225	175
Model 15, .357 Magnum, Various Barrel Lengths, Double Action, Blue, Adjustable Sights, Modern	200	250	175
Model 15, .38 Special, Various Barrel Lengths, Double Action, Nickel Plated, Adjustable Sights, Modern	175	250	175
Model 15, .38 Special, Various Barrel Lengths, Double Action, Satin Blue, Adjustable Sights, Modern	150	200	150
Model 15, .38 Special, Various Barrel Lengths, Double Action, Blue, Adjustable Sights, Modern	175	225	150
Model 15–2, .357 Magnum or .22 L.R.R.F., Double Action, 4–Barrel Set, Blue, Adjustable Sights, Modern	275	350	350
Model 15–2, .357 Magnum or .22 L.R.R.F., Various Barrel Lengths, Double Action, Blue, Adjustable Sights, Modern	150	200	200
Model 15–2H, .357 Magnum or .22 L.R.R.F., Double Action, 4–Barrel Set, Blue, Adjustable Sights, Heavy Barrel, Modern	275	350	350
Model 15–2H, .357 Magnum or .22 L.R.R.F., Various Barrel Lengths, Double Action, Blue, Adjustable Sights, Heavy Barrel, Modern	150	225	225
Model 15–2V, .357 Magnum or .22 L.R.R.F., Double Action, 4–Barrel Set, Blue, Adjustable Sights, Vent Rib, Modern	325	400	400
Model 15–2V, .357 Magnum or .22 L.R.R.F., Various Barrel Lengths, Double Action, Blue, Adjustable Sights, Vent Rib, Modern	150	225	225
Model 15–2VH, .357 Magnum or .22 L.R.R.F., Double Action, 4–Barrel, Vent Rib, Modern	300	375	375
Model 15–2VH, .357 Magnum or .22 L.R.R.F., Various Barrel Lengths, Double Action, Adjustable Sights, Heavy Barrel, Vent Rib, Modern	200	275	225
Model 44–V, .44 Magnum, Double Action, 4–Barrel Set, Blue, Adjustable Sights, Vent Rib, Modern	350	750	450
Model 44–V, .44 Magnum, Various Barrel Lengths, Double Action, Blue, Adjustable Sights, Vent Rib, Modern	500	650	350
Model 44–VH, .44 Magnum, Double Action, 4–Barrel Set, Blue, Adjustable Sights, Heavy Barrel, Vent Rib, Modern	700	475	450
Model 44–VH, .44 Magnum, Various Barrel Lengths, Double Action, Adjustable Sights, Heavy Barrel, Vent Rib, Modern	450	675	350
Model 714, .357 Magnum, Double Action, 4–Barrel Set, Stainless Steel, Fixed Sights, Modern	300	400	300
Model 714, .357 Magnum, Various Barrel Lengths, Double Action, Stainless Steel, Fixed Sights, Modern	250	300	175
Model 715-2, .357 Magnum, Double Action, 4–Barrel Set, Stainless Steel, Adjustable Sights, Modern	325	400	400
Model 715-2, .357 Magnum, Various Barrel Lengths, Double Action, Stainless Steel, Adjustable Sights, Modern	225	275	250
Model 715-2V, .357 Magnum, Double Action, 4–Barrel Set, Stainless Steel, Adjustable Sights, Vent Rib, Modern	400	475	475

	V.G.	Exc	Prior Edition
Model 715-2V, .357 Magnum, Various Barrel Lengths, Double Action, Stainless Steel, Adjustable Sights, Vent Rib, Modern..................	$275	$350	$275
Model 715-2VH, .357 Magnum, Double Action, 4–Barrel Set, Stainless Steel, Adjustable Sights, Vent Rib, Heavy Barrel, Modern..........	400	500	500
Model 744–V, .44 Magnum, Double Action, 4–Barrel Set, Stainless, Adjustable Sights, Vent Rib, Modern.......................	700	900	450
Model 744–V, .44 Magnum, Various Barrel Lengths, Double Action, Stainless, Adjustable Sights, Vent Rib, Modern..........	600	725	325
Model 744–VH, .44 Magnum, Various Barrel Lengths, Double Action, Adjustable Sights, Stainless, Heavy Barrel, Vent Rib, Modern..........	650	800	350
Model 744–VH, .44 Magnum, Various Barrel Lengths, Double Action, Adjustable Sights, Stainless, Heavy Barrel, Vent Rib, Modern..........	725	925	525

DANIELS, HENRY & CHARLES Chester, Conn., 1835–1850.

RIFLE, PERCUSSION

Turret Rifle, .40, Underhammer, 8 Shot, Manual Repeater, Octagon Barrel, Antique................................	6,500	7,500	7,500

DANISH MILITARY

HANDGUN, REVOLVER

9.1mm Ronge 1891, Military, Top Break, Hammer–Like Latch, Antique..........	400	450	375

HANDGUN, SEMI-AUTOMATIC

M1910, 9mm B, Made By Pieper, Clip Fed, Curio....................	475	650	650
M1910/21, 9mm B, Converted From M1910, Clip Fed, Curio................	400	450	525
M1910/21, 9mm B, Made by Danish Army Arsenal, Clip Fed, Curio..........	500	550	725
S.L.G. SG/8 9mm Luger, Clip Fed, Military, Curio................	1,000	1,250	1,375

RIFLE, BOLT ACTION

M1889 Krag, 8 x 54 Krag–Jorgensen, Carbine, Antique..........	650	750	575
M98 Mauser, 6.5 x 57, Haerens Vabenarsenal, Curio..............	250	350	350

RIFLE, SINGLESHOT

M1867, Remington Rolling Block, Full Stock, Antique..........	850	950	650

	V.G.	Exc	Prior Edition

DANTON   Made By Gabilondo y Cia., Elgoibar, Spain, 1925–1933.

HANDGUN, SEMI-AUTOMATIC

Pocket, .25 ACP, Clip Fed, Curio..	$100	$150	$150

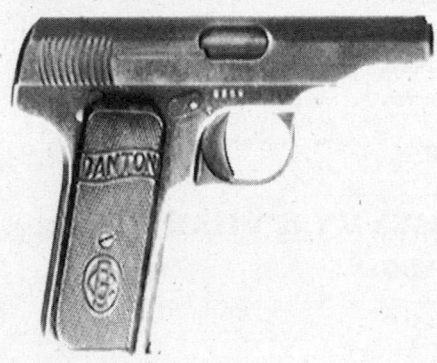

Danton .25

Pocket, .25 ACP, Grip Safety, Clip Fed, Curio..	125	175	175
Pocket, .32 ACP, Clip Fed, Curio..	100	175	175
Pocket, .32 ACP, Grip Safety, Clip Fed, Curio..	125	175	175

DARDICK   Hamden, Conn., 1954–1962.

HANDGUN, REVOLVER

Series 1100, .38 Dardick Tround, Double Action, Clip Fed, 3" Barrel, 11 Shot, Modern..	550	750	750
Series 1500, .22, Double Action, Clip Fed, 2" and 11" Barrels, Modern...	750	950	950
Series 1500, .30, Double Action, Clip Fed, 4¾" Barrel, Modern..............	750	950	950
Series 1500, .38 Dardick Tround, Double Action, Clip Fed, 6" Barrel, 15 Shot, Modern...	450	650	650
For Carbine Conversion Unit .22, Add $25.00–$395.00			
For Carbine Conversion Unit .38, Add $215.00–$325.00			

DARNE   St. Etienne, France.

SHOTGUN, DOUBLE BARREL, SIDE-BY-SIDE

Bird Hunter, Various Gauges, Sliding Breech, Ejectors, Double Triggers, Checkered Stock, Modern...	800	1,000	1,000
Hors Serie #1, Various Gauges, Sliding Breech, Ejectors, Fancy Engraving, Checkered Stock, Modern...	3,200	4,500	4,500
Magnum, 12 or 20 Gauges 3", Sliding Breech, Ejectors, Double Triggers, Checkered Stock, Modern...	2,250	3,250	3,250
Pheasant Hunter, Various Gauges, Sliding Breech, Ejectors, Light Engraving, Checkered Stock, Modern...	2,000	2,500	2,500

	V.G.	Exc	Prior Edition
Quail Hunter, Various Gauges, Sliding Breech, Ejectors, Engraved, Checkered Stock, Modern......	$2,750	$3,750	$3,750

DAVENPORT, W. H. Providence, R.I. 1880–1883, Norwich, Conn. 1890–1900.

SHOTGUN, DOUBLE BARREL, SIDE-BY-SIDE

8 Ga., Modern......	250	300	300

SHOTGUN, SINGLESHOT

Various Gauges, Hammer, Steel Barrel, Modern......	150	200	200

DAVIDSON Spain Mfg. by Fabrica de Armas, Imported by Davidson Firearms Co., Greensboro, N.C.

SHOTGUN, DOUBLE BARREL, SIDE-BY-SIDE

73 Stagecoach, 12 or 20 Gauges, Magnum, Checkered Stock, Modern......	225	275	275
Model 63B, 12 and 20 Gauges, Magnum, Engraved, Nickel Plated, Checkered Stock, Modern......	175	250	250
Model 63B, Various Gauges, Engraved, Nickel Plated, Checkered Stock, Modern......	125	200	200
Model 673B, 10 Ga. 3½", Magnum, Engraved, Nickel Plated, Checkered Stock, Modern......	200	275	275
Model 69 SL, 12 and 20 Gauges, Sidelock, Light Engraving, Checkered Stock, Modern......	325	400	400

DAVIS INDUSTRIES Current manufacturer in Chino, Calif.

HANDGUN, DOUBLE BARREL, OVER-UNDER

Model D–22, .22 L.R.R.F., Remington Derringer Style, Chrome, Modern......	50	75	50
Model D–22, .22 L.R.R.F., Remington Derringer Style, Black, Teflon, Modern......	50	75	50
Model D–22, .25 ACP, Remington Derringer Style, Black Teflon, Modern......	50	75	50
Model D–22, .25 ACP, Remington Derringer Style, Chrome, Modern......	50	75	50

DAVIS, N. R. & CO. Freetown Mass. 1853–1917. Merged with Warner Co. of Norwich, Conn. and became Davis–Warner Arms Co. It was not active between 1920–1922, but in 1930 started again as Crescent–Davis Arms Co., Norwich. This included Crescent Firearms Co. They relocated in Springfield, Mass. 1931–1932 and were taken over in 1932 by Stevens Arms.

RIFLE, PERCUSSION

.45, Octagon Barrel, Antique......	400	675	675

	V.G.	Exc	Prior Edition

SHOTGUN, PERCUSSION

#1 Various Gauges, Double Barrel, Side by Side, Damascus Barrel,
Outside Hammers, Antique.. $325 $475 $475
#3 Various Gauges, Double Barrel, Side by Side, Damascus Barrel,
Outside Hammers, Antique.. 275 400 400

SHOTGUN, DOUBLE BARREL, SIDE-BY-SIDE

Various Gauges, Hammerless, Damascus Barrel, Modern...................... 100 175 175
Various Gauges, Hammerless, Steel Barrel, Modern............................... 125 200 200
Various Gauges, Outside Hammers, Damascus Barrel, Modern.............. 100 175 175
Various Gauges, Outside Hammers, Steel Barrel, Modern...................... 100 200 200

SHOTGUN, SINGLE BARREL

Various Gauges, Hammer, Steel Barrel, Modern..................................... 50 100 80

DAY ARMS CO. San Antonio, Tex.

HANDGUN, SEMI-AUTOMATIC

Conversion Unit Only, .22 L.R.R.F., For Colt M1911, Clip Fed 125 150 150

DEAD SHOT L. W. Pond Co.

HANDGUN, REVOLVER

.22 Long R.F., 6 Shot, Single Action, Solid Frame, Spur Trigger,
Antique.. 225 275 275

DEANE, ADAMS & DEANE See Adams.

DEBATIR

HANDGUN, SEMI-AUTOMATIC

.25 ACP, Clip Fed, Curio.. 150 225 225

Debatir .25

.32 ACP, Clip Fed, Curio... 175 250 250

DEBERIERE, HENRY Phila., Pa. 1769–1774, See Kentucky Rifles & Pistols.

DECKER, WILHELM Zella St. Blasii, Germany, c. 1913.

HANDGUN, REVOLVER

	V.G.	Exc	Prior Edition
Decker, .25 ACP, Hammerles, 6 Shot, Curio	$650	$875	$875
Mueller Special, .25 ACP, Hammerles, 6 Shot, Curio	675	975	975

DEFENDER Made by Iver–Johnson, Sold by J.P. Lovell Arms 1875–1895.

HANDGUN, REVOLVER

	V.G.	Exc	Prior Edition
#89, .22 Short R.F., 7 Shot, Spur Trigger, Solid Frame, Single Action, Antique	100	150	150
#89, .32 Short R.F., 5 Shot, Spur Trigger, Solid Frame, Single Action, Antique	125	175	175
.22 Short R.F., 7 Shot, Spur Trigger, Solid Frame, Single Action, Antique	100	175	175
.32 Short R.F., 5 Shot, Spur Trigger, Solid Frame, Single Action, Antique	125	175	175

DEFENDER N. Shore & Co., Chicago, Ill., c. 1922.

HANDGUN, KNIFE PISTOL

	V.G.	Exc	Prior Edition
#215, .22 R.F., 3" Over All Length, 1 Blade	100	175	175

DEFIANCE Made By Norwich Falls Pistol Co., c. 1880.

HANDGUN, REVOLVER

	V.G.	Exc	Prior Edition
.22 Short R.F., 7 Shot, Spur Trigger, Solid Frame, Single Action, Antique	100	175	175

DEHUFF, ABRAHAM Lancaster, Pa., c. 1779. See Kentucky Rifles & Pistols.

DEK–DU Tomas de Urizar y Cia., Eibar, Spain, c. 1910.

HANDGUN, REVOLVER

	V.G.	Exc	Prior Edition
Velo Dog, .25 ACP, 12 Shots, Folding Trigger, Curio	125	175	175
Velo Dog, 5.5mm Velo Dog, 12 Shots, Folding Trigger, Curio	100	150	150

DELPHIAN Made by Stevens Arms.

SHOTGUN, SINGLESHOT

	V.G.	Exc	Prior Edition
Model 90, Various Gauges, Takedown, Automatic Ejector, Plain Hammer, Modern	50	75	75

	V.G.	Exc	Prior Edition

DELU Fab. d' Armes Delu & Co.

HANDGUN, SEMI-AUTOMATIC

	V.G.	Exc	Prior Edition
.25 ACP, Clip Fed, Curio..	$150	$175	$175

DEMRO Manchester, Conn.

HANDGUN, SEMI-AUTOMATIC

T.A.C. XF–7 Wasp, .45 ACP or 9mm Luger, Clip Fed, Modern............	300	350	350

RIFLE, SEMI-AUTOMATIC

T.A.C. Model 1 Carbine, .45 ACP or 9mm Luger, Clip Fed, Fixed Stock, Modern...............	225	350	350
T.A.C. XF–7 Wasp Carbine, .45 ACP or 9mm Luger, Clip Fed, Folding Stock, Modern............	350	400	400

DERINGER RIFLE AND PISTOL WORKS Philadelphia, Pa. 1870–1880.

HANDGUN, REVOLVER

Centennial '76, .38 Long R.F., 5 Shot, Single Action, Spur Trigger, Tip–up, Antique............	350	400	400
Model 1, .22 Short R.F., 7 Shot, Spur Trigger, Tip–up, Antique.............	300	375	400
Model 2, .22 Short R.F., 7 Shot, Spur Trigger, Tip–up, Antique.............	200	275	375
Model 2, .32 Long R.F., 5 Shot, Single Action, Spur Trigger, Tip–up, Antique............	200	275	375

DERINGER, HENRY, JR. Philadelphia, Pa. 1806–1868. Also see U.S. Military.

HANDGUN, PERCUSSION

Dueller, .41, Back Lock, German Silver Mounts, Antique.....................	2,000	2,500	2,500
Medium Pocket, .41, Back Lock, German Silver Mounts, Antique.........	1,000	1,500	1,500
Pocket, .41, Back Lock, German Silver Mounts, Antique........................	750	1,250	1,250

DERINGER, HENRY, SR. Richmond, Va. & Philadelphia, Pa. 1768–1814. See Kentucky Rifles & Pistols; U.S. Military.

DERR, JOHN Lancaster, Pa. 1810–1844. See Kentucky Rifles & Pistols.

DESPATCH Made by Hopkins & Allen, c. 1875.

HANDGUN, REVOLVER

.22 Short R.F., 7 Shot, Spur Trigger, Solid Frame, Single Action, Antique......................	125	175	175

	V.G.	Exc	Prior Edition

DESTROYER Made in Spain by Isidro Gaztanaga 1914–1933, reorganized as Gaztanaga, Trocoala y Ibarzabal 1933–1936.

HANDGUN, SEMI-AUTOMATIC

Destroyer, .25 ACP, Clip Fed, Curio..	$125	$175	$175

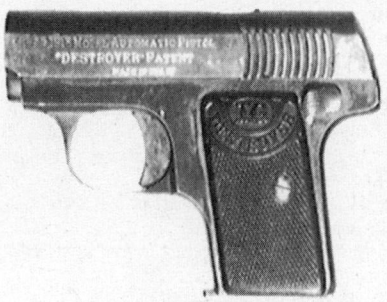

Destroyer .25

Destroyer, .32 ACP, Clip Fed, Long Grip, Curio.....................................	150	200	200

Destroyer .32

Model 1913, .25 ACP, Clip Fed, Modern..	125	175	175
Model 1919, .32 ACP, Clip Fed, Modern..	125	175	175
Super Destroyer, .32 ACP, Clip Fed, Modern...	175	225	225

DESTRUCTOR Iraola Salaverria, Eibar, Spain.

HANDGUN, SEMI-AUTOMATIC

.25 ACP, Clip Fed, Modern..	100	150	150

	V.G.	Exc	Prior Edition
.32 ACP, Clip Fed, Modern..	$125	$175	$175

DETONICS Seattle, Washington.

HANDGUN, SEMI-AUTOMATIC

	V.G.	Exc	Prior Edition
Mark I, .45 ACP, Combat Modifications, Clip Fed, Pocket Pistol, Matt Blue, Modern..	450	575	575
Mark II, 9mm P., Combat Modifications, Clip Fed, Pocket Pistol, Matt Blue, Modern..	375	450	675
Mark III, .38 Super, Combat Modifications, Clip Fed, Pocket Pistol, Matt Blue, Modern..	400	500	675
Combat Master, .45 ACP, Combat Modifications, Clip Fed, Pocket Pistol, Matt Blue, Modern..	675	750	600
Combat Master, .45 ACP, Combat Modifications, Clip Fed, Pocket Pistol, Matt Blue, Adjustable Sights, Modern...............................	725	800	550
Combat Master Mk. V, .38 Super, Combat Modifications, Clip Fed, Pocket Pistol, Matt Stainless, Modern...	700	775	775
Combat Master Mk. V, .45 ACP, Combat Modifications, Clip Fed, Pocket Pistol, Matt Stainless, Modern...	600	750	750
Combat Master Mk. V, 9mm P., Combat Modifications, Clip Fed, Pocket Pistol, Matt Stainless, Modern..............................	700	775	775
Combat Master Mk. VI, .45 ACP, Combat Modifications, Clip Fed, Pocket Pistol, Polished Stainless, Adjustable Sights, Modern...........	725	800	800

Detonics Mark VI

	V.G.	Exc	Prior Edition
Combat Master Mk. VI, .451 Mag., Combat Modifications, Clip Fed, Pocket Pistol, Polished Stainless, Adjustable Sights, Modern...........	800	975	875
Combat Master Mk. VI, 9mm P., Combat Modifications, Clip Fed, Pocket Pistol, Polished Stainless, Adjustable Sights, Modern..................	750	825	825
Combat Master Mk. VII, .38 Super, Combat Modifications, Clip Fed, Pocket Pistol, Matt Stainless, No Sights, Lightweight, Modern........	850	925	925
Combat Master Mk. VII, .45 ACP, Combat Modifications, Clip Fed, Pocket Pistol, Matt Stainless, No Sights, Lightweight, Modern................	825	900	900

	V.G.	Exc	Prior Edition
Combat Master Mk. VII, .451 Mag., Combat Modifications, Clip Fed, Pocket Pistol, Matt Stainless, No Sights, Lightweight, Modern........	$900	$1,200	$1,200
Combat Master Mk. VII, 9mm P., Combat Modifications, Clip Fed, Pocket Pistol, Matt Stainless, No Sights, Lightweight, Modern...............	850	925	925
MC2 Military Combat, .38 Super, Clip Fed, Pocket Pistol, Matt Stainless, Modern......	600	650	650
MC2 Military Combat, .45 ACP, Clip Fed, Pocket Pistol, Matt Stainless, Modern......	575	625	625
MC2 Military Combat, 9mm P., Clip Fed, Pocket Pistol, Matt Stainless, Modern......	600	650	650
Scoremaster, .45 ACP, I.P.S.C. Target Pistol, Target Sights, Stainless Steel, Modern.................	750	950	1,150
Scoremaster, .451 Mag., I.P.S.C. Target Pistol, Target Sights, Stainless Steel, Modern........	1,000	1,250	1,150

DIAMOND Made by Stevens Arms.

SHOTGUN, SINGLESHOT

Model 89 Dreadnaught, Various Gauges, Hammer, Modern.................	75	100	100
Model 90, Various Gauges, Takedown, Automatic Ejector, Plain Hammer, Modern........	50	75	75
Model 95, 12 and 16 Gauge, Takedown, Modern.....................	50	75	75

DIANE Erquiaga, Muguruzu, y Cia., Eibar, Spain, c. 1923.

HANDGUN, SEMI-AUTOMATIC

.25 ACP, Clip Fed, Blue, Curio................	225	275	275

DIANE Made by Wilkinson Arms, Covina, Calif.

HANDGUN, SEMI-AUTOMATIC

Standard Model, .25 ACP, Clip Fed, Modern.........................	100	125	125

DICKINSON, J. & L. Also E. L. & J. Dickinson, Springfield, Mass. 1863–1880.

HANDGUN, SINGLESHOT

.22 R.F., Brass Frame, Pivoting Barrel, Rack Ejector, Antique.................	350	400	400
.32 R.F., Brass Frame, Pivoting Barrel, Rack Ejector, Antique.................	250	300	300

DICKSON Made in Italy for American Import Co. until 1968.

HANDGUN, SINGLESHOT

Detective, .25 ACP, Clip Fed, Modern....................................	100	125	125

DICTATOR Made by Hopkins & Allen, c. 1880.

HANDGUN, REVOLVER

.22 Short R.F., 7 Shot, Spur Trigger, Solid Frame, Single Action, Antique........	125	175	175

	V.G.	Exc	Prior Edition
.32 Short R.F., 5 Shot, Spur Trigger, Solid Frame, Single Action, Antique	$125	$175	$175
#2, .32 Short R.F., 5 Shot, Spur Trigger, Solid Frame, Single Action, Antique	150	200	200

DIXIE GUN WORKS Union City, Tenn.

HANDGUN, FLINTLOCK

Tower, .67, Brass Furniture, Reproduction	25	50	50

HANDGUN, PERCUSSION

Army, .44 Revolver, Buntline, Reproduction	125	150	150
Navy, .36 Revolver, Buntline, Brass Frame, Engraved, Reproduction	175	225	225
Navy, .36 Revolver, Buntline, Brass Frame, Reproduction	150	200	200
Spiller & Burr, .36 Revolver, Buntline, Brass Frame, Reproduction	75	100	100
Wyatt Earp, .44 Revolver, Buntline, Brass Frame, Reproduction	75	100	100
Wyatt Earp, .44 Revolver, Buntline, Brass Frame, With Shoulder Stock, Reproduction	150	175	175

RIFLE, LEVER ACTION

Win. 73 (Italian), .44–40 WCF, Tube Feed, Octagon Barrel, Carbine, Modern	475	600	600
Win. 73 (Italian), .44–40 WCF, Tube Feed, Octagon Barrel, Color Cased Hardened Frame, Engraved, Modern	475	600	600

RIFLE, FLINTLOCK

1st. Model Brown Bess, .75, Military, Reproduction	325	400	400
2nd. Model Brown Bess, .74, Military, Reproduction	425	500	500
Coach Guard, .95, Blunderbuss, Brass Furniture, Reproduction	100	150	150
Day Rifle, .45, Double Barrel, Over–under, Swivel Breech, Brass Furniture, Reproduction	300	375	375
Deluxe Pennsylvania, .45, Kentucky Rifle, Full–Stocked, Brass Furniture, Light Engraving, Reproduction	275	350	350
Deluxe Pennsylvania, .45, Kentucky Rifle, Full–Stocked, Brass Furniture, Reproduction	250	325	325
Kentuckian, .45, Kentucky Rifle, Full–Stocked, Brass Furniture, Reproduction	100	150	150
Kentuckian, .45, Kentucky Rifle, Full–Stocked, Brass Furniture, Reproduction, Carbine	150	225	225
Musket, .67, Smoothbore, Reproduction, Carbine	75	125	125
Squirel Rifle, .45, Kentucky Rifle, Full–Stocked, Brass Furniture, Reproduction	275	375	375
York County, .45, Kentucky Rifle, Full–Stocked, Brass Furniture, Reproduction	150	175	175

RIFLE, PERCUSSION

Day Rifle, .45, Double Barrel, Over–under, Swivel Breech, Brass Furniture, Reproduction	225	275	275
Deluxe Pennsylvania, .45, Kentucky Rifle, Full–Stocked, Brass Furniture, Reproduction	275	325	325
Deluxe Pennsylvania, .45, Kentucky Rifle, Full–Stocked, Brass Furniture, Light Engraving, Reproduction	275	350	350

	V.G.	Exc	Prior Edition
Dixie Hawkin, .45, Half–Stocked, Octagon Barrel, Set Trigger, Brass Furniture, Reproduction	$150	$200	$200
Dixie Hawkin, .50, Half–Stocked, Octagon Barrel, Set Trigger, Brass Furniture, Reproduction	150	200	200
Enfield Two–Band, .577, Musketoon, Military, Reproduction	125	200	200
Kentuckian, .45, Kentucky Rifle, Full–Stocked, Brass Furniture, Reproduction	125	175	175
Kentuckian, .45, Kentucky Rifle, Full–Stocked, Brass Furniture, Reproduction, Carbine	200	250	250
Musket, .66, Smoothbore, Reproduction	125	175	175
Plainsman, .45, Half–Stocked, Octagon Barrel, Reproduction	200	250	250
Plainsman, .50, Half–Stocked, Octagon Barrel, Reproduction	150	275	275
Squirrel Rifle, .45, Kentucky Rifle, Full–Stocked, Brass Furniture, Reproduction	300	375	375
Target, .45, Half–Stocked, Octagon Barrel, Reproduction	75	125	125
York County, .45, Kentucky Rifle, Full–Stocked, Brass Furniture, Reproduction	125	175	175
Zouave M 1863, .58, Military, Reproduction	175	250	250

SHOTGUN, PERCUSSION

	V.G.	Exc	Prior Edition
12 Gauge, Double Barrel, Side by Side, Double Trigger, Reproduction	75	100	100
28 Gauge, Single Barrel, Reproduction	75	100	100

SHOTGUN, FLINTLOCK

	V.G.	Exc	Prior Edition
Fowling Piece, 14 Gauge, Single Barrel, Reproduction	100	105	105

DOBSON T. London, England, c. 1780.

HANDGUN, FLINTLOCK

	V.G.	Exc	Prior Edition
.64, Presentation, Holster Pistol, Gold Inlays, Engraved, Half–Octagon Barrel, High Quality, Antique	2,500	4,000	4,000

DOMINO Made in Italy, Imported by Mandell Shooting Sports. Also see Beeman.

HANDGUN, SEMI-AUTOMATIC

	V.G.	Exc	Prior Edition
Model O.P. 601, .22 Short, Target Pistol, Adjustable Sights, Target Grips, Modern	900	1,100	725
Model O.P. 602, .22 L.R., Target Pistol, Adjustable Sights, Target Grips, Modern	1,000	1,200	800

DREADNAUGHT Made by Hopkins & Allen c. 1880.

HANDGUN, REVOLVER

	V.G.	Exc	Prior Edition
.22 Short R.F., 7 Shot, Spur Trigger, Solid Frame, Single Action, Antique	100	150	150
.32 Short R.F., 5 Shot, Spur Trigger, Solid Frame, Single Action, Antique	125	175	175

	V.G.	Exc	Prior Edition

DREYSE Dreyse Rheinische Metallwaren Machinenfabrik, Sommerda, Germany since 1889. In 1936 merged and became Rheinmetall–Borsig, Dusseldorf, Germany.

HANDGUN, SEMI-AUTOMATIC

	V.G.	Exc	Prior Edition
M1907, .32 ACP, Clip Fed, Curio	$125	$175	$175

Dreyse Model 1907 Late

	V.G.	Exc	Prior Edition
M1907, .32 ACP, Clip Fed, Early Model, Curio	150	200	200
M1910, 9mm Luger, Clip Fed, Curio	2,500	3,000	2,500
Rheinmetall, .32 ACP, Clip Fed, Curio	225	275	275
Vest Pocket, .25 ACP, Clip Fed, Curio	150	200	200
Vest Pocket, .25 ACP, Clip Fed, Early, Curio	175	225	225

RIFLE, SEMI-AUTOMATIC

	V.G.	Exc	Prior Edition
Carbine, .32 ACP, Clip Fed, Checkered Stock, Curio	375	450	450

DRIPPARD, F. Lancaster, Pa., 1767–1773, See Kentucky Rifles & Pistols.

DRISCOLL, J. B. Springfield, Mass., c. 1870.

HANDGUN, SINGLESHOT

	V.G.	Exc	Prior Edition
.22 R.F., Brass Frame, Spur Trigger, Antique	300	350	350

DUBIEL ARMS CO. Sherman, Tex. since 1975.

RIFLE, BOLT ACTION

	V.G.	Exc	Prior Edition
Custom Rifle, Various Calibers, Various Styles, Fancy Wood, Modern	2,000	2,500	2,250

	V.G.	Exc	Prior Edition

DUMARESD, B. Marseille, France, probably c. 1730.

HANDGUN, FLINTLOCK

Holster Pistol, Engraved, Horn Inlays, Ornate, Silver Furniture,
Antique.. $1,500 $2,000 $2,000

DUMOULIN FRERES ET CIE Milmort, Belgium since 1849.

RIFLE, BOLT ACTION

African Pro, Various Calibers, Fancy Checkering, Fancy Engraving,
Fancy Wood, Modern... 4,000 4,500 3,750
Safari Sportsman, Various Calibers, Fancy Checkering, Engraved,
Fancy Wood, Modern... 3,000 3,500 2,000
Safari, Various Calibers, Fancy Checkering, Engraved,
Modern... 2,000 2,500 1,750

RIFLE, DOUBLE BARREL, SIDE-BY-SIDE

Europa, Various Calibers, Fancy Checkering, Engraved, Fancy Wood,
Modern... 3,500 3,800 3,800

DUO FRANTISEK DUSEK Opocno, Czechoslovakia 1926–1948.
Ceska Zbrojovka from 1948 to date.

HANDGUN, SEMI-AUTOMATIC

Duo, .25 ACP, Clip Fed, Modern.. 200 250 175

DUTCH MILITARY

HANDGUN, REVOLVER

Model 1871 Hemberg, 9.4mm, Military, Antique...................... 300 350 175

RIFLE, BOLT ACTION

Beaumont–Vitale M1871/88, Military, Antique.......................... 150 200 200
Model 95, 6.5mm Mannlicher, Carbine, Full Stock, Curio...... 100 125 75
Model 95, 6.5mm Mannlicher, Full Stock, Curio..................... 125 150 100

RIFLE, FLINTLOCK

.70, Officers Type, Musket, Brass Furniture, Antique............... 1,250 1,500 1,500

DUTTON, JOHN S. Jaffrey, N.H. 1855–1870.

RIFLE, PERCUSSION

.36, Target Rifle, Swiss Buttplate, Octagon Barrel, Target
Sights, Antique... 900 1,600 1,600

	V.G.	Exc	Prior Edition

DWM Deutsche Waffen und Munitionsfabrik, Berlin, Germany 1896–1945.
Also see Luger and Borchardt.

HANDGUN, SEMI-AUTOMATIC

	V.G.	Exc	Prior Edition
Pocket, .32 ACP, Clip Fed, Curio...	$250	$350	$350

E

E.A. Echave y Arizmendi, Eibar, Spain 1911–1975. Also see Echasa and MAB.

HANDGUN, SEMI-AUTOMATIC

	V.G.	Exc.	Prior Edition
1916 Model, .25 ACP, Clip Fed, Curio...	$75	$125	$125

E.A. Eulogio Arostegui, Eibar, Spain, c. 1930.

HANDGUN, SEMI-AUTOMATIC

.25 ACP, Clip Fed, Blue, Dog Logo on Grips, Modern............................	75	125	125

EAGLE Made by Iver–Johnson, c. 1879–1886.

HANDGUN, REVOLVER

.22 Short F.F., 7 Shot, Spur Trigger, Solid Frame, Single Action, Antique....................	100	150	150
.32 Short R.F., 5 Shot, Spur Trigger, Solid Frame, Single Action, Antique....................	100	150	150
.38 Short R.F., 5 Shot, Spur Trigger, Solid Frame, Single Action, Antique....................	125	175	175
.44 Short R.F., 5 Shot, Spur Trigger, Solid Frame, Single Action, Antique....................	200	275	275

EAGLE ARMS CO. N.Y.C., c. 1865. Marketed by Plant's Manufacturing Company, New Haven, Conn.

HANDGUN, REVOLVER

.30 Cup Primed Cartridge, 6 Shot, Single Action, Spur Trigger, Solid Frame, Antique....................	400	500	500

	V.G.	Exc	Prior Edition
.30 Cup Primed Cartridge, 6 Shot, Single Action, Spur Trigger, Tip–up, Antique..	$525	$650	$650

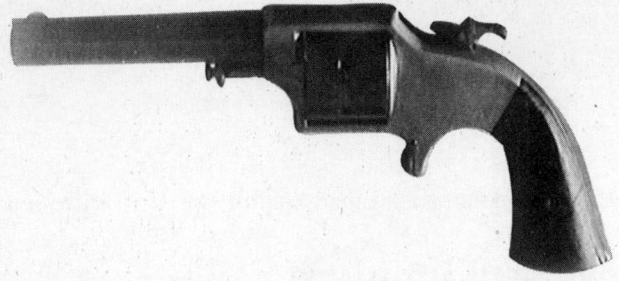

Eagle Arms Plants Patent, .30 Caliber Revolver

.42 Cup Primed Cartridge, 6 Shot, Single Action, Spur Trigger, Iron Frame, Antique..	850	950	950
.42 Cup Primed Cartridge, 6 Shot, Single Action, Spur Trigger, Tip–up, Antique..	950	1,150	1,150

EARLHOOD Made by E. L. Dickinson Co. Springfield, Mass. 1870–1880.

HANDGUN, REVOLVER

.32 Short R.F., 5 Shot, Spur Trigger, Solid Frame, Single Action, Antique..	125	175	175

EARLY, AMOS Dauphin Co. Pa. See Kentucky Rifles.

EARLY, JACOB Dauphin Co. Pa. See Kentucky Rifles.

EARTHQUAKE Made by E. L. Dickinson Co. Springfield, Mass. 1870–1880.

HANDGUN, REVOLVER

.32 Short R.F., 5 Shot, Spur Trigger, Solid Frame, Single Action, Antique..	100	175	175

EASTERN Made by Stevens Arms.

SHOTGUN, DOUBLE BARREL, SIDE-BY-SIDE

Model 311, Various Gauges, Hammerless, Steel Barrel, Modern............	150	175	175

SHOTGUN, SINGLESHOT

Model 94, Various Gauges, Takedown, Automatic Ejector, Plain Hammer, Modern..	50	75	75

	Prior
V.G.	Exc	Edition

EASTERN ARMS CO. Made by Meriden Firearms and sold by Sears–Roebuck.

HANDGUN, REVOLVER

	V.G.	Exc	Prior Edition
.32 S & W, 5 Shot, Double Action, Top Break, Modern............................	$75	$100	$100
.38 S & W, 5 Shot, Double Action, Top Break, Modern............................	100	125	125

EASTFIELD See Smith & Wesson.

ECHABERRIA, ARTURA Spain, c. 1790.

HANDGUN, MIQUELET-LOCK

Pair, Holster Pistol, Plain, Brass Furniture, Antique................................	3,500	4,500	4,500

ECHASA Tradename used in the 1950's by Echave, Arizmendi y Cia., Eibar, Spain.

HANDGUN, SEMI-AUTOMATIC

Model GZ MAB, .22 L.R.R.F., Clip Fed, Hammer, Modern....................	100	150	150

Echasa GZ-MAB

Model GZ MAB, .25 ACP, Clip Fed, Hammer, Modern...........................	125	150	150
Model GZ MAB, .32 ACP, Clip Fed, Hammer, Modern........................	125	175	175

ECLIPSE Made by Johnson, Bye & Co., c. 1875.

HANDGUN, SINGLESHOT

.25 Short R.F., Derringer, Spur Trigger, Antique......................................	75	125	125

	V.G.	Exc	Prior Edition

EDGESON Lincolnshire, England, 1810–1830.

HANDGUN, FLINTLOCK

	V.G.	Exc	Prior Edition
.45, Pair, Box Lock, Screw Barrel, Pocket Pistol, Folding Trigger, Plain, Antique	$1,000	$1,800	$1,800

EDMONDS, J. See Kentucky Rifles.

EGG, CHARLES London, England, c. 1850.

HANDGUN, PERCUSSION

	V.G.	Exc	Prior Edition
Pepperbox, .36, 6 Shot, 3½" Barrels, Antique	325	375	400

EGG, DURS London, England 1770–1840. Also see British Military.

HANDGUN, FLINTLOCK

	V.G.	Exc	Prior Edition
.50, Duelling Type, Holster Pistol, Octagon Barrel, Steel Furniture, Light Ornamentation, Antique	1,500	1,750	1,800

HANDGUN, PERCUSSION

	V.G.	Exc	Prior Edition
6 Shot, Pepperbox, Fluted Barrel, Pocket Pistol, Engraved, Antique	1,500	2,000	2,000

EGYPTIAN MILITARY

HANDGUN, SEMI-AUTOMATIC

	V.G.	Exc	Prior Edition
Tokagypt M–58, 9mm Luger, Clip Fed, Curio	300	350	350

RIFLE, SEMI-AUTOMATIC

	V.G.	Exc	Prior Edition
Hakim, .22 L.R.R.F., Training Rifle, Military, Modern	250	275	375
Hakim, 8mm Mauser, Military, Modern	300	350	650

84 GUN CO. Eighty Four, Pa. c. 1973.

RIFLE, BOLT ACTION

	V.G.	Exc	Prior Edition
Classic Rifle, Various Calibers, Checkered Stock, Grade 1, Modern	250	300	250
Classic Rifle, Various Calibers, Checkered Stock, Grade 2, Modern	500	600	325
Classic Rifle, Various Calibers, Checkered Stock, Grade 3, Modern	550	650	600
Classic Rifle, Various Calibers, Checkered Stock, Grade 4, Modern	1,000	1,200	675
Lobo Rifle, Various Calibers, Checkered Stock, Grade 1, Modern	375	400	275
Lobo Rifle, Various Calibers, Checkered Stock, Grade 2, Modern	500	575	525
Lobo Rifle, Various Calibers, Checkered Stock, Grade 3, Modern	1,000	1,200	1,050
Lobo Rifle, Various Calibers, Checkered Stock, Grade 4, Modern	1,500	1,800	1,550
Pennsy Rifle, Various Calibers, Checkered Stock, Grade 1, Modern	350	400	400
Pennsy Rifle, Various Calibers, Checkered Stock, Grade 2, Modern	450	600	600
Pennsy Rifle, Various Calibers, Checkered Stock, Grade 3, Modern	950	1,250	1,250
Pennsy Rifle, Various Calibers, Checkered Stock, Grade 4, Modern	1,250	1,750	1,750
Pennsy Rifle, Various Calibers, Checkered Stock, Standard Grade, Modern	250	325	325

	V.G.	Exc	Prior Edition

EL FAISAN

SHOTGUN, DOUBLE BARREL, SIDE-BY-SIDE

	V.G.	Exc	Prior Edition
El Faisan, .410 Gauge, Folding Gun, Double Trigger, Outside Hammers, Modern....	$75	$100	$100

EL TIGRE

RIFLE, LEVER ACTION

Copy of Winchester M1892, 44–40 WCF, Tube Feed, Modern............	200	275	275

ELECTOR Made by Hopkins & Allen, c. 1880.

HANDGUN, REVOLVER

.22 Short R.F., 7 Shot, Spur Trigger, Solid Frame, Single Action, Antique....	100	150	150
.32 Short R.F., 5 Shot, Spur Trigger, Solid Frame, Single Action, Antique....	125	175	175

ELECTRIC Made by Forehand & Wadsworth 1871–1880.

HANDGUN, REVOLVER

.32 Short R.F., 5 Shot, Spur Trigger, Solid Frame, Single Action, Antique....	125	175	175

ELGIN ARMS CO. Made by Crescent for Fred Bifflar & Co., Chicago, Ill.

SHOTGUN, DOUBLE BARREL, SIDE-BY-SIDE

Various Gauges, Hammerless, Damascus Barrel, Modern....	100	150	150
Various Gauges, Hammerless, Steel Barrel, Modern....	125	175	175
Various Gauges, Outside Hammers, Damascus Barrel, Modern....	100	175	175
Various Gauges, Outside Hammers, Steel Barrel, Modern....	150	200	200

SHOTGUN, SINGLESHOT

Various Gauges, Hammer, Steel Barrel, Modern....	50	75	75

ELGIN CUTLASS PISTOLS Springfield, Mass. Made by C.B. Allen, and Morill, Mosman & Blair. Blades made by Ames Sword Co. c. 1835.

HANDGUN, PERCUSSION

Allen Small Frame, 35–41 Cal., 4"- 5" Octagonal Barrel and 7½" - 10" Blade, Antique....	5,000	6,000	5,500
M.M.&B. Medium Frame, 31–36 Cal., 4" Round Barrel and 8¾" - 9½" Blade, Antique....	4,500	5,500	5,250

	V.G.	Exc	Prior Edition
U.S. Navy Model (Allen), 54 Cal., 5" Octagonal Barrel and 11" Blade, Antique	$12,500	$15,000	$12,500

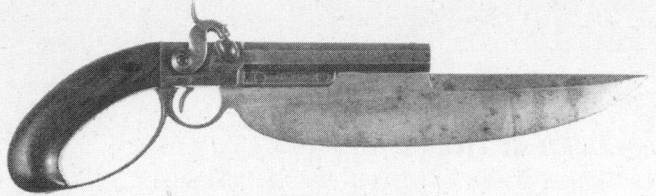

Elgin Cutlass Pistol, .54 Caliber

ELLIS, REUBEN Albany, N.Y. 1808–1829.

RIFLE, FLINTLOCK

Ellis–Jennings, .69, Sliding Lock for Multiple Loadings, 4 shot, Antique	15,000	20,000	20,000
Ellis–Jennings, .69, Sliding Lock for Multiple Loadings, 10 shot, Antique	25,000	30,000	30,000

E.M.F. (Early and Modern Firearms Co., Inc.) Studio City, Calif.

HANDGUN, REVOLVER

California Dragoon, .44 Magnum, Single Action, Western Style, Engraved, Modern	225	275	275
Dakota, Various Calibers, Single Action, Western Style, Modern	175	225	225
Dakota, Various Calibers, Single Action, Western Style, Engraved, Modern	250	325	325
Dakota, Various Calibers, Single Action, Western Style, Nickel Plated, Modern	200	275	275
Dakota, Various Calibers, Single Action, Western Style, Nickel Plated, Engraved, Modern	275	350	350
Dakota Buntline, Various Calibers, 12" Barrel, Single Action, Western Style, Modern	200	250	250

E.M.F. Dakota Buntline

Dakota Buckhorn, Various Calibers, 16¼" Barrel, Single Action, Western Style, Modern	200	275	275

	V.G.	Exc	Prior Edition
Dakota Buckhorn, Various Calibers, 16¼" Barrel, Single Action, Western Style, with Shoulder Stock, Modern..	$200	$300	$300
Dakota Sheriff, Various Calibers, Single Action, Western Style, Modern...	225	275	275
Super Dakota, Various Calibers, Single Action, Western Style, Magnum, Modern...	225	300	235
Outlaw 1875, Various Calibers, Single Action, Remington Style, Engraved, Modern...	175	250	250
Outlaw 1875, Various Calibers, Single Action, Remington Style, Engraved, Modern...	225	325	325
Thermodynamics, .357 Magnum, Solid Frame, Swing–out Cylinder, Vent Rib, Stainless Steel, Modern..	150	225	225

HANDGUN, SINGLESHOT

	V.G.	Exc	Prior Edition
Baron, .22 Short R.F., Derringer, Gold Frame, Blue Barrel, Wood Grips, Modern..	50	75	75
Baron, Count, Etc., Derringer, if Cased Add $10.00–$15.00			
Baroness, .22 Short R.F., Derringer, Gold Plated, Pearl Grips, Modern..	50	75	75
Count, .22 Short R.F., Derringer, Blue, Wood Grips, Modern..................	25	50	50
Rolling Block, .357 Magnum, Remington Copy, Modern........................	100	150	150

RIFLE, LEVER ACTION

	V.G.	Exc	Prior Edition
1866 Yellowboy Carbine, Various Calibers, Brass Frame, Winchester Modern...	375	450	400
1866 Yellowboy Carbine, Various Calibers, Brass Frame, Winchester Engraved, Modern..	450	600	450
1873 Carbine, Various Calibers, Winchester Copy, Modern....................	375	450	450
1873 Rifle, Various Calibers, Winchester Copy, Modern........................	500	600	475
1873 Rifle, Various Calibers, Winchester Copy, Engraved, Modern...	450	650	550

EM–GE Gerstenberger & Eberwein, Gussenstadt, West Germany.

HANDGUN, REVOLVER

	V.G.	Exc	Prior Edition
Model 220 KS, .22 L.R.R.F., Double Action, Modern.............................	50	75	50
Model 223, .22 W.M.R., Double Action, Modern....................................	50	75	50
Target Model 200, .22 L.R.R.F., Double Action, Target Sights, Vent Rib, Modern..	75	100	75

EMPIRE Made by Jacob Rupertus 1858–1888.

HANDGUN, REVOLVER

	V.G.	Exc	Prior Edition
.22 Short R.F., 7 Shot, Spur Trigger, Solid Frame, Single Action, Antique...	100	175	175
.38 Short R.F., 5 Shot, Spur Trigger, Solid Frame, Single Action, Antique...	150	200	200
.41 Short R.F., 5 Shot, Spur Trigger, Solid Frame, Single Action, Antique...	175	225	225

	V.G.	Exc	Prior Edition

EMPIRE ARMS Made by Meriden, and distributed by H. & D. Folsom.

HANDGUN, REVOLVER

	V.G.	Exc	Prior Edition
.32 S & W, 5 Shot, Double Action, Top Break, Modern............................	$75	$125	$125
.38 S & W, 5 Shot, Double Action, Top Break, Modern............................	75	125	125

EMPIRE ARMS CO. Made by Crescent for Sears Roebuck & Co., c. 1900.

SHOTGUN, DOUBLE BARREL, SIDE-BY-SIDE

Various Gauges, Hammerless, Damascus Barrel, Modern......................	100	150	150
Various Gauges, Hammerless, Steel Barrel, Modern.............................	125	175	175
Various Gauges, Outside Hammers, Damascus Barrel, Modern.............	100	150	150
Various Gauges, Outside Hammers, Steel Barrel, Modern.....................	125	175	175

SHOTGUN, SINGLESHOT

Various Gauges, Hammer, Steel Barrel, Modern....................................	50	75	75

EMPIRE STATE Made by Meriden Firearms, and distributed by H & D Folsom.

HANDGUN, REVOLVER

.32 S & W, 5 Shot, Double Action, Top Break, Modern..........................	75	100	100
.38 S & W, 5 Shot, Double Action, Top Break, Modern..........................	75	100	100

EMPRESS Made by Jacob Rupertus 1858–1888.

HANDGUN, REVOLVER

.32 Short R.F., 5 Shot, Spur Trigger, Solid Frame, Single Action, Antique..	125	150	150

ENCORE Made by Johnson–Bye, also by Hopkins & Allen 1847–1887.

HANDGUN, REVOLVER

.22 Short R.F., 7 Shot, Spur Trigger, Solid Frame, Single Action, Antique..	100	150	150
.32 Short R.F., 5 Shot, Spur Trigger, Solid Frame, Single Action, Antique..	125	175	175
.38 R.F., 5 Shot, Spur Trigger, Solid Frame, Single Action, Antique..	150	200	200

ENDERS OAKLEAF Made by Crescent for Shapleigh Hardware Co., St. Louis, Mo.

SHOTGUN, DOUBLE BARREL, SIDE-BY-SIDE

Various Gauges, Hammerless, Damascus Barrel, Modern......................	100	150	150
Various Gauges, Hammerless, Steel Barrel, Modern.............................	125	175	175
Various Gauges, Outside Hammer, Steel Barrel, Modern......................	125	175	175

	V.G.	Exc	Prior Edition
Various Gauges, Outside Hammers, Damascus Barrel, Modern.............	$100	$150	$150

SHOTGUN, SINGLESHOT

	V.G.	Exc	Prior Edition
Various Gauges, Hammer, Steel Barrel, Modern.....................................	50	75	75

ENTERPRISE Made by Enterprise Gun Works, Pittsburgh, Pa., c. 1875.

HANDGUN, REVOLVER

	V.G.	Exc	Prior Edition
#1, .22 Short R.F., 7 Shot, Spur Trigger, Solid Frame, Single Action, Antique..........	125	175	175
#2, .32 Short R.F., 5 Shot, Spur Trigger, Solid Frame, Single Action, Antique..........	150	200	200
#3, .38 Short R.F., 5 Shot, Spur Trigger, Solid Frame, Single Action, Antique..........	175	225	225
#4, .41 Short R.F., 5 Shot, Spur Trigger, Solid Frame, Single Action, Antique..........	200	250	250

ERBI

SHOTGUN, DOUBLE BARREL, SIDE-BY-SIDE

	V.G.	Exc	Prior Edition
Deluxe Ejector Grade, 12 and 20 Gauge, Raised Matted Rib, Double Trigger, Checkered Stock, Beavertail Forend, Automatic Ejector, Modern....................	175	250	250
Field Grade, 12 and 20 Gauge, Raised Matted Rib, Double Trigger, Checkered Stock, Modern........................	150	200	200

ERIKA Francios Pfannl, Krems, Austria 1913–1926.

HANDGUN, SEMI-AUTOMATIC

	V.G.	Exc	Prior Edition
4.25mm, Clip Fed, Blue, Curio................................	450	650	650

ERMA Erfurter Maschinen u. Werkzeugfabrik, Erfurt, Germany prior to WWII, and after the war became Erma–Werke, Munich–Dachau, West Germany. Imported by Excam, Miami, Fla.

HANDGUN, REVOLVER

	V.G.	Exc	Prior Edition
Model 440, .38 Spec., Double Action, Swing–Out Cylinder, Stainless, Modern............................	175	225	225
Model 442, .22 L.R.R.F., Double Action, Swing–Out Cylinder, Blue, Modern............................	125	175	175
Model 443, .22 W.M.R., Double Action, Swing–Out Cylinder, Blue, Modern............................	125	175	175

HANDGUN, SEMI-AUTOMATIC

	V.G.	Exc	Prior Edition
EP–22, .22 L.R.R.F., Clip Fed, Modern.............................	150	275	275
EP–25, .25 ACP, Clip Fed, Modern.............................	175	250	250
ET–22 Luger, .22 L.R.R.F., Clip Fed, Modern.....................	275	350	350
ET–22 Luger, .22 L.R.R.F., Clip Fed, With Conversion Kit, Cased with Accessories, Modern.....................	350	425	425
FB–1, .25 ACP, Clip Fed, Modern.............................	75	125	125
KGP–68 (Baby), .32 ACP, Clip Fed, Modern.......................	250	325	325

	V.G.	Exc	Prior Edition
KGP–68 (Baby), .380 ACP, Clip Fed, Modern	$275	$350	$350
KGP–69, .22 L.R.R.F., Clip Fed, Modern	275	350	350
LA–22 PO 8, .22 L.R.R.F., Clip Fed, Modern	200	275	275
New Model Target, .22 L.R.R.F., Clip Fed, Modern	250	275	275
Old Model Target, .22 L.R.R.F., Clip Fed, Modern	225	250	250
RX–22, .22 L.R.R.F., Double Action, Clip Fed, Modern	175	200	200

RIFLE, BOLT ACTION

	V.G.	Exc	Prior Edition
EG–61, .22 L.R.R.F., Singleshot, Open Sights, Modern	75	100	100
M1957 KK, .22 L.R.R.F., Military Style Training Rifle, Modern	75	100	100
M98 Conversation Unit, .22 L.R.R.F., Clip Fed, Cased, Modern	250	325	325
Master Target, .22 L.R.R.F., Checkered Stock, Peep Sights, Modern	125	175	175

RIFLE, LEVER ACTION

	V.G.	Exc	Prior Edition
EG–71, .22 L.R.R.F., Tube Feed, Modern	100	150	150
EG–712, .22 L.R.R.F., Tube Feed, Modern	125	175	175
EG–712 L, .22 L.R.R.F., Tube Feed, Octagon Barrel, Nickel Silver Receiver, Modern	200	275	275
EG–73, .22 W.M.R., Tube Feed, Modern	150	200	200

RIFLE, SEMI-AUTOMATIC

	V.G.	Exc	Prior Edition
EGM–1, .22 L.R.R.F., Clip Fed, Modern	125	150	150
EM–1, .22 L.R.R.F., Clip Fed, Modern	125	150	150
ESG22, .22 L.R.R.F., Clip Fed, Modern	125	150	150
ESG22, .22 W.M.R., Clip Fed, Modern	175	250	250

ESSEX Made by Crescent for Belknap Hardware Co. Louisville, Ky.

SHOTGUN, DOUBLE BARREL, SIDE-BY-SIDE

	V.G.	Exc	Prior Edition
Various Gauges, Hammerless, Damascus Barrel, Modern	100	150	150
Various Gauges, Hammerless, Steel Barrel, Modern	125	175	175
Various Gauges, Outside Hammers, Damascus Barrel, Modern	100	150	150
Various Gauges, Outside Hammers, Steel Barrel, Modern	125	175	175

SHOTGUN, SINGLESHOT

	V.G.	Exc	Prior Edition
Various Gauges, Outside Hammers, Steel Barrel, Modern	50	75	75

ESSEX Made by Stevens Arms.

RIFLE, BOLT ACTION

	V.G.	Exc	Prior Edition
Model 50, .22 L.R.R.F., Singleshot, Takedown, Modern	25	50	50
Model 53, .22 L.R.R.F., Singleshot, Takedown, Modern	25	50	50
Model 56 Buckhorn, .22 L.R.R.F., 5 Shot Clip, Open Rear Sights, Modern	25	50	50

SHOTGUN, DOUBLE BARREL, SIDE-BY-SIDE

	V.G.	Exc	Prior Edition
Model 515, Various Gauges, Hammerless, Modern	100	150	150

ESSEX Makers of pistol frames in Island Pond, Vt.

HANDGUN, SEMI-AUTOMATIC

	V.G.	Exc	Prior Edition
Colt M1911 Copy, .45 ACP, Parts Gun, Modern	200	275	275

	V.G.	Exc	Prior Edition

ESTEVA, PEDRO Spain, c. 1740.

HANDGUN, FLINTLOCK

Pair, Belt Pistol, Silver Inlay, Silver Furniture, Engraved, Half-Octagon Barrel, Antique.. $7,500 $9,000 $9,000

EVANS RIFLE MFG. CO. Mechanic Falls, Maine 1868–1880.

RIFLE, LEVER ACTION

New Model, .44 C.F., Tube Feed, Dust Cover, Carbine, Antique............ 750 900 900
New Model, .44 C.F., Tube Feed, Dust Cover, Military Musket, Antique... 1,000 1,250 1,100
New Model, .44 C.F., Tube Feed, Dust Cover, Sporting Rifle, Antique... 650 750 600
Old Model, .44 C.F., Upper Buttstock Only, Tube Feed, Sporting Rifle, Antique.. 1,000 1,250 1,100

EVANS, STEPHEN Valley Forge, Pa. 1742–1797. See Kentucky Rifles and U. S. Military.

EVANS, WILLIAMS London, England 1883–1900.

SHOTGUN, DOUBLE BARREL, SIDE-BY-SIDE

Pair, 12 Gauge, Double Trigger, Plain, Cased, Modern........................... 5,000 6,000 6,000
Pair, 12 Gauge, Double Trigger, Straight Grip, Cased, Modern............... 6,000 7,000 7,000

EXCAM Importers, Hialeah, Fla. Also see Erma and Tanarmi.

HANDGUN, DOUBLE BARREL, OVER-UNDER

TA–38, .38 Special, 2 Shot, Derringer, Modern....................................... 75 85 75

HANDGUN, REVOLVER

Buffalo Scout TA–22, .22 L.R.R.F., Western Style, Single Action, Brass Backstrap, Modern... 65 75 50
Buffalo Scout TA–22, .22 LR/.22 WMR Combo, Western Style, Single Action, Brass Backstrap, Modern..................................... 85 100 75
Buffalo Scout TA–22, .22 LR/.22 WMR Combo, Western Style, Single Action, Brass Backstrap, Target Sights, Modern........................... 80 100 75
Buffalo Scout TA–76, .22 L.R.R.F., Western Style, Single Action, Modern.. 70 85 75
Buffalo Scout TA–76, .22 LR/.22 WMR Combo, Western Style, Single Action, Modern... 70 85 75
Warrior, .22 L.R.R.F., Double Action, Blue, Vent Rib, Modern............ 50 75 75
Warrior, .22 LR/.22 WMR Combo, Double Action, Blue, Vent Rib, Modern.. 100 125 125
Warrior, .357 Magnum, Double Action, Blue, Vent Rib, Target Sights, Modern.. 100 150 150
Warrior, .38 Spec., Double Action, Blue, Vent Rib, Target Sights, Modern.. 75 100 100

	V.G.	Exc	Prior Edition

HANDGUN, SEMI-AUTOMATIC

	V.G.	Exc	Prior Edition
GT–22, .22 L.R.R.F., Clip Fed, Modern	$75	$150	$150
GT–26, .25 ACP, Clip Fed, Steel Frame, Modern	25	50	50
GT–27, .25 ACP, Clip Fed, Modern	25	50	50
GT–27, .25 ACP, Clip Fed, Steel Frame, Modern	50	75	75
GT–32, .32 ACP, Clip Fed, Modern	125	150	150
GT–32, .32 ACP, Clip Fed, 12 Shot, Modern	125	150	150
GT–380, .25 ACP, Clip Fed, Engraved, Modern	125	150	150
GT–380, .380 ACP, Clip Fed, Modern	100	125	125
GT–380, .380 ACP, Clip Fed, 11 Short, Modern	125	150	150
RX–22, .22 L.R.R.F., Clip Fed, Modern	100	125	125

EXCELSIOR Made by Norwich Pistol Co., c. 1880.

HANDGUN, REVOLVER

	V.G.	Exc	Prior Edition
.32 Short R.F., 5 Shot, Spur Trigger, Solid Frame, Single Action, Antique	125	175	175

EXCELSIOR Made in Italy.

SHOTGUN, DOUBLE BARREL, SIDE-BY-SIDE

	V.G.	Exc	Prior Edition
Super 88, 12 Ga. Mag 3", Boxlock, Checkered Stock, Modern	275	350	350

EXPRESS Made by Bacon Arms Co., c. 1880.

HANDGUN, REVOLVER

	V.G.	Exc	Prior Edition
.22 Short R.F., 7 Shot, Spur Trigger, Solid Frame, Single Action, Antique	125	175	175

EXPRESS Tomas de Urizar y Cia., Eibar, Spain, c. 1905–1921

HANDGUN, SEMI-AUTOMATIC

	V.G.	Exc	Prior Edition
Type 1, .25 ACP, Clip Fed, Fixed Ribbed Barrel, Curio	200	250	250
Type 1, .32 ACP, Clip Fed, 4" Fixed Barrel, Curio	175	225	225
Type 2, .25 ACP, Clip Fed, Hammerless, Eibar Style, Curio	100	125	125
Type 2, .32 ACP, Clip Fed, Hammerless, Eibar Style, Curio	100	150	150
Type 3, .25 ACP, Clip Fed, Hammer, Eibar Style, Curio	100	150	150
Type 3, .32 ACP, Clip Fed, Hammer, Eibar Style, Curio	100	150	150

F

	V.G.	Exc.	Prior Edition

F.I.E. Firearms Import & Export Corp., Miami, Fla.

HANDGUN, DOUBLE BARREL, OVER-UNDER

	V.G.	Exc.	Prior Edition
D 38, .38 Special, Derringer, Modern	$50	$65	$50
D 86, .38 Special, Derringer, Modern	70	85	75

HANDGUN, FLINTLOCK

	V.G.	Exc.	Prior Edition
Kentucky, .44, Belt Pistol, Engraved, Reproduction	25	50	50
Kentucky, .44, Belt Pistol, Reproduction	25	50	50
Tower, .69	25	25	25

HANDGUN, PERCUSSION

	V.G.	Exc.	Prior Edition
Baby Dragoon, .31, Revolver, Engraved, Reproduction	25	50	50
Baby Dragoon, .31, Revolver, Reproduction	25	50	50
Kentucky, .44, Belt Pistol, Engraved, Reproduction	25	50	50
Kentucky, .44, Belt Pistol, Reproduction	25	50	50
Navy, .36, Revolver, Engraved, Reproduction	25	50	50
Navy, .36, Revolver, Reproduction	25	25	25
Navy, .44, Revolver, Engraved, Reproduction	25	50	50
Navy, .44, Revolver, Reproduction	25	50	50
Remington, .36, Revolver, Engraved, Reproduction	25	50	50
Remington, .36, Revolver, Reproduction	25	50	50
Remington, .44, Revolver, Engraved, Reproduction	25	50	50
Remington, .44, Revolver, Reproduction	25	50	50

HANDGUN, REVOLVER

	V.G.	Exc.	Prior Edition
Arminius, .22 L.R.R.F., Double Action, Swing–out Cylinder, Fixed Sights, Chrome, Modern	75	100	75
Arminius, .22 L.R.R.F., Double Action, Swing–out Cylinder, Adjustable Sights, Blue, Modern	50	75	70
Arminius, .22 L.R.R.F., Double Action, Swing–out Cylinder, Adjustable Sights, Chrome, Modern	75	100	100
Arminius, .22 L.R.R.F., Double Action, Swing–out Cylinder, Adjustable Sights, Blue, Target, Modern	75	100	100
Arminius, .22 L.R.R.F., Double Action, Swing–out Cylinder, Adjustable Sights, Chrome, Target, Modern	75	100	100
Arminius, .22 LR/.22 WMR Combo, Double Action, Swing–out Cylinder, Fixed Sights, Chrome, Modern	75	100	100
Arminius, .22 LR/.22 WMR Combo, Double Action, Swing–out Cylinder, Adjustable Sights, Chrome, Modern	75	100	100
Arminius, .22 LR/.22 WMR Combo, Double Action, Swing–out Cylinder, Adjustable Sights, Blue, Modern	75	100	100

	V.G.	Exc	Prior Edition
Arminius, .22 LR/.22 WMR Combo, Double Action, Swing–out Cylinder, Adjustable Sights, Blue, Target, Modern...................................	$50	$75	$75
Arminius, .32 S & W, Double Action, Swing–out Cylinder, Adjustable Sights, Blue, Target, Modern...............................	75	100	100
Arminius, .32 S & W, Double Action, Swing–out Cylinder, Adjustable Sights, Chrome, Target, Modern............................	75	100	100
Arminius, .357 Magnum, Double Action, Swing–out Cylinder, Adjustable Sights, Chrome, Target, Modern............................	100	125	125
Arminius, .357 Magnum, Double Action, Swing–out Cylinder, Adjustable Sights, Blue, Target, Modern...............................	100	125	125
Arminius, .38 Special, Double Action, Swing–out Cylinder, Adjustable Sights, Blue, Target, Modern...............................	75	100	100
Arminius, .38 Special, Double Action, Swing–out Cylinder, Adjustable Sights, Chrome, Target, Modern............................	75	100	100
Arminius, .38 Special, Double Action, Swing–out Cylinder, Blue, Modern...	50	75	75
Arminius, .38 Special, Double Action, Swing–out Cylinder, Chrome, Modern...	50	75	75
Buffalo Scout, .22LR/.22 WMR Combo, Single Action, Western Style, Modern...	65	75	50
Buffalo, .22 L.R.R.F., Single Action, Western Style,., Modern...............	25	50	50
Guardian, .22 L.R.R.F., Double Action, Swing–out Cylinder, Modern...	25	50	50
Guardian, .22 L.R.R.F., Double Action, Swing–out Cylinder, Chrome, Modern...	25	50	50
Guardian, .32 S & W, Double Action, Swing–out Cylinder, Modern...	25	50	50
Guardian, .32 S & W, Double Action, Swing–out Cylinder, Chrome, Modern...	25	50	50
Hombre, .357 Magnum, Single Action, Western Style, Steel Frame, Modern..	150	200	125
Hombre, .44 Mag, Single Action, Western Style, Steel Frame, Modern..	150	200	150
Hombre, .45 L.C., Single Action, Western Style, Steel Frame, Modern..	150	200	125
Legend, .22 L.R.R.F., Single Action, Western Style, Steel Frame, Modern..	85	100	75
Legend, .22LR/.22 WMR Combo, Single Action, Western Style, Steel Frame, Modern..	85	100	75
Texas Ranger, .22LR/.22 WMR Combo, Single Action, Western Style, Steel Frame, Modern...	65	75	50

HANDGUN, SEMI-AUTOMATIC

	V.G.	Exc	Prior Edition
Best, .25 ACP, Hammer, Steel Frame, Blue, Modern.............................	75	100	100
Guardian, .25 ACP, Hammer, Blue, Modern....................................	25	50	50
Guardian, .25 ACP, Hammer, Chrome, Modern................................	25	50	50
Guardian, .25 ACP, Hammer, Gold Plated, Modern............................	25	50	50
Interdynamics KG–9, 9mm Luger, Clip Fed, Modern............................	325	350	350
Interdynamics Mini–99, 9mm Luger, Clip Fed, Modern........................	200	225	225
Super Titan II, .32 ACP, Hammer, Steel Frame, Blue, 13 Shot, Modern..	100	125	125
Super Titan II, .380 ACP, Hammer, Steel Frame, Blue, 12 Shot, Modern..	125	150	150
Titan, .25 ACP, Hammer, Blue, Modern..	25	50	50
Titan, .25 ACP, Hammer, Chrome, Modern......................................	25	50	50

	V.G.	Exc	Prior Edition
Titan, .32 ACP, Hammer, Steel Frame, Blue, Modern	$75	$100	$100
Titan, .32 ACP, Hammer, Steel Frame, Chrome, Modern	75	100	100
Titan, .32 ACP, Hammer, Steel Frame, Engraved, Blue, Modern	75	100	100
Titan, .32 ACP, Hammer, Steel Frame, Engraved, Chrome, Modern	75	100	100
Titan, .380 ACP, Hammer, Steel Frame, Blue, Modern	75	100	100
Titan, .380 ACP, Hammer, Steel Frame, Chrome, Modern	100	125	125
Titan, .380 ACP, Hammer, Steel Frame, Engraved, Blue, Modern	125	150	150
Titan, .380 ACP, Hammer, Steel Frame, Engraved, Chrome, Modern	125	150	150
TZ–75, 9mm. Luger, Clip Fed, Double Action, Hammer, Adjustable Sights, Wood Grips, Modern	225	250	250

RIFLE, FLINTLOCK

	V.G.	Exc	Prior Edition
Kentucky, .45, Engraved, Reproduction	50	75	75
Kentucky, .45, Reproduction	50	75	75

RIFLE, PERCUSSION

	V.G.	Exc	Prior Edition
Berdan, .45, Reproduction	50	75	75
Kentucky, .45, Engraved, Reproduction, Antique	50	75	75
Kentucky, .45, Reproduction, Antique	50	75	75
Zoave, .58, Reproduction, Antique	75	100	100

COMBINATION WEAPON, OVER-UNDER

	V.G.	Exc	Prior Edition
Combo, 30/30–20 Ga., Modern	75	100	100

SHOTGUN, DOUBLE BARREL, OVER-UNDER

	V.G.	Exc	Prior Edition
OU, 12 and 20 Ga., Field Grade, Vent Rib, Modern	150	175	175
OU 12 T, 12 Ga., Trap Grade, Vent Rib, Modern	150	175	175
OU–S, 12 and 20 Ga., Skeet Grade, Vent Rib, Modern	150	175	175

SHOTGUN, DOUBLE BARREL, SIDE-BY-SIDE

	V.G.	Exc	Prior Edition
Brute, Various Gauges, Short Barrels, Short Stock, Modern	100	175	175
DB, Various Gauges, Hammerless, Modern	75	125	125
DB Riot, Various Gauges, Hammerless, Modern	75	150	150

SHOTGUN, SINGLESHOT

	V.G.	Exc	Prior Edition
S.O.B., 12 and 20 Gauges, Short Barrel, Short Stock, Modern	25	50	50
SB 12 16 20 .410, Various Gauges, Hammer, Modern	25	50	50
SB 40, 12 Ga., Hammer, Button Break, Modern	25	50	50
SB 41, 20 Ga., Hammer, Button Break, Modern	25	50	50
SB 42, .410 Ga., Hammer, Button Break, Modern	25	50	50
SB Youth, Various Gauges, Hammer, Modern	25	50	50

FABRIQUE D'ARMES DE GUERRE Spain, c. 1900.

HANDGUN, SEMI-AUTOMATIC

	V.G.	Exc	Prior Edition
Paramount, .25 ACP, Clip Fed, Modern	125	150	150

	V.G.	Exc	Prior Edition

FABRIQUE D'ARMES DE GUERRE DE GRAND PRECISION Tradename used by Etxezagarra & Abitua, Eibar, Spain, c. 1920.

HANDGUN, SEMI-AUTOMATIC

	V.G.	Exc	Prior Edition
Bulwak, .25 ACP, Clip Fed, Modern	$125	$150	$150
Colonial, .25 ACP, Clip Fed, Modern	150	175	175
Colonial, .32 ACP, Clip Fed, Modern	175	200	200
Helvece, .25 ACP, Clip Fed, Modern	125	150	150
Jupiter, .32 ACP, Clip Fed, Modern	125	150	150
Libia, .32 ACP, Clip Fed, Modern	150	175	175
Looking Glass, .32 ACP, Clip Fed, Modern	150	175	175
Looking Glass, .32 ACP, Clip Fed, Grip Safety, Modern	175	200	200
trust, .25 ACP, Clip Fed, Modern	125	150	150

FABRIQUE NATIONALE Herstal, Belgium from 1889. Also see Browning and Belgian Military.

RIFLE, BOLT ACTION

	V.G.	Exc	Prior Edition
Mauser 98 Military Style, 30/06, Military Finish, Military Stock, Commercial, Modern	200	250	250
Mauser 98 Military Style, Various Military Calibers, Military Finish, Military Stock, Commercial, Modern	125	150	150
Mauser Deluxe Presentation, Various Calibers, Sporting Rifle, Fancy Wood, Engraved, Modern	850	1,000	850
Mauser Deluxe, Various Calibers, Sporting Rifle, Checkered Stock, Engraved, Modern	525	600	450
Mauser Supreme, Various Calibers, Sporting Rifle, Checkered Stock, Modern	500	575	525
Mauser Supreme, Various Calibers, Sporting Rifle, Checkered Stock, Magnum, Modern	575	650	500
Model 1925 Deluxe, .22 L.R.R.F., Singleshot, Checkered Stock, Modern	75	100	100
Model 1925, .22 L.R.R.F., Singleshot, Modern	50	75	75

RIFLE, SEMI-AUTOMATIC

	V.G.	Exc	Prior Edition
FN FAL, .308 Win., Clip Fed, Commercial, Modern	750	950	950
FN LAR Competition, .308 Win., Clip Fed, Commercial, Flash Hider, Modern	1,400	1,650	1,600
FN LAR Heavy Barrel, .308 Win., Clip Fed, Commercial, Synthetic Stock, Bipod, Modern	1,650	1,850	1,850
FN LAR Heavy Barrel, .308 Win., Clip Fed, Commercial, Wood Stock, Bipod, Modern	1,750	2,000	1,950
FN LAR Paratrooper, .308 Win., Clip Fed, Commercial, Folding Stock, Modern	800	950	850
FNC Competition, .223 Rem., Clip Fed, Commercial, Flash Hider, Modern	850	1,000	825
FNC Paratrooper, .223 Rem., Clip Fed, Commercial, Folding Stock, Modern	1,000	1,150	925
M–49 Egyptian, 8mm Mauser, Clip Fed, Military, Modern	275	325	325
Model 1949, 30/06, Clip Fed, Military, Modern	350	400	400

	V.G.	Exc	Prior Edition
Model 1949, 7mm or 9mm Mauser, Clip Fed, Military, Modern..............	$275	$325	$300

SHOTGUN, BOLT ACTION
9mm Shotshell, Modern..	125	150	150

FALCON FIREARMS Northridge, Ca.

HANDGUN, SEMI-AUTOMATIC
Portsider, .45 ACP, Clip Fed, Stainless Steel, Modern............................	400	475	75

FAMARS Brescia, Italy.

SHOTGUN, DOUBLE BARREL, SIDE-BY-SIDE
Hammer Gun, Various Gauges, Automatic Ejector, Fancy Wood, Fancy Engraving, Double Trigger, Modern...	7,000	7,750	7,500
Sidelock Gun, Various Gauges, Automatic Ejector, Double Trigger, Fancy Engraving, Fancy Wood, Modern..	9,000	10,500	10,000

FARNOT, FRANK Lancaster, Pa. 1779–1783. See Kentucky Rifles and Pistols.

FARNOT, FREDERICK Lancaster, Pa. 1779–1782. See Kentucky Rifles and Pistols.

FARROW ARMS CO. Holyoke, Mass. Established by William Farrow 1878–1885. Became Farrow Arms Co. About 1885 and moved to Mason, Tenn. in 1904, then to Washington, D.C. in 1904 and remained in business until 1917.

RIFLE, SINGLESHOT
#1, .30 Long R.F., Target Rifle, Octagon Barrel, Target Sights, Fancy Wood, Antique..	4,000	4,500	3,500
#2, .30 Long R.F., Target Rifle, Octagon Barrel, Target Sights, Antique...	3,000	3,500	2,500

FAST Echave, Arizmendi y Cia, Eibar, Spain.

HANDGUN, SEMI-AUTOMATIC
Model 221, .22 L.R.R.F., Clip Fed, Blue, Modern...................................	95	150	150
Model 221, .22 L.R.R.F., Clip Fed, Chrome, Modern.............................	150	175	175
Model 631, .25 ACP, Clip Fed, Blue, Modern...	125	150	150
Model 631, .25 ACP, Clip Fed, Chrome, Modern....................................	125	150	150
Model 761, ..32 ACP, Clip Fed, Blue, Modern...	150	175	175
Model 761, .32 ACP, Clip Fed, Chrome, Modern....................................	150	175	175
Model 901, ..380 ACP, Clip Fed, Blue, Modern.......................................	150	175	175
Model 901, .380 ACP, Clip Fed, Chrome, Modern...................................	150	175	175

	V.G.	Exc	Prior Edition

FAULTLESS GOOSE GUN Made by Crescent for John M.
Smythe Hdw. Co., Chicago, Ill.

SHOTGUN, DOUBLE BARREL, SIDE-BY-SIDE

	V.G.	Exc	Prior Edition
Various Gauges, Hammerless, Damascus Barrel, Modern	$125	$175	$175
Various Gauges, Hammerless, Steel Barrel, Modern	150	200	200
Various Gauges, Outside Hammers, Damascus Barrel, Modern	125	175	175
Various Gauges, Outside Hammers, Steel Barrel, Modern	150	200	200

SHOTGUN, SINGLESHOT

Various Gauges, Hammer, Steel Barrel, Modern	75	100	100

FAVORITE Made by Johnson–Bye Co., c. 1874–1884.

HANDGUN, REVOLVER

#1, .22 Short R.F., 7 Shot, Spur Trigger, Solid Frame, Single Action, Antique	125	175	175
#2, .32 Short R.F., 5 Shot, Spur Trigger, Solid Frame, Single Action, Antique	125	175	175
#3, .38 Short R.F., 5 Shot, Spur Trigger, Solid Frame, Single Action, Antique	150	200	200
#4, .41 Short R.F., 5 Shot, Spur Trigger, Solid Frame, Single Action, Antique	175	225	225

FAVORITE NAVY Made by Johnson–Bye Co., c. 1874–1884.

HANDGUN, REVOLVER

.44 Short R.F., 5 Shot, Spur Trigger, Solid Frame, Single Action, Antique	250	300	300

FAY, HENRY C. Lancaster, Mass., c. 1837.

RIFLE, PERCUSSION

.58, Military, Antique	2,750	3,500	3,500

FECHT, G. VAN DER Berlin, Germany, c. 1733.

RIFLE, FLINTLOCK

Yaeger, Half–Octagon Barrel, Brass Furniture, Engraved, Carved, Antique	4,500	5,000	5,000

FEDERAL ARMS Made by Meriden Firearms, sold by Sears–Roebuck.

HANDGUN, REVOLVER

.32 S & W, 5 Shot, Double Action, Top Break, Modern	75	100	100
.38 S & W, 5 Shot, Double Action, Top Break, Modern	75	100	100

FEMARU Made by Femaru Fegyver es Gepgyar (Fegyvergyar) Pre–War;
Post War Made by Femaru es Szerszamgepgyar, N.V., Budapest, Hungary.
Also see Frommer, Hungarian Military.

HANDGUN, SEMI-AUTOMATIC

	V.G.	Exc	Prior Edition
M 29, .380 ACP, Clip Fed, Military, Curio	$175	$225	$225
M 37, .32 ACP, Clip Fed, Nazi–Proofed, Modern	200	250	250
M 37, .380 ACP, Clip Fed, Military, Modern	200	250	250
M 37, .380 ACP, Clip Fed, Nazi–Proofed, Modern	225	275	275

FENNO Lancaster Pa. 1790–1800. See Kentucky Rifles and Pistols.

FERLACH Genossenschaft der Buchsenmachermeister, Ferlach, Austria.

RIFLE, DOUBLE BARREL, SIDE-BY-SIDE

	V.G.	Exc	Prior Edition
Standard Grade, Various Calibers, Boxlock, Engraved, Checkered Stock, Fancy Wood, Modern	3,000	3,500	3,500
Standard Grade, Various Calibers, Sidelock, Engraved, Checkered Stock, Fancy Wood, Modern	4,500	5,000	5,000

FERREE, JACOB Lancaster, Pa. 1774–1784, see Kentucky Rifles and U.S. Military.

FESIG, CONRAD Reading, Pa. 1779–1790, see Kentucky Rifles and Pistols.

FIALA Made for Fiala Arms & Equipment Co. by Blakslee Forging Co., New Haven, Conn.

HANDGUN, MANUAL REPEATER

	V.G.	Exc	Prior Edition
.22 L.R.R.F., Clip Fed, Target Pistol, Curio	400	450	400
.22 L.R.R.F., Clip Fed, Target Pistol, With Shoulder Stock, 20" Barrel, 3" Barrel, Cased, Curio	1,000	1,150	1,000

FIEHL & WEEKS FIRE ARMS MFG. CO. Philadelphia, Pa., c. 1895.

HANDGUN, REVOLVER

	V.G.	Exc	Prior Edition
.32 S & W, 5 Shot, Top Break, Hammerless, Double Action, Modern	75	100	100

FIEL Erquiaga, Muguruzu y Cia., Eibar, Spain, c., 1920.

HANDGUN, SEMI-AUTOMATIC

	V.G.	Exc	Prior Edition
Fiel #1, .25 ACP, Clip Fed, Eibar Style, Curio	125	150	150

	V.G.	Exc	Prior Edition
Fiel #1, .32 ACP, Clip Fed, Eibar Style, Curio..	$125	$150	$150
Fiel #2, .25 ACP, Clip Fed, Breech Bolt, Curio...	175	225	225

FIGTHORN, ANDREW Reading, Pa. 1779–1790, see Kentucky Rifles.

FINNISH LION Made by Valmet, Jyvaskyla, Finland.

RIFLE, BOLT ACTION

Champion, .22 L.R.R.F., Singleshot, Free Rifle, Thumbhole Stock, Target Sights, Heavy Barrel, Modern..	450	500	500
Match, .22 L.R.R.F., Singleshot, Target Rifle, Thumbhole Stock, Target Sights, Modern...	350	400	400
Standard, .22 L.R.R.F., Singleshot, Target Rifle, Target Stock, Target Sights, U.I.T. Rifle, Modern...	225	275	275

FIRARMS SPECIALTIES Owosso, Mich., c. 1972.

HANDGUN, REVOLVER

.45/70 Custom Revolver, Brass Frame, Single Action, Western Style, Modern...	500	550	550

FIREARMS CO. LTD. Made in England for Mandall Shooting Supplies.

RIFLE, BOLT ACTION

Alpine Custom, Various Calibers, Checkered Stock, Recoil Pad, Open Rear Sight, Modern..	275	325	325
Alpine Standard, Various Calibers, Checkered Stock, Recoil Pad, Open Rear Sight, Modern..	250	300	300

FIREARMS, CUSTOM MADE This category covers some of the myriad special firearms that are built to an individual's specifications by a competent gunsmith, and not by the original factory. Most firearms in this class will appeal only to a person who happens to want the same special features, and because of this many of these guns will sell for less than the cost of the conversion.

HANDGUN, PERCUSSION

Target Revolver, Various Calibers, Tuned, Target Sights, Reproduction	—	250	—

HANDGUN, REVOLVER

"F.B.L." Conversion, .38 Special, Cut Trigger Guard, Spurless Hammer, Short Barrel, Modern...	—	400	—
P.P.C. Conversion, .38 Special, Heavy Barrel, Rib with Target Sights, Target Trigger, Target Grips, Modern...	—	500	—
Recoil Compensation Devices or Ports, Add $25.00–$45.00			

	V.G.	Exc	Prior Edition

HANDGUN, SEMI-AUTOMATIC

M1911A1, Combat Conversion, Extended Trigger Guard, Ambidextrous Safety, Special Slide Release, Ported, Combat Sights, Modern....................... — $550 —
M1911A1, Double Action Conversion, Add $95.00–$175.00
M1911A1, I.P.S.C. Conversion, Extended Trigger Guard, Ambidextrous Safety, Special Slide Release, Ported, Target Sights, Extended Grip Safety, Modern...................... — 650 —

HANDGUN, SINGLESHOT

Silhouette Pistol, Various Calibers, Bolt Action, Thumbhole Stock, Target Sights, Target Trigger, Modern...................... — 500 —

RIFLE, BOLT ACTION

Sporting Rifle, Various Calibers, Checkered Stock, Recoil Pad, Simple Military Conversion, Modern..................... — 225 —
Sporting Rifle, Various Calibers, Fancy Stock, High Quality Commercial Parts, Fancy Checkering, Stock Inlays, Modern.................. — 1,250 —
Sporting Rifle, Various Calibers, Fancy Stock, High Quality Commercial Parts, Fancy Checkering, Stock Inlays, Engraved, Modern..................... — 2,000 —
Sporting Rifle, Various Calibers, Fancy Stock, High Quality Commercial Parts, Fancy Checkering, Stock Inlays, Engraved, Gold Inlays, Modern..................... — 3,500 —
Sporting Rifle, Various Calibers, Fancy Wood, Recoil Pad, Fancy Military Conversion, Modern..................... — 600 —
Sporting Rifle, Various Calibers, Mauser 1871 Action, Checkered Stock, Antique..................... — 450 —
Sporting Rifle, Various Calibers, Plain Stock, Commercial Parts, Modern..................... — 350 —

RIFLE, SINGLESHOT

Target Rifle, Centerfire Calibers, Fancy, Target Sights, Built on Various Moving Block Actions, Modern..................... — 650 —
Target Rifle, Centerfire Calibers, Plain, Target Sights, Built on Various Bolt Actions, Modern..................... — 575 —
Target Rifle, Centerfire Calibers, Plain, Target Sights, Built on Various Moving Block Actions, Modern..................... — 400 —
Target Rifle, Rimfire Calibers, Plain, Target Sights, Built on Various Moving Block Actions, Modern..................... — 400 —

SHOTGUN, DOUBLE BARREL, OVER-UNDER

Trap Conversion, 12 Ga., Recoil Reducer in Stock, Release Triggers, Throated Chambers, Trap Pad, Add $275.00–$400.00

SHOTGUN, SLIDE ACTION

Combat Conversion, 12 Ga., Short Barrel, Extended Magazine Tube, Folding Stock, Rifle Sights, Modern..................... — 350 —
Competition Conversion, Various Gauges, High Rib, Recoil Reducer in Stock, Fancy Wood, Modern..................... — 525 —

	V.G.	Exc	Prior Edition

FIREARMS INTERNATIONAL Washington, D.D.

HANDGUN, REVOLVER

	V.G.	Exc	Prior Edition
Regent, .22 L.R.R.F., 7 Shot, Various Barrel Lengths, Blue, Modern	$75	$100	$100
Regent, .22 L.R.R.F., 8 Shot, Various Barrel Lengths, Blue, Modern	75	100	100

HANDGUN, SEMI-AUTOMATIC

Combo, .22 L.R.R.F., Unique Model L Pistol with Conversion Kit for Stocked Rifle, Modern	125	150	150
Model D, .380 ACP., Clip Fed, Adjustable Sights, Blue, Modern	125	175	175
Model D, .380 ACP., Clip Fed, Adjustable Sights, Chrome, Modern	150	175	175
Model D, .380 ACP., Clip Fed, Adjustable Sights, Matt Blue, Modern	125	175	175

SHOTGUN, DOUBLE BARREL, SIDE-BY-SIDE

Model 400, Various Gauges, Single Trigger, Checkered Stock, Modern.	175	225	225
Model 400E, Various Gauges, Single Selective Trigger, Checkered Stock, Selective Ejector, Vent Rib, Modern	225	275	275
Model 400E, Various Gauges, Single Selective Trigger, Selective Ejector, Modern	200	250	250

FIREBIRD Made by Femaru for German exporter for U.S. Sales.

HANDGUN, SEMI-AUTOMATIC

Tokagypt Type, 9mm Luger, Clip Fed, Blue, Modern	400	600	600

FITCH & WALDO New York City, c. 1862–67. Made by Bacon Mfg. Co., Norwich, Conn.

HANDGUN, REVOLVER

Pocket Model, .31, 5 Shot, Antique	400	475	275

Fitch & Waldo Pocker Revolver, .31 Caliber

	V.G.	Exc	Prior Edition

FLINTLOCK Examples.

HANDGUN, FLINTLOCK

	V.G.	Exc	Prior Edition
.28, English, Pocket Pistol, Queen Anne Style, Box Lock, Screw Barrel, Plain, Antique......................	$475	$575	$550
.40, Herdsman Pistol, Long Tapered Round Barrel, Silver Furniture, Antique......................	200	250	650
.45, French, Mid–1700's, Screw Barrel, Long Cannon Barrel, Silver Furniture	1,500	1,750	1,500
.60, Continental, Early 1700's, Holster Pistol, Half–Octagon Bar Engraved, High Quality	2,500	2,750	2,500
.60, Oval Bore, Box Lock, Pocket Pistol, Steel Furniture	750	1,000	950
.62, Crantham English, Holster Pistol, Brass Furniture, Plain	650	750	650
.63, Spanish, Mid–1600's, Holster Pistol, Silver Inlay, Engraved	4,000	4,250	4,500
.65, Arabian, Holster Pistol, Flared, Round Barrel, Low Quality	200	250	400
.68, Tower, Continental, Plain	350	400	400
English Lock, mid–1600's, Military, Holster Pistol, Iron Mounts, Plain	3,000	3,500	3,000
English, Early 1700's, Pocket Pistol, Box Lock, Double Barrel, Screw Barrel, Low Quality	600	650	700
English, Early 1700's, Pocket Pistol, Queen Anne Style, Box Lock, Screw Barrel, All Metal	800	850	750
English, Mid–1600's, Button Trigger, Brass Barrel, Octagon Fishtail Butt	2,500	3,000	3,000
French Officer's Type, c. 1650, Steel Furniture, Rifled	2,750	2,500	2,500
French Sedan Mid–1600's, Long Screw Barrel, Rifled, Plain	3,250	3,000	3,000

RIFLE, FLINTLOCK

	V.G.	Exc	Prior Edition
.64, Continental, Carbine, Musket, Brass Furniture,	600	675	650
.72, Continental, 1650, Musket, Brass Furniture, Plain	1,200	1,250	1,200

SHOTGUN, FLINTLOCK

	V.G.	Exc	Prior Edition
.65, American Hudson Valley	1,250	1,650	1,500

FOLGER, WILLIAM H. Barnsville, Ohio 1830–1854, also see Kentucky Rifles.

FOLK'S GUN WORKS Bryan, Ohio 1860–1891.

RIFLE, SINGLESHOT

	V.G.	Exc	Prior Edition
.32 L.R.R.F., Side Lever, Octagon Barrel, Antique......................	325	375	375

FONDERSMITH, JOHN Strasburg, Pa. 1749–1801. See Kentucky Rifles, U.S. Military.

FORBES, F. F. Made by Crescent, c. 1900.

SHOTGUN, DOUBLE BARREL, SIDE-BY-SIDE

	V.G.	Exc	Prior Edition
Various Gauges, Hammerless, Damascus Barrel, Modern......................	125	150	150
Various Gauges, Hammerless, Steel Barrel, Modern......................	150	175	175

	V.G.	Exc	Prior Edition
Various Gauges, Outside Hammers, Damascus Barrel, Modern............	$125	$150	$150
Various Gauges, Outside Hammers, Steel Barrel, Modern......................	125	175	175

SHOTGUN, SINGLESHOT

Various Gauges, Hammer, Steel Barrel, Modern....................................	50	75	75

FOREHAND & WADSWORTH   Worchester, Mass. Succes–

sors and sons-in-law to Ethan Allen 1871–1902. In 1872 the name was changed to Forehand & Wadsworth, in 1890 to Forehand Arms. Co.

HANDGUN, REVOLVER

.22 Short R.F. Side Hammer, 7 Shot, Single Action, Solid Frame, Antique...	175	200	275
.41 Short R.F. Center Hammer, Single Action, Spur Trigger, Solid Frame, Antique...	100	125	100
American Bulldog, .32 S & W, 6 Shot, Double Action, Solid Frame, Antique...	100	125	—
British Bulldog, .38 S & W, 6 Shot, Double Action, Solid Frame, Antique...	225	250	250
British Bulldog, .44 S & W, 6 Shot, Double Action, Solid Frame, Antique...	250	275	275
New Army, .44 Russian, 6 Shot, Single Action, Solid Frame, Antique...	1,200	1,450	200
Old Army, .44 Russian, 6 Shot, Single Action, Solid Frame, 7½" Barrel, Antique..	1,000	1,250	750
Swamp Angel, .41 Short R.F., 5 Shot, Single Action, Solid Frame, Spur Trigger, Antique..	125	175	200
Terror, .32 Short R.F., 5 Shot, Single Action, Solid Frame, Spur Trigger, Antique..	125	175	175

HANDGUN, SINGLESHOT DERINGER

.22 Short R.F., Spur Trigger, Side–swing Barrel, Antique......................	300	350	300
.41 Short R.F., Spur Trigger, Side–swing Barrel, Antique......................	550	650	450

	V.G.	Exc	Prior Edition

FOREHAND ARMS CO.

HANDGUN, REVOLVER

.32 S & W, 5 Shot, Double Action, Solid Frame, 2" Barrel, Antique........ $75 $100 $100

Forehand Arms Co., .32 S&W

.38 S & W, 5 Shot, Double Action, Solid Frame, 2" Barrel, Antique........	75	100	100
Perfection Automatic, .32 S & W, 5 Shot, Double Action, Top Break, Hammerless, Antique....................	125	150	150
Perfection Automatic, .32 S & W, 5 Shot, Double Action, Top Break, Antique....................	100	125	125

FOREVER YOURS Flaig's Lodge, Millvale, Pa.

SHOTGUN, DOUBLE BARREL, OVER-UNDER

Various Gauges, Automatic Ejector, Checkered Stock, Vent Rib, Double Trigger, Modern....................	550	650	650
Various Gauges, Automatic Ejector, Checkered Stock, Vent Rib, Single Trigger, Modern....................	550	700	700

FOULKES, ADAM Easton & Allentown, Pa. 1773–1794. See Kentucky Rifles and U.S. Military.

FOUR ACE CO. Brownsville, Texas.

HANDGUN, SINGLESHOT

Four Ace, Derringer, Presentation Case Add $10.00–$15.00

Four Ace Model 200, .22 Short R.F., Derringer, 4 Shot, Spur Trigger, Modern....................	25	50	50
Four Ace Model 200, .22 Short R.F., Derringer, 4 Shot, Spur Trigger, Nickel Plated, Gold Plated, Modern....................	25	50	50
Four Ace Model 202, .22 L.R.R.F., Derringer, 4 Shot, Spur Trigger, Nickel Plated, Gold Plated, Modern....................	50	75	75
Four Ace Model 202, .22 L.R.R.F., Derringer, 4 Shot, Spur Trigger, Modern....................	25	50	50

	V.G.	Exc	Prior Edition
Four Ace Model 204, .22 L.R.R.F., Derringer, 4 Shot, Spur Trigger, Stainless Steel, Modern..................	$50	$75	$75
Little Ace Model 300, .22 Short R.F., Derringer, Side–swing Barrel, Spur Trigger, Modern..................	25	50	50

FOX Foxco Products, Inc. Manchester, Conn. Also see Demro, T.A.C.

RIFLE, SEMI-AUTOMATIC

Model #1, 9mm Luger or .45 ACP, Carbine, Clip Fed, Modern..............	175	275	275

FOX, A.H. GUN CO. Philadelphia, Pa. Formerly Philadelphia Arms Co., From 1903. A subsidiary of Savage Arms Co., 1930–1942. Also see Savage Arms Co.

SHOTGUN, DOUBLE BARREL, SIDE-BY-SIDE

	V.G.	Exc	Prior Edition
Various Gauges, Beavertail Forend Add 10%–15%			
Various Gauges, For SingleTrigger Add $200.00–$300.00			
Various Gauges, For Vent Rib Add $295.00–$495.00			
Various Gauges, Single Selective Trigger Add $295.00–$495.00			
Various Grades, for 20 Ga. Add 50%–75%			
A Grade, Various Gauges, Box Lock, Light Engraving, Checkered Stock, Modern..................	1,150	1,400	1,400
AE Grade, Various Gauges, Box Lock, Light Engraving, Checkered Stock, Automatic Ejector, Modern..................	1,500	1,700	1,700
BE Grade, Various Gauges, Box Lock, Engraved, Checkered Stock, Automatic Ejector, Modern..................	2,000	2,500	2,500
CE Grade, Various Gauges, Box Lock, Engraved, Fancy Checkering, Automatic Ejector, Modern..................	4,500	6,000	3,000
DE Grade, Various Gauges, Box Lock, Fancy Engraving, Fancy Checkering, Fancy Wood, Automatic Ejector, Modern..................	7,000	9,000	8,000
FE Grade, Various Gauges, Box Lock, Fancy Engraving, Fancy Checkering, Fancy Wood, Automatic Ejector, Modern..................	10,000	12,500	20,000
HE Grade, 12 and 20 Gauge, Box Lock, Light Engraving, Checkered Stock, Automatic Ejector, Modern..................	2,200	2,500	2,500
SP Grade, Various Gauges, Box Lock, Checkered Stock, Modern..................	800	1,000	1,000
SP Grade, Various Gauges, Box Lock, Checkered Stock, Automatic Ejector, Modern..................	900	1,200	1,200
SP Grade, Various Gauges, Box Lock, Skeet Grade, Automatic Ejector, Checkered Stock, Modern..................	950	1,150	950
SP Grade, Various Gauges, Box Lock, Skeet Grade, Checkered Stock, Modern..................	750	950	875
Sterlingworth, Various Gauges, Box Lock, Checkered Stock, Hammerless, Modern..................	800	1,000	850
Sterlingworth, Various Gauges, Box Lock, Checkered Stock, Hammerless, Automatic Ejector, Modern..................	1,000	1,250	950
Sterlingworth, Various Gauges, Box Lock, Skeet Grade, Checkered Stock, Modern..................	—	850	—
Sterlingworth, Various Gauges, Box Lock, Skeet Grade, Checkered Stock, Automatic Ejector, Modern..................	—	1,450	—
Sterlingworth Deluxe, Various Gauges, Box Lock, Checkered Stock, Hammerless, Recoil Pad, Modern..................	1,000	1,250	1,600

	V.G.	Exc	Prior Edition
Sterlingworth Deluxe, Various Gauges, Box Lock, Checkered Stock, Hammerless, Recoil Pad, Automatic Ejector, Modern....................	$1,250	$1,500	$1,850
XE Grade, Various Gauges, Box Lock, Fancy Engraving, Fancy Checkering, Fancy Wood, Automatic Ejector, Modern.............................	5,500	6,500	5,000

SHOTGUN, SINGLESHOT

JE Grade, 12 Gauge, Trap Grade, Vent Rib, Automatic Ejector, Engraved, Fancy Checkering, Modern.......................................	1,475	1,775	1,775
KE Grade, 12 Gauge, Trap Grade, Vent Rib, Automatic Ejector, Engraved, Fancy Checkering, Modern.......................................	2,250	2,550	2,550
LE Grade, 12 Gauge, Trap Grade, Vent Rib, Automatic Ejector, Fancy Engraving, Fancy Checkering, Modern..........................	3,000	3,500	3,475
ME Grade, 12 Gauge, Trap Grade, Vent Rib, Automatic Ejector, Fancy Engraving, Fancy Checkering, Modern..........................	6,500	7,500	7,500

FRANCAIS France, Made by Manufacture D'Armes Automatiques Francaise.

HANDGUN, SEMI-AUTOMATIC

Prima, .25 ACP, Clip Fed, Modern..	100	125	125

FRANCHI Brescia, Italy, now imported by F.I.E.

RIFLE, SEMI-AUTOMATIC

Centennial, .22 L.R.R.F., Checkered Stock, Tube Feed, Takedown, Modern............	275	325	250
Centennial Deluxe, .22 L.R.R.F., Checkered Stock, Tube Feed, Takedown, Light Engraving, Modern...................	325	400	350
Centennial Gallery, .22 Short R.F., Checkered Stock, Tube Feed, Takedown, Modern..........	200	250	200

SHOTGUN, DOUBLE BARREL, OVER-UNDER

Alcione, 12 Ga., Field Grade, Automatic Ejectors, Single Selective Trigger, Vent Rib, Modern................	400	500	500
Alcione, 12, Vent Rib, Single Selective Trigger, Automatic Ejector, Engraved, Modern................	450	550	525
Alcione, 12, Vent Rib, Single Selective Trigger, Automatic Ejector, Engraved, Modern................	857	975	975
Aristocrat, 12 Ga., Imperial Grade, Automatic Ejectors, Single Selection Trigger, Vent Rib, Modern..............	1,800	2,100	2,100
Aristocrat, 12 Ga., Monte Carlo Grade, Automatic Ejectors, Single Selective Trigger, Vent Rib, Modern..................	2,500	3,000	3,000
Barrage Skeet, 12 Ga., Vent Rib, Single Selective Trigger, Automatic Ejector, Recoil Pad, Modern....................	900	1,100	1,100
Barrage Trap, 12 Ga., Vent Rib, Single Selective Trigger, Automatic Ejector, Recoil Pad, Modern....................	900	1,100	1,100
Dragon Skeet, 12 Ga., Vent Rib, Single Selective Trigger, Automatic Ejector, Recoil Pad, Modern....................	800	950	950
Dragon Trap, 12 Ga., Vent Rib, Single Selective Trigger, Automatic Ejector, Recoil Pad, Modern....................	800	950	650
Falconet Buckskin, 12 and 20 Ga., Vent Rib, Single Selective Trigger, Automatic Ejector, Modern.....................	475	550	550

	V.G.	Exc	Prior Edition
Falconet Ebony, 12 and 20 Ga., Vent Rib, Single Selective Trigger, Automatic Ejector, Modern...	$425	$500	$500
Falconet Peregrine 400, 12 and 20 Ga., Vent Rib, Single Selective Trigger, Automatic Ejector, Modern...	575	650	650
Falconet Peregrine 451, 12 and 20 Ga., Vent Rib, Single Selective Trigger, Automatic Ejector, Modern...	500	600	600
Falconet Pigeon, 12 Ga., Vent Rib, Single Selective Trigger, Automatic Ejector, Fancy Engraving, Fancy Checkering, Modern...........	1,000	1,200	1,200
Falconet Silver, 12 Ga., Vent Rib, Single Selective Trigger, Automatic Ejector, Modern..	550	625	625
Falconet Super, 12 Ga., Vent Rib, Single Selective Trigger, Automatic Ejector, Modern..	650	725	725
Falconet Super Deluxe, 12 Ga., Vent Rib, Single Selective Trigger, Automatic Ejector, Modern..	750	950	950
Model 2003, 12 Ga., Trap Grade, Vent Rib, Single Selective Trigger, Automatic Ejector, Modern..	1,075	1,250	1,250
Model 2005/2, 12 Ga., Trap Grade, Vent Rib, Single Selective Trigger, Automatic Ejector, Extra Shotgun Barrel, Modern......................	2,000	2,250	2,250
Model 2005/3, 12 Ga., Trap Grade, Vent Rib, Single Selective Trigger, Automatic Ejector, Extra Shotgun Barrel, Custom Choke, Modern..	2,250	2,500	2,500
Model 255, 12 Ga., Vent Rib, Single Selective Trigger, Automatic Ejector, Modern...	500	525	525

SHOTGUN, DOUBLE BARREL, SIDE-BY-SIDE

	V.G.	Exc	Prior Edition
Airone, 12 Ga., Box Lock, Hammerless, Checkered Stock, Automatic Ejector, Modern..	800	1,000	1,000
Astore, 12 Ga., Box Lock, Hammerless, Checkered Stock, Modern........	700	800	800
Astore 5, 12 Ga., Box Lock, Hammerless, Checkered Stock, Light Engraving, Modern..	1,500	1,700	1,700
Condor, Various Gauges, Sidelock, Engraved, Checkered Stock, Automatic Ejector, Modern..	5,000	6,000	6,000
Imperial, Various Gauges, Sidelock, Engraved, Checkered Stock, Automatic Ejector, Modern..	8,500	9,500	9,000
Imperial Monte Carlo #11, Various Gauges, Sidelock, Fancy Engraving, Fancy Checkering, Automatic Ejector, Modern......................	12,000	14,000	13,000
Imperial Monte Carlo #5, Various Gauges, Sidelock, Fancy Engraving, Fancy Checkering, Automatic Ejector, Modern	10,000	12,500	12,000
Imperial Monte Carlo Extra, Various Gauges, Sidelock, Fancy Engraving, Fancy Checkering, Automatic Ejector, Modern...................	15,000	18,000	16,000
Imperiales, Various Gauges, Sidelock, Engraved, Checkered Stock, Automatic Ejector, Modern..	8,500	9,500	9,000

SHOTGUN, SEMI-AUTOMATIC

	V.G.	Exc	Prior Edition
Dynamic (Heavy), 12 Ga., Checkered Stock, Slug, Open Rear Sight, Modern..	275	375	375
Dynamic (Heavy), 12 Ga., Plain Barrel, Modern.....................................	250	325	325
Dynamic (Heavy), 12 Ga., Skeet Grade, Vent Rib, Checkered Stock, Modern..	275	375	375
Dynamic (Heavy), 12 Ga., Vent Rib, Modern...	300	350	350
Eldorado, 12 and 20 Ga., Vent Rib, Engraved, Fancy Checkering, Lightweight, Modern..	350	450	450
Hunter, 12 and 20 Ga., Vent Rib, Engraved, Checkered Stock, Lightweight, Modern..	400	500	500
Model 500, 12 Ga., Vent Rib, Checkered Stock, Modern.........................	250	350	350

	V.G.	Exc	Prior Edition
Model 500, 12 Ga., Vent Rib, Checkered Stock, Engraved, Modern	$350	$450	$450
Slug Gun, 12 and 20 Ga., Open Rear Sights, Sling Swivels, Modern	350	450	450
SPAS 12, 12 gauge, Combat Shotgun, Folding Stock, Rifle Sights, Lightweight, Modern	400	500	500
Standard, 12 and 20 Ga., Plain Barrel, Lightweight, Checkered Stock, Modern	325	425	425
Standard, 12 and 20 Ga., Solid Rib, Lightweight, Checkered Stock, Modern	350	450	450
Standard, 12 and 20 Ga., Vent Rib, Lightweight, Checkered Stock, Modern	375	475	475
Standard Magnum, 12 and 20 Gauges, Vent Rib, Lightweight, Checkered Stock, Modern	250	350	350
Superange (Heavy), 12 and 20 Gauges, Magnum, Plain Barrel, Checkered Stock, Modern	250	350	350
Superange (Heavy), 12 and 20 Gauges, Magnum, Vent Rib, Checkered Stock, Modern	375	425	425
Wildfowler (Heavy), 12 and 20 Gauges, Magnum, Vent Rib, Checkered Stock, Engraved, Modern	375	450	450

SHOTGUN, SINGLESHOT

	V.G.	Exc	Prior Edition
Model 2004, 12 Ga., Trap Grade, Vent Rib, Automatic Ejector, Modern	900	1,050	1,200
Model 3000/2, 12 Ga., Trap Grade, Vent Rib, Automatic Ejector, with Choke Tubes, Modern	2,000	2,600	2,600

FRANCI, PIERO INZI Brescia, Italy, c. 1640.

HANDGUN, WHEEL-LOCK

	V.G.	Exc	Prior Edition
Octagon–Barrel, Dagger, Handle Butt, Antique	4,000	5,000	5,000

FRANCOTTE, AUGUST Liege, Belgium 1844 to date, also London, England 1877–1893.

HANDGUN, REVOLVER

	V.G.	Exc	Prior Edition
Bulldog, Various Calibers, Double Action, Solid Frame, Curio	100	150	150

Francotte Bulldog Revolver

	V.G.	Exc	Prior Edition
Military Style, Various Calibers, Double Action, Antique.......................	$100	$150	$150

HANDGUN, SEMI-AUTOMATIC
Vest Pocket, .25 ACP, Clip Fed, Curio..	200	250	350

HANDGUN, SINGLESHOT
Target Pistol, .22 L.R.R.F., Toggle Breech, Modern................................	300	375	375

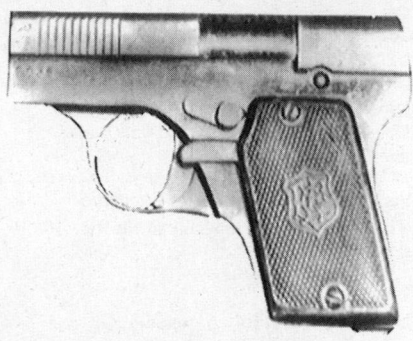

Francotte .25 ACP Pistol

RIFLE, DOUBLE BARREL, SIDE-BY-SIDE
Luxury Double, .458 Win., Sidelock, Hammerless, Double Triggers, Fancy Engraving, Curio...	17,500	20,000	20,000

SHOTGUN, DOUBLE BARREL, SIDE-BY-SIDE
A & F #14, Various Gauges, Box Lock, Automatic Ejector, Checkered Stock, Engraved, Hammerless, Curio....................	1,750	2,000	2,000
A & F #20, Various Gauges, Box Lock, Automatic Ejector, Checkered Stock, Engraved, Hammerless, Curio....................	2,750	3,250	3,000
A & F #25, Various Gauges, Box Lock, Automatic Ejector, Checkered Stock, Engraved, Hammerless, Curio....................	3,200	3,500	3,500
A & F #30, Various Gauges, Box Lock, Automatic Ejector, Checkered Stock, Engraved, Hammerless, Curio....................	3,800	4,500	4,500
A & F #45, Various Gauges, Box Lock, Automatic Ejector, Checkered Stock, Engraved, Hammerless, Curio....................	3,500	4,000	4,500
A & F Jubilee, Various Gauges, Box Lock, Automatic Ejector, Checkered Stock, Light Engraving, Hammerless, Curio..........................	1,250	1,500	1,500
A & F Knockabout, Various Gauges, Box Lock, Automatic Ejector, Checkered Stock, Hammerless, Curio..	1,000	1,250	1,250
Francotte Original, Various Gauges, Box Lock, Automatic Ejector, Checkered Stock, Hammerless, Engraved, Curio........................	2,000	3,000	3,000
Francotte Special, Various Gauges, Box Lock, Automatic Ejector, Checkered Stock, Hammerless, Light Engraving, Curio...........................	1,500	2,500	2,500
Model 10/18E/628, Various Gauges, Box Lock, Automatic Ejector, Checkered Stock, Hammerless, Light Engraving, Curio...........................	3,000	4,000	4,000
Model 10594, Various Gauges, Box Lock, Automatic Ejector, Checkered Stock, Hammerless, Engraved, Curio....................................	2,500	3,000	3,000
Model 11/18E, Various Gauges, Box Lock, Automatic Ejector, Checkered Stock, Hammerless, Engraved, Curio....................................	2,500	3,000	3,000

	V.G.	Exc	Prior Edition
Model 120.HE/328, Various Gauges, Sidelock, Automatic Ejector, Checkered Stock, Hammerless, Fancy Engraving, Curio.....................	$7,000	$8,500	$8,500
Model 4996, Various Gauges, Box Lock, Automatic Ejector, Checkered Stock, Hammerless, Light Engraving, Curio...........................	1,500	2,500	2,500
Model 6886, Various Gauges, Box Lock, Automatic Ejector, Checkered Stock, Hammerless, Curio......................................	1,500	2,500	2,500
Model 6930, Various Gauges, Box Lock, Automatic Ejector, Checkered Stock, Hammerless, Light Engraving, Curio...........................	1,500	2,500	2,500
Model 6982, Various Gauges, Box Lock, Automatic Ejector, Checkered Stock, Hammerless, Engraved, Curio..................................	2,500	3,500	3,500
Model 8455, Various Gauges, Box Lock, Automatic Ejector, Checkered Stock, Hammerless, Curio......................................	2,000	3,500	3,500
Model 8457, Various Gauges, Box Lock, Automatic Ejector, Checkered Stock, Hammerless, Engraved, Curio..................................	2,500	3,000	3,000
Model 9/40.SE, Various Gauges, Box Lock, Automatic Ejector, Checkered Stock, Hammerless, Fancy Engraving, Curio...............	7,000	9,500	9,500
Model 9/40E/38321, Various Gauges, Box Lock, Automatic Ejector, Checkered Stock, Hammerless, Engraved, Curio.................	3,000	4,000	4,000
Model SOB.E/11082, Various Gauges, Box Lock, Automatic Ejector, Checkered Stock, Hammerless, Engraved, Curio.................	5,000	6,000	6,000

FRANKLIN, C. W. Belgium, c. 1900.

SHOTGUN, DOUBLE BARREL, SIDE-BY-SIDE

Various Gauges, Hammerless, Damascus Barrel, Modern......................	125	175	175
Various Gauges, Hammerless, Steel Barrel, Modern.............................	150	200	200
Various Gauges, Outside Hammers, Damascus Barrel, Modern.............	125	175	175
Various Gauges, Outside Hammers, Steel Barrel, Modern.....................	125	175	175

SHOTGUN, SINGLESHOT

Various Gauges, Hammer, Steel Barrel, Modern...................................	75	100	100

FRANKONIA Franconia Jagd, arms dealers and manufacturers in West Germany.

RIFLE, BOLT ACTION

Favorit, Various Calibers, Set Triggers, Checkered Stock, Modern.........	275	325	325
Favorit Deluxe, Various Calibers, Set Triggers, Checkered Stock, Modern...............	350	425	475
Favorit Leichtmodell, Various Calibers, Lightweight, Set Triggers, Checkered Stock, Modern...............	400	450	450
Safari, Various Calibers, Target Trigger, Checkered Stock, Modern...............	425	475	475
Stutzen, Various Calibers, Carbine, Set Triggers, Full Stock, Modern...............	400	450	450

RIFLE, SINGLESHOT

Heeren Rifle, Various Calibers, Fancy Engraving, Fancy Wood, Octagon Barrel, Modern...............	2,500	3,250	3,000
Heeren Rifle, Various Calibers, Fancy Engraving, Fancy Wood, Round Barrel, Modern...............	2,200	2,500	2,500

	V.G.	Exc	Prior Edition

FRASER (formerly Bauer Firearms), Fraser, Mich.

HANDGUN, SEMI-AUTOMATIC

.25 ACP, Stainless Steel, Clip Fed, Hammerless, Browning Baby
Style, Modern... $100 $125 $125

FRASER, D. & J. Edinburgh, Scotland 1870–1900.

RIFLE, DOUBLE BARREL, SIDE-BY-SIDE

.360 N.E. #2, Automatic Ejector, Express Sights, Engraved, Extra
Set of Barrels, Cased with Accessories, Modern....................................... 8,500 10,000 8,500

FRAZIER, CLARK K. Rawson, Ohio.

RIFLE, PERCUSSION

Matchmate Offhand, Various Calibers, Under–Hammer, Thumbhole
Stock, Heavy Barrel, Reproduction, Antique... 450 650 650

FRAZIER, JAY Tyler, Wash. c. 1974.

RIFLE, SINGLESHOT

Creedmore Rifle, Various Calibers, Single Set Trigger, Vernier
Sights, Skeleton Buttplate, Pistol Grip Stock, Modern.............................. 600 800 800
Schuetzen Rifle, Various Calibers, Single Set Trigger, Vernier
Sights, Helm Buttplate, Palm Rest, False Muzzle, Modern....................... 600 800 800

FREEDOM ARMS Freedom, Wyo.

HANDGUN, REVOLVER

FA–BG, "Minute Man," .22 L.R.R.F., Spur Trigger, 3" Barrel,
Single Action, Modern.. 175 225 200
FA–S, "Bostonian," .22 L.R.R.F., Spur Trigger, 3" Barrel,
Single Action, Modern.. 175 250 225
FA–S, "Ironsides," .22 W.M.R., Matte Finish, Spur Trigger,
1" Barrel, Single Action, Modern.. 175 225 150
FA–S, "Patriot," .22 L.R.R.F., Matte Finish, Spur Trigger,
1" Barrel, Single Action, Modern.. 125 175 125
FA–S, .22 L.R.R.F., Stainless Steel, Matte Finish, Spur Trigger,
1¾" Barrel, Single Action, Buckel/Rev. Combo, Modern........................ 200 250 200
For High Gloss Finish, Add $5.00–$10.00

	V.G.	Exc	Prior Edition

FRENCH MILITARY

HANDGUN, FLINTLOCK

.69 AN XIII, Officer's Pistol, Made in France, Antique............................ $750 $1,000 $575

French Military AN XIII

.69 AN XIII, Officer's Pistol, Made in Occupied Country,
Antique... 750 1,000 650

.69 Charleville 1777, Cavalry Pistol, Brass Furniture, Belt Hook,
Antique... 1,050 1,200 1,200

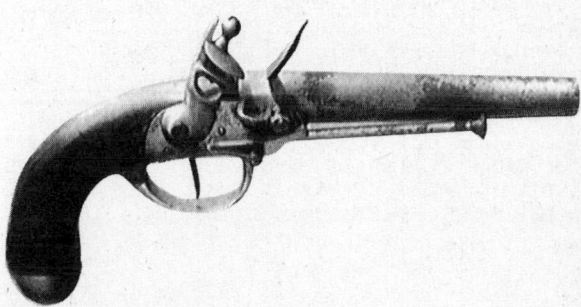

French Military M1777 Charleville

.69 Charleville 1810, Cavalry Pistol, Brass Furniture, Plain,
Antique... 800 900 900

.69 Charleville 1810, Cavalry Pistol, Brass Furniture, Converted
from Flintlock, Plain, Antique.. 400 550 550

.69 Model 1763, Belt Pistol, Military, Antique... 1,000 1,250 1,250

	V.G.	Exc	Prior Edition

HANDGUN, REVOLVER

Model 1873, 11mm French Ordnance, Double Action, Solid Frame, Antique... $200 $275 $275

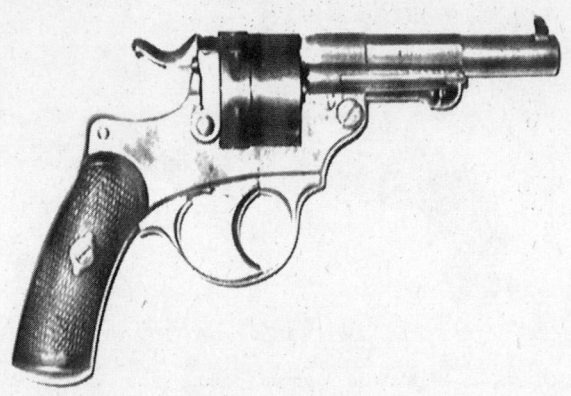

French Military M1873 Revolver

Model 1873 Officer's, 11mm French Ordnance, Double Action, Solid Frame, Antique.. 225 300 300

Model 1892, 8mm Lebel Revolver, Double Action, Solid Frame, Curio.. 150 200 175

Model 1915, 8mm Lebel Revolver, Double Action, Solid Frame, Spanish Contract, Curio.. 200 250 150

HANDGUN, SEMI-AUTOMATIC

M.A.B. Model C, 7.65mm, Clip Fed, Curio................................ 225 250 150

M.A.B. Model C, 7.65mm, Clip Fed, Nazi Proofed, Curio........ 325 350 200

M.A.B. Model D, 7.65mm, Clip Fed, Curio................................ 200 225 150

M.A.B. Model D, 7.65mm, Clip Fed, Nazi Proofed, Curio........ 250 300 200

	V.G.	Exc	Prior Edition
Model 1935–A, 7.65 MAS, Clip Fed, Black Paint, Curio........................	$125	$150	$125

French Military M1935A

	V.G.	Exc	Prior Edition
Model 1935–A, 7.65 MAS, Clip Fed, Blued, Curio.................................	150	175	150
Model 1935–A, 7.65 MAS, Clip Fed, Nazi Proofed, Curio......................	225	250	225
Model 1935–A, 7.65 MAS, M.A.C., Clip Fed, Curio.............................	250	300	175
Model 1935–S, 7.65 MAS, M.A.C. M–1, Clip Fed, Curio........................	325	350	125
Model 1935–S, 7.65 MAS, M.A.C., Clip Fed, Nazi Proofed, Curio...	400	450	200
Model 1935–S, 7.65 MAS, SACM, Clip Fed, Curio................................	200	225	150
Model 1935–S, 7.65 MAS, SAGEM M–1, Clip Fed, Nazi Proofed, Curio...	250	300	200
Model 1950, 9mm Luger, M.A.S., Clip Fed, Modern............................	350	475	475

French Military M1950

	V.G.	Exc	Prior Edition

RIFLE, BOLT ACTION

6.5 X 53.5 Daudetau, Carbine, Curio.. $100 $150 $150

French Military Daudetau Rifle

Model 1874, 11 X 59R Gras, Antique...	125	175	175
Model 1874, 11 X 59R Gras, Carbine, Antique...	150	200	200
Model 1886/93 Lebel, 8 X 50R Lebel, Curio...	75	100	100
Model 1907/15 Remington, 8 X 50R Lebel, Curio...................................	100	125	125
Model 1916 St. Etienne, 8 X 50R Lebel, Carbine, Curio.........................	125	150	150

French Military Model 1916 St. Etienne Rifle

Model 1936 MAS, 7.5 X 54 MAS, with Bayonet, Curio.......................... 100 125 175

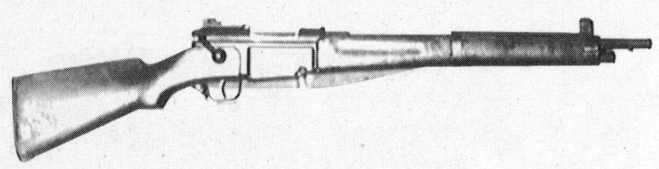

French Military Model 1935 MAS Rifle

RIFLE, FLINTLOCK

.69, Model 1763 Charleville 1st. Type, Musket, Antique........................... 1,500 1,850 1,850
Model 1763/66 Charleville, Musket, Antique... 850 1,200 1,200

RIFLE, PERCUSSION

Model 1840, Short Rifle, Antique.. 700 850 850

FROMMER Made by Femaru–Fegyver–Es Gepgyar R.T. (Fegyvergyar), Budapest, Hungary. Also see Femaru.

HANDGUN, SEMI-AUTOMATIC

Baby Pocket, .32 ACP, Clip Fed, Curio... 150 200 150

	V.G.	Exc	Prior Edition
Baby Pocket, .380 ACP, Clip Fed, Curio...	$175	$225	$175
Liliput, .22 L.R.R.F., Clip Fed, Curio...	—	RARE	—

Frommer Liliput

Liliput, .25 ACP, Clip Fed, Curio...	200	250	200
Roth–Frommer Model 1901, 8mm Roth Sauer, Fixed Magazine, Commercial, Curio..	1,500	1,750	1,750
Roth–Frommer Model 1901, 8mm Roth Sauer, Fixed Magazine, Military Test, Curio..	—	RARE	—
Roth–Frommer Model 1906, 7.65mm Roth Sauer, Clip Fed, Commercial, Curio..	1,250	1,500	1,500
Roth–Frommer Model 1906, 7.65mm Roth Sauer, Fixed Magazine, Commercial, Curio..	1,100	1,300	1,300
Roth–Frommer Model 1910, .32 ACP, Fixed Magazine, Commercial, Curio..	1,250	1,500	1,400

Frommer Roth Frommer 1910

Roth–Frommer Model 1910, .32 ACP, Fixed Magazine, Police, Curio...	1,500	1,750	1,600

	V.G.	Exc	Prior Edition
Stop Pocket, .32 ACP, Commercial, Clip Fed, Curio..............................	$200	$250	$250

Frommer Stop Pocket

Stop Pocket, .32 ACP, M–19 Military, Clip Fed, Curio............................	175	225	225
Stop Pocket, .32 ACP, Police, Clip Fed, Curio..	225	275	250
Stop Pocket, .32 ACP, WW–1 Military, Clip Fed, Curio.........................	175	225	225
Stop Pocket, .380 ACP, Military, Clip Fed, Curio....................................	275	325	325

FRONTIER Made by Norwich Falls Pistol Co., c. 1880.

HANDGUN, REVOLVER

.32 Short R.F., 5 Shot, Spur Trigger, Solid Frame, Single Action, Antique...	100	175	175

FRYBERG, ANDREW Hopkintown, Mass., c. 1905.

HANDGUN, REVOLVER

.32 S & W, 5 Shot, Top Break, Double Action, Modern............................	100	125	100
.32 S & W, 5 Shot, Top Break, Hammerless, Double Action, Modern.....	100	125	100
.38 S & W, 5 Shot, Top Break, Double Action, Modern............................	100	125	100
.38 S & W, 5 Shot, Top Break, Hammerless, Double Action, Modern.....	100	125	100

FTL Covina, Calif.

HANDGUN, SEMI-AUTOMATIC

.22 L.R.R.F., Clip Fed, Chrome Plated, Modern.......................................	100	150	150

G

GALAND, CHARLES FRANCIOS From 1865 until about

1910 with plants in London, England, Paris, France, and Liege, Belgium.

HANDGUN, REVOLVER

	V.G.	Exc.	Prior Edition
Galand, Various Calibers, Double Action, Underlever Extraction, Curio	$275	$325	$325
Galand–Perrin, Various Calibers, Double Action, Underlever Extraction, Curio	250	300	300
Galand–Sommerville, 7–12mm, Double Action, Underlevel Extraction, Curio	275	325	325
Galand–Sommerville, 7–12mm, Double Action, Underlever Extraction, Curio	300	350	350
Le Novo, .25 ACP, Double Action, Folding Trigger, Curio	150	200	200

SHOTGUN, PERCUSSION

	V.G.	Exc.	Prior Edition
Various Gauges, Checkered Stock, Double Barrel, Plain, Antique	200	250	250

SHOTGUN, DOUBLE BARREL, SIDE-BY-SIDE

	V.G.	Exc.	Prior Edition
Various Gauges, Checkered Stock, Plain, Hammers, Curio	125	175	175

GALEF Importers in N.Y.C.

HANDGUN, REVOLVER

	V.G.	Exc.	Prior Edition
Stallion, 22LR/.22 WMR Combo, Western Style, Single Action, Modern	75	100	100

HANDGUN, SEMI-AUTOMATIC

	V.G.	Exc.	Prior Edition
Brigadier, 9mm Luger, Beretta, Clip Fed, Modern	200	300	300
Cougar, .380 ACP, Beretta, Clip Fed, Modern	175	225	225
Jaguar, .22 L.R.R.F., Beretta, Clip Fed, Modern	150	200	200
Puma, .32 ACP, Beretta, Clip Fed, Modern	150	200	200
Sable, .22 L.R.R.F., Beretta, Clip Fed, Adjustable Sights, Modern	150	225	225

RIFLE, BOLT ACTION

	V.G.	Exc.	Prior Edition
BSA Monarch, Various Calibers, Checkered Stock Magnum Action, Modern	225	275	275
BSA Monarch, Various Calibers, Checkered Stock, Modern	200	250	250
BSA Monarch Varmint, Various Calibers, Checkered Stock, Heavy Barrel, Modern	250	300	300

	V.G.	Exc	Prior Edition

SHOTGUN, DOUBLE BARREL, OVER-UNDER

	V.G.	Exc	Prior Edition
Golden Snipe, 12 and 20 Gauges, Beretta, Single Selective Trigger, Automatic Ejector, Engraved, Fancy Checkering, Modern......................	$425	$475	$475
Golden Snipe, 12 and 20 Gauges, Beretta, Single Trigger, Automatic Ejector, Engraved, Fancy Checkering, Modern......................	350	400	400
Golden Snipe, 12 and 20 Gauges, Skeet Grade, Single Trigger, Automatic Ejector, Engraved, Checkered Stock, Modern........................	450	500	500
Golden Snipe, 12 Ga., Trap Grade, Single Trigger, Automatic Ejector, Engraved, Checkered Stock, Modern............................	450	500	500
Golden Snipe Deluxe, 12 and 20 Gauges, Beretta, Single Selective Trigger, Automatic Ejector, Fancy Engraving, Fancy Checkering, Modern........................	475	525	525
Silver Snipe, 12 and 20 Gauges, Beretta, Single Selective Trigger, Checkered Stock, Light Engraving, Modern............................	325	375	375
Silver Snipe, 12 and 20 Gauges, Beretta, Single Trigger, Checkered Stock, Modern........................	300	350	350
Silver Snipe, 12 and 20 Gauges, Skeet Grade, Single Trigger, Vent Rib, Engraved, Checkered Stock, Modern............................	375	425	425
Silver Snipe, 12 Ga., Trap Grade, Single Trigger, Vent Rib, Engraved, Checkered Stock, Modern............................	375	425	425
Zoli Golden Snipe, 12 and 20 Gauges, Vent Rib, Single Trigger, Adjustable Choke, Engraved, Checkered Stock, Modern........................	400	450	450
Zoli Silver Snipe, 12 and 20 Gauges, Vent Rib, Single Trigger, Engraved, Checkered Stock, Modern............................	350	400	400

SHOTGUN, DOUBLE BARREL, SIDE-BY-SIDE

	V.G.	Exc	Prior Edition
M213CH, 10 Ga. 3½", Double Trigger, Checkered Stock, Light Engraving, Recoil Pad, Modern............................	200	250	250
M213CH, Various Gauges, Double Trigger, Checkered Stock, Light Engraving, Recoil Pad, Modern........................	125	175	175
Silver Hawk, 10 Ga. 3½", Beretta, Double Trigger, Magnum, Modern............................	450	500	500
Silver Hawk, 12 and 20 Gauges, Double Trigger, Engraved, Checkered Stock, Modern............................	325	375	375
Silver Hawk, 12 Ga. Mag. 3", Beretta, Double Trigger, Magnum, Modern............................	325	375	375
Silver Hawk, 12 Ga. Mag. 3", Beretta, Single Trigger, Magnum, Modern............................	375	425	425
Silver Hawk, Various Gauges, Beretta, Double Trigger, Lightweight, Modern............................	275	325	325
Silver Hawk, Various Gauges, Beretta, Double Trigger, Lightweight, Modern............................	350	400	400
Zabala 213, 10 Ga. 3½", Double Trigger, Modern............................	150	200	200
Zabala 213, 12 and 20 Gauges, Double Trigger, Modern........................	125	175	175
Zabala 213, 12 and 20 Gauges, Double Trigger, Vent Rib, Modern........	125	175	175
Zabala Police, 12 and 20 Gauges, Double Trigger, Modern....................	125	175	175

SHOTGUN, SEMI-AUTOMATIC

	V.G.	Exc	Prior Edition
Gold Lark, 12 Ga., Beretta, Vent Rib, Light Engraving, Checkered Stock, Modern............................	200	250	250
Ruby Lark, 12 Ga., Beretta, Vent Rib, Fancy Engraving, Fancy Checkering, Modern............................	300	350	350
Silver Gyrfalcon, 12 Ga., Beretta, Checkered Stock, Modern................	100	125	125
Silver Lark, 12 Ga., Beretta, Checkered Stock, Modern....................	125	150	150

	V.G.	Exc	Prior Edition

SHOTGUN, SINGLESHOT

	V.G.	Exc	Prior Edition
Companion, Various Gauges, Folding Gun, Checkered Stock, Modern	$50	$75	$75
Companion, Various Gauges, Folding Gun, Checkered Stock, Vent Rib, Modern	50	75	75
Monte Carlo, 12 Ga., Trap Grade, Vent Rib, Engraved, Checkered Stock, Modern	175	225	225

SHOTGUN, SLIDE ACTION

	V.G.	Exc	Prior Edition
Gold Pigeon, 12 Ga., Beretta, Vent Rib, Fancy Engraving, Fancy Checkering, Modern	300	350	350
Ruby Pigeon, 12 Ga., Beretta, Vent Rib, Fancy Engraving, Fancy Checkering, Modern	400	450	450
Silver Pigeon, 12 Ga., Beretta, Light Engraving, Checkered Stock, Modern	125	150	150

GALESI Industria Armi Galesi, Brescia, Italy since 1910.

HANDGUN, SEMI-AUTOMATIC

	V.G.	Exc	Prior Edition
Galesi, 6.35mm, Clip Fed, Curio	200	250	225
Model 30, 6.35mm, Clip Fed, Curio	200	250	200
Model 30, 7.65mm, Clip Fed, Curio	200	250	200
Model 9, .22 L.R.R.F., Clip Fed, Curio	150	175	150

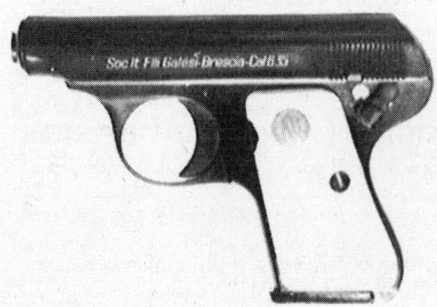

Galesi Model 9 Pistol

	V.G.	Exc	Prior Edition
Model 9, .32 ACP, Clip Fed, Curio	125	150	175
Model 9, .380 ACP, Clip Fed, Curio	150	175	150

GALLATIN, ALBERT See Kentucky Rifles and Pistols.

GALLUS Retoloza Hermanos, Eibar, Spain, c. 1920.

HANDGUN, SEMI-AUTOMATIC

	V.G.	Exc	Prior Edition
.25 ACP, Clip Fed, Blue, Curio	100	125	130

	V.G.	Exc	Prior Edition

GAMBA Renato Gamba, Brescia, Italy.

RIFLE, SINGLESHOT

Mustang, Various Calibers, Holland Type Sidelock Action, Set
Triggers, Checkered Stock, Engraved, Zeiss Scope, Modern.................... $7,000 $10,000 $10,000

RIFLE, DOUBLE BARREL, OVER-UNDER

Safari, Various Calibers, Boxlock, Checkered Stock, Engraved,
Double Triggers, Modern... 3,000 4,000 4,000

SHOTGUN, DOUBLE BARREL, SIDE-BY-SIDE

London, 12 or 20 Ga., Sidelock, Checkered Stock, Engraved,
Modern... 6,500 8,000 4,500
Oxford, 12 or 20 Ga., Boxlock, Checkered Stock, Engraved,
Modern... 2,500 3,000 1,700

GANDER, PETER Lancaster, Pa. 1779–1782, see Kentucky Rifles.

GARATE, ANITUA Eibar, Spain, c. 1915.

HANDGUN, REVOLVER

Pistol O.P. #Mk.I, .455 Webley, British Military, Curio......................... 250 275 275

HANDGUN, SEMI-AUTOMATIC

.32 ACP, Clip Fed, Long Grip, Curio.. 125 150 150

GARBI Amas Garbi, Eibar, Spain.

SHOTGUN, DOUBLE BARREL, SIDE-BY-SIDE

Model 51–A, Various Gauges, Boxlock, Checkered Stock, Engraved,
Modern... 400 450 350
Model 60–A, Various Gauges, Sidelock, Checkered Stock, Engraved,
Modern... 550 650 525
Model 60–B, Various Gauges, Sidelock, Checkered Stock, Engraved,
Automatic Ejectors, Modern.. 1,250 1,500 800

GARRISON Made by Hopkins & Allen, c. 1880–1890.

HANDGUN, REVOLVER

.22 Short R.F., 7 Shot, Spur Trigger, Solid Frame, Single Action,
Antique... 125 175 175

GARRUCHA Made by Amadeo Rossi, Sao Leopoldo, Brazil.

HANDGUN, DOUBLE BARREL, SIDE-BY-SIDE

.22 L.R.R.F., Double Triggers, Outside Hammers, Modern.................... 50 75 75

	V.G.	Exc	Prior Edition

GASSER Leopold Gasser, Vienna, Austria.

HANDGUN, REVOLVER

Montenegrin Gasser, 10.7mm Montenegrin, Double Action, Break

Top, Ring Extractor, Antique.....................	$375	$425	$400
Rast & Gasser, 8mm R&G, Double Action, Solid Frame, Curio.............	200	250	275

GASTINE RENETTE Paris, France since 1812.

RIFLE, DOUBLE BARREL, SIDE-BY-SIDE

Chapuis Standard, Various Calibers, Boxlock Action, Engraved, Checkered Stock, Double Trigger, Open Sights, Modern..........................	2,000	2,200	2,200
Chapuis de Luxe, Various Calibers, Boxlock Action With Sideplates, Fancy Engraving, Checkered Stock, Double Trigger Open Sights, Modern...	2,250	2,600	2,600
Chapuis President, Various Calibers, Boxlock Action With Sideplates, Engraved, Gold Inlays, Checkered Stock, Double Trigger, Open Sights, Modern........................	2,500	3,200	3,200

Chapuis, For Claw Mounts Add $150.00–$250.00
Chapuis, With 20 Gauge Barrels Add $550.00–$850.00

SHOTGUN, DOUBLE BARREL, OVER-UNDER

Bretton Baby Luxe, Lightweight, Double Trigger, Checkered Stock, Engraved, Chrome Frame, Modern..............................	400	450	450
Bretton Baby Standard, Lightweight, Double Trigger, Checkered Stock, Modern........	350	400	400
Bretton Baby–Elite, Lightweight, Double Trigger, Checkered Stock, Modern........	375	425	425

SHOTGUN, DOUBLE BARREL, SIDE-BY-SIDE

Model 105, 12 or 20 Gauge, Boxlock Action, Engraved, Fancy Wood, Checkered Stock, Double Trigger, Modern...................................	1,250	1,500	1,400
Model 202, 12 or 20 Gauge, Boxlock Action With Sideplates, Fancy Engraving, Fancy Wood, Checkered Stock, Double Trigger, Modern..	3,500	4,000	4,000
Model 353, 12 or 20 Gauge, Sidelock Action, Fancy Engraving, Fancy Wood, Checkered Stock, Double Trigger, Modern.........................	10,000	14,000	14,000
Model 98, 12 or 20 Gauge, Boxlock Action, Engraved, Fancy Wood, Checkered Stock, Double Trigger, Modern...................................	2,000	2,250	2,000

GATLING ARMS & AMMUNITION CO Birmingham, England, c. 1890.

HANDGUN, REVOLVER

Dimancea, .38 & .45 Caliber, Hammerless, Twist Opening, Double Action, Antique........................	800	900	900

	V.G.	Exc	Prior Edition

GAULOIS Tradename used by Mrs. Francaise de Armes et Cycles de St. Etienne, France 1897–1910.

HANDGUN, MANUAL REPEATER

Palm Pistol, 8mm, Engraved, Curio... $500 $650 $650

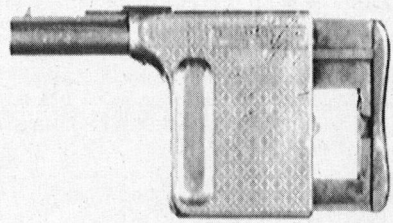

Gaulois Palm Pistol

GAUTEC, PETER Lancaster, Pa. c. 1780 Kentucky Rifles & Pistols.

GAVAGE Fab. d'Armes de Guerre de Haute Precision Armand Gavage, Leige, Belgium, c. 1940.

HANDGUN, SEMI-AUTOMATIC

7.65mm, Clip Fed, Blue, Curio.. 300   350   350

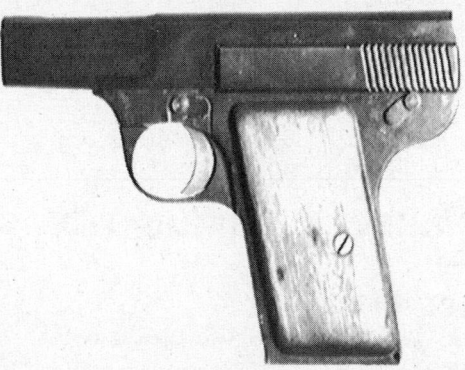

Gavage .32 Pistol

7.65mm, Clip Fed, Blue, Nazi–Proofed, Curio... 400   450   450

	V.G.	Exc	Prior Edition

GECADO Suhl, Germany, by G. C. Dornheim.
HANDGUN, SEMI-AUTOMATIC
Model 11, .25 ACP, Clip Fed, Modern.. $100 $125 $125

GECO Tragename used by Gustav Genschow, Hamburg, Germany.
HANDGUN, REVOLVER
Bulldog, .32 ACP, Double Action, Modern... 100 125 125
Velo Dog, .25 ACP, Double Action, Modern.. 100 125 125
SHOTGUN, DOUBLE BARREL, SIDE-BY-SIDE
12 Gauge, Checkered Stock, Double Triggers, Plain, Modern................. 125 175 175

GEM Made by Bacon Arms Co., c. 1880.
HANDGUN, REVOLVER
.22 Short R.F., 7 Shot, Spur Trigger, Solid Frame, Single Action, Antique.. 175 225 225

GEM Made by J. Stevens Arms & Tool, Chicopee Falls, Mass.
HANDGUN, SINGLESHOT
.22 or .30 R.F., Side–Swing Barrel, Spur Trigger, Antique...................... 125 175 175

GERMAN MILITARY Also see: Walther, Mauser, Luger.
HANDGUN, FLINTLOCK
Model 1830, .63, Military, Antique.. 900 950 650
HANDGUN, PERCUSSION
Model 1860, .63, Military, Antique.. 550 600 425

	V.G.	Exc	Prior Edition

HANDGUN, REVOLVER

Model 1879 Troopers Model, 11mm German Service, Solid
Frame, Single Action, Safety, 7" Barrel, 6 Shot, Antique............................ $375 $425 $425

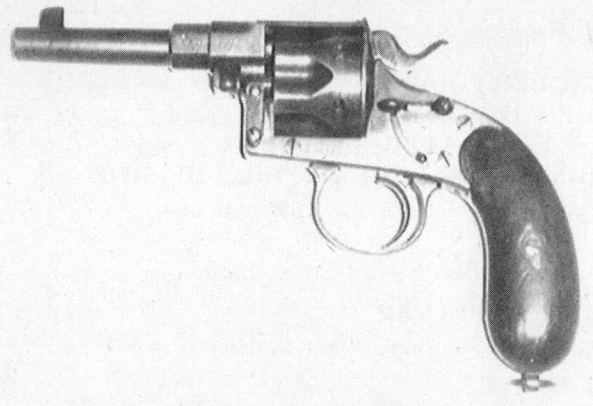

German Military Model 1879 Revolver

Model 1883 Officers' Model, 11mm German Service, Solid
Frame, Single Action, Safety, 5" Barrel, 6 Shot, Antique......................... 300 375 375

German Military Model 1883 Revolver

RIFLE, BOLT ACTION

	V.G.	Exc	Prior Edition
GEW 88 Commission, 8 x 57 JRS, Clip Fed, Antique............................	75	125	125
GEW 98 (Average), 8mm Mauser Military, Curio....................................	175	250	250
GEW 98 Sniper, 8mm Mauser, Scope Mounted, Military, Curio............	650	750	750
K98K Sniper, 8mm Mauser, Scope Mounted, Military, Curi...................	475	550	550
KAR 98 (Average), 8mm Mauser Military, Carbine, Curio....................	150	175	175

	V.G.	Exc	Prior Edition
KAR 98A (Average), 8mm Mauser Military, Carbine, Curio................	$150	$175	$175
M–95, 8mm Mauser, Steyr–Mannlicher, German Military, Nazi–Proofed, Curio........................	125	150	150
M–95, 8mm Mauser, Steyr–Mannlicher, German Military, Carbine Nazi–Proffed, Curio........................	100	125	125
Model 1871 Mauser, .43 Mauser, Carbine, Singleshot, Military, Antique........................	400	475	475
Model 1871 Mauser, .43 Mauser, Singleshot, Military, Antique............	300	350	350

German Military Model 1871 Rifle

Model 1936 Falke KK, .22 L.R.R.F., Training Rifle, Military, Curio........................	75	100	100
Model 29/40, 8mm Mauser, Nazi–Proofed, Military, Curio....................	100	150	150
Model 3¾40, 8mm Mauser, Nazi–Proofed, Military, Curio...................	125	175	175
Model 45 Mauser, .22 L.R.R.F., Training Rifle, Military, Curio...........	150	175	175
Model 71/84 Mauser, .43 Mauser, Tube Feed, Military, Antique...........	325	375	375

German Military Model 1871/84 Rifle

Needle Gun, 11mm, Singleshot, Military, Antique....................	525	600	600
VK–98, 8mm Mauser, Nazi–Proofed, Military, Curio..............................	175	200	200
VZ–24 BRNO, 8mm Mauser, Nazi–Proofed, Military, Curio................	125	150	150

RIFLE, PERCUSSION

M1839, .69, Musket, Brass Furniture, Military, Antique..........................	400	450	450
M1842, .75, Musket, Brass Furniture, Military, Antique........................	325	375	375

RIFLE, SEMI-AUTOMATIC

G43, 8mm Mauser, Clip Fed, 10 Shot, Military, Curio............................	275	325	325
GEW 41, 8mm Mauser, 10 Shot, Military, Curio.....................................	425	475	475
GEW 41(W), 8mm Mauser, 10 Shot, Military, Curio............................	375	450	450
KAR 43 Sniper, 8mm Mauser, Scope Mounted, Clip Fed, 10 Shot, Military, Curio........................	675	750	750
VG 2, 8mm Mauser, Clip Fed, 10 Shot, Military, Curio........................	300	375	375

RIFLE, SINGLESHOT

Model 1869 Werder, 11.5mm, Bavarian, Antique..................................	700	850	850

	V.G.	Exc	Prior Edition

GESSCER, GEORG Saxony, 1591–1611.

HANDGUN, WHEEL-LOCK

Pair, Military, Inlays, Pear Pommel, Medium Ornamentation,
Antique...$15,000 $20,000 $20,000

GEVARM Gevelot, St. Etienne, France.

RIFLE, SEMI-AUTOMATIC

Model A3, .22 L.R.R.F., Target Sights, Clip Fed, Modern........................	100	150	150
Model A6, .22 L.R.R.F., Open Sights, Clip Fed, Modern........................	100	125	125
Model A7, .22 L.R.R.F., Target Sights, Clip Fed, Modern.......................	100	150	175

GIBRALTER Made by Stevens Arms.

SHOTGUN, SINGLESHOT

Model 116, Various Gauges, Hammer, Automatic Ejector, Raised
Matted Rib, Modern... 50   75   75

GILL, THOMAS London, England 1770–1812.

HANDGUN, FLINTLOCK

.68, Pocket Pistol, Octagon Barrel, Plain, High Quality, Antique............. 800 1,000 1,000

GLASER WAFFEN Zurich, Switzerland.

HANDGUN, SINGLESHOT

Target Pistol, .22 L.R.R.F., Toggle Breech, Francotte, Modern.............. 350 400 400

RIFLE, BOLT ACTION

Custom Rifle, Various Calibers, Fancy Wood, Modern........................... 1,000 1,200 1,200

RIFLE, SINGLESHOT

Heeren Rifle, Various Calibers, Engraved, Fancy Wood, Modern.......... 2,000 2,500 2,500

GLASSBRENNER, DAVID Lancaster, Pa., c. 1800. See Kentucky Rifles.

GLAZIER, JOHN Belleville, Ind., c. 1820. See Kentucky Rifles.

GLENFIELD See Marlin.

	V.G.	Exc	Prior Edition

GLENN, ROBERT Edinburgh, Scotland, c. 1860. Made fine copies of Highland Pistols.

HANDGUN, SNAPHAUNCE

Replica Highland, All Brass, Engraved, Ovoid Pommel, Antique...........	$2,500	$3,000	$3,000

GLISENTI Soc. Siderugica Glisenti, Turin, Italy, c. 1889–1930.

HANDGUN, REVOLVER

M1889, 10.4mm Glisenti, Double Action, Folding Trigger, Military, Curio......................	125	150	150
M1889, 10.4mm Glisenti, Double Action, Trigger Guard, Military, Curio......................	125	150	150

HANDGUN, SEMI-AUTOMATIC

Brixia, 9mm Glisenti, Clip Fed, Hard Rubber Grips, Curio......................	375	425	425
M1906, 7.63 Mauser, Clip Fed, Military, Curio......................	475	550	550
M1910 Army, 9mm Glisenti, Clip Fed, Wood Grips, Curio......................	500	550	550
M1910 Navy, 9mm Glisenti, Clip Fed, Hard Rubber Grips, Curio..........	575	650	650

GOFF, DANIEL London, England 1779–1810.

HANDGUN, FLINTLOCK

Duelling Pistols, .50, Cased pair, with Accessories, Antique...................	2,000	2,500	2,500

GOLCHER, JAMES Philadelphia, Pa. 1820–1833.

GOLCHER, JOHN Easton, Pa., c. 1775.

GOLCHER, JOSEPH Philadelphia, Pa., c. 1800.

GOLDEN EAGLE Nikko Arms Co. Ltd., Tochigi, Japan.

RIFLE, BOLT ACTION

Model 7000, Various African Calibers, Grade 1, Checkered Stock, Modern......................	475	550	550
Model 7000, Various African Calibers, Grade 2, Checkered Stock, Modern......................	625	700	700
Model 7000, Various Calibers, Grade 1, Checkered Stock, Modern.......	425	500	500
Model 7000, Various Calibers, Grade 2, Checkered Stock, Modern.......	575	650	650

SHOTGUN, DOUBLE BARREL, OVER-UNDER

Model 5000 Grandee, 12 and 20 Gauges, Field Grade 3, Vent Rib, Checkered Stock, Fancy Engraving, Gold Overlay, Modern.....................	2,250	2,750	2,250
Model 5000 Grandee, 12 and 20 Gauges, Skeet Grade 3, Vent Rib, Checkered Stock, Fancy Engraving, Gold Overlay, Modern.....................	2,000	2,250	2,500
Model 5000 Grandee, 12 and 20 Gauges, Trap Grade 3, Vent Rib, Checkered Stock, Fancy Engraving, Gold Overlay, Modern.....................	2,000	2,250	2,500

	V.G.	Exc	Prior Edition
Model 5000, 12 and 20 Gauges, Field Grade 2, Vent Rib, Checkered Stock, Light Engraving, Gold Overlay, Modern............................	$1,000	$1,250	$1,000
Model 5000, 12 and 20 Gauges, Field Grade, Vent Rib, Checkered Stock, Light Engraving, Gold Overlay, Modern........................	725	850	850
Model 5000, 12 and 20 Gauges, Skeet Grade 2, Vent Rib, Checkered Stock, Light Engraving, Gold Overlay, Modern....................	950	1,100	1,100
Model 5000, 12 and 20 Gauges, Skeet Grade, Vent Rib, Checkered Stock, Light Engraving, Gold Overlay, Modern......................	800	900	950
Model 5000, 12 and 20 Gauges, Trap Grade 2, Vent Rib, Checkered Stock, Light Engraving, Gold Overlay, Modern....................	950	1,050	1,050
Model 5000, 12 and 20 Gauges, Trap Grade, Vent Rib, Checkered Stock, Light Engraving, Gold Overlay, Modern........................	875	950	950

GONTER, PETER Lancaster, Pa. 1770–1778. See Kentucky Rifles.

GOOSE GUN Made by Stevens Arms.

SHOTGUN, SINGLESHOT

	V.G.	Exc	Prior Edition
Model 89 Dreadnaught, Various Gauges, Hammer, Modern.................	50	75	75

GOVERNOR Made by Bacon Arms Co.

HANDGUN, REVOLVER

	V.G.	Exc	Prior Edition
.22 Short R.F., 7 Shot, Spur Trigger, Solid Frame, Single Action, Antique..	125	175	175

GOVERNOR Various makers, c. 1880.

HANDGUN, REVOLVER

	V.G.	Exc	Prior Edition
.32 S & W, 5 Shot, Double Action, Top Break, Modern...........................	75	100	100
.38 S & W, 5 Shot, Double Action, Top Break, Modern...........................	75	125	125

GRAEFF, WM. Reading, Pa. 1751–1784. See Kentucky Rifles.

GRANT HAMMOND New Haven, Conn. 1915–1917.

HANDGUN, SEMI-AUTOMATIC

	V.G.	Exc	Prior Edition
U.S. Test, .45 ACP, Clip Fed, Hammer, Curio..	7,000	8,000	8,000

GRANT, W. L. Manufactured by Wm. Uhlinger, Phil., Penn.

HANDGUN, REVOLVER

	V.G.	Exc	Prior Edition
.22 Long R.F., 6 Shot, Single Action, Solid Frame, Spur Trigger, Antique..	200	350	250
.22 Short R.F., 6 Shot, Single Action, Solid Frame, Spur Trigger, Antique..	200	375	250

GRAVE, JOHN Lancaster, Pa. 1769–1773. See Kentucky Rifles.

GREAT WESTERN   Venice, Calif. Moved to North Hollywood, Calif. in 1959. Last address Los Angeles, Calif. 1953–1961.

HANDGUN, DOUBLE BARREL, OVER-UNDER

	V.G.	Exc	Prior Edition
Double Derringer, .38 Spec., Remington Copy, Modern.........................	$300	$350	$275

HANDGUN, REVOLVER

Buntline, Various Calibers, Single Action, Western Style, Modern.........	650	750	400
Deputy, .22 L.R.R.F., Single Action, Western Style, Modern..................	850	1,000	300
Frontier, .22 L.R.R.F., Target Model, Single Action, Western Style, Modern...	750	900	750
Frontier, Various Calibers, Single Action, Western Style, Modern.........	500	600	350

GREAT WESTERN GUN WORKS   Pittsburgh, Pa., 1860 to about 1923.

HANDGUN, REVOLVER

.22 Short R.F., 7 Shot, Spur Trigger, Solid Frame, Single Action, Antique..	125	175	175

RIFLE, PERCUSSION

No. 5, Various Calibers, Various Barrel Lengths, Plains Rifle, Octagon Barrel, Brass Fittings, Antique..	575	650	650

GREEK MILITARY

RIFLE, BOLT ACTION

M 1903 Mannlicher Schoenauer, 6.5mm M.S., Military, Curio.............	225	275	100
M 1903 Mannlicher Schoenauer, 8mm Mauser, Military, Curio...........	225	275	100
M 1930 F N Short Rifle, 8mm Mauser, Military, Curio.........................	250	300	125

GREENER, W. W.   Established in 1829 in Northumberland, England as W. Greener, moved to Birmingham, England in 1844; name changed to W. W. Greener in 1860, and to W. W. Greener & Son in 1879.

SHOTGUN, DOUBLE BARREL, SIDE-BY-SIDE

Various Gauges, Single Non–Selective Trigger Add $280.00–$400.00			
Various Gauges, Single Selective Trigger Add $385.00–$475.00			
Crown DH–55, Various Gauges, Box Lock, Automatic Ejector, Checkered Stock, Fancy Engraving, Modern...	3,000	3,250	3,500
Empire, 12 Ga., Mag. 3", Box Lock, Hammerless, Light Engraving, Checkered Stock, Modern...	1,250	1,500	1,750
Empire, 12 Ga., Mag. 3", Box Lock, Hammerless, Light Engraving, Checkered Stock, Automatic Ejector, Modern...	1,500	1,700	2,250
Empire Deluxe, 12 Ga., Mag. 3", Box Lock, Hammerless, Engraved, Checkered Stock, Modern...	1,400	1,600	2,250
Empire Deluxe, 12 Ga., Mag. 3", Box Lock, Hammerless, Engraved, Checkered Stock, Automatic Ejector, Modern...	1,550	1,800	2,300

	V.G.	Exc	Prior Edition
Farkiller F35, 10 Ga. 3½", Box Lock, Hammerless, Engraved, Checkered Stock, Modern	$2,500	$2,750	$2,500
Farkiller F35, 10 Ga. 3½", Box Lock, Hammerless, Engraved, Checkered Stock, Automatic Ejector, Modern	3,250	3,500	3,000
Farkiller F35, 12 Ga., Mag. 3", Box Lock, Hammerless, Engraved, Checkered Stock, Modern	2,250	2,500	2,750
Farkiller F35, 12 Ga., Mag. 3", Box Lock, Hammerless, Engraved, Checkered Stock, Automatic Ejector, Modern	3,000	3,250	2,900
Farkiller F35, 8 Ga., Box Lock, Hammerless, Engraved, Checkered Stock, Modern	2,500	2,750	2,750
Farkiller F35, 8 Ga., Box Lock, Hammerless, Engraved, Checkered Stock, Automatic Ejector, Modern	3,250	3,500	3,200
Jubilee DH–35, Various Gauges, Box Lock, Automatic Ejector, Checkered Stock, Engraved, Modern	2,000	2,250	2,500
Royal DH–75, Various Gauges, Box Lock, Automatic Ejector, Checkered Stock, Fancy Engraving, Modern	3,700	3,950	3,950
Sovereign DH–40, Various Gauges, Box Lock, Automatic Ejector, Checkered Stock, Engraved, Modern	2,150	2,600	2,800

SHOTGUN, SINGLESHOT

	V.G.	Exc	Prior Edition
G.P. Martini, 12 Ga., Checkered Stock, Takedown, Modern	300	350	350

GREGORY Mt. Vernon, Ohio 1837–1842. See Kentucky Rifles.

GREIFELT & CO Suhl, Germany from 1885.

COMBINATION WEAPON, DRILLING

	V.G.	Exc	Prior Edition
Various Calibers, Engraved, Checkered Stock, Curio	2,500	3,000	3,500
Various Calibers, Fancy Wood, Fancy Checkering, Engraved, Curio	3,500	4,000	4,500

RIFLE, BOLT ACTION

	V.G.	Exc	Prior Edition
Sport, .22 Hornet, Checkered Stock, Express Sights, Curio	850	950	950

COMBINATION WEAPON, OVER-UNDER

	V.G.	Exc	Prior Edition
Various Calibers, Solid Rib, Engraved, Checkered Stock, Curio	4,500	5,000	5,000
Various Calibers, Solid Rib, Engraved, Checkered Stock, Automatic Ejector, Curio	5,000	5,500	5,500

SHOTGUN, DOUBLE BARREL, OVER-UNDER

	V.G.	Exc	Prior Edition
Various Gauges, For Vent Rib Add $300.00–$400.00			
Various Gauges, Single Trigger, Add $350.00–$450.00			
#1, .410 & 28 Ga., Automatic Ejector, Fancy Engraving, Checkered Stock, Fancy Wood, Solid Rib, Modern	3,000	3,500	5,500
#1, Various Gauges, Automatic Ejector, Fancy Engraving, Checkered Stock, Fancy Wood, Solid Rib, Modern	2,750	3,250	3,500
#3, .410 & 28 Ga., Automatic Ejector, Engraved, Checkered Solid Rib, Modern	2,000	2,500	3,500
#3, Various Gauges, Automatic Ejector, Engraved, Checkered Stock, Solid Rib, Modern	1,750	2,250	2,750
Model 143E, Various Gauges, Automatic Ejector, Engraved, Checkered Stock, Solid Rib, Double Trigger, Modern	2,000	2,250	2,250
Model 143E, Various Gauges, Automatic Ejector, Engraved, Checkered Stock, Vent Rib, Single Selective Trigger, Modern	2,250	2,500	2,500

	V.G.	Exc	Prior Edition

SHOTGUN, DOUBLE BARREL, SIDE-BY-SIDE

Model 103, 12 and 16 Gauge, Box Lock, Double Trigger,
Checkered Stock, Light Engraving, Modern... $1,500 $1,750 $2,000
Model 103E, 12 and 16 Gauge, Box Lock, Double Trigger,
Checkered Stock, Light Engraving, Automatic Ejector, Modern.............. 1,600 1,850 2,250
Model 22, 12 and 16 Gauge, Box Lock, Double Trigger,
Checkered Stock, Engraved, Modern... 1,500 1,750 1,850
Model 22E, 12 and 16 Gauge, Box Lock, Double Trigger,
Checkered Stock, Engraved, Automatic Ejector, Modern........................ 1,750 2,000 2,250

GREYHAWK ARMS CORP. South El Monte, Calif., c. 1975.

RIFLE, SINGLESHOT

Model 74, Various Calibers, Rolling Block, Octagon Barrel, Open
Rear Sight, Reproduction, Modern.. 100 125 125

GRIFFEN & HOWE N.Y.C. 1923–1976, subsidiary of Abercrombie & Fitch 1930–1976, privately held company after 1976. Maker of custom rifles.

RIFLE, BOLT ACTION

Mauser 98, .30/06, Sporterized, Engraved, Fancy Wood, Fancy
Checkering, Modern.. — 2,250 —
Mauser 98, .30/06, Sporterized, Fancy Engraving, Fancy Wood,
Fancy Checkering, Gold Inlays, Modern.. — 5,500 —
Springfield, .30/06, Sporterized, Engraved, Fancy Wood, Fancy
Checkering, Modern... — 1,800 —
Springfield, .30/06, Sporterized, Fancy Engraving, Fancy Wood,
Fancy Checkering, Modern.. — 3,500 —
Winchester M70, .30/06, Sporterized, Engraved, Fancy Wood,
Fancy Checkering, Modern.. — 3,500 —

GROOM, RICHARD London, England, c. 1855.

HANDGUN, FLINTLOCK

.68, East India Company, Calvary Pistol, Military, Tapered Round
Barrel, Brass Furniture, Antique.. 1,800 2,000 2,000

GROSS ARMS CO. Tiffin, Ohio 1862–1865.

HANDGUN, POCKET REVOLVER

.25 Short R.F., 7 Shot, Spur Trigger, Tip–Up, Antique............................ 750 900 750
.30 Short R.F., 7 Shot, Spur Trigger, Tip–Up, Antique............................ 800 1,000 725

	V.G.	Exc	Prior Edition

GRUENEL   Gruenig & Elmiger, Malters, Switzerland.

RIFLE, BOLT ACTION

Match 300m, Various Calibers, Offhand Target Rifle, Target
Sights, Ventilated Forestock, Palm Rest, Hook Buttplate, Modern........... $1,000 $1,200 $1,200
Model K 31, .308 Win., U.I.T. Target Rifle, Target Sights,
Ventilated Forestock, Modern..   750   900   900
U.L.T. Standard, .308 Win., Target Rifle, Target Sights,
Ventilated Forestock, Modern..   700   800   800

GUARDIAN   Made by Bacon Arms Co., c. 1880.

HANDGUN, REVOLVER

.22 Short R.F., 7 Shot, Spur Trigger, Solid Frame, Single Action,
Antique..   125   175   175
.32 Short R.F., 5 Shot, Spur Trigger, Solid Frame, Single Action,
Antique..   150   200   200

GUMPH, CHRISTOPHER   Lancaster, Pa. 1779–1803. See Ken–
tucky Rifles and Pistols.

GUSTAF, CARL   See Husqvarna.

GUSTLOFF WERKE   Suhl, Germany.

HANDGUN, SEMI-AUTOMATIC

.32 ACP, Clip Fed, Hammer, Single Action, Modern..............................   1,200   1,500   1,500

Gustloff Werke .32 Pistol

.380 ACP, Clip Fed, Hammer, Single Action, Modern............................   2,500   3,000   3,000

	V.G.	Exc	Prior Edition

RIFLE, BOLT ACTION

Mauser M98, 8mm Mauser, Military, Curio.. $75 $100 $100

Model KKW, .22 L.R.R.F., Pre–WW2, Singleshot, Tangent Sights,
Military Style Stock, Modern.. 350 400 400

SHOTGUN, DOUBLE BARREL, SIDE-BY-SIDE

16 Ga., Engraved, Color Case Hardened Floor, Modern.......................... 400 500 500

GYROJET See M.B. Associates.

H

V.G.   Exc.   Prior Edition

	V.G.	Exc.	Prior Edition

H & D   Henrion & Dassy, Liege, Belgium, c. 1900.

HANDGUN, SEMI-AUTOMATIC

H & D Patent, .25 ACP, Clip Fed, Curio.. $400 $500 $625

HACKET, EDWIN AND GEORGE   London, England, c. 1870.

SHOTGUN, DOUBLE BARREL, SIDE-BY-SIDE

10 Ga. 2 7/8", Damascus Barrel, Plain, Antique....................................... 150   200   200

HADDEN, JAMES   Philadelphia, Pa. c. 1769. See Kentucky Rifles and Pistols.

HAEFFER, JOHN   Lancaster, Pa., c. 1800. See Kentucky Rifles and Pistols.

HAENEL, C. G. C. G. Haenel Waffen und Fahrradfabrik, Suhl, Germany 1840–1945.

HANDGUN, SEMI-AUTOMATIC

Schmiesser Model 1, .25 ACP, Clip Fed, Curio.. $225 $275 $275

Haenel Schmeisser Model I

Schmiesser Model 2, .25 ACP, Clip Fed, Curio.. 250   300   300

RIFLE, BOLT ACTION

Model 88, Various Calibers, Sporting Rifle, Half–Octagon Barrel,
Open Rear Sights, Curio.. 300   350   350

Model 88 Sporter, Various Calibers, 5 Shot Clip, Half–Octagon
Barrel, Open Rear Sights, Curio... 350   400   400

	V.G.	Exc	Prior Edition

HAFDASA Hispano Argentina Fab. de Automoviles, Buenos Aires, Argentina, c. 1935.

HANDGUN, SEMI-AUTOMATIC

.22 L.R.R.F., Blowback, Curio.. $375 $450 $450

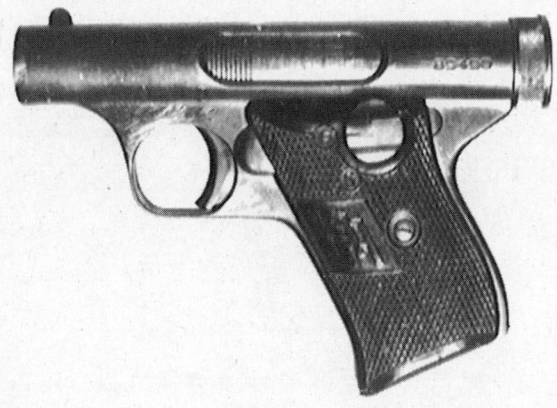

Hafdasa

HALF–BREED Made by Hopkins & Allen, c. 1880.

HANDGUN, REVOLVER

.32 Short R.F., 5 Shot, Spur Trigger, Solid Frame, Single Action,
Antique... 125 175 175

HAMMERLI Lenzburg, Switzerland.

HANDGUN, REVOLVER

Dakota, Various Calibers, Single Action, Western Style, Modern........... 250 275 275
Virginian, Various Calibers, Single Action, Western Style,
Modern... 225 250 250

HANDGUN, SEMI-AUTOMATIC

Model 200 Walther Olympia, .22 L.R.R.F., Target Pistol,
Modern... 600 625 625
Model 200 Walther Olympia, .22 L.R.R.F., Target Pistol,
Muzzle Brake, Modern... 650 675 675
Model 201 Walther Olympia, .22 L.R.R.F., Target Pistol,
Adjustable Grips, Modern... 600 625 625
Model 202 Walther Olympia, .22 L.R.R.F., Target Pistol,
Adjustable Grips, Modern... 700 750 750
Model 203 Walther Olympia, .22 L.R.R.F., Target Pistol,
Adjustable Grips, Modern... 650 700 700

	V.G.	Exc	Prior Edition
Model 203 Walther Olympia, .22 L.R.R.F., Target Pistol, Adjustable Grips, Muzzle Brake, Modern..	$725	$775	$775
Model 204 Walther Olympia, .22 L.R.R.F., Target Pistol, Modern..	700	750	750
Model 205 Walther Olympia, .22 L.R.R.F., Target Pistol, Fancy Wood, Modern..	775	850	850
Model 205 Walther Olympia, .22 L.R.R.F., Target Pistol, Fancy Wood, Muzzle Brake, Modern...	900	950	950
Model 206, .22 L.R.R.F., Target Pistol, Modern....................................	650	700	700
Model 207, .22 L.R.R.F., Target Pistol, Adjustable Grips, Modern..........	700	725	725
Model 208 Deluxe, .22 L.R.R.F., Target Pistol, Clip Fed, Adjustable Grips, Modern...	3,000	3,250	1,725
Model 208, .22 L.R.R.F., Target Pistol, Clip Fed, Adjustable Grips, Modern..	1,500	1,850	1,675
Model 209, .22 Short R.F., Target Pistol, 5 Shot Clip, Muzzle Brake, Modern..	700	775	775
Model 210, .22 L.R.R.F., Target Pistol, Adjustable Grips, Modern..........	800	875	875
Model 211, .22 L.R.R.F., Target Pistol, Clip Fed, Modern......................	1,500	1,800	1,800
Model 212, .22 L.R.R.F., Target Pistol, Clip Fed, Modern......................	1,500	1,600	1,600
Model 215, .22 L.R.R.F., Target Pistol, Clip Fed, Modern......................	850	900	900
Model 230, .22 Short R.F., Target Pistol, 5 Shot Clip, Modern...............	575	650	650
Model 232, .22 Short R.F., Target Pistol, 5 Shot Clip, Adjustable Grips, Modern...	625	675	675
Model 232, .22 Short R.F., Target Pistol, 5 Shot Clip, Adjustable Grips, Left Hand, Modern...	600	675	675
280, .22 L.R.R.F., Target Pistol, Clip Fed, Conversion Unit Only, Modern..	525	600	600
280, .22 Short, Clip Fed, Target Pistol, Cased with Accessories, Modern...	1,500	1,750	850
280, .32 Wadcutter, Clip Fed, Target Pistol, Cased with Accessories, Modern..	1,750	2,000	875

HANDGUN, SINGLESHOT

	V.G.	Exc	Prior Edition
Match Pistol, .22 L.R.R.F., Target Pistol, Round Barrel, Modern...........	500	600	950
Model 100, .22 L.R.R.F., Target Pistol, Modern....................................	750	800	800
Model 100 Deluxe, .22 L.R.R.F., Target Pistol, Modern........................	800	850	850
Model 101, .22 L.R.R.F., Target Pistol, Modern....................................	775	825	825
Model 102, .22 L.R.R.F., Target Pistol, Modern....................................	800	850	850
Model 102 Deluxe, .22 L.R.R.F., Target Pistol, Modern........................	825	875	875
Model 103, .22 L.R.R.F., Target Pistol, Carved, Modern.......................	850	925	925
Model 103, .22 L.R.R.F., Target Pistol, Carved, Inlays, Modern..............	1,000	1,250	900
Model 104, .22 L.R.R.F., Target Pistol, Round Barrel, Modern..............	750	850	950
Model 105, .22 L.R.R.F., Target Pistol, Octagon Barrel, Modern............	875	950	950
Model 107, .22 L.R.R.F., Target Pistol, Octagon Barrel, Modern...........	850	950	1,075
Model 107 Deluxe, .22 L.R.R.F., Target Pistol, Octagon Barrel, Engraved, Modern...	1,150	1,250	1,250
Model 120 H.B., .22 L.R.R.F., Target Pistol, Heavy Barrel, Left–Hand, Adjustable Grips, Modern...	550	500	500
Model 120–1, .22 L.R.R.F., Target Pistol, Heavy Barrel, Modern...........	400	450	450
Model 120–1, .22 L.R.R.F., Target Pistol, Heavy Barrel, Adjustable Grips, Modern...	400	475	475
Model 150, .22 L.R.R.F., Target Pistol, Modern....................................	1,500	1,750	1,500
Model 152 Electronic, .22 L.R.R.F., Target Pistol, Modern...................	1,750	2,000	1,600

	V.G.	Exc	Prior Edition

RIFLE, BOLT ACTION

Model 45, .22 L.R.R.F., Singleshot, Thumbhole Stock, Target
Sights, with Accessories, Modern... $500 | $550 | $550

Model 54, .22 L.R.R.F., Singleshot, Thumbhole Stock, Target
Sights, with Accessories, Modern... 525 | 575 | 575

Model 503, .22 L.R.R.F., Singleshot, Thumbhole Stock, Target
Sights, with Accessories, Modern... 500 | 550 | 550

Model 506, .22 L.R.R.F., Singleshot, Thumbhole Stock, Target
Sights, with Accessories, Modern... 550 | 600 | 600

Olympia 300 Meter, Various Calibers, Singleshot, Thumbhole
Stock, Target Sights, with Accessories, Modern.. 675 | 750 | 750

Sporting Rifle, Various Calibers, Set Triggers, Fancy Wood,
Checkered Stock, Open Sights, Modern... 525 | 600 | 600

Tanner, Various Calibers, Singleshot, Thumbhole Stock, Target
Sights, with Accessories, Modern... 750 | 825 | 825

HAMPTON, JOHN Dauphin Dounty, Pa. See Kentucky Rifles and Pistols.

HARD PAN Made by Hood Firearms, c. 1875.

HANDGUN, REVOLVER

.22 Short R.F., 7 Shot, Spur Trigger, Solid Frame, Single Action,
Antique... 100 | 150 | 150

.32 Short R.F., 5 Shot, Spur Trigger, Solid Frame, Single Action,
Antique... 125 | 175 | 175

HARPERS FERRY ARMS CO.

RIFLE, FLINTLOCK

.72 Lafayette, Musket, Reproduction .... 250 | 300 | 300

RIFLE, PERCUSSION

.51 Maynard, Carbine, Breech Loader, Reproduction .... 150 | 200 | 200
.58, 1861 Springfield, Rifled, Musket, Reproduction .... 150 | 200 | 200

HARRINGTON & RICHARDSON ARMS CO.

Worcester, Mass. Successors to Wesson & Harrington, 1874–1986. Also see the commemorative section.

HANDGUN, REVOLVER

Abilene Anniversary, .22 L.R.R.F., Commemorative, Curio.................. 75 | 100 | 100

	V.G.	Exc	Prior Edition
American, Various Calibers, Double Action, Solid Frame, Modern........	$50	$75	$75

Harrington & Richardson American .44

Auto Ejecting, Various Calibers, Top Break, Hammer, Double Action, Modern...	100	125	125

Harrington & Richardson Auto Ejecting

Bobby, Various Calibers, 6 Shot, Top Break, Double Action, Modern..	100	100	100
Bulldog, Various Calibers, Double Action, Solid Frame, Modern............	75	100	100
Defender, .38 S & W, Top Break, 6 Shot, Double Action, Adjustable Sights, Modern..	100	125	125
Expert, .22 L.R.R.F., Top Break, 9 Shot, Double Action, Wood Grips, Modern...	125	150	150
Expert, .22 W.R.F., Top Break, 9 Shot, Double Action, Wood Grips, Modern...	125	150	150
Hammerless, Various Calibers, Double Action, Solid Frame, Modern..	75	100	100
Hunter (Early), .22 L.R.R.F., 7 Shot, Solid Frame, Wood Grips, Double Action, Modern...	75	100	100
Hunter (Late), .22 L.R.R.F., 9 Shot, Solid Frame, Wood Grips, Double Action, Modern...	75	100	100
Model 4, Various Calibers, Double Action, Solid Frame, Modern...........	75	100	100

	V.G.	Exc	Prior Edition
Model 40, Various Calibers, Top Break, Hammerless, Double Action, Modern............	$100	$125	$125
Model 5, .32 S & W Double Action, 5 Shot, Solid Frame, Modern..........	75	100	100
Model 6, .22 L.R.R.F., Double Action, 7 Shot, Solid Frame, Modern............	75	100	100
Model 603, .22 W.M.R., 9 Shot, Solid Frame, Double Action, Swing–Out Cylinder, Adjustable Sights, Modern............	100	125	125
Model 604, .22 W.M.R., 9 Shot, Solid Frame, Double Action, Swing–Out Cylinder, Adjustable Sights, Modern............	125	150	100
Model 622, .22 L.R.R.F., Solid Frame, 6 Shot, Double Action, Modern............	50	75	75
Model 632, .32 S & W Long, Solid Frame, 6 Shot, Double Action, Modern............	75	100	100
Model 633, .32 S & W Long, Solid Frame, 6 Shot, Chrome, Double Action, Modern............	50	75	75
Model 649, .22LR/.22 W.M.R. Combo, Western Style, 9 Shot, Double Action, Adjustable Sights, Modern............	100	125	75

Harrington & Richardson M649, .22 Caliber

	V.G.	Exc	Prior Edition
Model 650, .22LR/.22 W.M.R. Combo, Western Style, 9 Shot, Double Action, Adjustable Sights, Modern............	125	150	75
Model 666, .22LR/.22 W.M.R. Combo, Solid Frame, 9 Shot, Double Action, Modern............	50	75	75
Model 676, .22LR/.22 W.M.R. Combo, Western Style, 9 Shot, Double Action, Adjustable Sights, Modern............	75	100	100
Model 676–12", .22LR/.22 W.M.R. Combo, Western Style, 9 Shot, Double Action, Adjustable Sights, Modern............	100	125	100
Model 686, .22LR/.22 W.M.R. Combo, Western Style, 9 Shot, Double Action, Adjustable Sights, Modern............	125	175	100
Model 732, .32 S & W Long, Solid Frame, 6 Shot, Double Action, Swing–Out Cylinder, Modern............	75	100	75
Model 733, .32 S & W Long, Solid Frame, 6 Shot, Double Action, Swing–Out Cylinder, Modern............	100	125	75
Model 766, .22 L.R.R.F., Top Break, 7 Shot, Double Action, Wood Grips, Modern............	100	125	150
Model 766, .22 W.M.F., Top Break, 7 Shot, Double Action, Wood Grips, Modern............	100	125	150
Model 826, .22 W.M.R., 6 Shot, Double Action, Adjustable Sights, Swing–Out Cylinder, Modern............	75	100	100
Model 829, .22 L.R.R.F., 9 Shot, Double Action, Adjustable Sights, Swing–Out Cylinder, Modern............	75	100	100

	V.G.	Exc	Prior Edition
Model 832, .32 S & W, 6 Shot, Double Action, Adjustable Sights, Swing–Out Cylinder, Modern...	$75	$100	$100
Model 900, .22 L.R.R.F., Solid Frame, 9 Shot, Double Action, Modern...	75	75	75

Harrington & Richardson M900, .22 Caliber

	V.G.	Exc	Prior Edition
Model 901, .22 L.R.R.F., Solid Frame, 9 Shot, Double Action, Modern...	75	100	75
Model 922 (Early), .22 L.R.R.F., 9 Shot, Solid Frame, Wood Grips, Octagon Barrel, Double Action, Modern..	75	100	100
Model 922 (Early), .22 L.R.R.F., 9 Shot, Solid Frame, Double Action, Modern...	50	75	100
Model 922 (Late), .22 L.R.R.F., 9 Shot, Solid Frame, Swing–Out Cylinder, Double Action, Modern..	50	75	75
Model 925, .22 L.R.R.F., 9 Shot, Solid Frame, Double Action, Swing–Out Cylinder, Modern...	75	100	75
Model 925, .38 S & W, Solid Frame, 5 Shot, Adjustable Sights, Modern...	75	100	100
Model 926, .22 L.R.R.F., 5 Shot, Solid Frame, Adjustable Sights, Modern...	100	125	100
Model 926, .38 S & W, Solid Frame, 5 Shot, Adjustable Sights, Modern...	75	100	100

	V.G.	Exc	Prior Edition
Model 929, .22 L.R.R.F., 9 Shot, Solid Frame, Double Action, Swing–Out Cylinder, Modern..	$50	$75	$75

Harrington & Richardson M929, .22 Caliber

	V.G.	Exc	Prior Edition
Model 930, .22 L.R.R.F., 9 Shot, Solid Frame, Double Action, Swing–Out Cylinder, Adjustable Sights, Modern.....................................	75	100	75
Model 939, .22 L.R.R.F., 9 Shot, Solid Frame, Double Action, Swing–Out Cylinder, Adjustable Sights, Modern.....................................	75	100	75
Model 940, .22 L.R.R.F., 9 Shot, Solid Frame, Double Action, Swing–Out Cylinder, Modern..	50	75	75
Model 949, .22 L.R.R.F., 9 Shot, Western Style, Double Action, Adjustable Sights, Modern..	75	100	75
Model 950, .22 L.R.R.F., 9 Shot, Western Style, Double Action, Adjustable Sights, Modern..	75	100	75
Model 976, .22 Checkered Grip, Case Hardened Frame, Modern............	50	75	75
Model 999 (Early), .22 L.R.R.F., 9 Shot, Top Break, Double Action, Adjustable Sights, Modern..	125	150	100
Model 999 (Early), .22 W.R.F., Top Break, 9 Shot, Double Action, Adjustable Sights, Modern..	125	150	150
Model 999 (Engraved), .22 L.R.R.F., Top Break, 9 Shot, Double Action, Adjustable Sights, Modern..	250	350	300
New Defender, .22 L.R.R.F., Top Break, 9 Shot, Double Action, Wood Grips, Adjustable Sights, Modern..	150	175	125
Special, .22 L.R.R.F., Top Break, 9 Shot, Double Action, Wood Grips, Modern..	100	125	125
Special, .22 W.R.F., Top Break, 9 Shot, Double Action, Wood Grips, Modern..	125	150	150
Sportsman No. 199, .22 L.R.R.F., Single Action, 9 Shot, Top Break Adjustable Sights, Modern..	75	100	100
Target (Early), .22 L.R.R.F., Top Break, 9 Shot, Double Action, Wood Grips, Modern...	100	125	125
Target (Early), .22 W.R.F., Top Break, 9 Shot, Double Action, Wood Grips, Modern...	100	125	150
Target (Hi Speed), .22 L.R.R.F., Top Break, 9 Shot, Double Action, Wood Grips, Modern...	125	150	150

	V.G.	Exc	Prior Edition
Target (Hi Speed), .22 W.R.F., Top Break, 9 Shot, Double Action, Wood Grips, Modern....................	$125	$150	$150
Trapper, .22 L.R.R.F., 7 Shot, Solid Frame, Wood Grips, Double Action, Modern....................	100	125	100
Vest Pocket, Various Calibers, Double Action, Solid Frame, Spurless Hammer, Modern....................	50	75	100
Young America, Various Calibers, Double Action, Solid Frame, Modern....................	50	75	100

HANDGUN, SEMI-AUTOMATIC

	V.G.	Exc	Prior Edition
Self–Loading, .25 ACP, Clip Fed, Modern....................	275	325	325
Self–Loading, .32 ACP, Clip Fed, Modern....................	225	275	275

Harrington & Richardson .32 Pistol

HANDGUN, SINGLESHOT

	V.G.	Exc	Prior Edition
U.S.R.A. Target, .22 L.R.R.F., Top Break, Adjustable Sights, Wood Grips, Modern....................	325	375	375

RIFLE, BOLT ACTION

	V.G.	Exc	Prior Edition
Model 250 Sportster, .22 L.R.R.F., 5 Shot Clip, Open Rear Sight, Modern....................	50	75	75
Model 251 Sportster, .22 L.R.R.F., 5 Shot Clip, Open Rear Sight, Modern....................	50	75	75
Model 265 Reg'lar, .22 L.R.R.F., Clip Fed, Peep Sights, Modern....................	50	75	75
Model 300, Various Calibers, Cheekpiece, Monte Carlo Stock, Checkered Stock, Modern....................	300	350	350
Model 301, Various Calibers, Checkered Stock, Mannlicher, Modern....................	350	400	400
Model 317, Various Calibers, Checkered Stock, Monte Carlo Stock, Modern....................	275	325	325
Model 317P, .223 Rem., Fancy Checkering, Monte Carlo Stock, Fancy Wood, Modern....................	450	500	500
Model 330, Various Calibers, Checkered Stock, Monte Carlo Stock, Modern....................	225	275	275
Model 333, Various Calibers, Monte Carlo Stock, Modern....................	225	275	275

	V.G.	Exc	Prior Edition
Model 340, Various Calibers, Monte Carlo Stock, Recoil Pad, Modern....................	$250	$300	$300
Model 365 ACE, .22 L.R.R.F., Singleshot, Peep Sights, Modern...........	50	50	50
Model 370, Various Calibers, Target Stock, Heavy Barrel, Modern....................	300	350	350
Model 450 Medalist, .22 L.R.R.F., 5 Shot Clip, No Sights, Target Stock, Modern....................	125	150	150
Model 451 Medalist, .22 L.R.R.F., 5 Shot Clip, Lyman Sights, Target Stock, Modern....................	125	175	175
Model 465 Targeteer, .22 L.R.R.F., Clip Fed, Peep Sights, Modern....................	75	100	100
Model 465 Targeteer Jr., .22 L.R.R.F., Clip Fed, Peep Sights, Modern....................	75	100	100
Model 5200 Match, .22 L.R.R.F., Target Rifle, Single Shot, Heavy Barrel, No Sights, Modern....................	225	275	275
Model 5200 Sporter, .22 L.R.R.F., Targert Rifle, Clip Fed, Target Sights, Checkered Stock, Modern....................	225	275	275
Model 750 Pioneer, .22 L.R.R.F., Singleshot, Open Rear Sight, Modern....................	50	50	50
Model 751 Pioneer, .22 L.R.R.F., Singleshot, Open Rear Sight, Mannlicher, Modern....................	50	75	75
Model 765 Pioneer, .22 L.R.R.F., Singleshot, Open Rear Sight, Modern....................	50	50	50
Model 852 Fieldsman, .22 L.R.R.F., Tube Feed, Open Rear Sight, Modern....................	50	75	75
Model 865 Plainsman, .22 L.R.R.F., 5 Shot Clip, Open Rear Sights, Modern....................	50	75	75
Model 866 Plainsman, .22 L.R.R.F., 5 Shot Clip, Open Rear Sight, Mannlicher, Modern....................	50	75	75

RIFLE, PERCUSSION

	V.G.	Exc	Prior Edition
Huntsman .45, Top Break, Side Lever, Rifled, Reproduction, Antique....................	75	100	100
Huntsman .50, Top Break, Side Lever, Rifled, Reproduction, Antique....................	75	100	100
Model 175, .45 or .58 Caliber, Springfield Style, Open Sights, Reproduction, Antique....................	125	175	175
Model 175 Deluxe, .45 or .58 Caliber, Springfield Style, Open Sights, Checkered Stock, Reproduction, Antique....................	225	275	275

RIFLE, SEMI-AUTOMATIC

	V.G.	Exc	Prior Edition
Model 150 Leatherneck, .22 L.R.R.F., 5 Shot Clip, Open Rear Sight, Modern....................	75	100	100
Model 151 Leatherneck, .22 L.R.R.F., 5 Shot Clip, Peep Sights, Modern....................	75	100	100
Model 165 Leatherneck, .22 L.R.R.F., Clip Fed, Heavy Barrel, Peep Sights, Modern....................	100	125	125
Model 308, Various Calibers, Checkered Stock, Monte Carlo Stock, Modern....................	275	325	325
Model 360, Various Calibers, Checkered Stock, Monte Carlo Stock, Modern....................	250	300	300
Model 361, Various Calibers, Checkered Stock, Monte Carlo Stock, Modern....................	275	325	325
Model 60 Reising, .45 ACP, Clip Fed, Carbine, Open Rear Sight, Modern....................	350	400	400

	V.G.	Exc	Prior Edition
Model 65 General, .22 L.R.R.F., Clip Fed, Heavy Barrel, Peep Sights, Modern.............................	$200	$250	$250
Model 700, .22 W.M.R., Monte Carlo Stock, 5 Shot Clip, Modern..........	125	150	150
Model 700 Deluxe, .22 W.M.R., Monte Carlo Stock, 5 Shot Clip, Modern................................	200	225	225
Model 800 Lynx, .22 L.R.R.F., Clip Fed, Open Rear Sight, Modern................................	75	100	100

RIFLE, SINGLESHOT

	V.G.	Exc	Prior Edition
1871 Springfield Deluxe, .45–70 Government, Trap Door Action, Carbine, Light Engraving, Modern......................	225	250	250
1871 Springfield Officers', .45–70 Government, Commemorative, Trap Door Action, Curio............	275	350	350
1871 Springfield Standard, .45–70 Government, Trap Door Action, Carbine, Modern...........	175	200	200
1873 Springfield Officers', .45–70 Government, Trap Door Action, Light Engraving, Peep Sights, Modern............	250	300	300
1873 Springfield Standard, .45–70 Government, Trap Door Action, Commemorative, Modern............	200	225	225
Custer Memorial Enlisted Model, .45–70 Government, Commemorative, Trap Door Action, Carbine, Fancy Engraving, Fancy Wood, Curio............	1,000	1,500	1,500
Custer Memorial Officers' Model, .45–70 Government, Commemorative, Trap Door Action, Carbine, Fancy Engraving, Fancy Wood, Curio............	2,000	2,750	2,750
Little Big Horn Springfield Standard, .45–70 Government, Commemorative, Trap Door Action, Carbine, Curio...........	300	350	350
Model 157, Various Calibers, Top Break, Side Lever, Automatic Ejector, Open Rear Sights, Mannlicher, Modern....................	50	75	75
Model 158 Topper, Various Calibers, Top Break, Side Lever, Automatic Ejector, Open Rear Sight, Modern............	50	75	75
Model 158 Topper, Various Calibers, Top Break, Side Lever, Automatic Ejector, Open Rear Sight, Extra Set of Rifle Barrels, Modern...........	75	100	100
Model 158 Topper, Various Calibers, Top Break, Side Lever, Automatic Ejector, Open Rear Sight, Extra Shotgun Barrel, Modern...........	75	100	100
Model 163, Various Calibers, Top Break, Side Lever, Automatic Ejector, Open Rear Sight, Modern...........	50	75	75
Model 172 Springfield, .45–70 Government, Trap Door Action, Carbine, Engraved, Silver Plated, Tang Sights, Checkered Sights, Modern...........	350	400	400
Model 755 Sahara, .22 L.R.R.F., Singleshot, Open Rear Sight, Mannlicher, Modern...........	50	75	75
Model 760 Sahara, .22 L.R.R.F., Singleshot, Open Rear Sight, Modern...........	50	50	50
Shikari, .44 Magnum, Top Break, Side Lever, Automatic Ejector, Modern...........	50	75	75
Shikari, .45–70 Government, Top Break, Side Lever, Automatic Ejector, Modern...........	75	100	100

RIFLE, SLIDE ACTION

	V.G.	Exc	Prior Edition
Model 422, .22 L.R.R.F., Tube Feed, Open Rear Sight, Modern..............	100	125	125

	V.G.	Exc	Prior Edition

SHOTGUN, BOLT ACTION

Model 348 Gamemaster, 12 and 16 Gauges, Tube Feed,
Takedown, Modern...... $50 $75 $75

Model 349 Deluxe, 12 and 16 Gauges, Tube Feed, Takedown,
Adjustable Choke, Modern...... 50 75 75

Model 351 Huntsman, 12 and 16 Gauges, Tube Feed, Takedown,
Monte Carlo Stock, Adjustable Choke, Modern...... 50 75 75

SHOTGUN, PERCUSSION

Huntsman 12 Ga., Top Break, Side Lever, Reproduction, Antique...... 75 100 100

SHOTGUN, DOUBLE BARREL, OVER-UNDER

Model 1212, 12 Ga., Field Grade, Vent Rib, Single Selective
Trigger, Modern...... 325 375 375

Model 1212 Waterfowl, Ga. Mag. 3", Field Grade, Vent Rib,
Single Selective Trigger, Modern...... 350 400 400

SHOTGUN, DOUBLE BARREL, SIDE-BY-SIDE

Model 404, Various Gauges, Hammerless, Modern...... 150 175 175

Model 404C, Various Gauges, Hammerless, Checkered Stock,
Modern...... 125 175 175

SHOTGUN, SEMI-AUTOMATIC

Model 403, .410 Ga., Takedown, Modern...... 150 200 200

SHOTGUN, SINGLESHOT

Folding Gun, Various Gauges, Top Break, Hammer, Automatic
Ejector, Modern...... 50 75 75

Model #1 Harrich, 12 Ga., Vent Rib, Engraved, Fancy
Checkering, Modern...... 1,250 1,550 1,550

Model 148, Various Gauges, Top Break, Side Lever, Automatic
Ejector, Modern...... 50 75 75

Model 158, Various Gauges, Top Break, Side Lever, Automatic
Ejector, Modern...... 50 75 75

Model 159, Various Gauges, Top Break, Side Lever, Automatic
Ejector, Modern...... 50 75 75

Model 162 Buck, 12 Ga., Top Break, Side Lever, Automatic
Ejector, Peep Sights, Modern...... 50 75 75

Model 176, 10 Ga. 3½", Top Break, Side Lever, Automatic
Ejector, Modern...... 50 75 75

Model 188 Deluxe, Various Gauges, Top Break, Side Lever,
Automatic Ejector, Modern...... 25 50 50

Model 198 Deluxe, Various Gauges, Top Break, Side Lever,
Automatic Ejector, Modern...... 25 50 50

Model 3, Various Gauges, Top Break, Hammerless, Automatic
Ejector, Modern...... 50 75 75

Model 459 Youth, Various Gauges, Top Break, Side Lever,
Automatic Ejector, Modern...... 50 75 75

Model 48, Various Gauges, Top Break, Hammer, Automatic
Ejector, Modern...... 50 50 50

Model 480 Youth, Various Gauges, Top Break, Side Lever,
Automatic Ejector, Modern...... 50 50 50

Model 488 Deluxe, Various Gauges, Top Break, Hammer,
Automatic Ejector, Modern...... 50 75 75

	V.G.	Exc	Prior Edition
Model 490 Youth, Various Gauges, Top Break, Side Lever, Automatic Ejector, Modern	$50	$50	$50
Model 5, Various Gauges, Top Break, Lightweight, Automatic Ejector, Modern	75	100	100
Model 6, Various Gauges, Top Break, Heavyweight, Automatic Ejector, Modern	75	100	100
Model 7, Various Gauges, Top Break, Automatic Ejector, Modern	50	75	75
Model 8 Standard, Various Gauges, Top Break, Automatic Ejector, Modern	50	75	75
Model 9, Various Gauges, Top Break, Automatic Ejector, Modern	50	75	75
Model 98, Various Gauges, Top Break, Side Lever, Automatic Ejector, Modern	50	75	75

SHOTGUN, SLIDE ACTION

	V.G.	Exc	Prior Edition
Model 400, Various Gauges, Solid Frame, Modern	150	175	175
Model 400, Various Gauges, Solid Frame, Vent Rib, Modern	150	175	175
Model 401, Various Gauges, Solid Frame, Adjustable Choke, Modern	150	175	175
Model 402, .410 Ga., Solid Frame, Modern	150	175	175
Model 440, Various Gauges, Solid Frame, Modern	150	175	175

HARRIS, HENRY Payton, Pa. 1779–1783. See Kentucky Rifles.

HARRISON ARMS CO. Made in Belgium for Sickles & Preston, Davenport, Iowa.

SHOTGUN, DOUBLE BARREL, SIDE-BY-SIDE

	V.G.	Exc	Prior Edition
Various Gauges, Hammerless, Damascus Barrel, Modern	100	150	150
Various Gauges, Hammerless, Steel Barrel, Modern	125	200	200
Various Gauges, Outside Hammers, Damascus Barrel, Modern	100	150	150
Various Gauges, Outside Hammers, Steel Barrel, Modern	150	225	200

SHOTGUN, SINGLESHOT

	V.G.	Exc	Prior Edition
Various Gauges, Hammer, Steel Barrel, Modern	50	75	75

HARTFORD ARMS & EQUIPMENT CO. Hartford, Conn. 1929–1932. Acquired by High Standard Arms Co. in 1932.

HANDGUN, MANUAL REPEATER

	V.G.	Exc	Prior Edition
.22 L.R.R.F., Single Shot Target, Clip Fed, Target Pistol, Curio	700	800	550

HANDGUN, SEMI-AUTOMATIC

	V.G.	Exc	Prior Edition
1st Model, .22 L.R.R.F., Clip Fed, Target Pistol, Curio	650	750	500
2nd Model, .22 L.R.R.F., Target Pistol, Curio	600	700	525

HARTFORD ARMS CO. Made by Crescent for Simmons Hard– ware Co., St. Louis, Mo.

SHOTGUN, DOUBLE BARREL, SIDE-BY-SIDE

	V.G.	Exc	Prior Edition
Various Gauges, Hammerless, Damascus Barrel, Modern	100	150	150
Various Gauges, Hammerless, Steel Barrel, Modern	150	175	200

	V.G.	Exc	Prior Edition
Various Gauges, Outside Hammers, Damascus Barrel, Modern..............	$125	$175	$175
Various Gauges, Outside Hammers, Steel Barrel, Modern......................	150	200	200

SHOTGUN, SINGLESHOT

Various Gauges, Hammer, Steel Barrel, Modern....................................	50	75	75

HARTFORD ARMS CO. Made by Norwich Falls Pistol Co., c. 1880.

HANDGUN, REVOLVER

.32 Short R.F., 5 Shot, Spur Trigger, Solid Frame, Single Action, Antique..	125	175	175

HARVARD Made by Crescent, c. 1900.

SHOTGUN, DOUBLE BARREL, SIDE-BY-SIDE

Various Gauges, Hammerless, Damascus Barrel, Modern......................	150	175	150
Various Gauges, Hammerless, Steel Barrel, Modern...............................	150	200	200
Various Gauges, Outside Hammers, Damascus Barrel, Modern............	125	175	175
Various Gauges, Outside Hammers, Steel Barrel, Modern......................	150	200	200

SHOTGUN, SINGLESHOT

Various Gauges, Hammer, Steel Barrel, Modern....................................	50	75	75

HAUCK, WILBUR West Arlington, Vt., c. 1950.

RIFLE, SINGLESHOT

Target Rifle, Various Calibers, Target Sights, Target Stock, Adjustable Trigger, Modern..	450	550	525

HAWES FIREARMS Van Nuys, Calif. Manufactured by J. P. Sauer und Sohn, Eckernforde, Germany.

HANDGUN, REVOLVER

Chief City Marshall, .25 Colt, Western Style, Single Action, Brass Grip Frame, Adjustable Sights, Modern..	125	200	200
Chief Marshall, .357 Magnum, Western Style, Single Action, Brass Grip Frame, Adjustable Sights, Modern..	125	200	200
Chief Marshall, .44 Magnum, Western Style, Single Action, Brass Grip Frame, Adjustable Sights, Modern..	125	200	200
Denver Marshall, .22 L.R.R.F., Western Style, Single Action, Brass Grip Frame, Adjustable Sights, Modern..	75	100	100
Denver Marshall, .22 L.R.R.F./.22 W.M.R. Combo, Western Style, Single Action, Adjustable Sights, Modern......................................	125	150	150
Montana Marshall, .22 L.R.R.F., Western Style, Single Action, Brass Grip Frame, Modern..	75	100	100
Montana Marshall, .22 L.R.R.F./.22 W.M.R. Combo, Western Style, Single Action, Brass Grip Frame, Modern......................................	100	125	125
Montana Marshall, .357 Magnum/9mm Combo, Western Style, Single Action, Brass Grip Frame, Modern..	175	225	225
Montana Marshall, .44 Magnum, Western Style, Single Action, Brass Grip Frame, Modern..	150	200	200

	V.G.	Exc	Prior Edition
Montana Marshall, .44 Magnum/.44–40 Combo, Western Style, Single Action, Brass Grip Frame, Modern	$175	$225	$225
Montana Marshall, .45 Colt, Western Style, Single Action, Brass Grip Frame, Modern	150	200	200
Montana Marshall, .45 Colt/.45 ACP Combo, Western Style, Single Action, Brass Grip Frame, Modern	175	250	250
Silver City Marshall, .22 L.R.R.F., Western Style, Single Action, Brass Grip Frame, Modern	75	100	100
Silver City Marshall, .22 L.R.R.F./.22 W.M.R., Western Style, Single Action, Brass Grip Frame, Modern	100	150	150
Silver City Marshall, .357 Magnum/9mm Combo, Western Style, Single Action, Brass Grip Frame, Modern	150	225	225
Silver City Marshall, .44 Magnum, Western Style, Single Action, Brass Grip Frame, Modern	150	225	225
Silver City Marshall, .44 Magnum/.44–40 Combo, Western Style, Single Action, Brass Grip Frame, Modern	150	225	225
Silver City Marshall, .45 Colt, Western Style, Single Action, Brass Grip Frame, Modern	125	200	200
Silver City Marshall, .45 Colt/.45 ACP Combo, Western Style, Single Action, Brass Grip Frame, Modern	150	250	250
Texas Marshall, .22 L.R.R.F., Western Style, Single Action, Nickel Plated, Modern	75	100	100
Texas Marshall, .22 L.R.R.F./.22 W.M.R., Combo, Western Style, Single Action, Nickel Plated, Modern	125	150	150
Texas Marshall, .357 Magnum, Western Style, Single Action, Nickel Plated, Modern	125	200	200
Texas Marshall, .357 Magnum/9mm Combo, Western Style, Single Action, Nickel Plated, Modern	150	225	225
Texas Marshall, .44 Magnum, Western Style, Single Action, Nickel Plated, Modern	125	200	200
Texas Marshall, .44 Magnum/.44–40 Combo, Western Style, Single Action, Nickel Plated, Modern	175	250	250
Texas Marshall, .45 Colt, Western Style, Single Action, Nickel Plated, Modern	125	200	200
Texas Marshall, .45 Colt/.45 ACP Combo, Western Style, Single Action, Nickel Plated, Modern	175	250	250

HANDGUN, SEMI-AUTOMATIC

.25 ACP, Clip Fed, Modern	100	125	125

HANDGUN, SINGLESHOT

Stevens Favorite Copy, .22 L.R.R.F., Tip–Up, Plastic Grips, Modern	100	125	125
Stevens Favorite Copy, .22 L.R.R.F., Tip–Up, Plastic Grips, Target Sights, Modern	100	125	125
Stevens Favorite Copy, .22 L.R.R.F., Tip–Up, Rosewood Grips, Modern	100	125	125

HAWKIN, J. & S. Jacob and Samuel Hawkin, St. Louis, Mo. 1822–1862. John Gemmer purchased the business and continued it until 1890.

RIFLE, PERCUSSION

Gemmer Plains Rifle, Various Calibers, Hawkin Style, Antique	20,000	RARE	—
Hawkin Plains Rifle, Various Calibers, Hawkin Style, Antique	25,000	RARE	—

	V.G.	Exc	Prior Edition

HAWKINS, HENRY Schenectady, N.Y. 1769–1775. See Kentucky Rifles.

H.D.H. Mrs. D'Armes HDH, Liege, Belgium, c. 1910.

HANDGUN, REVOLVER

	V.G.	Exc	Prior Edition
10 Shot, Various Calibers, Double Action, Curio......................................	$125	$200	$200
20 Shot, Various Calibers, Over–Under Barrels, Two Row Cylinder, Double Action, Curio.......................	225	275	275
Constabulary Type, Various Calibers, Double Action, Curio.................	125	150	150
Ordnance Type, Various Calibers, Double Action, Curio.......................	150	175	175
"Velo–Dog," Various Calibers, Folding Trigger, Double Action, Hammerless, Curio.......................	100	125	125

HECKERT, PHILIP York, Pa. 1769–1779. See Kentucky Rifles and Pistols.

HECKLER & KOCH Oberndorf/Neckar, Germany.

HANDGUN, SEMI-AUTOMATIC

	V.G.	Exc	Prior Edition
HK, Various Calibers, Clip Fed, Conversion Kit Only, Each....................	25	50	75
HK, Various Calibers, Clip Fed, Double Action, with Conversion Kits All 4 Calibers, Modern.......................	500	600	450
HK P–7(PSP), 9mm Luger, Squeeze Cocking, Modern..........................	575	675	550
HK P–9S, .45 ACP, Clip Fed, Double Action, Modern.......................	325	400	400
HK P–9S, .45 ACP, Target Model, Clip Fed, Double Action, Modern.......................	350	450	600

Heckler & Koch P-9S Sport Competition

	V.G.	Exc	Prior Edition
HK P–9S, .45 ACP, with Extra 8" Barrel, Clip Fed, Double Action, Modern	$400	$500	$725
HK–4, .22 L.R.R.F., Clip Fed, Double Action, Modern	400	475	325
HK–4, .25 ACP, Clip Fed, Double Action, Modern	275	350	300
HK–4, .32 ACP, Clip Fed, Double Action, Modern	225	300	250
HK–4, .32 ACP, Clip Fed, Double Action, French Made, Modern	250	300	275
HK–4, .32 ACP, Clip Fed, Double Action, German Police, Modern	300	400	400
HK–4, .380 ACP, Clip Fed, Double Action, Modern	375	450	325
P–9S, 9mm Luger, Clip Fed, Double Action 5½" Barrel, Target Sights, Modern	350	450	825
P–9S Combat, 9mm Luger, Clip Fed, Double Action 4" Barrel, Modern	425	500	550
P–9S Combat, 9mm Luger, Clip Fed, Double Action 4" Barrel with .30 Luger Conversion Kit, Modern	625	700	750
P–9S Competition Kit, 9mm Luger, Clip Fed, Double Action, Extra Barrel, Target Sights, Target Grips, Modern	650	750	850
VP–70Z, 9mm Luger, Clip Fed, Double Action, 18 Shot Clip, Modern	275	350	275

RIFLE, SEMI-AUTOMATIC

	V.G.	Exc	Prior Edition
HK 770, .308 Win., Sporting Rifle, Checkered Stock, Monte Carlo Stock, Modern	550	650	575
HK 91 A–2 Package, .308 Win., Clip Fed, Sporting Version of Military Rifle, with Compensator, Polygonal Rifling, Modern	1,500	1,750	750
HK 91 A–2, .308 Win., Clip Fed, Sporting Version of Military Rifle, with Compensator, Modern	1,000	1,250	950
HK 91 A–2, .308 Win., Clip Fed, Sporting Version of Military Rifle, Folding Stock with Compensator, Polygonal Rifling, Modern	1,250	1,500	900
HK 91 A–3, .308 Win., Clip Fed, Sporting Version of Military Rifle, Folding Stock with Compensator, Modern	1,250	1,500	1,400
HK 91, .22 L.R.R.F., Clip Fed, Conversion Kit Only,	600	750	350
HK 91/93, For Scope Mount Add $75.00–$120.00			
HK 91/93, Light Bipod, Add $40.00–$60.00			
HK 93 A–2, .223 Rem., Clip Fed, Sporting Version of Military Rifle, with Compensator, Modern	1,000	1,250	950
HK 93 A–3, .223 Rem., Clip Fed, Sporting Version of Military Rifle, Folding Stock with Compensator, Modern	1,250	1,500	1,000

Heckler & Koch HK 93 A-3

	V.G.	Exc	Prior Edition
HK 94 A–2, 9mm Luger, Clip Fed, Carbine, Standard Stock, Modern.........	$1,750	$2,000	$1,100

Heckler & Koch HK 94 A-2

	V.G.	Exc	Prior Edition
HK 94 A–3, 9mm Luger, Clip Fed, Carbine, Folding Stock, Modern.........	1,850	2,150	1,200
Model 270, .22 L.R.R.F., Clip Fed, Checkered Stock, Open Rear Sight, Modern.........	300	325	325
Model 300, .22 WMR, Clip Fed, Checkered Stock, Open Rear Sight, Modern.........	425	500	425
Model 630, .223 Rem., Clip Fed, Checkered Stock, Open Rear Sight, Modern.........	500	600	500
Model 940, .30/06, Clip Fed, Checkered Stock, Open Rear Sight, Modern.........	550	650	600

Heckler & Koch HK Model 940

	V.G.	Exc	Prior Edition
Model SL 6, .223 Rem., Clip Fed, Military Style Carbine, Open Rear Sight, Modern.........	450	575	525
Model SL 7, .308 Win., Clip Fed, Military Style Carbine, Open Rear Sight, Modern.........	425	550	525

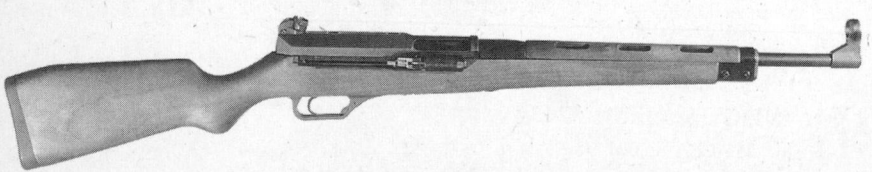

Heckler & Koch SL 7

HEGE
Tradename of Hebsacker Gesellschaft and Hege GmbH, established in 1959 in Schwabisch Halle, West Germany. Now in Uberlingen/Bodensee, West Germany. Also see Beeman's.

HANDGUN, PERCUSSION

	V.G.	Exc	Prior Edition
Silber Pistol, .33 Caliber, British Style, Engraved, Cased, Reproduction, Antique	$375	$425	$425
Silber Pistol, .33 Caliber, French Style, Engraved, Gold Inlays, Cased, Reproduction, Antique	600	650	650

HANDGUN, SEMI-AUTOMATIC

AP–63, .32 ACP, Clip Fed, Double Action, Modern	275	325	325

Hege AP-66 .32

AP–66, .32 ACP, Clip Fed, Double Action, Modern	225	275	275
AP–66, .380 ACP, Clip Fed, Double Action, Modern	250	300	300

COMBINATION WEAPON, OVER-UNDER

President, Various Calibers, Box Lock, Solid Rib, Double Trigger, Checkered Stock, Modern	675	725	725

RIFLE, MATCHLOCK

Zeughaus Musket, .63 Caliber, Heavy Swiss Style, Plain, Reproduction, Antique	250	300	300

HEINZELMANN, C.E.
Plochigen, Germany 1921–1928.

HANDGUN, SEMI-AUTOMATIC

Heim, .25 ACP, Clip Fed, Blue, Curio	200	250	225

	V.G.	Exc	Prior Edition

HELFRICHT Alfred Krauser Waffenfabrik, Zella Mehlis, Germany 1921–1929.

HANDGUN, SEMI-AUTOMATIC

	V.G.	Exc	Prior Edition
Model 1, .25 ACP, Clip Fed, Curio..	$425	$475	$475
Model 2, .25 ACP, Clip Fed, Curio..	400	450	450
Model 3, .25 ACP, Clip Fed, Curio..	400	450	450
Model 4, .25 ACP, Clip Fed, Curio..	350	400	400

HELVICE Fab. D'Armes de Guerre de Grand Precision, Eibar, Spain.

HANDGUN, SEMI-AUTOMATIC

.25 ACP, Clip Fed, Modern..	125	150	150

HENNCH, PETER Lancaster, Pa. 1770–1774. See Kentucky Rifles.

HENRY GUN CO. Belgium, c. 1900.

SHOTGUN, DOUBLE BARREL, SIDE-BY-SIDE

Various Gauges, Hammerless, Damascus Barrel, Modern......................	150	200	200
Various Gauges, Hammerless, Steel Barrel, Modern...............................	175	225	225
Various Gauges, Outside Hammers, Damascus Barrel, Modern.............	150	200	200
Various Gauges, Outside Hammers, Steel Barrel, Modern......................	150	200	200

SHOTGUN, SINGLESHOT

Various Gauges, Hammer, Steel Barrel, Modern....................................	75	100	100

HENRY, ALEXANDER Edinburgh, Scotland 1869–1895.

RIFLE, DOUBLE BARREL, SIDE-BY-SIDE

.500/450 Mag. BPE, Damascus Barrel, Engraved, Fancy Checkering, Ornate, Cased with Accessories, Hammerless, Antique...........................	4,750	5,250	5,000

HERCULES Made by Stevens Arms.

SHOTGUN, DOUBLE BARREL, SIDE-BY-SIDE

M 315, Various Gauges, Hammerless, Steel Barrel, Modern....................	150	175	175
Model 215, 12 and 16 Gauges, Outside Hammers, Steel Barrel, Modern...	150	175	175
Model 311, Various Gauges, Hammerless, Steel Barrel, Modern.............	175	200	200
Model 3151, Various Gauges, Hammerless, Recoil Pad, Front & Rear Bead Sights, Modern...	175	200	200
Model 5151, Various Gauges, Hammerless, Steel Barrel, Modern...........	175	200	200

SHOTGUN, SINGLESHOT

Model 94, Various Gauges, Takedown, Automatic Ejector, Plain Hammer, Modern..	50	75	75

	V.G.	Exc	Prior Edition

HERMETIC Tradename used by Bernadon–Martin, St. Etienne, France, c. 1912.

HANDGUN, SEMI-AUTOMATIC

	V.G.	Exc	Prior Edition
B.M., .32 ACP, Clip Fed, Curio..	$275	$325	$325

HERMITAGE Made by Stevens Arms.

SHOTGUN, SINGLESHOT

	V.G.	Exc	Prior Edition
Model 90, Various Gauges, Takedown, Automatic Ejector, Plain Hammer, Modern...	50	75	75

HERMITAGE ARMS CO. Made by Crescent for Grey & Dudley Hdw. Co., Nashville, Tenn.

SHOTGUN, DOUBLE BARREL, SIDE-BY-SIDE

	V.G.	Exc	Prior Edition
Various Gauges, Hammerless, Damascus Barrel, Modern......................	150	175	175
Various Gauges, Hammerless, Steel Barrel, Modern.............................	175	200	200
Various Gauges, Outside Hammers, Damascus Barrel, Modern.............	150	175	175
Various Gauges, Outside Hammers, Steel Barrel, Modern.....................	175	200	200

SHOTGUN, SINGLESHOT

	V.G.	Exc	Prior Edition
Various Gauges, Hammer, Steel Barrel, Modern....................................	50	75	75

HERO Made by Manhattan/American Standard.

HANDGUN, SINGLESHOT PISTOL

	V.G.	Exc	Prior Edition
.34 Caliber, American Standard, Spur Trigger, Solid Frame, Single Action, Antique..	200	275	250
.34 Caliber, Manhattan, Spur Trigger, Solid Frame, Single Action, Antique...	225	300	275

HEROLD Tradename of Franz Jager & Co., Suhl, Germany 1923–1939.

RIFLE, BOLT ACTION

	V.G.	Exc	Prior Edition
Herold Repetierbuchse, .22 Hornet, Set Triggers, Checkered Stock, Modern...	750	800	800

HERTERS Distributor & Importer in Waseca, Minn.

HANDGUN, REVOLVER

	V.G.	Exc	Prior Edition
Guide, .22 L.R.R.F., Swing–Out Cylinder, Double Action, Modern...	75	100	100
Power–Mag, .357 Magnum, Western Style, Single Action, Modern...	100	125	125
Power–Mag, .401 Herter Mag., Western Style, Single Action, Modern...	100	125	125
Power–Mag, .44 Magnum, Western Style, Single Action, Modern.........	125	150	150
Western, .22 L.R.R.F., Single Action, Western Style, Modern...............	50	75	75

	V.G.	Exc	Prior Edition

RIFLE, BOLT ACTION

Model J–9 Hunter, Various Calibers, Plain, Monte Carlo Stock, Modern.. $150 $200 $225

Model J–9 Presentation, Various Calibers, Checkered Stock, Monte Carlo Stock, Sling Swivels, Modern.............................. 175 225 250

Model J–9 Supreme, Various Calibers, Checkered Stock, Monte Carlo Stock, Sling Swivels, Modern......................... 200 250 250

Model U–9 Hunter, Various Calibers, Plain, Monte Carlo Stock, Modern... 125 175 225

Model U–9 Presentation, Various Calibers, Checkered Stock, Monte Carlo Stock, Sling Swivels, Modern.............................. 150 200 250

Model U–9 Supreme, Various Calibers, Checkered Stock, Sling Swivels, Monte Carlo Stock, Modern... 175 225 225

SHOTGUN, SEMI-AUTOMATIC

Model SL–18, 12 Ga. 3", Checkered Stock, Modern............................... 225 275 275

SHOTGUN, SINGLESHOT

Model 151, Various Gauges, Hammer, Modern.. 75 100 75

HESS, JACOB Stark Co., Ohio 1842–1860. See Kentucky Rifles.

HESS, SAMUEL Lancaster, Pa., c. 1771. See Kentucky Rifles.

HEYM Franz W. Heym, 1934–1945 in Suhl, Germany, now in Munnerstadt, West Germany.

COMBINATION WEAPON, DRILLING

Model 33, Various Calibers, Hammerless, Double Triggers, Engraved, Checkered Stock, Express Sights, Curio.................................. 4,500 5,500 5,500

Model 37, Various Calibers, Hammerless, Sidelock, Double Rifle Barrels, Engraved, Checkered Stock, Curio... 8,000 9,000 9,500

Model 37, Various Calibers, Hammerless, Sidelock, Engraved, Checkered Stock, Curio... 7,500 8,500 8,500

Model 37 Deluxe, Various Calibers, Hammerless, Sidelock, Double Rifle Barrels, Engraved, Checkered Stock, Curio....................... 8,500 9,500 9,700

RIFLE, BOLT ACTION

Model SR–20, Various Calibers, Fancy Wood, Double Set Triggers, Curio.. 1,000 1,250 1,000

Model SR–20 Hunter, Various Calibers, Fancy Wood, Double Set Triggers, Curio... 950 1,100 1,200

COMBINATION WEAPON, OVER-UNDER

Model 22S, Various Calibers, Single Set Trigger, Checkered Stock, Light Engraving, Curio... 2,000 2,500 2,250

Model 55BF (77BF), Various Calibers, Boxlock, Double Triggers, Checkered Stock, Engraved, Curio.. 4,000 5,000 4,500

Model 55BFSS (77BFSS), Various Calibers, Sidelock, Double Triggers, Checkered Stock, Curio... 3,000 3,500 3,000

	V.G.	Exc	Prior Edition

RIFLE, SINGLESHOT

Model HR–30, Various Calibers, Fancy Wood, Engraved, Single
Set Trigger, Ruger Action, Round Barrel, Curio $2,000 $2,500 $2,500

Model HR–38, Various Calibers, Fancy Wood, Engraved, Single
Set Trigger, Ruger Action, Octagon Barrel, Curio 2,500 3,000 3,000

RIFLE, DOUBLE BARREL, OVER-UNDER

Model 88–B, Various Calibers, Boxlock, Engraved,
Checkered Stock, Curio 7,500 9,000 8,500

Model 88–B Safari, Various Calibers, Sidelock, Engraved,
Checkered Stock, Curio 8,500 11,000 10,000

SHOTGUN, DOUBLE BARREL, OVER-UNDER

Model 55F (77F), Various Gauges, Boxlock, Engraved,
Checkered Stock, Double Triggers, Curio 3,750 4,250 3,750

Model 55FSS (77FSS), Various Gauges, Sidelock, Engraved,
Checkered Stock, Double Triggers, Curio 3,000 3,500 3,500

HIGGINS, J.C. Trade Name used by Sears–Roebuck. 1946–1962.

HANDGUN, REVOLVER

Model 88, .22 L.R.R.F., Modern	50	75	75
Model 88 Fisherman, .22 L.R.R.F., Modern	50	75	75
Ranger, .22 L.R.R.F., Modern	50	75	75

HANDGUN, SEMI-AUTOMATIC

Model 80, .22 L.R.R.F., Clip Fed, Hammerless, Modern	75	100	100
Model 85, .22 L.R.R.F., Clip Fed, Hammer, Modern	100	125	125

RIFLE, BOLT ACTION

Model 228, .22 L.R.R.F., Clip Fed, Modern	25	50	50
Model 229, .22 L.R.R.F., Tube Feed, Modern	25	50	50
Model 245, .22 L.R.R.F., Singleshot, Modern	25	50	50
Model 51, Various Calibers, Checkered Stock, Modern	175	225	225
Model 51 Special, Various Calibers, Checkered Stock, Light Engraving, Modern	225	275	275

RIFLE, LEVER ACTION

.22 WMR, Modern	50	75	75
Model 45, Various Calibers, Tube Feed, Carbine, Modern	50	75	75

RIFLE, SEMI-AUTOMATIC

Model 25, ..22 L.R.R.F., Clip Fed, Modern	25	50	50
Model 31, ..22 L.R.R.F., Tube Feed, Modern	50	75	75

RIFLE, SLIDE ACTION

Model 33, .22 L.R.R.F., Tube Feed, Modern	50	75	75

SHOTGUN, BOLT ACTION

Model 10, Various Gauges, Tube Feed, 5 Shot, Modern	50	75	75
Model 11, Various Gauges, Tube Feed, 3 Shot, Modern	50	50	50

SHOTGUN, DOUBLE BARREL, SIDE-BY-SIDE

Various Calibers, Plain, Takedown, Hammerless, Modern	150	175	175

	V.G.	Exc	Prior Edition
SHOTGUN, SEMI-AUTOMATIC			
Model 66, 12 Ga., Plain Barrel, Modern	$125	$175	$175
Model 66, 12 Ga., Plain Barrel, Adjustable Choke, Modern	150	175	175
Model 66, 12 Ga., Vent Rib, Adjustable Choke, Modern	150	175	175
Model 66 Deluxe, 12 Ga., Modern	150	175	175
SHOTGUN, SINGLESHOT			
Various Calibers, Takedown, Adjustable Choke, Plain, Hammer, Modern	50	75	75
SHOTGUN, SLIDE ACTION			
Model 20 Deluxe, 12 Ga., Modern	125	150	150
Model 20 Deluxe, 12 Ga., Vent Rib, Adjustable Choke, Modern	125	150	150
Model 20 Special, 12 Ga., Vent Rib, Adjustable Choke, Modern	150	200	200
Model 20 Standard, 12 Ga., Modern	100	150	150

HIGH STANDARD High Standard Mfg. Co. 1926 to the present, first in New Haven, Conn., then as High Standard Sporting Firearms in Hamden, Conn., now as High Standard, Inc. in East Hartford, Conn. All High Standard machinery was sold at auction October 5, 1984. Also see the commemorative section.

	V.G.	Exc	Prior Edition
HANDGUN, DOUBLE BARREL, OVER-UNDER			
Derringer, .22 L.R.R.F., Double Action, Top Break, Electroless, Nickel Plated, Hammerless, Walnut Grips, Cased, Modern	150	175	175
Derringer, .22 L.R.R.F., Double Action, Top Break, Nickel Plated, Hammerless, Cased, Modern	150	175	175
Derringer, .22 WMR, Double Action, 2 Shot, Modern	150	175	175
Derringer, .22 WMR, Double Action, Top Break, Electroless, Nickel Plated, Hammerless, Walnut Grips, Cased, Modern	175	200	200
Derringer, .22 WMR, Double Action, Top Break, Nickel Plated, Hammerless, Cased, Modern	175	200	200
Derringer, 22 L.R.R.F., Double Action, 2 Shot, Modern	125	150	150
Gold Derringer, .22 WMR, Double Action, 2 Shot, Modern	300	400	350
Silver Derringer, .22 WMR, Double Action, Top Break, Hammerless, Cased, Modern	250	350	225
HANDGUN, PERCUSSION			
.36, Griswald & Gunnison, Revolver, Commemorative, Cased, Reproduction, Antique	200	225	225
.36 Leech & Rigdon, Revolver, Commemorative, Cased, Reproduction, Antique	200	225	225
.36 Schneider & Glassick, Revolver, Commemorative, Cased, Reproduction, Antique	250	275	275
HANDGUN, REVOLVER			
For Nickel Plating, Add $7.50–$12.50			
Crusader, Deluxe Pair, .44 Mag. & .45 Colt, Commemorative, Double Action, Swing–Out Cylinder, Gold Inlays, Engraved, Modern	1,500	2,500	3,000
Double–Nine, .22 L.R.R.F., Double Action, Western Style, Modern	125	150	150

	V.G.	Exc	Prior Edition
Double–Nine, .22 LR/.22 WMR Combo, Double Action, Western Style, Alloy Frame, Modern...........................	$150	$175	$175
Double–Nine, .22 LR/.22 WMR Combo, Double Action, Western Style, Modern......................................	150	200	200
Double–Nine Deluxe, .22 LR/.22 WMR Combo, Double Action, Western Style, Adjustable Sights, Modern.......................	200	225	225
Durango, .22 L.R.R.F., Double Action, Western Style, Modern..............	100	125	125
High Sierra, .22 LR/.22 WMR Combo, Double Action, Western Style, Octagon Barrel, Modern........................	125	150	150
High Sierra Deluxe, .22 LR/.22 WMR Combo, Double Action, Western Style, Octagon Barrel, Adjustable Sights, Modern.....................	150	175	175
Kit Gun, .22 L.R.R.F., Double Action, 9 Shot, Swing–Out Cylinder, Adjustable Sights, Modern........................	125	175	175
Longhorn, .22 LR/.22 WMR Combo, Double Action, Adjustable Sights, Western Style, Modern............................	150	175	175
Longhorn, .22 LR/.22 WMR Combo, Double Action, Western Style, Alloy Frame, Modern............................	100	125	125
Longhorn, .22 LR/.22 WMR Combo, Double Action, Western Style, Modern............................	125	150	150

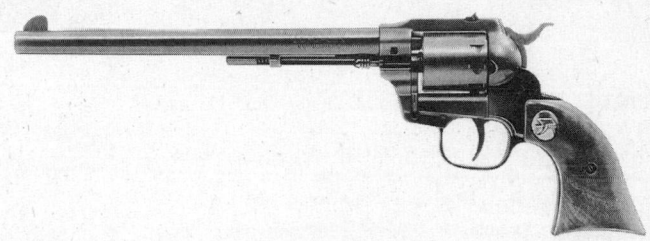

High Standard Longhorn

	V.G.	Exc	Prior Edition
Natchez, .22 LR/.22 WMR Combo, Double Action, Western Style, Birdshead Grip, Allow Frame, Modern...........................	75	100	100
Posse, .22 LR/.22 WMR Combo, Double Action, Western Style, Brass Gripframe, Modern............................	75	100	100
Sentinel, .22 L.R.R.F., Double Action, Swing–Out Cylinder, Modern............................	125	150	100
Sentinel Deluxe, .22 L.R.R.F., Double Action, Swing–Out Cylinder, Modern............................	150	175	125
Sentinel Imperial, .22 L.R.R.F., Double Action, Swing–Out Cylinder, Modern............................	150	175	125
Sentinel Mk I, .22 L.R.R.F., Double Action, Swing–Out Cylinder, Modern............................	125	175	100
Sentinel Mk I, .22 L.R.R.F., Double Action, Swing–Out Cylinder, Adjustable Sights, Modern............................	150	175	125
Sentinel Mk II, .357 Magnum, Double Action, Swing–Out Cylinder, Modern............................	100	125	150
Sentinel Mk III, .357 Magnum, Double Action, Swing–Out Cylinder, Adjustable Sights, Modern...........................	100	150	175

	V.G.	Exc	Prior Edition
Sentinel Mk IV, .22 L.R.R.F., Double Action, Swing–Out Cylinder, Adjustable Sights, Modern..	$125	$150	$175

High Standard Sentinel

	V.G.	Exc	Prior Edition
Sentinel Mk IV, .22 WMR, Double Action, Swing–Out Cylinder, Adjustable Sights, Modern........................	100	150	175
Sentinel Mk IV, .22 WMR, Double Action, Swing–Out Cylinder, Modern........................	100	125	125
Sentinel Snub, .22 L.R.R.F., Double Action, Swing–Out Cylinder, Modern........................	75	100	100

HANDGUN, SEMI-AUTOMATIC

	V.G.	Exc	Prior Edition
For Nickel Plating, Add $20.00–$35.00			
"Benner Olympic," .22 L.R.R.F., Supermatic, Military, Engraved, Curio........................	650	750	750
10–X Custom, .22 L.R.R.F., Heavy Barrel, Military Grip, Target Sights, Modern........................	1,500	1,750	950
Citation (Early), .22 L.R.R.F., Supermatic, Clip Fed, Hammerless, Tapered Barrel, Modern........................	350	450	455
Citation (Early), .22 L.R.R.F., Supermatic, Clip Fed, Hammerless, Heavy Barrel, Modern........................	375	475	400
Citation (Late), .22 L.R.R.F., Supermatic, Clip Fed, Hammerless, Frame–Mounted Rear Sight, Heavy Barrel, Modern........................	375	425	425
Citation (Late), .22 L.R.R.F., Supermatic, Military, Hammerless, Frame–Mounted Rear Sight, Fluted Barrel, Modern........................	350	425	475
Citation (Late), .22 L.R.R.F., Supermatic, Military, Hammerless, Frame–Mounted Rear Sight, Heavy Barrel, Modern........................	375	450	425
Duramatic, .22 L.R.R.F., Clip Fed, Hammerless, Modern........................	275	350	300
Field King, .22 L.R.R.F., Clip Fed, Hammerless, Heavy Barrel, Modern........................	300	350	375
Flight King, .22 Short R.F., Clip Fed, Hammerless, Modern........................	275	325	325
Flight King, .22 Short R.F., Clip Fed, Hammerless, Extra Barrel, Modern........................	300	350	350
Flight King, .22 Short R.F., Clip Fed, Hammerless, Lightweight, Modern........................	275	350	325

	V.G.	Exc	Prior Edition
Flight King, .22 Short R.F., Clip Fed, Hammerless, Lightweight, Extra Barrel, Modern................	$300	$375	$350
Model A, .22 L.R.R.F., Clip Fed, Hammerless, Curio................	400	450	450
Model B, .22 L.R.R.F., Clip Fed, Hammerless, Curio................	350	400	400
Model B, .22 L.R.R.F., Navy, Clip Fed, Hammerless, Curio................	475	550	550
Model C, .22 Short R.F., Clip Fed, Hammerless, Curio................	450	525	525
Model D, .22 L.R.R.F., Clip Fed, Hammerless, Heavy Barrel, Curio................	450	525	550
Model E, .22 L.R.R.F., Clip Fed, Hammerless, Heavy Barrel, Target Grips, Curio................	650	750	750
Model G–380, .380 ACP, Clip Fed, Hammer, Takedown, Curio................	425	500	500
Model G–B, .22 L.R.R.F., Clip Fed, Hammerless, Takedown, Curio................	400	450	450
Model G–B, .22 L.R.R.F., Clip Fed, Hammerless, Takedown, Extra Barrel, Curio................	450	525	525
Model G–D, .22 L.R.R.F., Clip Fed, Hammerless, Takedown, Curio................	500	600	550
Model G–D, .22 L.R.R.F., Clip Fed, Hammerless, Takedown, Extra Barrel, Curio................	550	650	575
Model G–E, .22 L.R.R.F., Clip Fed, Hammerless, Takedown, Extra Barrel, Curio................	800	950	850
Model G–E, .22 L.R.R.F., Clip Fed, Hammerless, Takedown, Curio................	750	900	800
Model G–O, .22 Short, Clip Fed, Hammerless, Takedown, Extra Barrel, Curio................	900	1,050	825
Model G–O, .22 Short, Clip Fed, Hammerless, Takedown, Curio................	850	1,000	775
Model H–A, .22 L.R.R.F., Clip Fed, Hammer, Curio................	550	650	550
Model H–B, .22 L.R.R.F., Clip Fed, Hammer, Curio................	375	450	525
Model H–D Military, .22 L.R.R.F., Clip Fed, Hammer, Heavy Barrel, Thumb Safety, Curio................	375	425	425
Model H–D, .22 L.R.R.F., Clip Fed, Hammer, Heavy Barrel, Curio................	850	1,000	600
Model H–E, .22 L.R.R.F., Clip Fed, Hammer, Heavy Barrel, Target Grips, Curio................	1,250	1,500	1,110
Model SB, .22 L.R.R.F., Clip Fed, Hammerless, Smoothbore, Class 3	400	475	475
Olympic I.S.U., .22 Short R.F., Clip Fed, Hammerless, Military, Frame–Mounted Rear Sights, Modern................	500	600	600
Olympic I.S.U., .22 Short R.F., Clip Fed, Hammerless, Frame–Mounted Rear Sights, Modern................	525	600	600
Olympic I.S.U., .22 Short R.F., Supermatic, Clip Fed, Hammerless, Military, Modern................	550	650	600
Olympic I.S.U., .22 Short R.F., Supermatic, Clip Fed, Hammerless, Modern................	525	600	575
Olympic, .22 Short R.F., Clip Fed, Hammerless, Modern................	475	550	500
Olympic, .22 Short R.F., Clip Fed, Hammerless, Extra Barrel, Modern................	575	650	525
Plinker, .22 L.R.R.F., Clip Fed, Hammer, Modern................	200	250	350
Sharpshooter (Late), .22 L.R.R.F., Military Grip, Clip Fed, Hammerless, Modern................	375	425	350

	V.G.	Exc	Prior Edition
Sharpshooter, .22 L.R.R.F., Clip Fed, Hammerless, Modern...........	$350	$400	$300

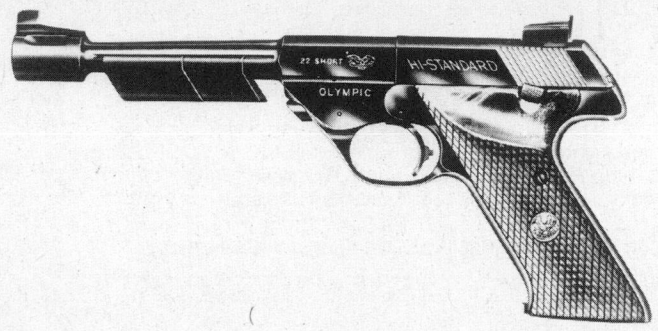

High Standard Sharpshooter

	V.G.	Exc	Prior Edition
Sport King (Late), .22 L.R.R.F., Military Grip, Clip Fed, Hammerless, Modern..........................	225	275	350
Sport King, .22 L.R.R.F., Clip Fed, Hammerless, Modern......................	200	300	300
Sport King, .22 L.R.R.F., Clip Fed, Hammerless, Extra Barrel, Modern..........................	250	325	300
Sport King, .22 L.R.R.F., Clip Fed, Hammerless, Lightweight, Modern..........................	225	300	275
Sport King, .22 L.R.R.F., Clip Fed, Hammerless, Lightweight, Extra Barrel, Modern........................	250	325	300
Supermatic, .22 L.R.R.F., Clip Fed, Hammerless, Modern....................	450	525	525
Supermatic, .22 L.R.R.F., Clip Fed, Hammerless, Extra Barrel, Modern..........................	450	550	550
Survival Pack, .22 L.R.R.F., Sharpshooter (Late), Electroless Nickel Plated, Cased with Accessories, Modern........................	375	450	450
Tournament, .22 L.R.R.F., Supermatic, Clip Fed, Hammerless, Modern..........................	375	425	425
Tournament, .22 L.R.R.F., Supermatic, Clip Fed, Hammerless, Military, Modern..........................	350	400	400
Trophy (Early), .22 L.R.R.F., Supermatic, Clip Fed, Hammerless, Modern..........................	475	525	525
Trophy (Late), .22 L.R.R.F., Supermatic, Military, Hammerless, Frame–Mounted Rear Sight, Fluted Barrel, Modern........................	400	500	500
Trophy (Late), .22 L.R.R.F., Supermatic, Military, Hammerless, Frame–Mounted Rear Sight, Heavy Barrel, Modern........................	500	575	575
Victor, .22 L.R.R.F., Heavy Barrel, Military Grip, Solid Rib, Target Sights, Modern........................	450	550	550
Victor, .22 L.R.R.F., Heavy Barrel, Military Grip, Vent Rib, Target Sights, Modern........................	500	575	575

RIFLE, BOLT ACTION

	V.G.	Exc	Prior Edition
Hi Power Deluxe, Various Calibers, Monte Carlo Stock, Checkered Stock, Modern........................	200	250	250
High Power, Various Calibers, Field Grade, Modern.............................	175	225	225

	V.G.	Exc	Prior Edition

RIFLE, SEMI-AUTOMATIC

	V.G.	Exc	Prior Edition
Sport King, .22 L.R.R.F., Field Grade, Carbine, Tube Feed, Modern	$75	$100	$100
Sport King, .22 L.R.R.F., Field Grade, Tube Feed, Modern	50	75	75
Sport King Deluxe, .22 L.R.R.F., Tube Feed, Monte Carlo Stock, Checkered Stock, Modern	100	150	125
Sport King Special, .22 L.R.R.F., Tube Feed, Monte Carlo Stock, Modern	75	100	100

RIFLE, SLIDE ACTION

	V.G.	Exc	Prior Edition
.22 L.R.R.F., Flight–King, Tube Feed, Monte Carlo Stock, Modern	75	100	100

SHOTGUN, DOUBLE BARREL, OVER-UNDER

	V.G.	Exc	Prior Edition
Shadow Indy, 12 Ga., Single Selective Trigger, Selective Ejectors, Checkered Stock, Engraved, Modern	650	750	750
Shadow Seven, 12 Ga., Single Selective Trigger, Selective Ejectors, Checkered Stock, Light Engraving, Modern	550	650	650

SHOTGUN, SEMI-AUTOMATIC

	V.G.	Exc	Prior Edition
12 Ga., Supermatic, Field Grade, Modern	150	175	175
20 Ga. Mag., Supermatic, Field Grade, Modern	150	175	175
20 Ga. Mag., Supermatic, Skeet Grade, Vent Rib, Modern	145	225	225
Deer Gun, 12 Ga., Supermatic, Open Rear Sight, Recoil Pad, Modern	175	200	200
Deluxe, 20 Ga. Mag., Supermatic, Recoil Pad, Modern	175	225	175
Deluxe, 20 Ga. Mag., Supermatic, Recoil Pad, Vent Rib, Modern	175	225	200
Deluxe, Recoil Pad, Modern	150	175	175
Deluxe, Recoil Pad, Vent Rib, Modern	175	200	200
Duck Gun, 12 Ga. Mag., 3", Supermatic, Recoil Pad, Field Grade, Modern	175	200	200
Duck Gun, 12 Ga. Mag., 3", Supermatic, Vent Rib, Recoil Pad, Modern	175	225	200
Model 10B, 12 Ga., Riot Gun, Modern	475	550	375
Skeet Grade, Vent Rib, Recoil Pad, Modern	225	250	250
Special, 12 Ga., Field Grade, Adjustable Choke, Modern	175	200	200
Special, 20 Ga. Mag., Supermatic, Field Grade, Adjustable Choke, Modern	175	200	200
Trap Grade, Vent Rib, Recoil Pad, Modern	200	225	225
Trophy, 20 Ga. Mag., Supermatic, Recoil Pad, Vent Rib, Adjustable Choke, Modern	200	225	225
Trophy, Recoil Pad, Vent Rib, Adjustable Choke, Modern	150	200	225

SHOTGUN, SLIDE ACTION

	V.G.	Exc	Prior Edition
.410 Ga. 3", Flight–King, Field Grade, Modern	125	150	150
.410 Ga. 3", Flight–King, Skeet Grade, Modern	150	175	175
12 and 20 Gauges, Flight–King, Field Grade, Modern	125	150	150
12 Ga., Flight King, Trap Grade, Vent Rib, Recoil Pad, Modern	150	175	175
12 Ga., Flight– King, Skeet Grade, Vent Rib, Recoil Pad, Modern	150	175	175
28 Ga., Flight–King, Field Grade, Modern	150	175	175
28 Ga., Flight–King, Skeet Grade, Vent Rib, Modern	150	175	175
Brush Gun, 12 Ga., Flight–King, Open Rear Sight, Modern	125	150	150
Deluxe, .28 Ga., Flight–King, Vent Rib, Modern	150	175	175
Deluxe, .410 Ga. 3", Flight–King, Vent Rib, Modern	150	175	175

	V.G.	Exc	Prior Edition
Deluxe, 12 and 20 Gauges, Flight–King, Recoil Pad, Vent Rib, Modern........	$150	$175	$175
Deluxe, 12 and 20 Gauges, Flight–King, Recoil Pad, Modern.........	125	150	150
Deluxe Brush Gun, 12 Ga., Flight–King, Peep Sights, Sling Swivels, Modern........	175	200	200
Riot, 12 Ga., Flight–King, Open Rear Sight, Modern........	150	175	175
Riot, 12 Ga., Flight–King, Plain Barrel, Modern........	150	175	175
Special, 12 and 20 Gauges, Flight–King, Field Grade, Adjustable Choke, Modern........	150	175	175
Trophy, 12 and 20 Gauges, Flight–King, Recoil Pad, Vent Rib, Adjustable Choke, Modern........	150	175	175

HIJO Tradename used by Sloan's of N.Y.C.

HANDGUN, SEMI-AUTOMATIC

Hijo, .25 ACP, Clip Fed, Modern........	75	100	100
Hijo Military, .22 L.R.R.F., Clip Fed, Modern........	100	125	125

HILL, S.W. See Kentucky Rifles and Pistols.

HILLEGAS, J. Pottsville, Pa. 1810–1830. See Kentucky Rifles.

HILLIARD, D.H. & GEORGE C. D. H. Hilliard, Cornish, New Hampshire, 1842–1877, taken over by George C. Hilliard and operated 1877–1880.

HANDGUN, PERCUSSION

.34, Underhammer Target Pistol, Antique........	700	850	450

HINO–KOMORO Kumaso Hino and Tomisiro Komoro, Tokyo, Japan, c. 1910.

HANDGUN, SEMI-AUTOMATIC

Blow–Forward, 7.65mm, Clip Fed, Curio........	3,000	3,250	3,250

HOCKLEY, JAMES Chester County, Pa. 1769–1771. See Kentucky Rifles.

HOLDEN, CYRUS B. Worchester, Mass, c. 1861–1880.

RIFLE, SINGLESHOT

Model 1862, .44 Henry, Octagon Barrel, Antique........	550	775	775
Tip–Up, .22 R.F., Nickel Plated Frame, Blued Barrel, Antique........	450	600	600

	V.G.	Exc	Prior Edition

HOLLAND & HOLLAND   London, England since 1835.

RIFLE, BOLT ACTION

	V.G.	Exc	Prior Edition
Best Quality, Various Calibers, Express Sights, Checkered Stock, Modern	—	$12,500	$7,500
Best Quality, Various Calibers, Express Sights, Fancy Checkering, Engraved, Modern	—	20,000	9,500

RIFLE, DOUBLE BARREL, SIDE-BY-SIDE

	V.G.	Exc	Prior Edition
#2, Various Calibers, Sidelock, Checkered Stock, Engraved, Hammerless, Modern	—	14,500	14,500
Deluxe, Various Calibers, Sidelock, Automatic Ejector, Fancy Engraving, Fancy Checkering, Double Trigger, Modern	—	50,000	45,000
Royal, Various Calibers, Sidelock, Automatic Ejector, Fancy Engraving, Fancy Checkering, Double Trigger, Modern	—	75,000	55,000

SHOTGUN, DOUBLE BARREL, OVER-UNDER

	V.G.	Exc	Prior Edition
Deluxe Royal, 12 Ga., Sidelock, Automatic Ejector, Fancy Engraving, Fancy Checkering, Double Triggers, Modern	35,000	40,000	40,000
Deluxe Royal, 12 Ga., Sidelock, Automatic Ejector, Fancy Engraving, Fancy Checkering, Single Trigger, Modern	40,000	45,000	50,000
Royal Model (Late), 12 Ga., Sidelock, Automatic Ejector, Fancy Engraving, Fancy Checkering, Double Triggers, Modern	22,500	25,000	25,000
Royal Model (Late), 12 Ga., Sidelock, Automatic Ejector, Fancy Engraving, Fancy Checkering, Single Trigger, Modern	25,000	27,500	27,500
Royal Model (Old), 12 Ga., Sidelock, Automatic Ejector, Fancy Engraving, Fancy Checkering, Double Triggers, Modern	17,500	20,000	20,000
Royal Model (Old), 12 Ga., Sidelock, Automatic Ejector, Fancy Engraving, Fancy Checkering, Single Trigger, Modern	20,000	22,000	22,000

SHOTGUN, DOUBLE BARREL, SIDE-BY-SIDE

	V.G.	Exc	Prior Edition
Badminton, Various Gauges, Sidelock, Automatic Ejector, Fancy Engraving, Fancy Checkering, Double Triggers, Modern	7,500	8,500	10,000
Badminton, Various Gauges, Sidelock, Automatic Ejector, Fancy Engraving, Fancy Checkering, Single Trigger, Modern	8,000	9,250	12,000
Centenary Royal, 12 Ga. 2", Sidelock, Automatic Ejector, Fancy Engraving, Fancy Checkering, Double Triggers, Modern	12,500	15,000	15,000
Deluxe, Various Gauges, Sidelock, Automatic Ejector, Fancy Engraving, Fancy Checkering, Double Triggers, Modern	12,500	15,000	12,500
Deluxe, Various Gauges, Sidelock, Automatic Ejector, Fancy Engraving, Fancy Checkering, Single Trigger, Modern	15,000	17,500	15,000
Dominion, 12 Ga. 2", Sidelock, Automatic Ejector, Engraved, Checkered Stock, Double Triggers, Modern	5,000	5,500	7,500
Dominion, Various Gauges, Sidelock, Automatic Ejector, Engraved, Checkered Stock, Double Triggers, Modern	4,000	4,500	10,000
Northwood, Various Gauges, Boxlock, Automatic Ejector, Checkered Stock, Engraved, Modern	4,500	5,000	2,700
Riviera, Various Gauges, Extra Shotgun Barrel, Automatic Ejector, Fancy Engraving, Fancy Checkering, Double Triggers, Modern	8,000	10,000	14,000
Royal, Various Gauges, Sidelock, Automatic Ejector, Fancy Engraving, Fancy Checkering, Double Triggers, Modern	7,500	10,000	14,000
Royal, Various Gauges, Sidelock, Automatic Ejector, Fancy Engraving, Fancy Checkering, Single Trigger, Modern	10,000	12,000	16,000

	V.G.	Exc	Prior Edition
Royal Ejector Grade, 12 Ga. Mag. 3", Single Selective Trigger, Vent Rib, Pistol–Grip Stock, Cased with Accessories, Modern..............	$10,000	$12,500	$12,500

SHOTGUN, SINGLESHOT

Standard Super Trap, 12 Ga., Boxlock, Automatic Ejector, Vent Rib, Fancy Engraving, Checkered Stock, Modern...........................	3,500	4,000	6,000
Deluxe Super Trap, 12 Ga., Boxlock, Automatic Ejector, Vent Rib, Fancy Engraving, Checkered Stock, Modern.....................................	5,500	6,500	7,500
Exhibition Super Trap, 12 Ga., Boxlock, Automatic Ejector, Vent Rib, Fancy Engraving, Checkered Stock, Modern...........................	7,500	8,000	9,000

HOLLIS, CHAS. & SONS London, England.

SHOTGUN, DOUBLE BARREL, SIDE-BY-SIDE

12 Ga., Hammerless, Engraved, Fancy Checkering, Fancy Wood, Modern..........	2,500	3,000	3,000

HOLLIS, RICHARD London, England 1800–1850.

HANDGUN, FLINTLOCK

.68, Holster Pistol, Round Barrel, Brass Furniture, Plain, Antique............	550	775	775

SHOTGUN, PERCUSSION

12 Ga., Double Barrels, Double Triggers, Hook Breech, Light Engraving, Checkered Stock, Antique.......................................	450	550	550

HOLMES, BILL Fayetteville, Ark.

SHOTGUN, SINGLESHOT

Supertrap, 12 Ga., Various Action Types, Checkered Stock, Modern..........	1,650	1,800	1,800

HOOD FIREARMS CO. Norwich, Conn., c. 1875.

HANDGUN, REVOLVER

.32 Short R.F., 5 Shot, Spur Trigger, Solid Frame, Single Action, Antique..........	125	175	175

HOPKINS & ALLEN Norwich, Conn. 1868–1914, taken over by Marlin–Rockwell in 1914. Also see Bacon Arms Co. and Merwin Hulbert & Co.

HANDGUN, PERCUSSION REVOLVER

Dictator, .36 Caliber, 5 Shot, Octagon Barrel, Antique..........	375	450	400

HANDGUN, REVOLVER

Model 1876 Army, .44–40 WCF, Solid Frame, Single Action, 6 Shot, Finger–Rest Trigger Guard, Antique.............................	550	650	650
Safety Police, .22 L.R.R.F., Top Break, Double Action, Various Barrel Lengths, Curio...	150	200	150

	V.G.	Exc	Prior Edition
Safety Police, .32 S & W, Top Break, Double Action, Various Barrel Lengths, Curio..	$125	$150	$150
Safety Police, .38 S & W, Top Break, Double Action, Various Barrel Lengths, Curio..	125	175	150
XL .30 Long, .30 Long R.F., Solid Frame, Spur Trigger, Single Action, 5 Shot, Antique..	150	175	175
XL 1 Double Action, .22 Short R.F., Solid Frame, Folding Hammer, Curio..	100	125	125
XL 3 Double Action, .32 S & W, Solid Frame, Folding Hammer, Curio..	75	100	100
XL Bulldog, .32 S & W, Solid Frame, Folding Hammer, Curio...............	100	125	125
XL Bulldog, .32 Short R.F., Solid Frame, Folding Hammer, Curio.........	75	100	100
XL Bulldog, .38 S & W, Solid Frame, Folding Hammer, Curio..............	75	100	100
XL CR .22 Short R.F., Solid Frame, SpurTrigger, Single Action, 7 Shot, Antique..	150	175	175
XL Double Action, .32 S & W, Solid Frame, Folding Hammer, Curio..	75	100	100
XL Double Action, .38 S & W, Solid Frame, Folding Hammer, Curio....	75	100	100
XL Navy, .38 Short R.F., Solid Frame, Single Action, 6 Shot, Antique...	500	650	500
XL No. 1, .22 Short R.F., Solid Frame, Spur Trigger, Single Action, 7 Shot, Antique..	150	175	175
XL No. 2, .30 Short R.F., Solid Frame, Spur Trigger, Single Action, 5 Shot, Antique..	175	200	200
XL No. 3, .32 Short R.F., Solid Frame, Spur Trigger, Single Action, 5 Shot, Safety Cylinder, Antique...............................	175	200	200
XL No. 4, .38 Short R.F., Solid Frame, Spur Trigger, Single Action, 5 Shot, Antique..	175	200	200
XL No. 5, .38 S & W, Solid Frame, Spur Trigger, Single Action, 5 Shot, Antique...	350	400	400
XL No. 5, .38 Short R.F., Solid Frame, Spur Trigger, Single Action, 5 Shot, Safety Cylinder, Engraved, Antique................................	300	350	350
XL No. 6, .41 Short R.F., Solid Frame, Spur Trigger, Single Action, 5 Shot, Antique..	175	225	225
XL No. 7, .41 Short R.F., Solid Frame, Spur Trigger, Single Action, 5 Shot, Swing–Out Cylinder, Antique..	225	275	275
XL No. 8 Army, .44 R.F., Solid Frame, Single Action, 6 Shot, Antique...	600	750	550
XL Police, .38 Short R.F., Solid Frame, Single Action, 6 Shot, Antique...	350	450	175

HANDGUN, SINGLESHOT

	V.G.	Exc	Prior Edition
New Model Target, .22 L.R.R.F., Top Break, 10" Barrel, Adjustable Sights, Target Grips	300	350	350
Single Shot Derringer, .22 Short R.F., 1¾" Barrel Pivots Downward for Loading, Folding Trigger, Single Action, Antique.............................	750	1,000	850
XL Derringer, .41 Short R.F., Spur Trigger, Single Action, Antique..	475	550	550

RIFLE, BOLT ACTION

	V.G.	Exc	Prior Edition
American Military, .22 L.R.R.F., Singleshot, Takedown, Open Rear Sight, Round Barrel, Curio...	200	250	200

RIFLE, FLINTLOCK

	V.G.	Exc	Prior Edition
"Kentucky," .31, Octagon Barrel, Full–Stocked, Brass Furniture, Reproduction, (Numrich), Antique...................................	175	200	200

	V.G.	Exc	Prior Edition
"Kentucky," .36, Octagon Barrel, Full–Stocked, Brass Furniture, Reproduction, (Numrich), Antique..............	$150	$200	$200
"Kentucky," .45, Octagon Barrel, Full–Stocked, Brass Furniture, Reproduction, (Numrich), Antique..............	175	200	200
"Minute Brush," .50, Octagon Barrel, Full–Stocked, Carbine Reproduction, (Numrich), Antique..............	175	200	200
"Minuteman Brush," .45, Octagon Barrel, Full–Stocked, Carbine Reproduction, (Numrich), Antique..............	175	200	200
"Minuteman," .31, Octagon Barrel, Full–Stocked, Brass Furniture, Reproduction, (Numrich), Antique..............	150	200	200
"Minuteman," .36, Octagon Barrel, Full–Stocked, Brass Furniture, Reproduction, (Numrich), Antique..............	150	175	175
"Minuteman," .45, Octagon Barrel, Full–Stocked, Brass Furniture, Reproduction, (Numrich), Antique..............	175	200	200
"Minuteman," .50, Octagon Barrel, Full–Stocked, Brass Furniture, Reproduction, (Numrich), Antique..............	175	200	200
"Pennsylvania," .31, Octagon Barrel, Half–Stocked, Brass Furniture, Reproduction, (Numrich), Antique..............	150	175	175
"Pennsylvania," .36, Octagon Barrel, Half–Stocked, Brass Furniture, Reproduction, (Numrich), Antique..............	150	175	175
"Pennsylvania," .45, Octagon Barrel, Half–Stocked, Brass Furniture, Reproduction, (Numrich), Antique..............	175	200	200
"Pennsylvania," .50, Octagon Barrel, Half–Stocked, Brass Furniture, Reproduction, (Numrich), Antique..............	150	175	175

RIFLE, PERCUSSION

	V.G.	Exc	Prior Edition
"Buggy Deluxe," .36, Under–Hammer, Octagon Barrel, Carbine, Reproduction, (Numrich), Antique..............	75	100	100
"Buggy Deluxe," .45, Under–Hammer, Octagon Barrel, Carbine, Reproduction, (Numrich), Antique..............	100	125	125
"Deer Stalker," .58, Under–Hammer, Octagon Barrel, Reproduction, (Numrich), Antique..............	75	100	100
"Heritage," .36, Under–Hammer, Octagon Barrel, Brass Furniture, Reproduction, (Numrich), Antique..............	100	125	125

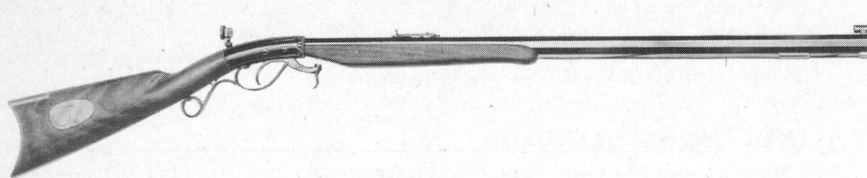

Hopkins & Allen Heritage Rifle

	V.G.	Exc	Prior Edition
"Heritage," .45, Under–Hammer, Octagon Barrel, Brass Furniture, Reproduction, (Numrich), Antique..............	100	125	125
"Kentucky," .31, Full–Stocked, Octagon Barrel, Brass Furniture, Reproduction, (Numrich), Antique..............	150	175	175
"Kentucky," .36, Full–Stocked, Octagon Barrel, Brass Furniture, Reproduction, (Numrich), Antique..............	150	175	175
"Kentucky," .45, Full–Stocked, Octagon Barrel, Brass Furniture, Reproduction, (Numrich), Antique..............	150	175	175
"Minuteman Brush," .45, Full–Stocked, Octagon Barrel, Carbine, Reproduction, (Numrich), Antique..............	150	175	175

	V.G.	Exc	Prior Edition
"Minuteman Brush," .50, Full–Stocked, Octagon Barrel, Carbine, Reproduction, (Numrich), Antique..........................	$175	$200	$200
"Minuteman," .31, Full–Stocked, Octagon Barrel, Brass Furniture, Reproduction, (Numrich), Antique..........................	150	175	175
"Minuteman," .36, Full–Stocked, Octagon Barrel, Brass Furniture, Reproduction, (Numrich), Antique..........................	150	175	175
"Minuteman," .45, Full–Stocked, Octagon Barrel, Brass Furniture, Reproduction, (Numrich), Antique..........................	150	175	175
"Minuteman," .50, Full–Stocked, Octagon Barrel, Brass Furniture, Reproduction, (Numrich), Antique..........................	125	175	175
"Offhand Deluxe," .36 Under–Hammer, Octagon Barrel, Reproduction, (Numrich), Antique..........................	75	100	100
"Offhand Deluxe," .45 Under–Hammer, Octagon Barrel, Reproduction, (Numrich), Antique..........................	75	100	100
"Offhand Deluxe," .45 Under–Hammer, Octagon Barrel, Reproduction, (Numrich), Antique..........................	75	100	100
"Pennsylvania," .31, Half–Stocked, Octagon Barrel, Brass Furniture, Reproduction, (Numrich), Antique..........................	125	150	150
"Pennsylvania," .36, Half–Stocked, Octagon Barrel, Brass Furniture, Reproduction, (Numrich), Antique..........................	150	175	175
"Pennsylvania," .45, Half–Stocked, Octagon Barrel, Brass Furniture, Reproduction, (Numrich), Antique..........................	150	175	175
"Pennsylvania," .50, Half–Stocked, Octagon Barrel, Brass Furniture, Reproduction, (Numrich), Antique..........................	150	175	175
"Target," .45, Under–Hammer, Octagon Barrel, Reproduction, (Numrich), Antique..........................	75	100	100
.45, Double Barrel, Over–Under, Swivel Breech, Brass Furniture, Reproduction, (Numrich), Antique..........................	100	125	125

RIFLE, SINGLESHOT

	V.G.	Exc	Prior Edition
Model 1881 (XL), Various Calibers, Falling Block, Takedown, Lever Action, Round Barrel, Open Rear Sight, Antique..........................	375	450	375
Model 1881 Junior, .22 L.R.R.F., Falling Block, Takedown, Lever Action, Round Barrel, Open Rear Sight, Antique..........................	350	500	150
No. 1922 New Model Junior, .22 L.R.R.F., Falling Block, Takedown, Lever Action, Octagon Barrel, Open Rear Sight, Curio..........................	200	225	225
No. 1925 New Model Junior, .25 Short R.F., Falling Block, Takedown, Lever Action, Octagon Barrel, Open Rear Sight, Curio..........................	250	275	275
No. 1932 New Model Junior, .32 Long R.F., Falling Block, Takedown, Lever Action, Octagon Barrel, Open Rear Sight, Curio..........................	225	250	250
No. 1938 New Model Junior, .38 S & W, Falling Block, Takedown, Lever Action, Octagon Barrel, Open Rear Sight, Curio..........................	250	275	275
No. 2922 New Model Junior, .22 L.R.R.F., Falling Block, Takedown, Lever Action, Octagon Barrel, Checkered Stock, Open Rear Sight, Curio..........................	225	250	250
No. 2925 New Model Junior, .25 Short R.F., Falling Block, Takedown, Lever Action, Octagon Barrel, Checkered Stock, Open Rear Sight, Curio..........................	250	275	275
No. 2932 New Model Junior, .32 Long R.F., Falling Block, Takedown, Lever Action, Octagon Barrel, Checkered Stock, Open Rear Sight, Curio..........................	250	275	275

	V.G.	Exc	Prior Edition
No. 2938 New Model Junior, .38 S & W, Falling Block, Takedown, Lever Action, Octagon Barrel, Checkered Stock, Open Rear Sight, Curio............	$275	$300	$300
No. 3922 Schuetzen Target, .22 L.R.R.F., Falling Block, Takedown, Lever Action, Octagon Barrel, Checkered Stock, Swiss Buttplate, Antique............	1,250	1,500	650
No. 3925 Schuetzen Target, .25–20 WCF, Falling Block, Takedown, Lever Action, Octagon Barrel, Checkered Stock, Swiss Buttplate, Antique............	1,000	1,250	750
No. 722, .22 L.R.R.F., Rolling Block, Takedown, Round Barrel, Open Rear Sight, Curio............	100	125	125
No. 822, .22 L.R.R.F., Rolling Block, Takedown, Lever Action, Round Barrel, Open Rear Sight, Curio............	125	150	150
No. 832, .32 Short R.F., Rolling Block, Takedown, Lever Action, Round Barrel, Open Rear Sight, Curio............	150	175	175
No. 922 New Model Junior, .22 L.R.R.F., Falling Block, Takedown, Lever Action, Round Barrel, Open Rear Sight, Curio............	150	175	175
No. 925 New Model Junior, .25 Short .R.F., Falling Block, Takedown, Lever Action, Round Barrel, Open Rear Sight, Curio............	150	175	175
No. 932 New Model Junior, .32 Long .R.F., Falling Block, Takedown, Lever Action, Round Barrel, Open Rear Sight, Curio............	125	175	175
No. 938 New Model Junior, .38 S & W, Falling Block, Takedown, Lever Action, Round Barrel, Open Rear Sight, Curio............	225	250	250

SHOTGUN, DOUBLE BARREL, SIDE-BY-SIDE

	V.G.	Exc	Prior Edition
No. 100, 12 and 16 Ga., Double Trigger, Outside Hammers, Checkered Stock, Steel Barrel, Curio............	125	150	150
No. 110, 12 and 16 Ga., Double Trigger, Hammerless, Checkered Stock, Steel Barrel, Curio............	150	175	175

SHOTGUN, SINGLESHOT

	V.G.	Exc	Prior Edition
New Model, Various Gauges, Hammer, Top Break, Damascus Barrel, Checkered Stock, Curio............	75	100	75
New Model, Various Gauges, Hammer, Top Break, Steel Barrel, Curio............	75	100	75
New Model, Various Gauges, Hammer, Top Break, Steel Barrel, Automatic Ejector, Checkered Stock, Curio............	75	100	75

HOPKINS, C. W. Made by Bacon Mfg. Co., Norwich, Conn.

HANDGUN, REVOLVER

	V.G.	Exc	Prior Edition
.32 Short R.F., Single Action, Solid Frame, Swing–Out Cylinder, Antique............	350	450	350
.38 Caliber (Navy), Single Action, Solid Frame, Swing–Out Cylinder, Antique............	575	625	625

HOROLT, LORENZ Nuremburg, Germany, c. 1600.

HANDGUN, WHEEL-LOCK

	V.G.	Exc	Prior Edition
Long Barreled, Holster Pistol, Hexagonal Ball Pommel, Light Ornamentation, Antique............	7,500	8,500	8,500

	V.G.	Exc	Prior Edition

HOUILLER, BLANCHAR Paris, France, c. 1845.

HANDGUN, PERCUSSION

Pepperbox, .48, 6 Shot, Antique	$375	$500	$500

HOWARD ARMS Made by Cresent for Fred Bifflar & Co.

SHOTGUN, DOUBLE BARREL, SIDE-BY-SIDE

Various Gauges, Hammerless, Damascus Barrel, Modern	150	175	175
Various Gauges, Hammerless, Steel Barrel, Modern	175	200	200
Various Gauges, Outside Hammers, Damascus Barrel, Modern	150	175	175
Various Gauges, Outside Hammers, Steel Barrel, Modern	150	175	175

SHOTGUN, SINGLESHOT

Various Gauges, Hammer, Steel Barrel, Modern	50	75	75

HOWARD ARMS Made by Meriden Firearms Co.

HANDGUN, REVOLVER

.32 S & W, 5 Shot, Double Action, Top Break, Modern	75	100	100
.38 S & W, 5 Shot, Double Action, Top Break, Modern	75	100	100

HOWARD BROTHERS Detroit, Mich., c. 1868.

RIFLE, SINGLESHOT

.44 Henry R.F., Round Barrel, Antique	375	500	500

HUMBERGER, PETER JR. Ohio 1791–1852. See Kentucky Rifles.

HUMBERGER, PETER SR. Pa. 1774–1791, then Ohio 1791–1811. See Kentucky Rifles.

HUMMER Belgium, for Lee Hdw., Kansas.

SHOTGUN, DOUBLE BARREL, SIDE-BY-SIDE

Various Gauges, Hammerless, Steel Barrel, Modern	175	200	200
Various Gauges, Outside Hammers, Damascus Barrel, Modern	150	175	175
Various Gauges, Outside Hammers, Steel Barrel, Modern	150	175	175

SHOTGUN, SINGLESHOT

Various Gauges, Hammer, Steel Barrel, Modern	50	75	75

HUNGARIAN MILITARY

HANDGUN, SEMI-AUTOMATIC

29M Femaru, 7.65mm, Clip Fed, Blue, Miltary, Curio	350	375	175

	V.G.	Exc	Prior Edition
37M Femaru, 7.65mm, Clip Fed, Blue, Miltary, Curio..........................	$250	$275	$150

Hungarian Military 37M Femaru

Frommer, Stop Pocket, .380 ACP, Clip Fed, Blue, Military, Curio........	225	250	225

RIFLE, BOLT ACTION

1935M, 8mm, Mannlicher, Military, Curio...	225	250	100
1943M, 8mm Mauser, Mannlicher, Military, Curio..................................	325	350	150

HUNTER ARMS See L. C. Smith.

HUNTING WORLD N.Y.C.

SHOTGUN, DOUBLE BARREL, SIDE-BY-SIDE

Royal Deluxe Game Gun, 12 or 20 Gauges, Sidelock, Fancy Wood, Engraved, Modern..	3,500	4,000	4,000

| | Prior |
| V.G. | Exc | Edition |

HUSQVARNA VAPENFABRIK AKITIEBOLAG

Husqvarna, Sweden.

HANDGUN, REVOLVER

Model 1887 Swedish Nagent, 7.5mm, Double Action, Blue,
Military, Antique.. $300 $350 $250

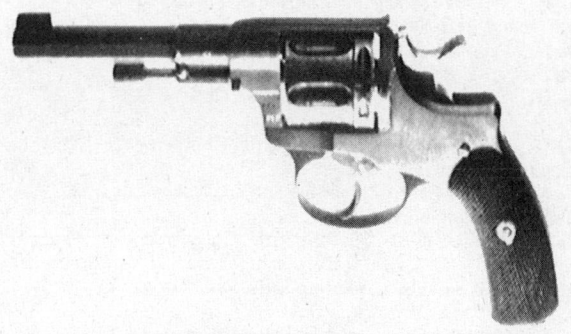

Husqvarna M1887 Revolver

HANDGUN, SEMI-AUTOMATIC

	V.G.	Exc	Prior Edition
Model 40 "Lahti," 9mm Browning Long, Clip Fed, Swedish Military, Curio.........	300	350	350
Model L-35 "Lahti," 9mm Browning Long, Clip Fed, Finnish Military Curio.........	700	850	375

RIFLE, BOLT ACTION

	V.G.	Exc	Prior Edition
1000 Super Grade, Various Calibers, Sporting Rifle, Checkered Stock, Monte Carlo Stock, Curio.........	300	350	325
1100 Deluxe, Various Calibers, Sporting Rifle, Checkered Stock, Curio.........	300	350	325
1622, .22 L.R.R.F., Clip Fed, Sling Swivels, Curio.........	100	150	100
1951, Various Calibers, Sporting Rifle, Checkered Stock, Curio.........	300	375	300
3000 Crown Grade, Various Calibers, Sporting Rifle, Checkered Stock, Monte Carlo Stock, Curio.........	350	375	375
3100 Crown Grade, Various Calibers, Sporting Rifle, Checkered Stock, Curio.........	325	375	375
4000, Various Calibers, Sporting Rifle, Checkered Stock, Lightweight, Monte Carlo Stock, Curio.........	350	375	375
4100, Various Calibers, Sporting Rifle, Checkered Stock, Lightweight, Curio.........	325	375	375
456, Various Calibers, Sporting Rifle, Checkered Stock, Lightweight, Full–Stocked, Curio.........	375	400	400
6000 Imperial, Various Calibers, Sporting Rifle, Checkered Stock, Fancy Wood, Express Sights, Curio.........	425	475	450
8000 Imperial Grade, Various Calibers, Sporting Rifle, Checkered Stock, Engraved, Monte Carlo Stock, Fancy Wood, Curio.........	425	500	475

	V.G.	Exc	Prior Edition
9000 Crown Grade, Various Calibers, Sporting Rifle, Checkered Stock, Monte Carlo Stock, Curio....................	$325	$375	$400
Gustav CG–T, Various Calibers, Singleshot, Target Stock, Heavy Barrel, Curio....................	250	275	275
Gustav Grade II, Various Calibers, Sporting Rifle, Checkered Stock, Curio....................	375	400	400
Gustav Grade II, Various Calibers, Sporting Rifle, Checkered Stock, Left–Hand, Curio....................	400	425	425
Gustav Grade II, Various Calibers, Sporting Rifle, Checkered Stock, Magnum Action, Curio....................	375	400	400
Gustav Grade III, Various Calibers, Sporting Rifle, Checkered Stock, Magnum Action, Left–Hand, Curio....................	400	425	425
Gustav Grade III, Various Calibers, Sporting Rifle, Checkered Stock, Magnum Action, Light Engraving, Left–Hand, Curio....................	400	475	475
Gustav Grade III, Various Calibers, Sporting Rifle, Checkered Stock, Magnum Action, Light Engraving, Curio....................	450	475	475
Gustav Grade III, Various Calibers, Sporting Rifle, Checkered Stock, Light Engraving, Curio....................	450	500	500
Gustav Grade III, Various Calibers, Sporting Rifle, Checkered Stock, Light Engraving, Left–Hand, Curio....................	425	475	475
Gustav Grade V, Various Calibers, Sporting Rifle, Checkered Stock, Engraved, Curio....................	600	650	650
Gustav Grade V, Various Calibers, Sporting Rifle, Checkered Stock, Engraved, Left–Hand, Curio....................	575	650	650
Gustav Grade V, Various Calibers, Sporting Rifle, Checkered Stock, Engraved, Magnum Action, Curio....................	600	675	675
Gustav Grade V, Various Calibers, Sporting Rifle, Checkered Stock, Engraved, Magnum Action, Left–Hand, Curio....................	625	675	675
Gustav Swede, Various Calibers, Sporting Rifle, Checkered Stock, Curio....................	300	325	325
Gustav Swede Deluxe, Various Calibers, Sporting Rifle, Checkered Stock, Light Engraving, Curio....................	300	350	350
Gustav V–T, Various Calibers, Varmint, Target Stock, Heavy Barrel, Curio....................	400	450	450
Hi Power, Various Calibers, Sporting Rifle, Checkered Stock, Curio....................	300	350	300
P 3000 Presentation, Various Calibers, Sporting Rifle, Checkered Stock, Engraved, Fancy Wood, Curio....................	625	650	650

HUTZ, BENJAMIN Lancaster, Pa. c. 1802. See Kentucky Rifles.

HVA See Husqvarna.

HY HUNTER Burbank, Calif.

HANDGUN, DOUBLE BARREL, OVER-UNDER

Automatic Derringer, .22 L.R.R.F., Blue, Modern....................	25	50	50

HANDGUN, REVOLVER

Chicago Cub, .22 Short, 6 Shot, Folding Trigger, Modern....................	25	50	50
Detective, .22 L.R.R.F., Double Action, 6 Shot, Modern....................	50	75	75
Detective, .22 W.M.R., Double Action, 6 Shot, Modern....................	50	75	75

	V.G.	Exc	Prior Edition
Frontier Six Shooter, .22 L.R.R.F., Single Action, Western Style, Modern	$50	$75	$75
Frontier Six Shooter, .22 LR/.22 WRF Combo, Single Action, Western Style, Modern	50	75	75
Frontier Six Shooter, .357 Mag., Single Action, Western Style, Modern	125	150	100
Frontier Six Shooter, .44 Mag., Single Action, Western Style, Modern	150	175	150
Frontier Six Shooter, .45 Colt, Single Action, Western Style, Modern	125	150	125

HANDGUN, SEMI-AUTOMATIC

Maxim, .25 ACP, Clip Fed, Modern	50	75	75
Militar, .22 L.R.R.F., Double Action, Hammer, Clip Fed, Blue, Modern	50	100	100
Militar, .32 ACP, Double Action, Hammer, Clip Fed, Blue, Modern	75	100	100
Militar, .380 ACP, Double Action, Hammer, Clip Fed, Blue, Modern	100	125	100
Panzer, .22 L.R.R.F., Clip Fed, Blue, Modern	50	75	75
Stingray, .25 ACP, Clip Fed, Blue, Modern	50	75	75
Stuka, .22 Long, Clip Fed, Blue, Modern	50	75	75

HANDGUN, SINGLESHOT

Accurate Ace, .22 Short, Flobert Type, Chrome Plated, Modern	25	50	50
Favorite, .22 L.R.R.F., Stevens Copy, Modern	50	75	75
Favorite, .22 W.M.R., Stevens Copy, Modern	50	75	75
Gold Rush Derringer, .22 L.R.R.F., Spur Trigger, Modern	25	50	50
Target, .22 L.R.R.F., Bolt Action, Modern	25	50	50
Target, .22 W.M.R., Bolt Action, Modern	25	50	50

HY SCORE ARMS Brooklyn, N.Y.

HANDGUN, REVOLVER

.22 L.R.R.F., Double Action, Modern	25	50	50

HYPER Jenks, Okla. Discontinued 1984.

RIFLE, SINGLESHOT

Hyper–Single Rifle, Various Calibers, Fancy Wood, No Sights, Falling Block, Fancy Checkering, Modern	1,750	2,000	2,000
Hyper–Single Rifle, Various Calibers, Fancy Wood, No Sights, Falling Block, Fancy Checkering, Stainless Steel Barrel, Modern	2,000	2,250	2,250

I

I G   Grey, of Dundee, c. 1630.

HANDGUN, SNAPHAUNCE

Belt Pistol, Engraved, Ovoid Pommel, All Metal, Antique......................$20,000 $25,000 $25,000

I P   German, 1580–1600.

RIFLE, WHEEL-LOCK

.60, German Style, Brass Furniture, Light Ornamentation, Horn
Inlays, Set Trigger, Antique.. 4,000   4,500   4,500

IAB SHOTGUNS   Brescia, Italy. Imported by Puccinelli Co., San Anselmo, Calif.

SHOTGUN, DOUBLE BARREL, OVER-UNDER

C–300 Super Combo, 12 Ga., Vent Rib, Single Selective Trigger,
Checkered Stock, with 2 Extra Single Barrels, Modern............................ 2,250   2,750   2,750
C–3000 Combo, 12 Ga., Vent Rib, Single Selective Trigger,
Checkered Stock, with 2 Extra Single Barrels, Modern............................ 1,750   2,000   1,750

SHOTGUN, SINGLESHOT

S–300, 12 Ga., Vent Rib, Checkered Stock, Trap Grade, Modern............ 1,000   1,250   950

IMPERIAL ARMS   Made by Hopkins & Allen, c. 1880.

HANDGUN, REVOLVER

.32 Short R.F., 5 Shot, Spur Trigger, Solid Frame, Single Action,
Antique.. 125   150   150
.38 Short R.F., 5 Shot, Spur Trigger, Solid Frame, Single Action,
Antique.. 150   175   175

IMPERIAL REVOLVER   c. 1880.

HANDGUN, REVOLVER

.22 Short R.F., 7 Shot, Spur Trigger, Solid Frame, Single Action,
Antique.. 125   150   150
.32 Short R.F., 5 Shot, Spur Trigger, Solid Frame, Single Action,
Antique.. 150   175   175

	V.G.	Exc	Prior Edition

I.N.A. Industria Nacional de Armas, Sao Paulo, Brazil.

HANDGUN, REVOLVER

	V.G.	Exc	Prior Edition
Tiger, .22 L.R.R.F., Single Action, Western Style, Modern.....................	$50	$75	$75
Tiger, .32 S&W Long, Single Action, Western Style, Modern.................	50	75	75

INDIA MILITARY

RIFLE, BOLT ACTION

	V.G.	Exc	Prior Edition
No. 1 Mk.III, S.M.L.E., .303 British, Clip Fed, Ishapore, Curio..............	150	175	100

INDIAN ARMS Detroit, Mich., c. 1976. Discontinued.

HANDGUN, SEMI-AUTOMATIC

	V.G.	Exc	Prior Edition
.380 ACP, Clip Fed, Stainless Steel, Vent Rib, Double Action, Modern..	300	375	475

INDIAN SALES Cheyenne, Wyo.

HANDGUN, REVOLVER

	V.G.	Exc	Prior Edition
HS–21, .22 L.R.R.F., Double Action, Blue, Modern...............................	25	50	50

HANDGUN, SEMI-AUTOMATIC

	V.G.	Exc	Prior Edition
Model 4, .25 ACP, Clip Fed, Blue, Modern...	50	75	75

INGRAM Invented by Gordon Ingram. Made by Police Ordnance Co., Los Angeles, Calif. and Military Armament Corp., Georgia. Discontinued 1982.

SEMI-AUTOMATIC WEAPON

	V.G.	Exc	Prior Edition
MAC 10, .45, ACP or 9mm, Clip Fed, Folding Stock, Open–Bolt, Modern...	650	750	750
MAC 10A1, 9mm Luger or .45 ACP, Clip Fed, Folding Stock, Closed Bolt, Modern...	250	275	275
MAC 11, .380 ACP, Clip Fed, Folding Stock, Smaller Version of MAC 10, Modern...	500	575	575

INGRAM, CHARLES Glasgow, Scotland, c. 1860.

SHOTGUN, DOUBLE BARREL, SIDE-BY-SIDE

	V.G.	Exc	Prior Edition
Extra Set of Rifle Barrels, High Quality, Cased with Accessories, Engraved, Checkered Stock, Antique..	6,500	7,500	7,500

INHOFF, BENEDICT Berks County, Pa. 1781–1783. See Kentucky Rifles.

	V.G.	Exc	Prior Edition

INTERCHANGEABLE Belgium, Trade Name Schoverlin–Daley & Gales, c. 1880.

SHOTGUN, DOUBLE BARREL, SIDE-BY-SIDE

Various Gauges, Outside Hammers, Damascus Barrel, Curio.................	$100	$150	$150

INTERDYNAMIC Miami, Fla., c. 1979. Sold by F.I.E.

HANDGUN, SEMI-AUTOMATIC

KG–99, 9mm Luger, Clip Fed, SMG Styling, Modern............................	475	550	650

INTERNATIONAL Made by Hood Firearms, c. 1875.

HANDGUN, REVOLVER

.22 Short R.F., 7 Shot, Spur Trigger, Solid Frame, Single Action, Antique..	125	175	175
.32 Short R.F., 5 Shot, Spur Trigger, Solid Frame, Single Action, Antique..	125	175	175

INTERNATIONAL DISTRIBUTORS Miami, Fla.

RIFLE, BOLT ACTION

Mauser Type, Various Calibers, Checkered Stock, Sling Swivels, Recoil Pad, Modern..	150	200	200

INTERSTATE ARMS CO. Made by Crescent for Townley Metal & Hdw., Kansas City, Mo.

SHOTGUN, DOUBLE BARREL, SIDE-BY-SIDE

Various Gauges, Hammerless, Damascus Barrel, Modern......................	175	200	200
Various Gauges, Hammerless, Steel Barrel, Modern.............................	175	200	200
Various Gauges, Outside Hammers, Damascus Barrel, Modern.............	150	175	175
Various Gauges, Outside Hammers, Steel Barrel, Modern.....................	150	175	175

SHOTGUN, SINGLESHOT

Various Gauges, Hammer, Steel Barrel, Modern....................................	50	75	75

ISRAELI MILITARY This list includes both military arms and the commercial arms made by Israeli Military Industries (I.M.I.). Also see Magnum Research, Inc. (M.R.I.).

HANDGUN, REVOLVER

S & W Model 10 Copy, 9mm Luger, Solid Frame, Swing–Out Cylinder, Double Action, Military, Modern..	500	575	575

RIFLE, SEMI-AUTOMATIC

Galil, .223 Rem., Clip Fed, Assault Rifle, Folding Stock, Modern..........	800	950	950
Galil, .308 Win., Clip Fed, Assault Rifle, Folding Stock, Modern............	900	1,050	1,050

	V.G.	Exc	Prior Edition
UZI, 9mm Luger, Clip Fed, Folding Stock, Commercial, Modern...........	$850	$950	$850

ITALGUNS INTERNATIONAL Cusago, Italy

HANDGUN, REVOLVER

Western Style, Various Calibers, Single Action, Modern.........................	125	150	150
Western Style, Various Calibers, Single Action, Automatic Hammer Safety, Modern..	125	150	150

COMBINATION WEAPON, OVER-UNDER

Various Calibers, Checkered Stock, Double Triggers, Modern..............	275	325	325

SHOTGUN, DOUBLE BARREL, OVER-UNDER

Model 125, 12 Gauge, Checkered Stock, Vent Rib, Double Triggers, Modern..	200	225	225
Model 150, 12 or 20 Gauges, Checkered Stock, Vent Rib, Single Trigger, Modern..	225	250	250

ITALIAN MILITARY Also See Beretta.

HANDGUN, REVOLVER

Service Revolver, 10.4mm, Double Action, 6 Shot, Folding Trigger, Curio..	100	125	125

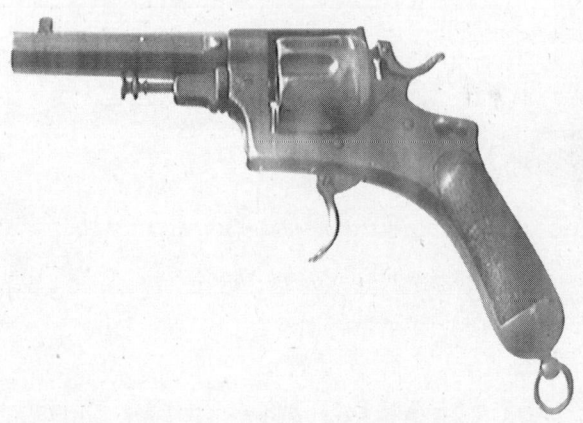

Italian Military Service Revolver Folding Trigger

Service Revolver, 10.4mm, Double Action, 6 Shot, Trigger Guard, Curio..	100	125	125

HANDGUN, SEMI-AUTOMATIC

Brixia, 9mm Glisenti, Clip Fed, Curio..	375	450	300

	V.G.	Exc	Prior Edition
M1910 Glisenti Army, 9mm, Clip Fed, Curio..	$300	$350	$300

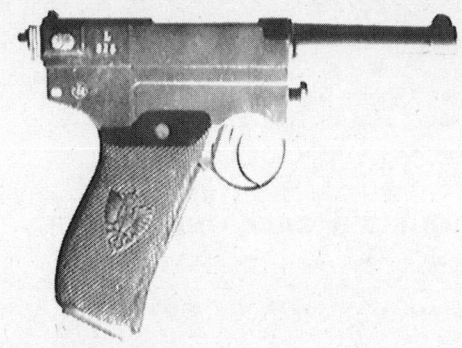

Italian Military M910

M1934 Beretta, .380 ACP, Clip Fed, Curio...	275	325	175

RIFLE, BOLT ACTION

M1891, 6.5 X 52 Mannlicher–Carcano, Curio...	75	100	100
M38, 7.35mm, Terni, Military, Curio..	75	100	75
M91 T.S., 6.5 X 52 Mannlicher–Carcano, Carbine, Folding Bayonet, Curio...	75	100	100

Italian Military M91 Rifle

M91 T.S. (Late), 6.5 X 52 Mannlicher–Carcano, Carbine, Folding Bayonet, Curio..	50	75	75
M91/24, 6.5 X 52 Mannlicher–Carcano, Curio..	50	75	75

Italian Military M91/24 Rifle

M91/24, 6.5 X 52 Mannlicher–Carcano, Carbine, Curio...........................	50	75	75
Vetterli M1870/1887, 10.4 X47R Italian Vetterli, Antique.....................	175	225	125
Vetterli M1870/87/15, 6.5 X 52 Mannlicher–Carcano, Antique..............	100	125	125

	V.G.	Exc	Prior Edition

ITHACA GUN CO. Ithaca, N.Y. 1883–1986. Absorbed Lefever Arms Co., Syracuse Arms Co., Union Firearms Co., and Wilkes Barre Gun Co. Also see the commemorative section.

RIFLE, BOLT ACTION

	V.G.	Exc	Prior Edition
LSA 55, Various Calibers, Monte Carlo Stock, Cheekpiece, Heavy Barrel, Modern..............	$350	$375	$375
LSA 55, Various Calibers, Monte Carlo Stock, Open Rear Sight, Modern..............	325	350	300
LSA 55 Deluxe, Various Calibers, Monte Carlo Stock, Cheekpiece, No Sights, Scope Mounts, Modern..............	350	400	400
LSA 65 Deluxe, Various Calibers, Monte Carlo Stock, Cheekpiece, No Sights, Scope Mounts, Modern..............	325	375	375
LSA–65, Various Calibers, Monte Carlo Stock, Open Rear Sight, Modern..............	300	350	350

RIFLE, LEVER ACTION

	V.G.	Exc	Prior Edition
Model 49, .22 L.R.R.F., Singleshot, Modern..............	75	100	75
Model 49, .22 WMR, Singleshot, Modern..............	75	100	75
Model 49 Deluxe, .22 L.R.R.F., Singleshot, Fancy Wood, Modern..........	100	125	75
Model 49 Presentation, .22 L.R.R.F., Singleshot, Engraved, Fancy Checkering, Modern..............	125	150	150
Model 49 R, .22 L.R.R.F., Tube Feed, Modern..............	75	100	100
Model 49 St. Louis, .22 L.R.R.F., Bicentennial, Fancy Wood, Singleshot, Curio..............	75	150	150
Model 49 Youth, .22 L.R.R.F., Singleshot, Modern..............	50	75	50
Model 72, .22 L.R.R.F., Tube Feed, Modern..............	100	125	125
Model 72, .22 WMR, Tube Feed, Modern..............	125	150	150
Model 72 Deluxe, .22 L.R.R.F., Tube Feed, Octagon Barrel, Modern..............	125	175	175

COMBINATION WEAPON, OVER-UNDER

	V.G.	Exc	Prior Edition
LSA 55 Turkey Gun, 12 Ga./.222, Open Rear Sight, Monte Carlo Stock, Modern..............	425	475	475

RIFLE, SEMI-AUTOMATIC

	V.G.	Exc	Prior Edition
X–15 Lightning, .22 L.R.R.F., Clip Fed, Modern..............	100	125	100
X5–C Light Lightning, .22 L.R.R.F., Clip Fed, Modern..............	75	100	100
X5–T Lightning, .22 L.R.R.F., Tube Feed, Modern..............	75	100	100

SHOTGUN, DOUBLE BARREL, OVER-UNDER

	V.G.	Exc	Prior Edition
Model 500, 12 and 20 Gauges, Field Grade, Selective Ejector, Vent Rib, Modern..............	350	400	400
Model 500, 12 Ga. Mag. 3", Field Grade, Selective Ejector, Vent Rib, Modern..............	375	425	425
Model 600, 12 and 20 Gauges, Field Grade, Selective Ejector, Vent Rib, Modern..............	400	475	475
Model 600, 12 and 20 Gauges, Skeet Grade, Selective Ejector, Vent Rib, Modern..............	475	525	525
Model 600, 12 Ga., Trap Grade, Selective Ejector, Vent Rib, Modern..............	450	525	525
Model 600, 12 Ga., Trap Grade, Selective Ejector, Vent Rib, Monte Carlo Stock, Modern..............	475	550	550

	V.G.	Exc	Prior Edition
Model 600, 28 and .410 Gauges, Skeet Grade, Selective Ejector, Vent Rib, Modern	$575	$650	$650
Model 600 Combo Set, Various Gauges, Skeet Grade, Selective Ejector, Vent Rib, Cased, Modern	950	1,350	1,350
Model 680 English, 12 and 20 Gauges, Field Grade, Selective Ejector, Vent Rib, Modern	575	625	625
Model 700, 12 and 20 Gauges, Skeet Grade, Selective Ejector, Vent Rib, Modern	675	750	750
Model 700, 12 Ga., Trap Grade, Selective Ejector, Vent Rib, Modern	675	750	750
Model 700, 12 Ga., Trap Grade, Selective Ejector, Vent Rib, Monte Carlo Stock, Modern	725	775	775
Model 700 Combo Set, Various Gauges, Skeet Grade, Selective Ejector, Vent Rib, Cased, Modern	1,500	1,750	1,750
Parazzi MT–6, 12 Ga., Skeet Grade, Automatic Ejector, Vent Rib, Cased, Modern	3,250	3,750	3,750
Parazzi MT–6, 12 Ga., Trap Grade, Automatic Ejector, Vent Rib, Cased, Modern	3,000	3,500	3,500
Perazzi Light Game Model, 12 Ga., Automatic Ejector, Vent Rib, Single Trigger, Modern	3,000	3,500	3,500
Perazzi Competition 1, 12 Ga., Skeet Grade, Automatic Ejector, Vent Rib, Single Trigger, Cased, Modern	3,000	3,500	3,500
Perazzi Competition 1, 12 Ga., Trap Grade, Automatic Ejector, Vent Rib, Single Trigger, Cased, Modern	1,750	2,000	2,250
Perazzi Mirage Special, 12 Ga., Trap Grade, Automatic Ejector, Vent Cased, Modern	4,500	5,000	4,750
Perazzi Mirage Special 4–Barrel Set, Various Gauges, Skeet Grade, Automatic Ejector, Vent Rib, Cased, Modern	8,000	9,000	6,500
Perazzi MX–7 Combo, 12 Ga., Trap Grade, Automatic Ejector, Vent RIb, Cased, Modern	4,000	4,500	3,950

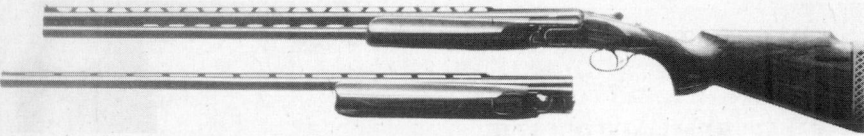

Ithaca Perazzi Combination

SHOTGUN, DOUBLE BARREL, SIDE-BY-SIDE

Early Model, Serial Numbers under 425,000, Deduct 50%
Outside Hammers, Deduct Another 20%–30%

	V.G.	Exc	Prior Edition
#2 Grade, 10 Ga. Magnum, Hammerless, Beavertail Forend, Double Trigger, Modern	1,500	1,750	1,225
#2 Grade, 12 Ga., Hammerless, Beavertail Forend, Double Trigger, Checkered Stock, Modern	1,050	1,100	1,025
#2 Grade, 16 Ga., Hammerless, Double Trigger, Checkered Stock, Modern	1,000	1,150	1,150
#2 Grade, 20 Ga., Hammerless, Double Trigger, Checkered Stock, Modern	1,200	1,350	925
#3 Grade, 10 Ga. Magnum, Hammerless, Beavertail Forend, Double Trigger, Modern	2,000	2,250	1,475

	V.G.	Exc	Prior Edition
#3 Grade, 12 Ga., Hammerless, Double Trigger, Engraved, Checkered Stock, Modern	$1,125	$1,325	$1,325
#3 Grade, 16 Ga., Hammerless, Beavertail Forend, Engraved, Checkered Stock, Double Trigger, Modern	1,050	1,250	1,250
#3 Grade, 20 Ga., Hammerless, Double Trigger, Engraved, Checkered Stock, Modern	1,500	1,750	1,550
#4 E Grade, 12 Ga., Hammerless, Automatic Ejector, Vent Rib, Beavertail Forend, Modern	2,750	3,000	3,250
#4 E Grade, 16 Ga., Hammerless, Automatic Ejector, Vent Rib, Fancy Checkering, Engraving, Modern	3,250	3,500	3,125
#4 E Grade, 20 Ga., Hammerless, Automatic Ejector, Beavertail Forend, Fancy Checkering, Engraving, Modern	3,500	3,750	2,875
#5 E Grade, 10 Ga. Mag., Hammerless, Automatic Ejector, Vent Rib, Beavertail Forend, Modern	—	RARE	—
#5 E Grade, 12 Ga., Hammerless, Automatic Ejector, Vent Rib, Fancy Checkering, Engraving, Modern	3,250	3,500	4,150
#5 E Grade, 16 Ga., Hammerless, Automatic Ejector, Beavertail Forend, Fancy Checkering, Fancy Engraving, Modern	3,250	3,500	3,750
#5 E Grade, 20 Ga., Hammerless, Automatic Ejector, Fancy Checkering, Fancy Engraving, Double Trigger, Modern	3,750	4,250	6,250
#7 E Grade, Various Gauges, Hammerless, Automatic Ejector, Vent Rib, Beavertail Forend, Modern	—	RARE	—
$1000 Grade, 12 Ga., Hammerless, Automatic Ejector, Single Selective Trigger, Vent Rib, Beavertail Forend, Curio	9,000	10,500	10,250
$1000 Grade, 16 and 20 Gauges, Hammerless, Curio	—	RARE	—
$2000 Grade, 12 Ga., Hammerless, Automatic Ejector, Single Selective Trigger, Ornate, Modern	8,500	9,500	9,500
$2000 Grade, 16 Ga., Hammerless, Automatic Ejector, Single Selective Trigger, Vent Rib, Ornate, Modern	—	RARE	—
$2000 Grade, 20 Ga., Hammerless, Automatic Ejector, Single Selective Trigger, Beavertail Forend, Ornate, Modern	—	RARE	—
Field Grade, Various Gauges, Hammerless, 10 Ga. Magnum, Beaverta Forend, Modern	1,750	2,000	725
Field Grade, Various Gauges, Hammerless, 10 Ga. Magnum, Double Trigger, Modern	1,500	1,750	650
Field Grade, Various Gauges, Hammerless, Beavertail Forend, Double Trigger, Modern	700	775	775
Field Grade, Various Gauges, Hammerless, Double Trigger, Checkered Stock, Modern	550	600	600

SHOTGUN, LEVER ACTION

	V.G.	Exc	Prior Edition
Model 66, Various Gauges, Singleshot, Modern	75	100	75
Model 66, Various Gauges, Singleshot, Ventilated Rib, Modern	100	125	75
Model 66 Youth, Various Gauges, Singleshot, Modern	50	75	75

SHOTGUN, PISTOL

	V.G.	Exc	Prior Edition
Auto Burglar, Various Gauges, Double Barrel, SIde by Side, Short Shotgun, Curio	650	850	850

SHOTGUN, SEMI-AUTOMATIC

	V.G.	Exc	Prior Edition
5KB 300 Standard, 12 and 20 Gauges, Modern	200	250	200
5KB 300 Standard, 12 and 20 Gauges, Vent Rib, Modern	225	275	225
5KB 300 XL Standard, 12 and 20 Gauges, Modern	275	300	225
5KB 300 XL Standard, 12 and 20 Gauges, Vent Rib, Modern	300	325	250
5KB 900 XL Deluxe, 12 and 20 Gauges, Vent Rib, Modern	275	300	250

	V.G.	Exc	Prior Edition
5KB 900 XL MR Deluxe, 12 and 20 Gauges, Vent Rib, Modern............	$250	$275	$325
5KB 900 XL Slug, 12 and 20 Gauges, Open Rear Sight, Modern............	275	300	250
5KB 900 XL, 12 and 20 Gauges, Skeet Grade, Modern..........................	325	350	250
5KB 900 XL, 12 Ga., Trap Grade, Modern...	325	350	275
5KB 900 XL, 12 Ga., Trap Grade, Monte Carlo Stock, Modern.............	350	375	275
Mag 10 Deluxe, 10 Ga. 3½", Takedown, Vent Rib, Fancy Wood, Checkered Stock, Modern...	800	950	525
Mag 10 Standard, 10 Ga. 3½", Takedown, Recoil Pad, Checkered Stock, Sling Swivels, Modern..	475	525	425
Mag 10 Standard, 10 Ga. 3½", Takedown, Vent Rib, Recoil Pad, Checkered Stock, Sling Swivels, Modern...	600	650	500
Mag 10 Supreme, 10 Ga. 3½", Takedown, Vent Rib, Fancy Wood, Engraved, Checkered Stock, Modern...	600	750	750
Model 51 Presentation, 12 and 20 Gauges, Skeet Grade, Takedown, Checkered Stock, Fancy Wood, Recoil Pad, Modern...........................	750	1,250	300
Model 51 Standard, 12 and 20 Gauges, Takedown, Checkered Stock, Modern..	225	275	225
Model 51 Standard, 12 and 20 Gauges, Takedown, Vent Rib, Checkered Stock, Modern...	300	375	250

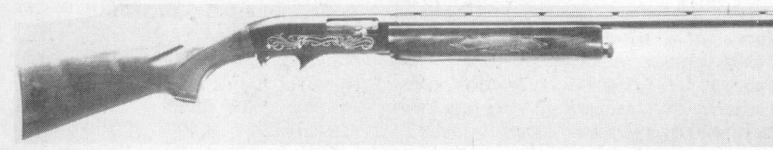

Ithaca Model 51

Model 51 Turkey Gun, 12 Ga., Trap Grade, Takedown, Checkered Stock, Fancy Wood, Recoil Pad, Modern.....................................	375	450	350
Model 51A Deerslayer, 12 Ga., Takedown, Open Rear Sight, Sling Swivels, Modern..	275	325	275
Model 51A Waterfowler, 12 Ga., Trap Grade, Monte Carlo Stock, Fan Wood, Recoil Pad, Modern...	325	350	350
Model 51A, Magnum 12 Gauge, Takedown, Vent Rib, Recoil Pad, Modern..	325	375	275

SHOTGUN, SINGLESHOT

$5000 Grade, 12 Ga., Trap Grade, Automatic Ejector, Ornate, Modern...	7,500	9,000	8,500
4 E Grade, 12 Ga., Trap Grade, Automatic Ejector, Engraved, Fancy Checkering, Modern...	1,000	1,200	1,200
5 E Grade, 12 Ga., Trap Grade, Automatic Ejector, Fancy Engraving, Fancy Checkering, Modern.......................................	2,000	2,250	2,200
7 E Grade, 12 Ga., Trap Grade, Automatic Ejector, Fancy Engraving, Fancy Checkering, Modern.......................................	4,000	4,500	3,250
Century 12 Ga., Trap Grade, Automatic Ejector, Engraved, Checkered Stock, Modern...	425	475	475
Century II, 12 Ga., Trap Grade, Automatic Ejector, Engraved, Checkered Stock, Modern...	475	525	500
Perazzi Competition, 12 Ga., Trap Grade, Automatic Ejector, Vent Rib, Cased, Modern..	950	1,250	1,250
Victory Grade, 12 Ga., Automatic Ejector, Checkered Stock, Vent Rib, Trap Grade, Modern..	725	800	750

	V.G.	Exc	Prior Edition

SHOTGUN, SLIDE ACTION

Model 37, Extra Vent Rib Barrel, Add $60.00–$85.00

Model 37, for Extra Barrel, Add $50.00–$75.00

Model 37 Deerslayer, Various Gauges, Takedown, Checkered Stock, Recoil Pad, Open Rear Sight, Modern.. $275 | $350 | $225

Model 37 Deerslayer, Various Gauges, Takedown, Fancy Wood, Checkered Stock, Recoil Pad, Open Rear Sight, Modern......................... 250 | 300 | 250

Model 37 DSPS, 12 Ga., Takedown, Checkered Stock, 5 Shot, Open Rear Sight, Modern.. 200 | 225 | 225

Model 37 DSPS, 12 Ga., Takedown, Checkered Stock, 8 Shot, Open Rear Sight, Modern.. 225 | 250 | 250

Model 37 English Ultralite, 12 or 20 Gauge, Takedown, Checkered Stock, Recoil Pad, Modern.. 250 | 300 | 225

Model 37 Field Grade, Various Gauges, Takedown, Plain, Modern....... 150 | 200 | 175

Model 37 Presentation, Various Gauges, Takedown, Skeet Grade, Fancy Wood, Checkered Stock, Modern.. 1,000 | 1,250 | 1,000

Model 37 Riotgun, 12 Ga., Takedown, Parkerized, 5 Shot, Modern........ 1,500 | 1,750 | 1,500

Model 37 Standard, Various Gauges, Takedown, Checkered Stock, Modern.. 200 | 225 | 225

Model 37 Trenchgun, 12 Ga., Takedown, Parkerized, 5 Shot, Modern... 3,000 | 3,500 | 3,250

Model 37, 12 Ga., Takedown, Bicentennial, Engraved, Fancy Wood, Checkered Stock, Modern.. 325 | 350 | 350

Model 37–$1000 Grade, Various Gauges, Takedown, Fancy Wood, Fancy Checkering, Fancy Engraving, Gold Inlays, Modern...................... 4,000 | 5,000 | 5,000

Model 37–$5000 Grade, Various Gauges, Takedown, Fancy Wood, Fancy Checkering, Fancy Engraving, Gold Inlays, Modern...................... 3,500 | 4,500 | 4,500

Model 37–D, Various Gauges, Takedown, Checkered Stock, Beavertail Forend, Modern... 225 | 250 | 250

Model 37–DV, Various Gauges, Takedown, Checkered Stock, Recoil Pad, Modern.. 225 | 275 | 200

Model 37–R Deluxe, Various Gauges, Takedown, Solid Rib, Fancy Wood, Checkered Stock, Modern.. 225 | 300 | 250

Model 37–R, Various Gauges, Takedown, Solid Rib, Checkered Stock, Modern.. 175 | 225 | 200

Model 37–R, Various Gauges, Takedown, Solid Rib, Plain, Modern.. 150 | 200 | 175

Model 37–S, Various Gauges, Takedown, Skeet Grade, Checkered Stock, Fancy Wood, Modern.. 325 | 400 | 375

Model 37–T, Various Gauges, Takedown, Trap Grade, Checkered Stock, Fancy Wood, Modern.. 325 | 400 | 375

Model 37–V Standard, Various Gauges, Takedown, Checkered Stock, Vent Rib, Modern.. 225 | 250 | 250

Model 37T Target, Various Gauges, Takedown, Trap Grade, Fancy Wood, Checkered Stock, Modern.. 350 | 400 | 400

	V.G.	Exc	Prior Edition

IVER JOHNSON Started as Johnson & Bye 1871 in Worcester, Mass. In 1883 became Iver Johnson's Arms & Cycle Works. 1891–1982 at Fitchburg, Mass., relocated to Jacksonville, Ark. in 1982. Acquired by American Military Arms in 1987. All operations ceased in 1993.

HANDGUN, PERCUSSION

	V.G.	Exc	Prior Edition
.36 1861 Navy, Revolver, Reproduction, Antique	$50	$75	$75
.36 New Model Navy, Revolver, Reproduction, Antique	50	75	75
.36 Pocket Model, Revolver, Reproduction, Antique	50	75	75
.36 Remington Army, Revolver, Reproduction, Antique	50	75	75
.44 1860 Army, Revolver, Reproduction, Antique	50	75	75
.44 Confederate Army, Revolver, Reproduction, Antique	50	75	75
.44 Remington Army, Revolver, Reproduction, Antique	75	100	100
.44 Remington Target, Revolver, Reproduction, Antique	75	100	100
Prince, .30, Singleshot, Spur Trigger, Various Barrel Lengths, Screw Barrel, Antique	300	325	325
Uncle Sam 1871, .30, Singleshot, Spur Trigger, Various Barrel Lengths, Antique	250	300	300

HANDGUN, REVOLVER

	V.G.	Exc	Prior Edition
.22 Supershot, .22 L.R.R.F., 7 Shot, Blue, Wood Grips, Top Break, Double Action, Modern	75	100	100
Armsworth M855, .22 L.R.R.F., 8 Shot, Single Action, Top Break, Adjustable Sights, Wood Grips, Modern	100	125	125
Buckhorn Buntline, .357 Magnum, Single Action, Western Style, with Detachable Shoulder Stock, Adjustable Sights, 18" Barrel, Modern	275	300	300
Buckhorn Buntline, .44 Magnum, Single Action, Western Style, with Detachable Shoulder Stock, Adjustable Sights, 18" Barrel, Modern	300	325	325
Buckhorn Buntline, .45 Colt, Single Action, Western Style, with Detachable Shoulder Stock, Adjustable Sights, 18" Barrel, Modern	275	300	300
Buckhorn, .357 Magnum, Single Action, Western Style, Color Case Hardened Frame, Adjustable Sights, 12" Barrel, Modern	175	200	200
Buckhorn, .357 Magnum, Single Action, Western Style, Color Case Hardened Frame, Adjustable Sights, Various Barrel Lengths, Modern	125	175	150
Buckhorn, .44 Magnum, Single Action, Western Style, Color Case Hardened Frame, Adjustable Sights, Various Barrel Lengths, Modern	175	200	200
Buckhorn, .45 Colt, Single Action, Western Style, Color Case Hardened Frame, Adjustable Sights, Various Barrel Lengths, Modern	150	175	175
Buckhorn, .45 Colt, Single Action, Western Style, Color Case Hardened Frame, Adjustable Sights, 12" Barrel, Modern	175	200	200
Cadet, .22 WMR, 8 Shot, Solid Frame, Double Action, Plastic Stock, Blue, Modern	50	75	75
Cadet, .32 S & W Long, 5 Shot, Solid Frame, Double Action, Plastic Stock, Nickel Plated, Modern	50	75	75

	V.G.	Exc	Prior Edition
Cadet, .32 S & W, 5 Shot, Solid Frame, Double Action, Plastic Stock, Blue, Modern..	$50	$75	$75
Cadet, .38 Special, 5 Shot, Solid Frame, Double Action, Plastic Stock, Blue, Modern..	50	75	75
Cadet, .38 Special, 5 Shot, Solid Frame, Double Action, Plastic Stock, Nickel Plated, Modern..	50	75	75
Cattleman, .357 Magnum, Single Action, Western Style, Color Case Hardened Frame, Various Barrel Lengths, Modern........................	150	175	150
Cattleman, .447 Magnum, Single Action, Western Style, Color Case Hardened Frame, Various Barrel Lengths, Modern........................	175	200	175
Cattleman, .45 Colt, Single Action, Western Style, Color Case Hardened Frame, Various Barrel Lengths, Modern.................................	125	150	150
Champion Target, .22 L.R.R.F., 8 Shot, Single Action, Top Break, Adjustable Sights, Wood Grips, Modern..	100	125	125
Model 1900 Target, .22 L.R.R.F., 7 Shot, Blue, Wood Grips, Solid Frame, Double Action, Modern...	125	150	175
Model 1900, .22 L.R.R.F., 7 Shot, Blue, Double Action, Solid Frame, Modern...	75	100	100
Model 1900, .22 L.R.R.F., 7 Shot, Nickel Plated, Double Action, Solid Frame, Modern...	75	100	100
Model 1900, .32 S & W Long, 6 Shot, Blue, Double Action, Solid Frame, Modern...	75	100	100
Model 1900, .32 S & W Long, 6 Shot, Nickel Plated, Double Action, Solid Frame, Modern...	75	100	100
Model 1900, .32 Short R.F., 6 Shot, Blue, Double Action, Solid Frame, Modern...	75	100	100
Model 1900, .32 Short R.F., 6 Shot, Nickel Plated, Double Action, Solid Frame, Modern...	100	125	125
Model 1900, .38 S & W, 5 Shot, Blue, Double Action, Solid Frame, Modern...	100	125	125
Model 1900, .38 S & W, 5 Shot, Nickel Plated, Double Action, Solid Frame, Modern...	100	125	150
Model 50A Sidewinder, .22 L.R.R.F., 8 Shot, Solid Frame, Double Action, Plastic Stock, Western Style, Modern..............................	50	75	75
Model 50A Sidewinder, .22 L.R.R.F., 8 Shot, Solid Frame, Double Action, Wood Grips, Western Style, Modern.............................	50	75	75
Model 55, .22 L.R.R.F., 8 Shot, Solid Frame, Double Action, Wood Grips, Blue, Modern...	50	75	75
Model 55–S Cadet, .32 S & W, 5 Shot, Solid Frame, Double Action, Plastic Stock, Blue, Modern...	50	75	75
Model 55–S Cadet, .38 S & W, 5 Shot, Solid Frame, Double Action, Plastic Stock, Blue, Modern...	50	75	75
Model 55–SA Cadet, .22 L.R.R.F., 8 Shot, Solid Frame, Double Action, Plastic, Blue, Modern..	50	75	75
Model 55–SA Cadet, .32 S & W, 5 Shot, Solid Frame, Double Action, Plastic Stock, Blue, Modern...	50	75	75
Model 55–SA Cadet, .38 S & W, 5 Shot, Solid Frame, Double Action, Plastic Stock, Blue, Modern...	50	75	75
Model 55A, .22 L.R.R.F., 8 Shot, Solid Frame, Double Action, Wood Grips, Blue, Modern...	75	100	100
Model 55A, .22 L.R.R.F., 8 Shot, Solid Frame, Double Action, Wood Grips, Blue, Modern...	75	100	100
Model 55A, .22 L.R.R.F., 8 Shot, Solid Frame, Double Action, Plastic Stock, Blue, Modern...	75	100	100

	V.G.	Exc	Prior Edition
Model 55S, .22 L.R.R.F., 8 Shot, Solid Frame, Double Action, Plastic Stock, Blue, Modern......................	$50	$75	$75
Model 57 Target, .22 L.R.R.F., 8 Shot, Solid Frame, Double Action, Plastic Stock, Adjustable Sights, Modern....................	75	100	100
Model 57 Target, .22 L.R.R.F., 8 Shot, Solid Frame, Double Action, Wood Grips, Adjustable Sights, Modern....................	75	100	100
Model 57–A Target, .22 L.R.R.F., 8 Shot, Solid Frame, Double Action, Plastic Stock, Adjustable Sights, Modern....................	75	100	100
Model 57–A Target, .22 L.R.R.F., 8 Shot, Solid Frame, Double Action, Wood Grips, Adjustable Sights, Modern....................	75	100	100
Model 66 Trailsman, .22 L.R.R.F., 8 Shot, Top Break, Double Action, Wood Grips, Adjustable Sights, Modern....................	75	100	100

Iver Johnson Trailsman

	V.G.	Exc	Prior Edition
Model 67 Viking, .22 L.R.R.F., 8 Shot, Top Break, Double Action, Plastic Stock, Adjustable Sights, Modern....................	75	100	100
Model 67S Viking, .32 S & W, 5 Shot, Top Break, Double Action, Plastic Stock, Adjustable Sights, Modern....................	75	100	100
Model 67S Viking, .38 S & W, 5 Shot, Top Break, Double Action, Plastic Stock, Adjustable Sights, Modern....................	50	75	75
Model 76S Viking, .22 L.R.R.F., 8 Shot, Top Break, Double Action, Plastic Stock, Adjustable Sights, Modern....................	75	100	100
Petite, .22 Short Nickel Plated, Folding Trigger, 5 Shot, "Baby" Style, Antique....................	200	250	250
Safety, .22 L.R.R.F., 7 Shot, Top Break, Double Action, Hammer, Blue, Modern....................	100	125	125
Safety, .22 L.R.R.F., 7 Shot, Top Break, Double Action, Hammer, Nickel Plated, Modern....................	125	150	150
Safety, .22 L.R.R.F., 7 Shot, Top Break, Double Action, Hammerless, Blue, Modern....................	125	150	150
Safety, .22 L.R.R.F., 7 Shot, Top Break, Double Action, Hammerless, Nickel Plated, Modern....................	125	150	150
Safety, .32 S & W Long, 6 Shot, Top Break, Double Action, Hammer, Blue, Modern....................	100	125	125
Safety, .32 S & W Long, 6 Shot, Top Break, Double Action, Hammer, Nickel Plated, Modern....................	100	125	125
Safety, .32 S & W Long, 6 Shot, Top Break, Double Action, Hammerless, Blue, Modern....................	100	125	125
Safety, .32 S & W, 5 Shot, Top Break, Double Action, Hammer, NIckel Plated, Modern....................	125	150	150

	V.G.	Exc	Prior Edition
Safety, .32 S & W, 5 Shot, Top Break, Double Action, Hammer, Blue, Modern................................	$100	$125	$125
Safety, .32 S & W, 5 Shot, Top Break, Double Action, Hammerless, Blue, Modern........................	125	150	150
Safety, .32 S & W, 5 Shot, Top Break, Double Action, Hammerless, Nickel Plated, Modern....................	125	150	150
Safety, .38 S & W, 5 Shot, Top Break, Double Action, Hammerless, Nickel Plated, Modern....................	125	150	150
Sealed 8 Protector, .22 L.R.R.F., 8 Shot, Blue, Wood Grips, Top Break, Double Action, Modern....................	125	150	150
Sealed 8 Supershot, .22 L.R.R.F., Adjustable Sights, Blue, Wood Grips, Top Break, Double Action, Modern....................	125	150	150
Sealed 8 Target, .22 L.R.R.F., 8 Shot, Blue, Wood Grips, Solid Frame, Double Action, Modern....................	100	125	125
Sidewinder, .22LR/.22 WMR Combo, Western Style, 4" Barrel, Adjustable Sights, Modern....................	75	100	100
Sidewinder, .22LR/.22 WMR Combo, Western Style, 6" Barrel, Adjustable Sights, Modern....................	75	100	100
Supershot 9, .22 L.R.R.F., 9 Shot, Adjustable Sights, Blue, Wood Grips, Top Break, Modern....................	100	125	125
Supershot M 844, .22 L.R.R.F., 8 Shot, Double Action, Top Break, Adjustable Sights, Wood Grips, Modern....................	75	100	100
Swing Out Model 1879, .38 S & W, 5 Shot, Swing Right, Forward Hinge, Solid Frame, Antique....................	275	300	300
Swing Out, .22 L.R.R.F., Swing-Out Cylinder, 4" Barrel, Double Action, Wood Grips, Blue, Modern....................	75	100	100
Swing Out, .22 L.R.R.F., Swing-Out Cylinder, 4" Barrel, Double Action, Adjustable Sights, Blue, Modern....................	125	150	150
Swing Out, .22 L.R.R.F., Swing-Out Cylinder, 6" Barrel, Double Action, Adjustable Sights, Blue, Modern....................	100	125	125
Swing Out, .22 L.R.R.F., Swing-Out Cylinder, Various Barrel Lengths, Double Action, Wood Grips, Blue, Modern....................	75	100	100
Swing Out, .22 WMR, Swing-Out Cylinder, 4" Barrel, Double Action, Wood Grips, Blue, Modern....................	75	100	100
Swing Out, .22 WMR, Swing-Out Cylinder, 4" Barrel, Double Action, Adjustable Sights, Blue, MOdern....................	125	150	150
Swing Out, .22 WMR, Swing-Out Cylinder, 6" Barrel, Double Action, Adjustable Sights, Blue, Modern....................	100	125	125
Swing Out, .22 WMR, Swing-Out Cylinder, Various Barrel, Lengths, Double Action, Wood Grips, Blue, Modern....................	75	100	100
Swing Out, .32 S & W Long, Swing-Out Cylinder, 4" Barrel, Double Action, Wood Grips, Blue, Modern....................	100	125	125
Swing Out, .32 S & W Long, Swing-Out Cylinder, 4" Barrel, Double Action, Adjustable Sights, Blue, Modern....................	125	150	150
Swing Out, .32 S & W Long, Swing-Out Cylinder, 6" Barrel, Double Action, Adjustable Sights, Blue, Modern....................	100	125	125
Swing Out, .32 S & W Long, Swing-Out Cylinder, Various Barrel Lengths, Double Action, Wood Grips, Blue, Modern....................	75	100	100
Swing Out, .32 S & W Long, Swing-Out Cylinder, Various Barrel Lengths, Double Action, Wood Grips, Nickel Plated, Modern....................	100	125	125
Swing Out, .38 Special, Swing-Out Cylinder, 4" Barrel, Double Action, Wood Grips, Blue, Modern....................	100	125	125
Swing Out, .38 Special, Swing-Out Cylinder, 4" Barrel, Double Action, Adjustable Sights, Blue, Modern....................	125	150	150

	V.G.	Exc	Prior Edition
Swing Out, .38 Special, Swing–Out Cylinder, 6" Barrel, Double Action, Adjustable Sights, Blue, Modern....................	$125	$150	$150
Swing Out, .38 Special, Swing–Out Cylinder, Various Barrel Lengths, Double Action, Wood Grips, Blue, Modern..............................	100	125	125
Swing Out, .38 Special, Swing–Out Cylinder, Various Barrel Lengths, Double Action, Wood Grips, Nickel Plated, Modern................	100	125	125
Target 9, .22 L.R.R.F., 9 Shot, Blue, Solid Frame, Wood Grips, Double Action, Modern........................	100	125	125
Trailblazer, .22LR/.22 WMR Combo, Single Action, Western Style, Color Case Hardened Frame, Adjustable Sights, Modern..........................	125	150	150
Trigger–Cocking, .22 L.R.R.F., 8 Shot, Single Action, Top Break, Adjustable Sights, Wood Grips, Modern......................	125	150	150

HANDGUN, SEMI-AUTOMATIC

	V.G.	Exc	Prior Edition
Model TP–22, .22 L.R.R.F., Double Action, Hammer, Clip Fed, Blue, Modern..........................	175	200	175
Model TP–25, .25 ACP, Double Action, Hammer, Clip Fed, Blue, Modern..........................	150	175	175
Pony, .380 ACP, Hammer, Clip Fed, Blue, Modern..................	200	250	225
Pony, .380 ACP, Hammer, Clip Fed, Nickel Plated, Modern..................	175	225	250
Pony, .380 ACP, Hammer, Clip Fed, Stainless, Modern..........................	225	275	225
PP30 Enforcer, .30 M1 Carbine, Clip Fed, Blue, Modern......................	200	225	225

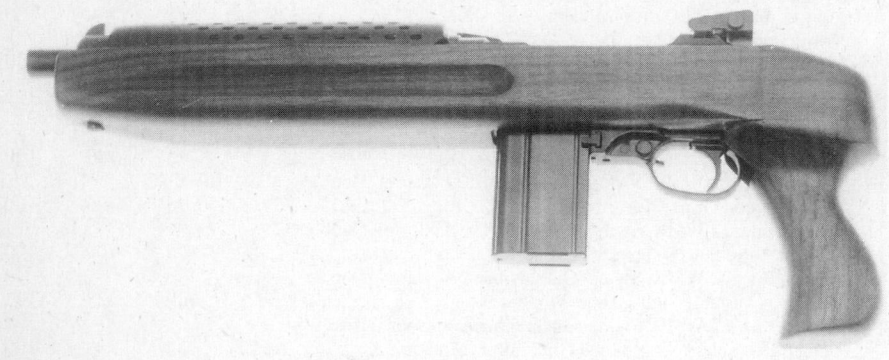

Iver Johnson Enforcer

	V.G.	Exc	Prior Edition
PP30S Enforcer, .30 M1 Carbine, Clip Fed, Stainless, Modern..............	225	250	250
Trailsman, .22 L.R.R.F., Clip Fed, Blue, Modern....................................	125	150	150

HANDGUN, SINGLESHOT

	V.G.	Exc	Prior Edition
Eclipse 1872, .22 R.F., Spur Trigger, Side–Swing Barrel, Hammer, Antique..........................	250	275	275

RIFLE, BOLT ACTION

	V.G.	Exc	Prior Edition
Model 2X, .22 L.R.R.F., Singleshot, Takedown, Modern........................	50	75	75
Model X, .22 L.R.R.F., Singleshot, Takedown, Modern........................	50	50	75

	V.G.	Exc	Prior Edition

RIFLE, SEMI-AUTOMATIC

PM30G, .30 Carbine, Clip Fed, Military Style, Carbine, Modern............. $150 $175 $200

Iver Johnson PM30G

PM30P, .30 Carbine, Clip Fed, Telescoping Stock, Carbine,
Modern.. 175 200 250

Iver Johnson PM30P

PM30PS Paratrooper, .30 M1 Carbine, Clip Fed, Stainless,
Modern.. 225 275 250
PM5.7 Spitfire, 5.7 Spitfire, Clip Fed, Military Style, Modern............... 150 175 175
SC30F, .30 Carbine, Clip Fed, Folding Stock, Carbine, Modern............. 175 200 250
SC30F, .30 Carbine, Clip Fed, Paratrooper, Carbine, Stainless,
Modern.. 200 250 275
SC30S, .30 Carbine, Clip Fed, Plastic Stock, Carbine, Stainless,
Modern.. 150 200 250

Iver Johnson SC30SS

SC5.7S, 5.7 Spitfire, Clip Fed, Carbine, Modern...................................... 150 200 275
SC5.7S, 5.7 Spitfire, Clip Fed, Folding Stock, Carbine, Modern.............. 150 175 225
SC5.7S, 5.7 Spitfire, Clip Fed, Plastic Stock, Modern.............................. 125 150 200

	V.G.	Exc	Prior Edition
SC5.7S, 5.7 Spitfire, Clip Fed, Plastic Stock, Stainless, Modern...............	$175	$225	$250

SHOTGUN, DOUBLE BARREL, OVER-UNDER

	V.G.	Exc	Prior Edition
Silver Shadow, 12 Gauge, Double Trigger, Checkered Stock, Modern..	250	300	275
Silver Shadow, 12 Gauge, Double Trigger, Checkered Stock, Light Engraving, Vent Rib, Modern..	300	350	275
Silver Shadow, 12 Gauge, Single Trigger, Checkered Stock, Modern..	350	400	325
Silver Shadow, 12 Gauge, Single Trigger, Checkered Stock, Light Engraving, Vent Rib, Modern..	375	425	300

SHOTGUN, DOUBLE BARREL, SIDE-BY-SIDE

	V.G.	Exc	Prior Edition
Hercules, Various Gauges, Double Trigger, Automatic Ejector, Hammerless, Checkered Stock, Modern.................................	400	475	475
Hercules, Various Gauges, Double Trigger, Checkered Stock, Hammerless, Modern...	375	375	450
Hercules, Various Gauges, Single Trigger, Automatic Ejector, Hammerless, Checkered Stock, Modern.................................	450	575	525
Hercules, Various Gauges, Single Trigger, Hammerless, Checkered Stock, Modern...	425	475	500
Knox–All, Various Gauges, Double Trigger, Hammer, Checkered Stock, Modern..	300	350	350
Skeeter, Various Gauges, Double Trigger, Hammerless, Modern............	700	800	650
Skeeter, Various Gauges, Skeet Grade, Single Selective Trigger, Hammerless, Modern...	800	950	700
Skeeter, Various Gauges, Skeet Grade, Single Selective Trigger, Automatic Ejector, Hammerless, Modern..............................	1,000	1,200	675
Skeeter, Various Gauges, Skeet Grade, Single Trigger, Hammerless, Modern...	800	950	675
Super, 12 Gauge, Trap Grade, Automatic Ejector, Hammerless, Modern..	700	750	750
Super, 12 Gauge, Trap Grade, Double Trigger, Hammerless, Modern..	600	650	650
Super, 12 Gauge, Trap Grade, Single Trigger, Hammerless, Modern..	700	750	700

SHOTGUN, SINGLESHOT

	V.G.	Exc	Prior Edition
Champion, Various Gauges, Automatic Ejector, Modern........................	50	75	75
Mat Rib Grade, Various Gauges, Raised Matted Rib, Automatic Ejector, Checkered Stock, Modern..	75	100	100
Side Snap, 12 Gauge, Damascus Barrel, Hammer, Antique....................	50	75	75
Side Snap, 12 Gauge, Steel Barrel, Hammer, Antique.............................	75	100	100
Top Snap, 12 Gauge, Steel Barrel, Hammer, Antique.............................	75	100	100
Trap Grade, 12 Gauge, Vent Rib, Checkered Stock, Modern................	125	150	175

IZARRA Made by Bonifacio Echeverra, Eibar, Spain, c. 1918.

HANDGUN, SEMI-AUTOMATIC

	V.G.	Exc	Prior Edition
.32 ACP, Clip Fed, Long Grip, Curio...	150	175	175

J

J & R Burbank, Calif.

RIFLE, SEMI-AUTOMATIC

Model 68, 9mm Luger, Clip Fed, Flash Hider, Takedown,
Modern.. $150 $175 $175

JACKRABBIT Continental Arms Corp., N.Y.C., c. 1960.

RIFLE, SINGLESHOT

Handy Gun, .44 Magnum, Detachable Shoulder Stock, Modern............ 75 100 100

SHOTGUN, SINGLESHOT

Handy Gun, .410, Detachable Shoulder Stock, Modern......................... 50 75 75

JACKSON ARMS CO. Made by Crescent for C. M. McClung & Co., Knoxville, Tenn.

SHOTGUN, DOUBLE BARREL, SIDE-BY-SIDE

Various Gauges, Hammerless, Damascus Barrel, Modern...................... 150 175 175
Various Gauges, Hammerless, Steel Barrel, Modern............................. 175 200 200
Various Gauges, Outside Hammers, Damascus Barrel, Modern............ 150 175 175
Various Gauges, Outside Hammers, Steel Barrel, Modern...................... 175 200 200

SHOTGUN, SINGLESHOT

Various Gauges, Hammer, Steel Barrel, Modern.................................... 55 75 75

JACKSON HOLE RIFLE CO. Jackson Hole, Wyo., c. 1970.

RIFLE, BOLT ACTION

Custom, Various Calibers, with 3 Interchangable Barrels, Fancy
Checkering, Fancy Wood, Modern... 850 950 900
Presentation, Various Calibers, with 3 Interchangable Barrels,
Fancy Checkering, Fancy Wood, Engraved, Modern............... 1,000 1,250 1,200
Sportsman, Various Calibers, with 3 Interchangable Barrels,
Checkered Stock, Modern... 750 850 800

JAGA Frantisek Dusek, Opocno, Czechoslovakia, c. 1930.

HANDGUN, SEMI-AUTOMATIC

.25 ACP, Clip Fed, Blue, Curio.. 125 150 150

	V.G.	Exc	Prior Edition

JAGER Germany, 1960–1975.

HANDGUN, REVOLVER

	V.G.	Exc	Prior Edition
Jager, .22LR/.22 WMR Combo, Single Action, Western Style, Adjustable Sights, Modern	$100	$125	$125
Jager, .22LR/.22 WMR Combo, Single Action, Western Style, Modern	75	100	100
Jager Centerfire, Various Calibers, Single Action, Western Style, Adjustable Sights, Modern	125	150	150
Jager Centerfire, Various Calibers, Single Action, Western Style, Modern	100	125	125

JAGER Suhl, Germany.

HANDGUN, SEMI-AUTOMATIC

	V.G.	Exc	Prior Edition
.32 ACP, Clip Fed, Commercial, Curio	350	375	375
.32 ACP, Clip Fed, MIlitary, Curio	400	450	450

JAGER, F. & CO. See Herold.

JANSSEN FRERES Liege, Belgium, c. 1925.

SHOTGUN, DOUBLE BARREL, SIDE-BY-SIDE

	V.G.	Exc	Prior Edition
Various Gauges, Hammerless, Steel Barrel, Curio	175	200	200

JAPANESE MILITARY

HANDGUN, REVOLVER

	V.G.	Exc	Prior Edition
Model 26, 9mm, Military, Curio	250	275	275

Japanese Military Type 26 Revolver

HANDGUN, SEMI-AUTOMATIC

	V.G.	Exc	Prior Edition
Baby Nambu, 7mm Nambu, "TGE," Clip Fed, Military, Curio	3,000	4,500	3,500
Baby Nambu, 7mm Nambu, Clip Fed, Military, Curio	2,250	2,500	2,500

	V.G.	Exc	Prior Edition
Type 14 Nambu, 8mm Nambu, Clip Fed, Large Trigger Guard, Military, Curio..............	$350	$375	$375
Type 14 Nambu, 8mm Nambu, Clip Fed, Small Trigger Guard, Military, Curio..............	425	475	475

Japanese Military Type 14 Pistol

	V.G.	Exc	Prior Edition
Type 1902 "Grandpa," 8mm Nambu, Tokyo Arsenal, Clip Fed, Military, Curio..............	3,000	3,500	3,000
Type 1904 "Papa," 8mm Nambu, TGE Commercial, Clip Fed, Curio..............	1,500	1,750	1,500
Type 1904 "Papa," 8mm Nambu, TGE Navy, Clip Fed, Military, Curio..............	1,250	1,500	1,400
Type 1904 "Papa," 8mm Nambu, Thailand, Clip Fed, Military, Curio..............	1,000	1,250	1,150
Type 1904 "Papa," 8mm Nambu, Tokyo Arsenal, Clip Fed, Military, Curio..............	1,000	1,250	1,175
Type 94, 8mm Nambu, Clip Fed, Military, Curio..............	225	250	250

RIFLE, BOLT ACTION

	V.G.	Exc	Prior Edition
Japanese "Siamese Mauser", 8 X 52R Cal., Made By Japan For The Government Of Siam In The Early 1920's. A Modified 98 Mauser, Bolt Action, 30–Inch Barrel, Curio..............	100	125	125
Model 38 (1905), 6.5 X 50 Arisaka, Military, Curio..............	125	150	150
Model 38 (1905), 6.5 X 50 Arisaka, Military, Carbine, Curio..............	150	175	175
Model 44 (1911), 6.5 X 50 Arisaka, Military, Carbine, Curio..............	225	275	275
Model 99 (1939), 7.7 X 58 Arisaka, Military, Open Rear Sight, Curio..............	125	150	150
Type 30 (1897), 6.5 Aisaka, Bolt Action, 31–Inch Barrel, Often Referred To As The "Hook Safety Rifle," Curio..............	150	175	175
Type 38 Carbine, 6.5 Cal., Aisaka, 19–Inch Barrel, Modified For Paratroop Use By The Edition Of A Hinge To The Wrist Of The Stock For Folding, Somewhat Rare, Curio..............	150	175	175
Type 38, 6.5 X 50 Arisaka, Late Model, Military, Curio..............	125	150	150
Type 44, 6.5 X 50 Arisaka, Folding Bayonet, Military, Curio..............	225	275	225

	V.G.	Exc	Prior Edition
Type 97 Sniper Rifle, Arisaka, 31–Inch Barrel, Specially Selected For Extreme Accuracy And Then Fitted With Telescopic Sight, Curio.......	$325	$375	$325
Type 99 Type 2 Take Down Rifle, 7.7 Cal., Arisaka, 25–Inch Barrel, A Standard Type 99 Rifle Modified To Break In Half For Compact Paratroop Use, Very Rare, Curio.....	275	325	275
Type 99, 7.7 Cal., Arisaka, 31–Inch Barrel, Five Shot Mauser Type Magazine, Bolt Action, Long Barrel Infantry Model, Becoming Scarce, Curio.....	125	150	150

Japanese Military Type 99 Rifle

	V.G.	Exc	Prior Edition
Type 99, 7.7 X 58 Arisaka, Aircraft Sights Dust Cover, Military, Curio.....	225	250	250

JENNINGS FIREARMS, INC. Carson City, Nv.

HANDGUN, SEMI-AUTOMATIC

Model J–22, .22 L.R.R.F., Clip Fed, Black Teflon Plate, Modern...........	50	50	50
Model J–22, .22 L.R.R.F., Clip Fed, Satin Nickel Plate, Modern...........	50	75	50

JEWEL Made by Hood Firearms Co., c. 1876.

HANDGUN, REVOLVER

#1, .22 Short R.F., 7 Shot, Spur Trigger, Solid Frame, Single Action, Antique.....	150	175	175

J.G.L. Jos. G. Landmann, Holstein, W. Germany, c. 1968.

RIFLE, SEMI-AUTOMATIC

JGL–68 Model 1, .22 L.R.R.F., Clip Fed, Carbine Style, Modern..........	50	75	75
JGL–68 Model 2, .22 L.R.R.F., Clip Fed, Vertical Grip & Foregrip, Modern.....	50	75	75
JGL–68 Model 3, .22 L.R.R.F., Clip Fed, Vertical Grip, Modern...........	50	75	75

JIEFFCO Mre. Liegoise d'Armes a Feu Robar et Cie, Liege, Belgium, c. 1912–1914.

HANDGUN, SEMI-AUTOMATIC

.25 ACP, Clip Fed, Blue, Curio.....	250	275	275
.32 ACP, Clip Fed, Blue, Curio.....	250	275	275

	V.G.	Exc	Prior Edition

JIEFFCO Tradename used by Davis–Warner on pistols made by Robar et Cie., c. 1920.

HANDGUN, SEMI-AUTOMATIC
New Model Melior, .25 ACP, Clip Fed, Curio.. $150 $175 $175

JO–JO–AR Hijos de Arrizabalaga, Eibar, Spain, c. 1920.

HANDGUN, SEMI-AUTOMATIC
.380 ACP, Tip–up, Clip Fed, Hammer, Spur Trigger, Military,
Curio..   200   250   250
9mm Bergmann, Tip–up, Clip Fed, Hammer, Spur Trigger,
Military, Curio..   150   200   200

JOFFRE Spain, c. 1900.

HANDGUN, SEMI-AUTOMATIC
M1916, .32 ACP, Clip Fed, Modern...   100   125   125

JOHNSON AUTOMATICS Providence, R.I. Also see U.S. Military.

RIFLE, BOLT ACTION
Diamond Cherry Featherweight, Various Calibers, Engraved,
Carved Cherry Stock, Muzzle Brake, Modern...   1,000   1,250   1,250
Honey Featherweight, Various Calibers, Engraved, Carved Stock,
Muzzle Brake, Gold and Silver Inlays, Modern.....................................   1,500   1,750   1,750
Laminar Sporter, Various Calibers, Laminated Stock, Modern...............   650   750   750

RIFLE, SEMI-AUTOMATIC
Model 1941, .30–06 Springfield, Miliatry, Curio....................................   1,000   1,250   775
Model 1941, 7mm Mauser, Military, Curio..   775   850   850

JONES, CHARLES Lancaster, Pa. 1780. See Kentucky Rifles.

JONES, J.N. & CO. London, England, c. 1760.

HANDGUN, FLINTLOCK
.60, George III, Navy Pistol, Brass Barrel, Brass Furniture,
Military, Antique...   1,250   1,500   1,500

HANDGUN, PERCUSSION
.58, Holster Pistol, Converted from Flintlock, Brass Furniture,
Plain, Antique..   750   100   100

JUPITER Fabrique d' Armes de Guerre de Grand Precision, Eibar, Spain.

HANDGUN, SEMI-AUTOMATIC
.32 ACP, Clip Fed, Blue, Curio...   125   150   150

K

KABA SPEZIAL Made by August Menz, Suhl, Germany, for Karl Bauer & Co., Berlin, Germany, c. 1925.

HANDGUN, SEMI-AUTOMATIC

	V.G.	Exc.	Prior Edition
Liliput, .25 ACP, Clip Fed, Blue, Modern..	$225	$250	$250
Liliput, .32 ACP, Clip Fed, Blue, Modern..	250	275	275

KABA SPEZIAL Made by Francisco Arizmendi, Eibar, Spain.

HANDGUN, SEMI-AUTOMATIC

.25 ACP, Clip Fed, Blue, Modern..	150	175	175

KART

HANDGUN, SEMI-AUTOMATIC

For Colt Government Target, .22 L.R.R.F., Conversion Unit Only	150	175	175
Target, .22 L.R.R.F., Clip Fed, M1911 Frame, 6" Barrel, Modern..........	575	650	650

KASSNAR IMPORTS Harrisburg, Pa.

RIFLE, BOLT ACTION

Model M–14S, .22 L.R.R.F., Clip Fed, Checkered Stock, Modern.........	50	75	75
Model M–15S, .22 WMR, Clip Fed, Checkered Stock, Modern.............	50	75	75
Model M–1400, .22 L.R.R.F., Clip Fed, Checkered Stock, Modern........	50	75	75
Model M–1500, .22 WMR, Clip Fed, Checkered Stock, Modern...........	75	100	100
Parker Hale Midland, Various Calibers, Checkered Stock, Open Sights, Modern...	200	225	225
Parker Hale Super, Various Calibers, Checkered Stock, Open Sights, Monte Carlo Stock, Modern...	250	300	300
Parker Hale Varmint, Various Calibers, Checkered Stock, Open Sights, Varmint Stock, Modern..	275	300	300

RIFLE, SEMI-AUTOMATIC

Model M–16, .22 L.R.R.F., Clip Fed, Military Style, Modern.................	50	75	75
Model M–20S, .22 L.R.R.F., Modern...	50	75	75

SHOTGUN, DOUBLE BARREL, OVER-UNDER

Fias SK–1, 12 and 20 Gauges, Double Trigger, Checkered Stock, Modern..	350	375	375

	V.G.	Exc	Prior Edition
Fias SK–3, 12 and 20 Gauges, Single Selective Trigger, Checkered Stock, Modern..	$350	$400	$400
Fias SK–4, 12 and 20 Gauges, Single Selective Trigger, Checkered Stock, Automatic Ejector, Modern..	375	450	450
Fias SK–4D, 12 and 20 Gauges, Single Selective Trigger, Fancy Checkering, Fancy Wood, Engraved, Automatic Ejector, Modern...........	400	475	475
Fias SK–4T, 12 Ga., Trap Grade, Single Selective Trigger, Automatic Ejector, Checkered Stock, Wide Vent Rib, Modern................	425	475	475

SHOTGUN, DOUBLE BARREL, SIDE-BY-SIDE

	V.G.	Exc	Prior Edition
Zabala, Various Gauges, Checkered Stock, Double Triggers, Modern...	325	375	375

SHOTGUN, SINGLESHOT

	V.G.	Exc	Prior Edition
Taiyojuki, Various Gauges, Top Break, Plain, Modern...........................	25	50	50

KEFFER, JACOB Lancaster, Pa., c. 1802. See Kentucky Rifles and Pistols.

KEIM, JOHN Reading, Pa. 1820–1839. See Kentucky Rifles and Pistols.

KENTUCKY RIFLES AND PISTOLS The uniquely American "Kentucky" (or, as some prefer, Pennsylvania") expressed in wood & metal, the attitude of strength and independence that fostered our young nation. For the most part Kentuckys are custom guns, and, aside from general similarities, virtually all are different, even those by the same maker. To add to the problem of price generalization, gunsmiths purchased parts from various makers and there maybe three different names on a single gun or none at all. The main considerations in determining value are: 1. Type of ignition; 2. Quality of workmanship; 3. Decoration; 4. Originality; 5. Condition.

RIFLE, FLINTLOCK

	V.G.	Exc	Prior Edition
High Quality, Fancy Decoration, Antique..	10,000	15,000	15,000
Moderate Quality, Medium Decoration, Antique....................................	5,000	10,000	10,000
Moderate Quality, Plain, Antique..	2,500	5,000	5,000
Over–Under, Swivel–Breech, High Quality, Antique...........................	20,000	25,000	20,000
Over–Under, Swivel–Breech, Medium Quality, Antique......................	17,500	15,000	10,000
Over–Under, Swivel–Breech, Plain, Antique...	7,500	10,000	7,500
Deduct 30%–40%, if Converted from Percussion			

RIFLE, PERCUSSION

	V.G.	Exc	Prior Edition
High Quality, Fancy Decoration, Antique..	7,500	10,000	10,000
Moderate Quality, Medium Decoratin, Antique.....................................	2,000	5,000	5,000
Moderate Quality, Plain, Antique..	2,000	2,500	1,500
Over–Under, High Quality, Swivel Breech, Antique.............................	10,000	12,500	12,500
Over–Under, Medium Quality, Swivel Breech, Antique........................	5,000	8,500	8,500
Over–Under, Medium Quality, Swivel Breech, Plain, Antique..............	3,500	5,000	2,500

	V.G.	Exc	Prior Edition

Add 20%, If Converted From Flintlock Percussion

PISTOLS, FLINTLOCK

	V.G.	Exc	Prior Edition
High Quality, Fancy Decoration, Antique	$8,000	$10,000	$10,000
Moderate Quality, Medium Decoration, Antique	6,500	7,500	5,000

PISTOL, PERCUSSION (ORIGINAL)

High Quality, Fancy Decoration, Antique	3,000	3,500	3,250
Moderate Quality, Medium Decoration, Antique	1,500	2,000	1,250

PISTOLS, PERCUSSION (CONVERTED FLINTLOCK)

High Quality, Fancy Decoration, Antique	4,000	4,500	4,500
Moderate Quality, Medium Decoration, Antique	3,000	3,500	3,500

KETLAND & CO Birmingham & London, England 1760–1831. Also See Kentucky Rifles.

HANDGUN, FLINTLOCK

.58, Holster Pistol, Plain, Tapered Round Barrel, Brass Furniture Antique	1,500	2,000	1,250
.62 , Belt Pistol, Brass Barrel, Brass Furniture, Light Ornamentation, Antique	2,000	2,500	1,500

KETLAND, T. Birmingham, England 1750–1829.

HANDGUN, FLINTLOCK

.69, Pair, Belt Pistol, Brass Furniture, Plain, Antique	2,250	2,500	2,500

RIFLE, FLINTLOCK

.65, Officers Model Brown Bess, Musket, Military, Antique	3,000	3,500	3,500
.73, 2nd. Model Brown Bess, Musket, Military, Antique	2,250	2,500	2,500

KETLAND, WILLIAM & CO.

HANDGUN, FLINTLOCK

.63, Holster Pistol, Round Barrel, Plain, Antique	1,250	1,500	900

KETTNER, ED Suhl, Thuringia, Germany 1922–1939.

COMBINATION WEAPON, DRILLING

12 X 12 X 10.75 X 65R Collath, Engraved, Checkered Stock, Sling Swivels, Curio	1,750	2,000	2,000

KIMBALL, J. M. ARMS CO. Detroit, Mich., c. 1955–1958.

HANDGUN, SEMI-AUTOMATIC

Combat Model, .30 Carbine, 3" Barrel, Clip Fed, Blue, Short Barrel, Modern	800	900	900
Target Model, .30 Carbine, 5" Barrel, Clip Fed, Blue, Adjustable Sight Modern	800	900	900
Standard Model, .22 Hornet, Clip Fed, Blue, Modern	—	RARE	—

KIMBER   Clackamas, Ore. 1980–1991.

RIFLE, BOLT ACTION

Model 82 Match, .22 L.R.R.F., Checkered Stock, Clip Fed, No
Sights, Modern... $1,250 $1,500 $550
Model 82 Varmint, .22 W.M.R., Checkered Stock, Clip Fed, No
Sights, Modern... 600   700   575
Model 82C Classic, .22 L.R.R.F., Checkered Stock, Clip Fed, No
Sights, Monte Carlo Stock, Modern.. 800   900   600
Model 82C Super America, .22 L.R.R.F., Checkered Stock, Clip Fed, 1
Sights, Monte Carlo Stock, Modern.. 850   950   625

KIMEL INDUSTRIES   Mathews, N.C.

HANDGUN, DOUBLE BARREL, OVER-UNDER

Twist, .22 Short R.F., Swivel Breech, Derringer, Spur Trigger,
Modern.. 50   75   50

KING NITRO   Made by Stevens Arms.

RIFLE, BOLT ACTION

Model 53, .22 L.R.R.F., Singleshot, Takedown, Modern........................... 250   50   50

SHOTGUN, DOUBLE BARREL, SIDE-BY-SIDE

M 315 Various Gauges, Hammerless, Steel Barrel, Modern.................. 125   150   175

KINGLAND 10–STAR   Made by Crescent for Geller, Wards, &
Hasner St. Louis, Mo. See Kingland Special.

KINGLAND SPECIAL   Made by Crescent for Geller, Wards &
Hasner St. Louis, Mo.

SHOTGUN, DOUBLE BARREL, SIDE-BY-SIDE

Various Gauges, Hammerless, Damascus Barrel, Modern...................... 150   175   175
Various Gauges, Hammerless, Steel Barrel, Modern............................... 175   200   200
Various Gauges, Outside Hammers, Damascus Barrel, Modern............. 150   175   175
Various Gauges, Outside Hammers, Steel Barrel, Modern..................... 150   175   175

SHOTGUN, SINGLESHOT

Various Gauges, Hammer, Steel Barrel, Modern..................................... 50   75   75

KIRIKKALE   Makina ve Kimya Endustrisi Kurumu Kirrikale, Ankara,
Turkey.

HANDGUN, SEMI-AUTOMATIC

MKE, 7.65mm & 9mmk, Clip Fed, Double Action, Modern.................... 325   375   350

	V.G.	Exc	Prior Edition

KITTEMAUG c. 1880.

HANDGUN, REVOLVER

.32 Short R.F., 5 Shot, Spur Trigger, Solid Frame, Single Action,
Antique.. $150 $175 $175

KLEINGUENTHER'S Seguin, Texas.

HANDGUN, REVOLVER

Reck R–18, .357 Magnum, Adjustable Sights, Western Style, Single
Action, Modern... 100 125 125

RIFLE, BOLT ACTION

K–10, .22 L.R.R.F., Single Shot, Tangent Sights, Modern........................	50	50	50
K–12, .22 L.R.R.F., Clip Fed, Checkered Stock, Modern.....................	50	75	75
K–13, .22 W.M.R., Clip Fed, Checkered Stock, Modern.........................	100	125	125
K–14 Insta–fire, Various Calibers, Checkered Stock, No Sights, Recoil Pad, Modern.....	700	800	800
K–15, .22 L.R.R.F., Clip Fed, Checkered Stock, Modern........................	100	125	125
K–15 Insta–fire, Various Calibers, Checkered Stock, No Sights, Recoil Pad, Modern.......	800	1,000	1,000
V2130, Various Calibers, Checkered Stock, Recoil Pad, Modern............	200	225	225

RIFLE, DOUBLE BARREL, OVER-UNDER

Model 222, .22 W.M.R., Plain, Modern...................................... 125 150 150

SHOTGUN, DOUBLE BARREL, OVER-UNDER

Condor, 12 Gauge, Single Selective Trigger, Automatic Ejector,
Vent Rib, Modern.. 375 425 425
Condor, 12 Gauge, Skeet Grade, Single Selective Trigger,
Automatic Ejector, Wide Vent Rib, Modern.. 400 450 450

SHOTGUN, DOUBLE BARREL, SIDE-BY-SIDE

Brescia, 12 Gauge, Hammerless, Light Engraving, Double Trigger,
Modern.. 200 250 250

SHOTGUN, SEMI-AUTOMATIC

12 Ga., Checkered Stock, Vent Rib, Engraved, Left Hand,
Modern.. 200 225 225
12 Ga., Checkered Stock, Vent Rib, Engraved, Right Hand,
Modern.. 175 200 200

KLETT, SIMON Lepzig, c. 1620.

RIFLE, WHEEL-LOCK

.54, Rifled, Octagon Barrel, Brass Furniture, Medium
Ornamentation, Engraved, High Quality, Antique..................................... 10,000 12,000 12,000

KNICKERBOCKER Made by Crescent H & D Folsom, c. 1900.

SHOTGUN, DOUBLE BARREL, SIDE-BY-SIDE

Various Gauges, Hammerless, Modern... 150 175 175

	V.G.	Exc	Prior Edition
Various Gauges, Outside Hammers, Modern..	$175	$200	$200

KNICKERBOCKER Made by Stevens Arms.

SHOTGUN, DOUBLE BARREL, SIDE-BY-SIDE

Model 311, Various Gauges, Hammerless, Steel Barrel, Modern.............	150	175	175

KNOCKABOUT Made by Stevens Arms.

SHOTGUN, DOUBLE BARREL, SIDE-BY-SIDE

Model 311, Various Gauges, Hammerless, Steel Barrel, Modern.............	150	175	175

KNOXALL Made by Crescent, c. 1900.

SHOTGUN, DOUBLE BARREL, SIDE-BY-SIDE

Various Gauges, Hammerless, Steel Barrel, Modern................................	175	200	200
Various Gauges, Outside Hammers, Steel Barrel, Modern.....................	150	175	175

KODIAK MFG. CO. North Haven, Conn., c. 1965.

RIFLE, BOLT ACTION

Model 98 Brush Carbine, Various Calibers, Checkered Stock, Modern...	150	175	175
Model 99 Deluxe Brush Carbine, Various Calibers, Checkered Stock, Modern...	150	175	175
Model 100 Deluxe Rifle, Various Calibers, Checkered Stock, Modern...	175	200	200
Model 100M Deluxe Rifle, Various Magnum Calibers, Checkered Stock, Modern...	175	200	200
Model 101 Ultra, Various Calibers, Monte Carlo Stock, Modern...........	175	200	200
Model 101M Ultra, Various Magnum Calibers, Monte Carlo Stock, Modern...	200	225	225
Model 102 Ultra Varmint, Various Calibers, Heavy Barrel, Modern...	200	225	225

RIFLE, SEMI-AUTOMATIC

Model 260 Autoloader, .22 L.R.R.F., Tube Feed, Open Sights, 22" Barrel, Modern...	200	250	100
Model 260 Autoloader Carbine, .22 L.R.R.F., Tube Feed, Open Sights, 20" Barrel, Modern..	225	275	100
Model 260 Magnum, .22 W.M.R., Tube Feed, Open Sights, 22" Barrel, Modern..	250	300	150
Model 260 Magnum Carbine, .22 W.M.R., Tube Feed, Open Sights, 20" Barrel, Modern..	225	275	150

KOHOUT & SPOL Kdyne, Czechoslovakia. 1928–1945.

HANDGUN, SEMI-AUTOMATIC

Mars, 6.35mm, Clip Fed, Curio...	175	225	175
Mars, 7.65mm, Clip Fed, Curio...	200	250	200

	V.G.	Exc	Prior Edition

KOMMER, THEODOR Zella Mehlis, Germany, c. 1920.

HANDGUN, SEMI-AUTOMATIC

Model I, 6.35mm, Clip Fed, Curio... $275 $300 $300

Kommer Model I

Model II, 6.35mm, Clip Fed, Curio... 250 275 275

Kommer Model 2

Model III, 6.35mm, Clip Fed, Curio... 225 250 250

	V.G.	Exc	Prior Edition
Model IV, 7.65mm, Clip Fed, Curio..	$300	$325	$325

Kommer Model 4

KORTH Wliheim Korth Waffenfabrik, Ratzburg, West Germany.

HANDGUN, REVOLVER

Target, Various Calibers, 6 Shot, Modern..	1,750	2,000	1,800

KRAFT, JACOB Lancaster, Pa. 1771–1782. See Kentucky Rifles and Pistols.

KRICO Stuttgart, West Germany. Also see Beeman's.

RIFLE, BOLT ACTION

.22 Rem. Carbine, Checkered Stock, Double Set Triggers, Modern..	575	625	625
.22 Rem. Rifle, Checkered Stock, Double Set Triggers, Modern.............	550	600	600
Model 302, .22 L.R.R.F., Clip Fed, Checkered Stock, Open Sights, Modern..	625	675	675
Model 304, .22 L.R.R.F., Clip Fed, Checkered Stock, Mannlicher Stock, Set Triggers, Open Sights, Modern...........................	625	675	675
Model 311, .22 L.R.R.F., Checkered Stock, Double Set Trigger, Modern..	300	325	325
Model 340, .22 L.R.R.F., Metallic Silhouette Match Rifle, Clip Fed, Checkered Stock, Target Stock, Modern.................................	600	650	650
Model 340, .22 L.R.R.F., Mini–Sniper Match Rifle, Clip Fed, Checkered Stock, Target Stock, Modern.................................	650	700	700
Model 351, .22 WMR, Checkered Stock, Double Set Triggers, Modern..	500	550	550
Model 354, .22 WMR, Checkered Stock, Double Set Triggers, Modern..	600	650	650
Model 400, .22 Hornet, Clip Fed, Checkered Stock, Open Sights, Modern..	625	700	700

	V.G.	Exc	Prior Edition
Model 420, .22 Hornet, Clip Fed, Checkered Stock, Set Triggers, Mannlicher Stock, Open Sights, Sling Swivels, Modern..........	$800	$875	$875
Model 600, Various Calibers, Clip Fed, Checkered Stock, Open Sights, Sling Swivels, Recoil Pad, Modern......................	800	1,000	1,000
Model 600 Export, Various Calibers, Checkered Stock, Double Set Triggers, Modern...............................	400	450	450
Model 600 Luxus, Various Calibers, Checkered Stock, Double Set Triggers, Modern...............................	475	525	525
Model 620, Various Calibers, Clip Fed, Checkered Stock, Set Triggers, Mannlicher Stock, Open Sights, Sling Swivels, Modern....................	900	1,150	1,150
Model 620 Luxus, Various Calibers, Checkered Stock, Double Set Triggers, Modern...............................	550	625	625
Model 640, Various Calibers, Deluxe Varmint Rifle, Clip Fed, Checkered Stock, Target Stock, Modern.....................	1,025	1,175	1,175
Model 650, Various Calibers, Sniper/Match Rifle, Clip Fed, Checkered Stock, Target Stock, Modern.....................	950	1,200	1,200
Model 700, Various Calibers, Clip Fed, Checkered Stock, Open Sights, Sling Swivels, Recoil Pad, Modern......................	750	900	900
Model 700 Export, Various Calibers, Checkered Stock, Double Set Triggers, Modern...............................	550	650	650
Model 700 Luxus, Various Calibers, Checkered Stock, Double Set Triggers, Modern...............................	6,500	675	675
Model 720, Various Calibers, Clip Fed, Checkered Stock, Set Triggers, Mannlicher Stock, Open Sights, Sling Swivels, Modern....................	950	1,100	1,100
Model 720 Luxus, Various Calibers, Checkered Stock, Double Set Triggers, Modern...............................	775	850	850
Model DJV, .22 Various Calibers, Checkered Target Stock, Double Set Triggers, Modern............................	500	550	550
Special Varmint, .222 Rem., Checkered Stock, Heavy Barrel, Double Set Triggers, Modern............................	550	600	600

KRIEGHOFF GUN CO. Suhl, Germany 1886–1945, and from 1945 to date in Ulm, West Germany. Also see Shotguns of Ulm.

COMBINATION WEAPON, DRILLING

Neptun, Various Calibers, Hammerless, Engraved, Fancy Checkering, Sidelock, Modern...............................	8,000	10,000	12,000

Krieghoff Neptun

Neptun Dural, Various Calibers, Hammerless, Engraved, Fancy Checkering, Sidelock, Modern...............................	8,000	10,000	12,500

	V.G.	Exc	Prior Edition
Neptun Primus, Various Calibers, Hammerless, Fancy Checkering, Fancy Engraving, Sidelock, Modern	$12,000	$15,000	$15,000
Neptun Primus Dural, Various Calibers, Hammerless, Fancy Checkering, Fancy Engraving, Sidelock, Lightweight, Modern	12,500	15,500	15,500
Trumpf, Various Calibers, Hammerless, Engraved, Fancy Checkering, Modern	6,000	6,500	6,500

Krieghoff Trumpf

	V.G.	Exc	Prior Edition
Trumpf Dural, Various Calibers, Hammerless, Engraved, Fancy Checkering, Lightweight, Modern	6,200	6,700	6,700

RIFLE, DOUBLE BARREL, OVER-UNDER

	V.G.	Exc	Prior Edition
Teck, Various Calibers, Hammerless, Engraved, Fancy Checkering, Modern	5,500	6,500	4,500
Teck Dural, Various Calibers, Hammerless, Engraved, Fancy Checkering, Lightweight, Modern	6,000	7,000	4,600
Ulm, Various Calibers, Hammerless, Engraved, Fancy Checkering, Sidelock, Modern	7,500	8,500	7,500

Krieghoff Ulm

	V.G.	Exc	Prior Edition
Ulm Dural, Various Calibers, Hammerless, Engraved, Fancy Checkering, Sidelock, Modern	8,000	9,000	7,700
Ulm Primus, Various Calibers, Hammerless, Engraved, Fancy Checkering, Sidelock, Modern	8,000	10,000	10,000
Ulm Primus Dural, Various Calibers, Hammerless, Engraved, Fancy Checkering, Sidelock, Lightweight, Modern	8,500	10,500	10,500

SHOTGUN, DOUBLE BARREL, OVER-UNDER

	V.G.	Exc	Prior Edition
Crown, 12 Gauge, Trap Grade, Modern	15,000	18,000	18,000
Exhibition, 12 Gauge, Trap Grade, Modern	25,000	30,000	30,000
Extra Barrel, Add $800.00–$1,000.00			
Monte Carlo, 12 Gauge, Trap Grade, Modern	10,000	13,000	13,000
Munchen, Various Gauges, Skeet Grade, Modern	5,000	7,000	7,000
San Remo, 12 Gauge, Trap Grade, Modern	6,000	8,000	8,000

	V.G.	Exc	Prior Edition
Standard, 12 Gauge, Field Grade, Modern...	$3,500	$4,000	$4,000

Krieghoff Standard

Standard, 12 Gauge, Trap Grade, Modern...	4,500	5,000	5,000
Standard, Various Gauges, Skeet Grade, Modern...................................	3,500	4,000	4,000
Super Crown, 12 Gauge, Trap Grade, Modern..	15,000	17,000	17,000

KROYDEN Tradename used by Savage Arms Corp.

RIFLE, SEMI-AUTOMATIC

.22 L.R.R.F., Tube Feed, Plain Stock, Modern..	50	75	75

KRUSCHITZ Vienna, Austria.

RIFLE, BOLT ACTION

Mauser 98, .30/06, Checkered Stock, Double Set Triggers, Modern..	250	300	300

KYNOCH GUN FACTORY Birmingham, England. Late 1880's.

HANDGUN, REVOLVER

Schlund, .32, .38 & .45 Calibers, Concealed Hammer, Top Break, Double Trigger, Cocking, Antique...	850	1,000	900

Kynoch Schlund Revolver

L

LA SALLE Tradename used by Manufrance.

SHOTGUN, SEMI-AUTOMATIC

	V.G.	Exc.	Prior Edition
Custom, 12 Ga., Checkered Stock, Modern..	$250	$300	$300

SHOTGUN, SLIDE ACTION

12 Gauge, Checkered Stock, Fancy Wood, Modern.................................	250	275	275
12 Gauge, Field Grade, Plain, Modern..	225	250	250
20 Gauge, Field Grade, Plain, Modern..	150	200	150

LAHTI Developed and made by Valtion Kivaarithedas, Jyvaskyla, Finland. Also made by Husqvarna in Sweden.

HANDGUN, SEMI-AUTOMATIC

L–35 Finnish, 9mm Luger, Clip Fed, Military, Curio...............................	750	850	1,250
M 40 Swedish, 9mm Luger, Clip Fed, Military, Modern.........................	275	325	250

LAKESIDE Made by Crescent for Montgomery Ward & Co., c. 1900.

SHOTGUN, DOUBLE BARREL, SIDE-BY-SIDE

Various Gauges, Hammerless, Damascus Barrel, Modern......................	125	150	150
Various Gauges, Hammerless, Steel Barrel, Modern..............................	150	200	200
Various Gauges, Outside Hammers, Damascus Barrel, Modern.............	150	175	175
Various Gauges, Outside Hammers, Steel Barrel, Modern.....................	175	200	200

SHOTGUN, SINGLESHOT

Various Gauges, Hammer, Steel Barrel, Modern....................................	50	75	75

LAMES Chiavari, Italy.

SHOTGUN, DOUBLE BARREL, OVER-UNDER

California, 12 Gauge, Trap Grade, Automatic Ejector, Single Selective Trigger, Vent Rib, Checkered Stock, Modern.................	675	725	725
Field Grade, 12 Gauge, Automatic Ejector, Single Selective Trigger, Vent Rib, Checkered Stock, Modern...........................	350	400	400
Skeet Grade, 12 Gauge, Automatic Ejector, Single Selective Trigger, Vent Rib, Checkered Stock, Modern...........................	500	575	575
Trap Grade, 12 Gauge, Automatic Ejector, Single Selective Trigger, Vent Rib, Monte Carlo Stock, Modern.......................	625	600	600

	V.G.	Exc	Prior Edition

LANBER Lanber Armas, S.A., Zaldibar, Spain.

SHOTGUN, DOUBLE BARREL, OVER-UNDER

	V.G.	Exc	Prior Edition
Model 844 ST, 12 Gauge, Double Triggers, Checkered Stock, Light Engraving, Modern....................	$275	$325	$425
Model 844 MST, 12 Gauge 3", Double Triggers, Checkered Stock, Light Engraving, Modern....................	300	350	425
Model 844 EST, 12 Gauge, Automatic Ejector, Double Triggers, Checkered Stock, Light Engraving, Modern....................	350	400	475
Model 844 EST CHR, 12 Gauge, Automatic Ejector, Double Triggers, Checkered Stock, Light Engraving, Modern....................	400	450	400
Model 2004 LCH, 12 Gauge, Trap Grade, Automatic Ejector, Single Trigger, Checkered Stock, Light Engraving, Lanber Choke, Modern....................	450	600	850
Model 2004 LCH, 12 Gauge, Skeet Grade, Automatic Ejector, Single Trigger, Checkered Stock, Light Engraving, Lanber Choke, Modern....................	450	600	775
Model 2004 LCH, 12 Gauge, Automatic Ejector, Single Trigger, Checkered Stock, Light Engraving, Lanber Choke, Modern....................	450	600	725

LANCASTER, CHARLES London, England 1889–1936.

RIFLE, BOLT ACTION

	V.G.	Exc	Prior Edition
Various Calibers, Sporting Rifle, Checkered Stock, Curio....................	1,000	1,250	900

LANCELOT

HANDGUN, SEMI-AUTOMATIC

	V.G.	Exc	Prior Edition
.25 ACP, Clip Fed, Blue, Modern....................	150	175	175

LANE & READ Boston, Mass. 1826–1835.

SHOTGUN, PERCUSSION

	V.G.	Exc	Prior Edition
28 Gauge, Double Barrel, Side by Side, Light Engraving, Checkered Stock, Antique....................	400	475	475

LANG, JOSEPH London, England, established in 1821.

HANDGUN, PERCUSSION

	V.G.	Exc	Prior Edition
Pair, Double Barrel, Over–Under, Officer's Belt Pistol, Light Engraving, Cased With Accessories, Antique....................	4,000	4,750	4,500

SHOTGUN, SINGLESHOT

	V.G.	Exc	Prior Edition
12 Gauge, Plain, Trap Grade, Modern....................	1,200	1,500	1,500

LANGENHAN   Friedrich Langenhan Gewehr u. Fahrradfabrik, Zella Mehlis, Germany.

HANDGUN, SEMI-AUTOMATIC

Model I, 7.65mm, Clip Fed, Military, Modern.. $225 $250 $250

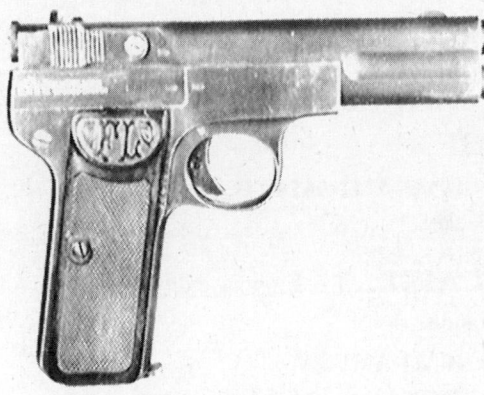

Langenhan Model I

Model II, 6.35mm, Clip Fed, Modern... 275   300   300
Model III, 6.35mm, Clip Fed, Modern....................................... 275   325   325

Langenhan Model III

	V.G.	Exc	Prior Edition

LAURONA Spain.

SHOTGUN, DOUBLE BARREL, OVER-UNDER

Model 67–G, 12 Gauge 3", Checkered Stock, Vent Rib, Double
Triggers, Modern.. $150 $225 $225

LE BARON

RIFLE, FLINTLOCK

.69 Presentation, Silver Furniture, Fancy Wood, Fancy
Checkering, Fancy Engraving, Antique.. 4,000 4,500 4,500

LE BASQUE

HANDGUN, SEMI-AUTOMATIC

7.65mm, Clip Fed, Blue, Modern.. 150 200 200

LE FRANCAISE Mre. Francaise de Armes et Cycles de St. Etienne, St. Etienne, France.

HANDGUN, SEMI-AUTOMATIC

Army Model, 9mm French Long, Clip Fed, Curio.................................... 800 950 850
Champion, 6.35mm, Clip Fed, Long Grip, Curio............................. 250 275 275
Le Francais, 7.65mm, Clip Fed, Curio.. 350 400 400
Pocket Model, 6.35mm, Clip Fed, Curio.. 175 200 200
Policeman, 6.35mm, Clip Fed, Curio.. 650 750 275

Le Francaise Policeman

Staff Officer's, 6.35mm, Clip Fed, Curio,................................. 300 350 350

	V.G.	Exc	Prior Edition

LE MARTINY
HANDGUN, SEMI-AUTOMATIC
6.35mm, Clip Fed, Blue, Curio.. $100 $125 $125

LE MONOBLOC Jules Jacquemart, Liege, Belgium, c. 1910.
HANDGUN, SEMI-AUTOMATIC
6.35mm, Clip Fed, Curio.. 200 250 375

LE PAGE Made by Manufacter D' Armes Le Page, Liege, Belgium.
HANDGUN, SEMI-AUTOMATIC
7.65mm, Clip Fed, Curio.. 375 400 400

Le Page

9mm Browning Long, Clip Fed, Adjustable Sights, Curio...................... 450 600 600
9mm Browning Long, Clip Fed, Adjustable Sights, Detachable
Shoulder Stock, Curio.. 800 900 900
9mm Short, Clip Fed, Adjustable Sights, Curio....................................... 400 450 450

LE SANS PARIEL Mre. d'Armes des Pyrenees.
HANDGUN, SEMI-AUTOMATIC
6.35mm, Clip Fed, Blue, Curio.. 125 150 150

LE TOUTACIER Mre. d'Armes des Pyrenees.
HANDGUN, SEMI-AUTOMATIC
6.35mm, Clip Fed, Blue, Curio.. 125 150 150

	V.G.	Exc	Prior Edition

LEADER Possibly Hopkins & Allen, c. 1880.

HANDGUN, REVOLVER

.22 Short R.F., 7 Shot, Spur Trigger, Solid Frame, Single Action,
Antique.. $150 $175 $175
.32 Short R.F., 5 Shot, Spur Trigger, Solid Frame, Single Action,
Antique.. 150 175 175

LEADER GUN CO. Made by Crescent for Charles William Stores Inc., c. 1900.

SHOTGUN, DOUBLE BARREL, SIDE-BY-SIDE

Various Gauges, Hammerless, Damascus Barrel, Modern...................... 125 175 175
Various Gauges, Hammerless, Steel Barrel, Modern............................... 175 200 200
Various Gauges, Outside Hammers, Damascus Barrel, Modern............. 150 175 175
Various Gauges, Outside Hammers, Steel Barrel, Modern...................... 150 200 200

SHOTGUN, SINGLESHOT

Various Gauges, Hammer, Steel Barrel, Modern.................................... 50 75 75

LEATHER, JACOB York, Pa. 1779–1802. See U.S. Military, Kentucky Rifles.

LEBEAU–COURALLY Lebeau–Couraly Continental Firearms, Liege, Belgium since 1865.

RIFLE, DOUBLE BARREL, SIDE-BY-SIDE

Ardennes, Various Calibers, Fancy Engraving, Double Triggers,
Checkered Stock, Automatic Ejector, Boxlock, Fancy Wood,
Modern.. 11,500 14,000 14,000
St. Hubert, Various Calibers, Fancy Engraving, Double Triggers,
Checkered Stock, Automatic Ejector, Sidelocks, Fancy Wood,
Modern.. 20,000 25,000 25,000

SHOTGUN, DOUBLE BARREL, SIDE-BY-SIDE

Grand Russe, 12 Gauge, Fancy Engraving, Double Triggers,
Checkered Stock, Automatic Ejector, Boxlock, Fancy Wood,
Modern.. 7,500 10,000 10,000
Sologne, 12 Gauge, Medium Engraving, Double Triggers,
Checkered Stock, Automatic Ejector, Boxlock with Sideplates,
Fancy Wood, Modern.. 9,500 12,000 12,000

LEE ARMS CO. Wilkes–Barre, Pa. c. 1870. Also See Red Jacket.

HANDGUN, REVOLVER

.22 Short R.F., 7 Shot, Spur Trigger, Solid Frame, Single Action,
Antique.. 150 175 175
.32 Short R.F., 5 Shot, Spur Trigger, Solid Frame, Single Action,
Antique.. 150 175 175

	V.G.	Exc	Prior Edition
.32 Short R.F., Spur Trigger, Nickel Plated, Antique	$125	$150	$150

LEE SPECIAL   Made by Crescent for Lee Hardware, Salinas, Kans. c. 1900.

SHOTGUN, DOUBLE BARREL, SIDE-BY-SIDE

Various Gauges, Hammerless, Damascus Barrel, Modern	150	175	175
Various Gauges, Hammerless, Steel Barrel, Modern	175	200	200
Various Gauges, Outside Hammers, Damascus Barrel, Modern	150	175	175
Various Gauges, Outside Hammers, Steel Barrel, Modern	150	175	175

SHOTGUN, SINGLESHOT

Various Gauges, Hammer, Steel Barrel, Modern	50	75	75

LEFAUCHEUX   Paris, France. c. 1865.

HANDGUN, REVOLVER

12mm Pinfire, Model 1863, Double Action, Finger Rest Trigger Guard, Antique	400	450	325
9mm Pinfire, Double Action, Folding Trigger, Belgian, Antique	200	250	175
9mm Pinfire, Double Action, Paris, Antique	250	300	300

SHOTGUN, DOUBLE BARREL, SIDE-BY-SIDE

Various Pinfire Gauges, Double Triggers, Hammers, Antique	125	150	150

LEFEVER SONS & CO.   Syracuse, N.Y. Nichols & Lefever, 1876–1878; D. M. Lefever, 1879–1889; Lefever Arms Co. 1889–1899; Lefever, Sons & co. 1899–1926. Purchased by Ithaca Gun Co. 1926. Lefever marked guns manufactured until 1948.

SHOTGUN, DOUBLE BARREL, SIDE-BY-SIDE

B, Various Gauges, Sidelock, Hammerless, Fancy Checkering, Fancy Engraving, Monte Carlo Stock, Curio	5,500	6,500	4,500
BE, Various Gauges, Sidelock, Hammerless, Fancy Checkering, Fancy Engraving, Monte Carlo Stock, Automatic Ejector, Curio	8,500	9,500	8,000
C, Various Gauges, Sidelock, Hammerless, Fancy Checkering, Fancy Engraving, Monte Carlo Stock, Curio	3,500	4,000	3,000
CE, Various Gauges, Sidelock, Hammerless, Fancy Checkering, Fancy Engraving, Monte Carlo Stock, Automatic Ejector, Curio	4,500	5,500	5,000
D, Various Gauges, Sidelock, Hammerless, Fancy Checkering, Engraved, Monte Carlo Stock, Curio	2,500	2,750	1,800
DE, Various Gauges, Sidelock, Hammerless, Fancy Checkering, Engraved, Monte Carlo Stock, Automatic Ejector, Curio	2,750	3,000	2,500
DS, Various Gauges, Sidelock, Hammerless, Checkered Stock, Curio	850	1,000	900
DSE, Various Gauges, Sidelock, Hammerless, Checkered Stock, Automatic Ejector, Curio	1,250	1,500	1,200
E, Various Gauges, Sidelock, Hammerless, Fancy Checkering, Engraved, Curio	1,750	2,000	1,550
EE, Various Gauges, Sidelock, Hammerless, Fancy Checkering, Engraved, Curio	2,250	2,500	2,000

	V.G.	Exc	Prior Edition
F, Various Gauges, Sidelock, Hammerless, Checkered Stock, Engraved, Curio	$1,000	$1,250	$1,400
FE, Various Gauges, Sidelock, Hammerless, Checkered Stock, Engraved, Automatic Ejector, Curio	1,250	1,500	1,800
G, Various Gauges, Sidelock, Hammerless, Checkered Stock, Light Engraving, Curio	1,250	1,500	1,300
GE, Various Gauges, Sidelock, Hammerless, Checkered Stock, Light Engraving, Automatic Ejector, Curio	1,500	1,750	1,600
H, Various Gauges, Sidelock, Hammerless, Checkered Stock, Light Engraving, Curio	1,000	1,250	1,000
HE, Various Gauges, Sidelock, Hammerless, Checkered Stock, Light Engraving, Automatic Ejector, Curio	1,250	1,500	1,500
Nitro Special, Various Gauges, Boxlock, Double Triggers, Checkered Stock, Curio	425	500	375
Nitro Special, Various Gauges, Boxlock, Single Triggers, Checkered Stock, Curio	500	575	500

SHOTGUN, SINGLESHOT

	V.G.	Exc	Prior Edition
A Grade Skeet, 12 Gauge, Hammerless, Vent Rib, Checkered Stock, Automatic Ejector, Curio	1,000	1,250	1,200
Long Range, Various Gauges, Field Grade, Hammerless, Checkered Stock, Curio	300	350	350
Trap Grade, 12 Gauge, Hammerless, Vent Rib, Checkered Stock, Automatic Ejector, Curio	500	550	550

LEFEVRE, PHILIP Beaver Valley, Pa. 1731–1756. See Kentucky Rifles.

LEFEVRE, SAMUEL Strasbourg, Pa. 1770–1771. See Kentucky Rifles.

LEIGH, HENRY Belgium, c. 1890.

SHOTGUN, DOUBLE BARREL, SIDE-BY-SIDE

	V.G.	Exc	Prior Edition
Various Gauges, Outside Hammers, Damascus Barrel, Curio	100	150	150

LEITNER, ADAM York Co, Pa. See Kentucky Rifles and Pistols.

LENNARD Lancaster, Pa. 1770–1772. See Kentucky Rifles and Pistols.

LEONHARDT H. M. Gering & Co., Arnstadt, Germany, c. 1917.

HANDGUN, SEMI-AUTOMATIC

	V.G.	Exc	Prior Edition
Army, 7.65 ACP, Clip Fed, Curio	175	200	200

	V.G.	Exc	Prior Edition
Gering, 7.65 ACP, Clip Fed, Curio..	$220	$225	$225

Leonhardt Gering

LEPCO

HANDGUN, SEMI-AUTOMATIC

6.35mm , Clip Fed, Blue, Modern...	100	125	125

Lepco

L.E.S. Skokie, Ill.

HANDGUN, SEMI-AUTOMATIC

P–18, 9mm Luger, Matte Stainless Steel, Clip Fed, Hammer, Double Action, Modern..	225	275	275
P–18 Deluxe, 9mm Luger, Polished Stainless Steel, Clip Fed, Hammer, Double Action, Modern...	250	325	325

LESCHER Philadelphia, Pa., c. 1730. See Kentucky Rifles and Pistols.

	V.G.	Exc	Prior Edition

LESCONNE, A.   French, c. 1650.

HANDGUN, FLINTLOCK

Pair, Engraved, Silver Inlay, Long Screw Barrel, Rifled, Belt
Hook, Antique.. $7,500 $10,000 $10,000

LIBERTY   Made by Hood Firearms, 1880–1900.

HANDGUN, REVOLVER

.22 Short R.F., 7 Shot, Spur Trigger, Solid Frame, Single Action,
Antique... 150   175   175
.32 Short R.F., 5 Shot, Spur Trigger, Solid Frame, Single Action,
Antique... 150   175   175

LIBERTY   Montrose, Calif.

HANDGUN, REVOLVER

Mustang, .22L.R.R.F., Single Action, Western Style, Adjustable
Sights, Modern.. 50   75   50
Mustang, .22LR/.22 WMR Combo, Single Action, Western Style,
Adjustable Sights, Modern.. 50   75   50

LIBERTY   Retolaza Hermanos, Eibar, Spain, c. 1920.

HANDGUN, SEMI-AUTOMATIC

M1924, 6.35mm, Clip Fed, Curio.. 125   150   150

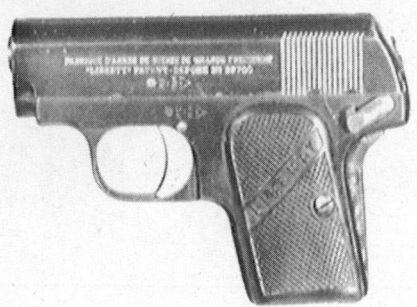

Liberty M1924

Model 1914, 7.65mm, Clip Fed, Blue, Curio... 150   175   175

	V.G.	Exc	Prior Edition
Model 1914, 7.65mm, Clip Fed, Blue, Long Grip, Curio.............	$150	$175	$175

Liberty Long Grip

LIBERTY CHIEF Miroku Firearms, Kochi, Japan.
HANDGUN, REVOLVER

Model 6, .38 Spec., Double Action, Blue, Modern....................	125	150	150

LIBIA Made by Beistegui Hermanos, c. 1920.
HANDGUN, SEMI-AUTOMATIC

6.35mm, Clip Fed, Blue, Curio................	175	200	200
7.65mm, Clip Fed, Blue, Curio................	200	225	225

LIEGEOISE D'ARMES A FEU Robar et Cie., Liege, Belgium, c. 1920.
HANDGUN, SEMI-AUTOMATIC

New Model Melior, 6.35mm, Clip Fed, Blue, Curio..............	150	175	175
Spanish Copy, 6.35mm, Blue, Clip Fed, Curio................	100	125	125
Spanish Copy, 7.65mm, Blue Clip Fed, Curio................	125	150	150

LIGHTNING Echave y Arizmendi, Eibar, Spain, c. 1920.
HANDGUN, SEMI-AUTOMATIC

6.35mm, Clip Fed, Blue, Curio................	125	150	150

	V.G.	Exc	Prior Edition

LIGNITZ, I. H. Continental, c. 1650.

HANDGUN, WHEEL-LOCK

Brass Barrel, Holster Pistol, Medium Ornamentation, Antique............... $6,500 $7,500 $7,500

LIGNOSE   Successors to Theodor Bergmann, Suhl, Germany, c. 1925.

HANDGUN, SEMI-AUTOMATIC

For Original Wood Grips, Add 10%–15%

Model 2, 6.35mm, Clip Fed, Curio.. 150   200   200

Model 2A, 6.35mm, Clip Fed, Einhand, Steel Cocking Piece,
Curio.. 200   250   250

Lignose 2A

Model 3A, 6.35mm, Clip Fed, Long Grip, Einhand, Brass
Cocking Piece, Curio.. 200   250   250

Lignose 3A

	V.G.	Exc	Prior Edition

LILIPUT August Menz, Suhl, Germany, c. 1920.

HANDGUN, SEMI-AUTOMATIC

	V.G.	Exc	Prior Edition
4.25mm Liliput, Clip Fed, Blue, Curio...	$400	$450	$450
6.35mm, Clip Fed, Blue, Curio...	125	150	150

LION Made by Johnson Bye & Co., c. 1870–1880. Sold by J. P. Lovell, Boston, Mass.

HANDGUN, REVOLVER

	V.G.	Exc	Prior Edition
#1, .22 Short R.F., 7 Shot, Spur Trigger, Solid Frame, Single Action, Antique..	150	175	175
#2, .32 Short R.F., 5 Shot, Spur Trigger, Solid Frame, Single Action, Antique..	150	175	175
#3, .38 Short R.F., 5 Shot, Spur Trigger, Solid Frame, Single Action, Antique..	150	175	175
#4, .41 Short R.F., 5 Shot, Spur Trigger, Solid Frame, Single Action, Antique..	175	200	200

LITTLE GIANT Made by Bacon Arms Co., c. 1880.

HANDGUN, REVOLVER

	V.G.	Exc	Prior Edition
.22 Short R.F., 7 Shot, Spur Trigger, Solid Frame, Single Action, Antique..	150	175	175

LITTLE JOHN Made by Hood Firearms., c. 1876.

HANDGUN, REVOLVER

	V.G.	Exc	Prior Edition
.22 Short R.F., 7 Shot, Spur Trigger, Solid Frame, Single Action, Antique..	150	175	175

LITTLE JOKER Made by John M. Marlin, New Haven, Conn. 1873–1875.

HANDGUN, REVOLVER

	V.G.	Exc	Prior Edition
.22 Short R.F., 7 Shot, Spur Trigger, Solid Frame, Single Action, Antique..	175	200	200

LITTLE PET Made by Stevens Arms.

SHOTGUN, SINGLESHOT

	V.G.	Exc	Prior Edition
Model 958, .410 Gauge, Automatic Ejector, Hammer, Modern...............	50	75	75
Model 958, 32 Gauge, Automatic Ejector, Hammer, Modern..................	50	75	75

LITTLE TOM Alois Tomiska, Pilsen, Czechoslovakia 1909–1918.

HANDGUN, SEMI-AUTOMATIC

	V.G.	Exc	Prior Edition
6.35mm, Clip Fed, Blue, Hammer, Curio..	300	375	425
7.65mm, Clip Fed, Blue, Hammer, Curio..	350	425	500

	V.G.	Exc	Prior Edition

LITTLE TOM Wiener Waffenfabrik, Vienna, Austria 1918–1925.

HANDGUN, SEMI-AUTOMATIC

	V.G.	Exc	Prior Edition
6.35mm, Clip Fed, Blue, Hammer, Curio..	$275	$325	$375

LJUTIC INDUSTRIES, INC. Yakima, Wash.

SHOTGUN, DOUBLE BARREL, OVER-UNDER

Bi–Gun, 12 Gauge, Vent Rib, Trap Grade, Checkered Stock, Modern............	6,500	7,500	4,250
Bi–Gun Set, Various Calibers, Vent Rib, Skeet Grade, Checkered Stock, With 4 Sets of Barrels, Modern..	10,000	12,500	9,000

SHOTGUN, SEMI-AUTOMATIC

Bi Matic, 12 Gauge, Vent Rib, Trap Garde, Checkered Stock, Modern..........	1,800	2,000	2,000

SHOTGUN, SINGLESHOT

Dyn–A–Trap, 12 Gauge, Trap Grade, Checkered Stock, Vent Rib, Modern......	1,800	2,000	2,000
Dyn–A–Trap, 12 Gauge, for Custom Stock Add $170.00–$300.00			
Dyn–A–Trap, 12 Gauge, Release Trigger, Add $150.00–$250.00			
Mono–Gun, 12 Gauge, Trap Grade, Checkered Stock, Olympic Rib, Modern...	3,500	4,000	5,000
Mono–Gun, 12 Gauge, Trap Grade, Checkered Stock, Vent Rib, Modern.........	3,000	3,500	3,500
Mono–Gun, 12 Gauge, For Extra Barrel Add $565.00–$750.00			
Mono–Gun, 12 Gauge, Release Trigger Add $220.00–$300.00			
X–73, 12 Gauge, Trap Grade, Checkered Stock, Vent Rib, Modern........	2,000	2,500	2,500
X–73, 12 Gauge, For Extra Barrel Add $435.00–$600.00			
X–73, 12 Gauge, Release Trigger Add $220.00–$300.00			

LLAMA Gabilondo y Cia., Elgoibar, Spain from 1930 to date. Imported by Stoegar Arms.

HANDGUN, REVOLVER

Chrome Plate, Add 20%–30%			
Commanche I, .22 L.R.R.F., Swing–Out Cylinder, Double Action, Blue, Modern..........	175	200	175
Commanche II, .38 Special, Swing–Out Cylinder, Double Action, Blue, Modern..........	175	200	200
Commanche III, .357 Magnum, Swing–Out Cylinder, Double Action, Blue, Modern.........	200	225	225
Engraving, Add 25%–35%			
Gold Damascening, Add 300%–400%			
Martial, .38 Special, Swing–Out Cylinder, Double Action, Blue, Modern........	150	175	175
Super Commanche IV, .44 Magnum, Swing–Out Cylinder, Double Action, Blue, Modern........	250	275	275
Super Commanche V, .357 Magnum, Swing–Out Cylinder, Double Action, Blue, Modern........	225	250	250

	V.G.	Exc	Prior Edition

HANDGUN, SEMI-AUTOMATIC

Chrome Plate, Add 20%–30%
Engraving, Add 25%–35%
Gold Damascening, Add 300%–400%

	V.G.	Exc	Prior Edition
Model I, .32 ACP. Clip Fed, Blue, Modern	$175	$200	$200
Model II, .380 ACP. Clip Fed, Blue, Modern	200	225	225
Model III, .380 ACP. Clip Fed, Blue, Modern	175	200	200
Model IIIA, .380 ACP. Clip Fed, Grip Safety, Blue, Modern	200	225	225
Model IV, 9mm Bergmann, Clip Fed, Blue, Modern	175	200	200
Model IX, .45 ACP. Clip Fed, Blue, Modern	275	300	300
Model IXA, .45 ACP. Clip Fed, Blue, Modern	275	300	300
Model V, .38 ACP. Clip Fed, Blue, Modern	175	200	200
Model VII, .38 ACP. Clip Fed, Blue, Modern	225	250	250
Model VIII, .38 ACP. Grip Safety, Blue, Modern	250	275	275
Model X, .32 ACP. Clip Fed, Blue, Modern	175	200	200
Model XA, .32 ACP. Clip Fed, Grip Safety, Blue, Modern	200	225	225
Model XI, 9mm Luger, Clip Fed, Blue, Modern	275	300	300
Model XV, .22 L.R.R.F., Clip Fed, Grip Safety, Blue, Modern	225	250	250
Omni, 9mm Luger or .45 ACP, Clip Fed, Double Action, Blue, Military, Antique	350	375	375

LOBINGER, JOHANN Vienna, Austria, c. 1780.

RIFLE, FLINTLOCK

	V.G.	Exc	Prior Edition
Yaeger, Smoothbore, Half–Octagon Barrel, Silver Furniture, Carved, Antique	3,500	4,000	4,000

LONG RANGE WONDER Tradename used by Sears, Roebuck & Co.

SHOTGUN, SINGLESHOT

	V.G.	Exc	Prior Edition
12 Ga., Hammer, Break–Open, Modern	50	75	75

LONG TOM Made by Stevens Arms.

SHOTGUN, SINGLESHOT

	V.G.	Exc	Prior Edition
Model 90, Various Gauges, Tkedown, Automatic Ejector, Plain, Hammer, Curio	50	75	75
Model 95, 12 and 16 Gauges, Hammer, Automatic Ejector, Curio	50	75	75

	V.G.	Exc	Prior Edition

LONGINES Cooperative Orbea, Eibar, Spain, c. 1920.

HANDGUN, SEMI-AUTOMATIC

7.65mm, Clip Fed, Curio... $175 $200 $200

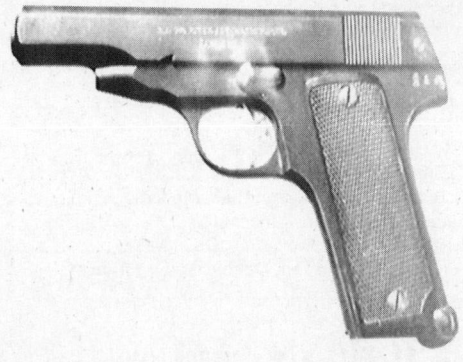

Longines

LOOKING GLASS Domingo Acha and Acha Hermanos, Ermua, Spain, c. 1920.

HANDGUN, SEMI-AUTOMATIC

6.35mm, Clip Fed, Hammer, Curio.....................................	125	150	150
6.35mm, Clip Fed, Hammerless, Curio.............................	100	125	125
7.65mm, Clip Fed, Long Grip, Hammer, Curio.....................	150	175	17
7.65mm, Clip Fed, Long Grip, Hammerless, Curio.................	125	150	150

LORD, J. Orwigsburg, Pa. 1842–55. See Kentucky Rifles.

LOWELL ARMS CO. Lowell, Mass. 1854–68.

HANDGUN, REVOLVER

.22 Short R.F., 7 Shot, Spur Trigger, Tip–up, Antique............................	300	350	350
.32 Long R.F., 6 Shot, Spur Trigger, Tip–up, Single Action,			
.38 Long R.F., 6 Shot, Spur Trigger, Tip–up, Single Action, Antique.....	250	275	275
Antique..	350	400	400

RIFLE, SINGLESHOT

.38 Long R.F., Antique...	350	375	375

	V.G.	Exc	Prior Edition

LOWER, J. P. Philadelphia, Pa., c. 1875.

HANDGUN, REVOLVER

	V.G.	Exc	Prior Edition
.22 Long R.F., 7 Shot, Single Action, Solid Frame, Spur Trigger, Antique	$225	$275	$175
.32 Long R.F., 7 Shot, Single Action, Solid Frame, Spur Trigger, Antique	325	375	200

LUGER Made by various companies for commercial and military use from 1900–45. Also see Mauser and German Military.

HANDGUN, SEMI-AUTOMATIC

	V.G.	Exc	Prior Edition
1900 Bulgarian, .30 Luger, Curio	3,500	8,000	7,500
1900 Commercial, .30 Luger, Curio	2,225	2,500	2,500
1900 Eagle, .30 Luger, Curio	2,000	2,250	2,250
1900 Swiss Commercial, .30 Luger, Curio	2,250	2,500	2,500
1900 Swiss Military, .30 Luger, Curio	2,250	2,500	2,250
1900 Swiss Military, .30 Luger, Wide Trigger, Curio	2,500	3,000	2,600
1902 Commercial, 9mm Luger, Curio	5,500	6,500	4,500

Luger 1902 Commercial

	V.G.	Exc	Prior Edition
1902 Eagle, 9mm Luger, Curio	5,000	5,500	5,500
1902 Prototype, .30 Luger and 9mm Luger, Curio	—	RARE	—
1902 Test, .30 Luger and 9mm Luger, Curio	6,000	7,000	4,000
1902, .30 Luger and (mm Luger, Carbine, Blue, Curio Add 50% For Stock,	6,500	7,500	5,000
1902, 9mm Luger, Cartridge Counter, Curio	12,500	15,000	15,000
1902–3 Presentation, .30 Luger, Carbine, Curio	—	RARE	—
1903 Commercial, .30 Luger, Curio	6,500	8,000	8,000
1904 Navy, 9mm Luger, Curio	10,000	12,500	12,500
1906 Brazilian, .30 Luger, Curio	1,200	1,650	1,500
1906 Bulgarian, .30 Luger, Curio	3,750	4,500	3,500
1906 Bulgarian, 9mm Luger, Curio	3,000	3,500	3,000

		V.G.	Exc	Prior Edition
1906 Commercial, .30 Luger, Curio		$1,500	$1,750	$1,500

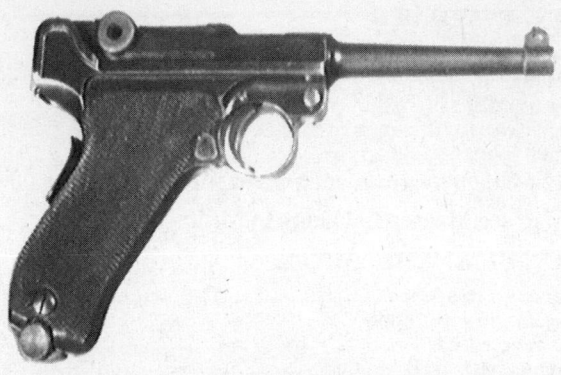

Luger 1906 Commercial

		V.G.	Exc	Prior Edition
1906 Commercial, 9mm Luger, Curio		1,750	2,100	2,000
1906 Dutch, 9mm Luger, Curio		1,500	1,950	1,600
1906 Eagle, .30 Luger, Curio		1,500	1,750	2,000
1906 Eagle, 9mm Luger, Curio		1,750	2,000	2,250
1906 French, .30 Luger, Curio		2,500	3,500	1,800
1906 Navy Commercial, 9mm Luger, Curio		3,000	4,000	3,000

Luger 1906 Navy

		V.G.	Exc	Prior Edition
1906 Navy Military, 9mm Luger, Curio		2,500	3,000	2,500
1906 Portuguese Army, .30 Luger, Curio		1,250	1,500	1,200
1906 Portuguese Navy , .30 Luger, Curio		6,500	7,000	7,000
1906 Portuguese Navy Crown, .30 Luger and 9mm Luger, Curio		6,500	7,250	7,250
1906 Russian, 9mm Luger, Curio		7,500	9,500	9,500
1906 Swiss Commercial, .30 Luger, Curio		2,000	2,350	2,350
1906 Swiss Military, .30 Luger, Curio		1,900	2,250	2,250
1906 Swiss Police, .30 Luger, Curio		2,250	2,500	2,500
1908 Bolivian, 9mm Luger, Curio		3,500	4,000	2,750

	V.G.	Exc	Prior Edition
1908 Bulgarian, 9mm Luger, Curio..........	$2,000	$2,500	$1,750
1908 DWM Commercial, 9mm Luger, Curio..........	750	900	700
1908 Military, 9mm Luger, Curio..........	575	650	650
1908 Navy Commercial, .30 Luger, Curio..........	3,000	3,500	3,500
1908 Navy Military, 9mm Luger, Curio..........	2,250	2,500	2,000
1913 Commercial, 9mm Luger, Curio..........	1,400	1,650	1,650
1914 Artillery, 9mm Luger, Curio..........	1,250	1,500	1,500
1914 Commercial, 9mm Luger, Curio..........	1,000	1,250	900
1914 Military, 9mm Luger, Curio..........	750	850	1,000
1914 Navy, 9mm Luger, Curio..........	2,450	2,600	2,600
1918 Spandau, 9mm Luger, Curio..........	—	RARE	—
1920 Abercrombie & Fitch, .30 Luger and 9mm Luger, Curio..........	4,000	4,500	4,500
1920 Artillery, 9mm Luger, Curio..........	1,000	1,300	1,300
1920 Commercial, .30 Luger and 9mm Luger, Curio..........	550	600	600
1920 Navy, 9mm Luger, Curio..........	1,800	2,000	2,000
1920 Simson, 9mm Luger, Curio..........	700	800	800
1920 Swiss Commercial, .30 Luger and 9mm Luger, Curio..........	1,250	1,500	1,500
1920 Swiss Rework, .30 Luger and 9mm Luger, Curio..........	1,200	1,550	1,550
1920–21, .30 Luger and 9mm Luger, Curio..........	500	650	650
1921 Krieghoff, .30 Luger, Curio..........	2,500	2,800	2,800
1923 Commercial "Safe–Loaded," .30 Luger and 9mm Luger, Curio..........	1,000	1,250	1,250
1923 Commercial Krieghoff, 9mm Luger, Curio..........	1,250	1,500	1,500
1923 Commercial, .30 Luger and 9mm Luger, Curio..........	650	750	750
1923 Dutch, 9mm Luger, Curio..........	1,200	1,450	1,450
1923 Finnish Army, 9mm Luger, Curio..........	550	600	600
1923 Simson Commercial, 9mm Luger, Curio..........	1,800	2,000	2,000
1923 Simson Military, 9mm Luger, Curio..........	2,000	2,250	2,250
1923 Stoeger, .30 Luger and 9mm Luger, Curio..........	2,250	2,750	2,250
1924 Bern, .30 Luger, Curio..........	1,500	2,500	2,250
1924–7 Simson, 9mm Luger, Dated Chamber, Curio..........	2,500	3,000	2,000
1929 Bern, .30 Luger and 9mm Luger, Curio..........	1,750	2,000	1,500
1930–33 Death Head, 9mm Luger, Curio..........	1,250	1,500	1,500
1933 K.I., 9mm Luger, Curio..........	850	1,000	1,000
1933–35 Dutch, 9mm Luger, Royal Dutch Air Force, Curio..........	1,450	1,650	1,650
1933–35 Mauser Commercial, 9mm Luger, Curio..........	1,250	1,500	1,500
1934 P Commercial Krieghoff, .30 Luger and 9mm Luger, Curio..........	2,250	2,500	2,500
1934 P Commercial, Krieghoff, 9mm Luger, Curio..........	2,000	2,250	2,250
1934 Sideframe, Krieghoff, 6" Barrel, 9mm Luger, Curio..........	2,500	3,000	3,000
1935 Portuguese, "GNR," .30 Luger, Curio..........	1,750	2,000	2,000
1936 Persian, 9mm Luger, Curio..........	3,000	3,500	3,500
1936–37, 9mm Luger, Krieghoff, Curio..........	1,750	2,250	3,000
1936–39, .30 Luger and 9mm Luger, 4" Barrel, Curio..........	750	900	900
1936–40 Dutch Banner, 9mm Luger, Curio..........	1,500	1,750	1,500
1936–9 S/42, 9mm Luger, Curio..........	750	875	875
1937–39 Banner Commercial, .30 Luger, 4" Barrel, Curio..........	1,500	1,750	1,600
1938, 9mm Luger, Curio..........	2,500	2,650	2,650

	V.G.	Exc	Prior Edition
1939–40 42, 9mm Luger, Curio...	$625	$750	$750

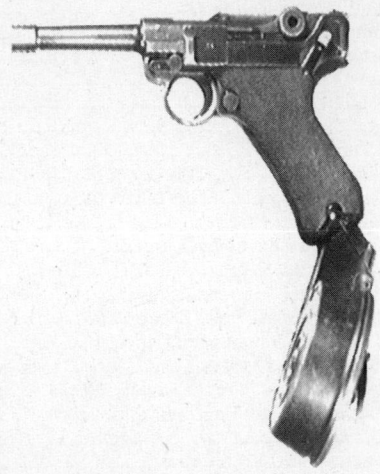

Luger 1940–42 with Snail Drum

1940 42/44 byf, 9mm Luger, Curio..	600	750	750
1940 Mauser Banner, .30 Luger and 9mm Luger, Curio.........................	1,250	1,500	1,500
1940, 9mm Luger, Krieghoff, Curio...	2,250	2,500	2,500
1941–2 byf, 9mm Luger, Curio...	750	900	900

Luger 1941–42 byf

1941–4, 9mm Luger, Krieghoff, Curio..	2,250	2,750	2,100
1945, 9mm Luger, Krieghoff, Curio...	5,000	7,500	9,500
36, 9mm Luger, Krieghoff, Curio..	2,500	3,000	2,500
41 & 42 Banner, 9mm Luger, Curio...	1,450	1,650	1,200
42/41, 9mm Luger, Curio...	800	950	950

	V.G.	Exc	Prior Edition
Artillery, Stock Only, Curio	$300	$350	$350
Austrian Banner, 9mm Luger, Curio	1,500	1,850	1,850
Banner Commercial, .30 Luger, 4" Barrel, Curio	1,500	1,750	1,450
Double Date, 9mm Luger, Curio	550	700	700
G.L. Baby, 9mm Luger, Curio	—	RARE	—
G–S/42, 9mm Luger, Curio	650	800	800
Ideal, Holster Stock, Curio	1,000	1,250	1,250
K U, 9mm Luger, Curio	1,200	1,500	1,650
K–S/42 Navy, 9mm Luger, Curio	2,250	2,800	3,500
K–S/42, 9mm Luger, Curio	2,000	2,500	3,000
Mauser Banner Commercial, 9mm Luger, Curio	1,250	1,750	1,000
Navy Stock Only,	500	650	650
Post War, 9mm Luger, Krieghoff, Curio	1,500	1,750	1,750
S/42 Navy, 9mm Luger, Curio	850	1,000	1,000
Snail Drum, Magazine, Curio	500	600	600
Stoeger Luger Carbine, .22 L.R.R.F., Clip Fed, Alloy Frame, Modern	375	475	150
Stoeger Luger, .22 L.R.R.F., Clip Fed, Alloy Frame, Modern	225	300	125
Stoeger Luger, .22 L.R.R.F., Clip Fed, Alloy Frame, Checkered Wood Grips, Early, Modern	250	325	150
Stoeger Target Luger, .22 L.R.R.F., Clip Fed, Alloy Frame, Modern	250	325	150
U.S. Test Eagle 1900, .30 Luger, Curio	2,500	3,000	3,000
Vickers Commercial, 9mm Luger, Curio	3,000	3,500	3,500
Vickers Military, 9mm Luger, Curio	2,000	2,500	2,500
VOPO, 9mm Luger, Clip Fed, Modern	1,250	1,450	1,450

Luger VOPO

	V.G.	Exc	Prior Edition

LUR-PANZER Echave y Arizmendi, Eibar, Spain.
HANDGUN, SEMI-AUTOMATIC
	V.G.	Exc	Prior Edition
Luger Type, .22 L.R.R.F., Toggle Action, Clip Fed, Modern..................	$125	$150	$150

LYMAN GUN SIGHT CORP. Middlefield, Conn.
HANDGUN, PERCUSSION
	V.G.	Exc	Prior Edition
.36 1851 Navy, Color Case Hardened Frame, Engraved Cylinder, Reproduction,	100	125	125
.36 New Model Navy, Brass Trigger Guard, Solid Frame, Reproduction,	75	100	100
.44 1860 Army, Color Case Hardened Frame, Engraved Cylinder, Reproduction,	100	125	125
.44 New Model Army, Brass Trigger Guard, Solid Frame, Reproduction,	100	125	125

RIFLE, FLINTLOCK
	V.G.	Exc	Prior Edition
Plains Rifle, Various Calibers, Brass Furniture, Set Trigger, Reproduction	200	225	225

RIFLE, PERCUSSION
	V.G.	Exc	Prior Edition
Plains Rifle, Various Calibers, Brass Furniture, Set Trigger, Reproduction	150	175	175
Trade Rifle, Various Calibers, Brass Furniture, Set Trigger, Reproduction	125	150	150

RIFLE, SINGLESHOT
	V.G.	Exc	Prior Edition
Centennial, 45/70 Government, Ruger #1, Commemorative, Cased with Accessories, Modern.................	1,200	1,450	1,450

M

MAADI

RIFLE, SEMI-AUTOMATIC

Paratrooper AKM, 7.62 X 39mm, Clip Fed, Assault Rifle,
Modern.. $750 $1,050 $1,050

Standard AKM, 7.62 X 39mm, Clip Fed, Assault Rifle,
Modern.. 750 950 950

MAB Mre. d'Armes Automatiques Bayonne, Bayonne, France since 1921.

HANDGUN, SEMI-AUTOMATIC

Modele A, 6.35mm, Clip Fed, Modern.. 150 175 150

MAB Modele A

	V.G.	Exc.	Prior Edition
Modele B, 6.35mm, Clip Fed, Modern......................	225	250	250
Modele C, .380 ACP, Clip Fed, Modern..................................	225	250	250
Modele C, 7.65mm, Clip Fed, Modern..................................	200	225	225
Modele C/D, .380 ACP, Clip Fed, Modern............................	175	200	200
Modele C/D, 7.65mm, Clip Fed, Modern............................	150	175	175
Modele D, .380 ACP, Clip Fed, Modern..............................	175	200	225
Modele D, 7.65mm, Clip Fed, Modern..............................	150	175	175
Modele D, 7.65mm, Clip Fed, French Military, Curio.............................	225	250	250

	V.G.	Exc	Prior Edition
Modele E, 6.35mm, Clip Fed, Long Grip, Modern.....................................	$200	$225	$225

MAB Modele E

Modele F, .22 L.R.R.F., Clip Fed, Hammer, 3" Barrel, Modern...............	175	200	200

MAB Modele F

Modele F, .22 L.R.R.F., Clip Fed, Hammer, 5" Barrel, Modern...............	200	225	225
Modele GZ, 7.65mm, Clip Fed, Modern...	175	200	200
Modele Le Chasseur, .22 L.R.R.F., Clip Fed, Hammer, Target Grips, Modern..	200	225	225
Modele PA–15, 9mm Luger, Clip Fed, Hammer, Modern........................	350	375	375
Modele R Court, 7.65mm, Clip Fed, Hammer, Modern.........................	275	300	300
Modele R Longue, 7.65 MAS, Clip Fed, Hammer, Modern....................	250	275	275
Modele R Para, 9mm Luger, Clip Fed, Hammer, Curio...........................	350	400	400
Modele R, 7.65mm, Clip Fed, Modern...	250	275	150

Nazi Navy Proofs, Add 40%–50%
Nazi Proofs, Add 20%–30%

	V.G.	Exc	Prior Edition

W.A.C. Markings, Deduct 5%–10% (Importer Winfield Arms Co., Los Angeles, Cal.)

M.A.C. (Military Armament Corp.) See Ingram.

MACLOED Doune, Scotland 1711–1750.

HANDGUN, FLINTLOCK

.54, All Steel, Engraved, Ram's Horn Butt, Antique................................... $3,000 $3,500 $3,500

MAGNUM RESEARCH INC. Minneapolis, Minn. Also see Israeli Military.

HANDGUN, SEMI-AUTOMATIC

Desert Eagle, .357 Magnum, Clip Fed, Interchangeable Barrels, Gas Operated, Blue, Modern... 500 550 550

MAICHE, A. France.

HANDGUN, FLINTLOCK

.56, Brass Mountings, Holster Pistol, Antique... 400 575 575

MALTBY–CURTIS Agent for Norwich Pistol Co. 1875–1881.

HANDGUN, REVOLVER

.22 Short R.F., 7 Shot, Spur Trigger, Solid Frame, Single Action, Antique... 150 175 175

.32 Short R.F., 5 Shot, Spur Trigger, Solid Frame, Single Action, Antique... 150 175 175

MALTY–HENLEY & CO. N.Y.C. 1878–1899. Made by Columbia Armory, Tenn.

HANDGUN, REVOLVER

Spencer Safety Hammerless, .32 S & W, 5 Shot, Top Break, Hammerless, Double Action, Curio.. 200 275 100

MAMBA Made by Relay Products in Johannesburg, South Africa, and Navy Arms in the U.S.

HANDGUN, SEMI-AUTOMATIC

Navy Mamba, 9mm Luger, Stainless, Double Action, Modern.............. 300 325 325

Relay Mamba, 9mm Luger, Stainless, Double Action, Modern.............. 425 475 475

Rhodesian Mamba, 9mm Luger, Stainless, Double Action, Modern... 1,500 2,000 2,000

	V.G.	Exc	Prior Edition

MANHATTAN FIREARMS MFG. CO. N.Y.C. & Newark,
N.J. 1849–1864.

HANDGUN, PERCUSSION

Bar Hammer, Double Action, Screw Barrel, Singleshot, Antique........... $300 $350 $250

Manhattan Bar Hammer, .31 Caliber

Hero, Singleshot, Derringer, Antique..	250	300	250
Pepperbox, .28, 3 Shot, Double Action, Antique.....................................	650	750	600
Pepperbox, .28, 6 Shot, Double Action, Antique.....................................	550	650	500
Revolver, .31, Pocket Model, Single Action, Antique..............................	400	475	450
Revolver, .36, Navy Model, Single Action, Antique................................	700	850	700
Revolver, Pocket, .22 Cal. Cartridge, Antique..	375	425	350

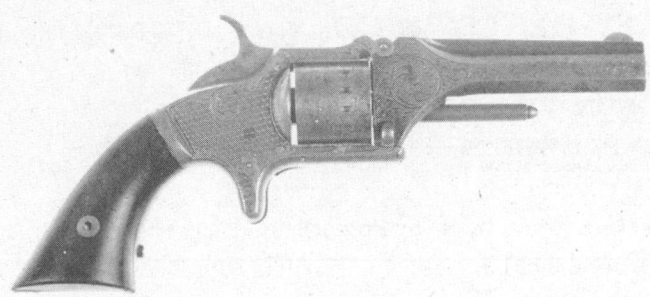

Manhattan Second Model, .22 Caliber

	V.G.	Exc	Prior Edition

MANHURIN   Mre. de Machines du Haut–Rhin, Mulhouse–Bourtzwiller, France. Also see Walther.

HANDGUN, REVOLVER

Model 73 Police, .357 Magnum, Double Action, Swing–Out Cylinder,
Modern... $900 $1,200 $1,200
Model 73 Sport, .357 Magnum, Double Action, Swing–Out Cylinder,
Modern... 1,000   1,300   1,300

MANN   Fritz Mann Werkzeugfabrik, Suhl, Germany 1919–1924.

HANDGUN, SEMI-AUTOMATIC

Pocket, .25 ACP, Clip Fed, Curio... 300   325   325

Mann Pocket

Pocket, .32 ACP, Clip Fed, Curio... 300   350   350
Pocket, .380 ACP, Clip Fed, Curio... 325   375   375

MANN, MICHEL   Uhlenberg, Germany, c. 1630.

HANDGUN, WHEEL-LOCK

Miniature, All Metal, Gold Damascened, Ball Pommel,
Antique.. 3,500   4,000   4,000

MANNLICHER–SCHOENAUER   Steyr–Daimler–Puch, Steyr, Austria.

RIFLE, BOLT ACTION

Alpine, Various Calibers, Sporting Rifle, Full–Stocked, Modern............. 425   475   475
Custom M–S, Various Calibers, Sporting Rifle, Scope Mounted,
Carbine, Modern.. 650   700   700
Custom M–S, Various Calibers, Sporting Rifle, Scope Mounted,
Modern... 675   725   725

	V.G.	Exc	Prior Edition
High Velocity, Various Calibers, Sporting Rifle, Set Trigger, Modern....................	$750	$825	$825
High Velocity, Various Calibers, Sporting Rifle, Takedown, Set Trigger, Modern....................	775	875	875
M–72 LM, Various Calibers, Sporting Rifle, Full–Stocked, Modern....................	750	800	800
M–72 S, Various Calibers, Sporting Rifle, Modern....................	775	850	850
M–72 T, Various Calibers, Sporting Rifle, Modern....................	800	875	875
Magnum M–S, Various Calibers, Sporting Rifle, Monte Carlo Stock, Set Trigger, Modern....................	825	875	875
MCA, Various Calibers, Sporting Rifle, Carbine, Monte Carlo Stock, Modern....................	875	950	950
MCA, Various Calibers, Sporting Rifle, Monte Carlo Stock, Modern....................	850	950	950
Model 1903, Various Calibers, Sporting Rifle, Carbine, Set Trigger, Full–Stocked, Modern....................	900	950	950
Model 1905, 9 X 56 M.S., Sporting Rifle, Carbine, Set Trigger, Full–Stocked, Modern....................	900	1,200	1,200
Model 1908, Various Calibers, Sporting Rifle, Carbine, Set Trigger, Full–Stocked, Modern....................	925	975	975
Model 1910, 9.5 X 57 M.S., Sporting Rifle, Carbine, Set Trigger, Full–Stocked, Modern....................	950	1,025	1,025
Model 1924, .30–06 Springfield, Sporting Rifle, Carbine, Set Trigger, Full–Stocked, Modern....................	1,000	1,175	1,175
Model 1950, 6.5 X 54 M.S., Sporting Rifle, Carbine, Set Trigger, Full–Stocked, Modern....................	850	975	975
Model 1950, Various Calibers, Sporting Rifle, Carbine, Set Trigger, Full–Stocked, Modern....................	850	950	950
Model 1950, Various Calibers, Sporting Rifle, Set Trigger, Modern....................	750	825	825
Model 1952, 6.5 X 54 M.S., Sporting Rifle, Carbine, Set Trigger, Full–Stocked, Modern....................	900	1,050	1,050
Model 1952, Various Calibers, Sporting Rifle, Carbine, Set Trigger, Full–Stocked, Modern....................	800	1,000	1,000
Model 1952, Various Calibers, Sporting Rifle, Set Trigger, Modern....................	650	800	800
Model 1956, Various Calibers, Sporting Rifle, Carbine, Set Trigger, Full–Stocked, Modern....................	750	800	800
Model 1956, Various Calibers, Sporting Rifle, Set Trigger, Modern....................	725	800	800
Model L Varmint, Various Calibers, Checkered Stock, Set Trigger, Modern....................	475	525	525
Model M, Various Calibers, Checkered Stock, Set Trigger, Modern....................	550	600	600
Model M Professional, Various Calibers, Checkered Stock, Set Trigger, Modern....................	375	425	425
Model ML 79, Various Calibers, Checkered Stock, Set Trigger, Modern....................	700	750	750
Model S, Various Calibers, Checkered Stock, Set Trigger, Modern....................	625	675	675
Model S/T Magnum, Various Calibers, Checkered Stock, Set Trigger, Modern....................	650	675	675
Model SSG Match, .308 Win., Synthetic Target Stock, Set Triggers, Walther Peep Sights, Modern....................	575	650	650

	V.G.	Exc	Prior Edition
Model SSG, .308 Win., Synthetic Target Stock, Set Triggers, Modern................	$450	$500	$500
Premier, Varius Calibers, Sporting Rifle, Fancy Checkering, Engraved, Modern................	575	650	650
Premier, Varius Calibers, Sporting Rifle, Magnum Action, Fancy Checkering, Engraved, Modern................	1,250	1,400	1,400

RIFLE, DOUBLE BARREL, SIDE-BY-SIDE

	V.G.	Exc	Prior Edition
Mustang, Various Calibers, Standard, Checkered Stock, Sidelock, Modern................	5,000	6,000	6,000
Mustang, Various Calibers, Standard, Checkered Stock, Sidelock, Engraved, Modern................	5,500	6,500	6,500

RIFLE, DOUBLE BARREL, OVER-UNDER

	V.G.	Exc	Prior Edition
Safari 72, .375 H & M Mag., Checkered Stock, Engraved, Double Trigger, Modern................	3,000	3,500	3,500
Safari 77, Various Calibers, Checkered Stock, Engraved, Double Trigger, Automatic Ejector, Modern................	4,000	4,500	4,500

SHOTGUN, DOUBLE BARREL, OVER-UNDER

	V.G.	Exc	Prior Edition
Edinbourgh, 12 Ga., Checkered Stock, Vent Rib, Modern................	1,250	1,500	1,500

SHOTGUN, DOUBLE BARREL, SIDE-BY-SIDE

	V.G.	Exc	Prior Edition
Ambassador English, 12 and 20 Gauges, Checkered Stock, Sidelock, Automatic Ejectors, Engraved, Modern................	7,000	7,500	7,500
Ambassador Executive, 12 and 20 Gauges, Checkered Stock, Sidelock, Automatic Ejectors, Fancy Engraving, Modern................	12,000	15,000	15,000
Ambassador Extra, 12 and 20 Gauges, Checkered Stock, Sidelock, Automatic Ejectors, Engraved, Modern................	6,500	7,250	7,250
Ambassador Golden Black, 12 and 20 Gauges, Checkered Stock, Sidelock, Automatic Ejectors, Engraved, Gold Inlays, Modern................	8,500	9,500	9,500
London, 12 and 20 Gauges, Checkered Stock, Sidelock, Automatic Ejectors, Engraved, Cased, Modern................	2,250	2,500	2,450
Oxford Field, 12 and 20 Gauges, Checkered Stock, Automatic Ejectors, Engraved, Modern................	1,000	1,300	1,300

MANTON J. & CO. Belgium, c. 1900.

SHOTGUN, DOUBLE BARREL, SIDE-BY-SIDE

	V.G.	Exc	Prior Edition
Various Gauges, Hammerless, Damascus Barrel, Modern................	150	175	175
Various Gauges, Hammerless, Steel Barrel, Modern................	150	200	200
Various Gauges, Outside Hammers, Damascus Barrel, Modern................	150	175	175
Various Gauges, Outside Hammers, Steel Barrel, Modern................	150	175	175

SHOTGUN, SINGLESHOT

	V.G.	Exc	Prior Edition
Various Gauges, Hammer, Steel Barrel, Modern................	50	75	75

MANTON, JOSEPH London, England 1795–1835.

HANDGUN, FLINTLOCK

	V.G.	Exc	Prior Edition
Pair, Octagon Barrel, Duelling Pistols, Gold Inlays, Light Engraving, Cased with Accessories, Antique................	4,000	5,000	5,000

	V.G.	Exc	Prior Edition

HANDGUN, PERCUSSION

.55, Pair, Duelling Pistols, Octagon Barrel, Light Ornamentation,
Cased with Accessories, Antique... $4,000 $5,000 $5,000

SHOTGUN, PERCUSSION

12 Ga. Double Barrel, Side by Side, Damascus Barrels, Light
Engraving, Gold Inlays, Antique... 500 650 650

MANUFRANCE Manufacture Francaise de Armes et Cycles de St. Etienne, St. Etienne, France. Also see Le Francaise. 1902–Date.

HANDGUN, SEMI-AUTOMATIC

Model 1911 Astra–Manufacture, .32 ACP, Clip Fed, Blue, Curio........ 125 175 175

RIFLE, BOLT ACTION

Buffalo Match, .22 L.R.R.F., Target Rifle, Modern..................................	150	175	175
Club, .22 L.R.R.F., Singleshot, Carbine, Modern......................................	75	100	100
Club, .22 L.R.R.F., Singleshot, Carbine, Checkered Stock, Modern..	100	125	125
Mauser K98 Sporter, .270 Win., Sporterized, Checkered Stock, Modern..	125	150	150
Mauser K98 Sporter, .270 Win., Sporterized, Plain, Modern.................	100	150	150
Rival, 375 H & H Mag., Checkered Stock, Modern.................................	250	300	300

RIFLE, SEMI-AUTOMATIC

Reina, .22 L.R.R.F., Carbine, Clip Fed, Modern.....................................	90	150	150
Sniper, .22 W.M.R., Carbine, Clip Fed, Modern.....................................	150	200	200

SHOTGUN, DOUBLE BARREL, OVER-UNDER

Falcor Field, 12 Ga., Vent Rib, Automatic Ejector, Single Selective Trigger, Checkered Stock, Modern......................................	575	650	650
Falcor Sport, 12 Ga., Vent Rib, Automatic Ejector, Single Selective Trigger, Checkered Stock, Extra Barrels, Modern....................	725	775	775
Falcor Trap, 12 Ga., Vent Rib, Automatic Ejector, Single Selective Trigger, Checkered Stock, Modern......................................	625	675	675

SHOTGUN, DOUBLE BARREL, SIDE-BY-SIDE

Ideal DeLuxe, 12 Ga. 3", Fancy Engraving, Checkered Stock, Double Triggers, Modern..	1,750	1,950	1,950
Ideal Prestige, 12 Ga. 3", Fancy Engraving, Checkered Stock, Double Triggers, Modern..	2,500	2,750	2,750
Robust, 12 Ga. 3", Checkered Stock, Double Triggers, Modern.............	350	375	375
Robust Luxe, 12 Ga. 3", Engraved, Automatic Ejectors, Checkered Stock, Double Triggers, Modern..	600	650	650

SHOTGUN, SEMI-AUTOMATIC

Perfex Special, 12 Ga., Open Sights, Short Barrel, Checkered Stock, Modern..	325	375	375
Perfex, 12 Ga., Checkered Stock, Modern...	300	350	350

SHOTGUN, SINGLESHOT

Simplex, 12 Gauge, Sling Swivels, Modern... 125 150 150

	V.G.	Exc	Prior Edition

SHOTGUN, SLIDE ACTION

Rapid, 12 or 16 Gauges, Plain, Modern.. $150 $175 $175

MARK X Made in Zestavia, Yugoslovia. Imported by Interarms.

RIFLE, BOLT ACTION

Alaskan, Various Calibers, Magnum, Open Rear Sights, Checkered
Stock, Sling Swivels, Modern.. 250 300 300
Cavalier, Various Calibers, Cheekpiece, Checkered Stock, Open
Rear Sight, Sling Swivels, Modern.. 225 275 275
Mannlicher, Various Calibers, Carbine, Full–Stocked, Checkered
Stock, Open Rear Sight, Sling Swivels, Modern...................................... 250 300 300
Marquis, Various Calibers, Carbine, Mauser Action, Modern.................. 425 475 475
Standard, Various Calibers, Checkered Stock, Open Rear Sight,
Sling Swivels, Modern... 225 250 250
Viscount, Various Calibers, Plain, Open Rear Sight, Checkered
Stock, Sling Swivels, Modern... 175 200 200

MARKWELL ARMS CO. Chicago, Ill.

HANDGUN, PERCUSSION

.41 Derringer, Singleshot, Brass Furniture, Reproduction...................... 25 50 50
.44 C S A 1860, Revolver, 6 Shot, Brass Frame, Reproduction.............. 50 75 75
.44 New Army, Revolver, 6 Shot, Brass Trigger Guard,
Reproduction... 50 75 75
.45 Colonial, Singleshot, Brass Furniture, Reproduction...................... 25 50 50
.45 Kentucky, Singleshot, Brass Furniture, Reproduction...................... 25 50 50
.45 Loyalist, Singleshot, Brass Furniture, Set Trigger, Adjustable
Sights, Reproduction.. 50 75 75

RIFLE, PERCUSSION

.45 Hawken, Brass Furniture, Reproduction.. 75 100 100
.45 Kentucky, Brass Furniture, Reproduction.. 50 75 75
.45 Super Kentucky, Brass Furniture, Set Trigger, Reproduction.......... 100 125 125

MARLIN FIREARMS CO. New Haven, Conn. J. M. Marlin, from
1870–1881. Marlin Firearms from 1881–1915. Marlin–Rockwell Corp.
1915–1926. From 1926 to date as Marlin Firearms Co., North Haven, Ct.
Also see Ballard. Also see the Commemorative Section.

HANDGUN, REVOLVER

Model 1887, .32 and .38, Double Action, Top Break, Antique.................. 300 350 350
Standard 1875, .30 R.F., Tip Up, Spur Trigger, Antique........................ 225 250 225

	V.G.	Exc	Prior Edition
XX Standard 1873, .22 R.F., Tip Up, Spur Trigger, Antique..................	$425	$475	$300

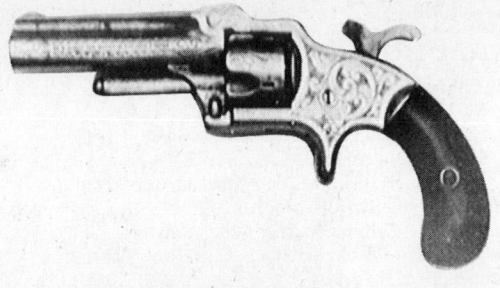

Marlin XX Standard 1873

	V.G.	Exc	Prior Edition
XX Standard 1873, .22 R.F., Tip Up, Spur Trigger, Octagon Barrel, Antique..............	375	425	350
XXX Standard 1872, .30 R.F., Tip Up, Spur Trigger, Antique...............	375	450	350

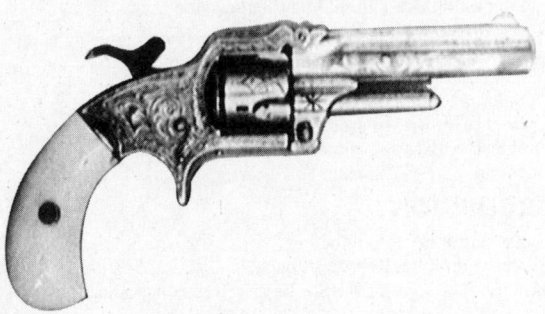

Marlin XXX Standard 1872

	V.G.	Exc	Prior Edition
XXX Standard 1872, .30 R.F., Tip Up, Spur Trigger, Octagon Barrel, Antique.................	350	400	375

RIFLE, BOLT ACTION

	V.G.	Exc	Prior Edition
Glenfield M10, .22 L.R.R.F., Singleshot, Modern..................	25	50	50
Glenfield M20, .22 L.R.R.F., Clip Fed, Modern..................	50	75	75
Model 100, .22 L.R.R.F., Singleshot, Open Rear Sight, Takedown, Modern..................	250	50	50
Model 100–S, .22 L.R.R.F., Singleshot, Peep Sights, Takedown, Modern..................	75	100	100
Model 100–SB, .22 L.R.R.F., Singleshot, Smoothbore, Takedown, Modern..................	25	50	50
Model 101, .22 L.R.R.F., Singleshot, Open Rear Sight, Takedown, Beavertail Forend, Modern..................	50	75	75
Model 101–DL, .22 L.R.R.F., Singleshot, Takedown, Peep Sights, Beavertail Forend, Modern..................	50	75	75

	V.G.	Exc	Prior Edition
Model 122, .22 L.R.R.F., Singleshot, Open Rear Sight, Monte Carlo Stock, Modern	$50	$75	$75
Model 322 (Sako), .222 Rem., Clip Fed, Peep Sights, Checkered Stock, Modern	275	325	325
Model 455 (FN), Various Calibers, Peep Sights, Monte Carlo Stock, Checkered Stock, Modern	300	325	325
Model 65, .22 L.R.R.F., Singleshot, Open Rear Sight, Modern	50	75	75
Model 65E, .22 L.R.R.F., Singleshot, Peep Sights, Modern	50	75	75
Model 780, .22 L.R.R.F., Clip Fed, Open Rear Sight, Modern	75	100	100

Marlin 780 with 200 Scope

Model 781, .22 L.R.R.F., Tube Feed, Open Rear Sight, Modern	75	100	100
Model 782, .22 WMR., Clip Fed, Open Rear Sight, Modern	75	100	100
Model 783, .22 WMR, Tube Feed, Open Rear Sight, Modern	100	125	125

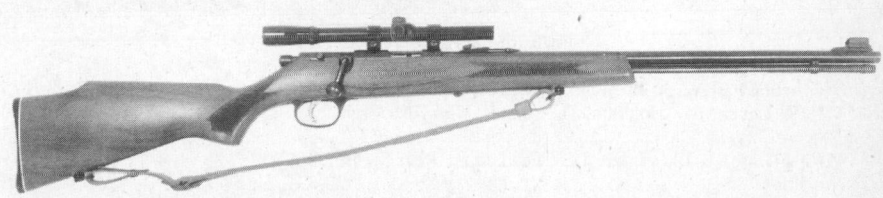

Marlin 783 with 200 Scope

Model 80, .22 L.R.R.F., Clip Fed, Open Rear Sight, Takedown, Modern	50	75	75
Model 80 DL, .22 L.R.R.F., Clip Fed, Beavertail Forend, Takedown, Peep Sights, Modern	50	75	75
Model 80C, .22 L.R.R.F., Clip Fed, Beavertail Forend, Takedown, Open Rear Sight, Modern	50	75	75
Model 80E, .22 L.R.R.F., Clip Fed, Peep Sights, Takedown, Modern	50	75	75
Model 81, .22 L.R.R.F., Tube Feed, Takedown, Open Rear Sight, Modern	50	75	75
Model 81C, .22 L.R.R.F., Tube Feed, Takedown, Open Rear Sight, Beavertail Forend, Modern	50	75	75
Model 81DL, .22 L.R.R.F., Tube Feed, Takedown, Peep Sights, Beavertail Forend, Modern	50	75	75
Model 81E, .22 L.R.R.F., Tube Feed, Takedown, Peep Sights, Modern	50	75	75
Model 81G, .22 L.R.R.F., Tube Feed, Takedown, Open Rear Sight, Beavertail Forend, Modern	50	75	75

	V.G.	Exc	Prior Edition
Model 980, .22 WMR, Clip Fed, Monte Carlo Stock, Open Rear Sight, Modern..	$75	$100	$100

RIFLE, LEVER ACTION

	V.G.	Exc	Prior Edition
Centennial Set 336–39 (1970), Fancy Checkering, Fancy Wood, Engraved, Brass Furniture, Curio..	1,000	1,250	1,250

Marlin Cased Centennial Pair

	V.G.	Exc	Prior Edition
Glenfield M 30 A, .30–30 Win., Tube Feed, Modern................................	125	175	175
M1894 (Late), .357 Magnum, Tube Feed, Open Rear Sight, Modern..	200	250	225
M1894 (Late), .41 Magnum, Tube Feed, Open Rear Sight, Modern..	200	250	200
M1894 (Late), .44 Magnum, Tube Feed, Open Rear Sight, Modern..	225	275	200
M1895 (Late), .45–70 Government, Tube Feed, Open Rear Sight, Modern..	250	300	225
Model 1881 Standard, Various Calibers, Tube Feed, Open Rear Sight, Antique..	1,000	1,250	775
Model 1888, Various Calibers, Tube Feed, Open Rear Sight, Antique..	2,000	2,250	950
Model 1889 Standard, Various Calibers, Tube Feed, Open Rear Sight, Antique..	650	800	575

	V.G.	Exc	Prior Edition
Model 1891, .22 L.R.R.F., Tube Feed, Open Rear Sight, Antique	$1,250	$1,500	$450

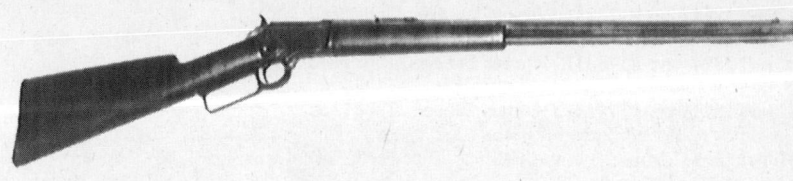

Marlin Model 1891

	V.G.	Exc	Prior Edition
Model 1892, Various Calibers, Tube Feed, Open Rear Sight, Antique	750	1,000	450
Model 1892 Over #177382, Various Calibers, Tube Feed, Modern	500	650	400
Model 1893, Various Calibers, Tube Feed, Musket, with Bayonet, Antique	3,000	4,500	3,250
Model 1893, Various Calibers, Tube Feed, Solid Frame, Octagon Barrl, Antique	750	850	550
Model 1893, Various Calibers, Tube Feed, Solid Frame, Round Barrel, Antique	650	750	475
Model 1893, Various Calibers, Tube Feed, Solid Frame, Round Barrel, Carbine, Antique	800	950	650
Model 1893, Various Calibers, Tube Feed, Sporting Carbine, 5 Shot, Antique	750	1,000	750
Model 1893, Various Calibers, Tube Feed, Sporting Carbine, Takedown, 5 Shot, Antique	1,000	1,250	825
Model 1893, Various Calibers, Tube Feed, Takedown, Octagon Barrel, Antique	8,000	950	675
Model 1893, Various Calibers, Tube Feed, Takedown, Round Barrel, Antique	800	900	575
Model 1893 over #177304, Various Calibers, Tube Feed, Solid Frame, Octagon Barrel, Modern	500	650	550
Model 1893 over #177304, Various Calibers, Tube Feed, Solid Frame, Round Barrel, Modern	450	550	450
Model 1893 over #177304, Various Calibers, Tube Feed, Solid Frame, Round Barrel, Carbine, Modern	600	750	550
Model 1893 over #177304, Various Calibers, Tube Feed, Takedown, Octagon Barrel, Modern	600	750	525
Model 1893 over #177304, Various Calibers, Tube Feed, Takedown, Round Barrel, Modern	550	700	450
Model 1893 over #177304, Various Calibers, Tube Feed, Sporting Carbine, 5 Shot, Modern	650	800	550
Model 1893 over #177304, Various Calibers, Tube Feed, Sporting Carbine, Takedown, 5 Shot, Modern	800	1,050	750
Model 1893 over #177304, Various Calibers, Tube Feed, Full–Stocked, with Bayonet, Modern	2,500	3,000	1,850
Model 1894, Various Calibers, Tube Feed, Solid Frame, Octagon Barrel, Antique	700	800	575
Model 1894, Various Calibers, Tube Feed, Solid Frame, Round Barrel, Antique	650	750	525
Model 1894, Various Calibers, Tube Feed, Takedown, Octagon Barrel, Antique	700	900	675

	V.G.	Exc	Prior Edition
Model 1894, Various Calibers, Tube Feed, Takedown, Round Barrel, Antique	$650	$850	$650
Model 1894 over #175431, Various Calibers, Tube Feed, Takedown, Octagon Barrel, Modern	550	700	700
Model 1894 over #175431, Various Calibers, Tube Feed, Takedown, Round Barrel, Modern	500	650	550
Model 1894 over #175431, Various Calibers, Tube Feed, Solid Frame, Octagon Barrel, Modern	475	600	575
Model 1894 over #175431, Various Calibers, Tube Feed, Solid Frame, Round Barrel, Modern	475	550	525
Model 1895 Carbine, Various Calibers, Tube Feed, Takedown, Octagon Barrel, Antique	3,500	4,500	975
Model 1895 Carbine over #167531, Various Calibers, Tube Feed, Takedown, Octagon Barrel, Modern	3,000	3,500	950
Model 1895 Lightweight, Various Calibers, Tube Feed, Solid Frame, Antique	1,000	1,500	850
Model 1895 Lightweight over #167531, Various Calibers, Tube Feed, Solid Frame, Octagon Barrel, Modern	1,000	1,250	875
Model 1895 Standard, Various Calibers, Tube Feed, Solid Frame, Antique	1,500	2,000	950
Model 1895 Standard over #167531, Various Calibers, Tube Feed, Solid Frame, Round Barrel, Modern	1,250	1,500	825
Model 1897, .22 L.R.R.F., Tube Feed, Takedown, Antique	700	950	525
Model 1897 over #177197, >22 L.R.R.F., Tube Feed, Takedown, Modern	650	850	475
Model 336, .219 Zipper, Tube Feed, Sporting Crabine, Open Rear Sight, 5 Shot, Modern	400	475	475
Model 336, Various Calibers, Tube Feed, Sporting Carbine, Open Rear Sight, 5 Shot, Modern	225	275	275
Model 336 Marauder, Various Calibers, Tube Feed, Carbine, Open Rar Sight, Straight Grip, Modern	300	350	350
Model 336 Zane Grey, .30–.30 Win., Tube Feed, Octagon Barrel, Open Rear Sight, Modern	300	350	350
Model 336A, Various Calibers, Tube Feed, Sporting Rifle, Open Rear Sight, 5 Shot, Modern	225	275	275

Marlin 336A

	V.G.	Exc	Prior Edition
Model 336A–DL, Various Calibers, Tube Feed, Sporting Rifle, Open Rear Sight, 5 Shot, Checkered Stock, Modern	175	225	225
Model 336C, Various Calibers, Tube Feed, Carbine, Open Rear Sight, Modern	175	225	225
Model 336T, .44 Magnum, Tube Feed, Carbine, Open Rear Sight, Straight Grip, Modern	175	225	225

	V.G.	Exc	Prior Edition
Model 336T, Various Calibers, Tube Feed, Carbine, Open Rear Sight, Straight Grip, Modern......................	$175	$225	$225
Model 36, Various Calibers, Tube Feed, Beavertail Forend, Open Rear Sight, Carbine, Modern........................	225	275	275
Model 36, Various Calibers, Tube Feed, Beavertail Forend, Open Rear Sight, Sporting Carbine, 5 Shot, Modern........................	250	300	300
Model 36A, Various Calibers, Tube Feed, Beavertail Forend, Open Rear Sight, 5 Shot, Modern........................	225	275	275
Model 36DL, Various Calibers, Tube Feed, Fancy Checkering, Open Rar Sight, 5 Shot, Modern........................	350	350	350
Model 39, .22 L.R.R.F., Takedown, Hammer, Octagon Barrel, Modern........................	325	350	350
Model 39 Article II, .22 L.R.R.F., Takedown, Tube Feed, Hammer, Octagon Barrel, Modern........................	275	325	325
Model 39 Article II, .22 L.R.R.F., Takedown, Tube Feed, Hammer, Octagon Barrel, Carbine, Modern........................	325	350	350
Model 39 Century, .22 L.R.R.F., Takedown, Tube Feed, Hammer, Octagon Barrel, Modern........................	300	325	325

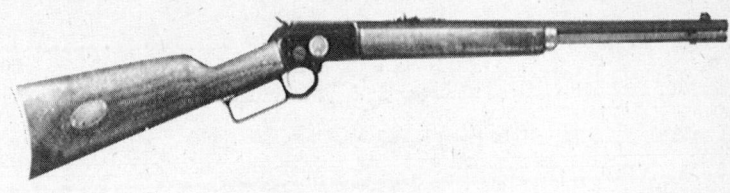

Marlin 39 Century Ltd.

Model 39 M, .22 L.R.R.F., Takedown, Tube Feed, Hammer, Round Barrel, Carbine, Modern........................	275	250	250
Model 39A Mountie, .22 L.R.R.F., Takedown, Tube Feed, Hammer, Round Barrel, Modern........................	175	200	200
Model 39A, .22 L.R.R.F., Takedown, Tube Feed, Hammer, Round Barrel, Modern........................	200	225	225

Marlin 39A

Model 444, .444 Marlin, Tube Feed, Monte Carlo Stock, Open Rear Sight, Straight Grip, Modern........................	225	250	250
Model 56, .22 L.R.R.F., Clip Fed, Open Rear Sight, Monte Carlo Stock, Modern........................	125	150	150
Model 57, .22 L.R.R.F., Tube Feed, Open Rear Sight, Monte Carlo Stock, Modern........................	125	150	150

	V.G.	Exc	Prior Edition
Model 57M, .22 WMR., Tube Feed, Open Rear Sight, Monte Carlo Stock, Modern.................	$150	$175	$175
Model 62, Various Calibers, Clip Fed, Open Rear Sight, Monte Carlo Stock, Modern.................	200	225	225

RIFLE, SEMI-AUTOMATIC

	V.G.	Exc	Prior Edition
Glenfield M40, .22 L.R.R.F., Tube Feed, Modern.................	100	125	125
Glenfield M60, .22 L.R.R.F., Tube Feed, Modern.................	50	75	75
Model 49 DL, .22 L.R.R.F., Tube Feed, Open Rear Sight, Modern.................	75	100	100

Marlin Model 49 DL

	V.G.	Exc	Prior Edition
Model 50, .22 L.R.R.F., Clip Fed, Open Rear Sight, Takedown, Modern.................	75	100	100
Model 50E, .22 L.R.R.F., Clip Fed, Peep Sights, Takedown, Modern.................	75	100	100
Model 88C, .22 L.R.R.F., Tube Feed, Takedown, Open Rear Sight, Modern.................	75	100	100
Model 88DL, .22 L.R.R.F., Tube Feed, Takedown, Peep Sights, Modern.................	100	125	125
Model 89C, .22 L.R.R.F., Clip Fed, Takedown, Open Rear Sight, Modern.................	75	100	100
Model 89DL, .22 L.R.R.F., Clip Fed, Takedown, Peep Sights, Modern.................	100	125	125
Model 98, .22 L.R.R.F., Tube Feed, Solid Frame, Open Rear Sight, Monte Carlo Stock, Modern.................	75	100	100
Model 989 G, .22 L.R.R.F., Clip Fed, Open Rear Sight, Monte Carlo Stock, Modern.................	50	75	75
Model 989, .22 L.R.R.F., Clip Fed, Open Rear Sight, Monte Carlo Stock, Modern.................	50	75	75

Marlin Model 989 M-2

	V.G.	Exc	Prior Edition
Model 99 M–1, .22 L.R.R.F., Tube Feed, Open Rear Sight, Monte Carlo Stock, Modern..	$50	$75	$75

Marlin Model 99 M-1

Model 99 M–2, .22 L.R.R.F., Clip Fed, Open Rear Sight, Modern.........	50	75	75
Model 99, .22 L.R.R.F., Tube Feed, Open Rear Sight, Modern..............	50	75	75
Model 990, .22 L.R.R.F., Tube Feed, Open Rear Sight, Monte Carlo Stock, Modern..	50	75	75
Model 995, .22 L.R.R.F., Clip Fed, Open Rear Sight, Modern...............	50	75	75
Model 99C, .22 L.R.R.F., Tube Feed, Open Rear Sight, Monte Carlo Stock, Modern..	50	75	75
Model 99DL , .22 L.R.R.F., Tube Feed, Open Rear Sight, Monte Carlo Stock, Modern..	50	75	75
Model A–1, .22 L.R.R.F., Clip Fed, Takedown, Open Rear Sight, Modern..	50	75	75
Model A–1E, .22 L.R.R.F., Clip Fed, Takedown, Peep Sights, Modern..	50	75	75

RIFLE, SLIDE ACTION

Model 18, .22 L.R.R.F., Solid Frame, Tube Feed, Hammer, Modern..	250	275	275
Model 20, .22 L.R.R.F., Takedown, Tube Feed, Hammer, Octagon Barrel, Modern...	225	250	250
Model 25, .22 Short R.F., Takedown, Tube Feed, Hammer, Modern..	250	300	350
Model 27, Various Calibers, Takedown,Tube Feed, Hammer, Octagon Barrel, Modern..	200	250	300
Model 27–S, Various Calibers, Takedown,Tube Feed, Hammer, Round Barrel, Modern...	200	250	300
Model 29, .22 L.R.R.F., Takedown, Tube Feed, Hammer, Round Barrel, Modern...	225	275	275
Model 32, .22 L.R.R.F., Takedown, Tube Feed, Hammerless, Octagon Barrel, Modern..	250	275	275
Model 38, .22 L.R.R.F., Takedown, Tube Feed, Hammerless, Octagon Barrel, Modern..	250	275	275

SHOTGUN, BOLT ACTION

Glenfield, 12 Ga. 3", Clip Fed, Modern................................	75	100	100

	V.G.	Exc	Prior Edition
Model 55, 12 Ga. 3", Clip Fed, Adjustable Choke, Modern......................	$100	$125	$125

Marlin Model 55 Slug Gun

Model 55, Various Gauges, Clip Fed, Modern...	75	100	100
Model 55, Various Gauges, Clip Fed, Adjustable Choke, Modern...........	100	125	125
Model 55 Goose Gun, 12 Ga. 3", Clip Fed, Modern................................	150	175	175
Model 55S, 12 Ga. 3", Clip Fed, Modern...	125	150	150
Model Super Goose, 10 Ga. 3½", Clip Fed, Modern...............................	175	200	200

SHOTGUN, DOUBLE BARREL, OVER-UNDER

Model 90, 12 and 16 Gauges, Checkered, Double Triggers, Modern..	350	400	400
Model 90, 12 and 16 Gauges, Checkered, Single Triggers, Modern..	400	450	450
Model 90, 20 and .410 Gauges, Checkered Stock, Double Triggers, Modern..	425	475	475
Model 90, 20 and .410 Gauges, Checkered Stock, Single Triggers, Modern..	475	525	525

SHOTGUN, LEVER ACTION

Four–Tenner, .410 Ga., Tube Feed, Modern..	500	625	625

SHOTGUN, SLIDE ACTION

Glenfield Model 778, 12 Ga., Hammerless, Tube Feed, Modern...........	175	225	225
Model 120, 12 Ga. 3", Hammerless, Tube Feed, Modern.......................	250	300	300
Model 16 A, 12 Ga., Hammer, Tube Feed, Modern................................	250	275	275
Model 16 B, 12 Ga., Hammer, Tube Feed, Checkered Stock, Modern..	350	400	400
Model 16 C, 12 Ga., Hammer, Tube Feed, Checkered Stock, Fancy Wood, Light Engraving, Modern......	450	500	500
Model 16 D, 12 Ga., Hammer, Tube Feed, Checkered Stock, Fancy Wood, Engraved, Modern..	850	1,000	1,000
Model 17, 12 Ga., Hammer, Tube Feed, Modern....................................	400	450	450
Model 1898 A, 12 Ga., Hammer, Tube Feed, Modern.............................	325	375	375
Model 1898 B, 12 Ga., Hammer, Tube Feed, Checkered Stock, Modern..	375	425	425
Model 1898 C, 12 Ga., Hammer, Tube Feed, Checkered Stock, Fancy Wood, Light Engraving, Modern...	775	800	800
Model 1898 D, 12 Ga., Hammer, Tube Feed, Checkered Stock, Fancy Wood, Engraved, Modern..	1,500	1,750	1,750
Model 19 A, 12 Ga., Hammer, Tube Feed, Modern................................	275	300	300
Model 19 B, 12 Ga., Hammer, Tube Feed, Checkered Stock, Modern..	350	400	400
Model 19 C, 12 Ga., Hammer, Tube Feed, Checkered Stock, Fancy Wood, Light Engraving, Modern...	450	500	500

	V.G.	Exc	Prior Edition
Model 19 D, 12 Ga., Hammer, Tube Feed, Checkered Stock, Fancy Wood, Engraved, Modern............................	$900	$1,050	$1,050
Model 21 B, 12 Ga., Hammer, Tube Feed, Checkered Stock, Modern..	350	400	400
MOdel 21 C, 12 Ga., Hammer, Tube Feed, Checkered Stock, Fancy Wood, Light Engraving, Modern.....................	350	500	500
Model 21 D, 12 Ga., Hammer, Tube Feed, Checkered Stock, Fancy Wood, Engraved, Modern...........................	875	1,050	1,050
Model 21 Field, 12 Ga., Hammer, Tube Feed, Modern...........................	250	275	275
Model 24 B, 12 Ga., Hammer, Tube Feed, Checkered Stock, Modern..	350	400	400
Model 24 C, 12 Ga., Hammer, Tube Feed, Checkered Stock, Fancy Wood, Light Engraving, Modern.....................	500	550	550
Model 24 D, 12 Ga., Hammer, Tube Feed, Checkered Stock, Fancy Wood, Engraved, Modern...........................	1,025	1,100	1,100
Model 24 Field, 12 Ga., Hammer, Tube Feed, Modern..........................	250	300	300
Model 26 Field, 12 Ga., Hammer, Tube Feed, Modern..........................	225	275	275
Model 28 A, 12 Ga., Hammerless, Tube Feed, Modern...........................	250	275	275
Model 28 B, 12 Ga., Hammerless, Tube Feed, Checkered Stock, Modern..	350	400	400
Model 28 C, 12 Ga., Hammerless, Tube Feed, Checkered Stock, Fancy Wood, Light Engraving, Modern.....................	425	500	500
Model 28 D, 12 Ga., Hammerless, Tube Feed, Checkered Stock, Fancy Wood, Engraved, Modern...........................	850	1,000	1,000
Model 28 Trap, 12 Ga., Hammerless, Tube Feed, Modern.....................	275	300	300
Model 30 A, 12 Ga., Hammer, Tube Feed, Modern.............................	275	300	300
Model 30 B, 12 Ga., Hammer, Tube Feed, Checkered Stock, Modern..	350	400	400
Model 30 C, 12 Ga., Hammer, Tube Feed, Checkered Stock, Fancy Wood, Light Engraving, Modern.....................	450	500	500
Model 30 D, 12 Ga., Hammer, Tube Feed, Checkered Stock, Fancy Wood, Engraved, Modern...........................	850	1,000	1,000
Model 31 B, 12 Ga., Hammerless, Tube Feed, Checkered Stock, Modern..	350	400	400
Model 31 D, 12 Ga., Hammerless, Tube Feed, Checkered Stock, Fancy Wood, Engraved, Modern...........................	1,000	1,200	1,200
Model 31 Field, 12 Ga., Hammerless, Tube Feed, Modern.....................	250	275	275
Model 31C, 12 Ga., Hammerless, Tube Feed, Checkered Stock, Fancy Wood, Light Engraving, Modern.....................	450	500	500
Model 44 Field, 12 Ga., Hammerless, Tube Feed, Modern.....................	350	375	375
Model 63 Field, 12 Ga., Hammerless, Tube Feed, Modern.....................	325	350	350
Premier Mark I, 12 Ga., Hammerless, Tube Feed, Modern....................	200	225	225
Premier Mark II, 12 Ga., Hammerless, Tube Feed, Modern...................	225	250	250
Premier Mark IV, 12 Ga., Hammerless, Tube Feed, Vent Rib, Modern..	250	300	300

MAROCCINI Frabricca Fucili da Caccia di Luciano Maroccini, Gardone Val Trompia, Italy.

SHOTGUN, DOUBLE BARREL, OVER-UNDER

	V.G.	Exc	Prior Edition
Field Master Commander, 12 Gauge Magnum, Police Style, Detachable Buttstock, Double Triggers, Boxlock, Modern......................	425	475	200
Field Master I, Various Gauges, Checkered Stock, Sling Swivels, Double Triggers, Boxlock, Modern...	325	375	175

	V.G.	Exc	Prior Edition
Field Master II, Various Gauges, Checkered Stock, Single Trigger, Boxlock, Automatic Ejectors, Modern.....................	$350	$425	$250

SHOTGUN, DOUBLE BARREL, SIDE-BY-SIDE

| **Mondial,** 12 Gauge, Checkered Stock, Sling Swivels, Double Triggers, Boxlock, Modern....................... | 100 | 150 | 200 |

MARQUIS OF LORNE Made by Hood Arms Co. Norwich, Conn. c. 1880.

HANDGUN, REVOLVER

| **.22 Short R.F.,** 7 Shot, Spur Trigger, Solid Frame, Single Action, Antique........................ | 150 | 175 | 175 |
| **.32 Short R.F.,** 5 Shot, Spur Trigger, Solid Frame, Single Action, Antique........................ | 175 | 200 | 200 |

MARS Kohout & Spolecnost, Kydne, Czechoslovakia, c. 1925.

HANDGUN, SEMI-AUTOMATIC

| **Mars,** 6.35mm, Clip Fed, Blue, Curio........................ | 200 | 250 | 250 |
| **Mars,** 7.65mm, Clip Fed, Blue, Curio........................ | 250 | 300 | 300 |

MARS Spain, c. 1920.

HANDGUN, SEMI-AUTOMATIC

| **Automat Pistole Mars,** 6.35mm, Clip Fed, Curio.................... | 100 | 150 | 200 |

MARS AUTOMATIC PISTOL SYNDICATE Distributors of the Gabbet Fairfax pistol made by Webley & Scott, Birmingham, England, 1902–1904.

HANDGUN, SEMI-AUTOMATIC

| **.45 Long,** Clip Fed, Blue, Hammer, Curio................... | 12,000 | 15,000 | 15,000 |
| **9mm,** Clip Fed, Blue, Hammer, Curio...................... | 8,000 | 10,000 | 10,000 |

MARSHWOOD Made by Stevens Arms.

SHOTGUN, DOUBLE BARREL, SIDE-BY-SIDE

| **M 315,** Various Gauges, Hammerless, Steel Barrel, Modern.................. | 150 | 175 | 175 |

MARSTON, STANHOPE N.Y.C., c. 1850's.

HANDGUN, PERCUSSION

| **Swivel Breech,** .31, Two Barrels, Ring Trigger, Bar Hammer, Antique........................ | 850 | 1,000 | 850 |

	V.G.	Exc	Prior Edition

MARSTON, WILLIAM W. N.Y.C. 1850–1875.

HANDGUN, PERCUSSION

	V.G.	Exc	Prior Edition
Breech Loader, .35, Half Octagon Barrel, Engraved, Antique..............	$1,800	$2,100	$2,100
Pepperbox, .31, Double Action, 6 Shot, Bar Hammer, Antique...............	500	600	600
Pocket, .31, Bar Hammer, Double Action, Screw Barrel, Antique..	300	375	375
Single Shot, .36, Bar Hammer, Single Action, Screw Barrel, Antique..	350	425	425

MARTE Erquiaga, Muguruzu y Cia., Eibar, Spain, c. 1920.

HANDGUN, SEMI-AUTOMATIC

	V.G.	Exc	Prior Edition
.25 ACP, Clip Fed, Blue, Curio...	125	150	150

MARTIAN Martin a Bascaran, Eibar, Spain 1916–1927.

HANDGUN, SEMI-AUTOMATIC

	V.G.	Exc	Prior Edition
6.35mm, Clip Fed, Eibar Type, Curio.......................................	100	125	150

Martian

	V.G.	Exc	Prior Edition
6.35mm, Clip Fed, Trigger Guard Takedown, Curio................................	200	225	250
7.65mm, Clip Fed, Eibar Type, Curio..	125	150	175
7.65mm, Clip Fed, Trigger Guard Takedown, Curio..............................	225	250	275

MARTIAN COMMERCIAL Martin A Bascaran, Eibar, Spain
1919–1927.

HANDGUN, SEMI-AUTOMATIC

	V.G.	Exc	Prior Edition
6.35, Clip Fed, Eibar Type, Curio..	$125	$150	$150
6.35, Clip Fed, Eibar Type, Curio..	150	175	175

MARTIN, ALEXANDER Glasglow & Aberdeen, Scotland 1922–
1928.

RIFLE, BOLT ACTION

	V.G.	Exc	Prior Edition
.303 British, Sporting Rifle, Express Sights, Engraved, Fancy Wood, Cased, Curio..	950	1,350	1,350

MASSACHUSETTS ARMS Made by Stevens Arms.

SHOTGUN, DOUBLE BARREL, SIDE-BY-SIDE

	V.G.	Exc	Prior Edition
Model 311, Various Gauges, Hammerless, Steel Barrel, Modern.............	150	175	175

SHOTGUN, SINGLESHOT

	V.G.	Exc	Prior Edition
Model 90, Various Gauges, Takedown, Automatic Ejector, Plain, Hammer, Modern..	50	75	75
Model 94, Various Gauges, Takedown, Automatic Ejector, Plain, Hammer, Modern..	50	75	75

MASSACHUSETTS ARMS CO. Chicopee Falls, Mass. 1850–
1866. Also see Adams.

HANDGUN, PERCUSSION

	V.G.	Exc	Prior Edition
Maynard Belt Revolver, .31, 6 Shot, Antique...	800	950	950
Maynard Pocket Revolver, .28, 6 Shot, Antique......................................	600	750	750
Wesson & Leavitt Belt Revolver, .31, 6 Shot, Antique...........................	1,000	1,200	950
Wesson & Leavitt Dragoon Revolver, .40, 6 Shot, Antique...................	2,500	3,000	2,000

MATADOR Made in Spain for Firearms International, Washington, D.C.

SHOTGUN, DOUBLE BARREL, SIDE-BY-SIDE

	V.G.	Exc	Prior Edition
Matador II, 12 or 20 Gauges, Checkered Stock, Single Trigger, Selective Ejectors, Modern..	200	250	250

MATCHLOCK ARMS EXAMPLES

RIFLE, MATCHLOCK

	V.G.	Exc	Prior Edition
.45, India Mid–1600's, 4 Shot, Revolving Cylinder, Light Ornamentation, Brass Furniture, Antique...	4,500	5,000	2,000
.57, Japanese Full Stock Musket, Octagon Barrel, Silver Inlay, Brass Furniture, Antique..	1,000	1,200	750

MAUSER   Germany Gebruder Mauser et Cie from 1854–1890. From 1890 –1994 is known as Mauser–Werke. 1994–Date Mauser–Werke Oberndorf Waff Ensysteme GmbH. Also see German Military, Luger.

HANDGUN, REVOLVER

	V.G.	Exc	Prior Edition
Colt Type, .38 Spec., Double Action, 6 Shot, 2" Barrel, Curio	$125	$175	$175
M 78 Zig Zag, 10.6mm, Tip–Up, Antique	3,000	3,500	3,500

Mauser M 78 Zig Zag

	V.G.	Exc	Prior Edition
M 78 Zig Zag, 7.6mm, Tip–Up, Antique	2,500	3,000	3,000
M 78 Zig Zag, 9mm Mauser, Tip–Up, Antique	2,500	3,000	3,000
M 78 Zig Zag, Tip–Up, Fancy Engraving, Antique	3,500	5,000	5,000

HANDGUN, SEMI-AUTOMATIC

	V.G.	Exc	Prior Edition
Chinese Shansei, .45 ACP, With Shoulder Stock, Curio	3,750	4,500	4,800
HSc 1 of 5,000, .380 ACP, Blue, Post–War, Cased, Modern	200	300	300
HSc Army, .32 ACP., Nazi–Proofed, Curio	325	375	375
HSc Navy, .32 ACP., Nazi–Proofed, Curio	500	575	575
HSc NSDAP SA, .32 ACP., Nazi–Proofed, Curio	600	750	750
HSc Police, .32 ACP., Nazi–Proofed, Curio	300	375	375
HSc Swiss, .32 ACP., Curio	950	1,200	1,200
HSc, .32 ACP, Nickel Plated, Post–War, Modern	275	300	275
HSc, .32 ACP, Post–War, Blue, Modern	250	275	250
HSc, .32 ACP. Pre–War, Nazi–Proofed, Commercial, Curio	425	500	325
HSc, .32 ACP. Pre–War, Prototype, Commercial, Curio	300	325	325
HSc, .380 ACP, Blue, Post–War, Modern	250	275	250
HSc, .380 ACP, Nickel Plated, Post–War, Modern	275	300	275
M 1896 (Early), 7.63 Mauser, Small Ring, Curio	3,000	3,500	2,400
M 1896 (Italian), 7.63 Mauser, Slabside, Curio	3,000	3,500	2,800
M 1896 Banner, 7.63 Mauser, Curio	2,000	2,250	2,250
M 1896 Bolo, 7.63 Mauser, Post–War, Curio	2,000	2,500	1,750
M 1896 French Police, 7.63 Mauser, Curio	1,500	1,750	2,100
M 1896 Persian, 7.63 Mauser, Curio	2,000	2,500	1,950
M 1896 Police, 7.63 Mauser, Curio	1,050	1,250	1,250
M 1896 System Mauser, 7.63 Mauser, With Conehammer, Curio	7,000	8,500	1,750

	V.G.	Exc	Prior Edition
M 1896 Turkish, 7.63 Mauser, Conehammer, Curio	$3,500	$4,000	$5,800
M 1896 WW I, 7.63 Mauser, Military, Curio	750	1,000	1,150

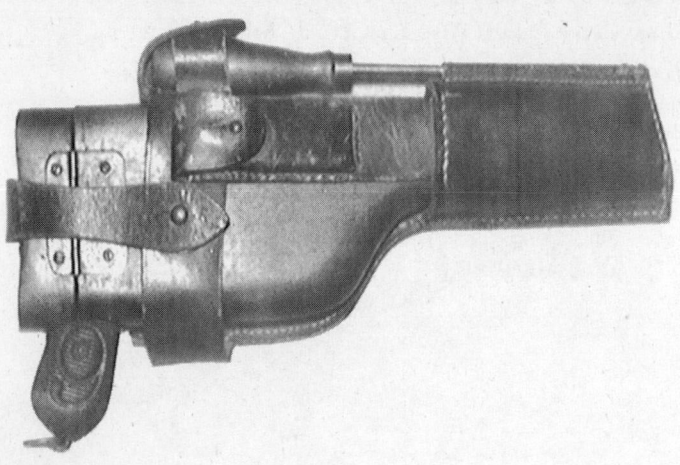

Mauser M 1896 WWI with Holster Stock

	V.G.	Exc	Prior Edition
M 1896 WW I, 9mm Luger, Military, Curio	1,000	1,250	1,450
M 1896, 7.63 Mauser, 10 Shot, Conehammer, Curio	2,500	2,750	4,500

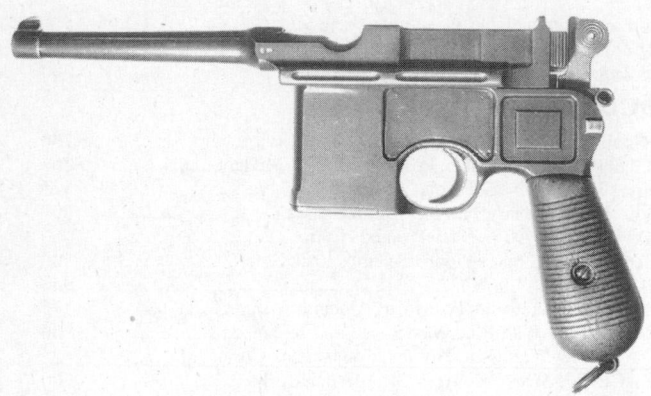

Mauser 1896 Conehammer

	V.G.	Exc	Prior Edition
M 1896, 7.63 Mauser, 10 Shot, Fixed Sight Conehammer, Curio	2,750	3,000	4,000
M 1896, 7.63 Mauser, Conehammer with Shoulder Stock, Curio	3,250	3,750	4,800
M 1896, 7.63 Mauser, Fixed Sight Conehammer with Shoulder Stock, Curio	3,750	4,250	4,300
M 1896, 7.63 Mauser, Flatside, Curio	2,000	2,200	2,200
M 1896, 7.63 Mauser, Pre–War, Commercial, Curio	1,000	1,250	1,400
M 1896, 7.63 Mauser, Transitional, Curio	2,250	2,500	2,500

	V.G.	Exc	Prior Edition

M 1896, Factory Engraving Add 300%
M 1896, Original Holster Stock Add 20%–35%
M 1896, 20–Shot Model Add 50%–80%
M 1896, 40–Shot Model Add 100%
M 1896, 6–Shot Model Add 75%–100%
M 1906/08, 7.63 Mauser, Clip Fed, Curio...\$25,000 \$30,000 \$30,000
M 1910, .25 ACP, Clip Fed, Curio.. 300 350 350

Mauser M 1910

M 1912/14, 9mm Luger, Clip Fed, Curio... 17,500 20,000 20,000

	V.G.	Exc	Prior Edition
M 1914 Army, .32 ACP, Clip Fed, Curio..	$275	$325	$450

Mauser M 1914

	V.G.	Exc	Prior Edition
M 1914 Early, .32 ACP, Clip Fed, Curio..	225	275	375
M 1914 Humpback, .32 ACP, Long Barrel, Clip Fed, Curio..................	2,500	2,700	2,700
M 1914 Navy, .32 ACP, Clip Fed, Curio...	300	350	800
M 1914 Post–War, .32 ACP, Clip Fed, Modern......................................	175	225	375
M 1914 War Commercial, .32 ACP, Clip Fed, Curio.............................	200	250	400
M 1934 Navy, .32 ACP, Clip Fed, Curio...	500	600	900
M 1934 Police, .32 ACP, Clip Fed, Curio...	300	350	750
M 1934, .32 ACP, Clip Fed, Curio..	250	300	425
New Model Carbine, 9mm Luger, 12" Barrel, Grip Safety, Modern.......	4,500	5,500	5,500
Parabellum Bulgarian, .30 Luger, Grip Safety, Commemorative, Modern...	1,000	1,250	1,500
Parabellum Cartridge Counter, 9mm Luger, Grip Safety, Commemorative, Modern...	2,000	2,500	3,000
Parabellum P.O8, .30 Luger, 6" Barrel, Grip Safety, Modern...............	450	500	650
Parabellum PO 8, .30 Luger, 4" Barrel, Grip Safety, Modern................	575	625	625
Parabellum PO 8, 9mm Luger, Various Barrel Lengths, Grip Safety, Modern...	500	600	600
Parabellum Russian, .30 Luger, Grip Safety, Commemorative, Modern...	1,000	1,250	1,500
Parabellum Sport, .30 or 9mm Luger, Heavy Barrel, Target Sights, Modern...	1,200	1,500	1,500
Parabellum Swiss, 7.65mm, 6" Barrel, Grip Safety, Modern..................	400	450	550
Parabellum Swiss, 9mm Luger, 4" Barrel, Grip Safety, Modern............	450	550	550

	V.G.	Exc	Prior Edition
W T P I, 6.35mm, Clip Fed, Modern...	$250	$300	$450

Mauser W T P

W T P II, 6.35mm, Clip Fed, Modern..	450	500	425

RIFLE, BOLT ACTION

Model 10 Varminter, .22–250 Post–War, Heavy Barrel, Monte Carlo Stock, Checkered Stock, Modern...	1,400	1,550	1,550
Model 2000, Various Calibers, Post–War, Monte Carlo Stock, Checkered Stock, Modern......................	300	350	350
Model 3000, Various Calibers, Post–War, Left–Hand, Magnum Action, Monte Carlo Stock, Checkered Stock, Modern............................	425	475	475
Model 3000, Various Calibers, Post–War, Left–Hand, Monte Carlo Stock, Checkered Stock, Modern................................	450	525	400
Model 3000, Various Calibers, Post–War, Magnum Action, Monte Carlo Stock, Checkered Stock, Modern......................................	475	550	425
Model 3000, Various Calibers, Post–War, Monte Carlo Stock, Modern..................	400	475	375
Model 4000, Various Calibers, Varmint, Checkering, Flared, Modern..................	350	400	400
Model 66S, Various Calibers, Post–War, Takedown, Monte Carlo Stock, Checkered Stock, Modern......................	1,250	1,500	1,200
Model 66S Safari, Various Calibers, Post–War, Takedown, Monte Carlo Stock, Checkered Stock, Magnum, Modern...................................	1,750	2,000	1,500
Model 98, Various Calibers, Sporting Rifle, Full–Stocked, Pre–WW2, Military, Commercial, Modern......................	325	375	375
Model A, Various Calibers, Sporting Rifle, Pre–WW2, Magnum Action, Curio..................	3,000	3,500	2,500
Model A, Various Calibers, Sporting Rifle, Pre–WW2, Short Action, Curio..................	3,250	3,500	3,500
Model A British, Various Calibers, Sporting Rifle, Express Sights, Pre–WW2, Curio..................	3,000	4,000	4,000
Model A British, Various Calibers, Sporting Rifle, Peep Sights, Pre–WW2, Octagon Barrel, Set Trigger, Curio...	2,800	4,500	4,500

	V.G.	Exc	Prior Edition
Model B, Various Calibers, Sporting Rifle, Pre–WW2, Octagon Barrel, Set Trigger, Curio	$2,000	$2,500	$3,000
Model B, Various Calibers, Sporting Rifle, Pre–WW2, Set Trigger, Express Sights, Curio	2,000	2,250	2,500
Model DSM 34, .22 L.R.R.F., Pre–WW2, Singleshot, Tangent Sights, Military Style, Stock, Curio	275	325	325
Model EL 320, .22 L.R.R.F., Pre–WW2, Singleshot, Sporting Rifle, Adjustable Sights, Curio	225	275	275
Model EN 310, .22 L.R.R.F., Pre–WW2, Singleshot, Open Rear Sight, Curio	200	250	250
Model ES 340, .22 L.R.R.F., Pre–WW2, Singleshot, Tangent Sights, Sporting Rifle, Curio	250	300	300
Model ES 340B, .22 L.R.R.F., Pre–WW2, Singleshot, Tangent Sights, Sporting Rifle, Curio	250	300	300
Model ES 340B, .22 L.R.R.F., Pre–WW2, Singleshot, Target Sights, Target Stock, Curio	350	400	400
Model ES 350, .22 L.R.R.F., Pre–WW2, Singleshot, Target Sights, Target Stock, Curio	400	450	450
Model K, Various Calibers, Sporting Rifle, Pre–WW2, Short Action, Curio	425	500	500
Model KKW, .22 L.R.R.F., Pre–WW2, Singleshot, Tangent Sights, Military Style Stock, Curio	350	400	400
Model M, Various Calibers, Express Sights, Carbine, Modern	550	700	700
Model M, Various Calibers, Sporting Rifle, Pre–WW2, Full–Stocked, Tangent Sights, Carbine, Curio	450	500	500
Model MM 410, .22 L.R.R.F., Pre–WW2, 5 Shot Clip, Tangent Sights, Sporting Rifle, Curio	300	375	300
Model MM 410B, .22 L.R.R.F., Pre–WW2, 5 Shot Clip, Tangent Sights, Sporting Rifle, Curio	350	425	375
Model MS 350B, .22 L.R.R.F., Pre–WW2, 5 Shot Clip, Target Sights, Target Stock, Curio	425	500	450
Model MS 420, .22 L.R.R.F., Pre–WW2, 5 Shot Clip, Tangent Sights, Sporting Rifle, Curio	275	350	275
Model MS 420B, .22 L.R.R.F., Pre–WW2, 5 Shot Clip, Tangent Sights, Target Stock, Curio	350	400	400
Model S, Various Calibers, Sporting Rifle, Pre–WW2, Full–Stocked, Set Trigger, Carbine, Curio	2,000	2,250	475
Standard, Various Calibers, Sporting Rifle, Set Trigger, Pre–WW1, Curio	2,500	2,750	500
Various Calibers, Sporting Rifle, Pre–WWI, Military, Commercial, Curio	1,500	1,750	1,750
Various Calibers, Sporting Rifle, Set Trigger, Pre–WWI, Short Action, Curio	2,500	3,250	3,250
Various Calibers, Sporting Rifle, Set Trigger, Pre–WWI, Carbine, Full–Stocked, Curio	1,750	2,250	2,250

RIFLE, SEMI-AUTOMATIC

	V.G.	Exc	Prior Edition
M 1896, 7.63 Mauser, Carbine, Curio	4,000	4,500	4,500

RIFLE, DOUBLE BARREL, OVER-UNDER

	V.G.	Exc	Prior Edition
Model Aristocrat, .375 H & H Magnum, Fancy Checkering, Engraved, Open Rear Sight, Cheekpiece, Double Trigger, Modern	1,750	2,000	1,500
Model Aristocrat, Various Calibers, Fancy Checkering, Engraved, Open Rear Sight, Checkpiece, Double Trigger, Modern	1,250	1,500	1,500

	V.G.	Exc	Prior Edition

SHOTGUN, BOLT ACTION

	V.G.	Exc	Prior Edition
16 Gauge, Modern	$100	$125	$125

SHOTGUN, DOUBLE BARREL, OVER-UNDER

	V.G.	Exc	Prior Edition
Model 610, 12 Gauge, Skeet Grade, with Conversion Kit, Vent Rib, Checkered Stock, Modern	1,500	1,600	1,600
Model 610, 12 Gauge, Trap Grade, Vent Rib, Checkered Stock, Modern	750	900	900
Model 620, 12 Gauge, Automatic Ejector, Double Trigger, Vent Rib, Fancy Wood, Modern	800	875	875
Model 620, 12 Gauge, Automatic Ejector, Single Selective Trigger, Vent Rib, Fancy Wood, Modern	850	1,000	1,000
Model 620, 12 Gauge, Automatic Ejector, Single Trigger, Vent Rib, Fancy Wood, Modern	700	950	950
Model 71E, 12 Gauge, Field Grade, Double Trigger, Checkered Stock, Modern	325	375	375
Model 72E, 12 Gauge, Skeet Grade, Checkered Stock, Light Engraving, Modern	450	500	500
Model 72E, 12 Gauge, Trap Grade, Checkered Stock, Light Engraving, Modern	450	500	500

SHOTGUN, DOUBLE BARREL, SIDE-BY-SIDE

	V.G.	Exc	Prior Edition
Model 496, 12 Gauge, Trap Grade, Vent Rib, Single Trigger, Checkered Stock, Box Lock, Modern	500	575	575
Model 545, 12 and 20 Gauges, Single Trigger, Recoil Pad, Checkered Stock, Box Lock, Modern	450	500	500
Model 580, 12 Gauge, Engraved, Fancy Checkering, Fancy Wood, Modern	800	975	975

SHOTGUN, SINGLESHOT

	V.G.	Exc	Prior Edition
Model 496, 12 Gauge, Trap Grade, Engraved, Checkered Stock, Modern	500	550	550
Model 496 Competition, 12 Gauge, Trap Grade, Engraved, Fancy Wood, Fancy Checkering, Modern	650	725	725

MAYER & SOEHNE Arnsberg, W. Germany.

HANDGUN, REVOLVER

	V.G.	Exc	Prior Edition
Target, .22 L.R.R.F., Break Top, 5 Shot, Target Sights, Double Action, Modern	100	125	125

MAYESCH Lancaster, Pa. 1760–1770. See Kentucky Rifles and Pistols.

MAYOR, FRANCOIS Lausanne, Switzerland.

HANDGUN, SEMI-AUTOMATIC

	V.G.	Exc	Prior Edition
Rochat, 6.35mm, Clip Fed, Modern	500	650	650

MBA San Ramon, Calif. 1965–1975.

HANDGUN, ROCKET PISTOL

Gyrojet, For Nickel Plating, Add 10%–15%

	V.G.	Exc	Prior Edition
Gyrojet, For U.S. Property Stamping Add 75%–100%			
Gyrojet Mark I Model A, Clip Fed, Modern...............................	$550	$650	$700
Gyrojet Mark I Model A Exp., Clip Fed, Modern..................................	800	950	1,350
Gyrojet Mark I Carbine Model B Exp., Clip Fed, Modern...................	1,000	1,250	1,000
Gyrojet Mark I Carbine Model B Snub, Clip Fed, Modern................	950	1,100	650
Gyrojet Mark I Carbine Model B, Clip Fed, Modern...........................	750	1,000	650
Gyrojet Mark I Carbine Model C, Clip Fed, Modern...........................	650	750	500
Gyrojet Mark I, Clip Fed, Presentation Cased with Accessories, Modern..	1,500	1,850	1,850

MCCOY, ALEXANDER Philadelphia, Pa. 1779. See Kentucky Rifles.

MCCOY, KESTER Lancaster, Pa. See Kentucky Rifles and Pistols.

MCCULLOUGH, GEORGE Lancaster, Pa. 1770–1773. See Kentucky Rifles.

MEIER, ADOLPHUS St. Louis, Mo. 1845–1850.

RIFLE, PERCUSSION

.58 Plains Type, Double Barrel, Side by Side, Half–Octagon Barrel, Rifled, Plain, Antique...	2,000	2,500	2,000

MELIOR Liege, Belgium, Made by Robar et Cie. 1900–1959.

HANDGUN, SEMI-AUTOMATIC

New Model Pocket, .22 L.R.R.F., Clip Fed, Modern................................	150	175	175
New Model Pocket, .380 ACP, Clip Fed, Modern....................................	150	175	175
New Model Pocket, 7.65mm, Clip Fed, Modern.....................................	125	150	150
New Model Vest Pocket, .22 Long R.F., Clip Fed, Modern.....................	125	150	150
New Model Vest Pocket, 6.35mm, Clip Fed, Modern.............................	150	175	175
Old Model Pocket, 7.65mm, Clip Fed, Modern......................................	150	175	175
Old Model Vest Pocket, 6.35mm, Clip Fed, Modern..............................	150	175	175
Target, .22 L.R.R.F., Clip Fed, Long Barrel, Modern..............................	200	250	250

MENDOZA Mexico City, Mexico.

HANDGUN, SINGLESHOT

K–62, .22 L.R.R.F., Modern...	100	125	125

RIFLE, BOLT ACTION

Modelo Conejo, .22 L.R.R.F., 2 Shot, Modern..	125	175	175

	V.G.	Exc	Prior Edition

MENTA Made by August Menz, Suhl, Germany, c. 1916.

HANDGUN, REVOLVER

7.65mm, Clip Fed, Commercial, Curio.. $250 $300 $225

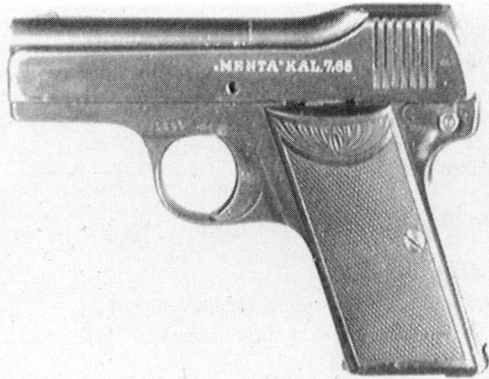

Menta .32

7.65mm, Clip Fed, Military, Curio... 300 350 250

MENZ, AUGUST Suhl, Germany 1912–1937. Also see Menta.

HANDGUN, SEMI-AUTOMATIC

Lilliput, 6.35mm, Clip Fed, Curio... 300 350 350
Model I, 7.65mm, Clip Fed, Curio... 250 300 300

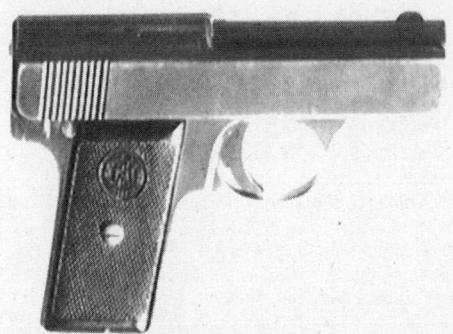

Menz Model I

Model II, 7.65mm, Clip Fed, Curio... 275 325 350
Model III, 7.65mm, Clip Fed, Hammer, Curio... 350 425 400

	V.G.	Exc	Prior Edition
P & B Special, .380 ACP, Clip Fed, Hammer, Double Action, Curio	$725	$825	$825
P & B Special, 7.65mm, Clip Fed, Hammer, Double Action, Curio	500	575	575

MERCURY Made by Robar et Cie., Liege, Belgium for Tradewinds.

RIFLE, SEMI-AUTOMATIC

	V.G.	Exc	Prior Edition
M 622 VP, .22 L.R.R.F., Clip Fed, Modern	100	300	300

SHOTGUN, DOUBLE BARREL, SIDE-BY-SIDE

	V.G.	Exc	Prior Edition
Mercury, 10 Gauge 3", Hammerless, Magnum, Checkered Stock, Double Trigger, Modern	170	350	350
Mercury, 12 and 20 Gauges, Hammerless, Magnum, Checkered Stock, Double Trigger, Modern	160	325	325

MERIDEN FIRE ARMS CO. Meriden, Conn. 1907–1909.

HANDGUN, REVOLVER

	V.G.	Exc	Prior Edition
.38 S & W, 5 Shot, Top Break, Hammerless, Double Action, Modern	100	125	125

RIFLE, SINGLESHOT

	V.G.	Exc	Prior Edition
Model 10, .22 L.R.R.F., Modern	50	75	75

RIFLE, SLIDE ACTION

	V.G.	Exc	Prior Edition
Model 15, .22 L.R.R.F., Tube Feed, Modern	200	225	225

MERKEL Gebruder Merkel, Suhl, Germany, from 1920. After WW II, VEB Fahrzeug u. Jagdwaffenwerk Ernst Thalmann, Suhl, East Germany.

COMBINATION WEAPON, DRILLING

	V.G.	Exc	Prior Edition
Model 142, Various Calibers, Pre–WW2, Double Trigger, Engraved, Checkered Stock, Curio	2,900	3,250	3,250
Model 142, Various Calibers, Pre–WW2, Double Trigger, Checkered Stock, Curio	3,000	3,500	3,500
Model 145, Various Calibers, Pre–WW2, Double Trigger, Engraved, Checkered Stock, Curio	2,500	2,750	3,000

COMBINATION WEAPON, OVER-UNDER

	V.G.	Exc	Prior Edition
Model 210, Various Calibers, Pre–WW2, Engraved, Checkered Stock, Curio	1,200	2,250	1,400
Model 211E, Various Calibers, Engraved, Checkered Stock, Automatic Ejector, Modern	3,000	3,500	2,250
Model 213E, Various Calibers, Sidelock, Fancy Checkering, Fancy Engraving, Automatic Ejector, Modern	5,500	6,500	3,800
Model 313E, Various Calibers, Sidelock, Fancy Checkering, Fancy Engraving, Automatic Ejector, Modern	6,750	7,250	7,250

RIFLE, DOUBLE BARREL, OVER-UNDER

	V.G.	Exc	Prior Edition
Model 220E, Various Calibers, Pre–WW2, Checkered Stock, Engraved, Curio	6,500	7,500	6,500

	V.G.	Exc	Prior Edition
Model 221E, Various Calibers, Engraved, Checkered Stock, Automatic Ejector, Curio	$6,500	$7,500	$9,000
Model 323E, Various Calibers, Sidelock, Fancy Checkering, Fancy Engraving, Automatic Ejector, Modern	15,000	17,500	15,000

SHOTGUN, DOUBLE BARREL, OVER-UNDER

	V.G.	Exc	Prior Edition
Model 100, Various Gauges, Pre–WW2, Plain Barrel, Checkered Stock, Curio	850	1,000	1,100
Model 100, Various Gauges, Pre–WW2, Raised Matted Rib, Checkered Stock, Curio	1,000	1,250	1,200
Model 101, Various Gauges, Pre–WW2, Raised Matted Rib, Checkered Stock, Light Engraving, Curio	1,050	1,250	1,250
Model 101E, Various Gauges, Pre–WW2, Raised Matted Rib, Checkered Stock, Light Engraving, Automatic Ejector, Curio	1,100	1,350	1,350
Model 200, Various Gauges, Pre–WW2, Raised Matted Rib, Checkered Stock, Light Engraving, Curio	950	1,200	1,200
Model 201, Various Gauges, Pre–WW2, Raised Matted Rib, Checkered Stock, Engraved, Curio	1,250	1,500	1,400
Model 201E, Various Gauges, Pre–WW2, Raised Matted Rib, Checkered Stock, Engraved, Automatic Ejector, Curio	1,500	1,750	1,500
Model 202, Various Gauges, Pre–WW2, Raised Matted Rib, Fancy Checkering, Fancy Engraving, Curio	2,000	2,250	2,200
Model 202E, Various Gauges, Pre–WW2, Raised Matted Rib, Fancy Checkering, Fancy Engraving, Automatic Engraving, Curio	2,250	2,500	2,600
Model 203E, Various Gauges, Sidelock, Fancy Checkering, Fancy Engraving, Automatic Ejector, Modern	2,650	3,000	3,000
Model 204E, Various Gauges, Pre–WW2, Sidelock, Fancy Checkering, Fancy Engraving, Automatic Ejector, Curio	4,250	4,700	4,700
Model 300, Various Gauges, Pre–WW2, Raised Matted Rib, Checkered Stock, Engraved, Curio	1,750	2,000	2,000
Model 300E, Various Gauges, Pre–WW2, Raised Matted Rib, Checkered Stock, Engraved, Automatic Ejector, Curio	1,950	2,200	2,200
Model 301, Various Gauges, Pre–WW2, Raised Matted Rib, Fancy Checkering, Engraved, Curio	3,500	4,000	4,000
Model 301E, Various Gauges, Pre–WW2, Raised Matted Rib, Fancy Checkering, Engraved, Automatic Ejector, Curio	4,500	5,000	5,000
Model 302, Various Gauges, Pre–WW2, Raised Matted Rib, Fancy Checkering, Fancy Engraving, Automatic Ejector, Curio	7,250	7,500	7,500
Model 303E, Various Gauges, Sidelock, Single Selective Trigger, Automatic Ejector, Fancy Engraving, Fancy Checkering, Modern	9,500	11,000	11,000

SHOTGUN, DOUBLE BARREL, SIDE-BY-SIDE

	V.G.	Exc	Prior Edition
Model 127, Various Gauges, Pre–WW2, Sidelock, Fancy Engraving, Fancy Checkering, Automatic Ejector, Curio	15,000	17,500	20,000
Model 130, Various Gauges, Pre–WW2, Fancy Engraving, Fancy Checkering, Automatic Ejector, Curio	8,500	10,000	10,000
Model 147E, Various Gauges, Fancy Checkering, Fancy Engraving, Modern	1,250	1,400	1,400
Model 147E, Various Gauges, Fancy Checkering, Fancy Engraving, Single Selective Trigger, Modern	1,450	1,600	1,600
Model 147S, Various Gauges, Fancy Checkering, Fancy Engraving, Sidelock, Modern	3,250	3,600	3,600
Model 147S, Various Gauges, Fancy Checkering, Fancy Engraving, Sidelock, Single Selective Trigger, Modern	4,000	4,600	4,600
Model 47E, Various Gauges, Checkered Stock, Engraved, Modern	850	1,000	1,000

	V.G.	Exc	Prior Edition
Model 47E, Various Gauges, Single Selective Trigger, Checkered Stock, Engraved, Modern....................	$950	$1,100	$1,100
Model 47S, Various Gauges, Sidelock, Checkered Stock, Engraved, Modern....................	2,500	2,800	2,800
Model 47S, Various Gauges, Sidelock, Single Selective Trigger, Checkered Stock, Engraved, Modern....................	2,750	3,000	3,000

MERRILL CO. Formerly in Rockwell City, Iowa, now in Fullerton, Calif.

HANDGUN, SINGLESHOT

Sportsman, For Extra 14" Barrel and Dies Add $125.00–$185.00
Sportsman, For Extra Barrel Add $75.00–$110.00
Sportsman, Wrist Attachment Add $15.00–$25.00

Sportsman, Various Calibers, Target Pistol, Top Break, Adjustable Sights, Vent Rib, Modern....................	300	350	450

MERRIMAC ARMS & MFG. CO. Newburyport, Mass. Absorbed by Brown Mfg. Co. Worcester, Mass. 1861–1866. Also see Ballard.

HANDGUN, SINGLESHOT

Southerner, .41 Short R.F., Derringer, Iron Frame, Light Engraving, Antique....................	500	550	475

RIFLE, DOUBLE BARREL, SIDE-BY-SIDE

Various Calibers, Octagon Barrel, Antique....................	950	1,200	1,200

SHOTGUN, SINGLESHOT

20 Gauge, Falling Block, Antique....................	250	300	300

MERVEILLEUX Rouchouse, Paris, France.

HANDGUN, MANUAL REPEATER

Palm Pistol, 6mm, Engraved, Nickel Plated, Curio....................	600	750	650

MERWIN & BRAY Worcester, Mass. 1864–1868. Became Merwin & Simpkins in 1868 and also Merwin–Taylor & Simpkins the same year, also within the same year became Merwin, Hulbert & Co. Also see Ballard, Merwin, Hulbert & Co.

HANDGUN, REVOLVER

"Navy," .32 Short R.F., 6 Shot, Single Action, Solid Frame, Finger–Rest Trigger Guard, Antique....................	400	475	475
"Navy," .38 Short R.F., 6 Shot, Single Action, Solid Frame, Finger–Rest Trigger Guard, Antique....................	475	550	550
"Original," .28 Cup Primed Cartridge, 6 Shot, Single Action, Spur Trigger, Tip–Up, Antique....................	600	675	675
"Original," .30 Cup Primed Cartridge, 6 Shot, Single Action, Spur Trigger, Tip–Up, Antique....................	650	725	725
"Original," .42 Cup Primed Cartridge, 6 Shot, Single Action, Spur Trigger, Tip–Up, Antique....................	700	775	775

	V.G.	Exc	Prior Edition
"Original," Various Cup–Primed Calibers, Extra Cylinder, Percussion, Add $95.00–$160.00			
.22 Short R.F., 7 Shot, Single Action, Solid Frame, Spur Trigger, Antique....................	$150	$200	$200
.28 Cup Primed Cartridge, 6 Shot, Single Action, Spur Trigger, Solid Frame, Antique....................	150	200	200
.30 Cup Primed Cartridge, 6 Shot, Single Action, Spur Trigger, Solid Frame, Antique....................	175	225	225
.31 R.F., 6 Shot, Single Action, Solid Frame, Spur Trigger, Antique....................	125	175	175
.32 Short R.F., 6 Shot, Single Action, Solid Frame, Spur Trigger, Antique....................	125	175	175
.42 Cup Primed Cartridge, 6 Shot, Single Action, Spur Trigger, Solid Frame, Antique....................	200	250	250
.42 Cup Primed Cartridge, 6 Shot, Single Action, Spur Trigger, Solid Frame, 6" Barrel, Antique....................	375	425	425
Reynolds, .25 Short R.F., 5 Shot, Single Action, Spur Trigger, 3" Barrel, Antique....................	175	200	200

HANDGUN, SINGLESHOT

	V.G.	Exc	Prior Edition
.32 Short R.F., Side–Swing Barrel, Brass Frame, 3" Barrel, Spur Trigger, Antique....................	225	275	200

MERWIN, HULBERT & CO. Successors to Merwin & Bray, et al. in 1868, and became Hulbert Bros. in 1892. Out of business in 1896.

HANDGUN, REVOLVER

	V.G.	Exc	Prior Edition
Army Model, "Safety Hammer," Add $65.00–$100.00			
Army Model, .44–40 WCF, Belt Pistol, 7" Barrel, Double Action, Round Butt, 6 Shot, Antique....................	750	900	700
Army Model, .44–40 WCF, Belt Pistol, 7" Barrel, Single Action, Square Butt, 6 Shot, Antique....................	900	1,250	750
Army Model, .44–40 WCF, Pocket Pistol, 3½" Barrel, Double Action, Round Butt, 6 Shot, Antique....................	600	750	650

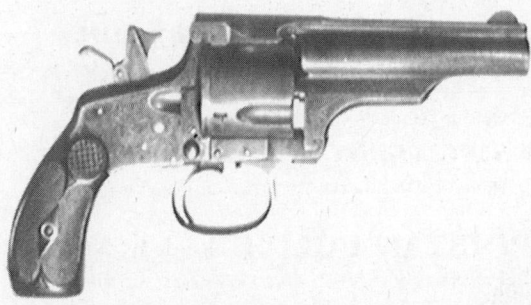

Merwin, Hulbert Pocket D.A.

	V.G.	Exc	Prior Edition

Army Model, .44–40 WCF, Pocket Pistol, 3½" Barrel, Single
Action, Square–Butt, 6 Shot, Antique.. $600 $675 $675

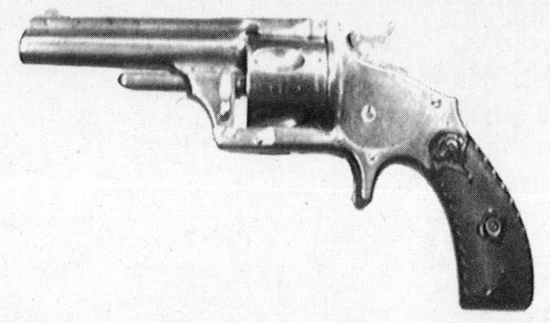

Merwin, Hulbert Pocket S.A.

Army Model, Extra Barrel, Add $200.00–$300.00
Pocket Model, .32 S & W, 5 Shot, Double Action, Antique..................... 300 350 250
Target Model, .32 S & W, 7 Shot, Double Action, Antique.................... 325 375 275

MESSERSMITH, JACOB Lancaster, Pa. 1779–1782. See Kentucky Rifles and Pistols.

METEOR Made by Stevens Arms.

RIFLE, BOLT ACTION
Model 52, .22 L.R.R.F., Singleshot, Takedown, Modern........................... 25 50 50

METROPOLITAN Made by Crescent for Siegel Cooper Co., N.Y.C., c. 1900.

SHOTGUN, DOUBLE BARREL, SIDE-BY-SIDE
Various Gauges, Hammerless, Damascus Barrel, Modern....................... 150 175 175
Various Gauges, Hammerless, Steel Barrel, Modern................................ 175 200 200
Various Gauges, Outside Hammers, Damascus Barrel, Modern............. 150 175 175

SHOTGUN, SINGLESHOT
Various Gauges, Hammer, Steel Barrel, Modern...................................... 50 75 75

METROPOLITAN POLICE Made by Norwich Falls Pistol Co. Norwich, Conn., c. 1885.

HANDGUN, REVOLVER
.32 Short R.F., 5 Shot, Spur Trigger, Solid Frame, Single Action,
Antique.. 125 175 175

	V.G.	Exc	Prior Edition

METZGER, J. Lancaster, Pa., c. 1728. See Kentucky Rifles.

MEUHIRTER, S. See Kentucky Rifles.

MEXICAN MILITARY

HANDGUN, SEMI-AUTOMATIC

	V.G.	Exc	Prior Edition
Obregon, .45 ACP, Clip Fed, Military, Modern	$1,750	$2,000	$375

RIFLE, BOLT ACTION

M1902 Mauser, 7mm, Military, Curio	275	300	175
M1936 Mauser, 7mm, Military, Curio	250	275	200

RIFLE, SEMI-AUTOMATIC

M1908 Mondragon, 7mm, Clip Fed, S.I.G., Curio	2,250	3,000	800

MIDLAND Imported from England by Jana International, c. 1973.

RIFLE, BOLT ACTION

Midland, Various Calibers, Checkered Stock, Open Sights, Modern	225	275	275

MIIDA Tradename of Marubeni America Corp. on Japanese shotguns.

SHOTGUN, DOUBLE BARREL, OVER-UNDER

Model 612, 12 Gauge, Field Grade, Checkered Stock, Light Engraving, Single Selective Trigger, Vent Rib, Modern	700	850	850
Model 2100, 12 Gauge, Skeet Grade, Checkered Stock, Engraved, Single Selective Trigger, Vent Rib, Modern	800	750	950
Model 2200 S, 12 Gauge, Skeet Grade, Checkered Stock, Engraved, Single Selective Trigger, wide Vent Rib, Modern	900	800	1,050
Model 2200 T, 12 Gauge, Trap Grade, Checkered Stock, Engraved, Single Selective Trigger, Wide Vent Rib, Modern	1,000	800	1,150
Model 2300 S, 12 Gauge, Skeet Grade, Fancy Wood, Engraved, Single Selective Trigger, Vent Rib, Modern	1,100	850	1,300
Model 2300 T, 12 Gauge, Trap Grade, Fancy Wood, Engraved, Single Selective Trigger, Vent Rib, Modern	1,250	850	1,400
Model Grandee, 12 Gauge, Fancy Engraving, Fancy Wood, Gold Inlays, Single Selective Trigger, Vent Rib, Modern	1,750	2,000	2,000

MIKROS Tradename of Manufacture D'Armes Des Pyrenees, Heydaye, France, 1934–1939, 1958 to date.

HANDGUN, SEMI-AUTOMATIC

6.35mm, Clip Fed, Magazine Disconnect, Modern	150	175	175
7.65mm, Clip Fed, Magazine Disconnect, Modern	150	175	175
KE, .22 Short R.F., Clip Fed, Hammer, Magazine Disconnect, 2" Barrel, Modern	125	150	140

	V.G.	Exc	Prior Edition
KE, .22 Short R.F., Clip Fed, Hammer, Magazine Disconnect, 4" Barrel, Modern	$125	$150	$150
KE, .22 Short R.F., Clip Fed, Hammer, Magazine Disconnect, 2" Barrel, Lightweight, Modern	100	125	125
KE, .22 Short R.F., Clip Fed, Hammer, Magazine Disconnect, 4" Barrel, Lightweight, Modern	100	125	125
KN, .25 ACP, Clip Fed, Hammer, Magazine Disconnect, 2" Barrel, Modern	100	125	125
KN, .25 ACP, Clip Fed, Hammer, Magazine Disconnect, 2" Barrel, Lightweight, Modern	100	125	125

MILITARY   Retolaza Hermanos, Eibar, Spain, c. 1915

HANDGUN, SEMI-AUTOMATIC

Model 1914, 7.65mm, Clip Fed, Curio	125	150	150

MILLER, MATHIAS   Easton, Pa. 1771–1788. See Kentucky Rifles.

MILLS, BENJAMIN   Charlottesville, N.C. 1784–1790, 1790–1814 at Harrodsburg, Ky. See Kentucky Rifles, U.S. Military.

MINNEAPOLIS FIREARMS CO.   Minneapolis, Minn., c. 1883.

HANDGUN, PALM PISTOL

The Protector, .32 Extra Short R.F., Nickel Plated, Antique	1,000	1,200	825

MIQUELET–LOCK EXAMPLES

HANDGUN, MIQUELET-LOCK

	V.G.	Exc	Prior Edition
.52 Arabian, Holster Pistol, Tapered Round Barrel, Low Quality, Antique	300	350	350
.55, Russian Cossack Type, Tapered Round Barrel, Steel Furniture, Silver Furniture, Antique	600	850	850
Central Italian 1700's, Holster Pistol, Brass Furniture, Brass Overlay Stock, Medium Quality, Antique	2,250	2,500	2,500
Pair Cominazzo Early 1700's, Steel Inlay, Medium Quality, Holster Pistol, Antique	3,250	3,500	3,500
Pair Late 1700's, Pocket Pistol, Medium Quality, Brass Furniture, Light Ornamentation, Antique	1,750	2,000	2,000
Pair Spanish Late 1600's, Belt Hook, Brass Overlay Stock, High Quality, Antique	—	RARE	—
Ripoll Type Late 1600's, Blunderbuss, Brass Inlay, Antique	4,250	4,500	4,500
Ripoll Type Late 1600's, Blunderbuss, Silver Inlay, Antique	7,000	7,500	7,500

RIFLE, MIQUELET--LOCK

	V.G.	Exc	Prior Edition
Mid–Eastern, Gold Inlays, Cannon Barrel, Front & Rear Bead Sights, Silver Overlay Stock, Silver Furniture, Antique	3,500	3,750	3,750
Mid–Eastern 1700's, Damascus Barrel, Gold Inlays, Many Semi–Precious Gem Inlays, Silver Furniture, Ornate, Antique	6,500	7,500	7,500

	V.G.	Exc	Prior Edition

MIROKU Tokyo, Japan.

HANDGUN, REVOLVER

Model 6, .38 Spec., Double Action, Swing–Out Cylinder, Modern.......... $125 $150 $150

RIFLE, LEVER ACTION

.22 L.R.R.F., Tube Feed, Plain, Modern.. 225 250 250

Miroku .22 Lever Action

Center Fire, Various Calibers, Checkered Stock, Clip Fed, Modern.. 200 225 225

RIFLE, SEMI-AUTOMATIC

.22 L.R.R.F., Takedown, Tube Feed Through Butt, Modern.................... 175 200 200

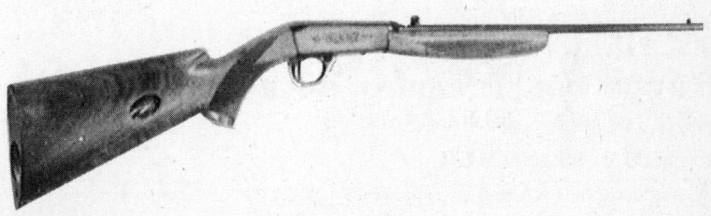

Miroku .22 Auto

RIFLE, SINGLESHOT

Model 78, Various Calibers, Checkered Stock, Falling Block, Modern.. 325 350 350

	V.G.	Exc	Prior Edition

SHOTGUN, DOUBLE BARREL, OVER-UNDER

Model 3800, 12 Ga., Checkered Stock, Vent Rib, Modern...................... $425 $475 $475

Miroku Model 3800

Model H.S.W. DeLuxe, 12 Ga., Checkered Stock, Vent Rib,
Engraved, Modern... 800   950   950

MISSISSIPPI VALLEY ARMS CO. Made by Crescent for
Shapleigh Hardware, St. Louis, Mo.

SHOTGUN, DOUBLE BARREL, SIDE-BY-SIDE

Various Gauges, Hammerless, Damascus Barrel, Modern......................	150	175	175
Various Gauges, Hammerless, Steel Barrel, Modern..............................	175	200	200
Various Gauges, Outside Hammer, Damascus Barrel, Modern..............	125	175	175
Various Gauges, Outside Hammers, Steel Barrel, Modern......................	150	175	175

SHOTGUN, SINGLESHOT

Various Gauges, Hammer, Steel Barrel, Modern.................................. 75   100   100

MITCHELL ARMS

HANDGUN, DOUBLE BARREL, OVER-UNDER

Derringer, .357 Magnum, Spur Trigger, Modern.................................... 125   150   100

HANDGUN, REVOLVER

Army, Various Calibers, Single Action, Western Style,
Modern.. 175   225   150

MITRAILLEUSE Mre. de Armes et Cycles de St. Etienne, St. Etienne,
France, c. 1893–1897.

HANDGUN, PALM PISTOL

Mitrailleuse, 8mm, Engraved, Nickel Plated, Antique............................ 600   700   700

MOHAWK Made by Crescent for Blish, Mize & Stillman, c. 1900.

SHOTGUN, DOUBLE BARREL, SIDE-BY-SIDE

Various Gauges, Hammerless, Damascus Barrel, Modern......................	150	175	175
Various Gauges, Hammerless, Steel Barrel, Modern..............................	175	200	200
Various Gauges, Outside Hammers, Damascus Barrel, Modern..............	150	175	175
Various Gauges, Outside Hammers, Steel Barrel, Modern......................	150	175	175

	V.G.	Exc	Prior Edition

SHOTGUN, SINGLESHOT

	V.G.	Exc	Prior Edition
Various Gauges, Hammer, Steel Barrel, Modern......................................	$75	$100	$100

MOLL, DAVID Hellerstown, Pa. 1814–1833. See Kentucky Rifles.

MOLL, JOHN Hellerstown, Pa. 1770–1794. See Kentucky Rifles.

MOLL, JOHN III Hellerstown, Pa. 1824–1863. See Kentucky Rifles.

MOLL, JOHN, JR. Hellerstown, Pa. 1794–1824. See Kentucky Rifles.

MOLL, PETER Hellerstown, Pa. 1804–1833 with Brother John Moll Jr. Made some of the Finest Kentucky Rifles in Pa. See Kentucky Rifles.

MONARCH c. 1880.

HANDGUN, REVOLVER

	V.G.	Exc	Prior Edition
.32 Short R.F., 5 Shot, Spur Trigger, Solid Frame, Single Action, Antique..	100	150	150

MONARCH Made by Hopkins & Allen, c. 1880.

HANDGUN, REVOLVER

	V.G.	Exc	Prior Edition
#1, .22 Short R.F., 7 Shot, Spur Trigger, Solid Frame, Single Action, Antique..	100	150	150
#2, .32 Short R.F., 5 Shot, Spur Trigger, Solid Frame, Single Action, Antique..	125	175	175
#3, .38 Short R.F., 5 Shot, Spur Trigger, Solid Frame, Single Action, Antique..	125	175	175
#4, .41 Short R.F., 5 Shot, Spur Trigger, Solid Frame, Single Action, Antique..	175	200	200

MONDIAL Gaspar Arrizaga, Eibar, Spain.

HANDGUN, SEMI-AUTOMATIC

	V.G.	Exc	Prior Edition
Model 1, 6.35mm, Clip Fed, Grip Safety, Magazine Disconnect, Modern..	200	250	250

	V.G.	Exc	Prior Edition
Model 2, 6.35mm, Clip Fed, Blue, Modern...	$150	$200	$200

Mondial Model 2

MONITOR Made by Stevens Arms.

SHOTGUN, DOUBLE BARREL, SIDE-BY-SIDE

Model 311, Various Gauges, Hammerless, Steel Barrel, Modern............	125	175	175

SHOTGUN, SINGLESHOT

Model 90, Various Gauges, Takedown, Automatic Ejector, Plain, Hammer, Modern...	50	75	75

MOORE PATENT FIRE ARMS CO. Brooklyn, N.Y/ 1863–1883.

HANDGUN, REVOLVER

.32 T.F., Spur Trigger, Single Action, Brass Frame, No Extractor, Antique..	300	350	500

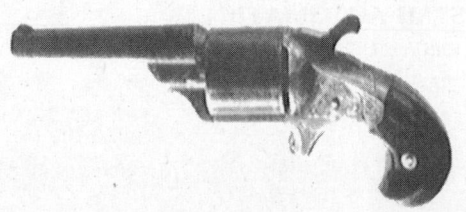

Moore .32 R.F

Williamson's Patent, .32 T.F., Brass Frame, Hook Extractor, Antique..	350	400	475

	Prior
V.G.	Exc Edition

HANDGUN, SINGLESHOT

.41 Short R.F., Derringer, Brass Frame, Antique...................................... $700 $850 $750

MORRONE Rhode Island Arms Co., Hope Valley, R.I., c. 1951.

SHOTGUN, DOUBLE BARREL, OVER-UNDER

Model 46, 12 Ga., Single Trigger, Plain Barrels, Checkered Stock,
Modern.. 750 950 950
Model 46, 20 Ga., Single Trigger, Vent Rib, Checkered Stock,
Modern.. 1,050 1,250 1,250

MORTIMER, H. W. & SON London, England 1800–1802.

HANDGUN, FLINTLOCK

.45, Barrel Duckfoot, Pocket Pistol, Steel Barrel and Frame,
Plain, Antique.. 4,000 4,500 4,500

MOSSBERG, O. F. & SONS New Haven, Conn. 1919 to date.

Fitchburg & Chicopee Falls, Mass, 1892–1919 as Oscar F. Mossberg.

HANDGUN, MANUAL REPEATER

Brownie, .22 L.R.R.F., Top Break, Double Action, Rotating Firing
Pin, 4 Barrels, 4 Shot, Modern.. 160 275 275

HANDGUN, REVOLVER

Abilene, .357 Mag., Single Action, Western Style, Adjustable
Sights, Various Barrel Lengths, Modern.. 275 325 225
Abilene, .44 Mag., Single Action, Western Style, Adjustable
Sights, Various Barrel Lengths, Modern.. 300 350 250

Mossberg Abilene, .44 Magnum

	V.G.	Exc	Prior Edition
Abilene Silhouette, .357 Mag., Single Action, Western Style, Adjustable Sights, 10" Barrel, Modern..	$325	$375	$275

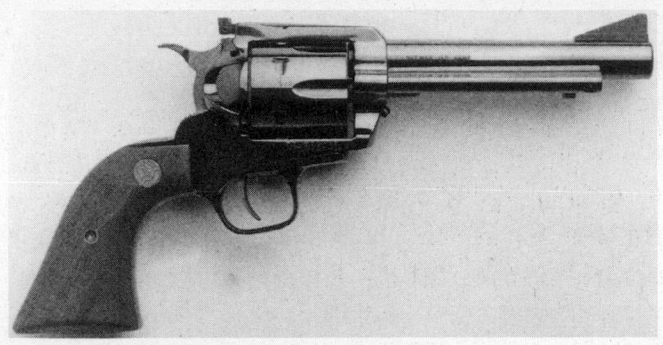

Mossberg Abilene, .357 Magnum

RIFLE, BOLT ACTION

	V.G.	Exc	Prior Edition
Model 10, .22 L.R.R.F., Singleshot, Takedown, Modern...........................	75	100	75
Model 14, .22 L.R.R.F., Singleshot, Takedown, Peep Sights, Modern..	75	100	75
Model 140B, .22 L.R.R.F., Clip Fed, Peep Sights, Monte Carlo Stock, Modern..	100	150	100
Model 140K, .22 L.R.R.F., Clip Fed, Open Rear Sights, Monte Carlo Stock, Modern...	75	100	100
Model 142A, .22 L.R.R.F., Clip Fed, Carbine, Monte Carlo Stock, Peep Sights, Modern..	125	150	100
Model 142A, .22 L.R.R.F., Clip Fed, Peep Sights, Modern.....................	100	125	100
Model 142K, .22 L.R.R.F., Clip Fed, Carbine, Monte Carlo Stock, Modern..	100	125	75
Model 142K, .22 L.R.R.F., Clip Fed, Open Rear Sights, Modern...........	75	100	100
Model 144, .22 L.R.R.F., Clip Fed, Heavy Barrel, Target Stock, Target Sights, Modern...	150	175	125
Model 144LS, .22 L.R.R.F., Clip Fed, Heavy Barrel, Lyman Sights, Target Stock, Modern..	175	225	150
Model 146B, .22 L.R.R.F., Takedown, Tube Feed, Monte Carlo Stock, Peep Sights, Modern...	125	150	100
Model 20, .22 L.R.R.F., Singleshot, Takedown, Modern......................	75	100	75
Model 25, .22 L.R.R.F., Singleshot, Takedown, Peep Sights, Modern..	75	100	75
Model 25A, .22 L.R.R.F., Singleshot, Takedown, Peep Sights, Modern..	100	125	100
Model 26B, .22 L.R.R.F., Singleshot, Takedown, Peep Sights, Modern..	75	100	75
Model 26C, .22 L.R.R.F., Singleshot, Takedown, Open Rear Sight, Modern..	75	100	75
Model 30, .22 L.R.R.F., Singleshot, Takedown, Peep Sights, Modern..	75	100	75
Model 320B, .22 L.R.R.F., Singleshot, Peep Sights, Modern..................	100	125	100
Model 320K, .22 L.R.R.F., Singleshot, Open Rear Sight, Monte Carlo Stock, Modern..	75	100	75

	V.G.	Exc	Prior Edition
Model 321K, .22 L.R.R.F., Singleshot, Open Rear Sight, Modern..........	$75	$100	$75
Model 340B, .22 L.R.R.F., Clip Fed, Peep Sights, Modern......................	100	125	100
Model 340K, .22 L.R.R.F., Clip Fed, Open Rear Sight, Modern.............	75	100	75
Model 340M, .22 L.R.R.F., Clip Fed, Full–Stocked, Carbine, Modern..	175	225	125
Model 341, .22 L.R.R.F., Clip Fed, Open Rear Sight, Modern...............	75	100	100
Model 342K, .22 L.R.R.F., Clip Fed, Open Rear Sight, Modern.............	75	100	75
Model 346B, .22 L.R.R.F., Tube Feed, Peep Sights, Monte Carlo Stock, Modern...	100	125	100
Model 346K, .22 L.R.R.F., Tube Feed, Monte Carlo Stock, Open Rear Sight, Modern...	100	125	100
Model 352K, .22 L.R.R.F., Clip Fed, Monte Carlo Stock, Open Rear Sight, Carbine, Modern...	75	100	100
Model 430, .22 L.R.R.F., Tube Feed, Monte Carlo Stock, Checkered Stock, Open Rear Sight, Modern.............................	75	100	100
Model 432, .22 L.R.R.F., Tube Feed, Western Style, Carbine, Modern...	75	100	100
Model 50, .22 L.R.R.F., Takedown, Tube Feed, Open Rear Sight, Modern...	125	150	100
Model 51, .22 L.R.R.F., Takedown, Tube Feed, Peep Sight, Modern...	125	150	100
Model 51M, .22 L.R.R.F., Takedown, Tube Feed, Peep Sight, Full–Stocked, Modern..	125	150	100

RIFLE, LEVER ACTION

	V.G.	Exc	Prior Edition
Model 400, .22 L.R.R.F., Tube Feed, Open Rear Sight, Modern.............	150	175	150
Model 402, .22 L.R.R.F., Tube Feed, Open Rear Sight, Monte Carlo Stock, Modern..	150	175	150
Model 472, Various Calibers, Pistol–Grip Stock, Tube Feed, Open Rear Sight, Modern..	125	175	175
Model 472C, Various Calibers, Straight Grip, Tube Feed, Open Rear Sight, Carbine, Modern..	125	150	200

RIFLE, SEMI-AUTOMATIC

	V.G.	Exc	Prior Edition
Model 151K, .22 L.R.R.F., Takedown, Tube Feed, Open Rear Sight, Modern..	100	125	125
Model 151M, .22 L.R.R.F., Takedown, Tube Feed, Peep Sights, Full–Stocked, Modern..	125	150	125
Model 152, .22 L.R.R.F., Clip Fed, Monte Carlo Stock, Peep Sights, Carbine, Modern..	125	150	125
Model 152K, .22 L.R.R.F., Clip Fed, Monte Carlo Stock, Open Rear Sight, Carbine, Modern..	100	125	150
Model 350K, .22 L.R.R.F., Clip Fed, Monte Carlo Stock, Open Rear Sight, Modern...	50	75	125
Model 351C, .22 L.R.R.F., Tube Feed, Monte Carlo Stock, Open Rear Sight, Carbine, Modern..	75	100	125
Model 351K, .22 L.R.R.F., Tube Feed, Monte Carlo Stock, Open Rear Sight, Modern...	100	100	100
Model 35, .22 L.R.R.F., Singleshot, Target Stock, Target Sights, Modern...	175	225	225
Model 35A, .22 L.R.R.F., Singleshot, Target Stock, Target Sights, Modern...	200	225	250
Model 35A–LS, .22 L.R.R.F., Singleshot, Target Stock, Lyman Sights, Modern..	225	250	275
Model 35B, .22 L.R.R.F., Singleshot, Target Sights, Heavy Barrel, Target Stock, Modern...	225	250	225

	V.G.	Exc	Prior Edition
Model 40, .22 L.R.R.F., Takedown, Tube Feed, Open Rear Sight, Modern	$75	$100	$100
Model 42, .22 L.R.R.F., Takedown, Clip Fed, Open Rear Sight, Modern	75	100	100
Model 42A, .22 L.R.R.F., Takedown, Clip Fed, Peep Sights, Modern	75	100	100
Model 42B, .22 L.R.R.F., Takedown, 5 Shot Clip, Peep Sights, Modern	75	100	100
Model 42C, .22 L.R.R.F., Takedown, 5 Shot Clip, Open Rear Sight, Modern	75	100	100
Model 42M, .22 L.R.R.F., Takedown, Clip Fed, Full–Stocked, Peep Sights, Modern	125	150	125
Model 42 MB (British), .22 L.R.R.F., Takedown, Clip Fed, Full–Stocked, Peep Sights, Modern	150	175	150
Model 43, .22 L.R.R.F., Clip Fed, Heavy Barrel, Target Sights, Target Stock, Modern	200	225	225
Model 44 US, .22 L.R.R.F., Clip Fed, Target Sights, Target Stock, Heavy Barrel, Modern	250	275	200
Model 44B, .22 L.R.R.F., Target Stock, Clip Fed, Target Sights, Modern	200	225	225
Model 45, .22 L.R.R.F., Takedown, Tube Feed, Peep Sights, Modern	125	150	150
Model 45A, .22 L.R.R.F., Takedown, Tube Feed, Peep Sights, Modern	125	150	150
Model 46, .22 L.R.R.F., Takedown, Tube Feed, Peep Sights, Modern	125	150	150
Model 46–ALS, .22 L.R.R.F., Takedown, Tube Feed, Lyman Sights, Modern	175	200	200
Model 46B, .22 L.R.R.F., Takedown, Tube Feed, Peep Sights, Modern	100	125	12
Model 46M, .22 L.R.R.F., Takedown, Tube Feed, Full–Stocked, Peep Sights, Modern	100	125	150
Model 46M, .22 L.R.R.F., Takedown, Tube Feed, Open Rear Sight, Modern	125	150	125
Model 46T, .22 L.R.R.F., Takedown, Tube Feed, Heavy Barrel, Target Stock, Peep Sights, Modern	150	175	175
Model 83D, .410 Ga., Takedown, 3 Shot, Modern	150	175	175
Model 85D, .20 Ga., Takedown, 3 Shot, Adjustable Choke, Modern	75	100	100
Model L45A, .22 L.R.R.F., Takedown, Tube Feed, Open Rear Sight, Modern	150	175	125

RIFLE, SINGLESHOT

	V.G.	Exc	Prior Edition
Model L, .22 L.R.R.F., Lever Action, Falling Block, Takedown, Modern	275	325	300

RIFLE, SLIDE ACTION

	V.G.	Exc	Prior Edition
Model K, .22 L.R.R.F., Takedown, Tube Feed, Hammerless, Modern	175	200	150
Model M, .22 L.R.R.F., Takedown, Tube Feed, Hammerless, Octagon Barrel, Modern	175	225	175

SHOTGUN, BOLT ACTION

	V.G.	Exc	Prior Edition
Model 173, .410 Ga., Takedown, Singleshot, Modern	75	100	75
Model 173Y, .410 Ga., Clip Fed, Singleshot, Modern	75	100	75
Model 183D, .410 Ga., Takedown, 3 Shot, Modern	75	100	75

	V.G.	Exc	Prior Edition
Model 183K, .410 Ga., Takedown, Adjustable Choke, Clip Fed, Modern	$75	$100	$75
Model 183T, .410 Ga., Clip Fed, Modern	75	100	75
Model 185D, .20 Ga., Takedown, 3 Shot, Modern	75	100	75
Model 185K, .20 Ga., Takedown, 3 Shot, Adjustable Choke, Modern	75	100	75
Model 190D, .16 Ga., Takedown, Clip Fed, Modern	75	100	75
Model 190K, .16 Ga., Takedown, Adjustable Choke, Clip Fed, Modern	75	100	75
Model 195D, .12 Ga., Takedown, Clip Fed, Modern	75	100	75
Model 195K, .12 Ga., Takedown, Adjustable Choke, Clip Fed, Modern	75	100	75
Model 385K, .20 Ga., Clip Fed, Adjustable Choke, Modern	75	100	75
Model 385T, 12 Ga. Mag. 3", Clip Fed, Adjustable Choke, Modern	75	100	75
Model 390K, .16 Ga., Clip Fed, Adjustable Choke, Modern	75	100	75
Model 390T, .16 Ga., Clip Fed, Modern	75	100	75
Model 395K, 12 Ga. Mag. 3", Clip Fed, Adjustable Choke,			

Mossberg 395K, 12 Gauge

	V.G.	Exc	Prior Edition
Modern	75	100	75
Model 395S, 12 Ga. Mag. 3", Clip Fed, Open Rear Sight, Modern	75	100	75
Model 395T, .12 Ga., Clip Fed, Modern	75	100	75
Model 73, .410 Ga., Takedown, Singleshot, Modern	75	100	75
Model 800, Various Calibers, Open Rear Sight, Monte Carlo Stock, Modern	175	200	200
Model 800D, Various Calibers, Monte Carlo Stock, Checkpiece, Checkered Stock, Open Rear Sight, Modern	200	225	225
Model 800M, Various Calibers, Open Rear Sight, Full–Stocked, Modern	200	225	225
Model 800SM, Various Calibers, Scope Mounted, Monte Carlo Stock, Modern	225	250	250
Model 800V, Various Calibers, No Sights, Monte Carlo Stock, Heavy Barrel, Modern	200	225	225
Model 810, Various Calibers, Magnum Action, Open Rear Sight, Monte Carlo Stock, Modern	200	225	225
Model 810, Various Calibers, Open Rear Sight, Long Action, Monte Carlo Stock, Modern	200	225	225
Model B, .22 L.R.R.F., Singleshot, Takedown, Modern	50	75	75
Model L42A, .22 L.R.R.F., Takedown, Clip Fed, Peep Sights, Left–Hand, Modern	75	100	100
Model L43, .22 L.R.R.F., Clip Fed, Heavy Barrel, Target Sights, Target Stock, Left–Hand, Modern	125	150	150
Model L45A, .22 L.R.R.F., Takedown, Tube Feed, Peep Sights, Modern	100	125	125

	V.G.	Exc	Prior Edition
Model L46A–LS, .22 L.R.R.F., Takedown, Tube Feed, Lyman Sights, Left–Hand, Modern	$125	$150	$150
Model R, .22 L.R.R.F., Takedown, Tube Feed, Open Rear Sight, Modern	50	75	75

SHOTGUN, SLIDE ACTION

	V.G.	Exc	Prior Edition
Cruiser, 12 Ga., One–Hand Grip, Nickel Plated, Modern	150	175	250
Model 200D, 12 Ga., Clip Fed, Adjustable Choke, Modern	100	125	125
Model 200K, 12 Ga., Clip Fed, Adjustable Choke, Modern	100	125	150
Model 500 Super, Checkered Stock, Vent Rib, Modern	200	250	200
Model 500A, 12 Ga. Mag. 3", Field Grade, Modern	175	200	175
Model 500AA, 12 Ga. Mag. 3", Trap Grade, Modern	225	275	225
Model 500AHTD, Trap Grade, High Vent Rib, with Choke Tubes, Modern	350	425	350
Model 500AK, Field Grade, Adjustable Choke, Modern	200	250	200
Model 500AKR, Field Grade, Adjustable Choke, Vent Rib, Modern	225	275	225
Model 500AM, Field Grade, Magnum, Modern	175	225	175
Model 500AMR, Field Grade, Magnum, Vent Rib, Modern	175	225	175
Model 500AR, Field Grade, Vent Rib, Modern	175	225	175
Model 500AS, Field Grade, Open Rear Sight, Modern	200	250	200
Model 500ATR, Trap Grade, Vent Rib, Modern	200	250	200
Model 500B, 16 Ga., Field Grade, Modern	200	250	200
Model 500BK, 16 Ga., Adjustable Choke, Modern	175	225	175
Model 500BS, 16 Ga., Open Rear Sight, Modern	175	225	175
Model 500C, 20 Ga., Field Grade, Modern	175	225	175
MOdel 500CK, 20 Ga., Field Grade, Adjustable Choke, Modern	175	225	175
Model 500CKR, 20 Ga., Field Grade, Vent Rib, Adjustable Choke, Modern	175	225	175
Model 500CR, 20 Ga., Field Grade, Vent Rib, Modern	175	225	175
Model 500CS, 20 Ga., Field Grade, Open Rear Sight, Modern	200	250	200
Model 500E, .410 Ga., Field Grade, Modern	175	225	175
Model 500EK, .410 Ga., Field Grade, Adjustable Choke, Modern	200	250	200
Model 500EKR, .410 Ga., Field Grade, Vent Rib, Adjustable Choke, Modern	175	225	175
Model 500ER, .410 Ga., Field Grade, Vent Rib, Modern	175	225	175

MOSTER, GEO. Lancaster, Pa. 1771–1779. See Kentucky Rifles and Pistols.

MOUNTAIN EAGLE Made by Hopkins & Allen, c. 1880.

HANDGUN, REVOLVER

	V.G.	Exc	Prior Edition
.32 Short R.F., 5 Shot, Spur Trigger, Solid Frame, Single Action, Antique	100	150	150

M.S. Modesto Santos, Eibar, Spain, c. 1920.

HANDGUN, SEMI-AUTOMATIC

	V.G.	Exc	Prior Edition
Action, 7.65mm, Clip Fed, Blue, Curio	125	150	150
Model 1920, .25 ACP, Clip Fed, Blue, Curio	100	125	125

	V.G.	Exc	Prior Edition

MT. VERNON ARMS Belgium, c. 1900.

SHOTGUN, DOUBLE BARREL, SIDE-BY-SIDE

	V.G.	Exc	Prior Edition
Various Gauges, Hammerless, Damascus Barrel, Modern..............	$150	$175	$175
Various Gauges, Hammerless, Steel Barrel, Modern...................	175	200	200
Various Gauges, Outside Hammers, Damascus Barrel, Curio...........	150	175	175
Various Gauges, Outside Hammers, Steel Barrel, Modern.............	150	175	175

SHOTGUN, SINGLESHOT

	V.G.	Exc	Prior Edition
Various Gauges, Hammer, Steel Barrel, Modern...................	50	75	75

MUGICA Jose Mugica, Eibar, Spain, tradename on Llama pistols. See Llama for equivilent models.

MUSGRAVE South Africa.

RIFLE, BOLT ACTION

	V.G.	Exc	Prior Edition
Mk. III, Various Calibers, Checkered Stock, Modern..............	275	325	325
Premier NR5, Various Calibers, Checkered Stock, Modern...........	300	350	350
Valiant NR6, Various Calibers, Checkered Stock, Modern...........	250	300	300

MUSKETEER Tradename used by Firearms International, Washington, D.C., c. 1968.

RIFLE, BOLT ACTION

	V.G.	Exc	Prior Edition
Carbine, Various Calibers, Monte Carlo Stock, Checkered Stock, Sling Swivels, Modern...................	300	325	325
Deluxe, Various Calibers, Monte Carlo Stock, Checkered Stock, Sling Swivels, Modern...................	325	350	350
Mannlicher, Various Calibers, Full Stock, Modern..............	275	325	325
Sporter, Various Calibers, Monte Carlo Stock, Checkered Stock, Sling Swivels, Modern...................	275	300	300

MUTTI, GEROLIMO Brescia, c. 1680.

HANDGUN, SNAPHAUNCE

	V.G.	Exc	Prior Edition
Pair, Belt Pistol, Brass Mounts, Engraved, Ornate, Antique..........	10,000	15,000	15,000

MUTTI, GIESU Brescia, c. 1790.

HANDGUN, SNAPHAUNCE

	V.G.	Exc	Prior Edition
Pair, Engraved, Belt Hook, Medium Ornamentation, Antique.........	7,500	10,000	10,000

N

NAPOLEON Made by Thomas Ryan, Jr., Pistol Mfg. Co., c. 1870–1876.

HANDGUN, REVOLVER

.22 Short R.F., 7 Shot, Spur Trigger, Solid Frame, Single Action,
Antique... $125 $150 $150
.32 Short R.F., 5 Shot, Spur Trigger, Solid Frame, Single Action,
Antique... 150   175   175

NATIONAL Made by Norwich Falls Pistol Co., c. 1880.

HANDGUN, REVOLVER

.32 Short R.F., 5 Shot, Spur Trigger, Solid Frame, Single Action,
Antique... 150   175   175
.38 Short R.F., 5 Shot, Spur Trigger, Solid Frame, Single Action,
Antique... 150   175   175

HANDGUN, SINGLESHOT

.41 Short R.F., Derringer, all Metal, Light Engraving, Antique.............. 225   275   275

NATIONAL ARMS CO. Made by Crescent, c. 1900.

SHOTGUN, DOUBLE BARREL, SIDE-BY-SIDE

Various Gauges, Hammerless, Damascus Barrel, Modern...................... 125   150   150
Various Gauges, Hammerless, Steel Barrel, Modern.............................. 175   200   200
Various Gauges, Outside Hammers, Damascus Barrel, Modern............. 150   175   175
Various Gauges, Outside Hammers, Steel Barrel, Modern..................... 150   175   175

SHOTGUN, SINGLESHOT

Various Gauges, Hammer, Steel Barrel, Modern.................................... 50   75   75

NATIONAL ORDNANCE South El Monte, Calif.

RIFLE, BOLT ACTION

1903A3, .30–06 Springfield, Modern... 125   150   150

RIFLE, SEMI-AUTOMATIC

Garand, .30–06 Springfield, Modern.. 400   450   450
M–1 Carbine, .30 Carbine, Clip Fed, Modern... 125   150   150
M–1 Carbine, .30 Carbine, Clip Fed, Folding Stock, Reweld,
Modern.. 150   175   175
Tanker Garand, .308 Win., Reweld, Military, Modern........................... 400   450   450

	V.G.	Exc	Prior Edition

NAVY ARMS Ridgefield, N.J. 1959–Date.

HANDGUN, FLINTLOCK

A Engraving Pistol, Add $115.00–$225.00
A Engraving Rifle, Add $145.00–$300.00
B Engraving Pistol, Add $140.00–$300.00
B Engraving Rifle, Add $215.00–$450.00
C Engraving Pistol, Add $265.00–$500.00
C Engraving Rifle, Add $495.00–$1000.00
Presentation Case Only, Add $25.00–$50.00
Tiffany Grips Only, Add $155.00–$350.00
Silver Plating, Add $95.00–$250.00

	V.G.	Exc	Prior Edition
.44 "Kentucky," Belt Pistol. Brass Furniture, Brass Barrel, Reproduction	$200	$250	$100
.44 "Kentucky," Belt Pistol. Brass Furniture, Reproduction	200	250	100
.577 Scotch Black Watch, Military, Belt Pistol, all Metal, Reproduction	225	275	125
.69 M1763 Charleville, Military, Belt Pistol, Reproduction	375	450	250
.69 M1763 Charleville, Military, Belt Pistol, Reproduction	225	275	125
.69 M1777 Charleville, Military, Belt Pistol, Reproduction	225	275	125
.69 Tower, Military, Belt Pistol, Reproduction	100	125	50

HANDGUN, PERCUSSION

	V.G.	Exc	Prior Edition
.36 M1851 New Navy, Revolver, Brass Grip Frame, Reproduction	200	250	100
.36 M1851 New Navy, Revolver, Silver–Plated Grip Frame, Reproduction	200	250	100
.36 M1853, Revolver, Pocket Pistol, 4½" Barrel, Reproduction	200	250	100
.36 M1853, Revolver, Pocket Pistol, 5½" Barrel, Reproduction	200	250	100
.36 M1853, Revolver, Pocket Pistol, 6½" Barrel, Reproduction	200	250	100
.36 M1860 Reb, Revolver, Brass Frame, Reproduction	200	250	100
.36 M1860 Sheriff, Revolver, Brass Frame, Reproduction	200	250	100
.36 M1861 Navy, Revolver, Engraved Cylinder, Reproduction	200	250	100
.36 M1861 Navy, Revolver, Fluted Cylinder, Reproduction	200	250	100
.36 M1861, Revolver, Sheriff's Model, with Short Barrel, Reproduction	200	250	100
.36 M1862 Police, Revolver, 5 Shot, Brass Grip Frame, Cased with Accessories, Reproduction	250	300	150
.36 M1862 Police, Revolver, 5 Shot, Brass Grip Frame, 4½" Barrel, Reproduction	200	250	100
.36 M1862 Police, Revolver, 5 Shot, Brass Grip Frame, 5½" Barrel, Reproduction	200	250	100
.36 M1862 Police, Revolver, 5 Shot, Brass Grip Frame, 6½" Barrel, Reproduction	200	250	100
.36 M1862 Police, Revolver, Fancy Engraving, Silver Plated, Gold Plated, Reproduction	800	950	500
.36 M1863, Revolver, Sheriff's Model, with Short Barrel, Reproduction	200	250	100
.36 Remington, Revolver, Target Pistol, Adjustable Sights, Reproduction	225	275	125
.36 Spiller & Burr, Revolver, Solid Frame, Reproduction	175	225	100
.44 "Kentucky," Belt Pistol, Brass Furniture, Brass Barrel, Reproduction	225	275	125
.44 "Kentucky," Belt Pistol, Brass Furniture, Reproduction	175	225	100

	V.G.	Exc	Prior Edition
.44 First Model Dragoon, Revolver, Brass Grip Frame, Reproduction	$225	$275	$125
.44 M1847 Walker, Revolver, Brass Grip Frame, Engraved, Gold Inlays, Reproduction	450	550	275
.44 M1847 Walker, Revolver, Brass Grip Frame, Reproduction	250	300	150
.44 M1860 Army, Revolver, Engraved Cylinder, Reproduction	150	200	100
.44 M1860 Army, Revolver, Fluted Cylinder, Reproduction	150	200	100
.44 M1860 Reb, Revolver, Shoulder Stock Only, Reproduction	50	75	50
.44 M1860 Sheriff, Revolver, Brass Frame, Reproduction	125	150	75
.44 M1860, Revolver, Sheriff's Model, with Short Barrel, Reproduction	175	225	100
.44 Remington Army, Revolver, Nickel Plated, Reproduction	225	275	150
.44 Remington, Revolver, Solid Frame, Reproduction	150	175	100
.44 Remington, Revolver, Stainless Steel, Reproduction	225	275	150

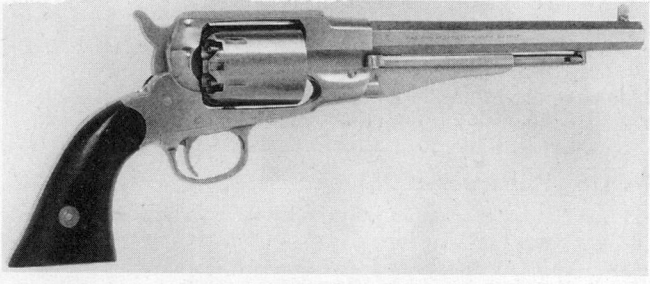

Navy Arms .44 Remington Stainless

.44 Remington, Revolver, Target Pistol, Adjustable Sights, Reproduction	225	275	150

Navy Arms .44 Remington Target

.44 Second Model, Dragoon, Revolver, Brass Grip Frame, Reproduction	300	375	125
.44 Third Model Dragoon, Revolver, Brass Grip Frame, with Detachable Shoulder Stock, Reproduction,	350	425	175
.44 Third Model Dragoon, Revolver, Brass Grip Frame, Reproduction,	325	375	150

	V.G.	Exc	Prior Edition
.44 Third Model Dragoon, Revolver, Buntline, with Detachable Shoulder Stock, Reproduction,	$350	$425	$200
.58 M1806, Harper's Ferry, Brass Furniture, Military, Belt Pistol, Reproduction,	150	175	100

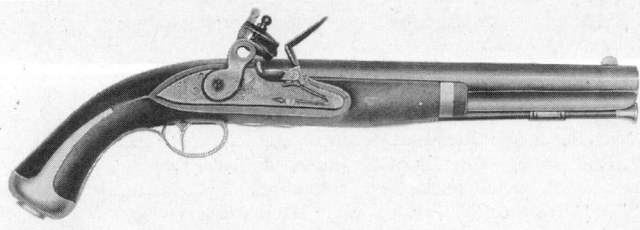

Navy Arms Harper's Ferry 1806

.58 M1855, Harper's Ferry, Holster Pistol, Military, with Detachable Shoulder Stock, Reproduction,	200	250	150
.58 M1855, Harper's Ferry, Shoulder Stock Only,	50	75	50

HANDGUN, REVOLVER

Cattleman, Various Calibers, Color Case Hardened Frame, Single Action, Western Style, Modern	300	350	175
Cattleman Buntline, .45 Colt, Color Case Hardened Frame, Single Action, Western Style, Adjustable Sights, with Detachable Shoulder Stock, Modern	425	400	225
Cattleman Carbine, Various Calibers, Color Case Hardened Frame, Single Action, Western Style, Adjustable Sights, Modern	400	475	175
Cattleman Target, .357 Magnum, Color Case Hardened Frame, Single Action, Western Style, Adjustable Sights, with Detachable Shoulder Stock, Modern	325	375	225
M1875 Remington, .357 Magnum, Color Case Hardened Frame, Western Style, Single Action, Modern	250	300	175
M1875 Remington, .357 Magnum, Nickel Plated, Western Style, Single Action, Modern	300	350	200
M1875 Remington, .44–40 WCF, Color Case Hardened Frame, Western Style, Single Action, Modern	300	350	175
M1875 Remington, .44–40 WCF, Nickel Plated, Western Style, Single Action, Modern	325	400	175
M1875 Remington, .45 Colt, Color Case Hardened Frame, Western Style, Single Action, Modern	275	325	175
M1875 Remington, .45 Colt, Nickel Plated, Western Style, Single Action, Modern	300	350	200
M1875 Remington, .45 Colt, Stainless Steel, Western Style, Single Action, Modern	325	375	200

HANDGUN, SINGLESHOT

Rolling Block, .22 Hornet, Half–Octagon Barrel, Color Case Hardened Frame, Adjustable Sights, Modern	250	300	150
Rolling Block, .22 L.R.R.F., Half–Octagon Barrel, Color Case Hardened Frame, Adjustable Sights, Modern	200	250	125
Rolling Block, .357 Magnum, Half–Octagon Barrel, Color Case Hardened Frame, Adjustable Sights, Modern	250	300	150

	V.G.	Exc	Prior Edition

RIFLE, BOLT ACTION

Mauser '98, .45–70 Government, Carbine, Checkered Stock,
Modern.. $225 $275 $150
Mauser '98, .45–70 Government, Checkered Stock, Modern.................. 225 275 150

RIFLE, LEVER ACTION

M1873 1 of 1000, .44–40 WCF, Blue Tube, Octagon Barrel, Steel
Buttplate, Engraved, Modern.. 675 750 750
M1873–".101," .22 L.R.R.F., Color Case Hardened Frame, Tube
Feed, Round Barrel, Steel Buttplate, Carbine, Modern............................ 500 600 225
M1873–".101," .44–40 WCF, Color Case Hardened Frame, Tube
Feed, Octagon Barrel, Steel Buttplate, Modern...................................... 550 650 250
M1873–".101," .44–40 WCF, Color Case Hardened Frame, Tube
Feed, Round Barrel, Steel Buttplate, Carbine, Modern............................ 600 700 225
M1873–".101," Trapper, .22 L.R.R.F., Color Case Hardened Frame,
Tube Feed, Round Barrel, Steel Buttplate, Modern................................. 450 550 225
M1873–".101," Trapper, .44–40 WCF, Color Case Hardened Frame,
Tube Feed, Round Barrel, Steel Buttplate, Modern................................. 425 500 225
Yellowboy Trapper, .22 L.R.R.F., Brass Frame, Tube Feed, Round
Barrel, Brass Buttplate, Modern.. 650 750 225
Yellowboy Trapper, .38 Special, Brass Frame, Tube Feed, Round
Barrel, Brass Buttplate, Modern.. 650 750 225
Yellowboy Trapper, .44–40 WCF, Brass Frame, Tube Feed,
Round Barrel, Brass Buttplate, Modern.. 700 800 225
Yellowboy, .22 L.R.R.F., Brass Frame, Tube Feed, Round Barrel,
Brass Buttplate, Saddle–Ring Carbine, Modern...................................... 525 625 225
Yellowboy, .38 Special, Brass Frame, Tube Feed, Octagon Barrel,
Brass Buttplate, Modern.. 550 650 225
Yellowboy, .38 Special, Brass Frame, Tube Feed, Round Barrel,
Brass Buttplate, Saddle–Ring Carbine, Modern...................................... 600 700 200
Yellowboy, .44–40 WCF, Brass Frame, Tube Feed, Octagon Barrel,
Brass Buttplate, Modern.. 600 700 225
Yellowboy, .44–40 WCF, Brass Frame, Tube Feed, Round Barrel,
Brass Buttplate, Saddle–Ring Carbine, Modern...................................... 600 700 225

RIFLE, FLINTLOCK

.45 "Kentucky," Carbine, Brass Furniture, Reproduction 300 350 175
.45 "Kentucky," Long Rifle, Brass Furniture, Reproduction 300 350 175
.58 M1803, Harper's Ferry, Brass Furniture, Military,
Reproduction 325 400 200

Navy Arms .58 1803 Harper's Ferry

.69 M1795 Springfield, Musket, Modern Reproduction 400 475 250
.69 M1809 Springfield, Musket, Modern Reproduction 400 475 250
.75 Brown Bess (Jap), Musket, Modern Reproduction 400 475 250

	V.G.	Exc	Prior Edition
.75 Brown Bess, Carbine, Modern Reproduction	$500	$575	$300
.75 Brown Bess, Musket, Modern Reproduction	500	575	300

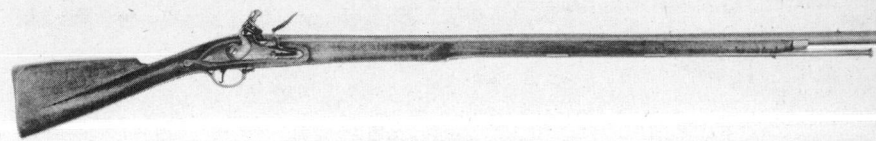

Navy Arms Brown Bess Rifle

RIFLE, PERCUSSION

.44 Remington, Revolving, Carbine, Brass Furniture, Reproduction	200	275	150
.45 "Kentucky," Carbine, Brass Furniture, Reproduction	275	325	175
.45 "Kentucky," Carbine, Brass Furniture, Reproduction	275	325	175
.45 "Kentucky," Long Rifle, Brass Furniture, Reproduction	275	325	175
.45 Hawken Hurricane, Octagon Barrel, Brass Furniture, Reproduction	300	375	200
.45 Morse, Octagon Barrel, Brass Frame, Reproduction	200	250	125
.50 Hawken Hurricane, Octagon Barrel, Brass Furniture, Reproduction	325	375	200
.50 Morse, Octagon Barrel, Brass Frame, Reproduction	225	275	150
.54 Gallagher, Carbine, Military, Steel Furniture, Reproduction	300	375	200
.577 M1853 3–Band, Military, Musket, (Parker–Hale), Reproduction	375	450	225
.577 M1858 2–Band, Military, Rifled, (Parker–Hale), Reproduction	325	375	200
.577 M1861, Military, Musketoon, (Parker–Hale), Reproduction	325	375	200
.58 Buffalo Hunter, Round Barrel, Brass Furniture, Reproduction	300	350	175

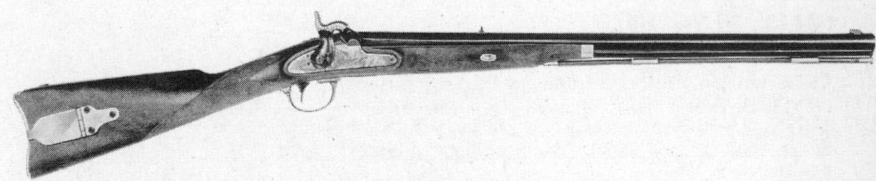

Navy Arms .58 Buffalo Hunter

.58 Hawken Hunter, Octagon Barrel, Brass Furniture, Reproduction	325	375	200
.58 J.P. Murray Artillery Carbine, Brass Furniture, Military, Reproduction	300	350	175
.58 M1841 Mississippi Rifle, Brass Furniture, Military, Reproduction	300	350	175

	V.G.	Exc	Prior Edition
.58 M1863 Springfield, Military, Rifled, Musket, Reproduction	$300	$350	$175

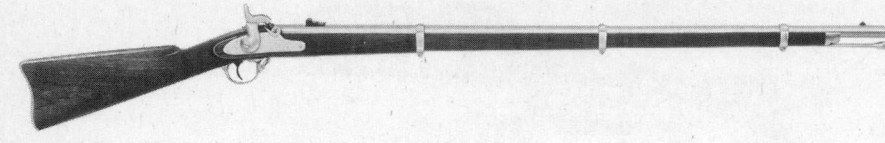

Navy Arms 1863 Springfield

.58 M1864 Springfield, Military, Rifled, Musket, Reproduction	325	375	200
.58 Morse, Octagon Barrel, Brass Frame, Reproduction	275	325	150
.58 Zouave 1864, Military, Carbine, Brass Furniture, Reproduction	300	350	175
.58 Zouave, Military, Reproduction	300	350	175

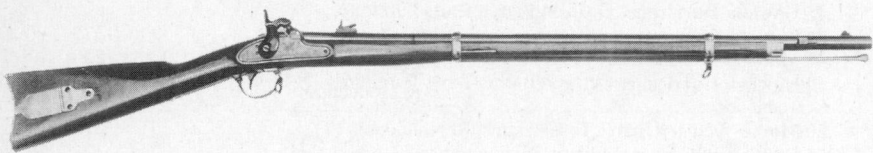

Navy Arms Zouave Rifle

RIFLE, SEMI-AUTOMATIC

AP–74, .22 L.R.R.F., Clip Fed, Plastic Stock, Modern..............................	150	175	100
AP–74, .22 L.R.R.F., Clip Fed, Wood Stock, Modern...............................	175	200	125
AP–74, .32 ACP, Clip Fed, Plastic Stock, Modern....................................	175	200	125
AP–74 Commando, .22 L.R.R.F., Clip Fed, Wood Stock, Modern..	150	175	100

RIFLE, SINGLESHOT

Buffalo, .45–70 Government, Rolling Block, Color Case Hardened Frame, Octagon Barrel, Open Rear Sights, Various Barrel Lengths, Modern..	200	250	175
Buffalo, .45–70 Government, Rolling Block, Color Case Hardened Frame, Half–Octagon Barrel, Open Rear Sights, Various Barrel Lengths, Modern..	200	250	175
Buffalo, .50 U.S. Carbine, Rolling Block, Color Case Hardened Frame, Octagon Barrel, Open Rear Sights, Various Barrel Lengths, Modern..	200	250	175
Buffalo, .50 U.S. Carbine, Rolling Block, Color Case Hardened Frame, Half–Octagon Barrel, Open Rear Sights, Various Barrel Lengths, Modern..	175	225	150
Creedmore, .45–70 Government, Rolling Block, Color Case Hardened Frame, Octagon Barrel, Vernier Sights, 30" Barrel, Modern..	350	425	225
Creedmore, .45–70 Government, Rolling Block, Color Case Hardened Frame, Half–Octagon Barrel, Vernier Sights, 30" Barrel, Modern...	325	375	200

	V.G.	Exc	Prior Edition
Creedmore, .50 U.S. Carbine, Rolling Block, Color Case Hardened Frame, Octagon Barrel, Vernier Sights, 30" Barrel, Modern.....	$325	$375	$200
Creedmore, .50 U.S. Carbine, Rolling Block, Color Case Hardened Frame, Half–Octagon Barrel, Vernier Sights, 30" Barrel, Modern.....	325	375	200
Creedmore, .50–140 Sharps, Rolling Block, Color Case Hardened Frame, Octagon Barrel, Vernier Sights, 30" Barrel, Modern.....	375	425	225
Martini, .45–70 Government, Color Case Hardened Frame, Half– Octagon Barrel, Open Rear Sight, Checkered Stock, Modern.....	400	450	250
Martini, .45–70 Government, Color Case Hardened Frame, Octagon Barrel, Open Rear Sight, Checkered Stock, Modern.....	400	450	250
Rolling Block, .22 Hornet, Carbine, Color Case Hardened Frame, Adjustable Sights, Modern.....	300	350	175
Rolling Block, .22 L.R.R.F., Carbine, Color Case Hardened Frame, Adjustable Sights, Modern.....	250	300	150
Rolling Block, .357 Magnum, Carbine, Color Case Hardened Frame, Adjustable Sights, Modern.....	250	300	150

SHOTGUN, PERCUSSION

Magnum Deluxe, 12 Ga., Double Barrel, Side by Side, Outside Hammers, Checkered Stock, Reproduction	200	225	200
Morse/Navy, 12 Ga., Singleshot, Brass Frame, Reproduction	150	175	150

Navy Arms Morse Navy Shotgun

Upland Deluxe, 12 Ga., Double Barrel, Side by Side, Outside Hammers, Checkered Stock, Reproduction	150	175	150
Zouave, 12 Ga., Brass Furniture, Reproduction	150	175	150

NEIHARD, PETER Northhampton, Pa. 1785–1787. See Kentucky Rifles.

NERO Made by Hopkins & Allen., c. 1880. Sold by C.L. Riker.

HANDGUN, REVOLVER

.22 Short R.F., 7 Shot, Spur Trigger, Solid Frame, Single Action, Antique.....	200	250	150
.32 Short R.F., 5 Shot, Spur Trigger, Solid Frame, Single Action, Antique.....	250	300	175

	V.G.	Exc	Prior Edition

NERO Made by J. Rupertus Arms Co., c. 1880. Sold by E. Tryon Co.

HANDGUN, REVOLVER

.22 Short R.F., 7 Shot, Spur Trigger, Solid Frame, Single Action,
Antique.. $250 $275 $175
.32 Short R.F., 5 Shot, Spur Trigger, Solid Frame, Single Action,
Antique.. 300 325 200

NEW CHIEFTAIN Made by Stevens Arms.

SHOTGUN, SINGLESHOT

Model 94, Various Gauges, Takedown, Automatic Ejector, Plain,
Hammer, Modern... 50 75 75

NEW NAMBU Shin Chuo Kogyo, Tokyo, Japan, c. 1960.

HANDGUN, REVOLVER

Model 58, .38 Special, Swing–Out Cylinder, Double Action,
Modern.. 100 125 125

HANDGUN, SEMI-AUTOMATIC

Model 57A, 9mm Luger, Clip Fed, Blue, Modern................................... 175 200 200
Model 57B, .32 ACP, Clip Fed, Blue, Modern... 150 175 175

NEW RIVAL Made by Crescent for Van Camp Hardware & Iron Co., Indianapolis, Ind.

SHOTGUN, DOUBLE BARREL, SIDE-BY-SIDE

Various Gauges, Hammerless, Damascus Barrel, Modern...................... 150 175 175
Various Gauges, Hammerless, Steel Barrel, Modern.............................. 175 200 200
Various Gauges, Outside Hammers, Damascus Barrel, Modern............. 150 175 175
Various Gauges, Outside Hammers, Steel Barrel, Modern..................... 150 175 175

SHOTGUN, SINGLESHOT

Various Gauges, Hammer, Steel Barrel, Modern.................................... 50 75 75

NEW YORK ARMS CO. Made by Crescent for Garnet Carter Co. Tenn., c. 1900.

SHOTGUN, DOUBLE BARREL, SIDE-BY-SIDE

Various Gauges, Hammerless, Damascus Barrel, Modern...................... 150 175 175
Various Gauges, Hammerless, Steel Barrel, Modern.............................. 175 200 200
Various Gauges, Outside Hammers, Damascus Barrel, Modern............. 150 175 175
Various Gauges, Outside Hammers, Steel Barrel, Modern..................... 175 200 200

SHOTGUN, SINGLESHOT

Various Gauges, Hammer, Steel Barrel, Modern.................................... 50 75 75

	V.G.	Exc	Prior Edition

NEW YORK PISTOL CO. N.Y.C., c. 1870.

HANDGUN, REVOLVER

	V.G.	Exc	Prior Edition
.22 Short R.F., 7 Shot, Spur Trigger, Solid Frame, Single Action, Antique	$150	$175	$165
.32 Short R.F., 5 Shot, Spur Trigger, Solid Frame, Single Action, Antique	125	150	150

NEWCOMER, JOHN Lancaster, Pa. 1770–1772. See Kentucky Rifles.

NEWHARDT, JACOB Allentown, Pa. 1770–1777. See Kentucky Rifles.

NEWPORT Made by Stevens Arms.

SHOTGUN, DOUBLE BARREL, SIDE-BY-SIDE

	V.G.	Exc	Prior Edition
Model 311, Various Gauges, Hammerless, Steel Barrel, Modern	125	150	175

NEWTON ARMS CO. Buffalo, N.Y. 1914–1918, reorganized 1918–1930 as Newton Rifle Corp.

RIFLE, BOLT ACTION

	V.G.	Exc	Prior Edition
1st Type, Various Calibers, Sporting Rifle, Set Trigger, Checkered Stock, Open Rear Sight, Curio	850	1,000	600
2nd Type, Various Calibers, Sporting Rifle, Set Trigger, Checkered Stock, Open Rear Sight, Curio	750	850	650
Newton–Mauser, Various Calibers, Sporting Rifle, Set Trigger, Checkered Stock, Open Rear Sight, Curio	675	775	525

NICHOLS, JOHN Oxford, England 1730–1775.

HANDGUN, FLINTLOCK

	V.G.	Exc	Prior Edition
Holster Pistol, Engraved, Brass Furniture, High Quality, Antique	3,000	3,500	3,500

NIKKO SPORTING FIREARMS Japan Imported by Kane–matsu–Gosho U.S.A. Inc., Arlington Heights, Ill. 1958–1989. Sold in the U.S. as "Golden Eagle."

RIFLE, BOLT ACTION

	V.G.	Exc	Prior Edition
Model 7000, Various African Calibers, Grade 1, Checkered Stock, Modern	300	575	350
Model 7000, Various Calibers, Grade 1, Checkered Stock, Modern	250	525	300

	V.G.	Exc	Prior Edition

SHOTGUN, DOUBLE BARREL, OVER-UNDER

Model 5000, 12 and 20 Gauge, Field Grade 2, Vent Rib,
Checkered Stock, Light Engraving, Gold Overlay, Modern...................... $775 $850 $575
Model 5000, 12 and 20 Gauge, Field Grade, Vent Rib, Checkered
Stock, Light Engraving, Gold Overlay, Modern.................................... 675 750 475
Model 5000, 12 and 20 Gauge, Skeet Grade 2, Vent Rib,
Checkered Stock, Light Engraving, Gold Overlay, Modern..................... 800 875 600
Model 5000, 12 and 20 Gauge, Skeet Grade, Vent Rib, Checkered
Stock, Light Engraving, Gold Overlay, Modern.................................... 700 775 575
Model 5000, 12 and 20 Gauge, Trap Grade 2, Vent Rib,
Checkered Stock, Light Engraving, Gold Overlay, Modern..................... 800 875 600
Model 5000, 12 and 20 Gauge, Trap Grade, Vent Rib, Checkered
Stock, Light Engraving, Gold Overlay, Modern.................................... 700 775 575
Model 5000 Grandee, 12 and 20 Gauge, Field Grade 3, Vent Rib,
Checkered Stock, Fancy Engraving, Gold Overlay, Modern.................... 1,750 2,000 2,000
Model 5000 Grandee, 12 and 20 Gauge, Skeet Grade 3, Vent Rib,
Checkered Stock, Fancy Engraving, Gold Overlay, Modern.................... 2,000 2,250 2,000
Model 5000 Grandee, 12 and 20 Gauge, Trap Grade 3, Vent Rib,
Checkered Stock, Fancy Engraving, Gold Overlay, Modern.................... 2,000 2,250 2,000

NITRO PROOF Made by Stevens Arms.

SHOTGUN, SINGLESHOT

Model 115, Various Gauges, Hammer, Automatic Ejector,
Modern.. 50 75 75

NIVA Kohout & Spolecnost, Kydne, Czechoslovakia.

HANDGUN, SEMI-AUTOMATIC

Niva, 6.35mm, Clip Fed, Blue, Modern...................................... 125 150 200

NOBLE Haydenville, Mass. 1950–1971.

RIFLE, BOLT ACTION

.98 Mauser, .30–06 Springfield, Monte Carlo Stock, Open Rear
Sight, Modern.. 100 125 125
Model 10, .22 L.R.R.F., Singleshot, Modern.. 25 50 50
Model 20, .22 L.R.R.F., Singleshot, Modern.. 25 50 50
Model 222, .22 L.R.R.F., Singleshot, Modern.. 50 75 75

RIFLE, LEVER ACTION

Model 275, .22 L.R.R.F., Tube Feed, Modern............................. 50 75 75

RIFLE, SEMI-AUTOMATIC

Model 285, .22 L.R.R.F., Tube Feed, Modern............................. 75 100 100

RIFLE, SLIDE ACTION

Model 235, .22 L.R.R.F., Wood Stock, Modern.. 75 100 100
Model 33, .22 L.R.R.F., Plastic Stock, Modern.. 50 75 75
Model 33A, .22 L.R.R.F., Wood Stock, Modern...................................... 75 100 100

	V.G.	Exc	Prior Edition

SHOTGUN, DOUBLE BARREL, SIDE-BY-SIDE

	V.G.	Exc	Prior Edition
Model 420, Various Gauges, Hammerless, Checkered Stock, Recoil Pad, Modern	$125	$150	$150
Model 420EK, Various Gauges, Hammerless, Checkered Stock, Recoil Pad, Fancy Wood, Modern	150	175	175
Model 450E, Various Gauges, Hammerless, Checkered Stock, Recoil Pad, Modern	200	250	250

SHOTGUN, SEMI-AUTOMATIC

	V.G.	Exc	Prior Edition
Model 80, .410 Ga., Modern	100	150	150

SHOTGUN, SLIDE ACTION

	V.G.	Exc	Prior Edition
Model 160 Deergun, 12 and 20 Gauges, Peep Sights, Modern	75	125	125
Model 166L Deergun, 12 and 16 Gauges, Peep Sights, Modern	75	125	125
Model 166LP Deergun, 12 and 16 Gauges, Peep Sights, Modern	75	125	125
Model 200, 20 Ga., Modern	75	125	125
Model 200, 20 Ga., Adjustable Choke, Modern	75	125	125
Model 200, 20 Ga., Trap Grade, Modern	75	125	125
Model 200, 20 Ga., Vent Rib, Adjustable Choke, Modern	75	125	125
Model 300, 12 Ga., Modern	75	125	125
Model 300, 12 Ga., Adjustable Choke, Modern	75	125	125
Model 300, 12 Ga., Trap Grade, Modern	100	150	150
Model 300, 12 Ga., Vent Rib, Adjustable Choke, Modern	125	150	150
Model 390, 12 Ga., Peep Sights, Modern	75	125	125
Model 40, 12 Ga., Hammerless, Solid Frame, Adjustable Choke, Modern	75	125	125
Model 400, .410 Ga., Modern	75	125	125
Model 400, .410 Ga., Adjustable Choke, Modern	75	125	125
Model 400, .410 Ga., Skeet Grade, Modern	75	125	125
Model 400, .410 Ga., Skeet Grade, Adjustable Choke, Modern	100	150	150
Model 50, 12 Ga., Hammerless, Solid Frame, Modern	50	100	100
Model 60, 12 and 16 Gauges, Hammerless, Solid Frame, Adjustable Choke, Modern	75	125	125
Model 60 RCLP, 12 and 16 Gauges, Hammerless, Solid Frame, Vent Rib, Adjustable Choke, Checkered Stock, Modern	75	125	125
Model 602, 20 Ga., Modern	75	125	125
Model 602CLP, 20 Ga., Adjustable Choke, Modern	75	125	125
Model 602RCLP, 20 Ga., Adjustable Choke, Vent Rib, Modern	100	150	150
Model 602RLP, 20 Ga., Vent Rib, Modern	75	125	125
Model 60ACP, 12 and 16 Gauges, Hammerless, Solid Frame, Adjustable Choke, Vent Rib, Modern	75	125	125
Model 60AF, 12 and 16 Gauges, Hammerless, Solid Frame, Vent, Rib, Adjustable Choke, Modern	75	125	125
Model 65, 12 and 20 Gauges, Hammerless, Solid Frame, Modern	50	100	100
Model 662CR, 20 Ga., Vent Rib, Modern	75	125	125
Model 66CLP, 12 and 16 Gauges, Adjustable Choke, Modern	75	125	125
Model 66RCLP, 12 and 20 Gauges, Hammerless, Solid Frame, Adjustable Choke, Vent Rib, Modern	75	125	125
Model 66RLP, 12 and 20 Gauges, Hammerless, Solid Frame, Vent Rib, Modern	75	125	125
Model 66XLP, 12 and 20 Gauges, Hammerless, Solid Frame, Modern	75	125	125
Model 70, .410 Ga., Modern	50	100	100
Model 70CLP, .410 Ga., Hammerless, Solid Frame, Adjustable Choke, Modern	75	125	125

	V.G.	Exc	Prior Edition
Model 70RL, .410 Ga., Modern	$75	$125	$125
Model 70X, .410 Ga., Modern	50	100	100
Model 70XL, .410 Ga., Modern	50	100	100
Model 757, 20 Ga., Adjustable Choke, Lightweight, Modern	100	150	150

NOCK, HENRY London & Birmingham, England 1760–1810.

RIFLE, FLINTLOCK

.65, Ellett Carbine, Musket, Military, Antique	1,750	2,000	2,000

SHOTGUN, PERCUSSION

Fowler, Converted from Flintlock, Patent Breech, Antique	600	750	750

NONPAREIL Made by Norwich Falls Pistols Co., c. 1880.

HANDGUN, REVOLVER

.32 Short R.F., 5 Shot, Spur Trigger, Solid Frame, Single Action, Antique	150	175	175

NORTH AMERICAN ARMS, INC. Provo, Ut.

HANDGUN, REVOLVER

.450 Magnum, Single Action, Western Style, High Polish Finish, 5 Shot, Modern	650	950	950
Mini, .22 L.R.R.F., 5 Shot, Single Action, Spur Trigger, 1" Barrel, Derringer, Modern	100	125	100
Mini, .22 L.R.R.F., 5 Shot, Single Action, Spur Trigger, 1½" Barrel, Derringer, Modern	100	125	100
Mini, .22 Short, 5 Shot, Single Action, Spur Trigger, 1" Barrel, Derringer, Modern	75	100	100
Mini, .22 W.M.R., 5 Shot, Single Action, Spur Trigger, 1" Barrel, Derringer, Modern	125	150	125

NORTHWESTERNER Made by Stevens Arms.

RIFLE, BOLT ACTION

Model 52, .22 L.R.R.F., Single Action, Takedown, Modern	25	50	50

SHOTGUN, SINGLESHOT

Model 94, Various Gauges, Takedown, Automatic Ejector, Plain, Hammer, Modern	50	75	75

NORTON See Budischowsky and Americam Arms & Ammunition Co.

NORWEGIAN MILITARY

HANDGUN, SEMI-AUTOMATIC

Mauser Model 1914, 7.65mm, Blue, Clip Fed, Curio	275	300	575
Model 1914, 11.25mm, Military, Clip Fed, Curio	700	800	350
Model 1914, 11.25mm, Military, Clip Fed, Nazi–Proofed, Curio	1,250	1,500	500

	V.G.	Exc	Prior Edition
RIFLE, BOLT ACTION			
Model 1894 Krag, 6.5 X 55mm, Military, Curio	$650	$750	$725
Model 1925 Krag Sniper, 6.5 X 55mm, Military, Curio	800	950	900

NORWICH PISTOL CO. Norwich, Conn. 1875–1881.

HANDGUN, REVOLVER

.22 Short R.F., 7 Shot, Spur Trigger, Solid Frame, Single Action, Antique	150	175	175
.32 Short R.F., 5 Shot, Spur Trigger, Solid Frame, Single Action, Antique	125	150	150

NOT–NAC MFG. CO. Made by Crescent for Belknap Hardware Co., Louisville, Ky.

SHOTGUN, DOUBLE BARREL, SIDE-BY-SIDE

Various Gauges, Hammerless, Damascus Barrel, Modern	150	175	175
Various Gauges, Hammerless, Steel Barrel, Modern	150	200	200
Various Gauges, Outside Hammers, Damascus Barrel, Modern	150	175	175
Various Gauges, Outside Hammers, Steel Barrel, Modern	150	175	175

SHOTGUN, SINGLESHOT

Various Gauges, Hammer, Steel Barrel, Modern	50	75	75

NOVA La France Specialties, San Diego, Calif.

HANDGUN, SEMI-AUTOMATIC

Nova, 9mm Luger, Clip Fed, "Electrofilm" Finish, Reduced M1911 Style, Modern	400	450	500

NOYS, R. Wiltshire, England 1800–1830.

HANDGUN, FLINTLOCK

Pocket Pistol, Screw Barrel, Box Lock, Steel Barrel and Frame, Plain, Antique	550	700	700

NUMRICH ARMS CO. West Hurley, N.Y. Also see Auto Ord–nance, Thompson, Hopkins & Allen.

HANDGUN, SEMI-AUTOMATIC

M1911A1, .45 ACP, Clip Fed, Blue, Military Style, Modern	200	250	250
Model ZG–51, .45 ACP, Clip Fed, Finned Barrel, Adjustable Sights, with Compensator, (Numrich), Modern	225	275	350

RIFLE, SEMI-AUTOMATIC

Model 27A1, .45 ACP, Clip Fed, without Compensator, Modern	375	450	350
Model 27A1, .45 ACP, Clip Fed, without Compensator, Cased with Accessories, Modern	550	650	475
Model 27A1 Deluxe, .45 ACP, Clip Fed, Finned Barrel, Adjustable Sights, with Compensator, Modern	450	525	375

	V.G.	Exc	Prior Edition
Model 27A3, .22 L.R.R.F., Clip Fed, Finned Barrel, Adjustable Sights, with Compensator, Modern..	$300	$350	$350

NUNNEMACHER, ABRAHAM York, Pa. 1779–1783. See Kentucky Rifles.

O

OAK LEAF Made by Stevens Arms.

SHOTGUN, SINGLESHOT

Model 90, Various Gauges, Takedown, Automatic Ejector, Plain, Hammer, Mpdern... $25 $50 $50

OCCIDENTAL Belgium, c. 1880.

SHOTGUN, DOUBLE BARREL, SIDE-BY-SIDE

Various Gauges, Outside Hammers, Damascus Barrel, Modern............ 100 150 150

OLD TIMER Made by Stevens Arms.

SHOTGUN, SINGLESHOT

Model 94, Various Gauges, Takedown, Automatic Ejector, Plain, Hammer, Modern... 25 50 50

OLYMPIC Made by Stevens Arms.

SHOTGUN, DOUBLE BARREL, SIDE-BY-SIDE

M 315, Various Gauges, Hamnmerless, Steel Barrel, Modern................. 150 175 175
Model 311, Various Gauges, Hamnmerless, Steel Barrel, Modern.......... 150 175 175

SHOTGUN, SINGLESHOT

Model 94, Various Gauges, Takedown, Automatic Ejector, Plain, Hammer, Modern... 25 50 50

O.M. Ojanguren y Marcaido, Eibar, Spain, c. 1920.

HANDGUN, REVOLVER

S & W Type, Various Calibers, Double Action, Swing–Out Cylinder, Blue, Curio... 75 100 100

OMEGA Armero Especialistas Reunidas, Eibar, Spain, c. 1925.

HANDGUN, SEMI-AUTOMATIC

6.35mm, Clip Fed, Curio... 100 125 125
7.65mm, Clip Fed, Grip Safety, Curio... 125 150 150

	V.G.	Exc	Prior Edition

OMEGA Tarrance, Calif. Made by Hi–Shear Corp. 1980's.
RIFLE, BOLT ACTION
Omega III, Various Calibers, no Sights, Fancy Wood, Adjustable
Trigger, Modern.. $375 $425 $425

ORBEA HERMANOS Orbea Hermanos and Orbea y Cia., Eibar, Spain, c. 1860–1935.
HANDGUN, REVOLVER
S & W Type, .44 Russian, Double Action, Top–Break, Antique.............. 100 125 125

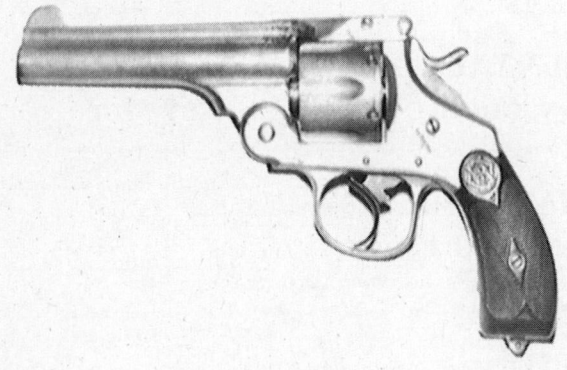

Orbea Hermanos .44

OREA Orechowsky, Graz, Austria, c. 1930.
RIFLE, SINGLESHOT
Heeren Rifle, Various Calibers, Checkered Stock, Engraved,
Fancy Wood, Modern.. 1,250 1,750 1,750

ORTGIES Germany, 1918–1921, 1921 Taken over by Deutsche–Werke, Er–furt, Germany.

HANDGUN, SEMI-AUTOMATIC

D Pocket, .380 ACP, Clip Fed, Curio.. $225 $275 $275

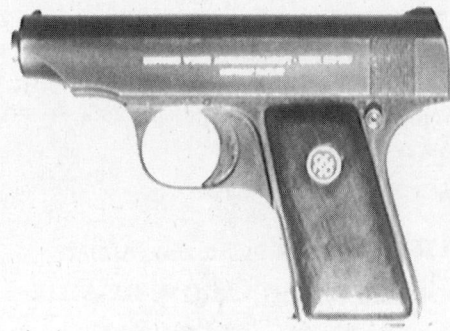

Ortgies D Pocket

D Pocket, 7.65mm, Clip Fed, Curio...	175	225	225
D Vest Pocket, 6.35mm, Clip Fed, Curio...	175	225	225
H O Pocket, .380 ACP, Clip Fed, Curio..	200	250	250
H O Vest Pocket, 6.35mm, Clip Fed, Curio...	175	225	225

Ortgies H O Vest Pocket

	V.G.	Exc	Prior Edition

OSGOOD GUN WORKS Norwich, Conn., c. 1880.

HANDGUN, REVOLVER

Duplex, .22/.32 R.F., 8 Shot .22, Singleshot .32, Two Barrels,
Spur Trigger, Antique... $650 $750 $500

OUR JAKE

HANDGUN, REVOLVER

.32 R.F., Spur Trigger, Solid Frame, Hammer, Antique............................ 125   150   150

OWA Oesterreichische Werke Anstalt, Vienna, Austria, c. 1920–1925.

HANDGUN, SEMI-AUTOMATIC

Model 1921 Standard, 6.35mm, Clip Fed, Curio..................................... 200   250   250

OXFORD ARMS Made by Stevens Arms.

SHOTGUN, DOUBLE BARREL, SIDE-BY-SIDE

Model 311, Various Gauges, Hammerless, Steel Barrel, Modern............. 150   175   175

OXFORD ARMS CO. Made by Crescent for Belknap Hdw. Co.,
Louisville, Ky.

SHOTGUN, DOUBLE BARREL, SIDE-BY-SIDE

Various Gauges, Hammerless, Damascus Barrel, Modern...................... 125   175   175
Various Gauges, Hammerless, Steel Barrel, Modern............................... 150   200   200
Various Gauges, Outside Hammers, Damascus Barrel, Modern............. 125   175   175
Various Gauges, Outside Hammers, Steel Barrel, Modern...................... 125   175   175

SHOTGUN, SINGLESHOT

Various Gauges, Hammer, Steel Barrel, Modern.................................... 50   75   75

P

P.A.F. Pretoria Arms Factory, Pretoria, South Africa, c. 1955.

HANDGUN, SEMI-AUTOMATIC

Junior, For Cocking Indicator Add 10%–15%
Junior, 6.35mm, High Slide, Clip Fed, Blue, Curio.................................. $225 $275 $300

P.A.F. Junior

Junior, 6.35mm, Low Slide, Clip Fed, Blue, Curio.................................... 250 300 325
Junior, 6.35mm, Sight Rib, Clip Fed, Blue, Curio.................................... 275 325 350

PAGE, T. Norwich, England, 1766–1776.

HANDGUN, FLINTLOCK

.60, Queen Anne Style, Pocket Pistol, Screw Barrel, Box Lock,
Brass Furniture, Engraved, Antique.. 1,200 1,600 1,600

PAGE–LEWIS ARMS CO. See Stevens, J. Arms & Tool Co. for similar listings.

PALMER, THOMAS Philadelphia, Pa. 1772–1776. See Kentucky Rifles and U.S. Military.

	V.G.	Exc	Prior Edition

PALMETTO Made by Stevens Arms.

SHOTGUN, SINGLESHOT

Model 90, Various Gauges, Takedown, Automatic Ejector, Plain,
Hammer, Curio.. $25 $50 $50
Model 94, Various Gauges, Takedown, Automatic Ejector, Plain,
Hammer, Modern.. 50 75 75

PANNABECKER, JEFFERSON Lancaster, Pa. 1790–1810. See Kentucky Rifles.

PANNABECKER, JESSE Lancaster, Pa. 1833–1860. See Kentucky Rifles.

PANTAX Tradename used by E. Woerther, Buenos Aires, Argentina.

PANZER G.M.F. Corp., Watertown, Ct.

HANDGUN, DOUBLE BARREL, OVER-UNDER

Panzer, .22 L.R.R.F., Twist Barrel, Spur Trigger, Modern...................... 50 75 50

PARAGON Made by Stevens Arms.

SHOTGUN, DOUBLE BARREL, SIDE-BY-SIDE

Model 311, Various Gauges, Hammerless, Steel Barrel, Modern............. 150 175 175

PARAGON Possibly made by Hopkins & Allen, c. 1880.

HANDGUN, REVOLVER

.32 Short R.F., 5 Shot, Spur Trigger, Solid Frame, Single Action,
Antique... 150 175 175

PARAMOUNT Retolaza Hermanos, Eibar, Spain, c. 1920.

HANDGUN, SEMI-AUTOMATIC

7.65mm, Clip Fed, Curio.. 100 125 125
M 1914, 7.65mm, Clip Fed, Long Grip, Curio........................... 125 150 150
Vest Pocket, 6.35mm, Clip Fed, Curio.................................... 100 125 125

PARKER BROTHERS Imported from Italy by Jana International.

SHOTGUN, DOUBLE BARREL, OVER-UNDER

California Trap Model, 12 Ga., Single Selective Trigger,
Automatic Ejectors, Checkered Stock, Engraved, Double
Vent Rib, Modern.. 475 550 550

	V.G.	Exc	Prior Edition
Field Model, 12 Ga. 3", Single Selective Trigger, Automatic Ejectors, Checkered Stock, Engraved, Vent Rib, Modern..........................	$300	$350	$350
Field Model, 12 Ga., Single Selective Trigger, Automatic Ejectors, Checkered Stock, Engraved, Vent Rib, Modern.......................................	275	325	325
Monte Carlo Stock, 12 Ga., Single Selective Trigger, Automatic Ejectors, Checkered Stock, Engraved, Vent Rib, Modern........................	300	375	375
Skeet Model, 12 Ga., Single Selective Trigger, Automatic Ejectors, Checkered Stock, Engraved, Vent Rib, Modern.......................................	300	350	350

PARKER BROTHERS Meriden, Conn. 1868–1934. In 1934 Parker Bros. was taken over by Remington Arms Co.

SHOTGUN, DOUBLE BARREL, SIDE-BY-SIDE

Beavertail Forend, for BHE through A–1 Add 20%
Beavertail Forend, VHE through CHE Add $300.00–$500.00
Extra Barrel, Add 30%–40%
For Damascus Barrel, Deduct 60%–75%
For Ejectors, Add 50% (E)
For Upgrades, Deduct 25%–30%
Outside Hammers with Steel Barrels, Deduct 20%–30%
Single Selective Trigger, Add 20%
Skeet Grade, Add 15%–25%
Trap Grade, Add 15%–25%

	V.G.	Exc	Prior Edition
A–1 Special, 12 Ga., Hammerless, Double Trigger, Automatic Ejector, Modern..	55,000	65,000	65,000
A–1 Special, 16 Ga., Hammerless, Double Trigger, Automatic Ejector, Modern..	55,000	65,000	65,000
A–1 Special, 20 Ga., Hammerless, Double Trigger, Automatic Ejector, Modern..	—	100,000	—
A–1 Special, 28 Ga., Hammerless, Double Trigger, Automatic Ejector, Modern..	—	RARE	—
AAHE, 12 Ga., Hammerless, Double Trigger, Automatic Ejector, Modern..	25,000	30,000	30,000
AAHE, 16 Ga., Hammerless, Double Trigger, Automatic Ejector, Modern..	27,500	32,500	32,000
AAHE, 20 Ga., Hammerless, Double Trigger, Automatic Ejector, Modern..	45,000	55,000	55,000
AAHE, 28 Ga., Hammerless, Double Trigger, Automatic Ejector, Modern..	—	75,000	75,000
AHE, .410 Ga., Hammerless, Double Trigger, Automatic Ejector, Modern..	—	RARE	—
AHE, 10 Ga., Hammerless, Double Trigger, Automatic Ejector, Modern..	—	RARE	—
AHE, 12 Ga., Hammerless, Double Trigger, Automatic Ejector, Modern..	15,000	17,500	18,000
AHE, 16 Ga., Hammerless, Double Trigger, Automatic Ejector, Modern..	17,500	20,000	19,000
AHE, 20 Ga., Hammerless, Double Trigger, Automatic Ejector, Modern..	20,000	25,000	25,000
AHE, 28 Ga., Hammerless, Double Trigger, Automatic Ejector, Modern..	—	50,000	45,000
BH, .410 Ga., Hammerless, Double Trigger, Automatic Ejector, Modern..	—	RARE	—

	V.G.	Exc	Prior Edition
BH, 10 Ga., Hammerless, Double Trigger, Automatic Ejector, Modern................	—	RARE	—
BH, 12 Ga., Hammerless, Double Trigger, Automatic Ejector, Modern................	$6,500	$7,500	$6,000
BH, 16 Ga., Hammerless, Double Trigger, Automatic Ejector, Modern................	6,000	8,000	6,500
BH, 20 Ga., Hammerless, Double Trigger, Automatic Ejector, Modern................	10,000	12,500	9,000
BH, 28 Ga., Hammerless, Double Trigger, Automatic Ejector, Modern................	20,000	25,000	25,000
CH, .410 Ga., Hammerless, Double Trigger, Automatic Ejector, Modern................	35,000	37,500	37,500
CH, 10 Ga., Hammerless, Double Trigger, Automatic Ejector, Modern................	—	RARE	—
CH, 12 Ga., Hammerless, Double Trigger, Automatic Ejector, Modern................	4,000	5,000	5,000
CH, 16 Ga., Hammerless, Double Trigger, Automatic Ejector, Modern................	4,500	5,500	5,700
CH, 20 Ga., Hammerless, Double Trigger, Automatic Ejector, Modern................	6,000	7,000	7,000
CH, 28 Ga., Hammerless, Double Trigger, Automatic Ejector, Modern................	12,500	15,000	15,000
DH, .410 Ga., Hammerless, Double Trigger, Automatic Ejector, Modern................	25,000	30,000	30,000
DH, 10 Ga., Hammerless, Double Trigger, Automatic Ejector, Modern................	—	RARE	—
DH, 12 Ga., Hammerless, Double Trigger, Automatic Ejector, Modern................	4,000	4,500	5,500
DH, 16 Ga., Hammerless, Double Trigger, Automatic Ejector, Modern................	4,000	4,500	6,000
DH, 20 Ga., Hammerless, Double Trigger, Automatic Ejector, Modern................	4,500	5,500	7,000
DH, 28 Ga., Hammerless, Double Trigger, Automatic Ejector, Modern................	7,500	10,000	12,000
Early Model, Various Gauges, Outside Hammers, Damascus Barrel, Under–Lever, Antique................	2,000	2,500	1,800
GH, .410 Ga., Hammerless, Double Trigger, Automatic Ejector, Modern................	17,500	20,000	24,000
GH, 10 Ga. 3½", Hammerless, Double Trigger, Automatic Ejector, Modern................	—	RARE	—
GH, 10 Ga. 3½", Hammerless, Double Trigger, Automatic Ejector, Modern................	—	RARE	—
GH, 12 Ga., Hammerless, Double Trigger, Automatic Ejector, Modern................	3,500	4,000	5,000
GH, 12 Ga., Hammerless, Double Trigger, Automatic Ejector, Modern................	3,500	4,000	5,000
GH, 16 Ga., Hammerless, Double Trigger, Automatic Ejector, Modern................	4,000	4,500	5,500
GH, 16 Ga., Hammerless, Double Trigger, Automatic Ejector, Moden................	4,000	4,500	5,500
GH, 20 Ga., Hammerless, Double Trigger, Automatic Ejector, Modern................	4,000	4,500	6,000
GH, 20 Ga., Hammerless, Double Trigger, Automatic Ejector, Modern................	4,000	4,500	6,000

	V.G.	Exc	Prior Edition
GH, 28 Ga., Hammerless, Double Trigger, Automatic Ejector, Modern	$17,500	$20,000	$24,000
GH, 28 Ga., Hammerless, Double Trigger, Automatic Ejector, Modern	6,500	7,500	9,000
Invincible , 12 Ga., Hammerless, Double Trigger, Automatic Ejector, Modern	—	RARE	—
Invincible , 16 Ga., Hammerless, Double Trigger, Automatic Ejector, Modern	—	RARE	—
Trojan, 12 and 16 Gauges, Hammerless, Double Trigger, Modern	1,500	1,750	1,500
Trojan, 16 Ga., Hammerless, Double Trigger, Modern	2,500	2,750	2,250
Trojan, 20 Ga., Hammerless, Double Trigger, Modern	2,000	2,250	2,250
Vent Rib, 20%–50%			
VH, .410 Ga., Hammerless, Double Trigger, Automatic Ejector, Modern	17,000	20,000	20,000
VH, 12 Ga., Hammerless, Double Trigger, Automatic Ejector, Modern	2,000	2,500	3,500
VH, 16 Ga., Hammerless, Double Trigger, Automatic Ejector, Modern	2,000	2,500	4,000
VH, 20 Ga., Hammerless, Double Trigger, Automatic Ejector, Modern	3,500	4,000	5,000
VH, 28 Ga., Hammerless, Double Trigger, Automatic Ejector, Modern	6,000	6,500	9,000

SHOTGUN, SINGLE BARREL TRAP

	V.G.	Exc	Prior Edition
S.A., 12 Ga., Hammerless, Vent Rib, Automatic Ejector, Modern	4,000	4,500	3,500
S.A.–1 Special, 12 Ga., Hammerless, Vent Rib, Automatic Ejector, Modern	12,500	15,000	17,000
S.A.A., 12 Ga., Hammerless, Vent Rib, Automatic Ejector, Modern	5,000	6,000	5,000
S.B., 12 Ga., Hammerless, Vent Rib, Automatic Ejector, Modern	3,500	4,000	2,800
S.C., 12 Ga., Hammerless, Vent Rib, Automatic Ejector, Modern	2,500	3,000	1,700

PARKER SAFETY HAMMERLESS Made by Columbia Armory, Tenn., c. 1890.

HANDGUN, REVOLVER

	V.G.	Exc	Prior Edition
.32 S & W, 5 Shot, Top Break, Hammerless, Double Action, Curio	75	100	100

PARKER, WILLIAM London, England 1790–1840.

SHOTGUN, PERCUSSION

	V.G.	Exc	Prior Edition
14 Ga, Single Barrel, Smoothbore, High Quality, Cased with Accessories, Antique	1,250	1,500	1,500

SHOTGUN, FLINTLOCK

	V.G.	Exc	Prior Edition
16 Ga., Double Barrel, Side by Side, Engraved, High Quality, Antique	3,500	4,000	4,000

	V.G.	Exc	Prior Edition

PARKER–HALE LTD. Birmingham, England. Purchased by Navy Arms in 1991.

HANDGUN, REVOLVER

S & W Victory, .22 L.R.R.F., Conversion, Adjustable Sights, Modern	$225	$250	$250

RIFLE, BOLT ACTION

Model 1200, Various Calibers, Checkered Stock, Open Rear Sight, Monte Carlo Stock, Modern	500	550	650
Model 1200M, Various Calibers, Magnum, Checkered Stock, Open Rear Sight, Monte Carlo Stock, Modern	550	600	700
Model 1200V, Various Calibers, Heavy Barrel, Checkered Stock, no Sights, Monte Carlo Stock, Modern	475	525	675

RIFLE, PERCUSSION

.451, Whitworth Military Target Rifle, 3 Bands, Target Sights, Checkered Stock, Reproduction	325	350	350
.54 Gallagher, Breech Loader, Carbine, Brass Furniture, Reproduction	150	175	175
.58 M1853 Enfield Rifle, Rifled, Brass Funiture, Reproduction	175	200	200
.58 M1853 Enfield, Musket, Rifled, 2 Bands, Brass Furniture, Reproduction	175	200	200
.58 M1861 Enfield, Musketoon, Rifled, 2 Bands, Brass Furniture, Reproduction	150	175	175

SHOTGUN, SEMI-AUTOMATIC

Model 640A, 12 Ga., Checkered Stock, Vent Rib, Modern	475	550	450
Model 640M, 10 Ga. 3", Checkered Stock, Vent Rib, Modern	600	700	500

PARKHILL, ANDREW Phila., Pa. 1778–1785. See Kentucky Rifles and Pistols.

PAROLE Made by Hopkins & Allen, c. 1880.

HANDGUN, REVOLVER

.22 Short R.F., 7 Shot, Spur Trigger, Solid Frame, Single Action, Antique	150	175	175

PARR, J. Liverpool, England, c. 1810.

RIFLE, FLINTLOCK

.75, 3rd Model Brown Bess, Musket, Military, Antique	1,200	1,500	1,500

PARSONS, HIRAM Baltimore, Md., c. 1819. See Kentucky Rifles.

	V.G.	Exc	Prior Edition

PATRIOT Made by Norwich Falls Pistol Co., c. 1880.

HANDGUN, REVOLVER

.32 Short R.F., 5 Shot, Spur Trigger, Solid Frame, Single Action,
Antique.. $150 $175 $175

PECK, ABIJAH Hartford, Conn. See U.S. Military.

PEERLESS Made by Crescent H. & D. Folsom, c. 1900.

SHOTGUN, DOUBLE BARREL, SIDE-BY-SIDE

	V.G.	Exc	Prior Edition
Various Gauges, Hammerless, Damascus Barrel, Modern......................	125	175	175
Various Gauges, Hammerless, Steel Barrel, Modern..............................	150	200	200
Various Gauges, Outside Hammers, Damascus Barrel, Modern.............	150	175	175
Various Gauges, Outside Hammers, Steel Barrel, Modern......................	150	200	200

SHOTGUN, SINGLESHOT

Various Gauges, Hammer, Steel Barrel, Modern.................................... 50   75   75

PEERLESS Made by Stevens.

RIFLE, BOLT ACTION

Model 056 Buckhorn, .22 L.R.R.F., 5 Shot Clip, Peep Sights,
Modern... 50   75   75
Model 066 Buckhorn, .22 L.R.R.F., Tube Feed, Peep Sights,
Modern... 50   75   75
Model 53, .22 L.R.R.F., Single Shot, Takedown, Modern....................... 25   50   50

PENCE, JACOB Lancaster, Pa. 1771. See Kentucky Rifles and Pistols.

PENETRATOR Made by Norwich Falls Pistol Co., c. 1880.

HANDGUN, REVOLVER

.32 Short R.F., 5 Shot, Spur Trigger, Solid Frame, Single Action,
Modern... 125   175   175

PENNYPACKER, DANIEL Berks County, Pa. 1773–1808. See Kentucky Rifles and Pistols.

PENNYPACKER, WM. Berks County, Pa. 1808–1858. See Kentucky Rifles and Pistols.

	V.G.	Exc	Prior Edition

PERCUSSION EXAMPLES

HANDGUN, PERCUSSION

	V.G.	Exc	Prior Edition
.40 English, 6 Shot, Pepperbox, Pocket Pistol, Light Engraving, German Silver Frame, Steel Barrel, Antique	$350	$500	$500
.45, Pair French, Target Pistol, Octagon Barrel, Single Set Trigger, Brass Furniture, Cased with Accessories, Antique	2,500	3,000	3,000
.70, French Sotiau, Belt Pistol, Steel Furniture, Rifled, Octagon Barrel, Antique	450	600	600
Boot Pistol, Bar Hammer, Screw Barrel, Antique	200	250	250
Boot Pistol, Boxlock, Screw Barrel, Antique	250	300	300
Boot Pistol, Sidelock, Derringer Style, Antique	200	250	250
Pair, Duelling Pistols, Octagon Barrel, Single Set Trigger, German Silver Furniture, Medium Quality, Cased with Accessories, Antique	2,000	2,500	2,500

HANDGUN, REVOLVER

	V.G.	Exc	Prior Edition
.36 , Navy Colt Type, Belgian Make, Medium Quality, Antique	200	250	250
.45, Adams Type, Double Action, Octagon Barrel, Plain, Cased with Accessories, Antique	850	1,000	1,000

RIFLE, PERCUSSION

	V.G.	Exc	Prior Edition
American Indian Trade Gun, Belgian, Converted from Flintlock, Brass Furniture, Antique	2,500	3,500	1,200
Benchrest, Various Calibers, Heavy Barrel, Set Triggers, Target Sights, Light Decoration, Antique	700	850	850

Percussion Arms, Unknown Maker Benchrest Rifle

	V.G.	Exc	Prior Edition
Benchrest, Various Calibers, Heavy Barrel, Set Triggers, Target Sights, Medium Decoration, Antique	800	1,000	1,000
German, Schutzen Rifle, Rifled, Ivory Inlays, Gold Inlays, Ornate, Antique	5,000	6,000	6,000

SHOTGUN, PERCUSSION

	V.G.	Exc	Prior Edition
English, 12 Ga., Doule Barrel, Side by Side, Light Ornamentation, Medium Quality, Antique	350	500	500
English, 12 Ga., Doule Barrel, Side by Side, Light Ornamentation, High Quality, Cased with Accessories, Antique	700	950	950

PERFECT Made by Foehl & Weeks. Phila., Pa., c. 1890.

HANDGUN, REVOLVER

	V.G.	Exc	Prior Edition
.38 S & W, 5 Shot, Double Action, Top Break, Modern	75	100	100

	V.G.	Exc	Prior Edition

PERFECTION Made by Crescent for H. & G. Lipscomb & Co., Nashville, Tenn.

SHOTGUN, DOUBLE BARREL, SIDE-BY-SIDE

	V.G.	Exc	Prior Edition
Various Gauges, Hammerless, Damascus Barrel, Modern......................	$150	$175	$175
Various Gauges, Hammerless, Steel Barrel, Modern..............................	150	200	200
Various Gauges, Outside Hammer, Damascus Barrel, Modern..............	125	175	175
Various Gauges, Outside Hammer, Steel Barrel, Modern.......................	150	200	200

SHOTGUN, SINGLESHOT

	V.G.	Exc	Prior Edition
Various Gauges, Hammer, Steel Barrel, Modern....................................	50	75	75

PERFECTION AUTOMATIC REVOLVER Made by Forehand Arms Co.

HANDGUN, REVOLVER

	V.G.	Exc	Prior Edition
.32 S & W, 5 Shot, Double Action, Top Break, Antique..........................	75	100	100
.32 S & W, 5 Shot, Double Action, Top Break, Hammerless, Antique...	100	125	12

PERLA Frantisek Dusek, Opocno, Czechoslovakia, c. 1935.

HANDGUN, SEMI-AUTOMATIC

	V.G.	Exc	Prior Edition
.25 ACP , Clip Fed, Blue, Modern...	175	225	225

PETTIBONE, DANIEL Philadelphia, Pa. 1799–1814. See Kentucky Rifles and Pistols.

PHILLIPINE MILITARY

SHOTGUN, SINGLESHOT

	V.G.	Exc	Prior Edition
WW 2 Guerrilla Weapon, 12 Ga., Modern...	125	150	75

PHOENIX Spain, Tomas de Urizar y Cia., c. 1920.

HANDGUN, SEMI-AUTOMATIC

	V.G.	Exc	Prior Edition
Vest Pocket, 6.35mm, Clip Fed, Curio..	125	150	150

	V.G.	Exc	Prior Edition

PHOENIX ARMS CO. Lowell Arms Co., Lowell, Mass., c. 1920.

HANDGUN, SEMI-AUTOMATIC

Vest Pocket, .25 ACP, Clip Fed, Curio.. $425 $475 $475

Phoenix Arms Co. .25

PIC Made in West Germany for Precise Imports Corp., Suffern, N.Y.

HANDGUN, REVOLVER

.22 L.R.R.F., Double Action, Blue, Modern.. 15   75   50

HANDGUN, SEMI-AUTOMATIC

Vest Pocket, .22 Short R.F., Clip Fed, Modern... 25   50   100
Vest Pocket, .25 ACP., Clip Fed, Modern... 25   50   100

PIC .25

PICKFATT, HUMPHREY London, England 1714–1730.

HANDGUN, FLINTLOCK

Pair, Holster Pistol, Engraved, Brass Furniture, High Quality,
Antique... $7,500 $8,500 $8,500
Pair, Queen Anne Style, Box Lock, Pocket Pistol, Silver Furniture,
Antique.. 2,500 3,000 3,000

PIEDMONT Made by Crescent for Piedmont Hdw. Danville, Pa.

SHOTGUN, DOUBLE BARREL, SIDE-BY-SIDE

	V.G.	Exc	Prior Edition
Various Gauges, Hammerless, Damascus Barrel, Modern......................	125	175	175
Various Gauges, Hammerless, Steel Barrel, Modern.............................	175	200	200
Various Gauges, Outside Hammers, Damascus Barrel, Modern.............	150	175	175
Various Gauges, Outside Hammers, Steel Barrel, Modern......................	150	200	200

SHOTGUN, SINGLESHOT

	V.G.	Exc	Prior Edition
Various Gauges, Hammer, Steel Barrel, Modern....................................	50	75	75

PIEPER Henry Pieper, Harstal, Belgium 1859. Became Nicolas Pieper in 1898, and in 1905 became Anciens Etablissments Pieper.

COMBINATION WEAPON, SIDE-BY-SIDE

	V.G.	Exc	Prior Edition
Various Calibers, Hammer, Open Rear Sight, Checkered Stock, Plain, Curio..	375	450	450

HANDGUN, SEMI-AUTOMATIC

	V.G.	Exc	Prior Edition
Bayard Model 1908 Pocket, .380 ACP, Blue, Clip Fed, Curio...............	150	175	175
Bayard Model 1908 Pocket, 6.35mm, Blue, Clip Fed, Curio.................	125	150	200
Bayard Model 1923 Pocket, 6.35mm, Blue, Clip Fed, Curio.................	150	175	175
Bayard Model 1923 Pocket, 7.65mm, Blue, Clip Fed, Curio.................	200	225	225
Bayard Model 1930 Pocket, 6.35mm, Blue, Clip Fed, Curio.................	200	225	225
Model A (Army), 7.65mm, Clip Fed, 7 Shot, Curio...............................	150	175	175
Model B, 7.65mm, Clip Fed, 6 Shot, Curio...	125	150	150
Model C, 6.35mm, Clip Fed, Curio..	125	150	150
Model C, 6.35mm, Clip Fed, Long Grip, Curio.....................................	150	175	175

	V.G.	Exc	Prior Edition
Model D (1920), 6.35mm, Clip Fed, Tip–Up, Curio................................	$150	$175	$175

Pieper Model D

Model Legia, 6.35mm, Clip Fed, Curio..	125	150	150

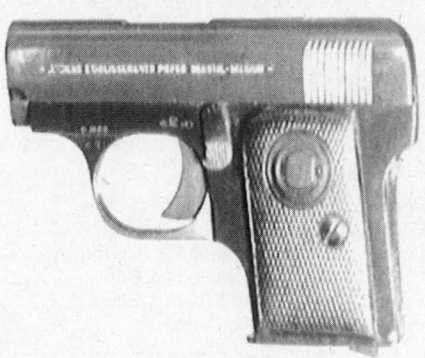

Pieper Legia

Model Legia, 6.35mm, Clip Fed, Long Grip, Curio...................................	150	175	175
Model N, 7.65mm, Clip Fed, Tip–Up, 7 Shot, Curio...............................	125	150	150
Model O, 7.65mm, Clip Fed, Tip–Up, 6 Shot, Curio...............................	125	150	150
Model P, 6.35mm, Clip Fed, Tip–Up, Curio..	150	175	175

RIFLE, BOLT ACTION

Singleshot, .22 L.R.R.F., Plain, Curio..	50	75	75

RIFLE, SEMI-AUTOMATIC

Pieper Carbine, .22 L.R.R.F., Checkered Stock, English Grip, Curio...	100	125	125
Pieper Musket, .22 L.R.R.F., Military Style Stock, Curio........................	100	125	125
Pieper Musket, .22 L.R.R.F., Military Style Stock, with Bayonet, Curio...	125	150	150

	V.G.	Exc	Prior Edition
Pieper/Bayard Carbine, .22 Long, Checkered Stock, Pistol Grip, Curio	$100	$125	$125
Pieper/Bayard Carbine, .22 Short, Checkered Stock, Pistol Grip, Curio	75	100	100

SHOTGUN, DOUBLE BARREL, SIDE-BY-SIDE

	V.G.	Exc	Prior Edition
Bayard, Various Gauges, Hammerless, Boxlock, Light Engraving, Checkered Stock, Modern	175	200	200
Hammer Gun, Various Gauges, Light Engraving, Steel Barrels, Modern	150	200	200
Hammer Gun, Various Gauges, Plain, Damascus Barrels, Modern	125	150	150
Hammer Gun, Various Gauges, Plain, Steel Barrels, Modern	150	175	175

PIEPER, ABRAHAM Lancaster, Pa. 1801–1803. See Kentucky Rifles and Pistols.

PIEPER, HENRY Also see Pieper.

COMBINATION WEAPON, SIDE-BY-SIDE

	V.G.	Exc	Prior Edition
Various Calibers, Double Trigger, Outside Hammers, Side Lever, Antique	375	450	450

PINAFORE Made by Norwich Falls Pistol Co., c. 1880.

HANDGUN, REVOLVER

	V.G.	Exc	Prior Edition
.22 Short R.F., 7 Shot, Spur Trigger, Solid Frame, Single Action, Antique	125	175	175

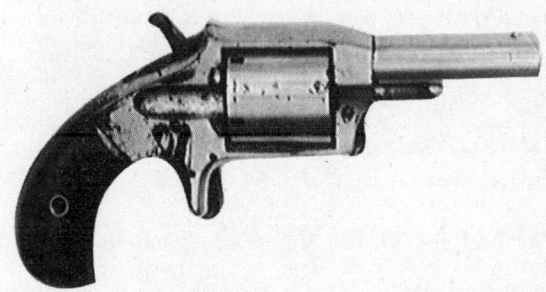

Pinafore

PINKERTON Gaspar Arizaga, Eibar, Spain, c. 1930.

HANDGUN, SEMI-AUTOMATIC

	V.G.	Exc	Prior Edition
Browning Type, 6.35mm, Clip Fed, Blue, Curio	125	150	150
Mondial Type, 6.35mm, Clip Fed, Blue, Curio	175	200	200

	V.G.	Exc	Prior Edition

PIONEER c. 1880.

HANDGUN, REVOLVER

.38 Short R.F., 5 Shot, Spur Trigger, Solid Frame, Single Action, Antique.. $150 $175 $175

PIONEER Made by Stevens Arms.

RIFLE, SEMI-AUTOMATIC

Model 87, .22 L.R.R.F., Tube Feed, Open Rear Sight, Modern............... 50 75 75

PIONEER ARMS CO. Made by Crescent for Kruse Hardware Co. Cincinatti, Ohio.

SHOTGUN, DOUBLE BARREL, SIDE-BY-SIDE

	V.G.	Exc	Prior Edition
Various Gauges, Hammerless, Damascus Barrel, Modern......................	150	175	175
Various Gauges, Hammerless, Steel Barrel, Modern...............................	150	175	175
Various Gauges, Outside Hammers, Damascus Barrel, Modern.............	150	175	175
Various Gauges, Outside Hammers, Steel Barrel, Modern.....................	150	175	175

SHOTGUN, SINGLESHOT

Various Gauges, Hammer, Steel Barrel, Modern.................................... 50 75 75

PIOTTI Brescia, Italy. Currently Imported by Ventura Imports.

SHOTGUN, DOUBLE BARREL, SIDE-BY-SIDE

Monte Carlo, 12 and 20 Gauges, Sideliock, Automatic Ejector, Single Selective Trigger, Fancy Checkering, Fancy Engraving, Modern.. 7,000 8,500 8,500
Westlake, 12 and 20 Gauges, Sideliock, Automatic Ejector, Double Trigger, Fancy Checkering, Fancy Engraving, Modern........................... 6,000 7,000 7,000

PJK Bradbury, Calif. 1960's.

RIFLE, SEMI-AUTOMATIC

M–68, 9mm Luger, Clip Fed, Carbine, Flash Hider, Modern.................. 150 200 200

PLAINFIELD MACHINE CO. Dunellen, N.J., Also see Iver Johnson.

HANDGUN, SEMI-AUTOMATIC

Super Enforcer, .30 Carbine, Clip Fed, Modern...................................... 175 225 225

RIFLE, SEMI-AUTOMATIC

M–1, .30 Carbine, Carbine, Modern... 150 200 200
M–1, .30 Carbine, Carbine, Sporting Rifle, Modern................................. 150 175 175
M–1, 5.7mm Carbine, Carbine, Modern.................................... 125 175 175
M–1 Deluxe, .30 Carbine, Carbine, Sporting Rifle, Monte Carlo Stock, Checkered Stock, Modern... 150 200 200

	V.G.	Exc	Prior Edition
M–1 Paratrooper, .30 Carbine, Carbine, Folding Stock, Modern...........	$200	$225	$225
M–1 Presentation, .30 Carbine, Carbine, Sporting Rifle, Monte Carlo Stock, Fancy Wood, Modern...............	200	225	225

PLAINFIELD ORDNANCE CO. Middlesex, N.J.

HANDGUN, SEMI-AUTOMATIC

Model 71, .22 L.R.R.F. and 25 ACP, Clip Fed, Stainless Steel, with Conversion Kit, Modern...............	175	200	150
Model 71, .22 L.R.R.F., Clip Fed, Stainless Steel, Modern...............	125	150	125
Model 71, 25 ACP, Clip Fed, Stainless Steel, Modern...............	100	125	150
Model 72, .22 ACP, Clip Fed, Lightweight, Modern...............	125	150	150
Model 72, .22 L.R.R.F. and 25 ACP, Clip Fed, Lightweight with Conversion Kit, Modern...............	175	225	175
Model 72, .22 L.R.R.F., Clip Fed, Lightweight, Modern...............	150	175	150

PLANT'S MFG. CO. New Haven, Conn. 1860–1866.

HANDGUN, REVOLVER

Army, .42 Cup Primed Cartridge, 6 Shot, Single Action, Spur Trigger, 1st Model, Antique...............	1,250	1,500	350

Plant's .42 C.P.

Army, .42 Cup Primed Cartridge, 6 Shot, Single Action, Spur Trigger, 2nd Model, Abntique...............	1,000	1,250	350
Army, .42 Cup Primed Cartridge, 6 Shot, Single Action, Spur Trigger, 3rd Model, Antique...............	750	100	475
Pocket, .30 Cup Primed Cartridge, 5 Shot, Single Action, Spur Trigger, Solid Frame, Antique...............	400	450	450

PLUS ULTRA Gabilondo y Cia., Eibar, Spain, c. 1930.

HANDGUN, SEMI-AUTOMATIC

7.65mm, Extra Long Grip, Military, Curio...............	425	500	500

	V.G.	Exc	Prior Edition

POND, LUCIUS W. Worcester, Mass., c. 1863–72.
HANDGUN, REVOLVER
Front Loader, .22, 7 Shot, 3½" bbl., Antique... $500 $600 $600

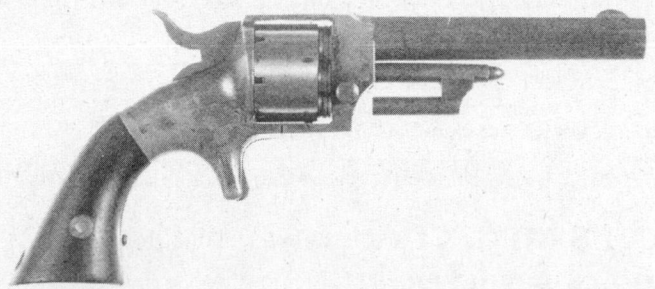

Lucius W. Pond Seven Shot Cartridge Revolver, .22 Caliber

Front Loader, .32, 7 Shot, 3½" bbl., Antique... 475 575 550

PORTER, PATRICK W. New York City, c. 1851–54.
HANDGUN, PERCUSSION
Patent Turret Pistol, .41, 9 Shot, Antique... 7,500 10,000 8,750

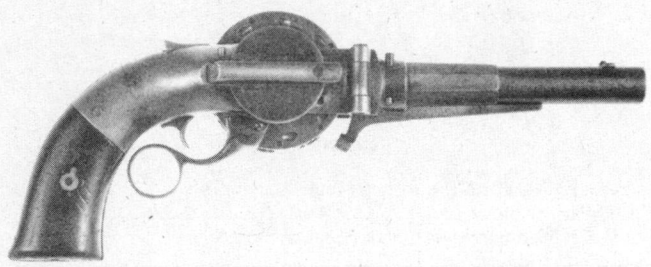

Patrick W. Porter Turret Pistol, .41 Caliber

PORTUGUESE MILITARY
RIFLE, BOLT ACTION
Kropatchek M1886, 8mm, Tube Feed, Antique... 200 250 125
Mauser–Vergueiro, 6.5mm, Rifle, Curio... 250 300 100

	V.G.	Exc	Prior Edition

POUS, EUDAL Spain, c. 1790.

HANDGUN, MIQUELET-LOCK

Pair, Holster Pistol, Low Quality, Light Brass Furniture, Antique........... $2,750 $3,000 $3,000

PRAGA Zbrojovka Praga, Prague, Czechoslovakia 1918–1926.

HANDGUN, SEMI-AUTOMATIC

Model 1921, 6.35mm, Clip fed, Folding Trigger, Curio.......................... 200 225 225

Praga Praha

Vz 21, 7.65mm, Clip Fed, Curio.. 275 325 275

PRAIRIE KING Made by Norwich Falls Pistol Co., c. 1880.

HANDGUN, REVOLVER

.22 Short R.F., 7 Shot, Spur Trigger, Soldi Frame, Single Action, Antique.. 125 150 150

PREMIER Brooklyn, N.Y.

SHOTGUN, DOUBLE BARREL, SIDE-BY-SIDE

Ambassador, Various Calibers, Checkered Stock, Hammerless, Double Trigger, Modern... 325 375 375

Brush King, 12 and 20 Gauges, Checkered Stock, Hammerless, Double Trigger, Modern... 225 275 275

Continental, Various Calibers, Checkered Stock, Outside Hammers, Double Trigger, Modern.. 200 250 250

Monarch, Various Calibers, Hammerless, Double Trigger, Checkered Stock, Engraved, Adjustable Choke, Modern......................... 375 450 450

Presentation, Various Calibers, Adjustable Choke, Double Trigger, Fancy Engraving, Fancy Checkering, Extra Shotgun Barrel, Modern...... 850 1,000 1,000

	V.G.	Exc	Prior Edition
Regent Magnum, 10 Ga. 3½", Checkered Stock, Hammerless, Double Trigger, Modern......	$275	$350	$350
Regent, Various Calibers, Checkered Stock, Hammerless, Double Trigger, Modern......	225	325	250
Regent, Various Calibers, Checkered Stock, Hammerless, Double Trigger, Extra Shotgun Barrel, Modern......	300	400	350

PREMIER   Made by Stevens Arms.

RIFLE, BOLT ACTION

Model 52, .22 L.R.R.F., Singleshot, Takedown, Modern......	25	50	50
Model 53, .22 L.R.R.F., Singleshot, Takedown, Modern......	50	75	75
Model 66 Buckhorn, .22 L.R.R.F., Tube Feed, Open Rear Sight, Modern......	50	75	75

RIFLE, SLIDE ACTION

Model 75, .22 L.R.R.F., Tube Feed, Hammerless, Modern......	125	175	175

PREMIER   Made by Thomas E. Ryan, Norwich, Conn., c. 1870–1876.

HANDGUN, REVOLVER

.22 Short R.F., 7 Shot, Spur Trigger, Solid Frame, Single Action, Antique......	125	175	175
.32 Long R.F., 6 Shot, Spur Trigger, Solid Frame, Single Action, Antique......	125	175	175

PREMIER   Tomas de Urizar y Cia., Eibar, Spain, c. 1920.

HANDGUN, SEMI-AUTOMATIC

6.35mm, Clip Fed, Blue, Modern......	100	125	125

PREMIER TRAIL BLAZER   Made by Stevens Arms.

RIFLE, SLIDE ACTION

Model 75, .22 L.R.R.F., Tube Feed, Hammerless, Modern......	125	175	175

PRESCOTT, E. A.   Worcester, Mass. 1860–1874.

HANDGUN, REVOLVER

"Navy" .38 Short R.F., 6 Shot, Single Action, Solid Frame, Finger–Rest Trigger Guard, Antique......	650	750	600
Belt .32 Short R.F., 6 Shot, Spur Trigger, Solid Frame, Single Action Antique......	500	600	450
Pocket .22 Short R.F., 7 Shot, Spur Trigger, Solid Frame, Single Action, Antique......	450	550	425
Pocket .31 Percussion, 6 Shot, Spur Trigger, Solid Frame, Single Action, Antique......	600	750	450

	V.G.	Exc	Prior Edition

PRICE, J. W. Made by Stevens Arms.
SHOTGUN, SINGLESHOT
Model 90 , Various Gauges, Takedown, Automatic Ejector, Plain,
Hammer, Modern.. $50 $75 $75

PRIMA Mre. d'Armes des Pyrenees, Hendaye, France.
HANDGUN, SEMI-AUTOMATIC
6.35mm, Clip Fed, Curio... 125   150   150

Prima

PRINCEPS Tomas de Urizar, Eibar, Spain, c. 1920.
HANDGUN, SEMI-AUTOMATIC
6.35mm, Clip Fed, Curio... 125   150   150

Princeps

	V.G.	Exc	Prior Edition

PRINCESS c. 1880.

HANDGUN, REVOLVER

.22 Short R.F., 7 Shot, Spur Trigger, Solid Frame, Single Action,
Antique.. $150 $175 $175

PROTECTION Made by Norwich Falls Pistol Co., c. 1860.

HANDGUN, REVOLVER

Pocket .28 Percussion, 6 Shot, Spur Trigger, Solid Frame, Single
Action, Antique.. 500 600 175

PROTECTOR ARMS CO. Spain, c. 1900.

HANDGUN, SEMI-AUTOMATIC

M 1918, 6.35mm, Clip Fed, Curio.. 125 150 150

PURDEY, JAMES

RIFLE, PERCUSSION

.52, Double Barrel, Side by Side, Damascus Barrel, Engraved,
Fancy Wood, Gold Inlays 6,500 7,500 7,500

RIFLE, DOUBLE BARREL, SIDE-BY-SIDE

.500 #2 Express, Damascus Barrel, Outside Hammers, Under–
Lever, Engraved, Ornate, Antique.. 4,000 5,000 5,000

PURDEY, JAS. & SONS London, England, 1814 to Date.

RIFLE, BOLT ACTION

Sporting Rifle, Various Calibers, Fancy Wood, Checkered Stock,
Express Sights, Modern... 5,500 6,000 6,000

RIFLE, DOUBLE BARREL, SIDE-BY-SIDE

Various Calibers, Sidelock, Fancy Engraving, Fancy Checkering,
Fancy Wood, Modern.. 50,000 60,000 50,000

SHOTGUN, DOUBLE BARREL, OVER-UNDER

12 Ga., Vent Rib, Single Selective trigger, Pistol–Grip Stock,
Modern.. 25,000 30,000 30,000
Purdy, Various Gauges, Sidelock, Automatic Ejector, Double
Trigger, Fancy Engraving, Fancy Checkering, Modern............... 20,000 25,000 25,000
Purdy, Various Gauges, Sidelock, Automatic Ejector, Single
Trigger, Fancy Engraving, Fancy Checkering, Modern............... 20,000 25,000 25,000
Various Gauges, Extra Barrels Ony $3,000.00–$5,000.00
Woodward, Various Gauges, Sidelock, Automatic Ejector, Double
Trigger, Fancy Engraving, Fancy Checkering, Modern............... 15,000 20,000 20,000
Woodward, Various Gauges, Sidelock, Automatic Ejector, Single
Trigger, Fancy Engraving, Fancy Checkering, Modern............... 25,000 30,000 30,000

	V.G.	Exc	Prior Edition

SHOTGUN, DOUBLE BARREL, SIDE-BY-SIDE

12 Ga., Extra Barrel, Vent Rib, Single Selective Trigger, Engraved, Cased with Accessories, Modern...$20,000 $25,000 $25,000

12 Ga., Extra Barrels, 10 Ga., Pistol–Grip Stock, Cased with Accesories, Modern... 20,000 25,000 25,000

Featherweight, Various Gauges, Sidelock, Automatic Ejector, Double Trigger, Fancy Engraving, Fancy Checkering, Modern................ 15,000 20,000 20,000

Featherweight, Various Gauges, Sidelock, Automatic Ejector, Single Trigger, Fancy Engraving, Fancy Checkering, Modern................. 17,500 22,500 22,500

Game Gun, Various Gauges, Sidelock, Automatic Ejector, Double Trigger, Fancy Engraving, Fancy Checkering, Modern............................ 15,000 20,000 20,000

Game Gun, Various Gauges, Sidelock, Automatic Ejector, Single Trigger, Fancy Engraving, Fancy Checkering, Modern............................ 17,500 22,750 22,750

Pigeon Gun, 12 Ga., Single Selective Trigger, Vent Rib, Cased Straight Grip, Modern.. 17,500 22,750 22,750

Pigeon Gun, Various Gauges, Sidelock, Automatic Ejector, Double Trigger, Fancy Engraving, Fancy Checkering, Modern................ 15,000 20,000 20,000

Pigeon Gun, Various Gauges, Sidelock, Automatic Ejector, Single Trigger, Fancy Engraving, Fancy Checkering, Modern............................ 15,000 20,000 20,000

Two–Inch, 12 Ga. 2", Sidelock, Automatic Ejector, Double Trigger, Fancy Engraving, Fancy Checkering, Modern... 12,500 15,000 15,000

Two–Inch, 12 Ga. 2", Sidelock, Automatic Ejector, Single Trigger, Fancy Engraving, Fancy Checkering, Modern... 15,000 20,000 20,000

Various Gauges, Extra Barrels Only $2,600.00–$3,750.00

SHOTGUN, SINGLESHOT

12 Ga., Vent Rig, Plain, Trap Grade, Modern... 12,500 15,000 15,000

PZK Kohout & Spolecnost, Kydne, Czechoslovakia.

HANDGUN, SEMI-AUTOMATIC

PZK, 6.35mm, Clip Fed, Modern.. 150 175 200

Q

	V.G.	Exc.	Prior Edition

QUACKENBUSH Herkimer, N.Y., c. 1880.

RIFLE, SINGLESHOT BOY'S RIFLE

	V.G.	Exc.	Prior Edition
.22 R.F., Side Swing Breech, Nickel Plated, Takedown, Curio................	$300	$350	$175

QUAIL Made by Crescent, c. 1900.

SHOTGUN, DOUBLE BARREL, SIDE-BY-SIDE

	V.G.	Exc.	Prior Edition
Various Gauges, Hammerless, Damascus Barrel, Modern......................	150	175	175
Various Gauges, Hammerless, Steel Barrel, Modern.............................	150	200	200
Various Gauges, Outside Hammers, Damascus Barrel, Modern.............	150	175	175
Various Gauges, Outside Hammers, Steel Barrel, Modern.....................	150	175	175

SHOTGUN, SINGLESHOT

	V.G.	Exc.	Prior Edition
Various Gauges, Hammer, Steel Barrel, Modern.....................................	50	75	75

QUAIL'S FARGO Tradename used by Dakin Gun Co. and Simmons Specialties.

SHOTGUN, DOUBLE BARREL, SIDE-BY-SIDE

	V.G.	Exc.	Prior Edition
12 Ga., Checkered Stock, Plain, Modern......................................	150	175	175

QUEEN CITY Made by Crescent for Elmira Arms Co., c. 1900.

SHOTGUN, DOUBLE BARREL, SIDE-BY-SIDE

	V.G.	Exc.	Prior Edition
Various Gauges, Hammerless, Damascus Barrel, Modern......................	150	175	175
Various Gauges, Hammerless, Steel Barrel, Modern.............................	150	200	200
Various Gauges, Outside Hammers, Damascus Barrel, Modern.............	150	175	175
Various Gauges, Outside Hammers, Steel Barrel, Modern.....................	150	175	175

SHOTGUN, SINGLESHOT

	V.G.	Exc.	Prior Edition
Various Gauges, Hammer, SteelBarrel, Modern.....................................	50	75	75

R

RADIUM Gabilondo y Urresti, Guernica, Spain, c. 1910.
HANDGUN, SEMI-AUTOMATIC
6.35mm, Fixed Magazine, Side Loading, Blue, Curio............................. $150 $175 $275

RADOM Fabryka Broni w Radomu, Radom, Poland, c. 1930 through WWII.
HANDGUN, REVOLVER
Ng 30, 7.62mm Nagant, Gas Seal, Double Action, Curio........................ 300 325 275
HANDGUN, SEMI-AUTOMATIC
VIS 1935, 9mm Luger, Clip Fed, Military, Nazi–Production, Early, Curio... 400 450 450

Radom, Early Nazi

VIS 1935, 9mm Luger, Clip Fed, Military, Nazi–Proofed, Early Type, Curio... 1,250 1,500 850

	V.G.	Exc	Prior Edition
VIS 1935 Navy, 9mm Luger, Clip Fed, Military, Nazi–Production, Late, Curio..	$1,000	$1,250	$850

Radom, Late Nazi

VIS 1935 Polish, 9mm Luger, Clip Fed, Military, Curio........................	1,000	1,250	800

Radom, Polish

	V.G.	Exc	Prior Edition

RANDALL Randall Firearms Mfg. Corp., Sun Valley, Calif.

HANDGUN, SEMI-AUTOMATIC

Compact Model, Various Calibers, Stainless Steel, M1911A1
Style, Herritt Grips, Adjustable Sights, Modern.. $550 $700 $350

Service Model, Various Calibers, Stainless Steel, M1911A1 Style,
Herritt Grips, Adjustable Sights, Modern... 600 800 400

Target Model, Various Calibers, Stainless Steel, M1911A1 Style,
Herritt Grips, Adjustable Sights with Rib, Modern.................................... 700 900 425

RANGER Made by E.L. Dickinson, Springfield, Mass.

HANDGUN, REVOLVER

#2, .32 Short R.F., 5 Shot, Spur Trigger, Solid Frame, Single
Action, Antique.. 125 175 175

RANGER Made by Hopkins & Allen, c. 1880.

HANDGUN, REVOLVER

.22 Short R.F., 7 Shot, Spur Trigger, Solid Frame, Single Action,
Antique... 150 175 175

.32 Short R.F., 6 Shot, Spur Trigger, Solid Frame, Single Action,
Antique... 150 175 175

RANGER Made by Stevens Arms.

RIFLE, SLIDE ACTION

Model 70, .22 L.R.R.F., Solid Frame, Hammer, Modern.......................... 125 175 175
Model 75, .22 L.R.R.F., Tube Feed, Hammerless, Modern...................... 150 175 175

SHOTGUN, DOUBLE BARREL, SIDE-BY-SIDE

Model 215, 12 and 16 Gauges, Steel Barrels, Outside Hammers,
Modern.. 125 175 175

Model 315, Various Gauges, Steel Barrels, Hammerless, Modern.......... 150 175 175

SHOTGUN, SINGLESHOT

Model 89 Dreadnaught, Various Gauges, Hammer, Modern................. 50 75 75

RANGER ARMS, INC. Gainesville, Tex., c. 1972.

RIFLE, BOLT ACTION

Bench Rest/Varminter, Various Calibers, Singleshot, Target
Rifle, Thumbhole Stock, Heavy Barrel, Recoil Pad, Modern.................... 425 500 500

Governor Grade, Various Calibers, Sporting Rifle, Fancy
Checkering, Fancy Wood, Recoil Pad, Sling Swivels, Modern................. 375 450 450

Governor Grade Magnum, Various Calibers, Sporting Rifle, Fancy
Checkering, Fancy Wood, Recoil Pad, Sling Swivels, Modern................. 400 475 475

Senator Grade, Various Calibers, Sporting Rifle, Fancy
Checkering, Recoil Pad, Sling Swivels, Modern....................................... 325 400 400

Senator Grade Magnum, Various Calibers, Sporting Rifle, Fancy
Checkering, Recoil Pad, Sling Swivels, Modern....................................... 350 425 425

	V.G.	Exc	Prior Edition
Statesman Grade, Various Calibers, Sporting Rifle, Checkered Stock, Recoil Pad, Sling Swivels, Modern..	$250	$325	$325
Statesman Grade Magnum, Various Calibers, Sporting Rifle, Checkered Stock, Recoil Pad, Sling Swivels, Modern..............................	300	350	350

RASCH Brunswick, Germany 1790–1810.

RIFLE, FLINTLOCK

Yaeger, Octagon Barrel, Brass Furniture, Engraved, Carved, Target Sights, Antique..	3,000	3,500	3,500

RATHFONG, GEORGE Lancaster, Pa. 1774–1809. See U.S. Military, Kentucky Rifles.

RATHFONG, JACOB Lancaster, Pa. 1810–1839. See Kentucky Rifles and Pistols.

RAVEN Raven Arms, Industry, Calif. 1970–1991.

HANDGUN, SEMI-AUTOMATIC

MP–25, .25 ACP, Clip Fed, Nickel, Modern...	25	50	75

Raven MP-25

MP–25, .25 ACP, Clip Fed, Teflon, Modern...	25	50	75
MP–25, .25 ACP, Clip Fed, Teflon, Modern...	25	50	75
P–25, .25 ACP, Clip Fed, Blue, Modern..	25	50	75
P–25, .25 ACP, Clip Fed, Chrome, Modern...	25	50	75
P–25, .25 ACP, Clip Fed, Nickel, Modern...	25	50	75

REASOR, DAVID Lancaster, Pa. 1749–1780. See Kentucky Rifles and Pistols.

RECK Reck Sportwaffenfabrik, Arnsberg, West Germany.

HANDGUN, REVOLVER
.22 L.R.R.F., Double Action, Blue, Modern... $25 $50 $50

HANDGUN, SEMI-AUTOMATIC
P–8, 6.35mm, Clip Fed, Blue, Modern... 50   75   75

RED CLOUD

HANDGUN, REVOLVER
.32 Long R.F., 5 Shot, Single Action, Solid Frame, Spur Trigger,
Antique.. 150   175   175

RED JACKET Made by Lee Arms, Wilkes–Barre, Pa., c. 1870.

HANDGUN, REVOLVER
.22 Long R.F., 7 Shot, Single Action, Solid Frame, Spur Trigger,
Antique.. 150   175   175
.32 Long R.F., 5 Shot, Single Action, Solid Frame, Spur Trigger,
Antique.. 150   175   175

REED, JAMES Lancaster, Pa. 1778–1780. See Kentucky Rifles.

REFORM August Schueler, Suhl, Germany. 1900–1905.

HANDGUN, MANUAL REPEATER
6mm R.F., 4 Barrel, Double Action, Hammer, Curio................................ 550   650   400

REFORM Spain, c. 1920.

HANDGUN, SEMI-AUTOMATIC
6.35mm, Clip Fed, Blue, Curio... 100   125   125

REGENT Gregorio Bolumburu, Eibar, Spain, c. 1925.

HANDGUN, SEMI-AUTOMATIC
6.35mm, Clip Fed, Blue, Curio... 100   125   125

REGENT Karl Burgsmuller, Kreiensen, West Germany.

HANDGUN, REVOLVER
.22 L.R.R.F., Double Action, Blue, Modern... 50   75   50

	V.G.	Exc	Prior Edition

REGINA Gregorio Bolumburu, Eibar, Spain, c. 1920.

HANDGUN, SEMI-AUTOMATIC

Pocket, 7.65mm, Clip Fed, Blue, Curio..	$125	$150	$150
Vest Pocket, 6.35mm, Clip Fed, Blue, Curio...	100	125	125

Regina Vest Pocket

REGNUM Tradename used by August Menz, Suhl, Germany.

HANDGUN, MANUAL REPEATER

6.35mm, 4 Barrels, Spur Trigger, Hammer, Curio......................................	400	450	250

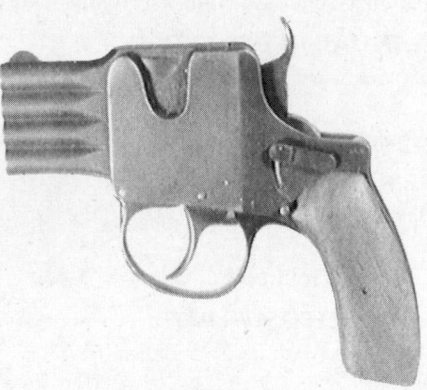

Regnum

	V.G.	Exc	Prior Edition

REID PATENT REVOLVERS Made by W. Irving for James
Reid, N.Y. 1862–1884.

HANDGUN, REVOLVER

	V.G.	Exc	Prior Edition
Model 1 .22 Short R.F., 7 Shot, Spur Trigger, Solid Frame, Single Action, Antique	$1,000	$1,200	$1,000
Model 2 .32 Short R.F., 7 Shot, Spur Trigger, Solid Frame, Single Action, Antique	800	1,000	1,200
My Friend .41 Short R.F., .22 R.F., Knuckleduster, 7 Shot, Antique	3,500	3,750	2,000
My Friend, .22 R.F., Knuckleduster, 7 Shot, Antique	750	850	675
My Friend, .32 R.F., Knuckleduster, 7 Shot, Antique	850	950	725

REIMS Azanza y Arrizabalaga, Eibar, Spain, c. 1914.

HANDGUN, SEMI-AUTOMATIC

	V.G.	Exc	Prior Edition
1914 Model, 6.35mm, Clip Fed, Curio	100	125	125
1914 Model, 7.65mm, Clip Fed, Curio	125	150	150

REINA Mre. d' Armes des Pyrenees, Hendaye, France, c. 1930.

HANDGUN, SEMI-AUTOMATIC

	V.G.	Exc	Prior Edition
7.65mm, Clip Fed, Blue, Curio	125	150	150

REISING Hartford, Conn. 1916–1924.

HANDGUN, SEMI-AUTOMATIC

	V.G.	Exc	Prior Edition
Target (Hartford), .22 L.R.R.F., Clip Fed, Hammer, Curio	525	575	375
Target (N.Y.), .22 L.R.R.F., Clip Fed, Hammer, Curio	600	650	450

REMINGTON ARMS CO. Eliphalet Remington, Herkimer County, N.Y. 1816–1831. Ilion, N.Y. 1831 to Date. 1856– E. Remington & Sons; 1888– Remington Arms Co.; 1910– Remington Arms U.M.C. Co.; 1925 to Date Remington Arms Co., Ilion, N.Y. Also see the Commemorative Section.

HANDGUN, DOUBLE BARREL, OVER-UNDER

"Over and Under" Derringer, 1st. Model, .41 Short R.F., Spur Trigger, Tip–Up, no Extractor, Markings on Side of Barrel, E. Remington & Sons, Antique.. $1,200 $1,500 $1,500

Remington Elliot Double Derringer

"Over and Under" Derringer, 2nd. Model, .41 Short R.F., Spur Trigger, Tip–Up, no Extractor, Markings on Side of Barrel, E.Remington & Sons, Antique.. 1,500   1,750   1,750

"Over and Under" Derringer, 3rd. Model, .41 Short R.F., Spur Trigger, Tip–Up, no Extractor, Markings on Top of Barrel, E. Remington & Sons, Antique.. 650   750   750

"Over and Under" Derringer, 4th. Model, .41 Short R.F., Spur Trigger, Tip–Up, no Extractor, Markings on Top of Barrel, Remington Arms Co., Curio.. 550   600   600

"Over and Under" Derringer, 5th. Model, .41 Short R.F., Spur Trigger, Tip–Up, with Extractor, Markings on Top of Barrel, Curio........ 550   600   600

"Over and Under" Derringer, 6th. Model, .41 Short R.F., Spur Trigger, Tip–Up, with Extractor, Remington Arms Co. #'s L75925–L99941, Curio.. 500   550   550

	V.G.	Exc	Prior Edition

HANDGUN, MANUAL REPEATER

Elliot Derringer, .22 Short R.F., 5 Shot, Double Action, Ring Trigger, Rotating Firing Block, Antique... $850 $950 $1,200

Remington Elliot Repeater

	V.G.	Exc	Prior Edition
Elliot Derringer, .32 Short R.F., 5 Shot, Double Action, Ring Trigger, Rotating Firing Block, Antique...	750	850	1,150
Rider Single Shot Derringer, .32 Extra Short R.F., Tube Feed, Spur Trigger, 5 Shot, Antique..	4,000	5,000	5,000

HANDGUN, PERCUSSION

	V.G.	Exc	Prior Edition
.31, Beals #1, Revolver, Pocket Pistol, 5 Shot, Octagon Barrel, 3" Barrel, Antique..............	750	900	900
.31, Beals #2, Revolver, Pocket Pistol, 5 Shot, Octagon Barrel, 3" Barrel, Spur Trigger, Antique...........	4,000	4,500	4,500
.31, Beals #3, Revolver, Octagon Barrel, 4" Barrel, Spur Trigger, with Loading Lever, Antique................	1,000	1,250	1,250
.31, New Model Pocket, Revolver, Safety Notches on Cylinder, Spur Trigger, 5 Shot, Octagon Barrel, Antique...	1,000	1,250	1,500
.31, Rider Pocket, Revolver, Double Action, 5 Shot, Octagon Barrel, 3" Barrel, Antique............	625	700	700
.36, Beals Navy, Revolver, Single Action, Octagon Barrel, 7½" Barrel, Antique...................	950	1,100	1,100
.36, Belt Model, Revolver, Safety Notches on Cylinder, Single Action, Octagon Barrel, 6½" Barrel, Antique...	1,000	1,200	1,200
.36, Belt Model, Revolver, Safety Notches on Cylinder, Double Action, Octagon Barrel, 6½" Barrel, Antique..	750	1,000	2,500
.36, Model 1861 Navy, Revolver, Channeled Loading Lever, Single Action, Octagon Barrel, 7½" Barrel, Antique..........................	1,250	1,600	1,600
.36, New Model Navy, Revolver, Safety Notches on Cylinder, Single Action, Octagon Barrel, 7½" Barrel, Antique..............................	1,050	1,300	1,300
.36, Police Model, Revolver, Single Action, Octagon Barrel, Various Barrel Lengths, 5 Shot, Antique.........................	900	975	975
.44, Beals Army, Revolver, Single Action, Octagon Barrel, 8" Barrel, Antique........................	2,500	2,750	2,750

	V.G.	Exc	Prior Edition
.44, Model 1861 Army, Revolver, Channeled Loading Lever, Single Action, Octagon Barrel, 8" Barrel, Antique..	$1,500	$1,800	$1,800

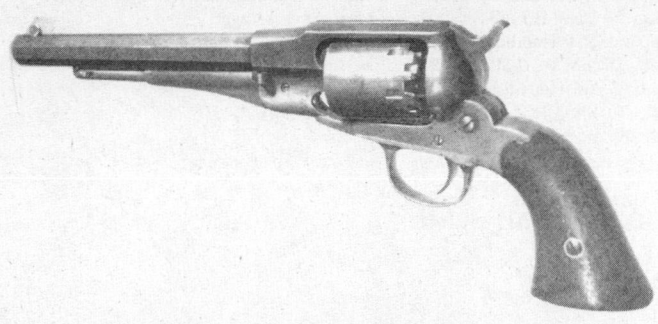

Remington .44 Model 1861 Army

.44, New Model Army, Revolver, Safety Notches on Cylinder, Single Action, Octagon Barrel, 7½" Barrel, Antique.................................	1,250	1,500	1,500

HANDGUN, REVOLVER

Iroquois, .22 L.R.R.F., 7 Shot, Solid Frame, Spur Trigger, Single Action, Fluted Cylinder, Antique..	400	450	400
Iroquois, .22 L.R.R.F., 7 Shot, Solid Frame, Spur Trigger, Single Action, Unfluted Cylinder, Antique..	450	500	450
Model 1875, .44–40 WCF, Single Action, Western Style, Solid Frame, Antique..	3,250	3,750	3,750
Model 1875, .45 Colt, Single Action, Western Style, Solid Frame, Antique..	3,000	3,500	3,500
Model 1890, .44–40 WCF, Single Action, Western Style, Solid Frame, Antique..	3,500	4,000	4,000
Smoot #1, .30 Short R.F., 5 Shot, Solid Frame, Spur Trigger, Single Action, Antique..	350	400	400

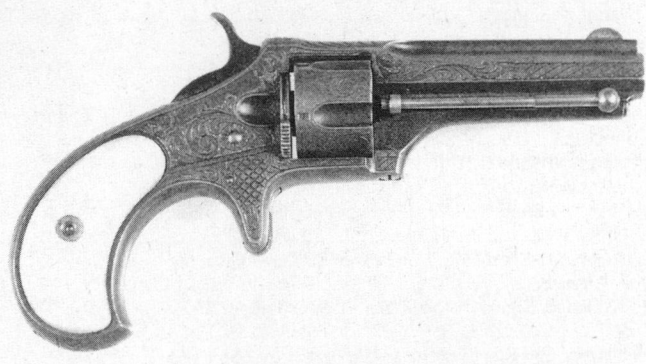

Remington Smoot #1

	V.G.	Exc	Prior Edition
Smoot #2, .32 Short R.F., 5 Shot, Solid Frame, Spur Trigger, Single Action, Antique........	$325	$375	$375
Smoot #3, .38 Long R.F., 5 Shot, Solid Frame, Spur Trigger, Single Action, Birdhead Grip, Antique........	400	450	450
Smoot #3, .38 Long R.F., 5 Shot, Solid Frame, Spur Trigger, Single Action, Saw Handle Grip, Antique........	450	500	500
Smoot #4, .38 S & W, 5 Shot, Solid Frame, Spur Trigger, Single Action, no Ejector Housing, Antique........	325	375	375
Smoot #4, .41 Short R.F., 5 Shot, Solid Frame, Spur Trigger, Single Action, no Ejector Housing, Antique........	350	400	400
Zig–Zag Derringer, .22 Short R.F., Pepperbox, Double Action, 6 Shot, Ring Trigger, Antique........	3,000	3,250	2,500

HANDGUN, SEMI-AUTOMATIC

	V.G.	Exc	Prior Edition
Model 51, .32 ACP, Early, Clip Fed, Grip Safety, Modern........	350	400	400

Remington 51

	V.G.	Exc	Prior Edition
Model 51, .32 ACP, Late, Clip Fed, Grip Safety, Modern........	325	375	375
Model 51, .380 ACP, Early, Clip Fed, Grip Safety, Modern........	400	450	450
Model 51, .380 ACP, Late, Clip Fed, Grip Safety, Modern........	375	425	425

HANDGUN, SINGLESHOT

	V.G.	Exc	Prior Edition
#1 Vest Pocket, .22 Short R.F., Iron Frame, no Breech Bolt, Spur Trigger, Antique........	500	650	700
#2 Vest Pocket, .30 Short R.F., Iron Frame, "Split Breech" Model, Spur Trigger, Antique........	775	850	850
#2 Vest Pocket, .41 Short R.F., Iron Frame, "Split Breech" Model, Spur Trigger, Antique........	850	1,000	1,200
Elliot Derringer, .41 Short R.F., Iron Frame, Birdhand Grip, no Breech Bolt, Antique........	1,175	1,400	1,400
Mark III, 10 Gauge, Signal Pistol, 9" Barrel, Spur Trigger, Brass Frame, Curio........	300	350	350
Model 1865 Navy, .50 Rem. Navy R.F., Rolling Block, Sour Trigger, 8½" Barrel, Antique........	2,000	2,500	2,500
Model 1867 Navy, .50 Rem. Rolling Block, 7" Barrel, Antique........	1,000	1,250	1,850
Model 1871 Army, .50 Rem. Rolling Block, 8" Barrel, Antique........	1,500	1,650	1,650

	V.G.	Exc	Prior Edition
Model 1891 Target, Rolling Block, 10" Barrel, Add 15%–20%			
Model 1891 Target, Rolling Block, 12" Barrel, Add 15%–20%			
Model 1891 Target, .22 L.R.R.F., Rolling Block, 8" Barrel, Half–Octagon Barrel, Plain Barrel, Antique	$1,750	$2,000	$2,000
Model 1891 Target, .25 Short R.F., Rolling Block, 8" Barrel, Half–Octagon Barrel, Plain Barrel, Antique	1,250	1,500	1,500
Model 1891 Target, .32 Long R.F., Rolling Block, 8" Barrel, Half–Octagon Barrel, Plain Barrel, Antique	1,400	1,600	1,600
Model 1891 Target, .32 S & W, Rolling Block, 8" Barrel, Half–Octagon Barrel, Plain Barrel, Antique	1,650	1,800	1,800
Model 1891 Target, .32–20 WCF, Rolling Block, 8" Barrel, Half–Octagon Barrel, Plain Barrel, Antique	2,000	2,250	2,250
Model 1901 Target, .22 L.R.R.F., Rolling Block, 10" Barrel, Checkered Stock, Half–Octagon Barrel, Modern	1,450	1,650	1,650
Model 1901 Target, .44 Russian, Rolling Block, 10" Barrel, Checkered Stock, Half–Octagon Barrel, Modern	1,800	2,050	2,050
XP–100, .221 Rem. Fireball, Bolt Action, Target Nylon Stock, 10½" Barrel, Vent Rib, Open Sights, Cased, Modern	300	350	275

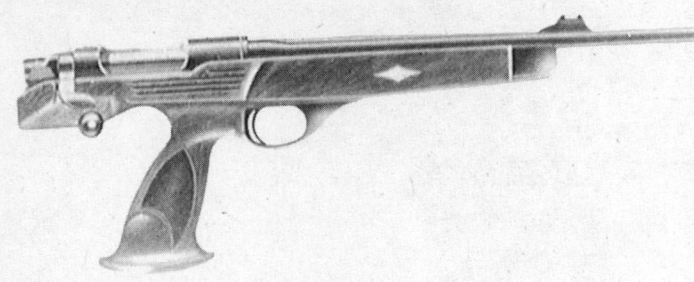

Remington XP-100

XP–100 Silhouette, 7mm BR Rem., Bolt Action, Target Nylon Stock, 15' Barrel, Vent Rib, Open Sights, Cased, Modern	375	425	425

RIFLE, BOLT ACTION

Enfield 1914, .303 British, Full–Stocked, Military, Curio	250	300	300
International (1961), Various Calibers, Singleshot, Target Stock, no Sights, with Accessories, Modern	400	450	450
Model 1907/15 French, 8 X 50R Lebel, Carbine, Military, Curio	300	350	200
Model 1907/15 French, 8 X 50R Lebel, Military, Curio	325	375	225
Model 1917 U.S., .30–06 Springfield, Full–Stocked, Military, Curio	300	350	350
Model 30A, Various Calibers, Sporting Rifle, Plain, Open Rear Sight, Modern	375	425	425
Model 30F Premier, Various Calibers, Sporting Rifle, Fancy Checkering, Fancy Engraving, Fancy Wood, Modern	650	725	725
Model 30R, Various Calibers, Sporting Rifle, Plain, Carbine, Open Rear Sights, Modern	425	475	475
Model 30S, Various Calibers, Sporting Rifle, Checkered Stock, Peep Sights, Modern	450	525	525
Model 33A, .22 L.R.R.F., Plain, Singleshot, Open Rear Sight, Modern	75	100	100

	V.G.	Exc	Prior Edition
Model 33A, .22 L.R.R.F., Plain, Singleshot, Peep Sights, Modern...........	$75	$100	$100
Model 33NRA, .22 L.R.R.F., Plain, Singleshot, Peep Sights, Sling Swivels, Modern....................	100	125	125
Model 341A, .22 L.R.R.F., Tube Feed, Takedown, Open Rear Sight, Modern....................	100	125	125
Model 341P, .22 L.R.R.F., Tube Feed, Takedown, Peep Sights, Modern....................	150	175	175
Model 341SB, .22 L.R.R.F., Tube Feed, Takedown, Smoothbore, Modern....................	100	125	125
Model 34A, .22 L.R.R.F., Tube Feed, Takedown, Lyman Sights, Modern....................	100	125	125
Model 34A, .22 L.R.R.F., Tube Feed, Takedown, Open Rear Sight, Modern....................	100	125	125
Model 34NRA, .22 L.R.R.F., Tube Feed, Takedown, Lyman Sights, Target, Modern....................	125	175	175
Model 37A, .22 L.R.R.F., 5 Shot Clip, Target Stock, Target Sights, Target Barrel, Modern....................	325	400	400
Model 37A, .22 L.R.R.F., 5 Shot Clip, Target Stock, Target Sights, Target Barrel, Fancy Wood, Modern....................	375	425	425
Model 37AX, .22 L.R.R.F., 5 Shot Clip, Target Stock, no Sights, Target Barrel, Modern....................	325	375	375
Model 40–XB CF–H2, Various Cailbers, Stainless Steel Barrel, Heavy Barrel, Target Stock, no Sights, Modern....................	1,000	1,100	850
Model 40–XB CF–S2, Various Cailbers, Stainless Steel Barrel, Target Stock, no Sights, Modern....................	1,150	1,250	875
Model 40–XB RF–H2, .22 L.R.R.F., Heavy Barrel, Target Stock, no Sights, Modern....................	850	950	575
Model 40–XB RF–S2, .22 L.R.R.F., Target Stock, no Sights, Modern....................	700	800	275
Model 40–XB–BR, Various Calibers, Stainless Steel, Heavy Barrel, Target Stock, no Sights, Modern....................	1,350	1,500	975

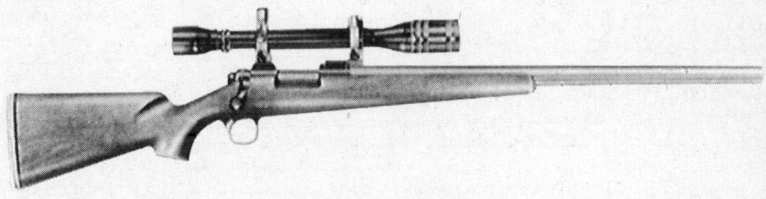

Remington 40-XB-BR

Model 40–XB–BR, For 2oz. Trigger, Add $40.00–$65.00
Model 40–XB–CF, For Repeater, Add $25.00

	V.G.	Exc	Prior Edition
Model 40X–CFH2, Various Calibers, SIngleshot, Target Stock, no Sights, Heavy Barrel, Modern....................	850	950	575
Model 40X–CFS2, Various Calibers, SIngleshot, Target Stock, no Sights, Modern....................	800	900	550
Model 40X–H1, .22 L.R.R.F., Singleshot, Target Stock, Target Sights, Heavy Barrel, Modern....................	800	900	550
Model 40X–H2, .22 L.R.R.F., Singleshot, Target Stock, no Sights, Heavy Barrel, Modern....................	750	850	525

	V.G.	Exc	Prior Edition
Model 40X–S1, .22 L.R.R.F., Singleshot, Target Stock, Target Sights, Modern.....................	$650	$750	$500
Model 40X–S2, .22 L.R.R.F., Singleshot, Target Stock, no Sights, Modern..........................	600	700	475
Model 40XB Sporter, .22 L.R.R.F., Modern........................	1,150	1,250	875
Model 40XC National Match, .308 Winchester, Target Stock, Target Sights, Modern........................	1,500	1,750	1,050
Model 40XR Position, .22 L.R.R.F., Target Stock, no Sights, Modern..........................	675	750	750
Model 41A, .22 L.R.R.F., Takedown, Singleshot, Plain, Open Rear Sight, Modern.....................	50	75	75
Model 41AS, .22 WRF, Takedown, Singleshot, Plain, Open Rear Sight, Modern.....................	125	150	150
Model 41P, .22 L.R.R.F., Takedown, Singleshot, Plain, Target Sights, Modern......................	50	75	75
Model 41SB, .22 L.R.R.F., Takedown, Singleshot, Plain, Smoothbore, Modern........................	150	175	175
Model 510A, .22 L.R.R.F., Singleshot, Open Rear Sight, Plain, Takedown, Modern.....................	50	75	75
Model 510C, .22 L.R.R.F., Singleshot, Carbine, Plain, Takedown, Modern............................	50	75	75
Model 510P, .22 L.R.R.F., Singleshot, Peep Sights, Plain, Takedown, Modern.....................	50	75	75
Model 510SB, .22 L.R.R.F., Singleshot, Smoothbore, Plain, Takedown, Modern.....................	100	125	125
Model 510X, .22 L.R.R.F., Singleshot, Plain, Modern..........................	75	100	100
Model 510X, .22 L.R.R.F., Singleshot, Plain, Smoothbore, Modern..........................	75	100	100
Model 511A, .22 L.R.R.F., Clip Fed, Open Rear Sight, Plain, Takedown, Modern.....................	75	100	100
Model 511P, .22 L.R.R.F., Clip Fed, Peep Sights, Plain, Takedown, Modern..........................	75	100	100
Model 511SB, .22 L.R.R.F., Clip Fed, Smoothbore, Plain, Takedown, Modern.....................	75	100	100
Model 511X, .22 L.R.R.F., Clip Fed, Plain, Modern..........................	75	100	100
Model 512A, .22 L.R.R.F., Tube Feed, Plain, Open Rear Sight, Modern..........................	75	100	100
Model 512P, .22 L.R.R.F., Tube Feed, Plain, Peep Sights, Modern..........................	75	100	100
Model 512SB, .22 L.R.R.F., Tube Feed, Plain, Smoothbore, Modern..........................	75	100	100
Model 512X, .22 L.R.R.F., Tube Feed, Plain, Modern..........................	75	100	100
Model 513SA, .22 L.R.R.F., Clip Fed, Sporting Rifle, Open Rear Sight, Takedown, Checkered Stock, Modern..........................	150	200	200
Model 513SP, .22 L.R.R.F., Clip Fed, Sporting Rifle, Peep Sights, Takedown, Checkered Stock, Modern..........................	175	200	200
Model 513TR, .22 L.R.R.F., Clip Fed, Target Stock, Target Sights, Takedown, Modern..........................	200	225	225
Model 513TX, .22 L.R.R.F., Clip Fed, Target Stock, no Sights, Takedown, Modern..........................	125	175	175
Model 514, .22 L.R.R.F., Singleshot, Plain, Open Rear Sight, Modern..........................	50	75	75
Model 514BR (Youth), .22 L.R.R.F., Singleshot, Plain, Open Rear Sight, Modern..........................	50	75	75

	V.G.	Exc	Prior Edition
Model 514P, .22 L.R.R.F., Singleshot, Plain, Peep Sights, Modern	$125	$150	$150
Model 521TL, .22 L.R.R.F., Takedown, Clip Fed, Target Stock, Lyman Sights, Modern	150	175	175
Model 540 XRJR Position, .22 L.R.R.F., Target Stock, no Sights, Modern	200	250	250
Model 540XR Position, .22 L.R.R.F., Target Stock, no Sights, Modern	225	275	275
Model 541–S, .22 L.R.R.F., Clip Fed, Checkered Stock, Fancy Wood, Modern	275	325	325
Model 580 BR (Youth), .22 L.R.R.F., Singleshot, Plain, Modern	75	100	100
Model 580 SB, .22 L.R.R.F., Singleshot, Plain, Smoothbore, Modern	50	75	75
Model 580, .22 L.R.R.F., Singleshot, Plain, Modern	75	100	100
Model 581, .22 L.R.R.F., Clip Fed, Plain, Modern	125	150	100
Model 581, .22 L.R.R.F., Clip Fed, Plain, Left–Hand, Modern	125	150	125
Model 582, .22 L.R.R.F., Tube Feed, Plain, Modern	125	150	100
Model 591, 5mm Rem. RFM, Clip Fed, Monte Carlo Stock, Plain, Modern	150	175	150
Model 592, 5mm Rem. RFM, Tube Feed, Monte Carlo Stock, Plain, Modern	250	300	150
Model 600 Montana Centennial, Trap Grade, Carbine, Checkered Stock, Commemorative, Curio	300	425	425
Model 600, Various Calibers, Vent Rib, Carbine, Checkered Stock, Modern	375	425	275
Model 600, Various Calibers, Vent Rib, Carbine, Magnum, Recoil Pad, Checkered Stock, Modern	400	450	350
Model 660, Various Calibers, Carbine, Checkered Stock, Modern	475	525	525
Model 660, Various Calibers, Carbine, Magnum, Recoil Pad, Checkered Stock, Modern	500	550	550
Model 700 Safari, Various Calibers, Magnum, Checkered Stock, Fancy Wood, Modern	675	750	750
Model 700ADL, Various Calibers, Checkered Stock, Modern	300	375	375
Model 700ADL, Various Calibers, Magnum, Checkered Stock, Modern	325	400	400
Model 700BDL, Various Calibers, Checkered Stock, Fancy Wood, Modern	350	400	400
Model 700BDL, Various Calibers, Checkered Stock, Fancy Wood, Magnum, Left–Hand, Modern	400	450	450
Model 700BDL, Various Calibers, Checkered Stock, Fancy Wood, Left–Hand, Modern	325	400	400
Model 700BDL, Various Calibers, Heavy Barrel, Varmint, Checkered Stock, Fancy Wood, Modern	400	450	450
Model 700BDL, Various Calibers, Magnum, Checkered Stock, Fancy Wood, Modern	375	425	425
Model 700C Custom, Various Calibers, Checkered Stock, Fancy Wood, Modern	775	850	850
Model 700D Peerless, Various Calibers, Fancy Checkering, Fancy Wood, Engraved, Modern	1,175	1,300	1,300
Model 700F Premier, Various Calibers, Fancy Checkering, Fancy Wood, Fancy Engraving, Modern	2,000	2,500	2,500
Model 720A, Various Calibers, Sporting Rifle, Open Rear Sight, Modern	950	1,200	1,200
Model 720A, Various Calibers, Sporting Rifle, Target Sights, Modern	1,050	1,300	1,300

	V.G.	Exc	Prior Edition
Model 720R, Various Calibers, Sporting Rifle, Open Rear Sight, Carbine, Modern........	$1,000	$1,250	$1,250
Model 720R, Various Calibers, Sporting Rifle, Target Sights, Carbine, Modern........	1,050	1,300	1,300
Model 720S, Various Calibers, Sporting Rifle, Target Sights, Modern........	1,050	1,300	1,300
Model 721, For .300 H & H Magnum, Add $20.00–$35.00			
Model 721 Peerless, Various Calibers, Long Action, Sporting Rifle, Fancy Wood, Engraved, Fancy Checkering, Modern........	575	750	750
Model 721 Premier, Various Calibers, Long Action, Sporting Rifle, Fancy Wood, Fancy Engraving, Fancy Checkering, Modern........	1,250	1,400	1,400
Model 721 Special, Various Calibers, Long Action, Sporting Rifle, Checkered Stock, Fancy Wood, Modern........	200	250	250
Model 721A, Various Calibers, Long Action, Sporting Rifle, Plain, Modern........	200	225	225
Model 721ADL, Various Calibers, Long Action, Sporting Rifle, Checkered Stock, Modern........	300	350	350
Model 721BDL, Various Calibers, Long Action, Sporting Rifle, Monte Carlo Stock, Checkered Stock, Fancy Wood, Modern........	375	450	450
Model 722, For .222 Rem. Add $25.00–$35.00			
Model 722A, Various Calibers, Short Action, Sporting Rifle, Plain, Modern........	200	225	225
Model 722ADL, Various Calibers, Short Action, Sporting Rifle, Checkered Stock, Modern........	300	350	350
Model 722BDL, Various Calibers, Short Action, Sporting Rifle, Checkered Stock, Fancy Wood, Modern........	325	400	400
Model 722D Peerless, Various Calibers, Short Action, Sporting Rifle, Fancy Wood, Fancy Checkering, Engraved, Modern........	950	1,200	1,200
Model 722F Premier, Various Calibers, Short Action, Sporting Rifle, Fancy Wood, Fancy Engraving, Fancy Checkering, Modern........	1,250	1,650	1,650
Model 725ADL, Various Calibers, Long Action, Magnum, Sporting Rifle, Checkered Stock, Fancy Wood, Modern........	450	500	500
Model 725ADL, Various Calibers, Long Action, Sporting Rifle, Checkered Stock, Fancy Wood, Modern........	350	400	400
Model 725D Peerless, Various Calibers, Long Action, Sporting Rifle, Engraved, Fancy Checkering, Fancy Wood, Modern........	1,000	1,225	1,225
Model 725F Premier, Various Calibers, Long Action, Sporting Rifle, Fancy Engraving, Fancy Checkering, Fancy Wood, Modern........	2,150	2,600	2,600
Model 788, Various Calibers, Clip Fed, Left–Hand, Plain, Modern........	225	250	250
Model 788, Various Calibers, Clip Fed, Plain, Modern........	200	225	225
Nylon 10, .22 L.R.R.F., Singleshot, Plastic Stock, Modern........	50	75	75
Nylon 10–SB, .22 L.R.R.F., Singleshot, Plastic Stock, Smoothbore, Modern........	200	225	225
Nylon 12, .22 L.R.R.F., Tube Feed, Plastic, Modern........	75	100	100

RIFLE, LEVER ACTION

	V.G.	Exc	Prior Edition
Nylon 76, .22 L.R.R.F., Tube Feed, Plastic Stock, Modern........	150	175	125

RIFLE, SEMI-AUTOMATIC

	V.G.	Exc	Prior Edition
Model Four, Various Calibers, Clip Fed, Sporting Rifle, Open Rear Sight, Checkered Stock, Fancy Wood, Modern........	300	350	350
Model 10C Mohawk, .22 L.R.R.F., Clip Fed, Plastic Stock, Modern........	75	100	100

	V.G.	Exc	Prior Edition
Model 16, .22 Rem. Automatic R.F., Takedown, Tube Feed, Modern............	$175	$225	$225
Model 16D, .22 Rem. Automatic R.F., Takedown, Tube Feed, Checkered Stock, Engraved, Modern...........	400	450	450
Model 16F, .22 Rem. Automatic R.F., Takedown, Tube Feed, Fancy Checkering, Fancy Engraving, Modern...........	950	1,200	1,200
Model 241A, .22 L.R.R.F., Tube Feed, Takedown, Open Rear Sight, Modern...........	225	275	275
Model 241A, .22 Short R.F., Tube Feed, Takedown, Open Rear Sight, Modern...........	200	250	250
Model 241D, .22 L.R.R.F., Tube Feed, Takedown, Fancy Checkering, Engraved, Modern...........	400	475	475
Model 241F, .22 L.R.R.F., Tube Feed, Takedown, Fancy Checkering, Fancy Engraving, Modern...........	750	850	850
Model 24A, .22 L.R.R.F., Takedown, Plain, Modern...........	150	175	175
Model 24A, .22 Short R.F., Takedown, Plain, Modern...........	150	175	175
Model 24C, .22 L.R.R.F., Takedown, Checkered Stock, Modern...........	175	200	200
Model 24D Peerless, .22 L.R.R.F., Takedown, Fancy Checkering, Engraved, Modern...........	500	550	550
Model 24F Premier, .22 L.R.R.F., Takedown, Fancy Checkering, Fancy Engraving, Modern...........	900	1,050	1,050
Model 550–2G, .22 Short R.F., Takedown, Open Rear Sight, Plain, Modern...........	125	150	150
Model 550A, .22 L.R.R.F., Takedown, Open Rear Sight, Plain, Modern...........	100	125	125
Model 550P, .22 L.R.R.F., Takedown, Peep Sights, Plain, Modern...........	100	125	125
Model 552A, .22 L.R.R.F., Tube Feed, Plain, Modern...........	100	125	125
Model 552BDL, .22 L.R.R.F., Tube Feed, Checkered Stock, Modern...........	125	150	150
Model 552C, .22 L.R.R.F., Tube Feed, Carbine, Plain, Modern...........	100	125	125
Model 552GS, .22 Short R.F., Tube Feed, Plain, Modern...........	125	150	150
Model 740 Peerless, Various Calibers, Clip Fed, Sporting Rifle, Open Rear Sight, Fancy Checkering, Engraved, Modern...........	1,550	1,800	1,800
Model 740A, Various Calibers, Clip Fed, Sporting Rifle, Open Rear Sight, Plain, Modern...........	200	250	250
Model 740ADL, Various Calibers, Clip Fed, Sporting Rifle, Open Rear Sight, Checkered Stock, Modern...........	225	275	275
Model 740BDL, Various Calibers, Clip Fed, Sportint Rifle, Open Rear Sight, Checkered Stock, Fancy Wood, Modern...........	275	325	325
Model 740F Premier, Various Calibers, Clip Fed, Sporting Rifle, Open Rear Sight, Fancy Checkering, Fancy Engraving,, Modern...........	3,000	3,500	3,500
Model 7400, Various Calibers, Clip Fed, Sporting Rifle, Open Rear Sight, Checkered Stock, Modern...........	325	350	350
Model 742, .30–.06 Springfield, Bicentennial, Clip Fed, Modern...........	300	325	325
Model 742, Various Calibers, Clip Fed, Sporting Rifle, Open Rear Sight, Checkered Stock, Modern...........	275	300	300
Model 742ADL, Various Calibers, Clip Fed, Sporting Rifle, Open Rear Sight, Checkered Stock, Modern...........	250	275	275
Model 742BDL, Various Calibers, Clip Fed, Sporting Rifle, Open Rear Sight, Checkered Stock, Fancy Wood, Modern...........	325	300	300
Model 742C, Various Calibers, Clip Fed, Sporting Rifle, Open Rear Sight, Carbine, Checkered Stock, Modern...........	250	300	300
Model 742CDL, Various Calibers, Clip Fed, Sporting Rifle, Open Rear Sight, Carbine, Fancy Wood, Modern...........	275	325	325

	V.G.	Exc	Prior Edition
Model 742 Canadian Centennial, Clip Fed, Sporting Rifle, Open Rear Sight, Checkered Stock, Commemorative, Curio..............................	$325	$350	$350
Model 742 Peerless, Various Calibers, Clip Fed, Sporting Rifle, Open Rear Sight, Fancy Checkering, Engraved, Modern..........................	1,700	1,900	1,900
Model 742 Premier, Various Calibers, Clip Fed, Sporting Rifle, Open Rear Sight, Fancy Checkering, Engraved, Modern..........................	3,500	4,000	4,000
Model 77, .22 L.R.R.F., Clip Fed, Plastic Stock, Modern......................	75	100	100
Model 81A, Various Calibers, Takedown, Plain, Modern........................	275	325	325
Model 81D Peerless, Various Calibers, Takedown, Fancy Checkering, Engraved, Modern...	625	700	700
Model 81F Premier, Various Calibers, Takedown, Fancy Checkering, Fancy Engraving, Fancy Wood, Modern.........................	1,150	1,400	1,400
Model 8A Standard, Various Calibers, Plain, Modern...........................	275	325	325
Model 8C Special, Various Calibers, Checkered Stock, Modern............	325	375	375
Model 8D Peerless, Various Calibers, Fancy Checkering, Light Engraving, Modern...	600	675	675
Model 8E Expert, Various Calibers, Fancy Checkering, Engraved, Modern...	875	950	950
Model 8F Premier, Various Calibers, Fancy Checkering, Fancy Engraving, Fancy Wood, Modern...	950	1,250	1,250
Nylon 11, .22 L.R.R.F., Clip Fed, Plastic Stock, Modern........................	50	75	75
Nylon 66, .22 L.R.R.F., Tube Feed, Bicentennial, Plastic Stock, Modern..	150	175	175
Nylon 66, .22 L.R.R.F., Tube Feed, Plastic Stock, Modern.....................	75	100	100
Nylon 66GS, .22 Short R.F., Tube Feed, Plastic Stock, Modern..	100	125	125

RIFLE, SINGLESHOT

	V.G.	Exc	Prior Edition
1867 Cadet Navy, 50/45 C.F., Military, Antique....................................	1,450	1,700	1,700
1867 Navy, 50/45 C.F., Military, Carbine, Antique.................................	1,150	1,200	1,200
Beals, .32 R.F., Sliding Barrel, Plain, Antique..	625	700	700
Hepburn #3, Various Calibers, Sporting Rifle, Checkered Stock, Hammer, Curio...	1,200	1,450	1,450
Model 1, Various Calibers, Rolling Block, Sporting Rifle, Adjustable Sights, Plain Stock, Curio..	750	1,000	1,000
Model 1, Various Calibers, Rolling Block, Target, Adjustable Sights, Checkered Stock, Curio..	2,100	2,500	2,500
Model 4, .22 L.R.R.F., Rolling Block, Takedown, Modern.....................	425	500	500
Model 4S Boy Scout, .22 L.R.R.F., Rolling Block, Full–Stocked, Curio..	725	800	800
Model 4S Boy Scout, .22 L.R.R.F., Rolling Block, Full–Stocked, with Bayonet, Curio..	775	900	900
Model 5, Various Calibers, Rolling Block, Sporting Rifle, Adjustable Sights, Plain Stock, Curio..	750	875	875
Model 6, .22 L.R.R.F., Rolling Block, Takedown, Modern.....................	300	350	350
Model 6, .32 Long Rifle, Rolling Block, Takedown, Modern..................	325	400	400
Model 7, Various Rimfires, Rolling Block, Target, Adjustable Sights, Checkered Stock, Curio..	2,100	2,500	2,500
Model 7, Various Rimfires, Rolling Block, Target, Swiss Buttplate, Checkered Stock, Adjustable Sights, Curio.....................	2,500	3,000	3,000
Model 7, Various Rimfires, Rolling Block, Target, Swiss Buttplate, Checkered Stock, Peep Sights, Curio...................................	2,750	3,250	3,250
Split Breech, .46 R.F., Military, Carbine, Antique..................................	1,500	1,750	650
Split Breech, .50 R.F., Military, Carbine, Antique..................................	750	850	850

	V.G.	Exc	Prior Edition

RIFLE, SLIDE ACTION

Model Six, Various Calibers, Clip Fed, Sporting Rifle, Open Rear Sight, Monte Carlo Stock, Checkered Stock, Modern............................. $350 · $375 · $325

Model 12A Standard, .22 L.R.R.F., Plain, Round Barrel, Tube Feed, Modern.............. 450 · 500 · 175

Model 12B Gallery, .22 Short R.F., Plain, Round Barrel, Tube Feed, Modern.............. 450 · 500 · 175

Model 12C, .22 L.R.R.F., Plain, Octagon Barrel, Tube Feed, Target, Modern.............. 400 · 450 · 225

Model 12C–NRA, .22 L.R.R.F., Plain, Octagon Barrel, Tube Feed, Peep Sights, Modern.............. 400 · 450 · 275

Model 12CS Special, .22 WRF, Plain, Octagon Barrel, Tube Feed, Modern.............. 450 · 500 · 250

Model 12D Peerless, .22 L.R.R.F., Checkered Stock, Octagon Barrel, Tube Feed, Light Engraving, Modern.............. 2,250 · 2,500 · 475

Model 12E Expert, .22 L.R.R.F., Fancy Checkering, Octagon Barrel, Tube Feed, Engraved, Modern.............. 2,500 · 2,750 · 675

Model 12F Premier, .22 L.R.R.F., Fancy Checkering, Octagon Barrel, Tube Feed, Fancy Engraving, Fancy Wood, Modern.............. 3,250 · 3,500 · 950

Model 121A, .22 L.R.R.F., Takedown, Tube Feed, Plain, Modern.............. 400 · 425 · 250

Model 121D Peerless, .22 L.R.R.F., Takedown, Tube Feed, Fancy Checkering, Engraved, Modern.............. 1,500 · 1,750 · 625

Model 121F Premier, .22 L.R.R.F., Takedown, Tube Feed, Fancy Checkering, Fancy Engraving, Modern.............. 2,500 · 2,750 · 950

Model 121S, .22 WRF., Takedown, Tube Feed, Plain, Modern.............. 625 · 700 · 225

Model 121SB, .22 L.R.R.F., Takedown, Tube Feed, Plain, Modern........ 500 · 550 · 200

Model 14, Various Calibers, Tube Feed, Plain, Modern.............. 325 · 375 · 250

Model 14 A, Various Calibers, Tube Feed, Short Action, Plain, Modern.............. 325 · 350 · 300

Model 14½, Various Calibers, Tube Feed, Short Action, Carbine, Plain Barrel, Modern.............. 400 · 425 · 350

Model 141A, Various Calibers, Takedown, Tube Feed, Plain, Modern.............. 375 · 400 · 275

Model 141D Peerless, Various Calibers, Takedown, Tube Feed, Fancy Checkering, Engraved, Modern.............. 800 · 950 · 650

Model 141F Premier, Various Calibers, Takedown, Tube Feed, Fancy Checkering, Fancy Engraving, Modern.............. 1,100 · 1,250 · 1,150

Model 141R, Various Calibers, Takedown, Tube Feed, Plain, Carbine, Modern.............. 350 · 375 · 275

Model 14C Special, Various Calibers, Tube Feed, Checkered Stock, Modern.............. 375 · 400 · 275

Model 14D Peerless, Various Calibers, Tube Feed, Fancy Checkering, Engraved, Modern.............. 450 · 500 · 600

Model 14F Premier, Various Calibers, Tube Feed, Fancy Checkering, Fancy Wood, Fancy Engraving, Modern.............. 850 · 1,000 · 1,200

Model 14R, Various Calibers, Tube Feed, Carbine, Plain, Modern.............. 350 · 400 · 550

Model 25A, Various Calibers, Takedown, Plain, Modern.............. 450 · 500 · 275

Model 25D Peerless, Various Calibers, Takedown, Checkered Stock, Engraved, Modern.............. 875 · 975 · 775

Model 25F Premier, Various Calibers, Takedown, Fancy Checkering, Fancy Engraving, Modern.............. 1,100 · 1,250 · 1,150

	V.G.	Exc	Prior Edition
Model 25R, Various Calibers, Takedown, Plain, Carbine, Modern......	$425	$475	$375
Model 572, .22 L.R.R.F., Tube Feed, Open Rear Sight, Lightweight, Fancy Checkering, Chrome, Modern.....	150	175	125
Model 572A, .22 L.R.R.F., Tube Feed, Open Rear Sight, Plain, Modern......	125	150	150
Model 572BDL, .22 L.R.R.F., Tube Feed, Open Rear Sight, Checkered Stock, Modern......	150	175	150
Model 572SB, .22 L.R.R.F., Tube Feed, Plain, Smoothbore, Modern......	125	150	150
Model 760, .30–06 Springfield, Bicentennial, Clip Fed, Modern.....	250	300	300
Model 760A, Various Calibers, Clip Fed, Sporting Rifle, Open Rear Sight, Plain, Modern......	225	275	275
Model 760ADL, Various Calibers, Clip Fed, Sporting Rifle, Open Rear Sight, Monte Carlo Stock, Checkered Stock, Modern......	275	325	325
Model 760BDL, Various Calibers, Clip Fed, Sporting Rifle, Open Rear Sight, Monte Carlo Stock, Checkered Stock, Modern......	200	275	275
Model 760C, Various Calibers, Clip Fed, Sporting Rifle, Open Rear Sight, Carbine, Plain, Modern......	250	325	325
Model 760CDL, Various Calibers, Clip Fed, Sporting Rifle, Open Rear Sight, Carbine, Checkered Stock, Modern......	300	375	375
Model 760D Peerless, Various Calibers, Clip Fed, Sporting Rifle, Open Rear Sight, Fancy Checkering, Engraved, Modern......	750	900	900
Model 760F Premier, Various Calibers, Clip Fed, Sporting Rifle, Open Rear Sight, Fancy Checkering, Fancy Engraving, Modern.....	1,650	1,850	1,850
Model 7600, Various Calibers, Clip Fed, Sporting Rifle, Open Rear Sight, Monte Carlo Stock, Checkered Stock, Modern......	300	375	375

SHOTGUN, DOUBLE BARREL, OVER-UNDER

	V.G.	Exc	Prior Edition
Model 32, Raised Solid Rib, Add $55.00–$150.00			
Model 32, for Vent Rib Add $95.00–$200.00			
Model 32, 12 Ga., Skeet Grade, Engraved, Fancy Checkering, Modern......	1,200	2,500	1,500
Model 32A, 12 Ga., Double Trigger, Automatic Ejector, Plain Barrel, Engraved, Checkered Stock, Modern......	800	2,250	950
Model 32A, 12 Ga., Single Selective Trigger, Automatic Ejector, Plain Barrel, Engraved, Checkered Stock, Modern......	1,250	2,500	1,500
Model 32D, 12 Ga., Fancy Checkering, Fancy Wood, Fancy Engraving, Modern......	2,250	3,250	2,700
Model 32E, 12 Ga., Fancy Checkering, Fancy Wood, Fancy Engraving, Modern......	3,500	4,000	4,000
Model 32F, 12 Ga., Fancy Checkering, Fancy Wood, Fancy Engraving, Modern......	5,000	6,500	500
Model 32TC, 12 Ga., Trap Grade, Single Selective Trigger, Engraved, Fancy Checkering, Modern......	2,500	2,750	2,750
Model 3200, 12 Ga. Mag 3", Field Grade, Automatic Ejector, Single Selective Trigger, Vent Rib, Checkered Stock, Modern......	800	950	950
Model 3200, 12 Ga., Field Grade, Automatic Ejector, Single Selective Trigger, Vent Rib, Checkered Stock, Modern......	775	850	850
Model 3200, 12 Ga., Skeet Grade, Automatic Ejector, Single Selective Trigger, Vent Rib, Checkered Stock, Modern......	875	950	950
Model 3200, 12 Ga., Trap Grade, Automatic Ejector, Single Selective Trigger, Vent Rib, Checkered Stock, Modern......	750	900	900
Model 3200 Competition, 12 Ga., Skeet Grade, Automatic Ejector, Single Selective Trigger, Vent Rib, Engraved, Modern......	750	1,000	1,000

	V.G.	Exc	Prior Edition
Model 3200 Competition, 12 Ga., Skeet Grade, Automatic Ejector, Single Selective Trigger, Vent Rib, Engraved, Extra Barrels, Modern.........	$3,750	$4,000	$3,800
Model 3200 Competition, 12 Ga., Trap Grade, Automatic Ejector, Ejector, Single Selective Trigger, Vent Rib, Engraved, Modern...............	1,050	1,350	1,350

SHOTGUN, DOUBLE BARREL, SIDE-BY-SIDE

	V.G.	Exc	Prior Edition
Model 1882, Various Gauges, Hammer, Damascus Barrel, Checkered Stock, Double Trigger, Antique.....................	900	975	975
Model 1883, Various Gauges, Hammer, Damascus Barrel, Checkered Stock, Double Trigger, Antique.....................	700	775	700
Model 1883, Various Gauges, Hammer, Steel Barrel, Checkered Stock, Double Trigger, Antique.....................	875	950	900
Model 1894–A, Various Gauges, Hammerless, Damascus Barrel, Plain, Checkered Stock, Double Trigger, Curio....................	600	700	700
Model 1894 AE, Various Gauges, Hammerless, Damascus Barrel, Automatic Ejector, Checkered Stock, Double Trigger, Curio....................	600	750	750
Model 1894 AEO, Various Gauges, Hammerless, Steel Barrel, Automatic Ejector, Checkered Stock, Double Trigger, Curio....................	775	850	850
Model 1894 AO, Various Gauges, Hammerless, Steel Barrel, Plain, Checkered Stock, Double Trigger, Curio....................	650	725	725
Model 1894 B, Various Gauges, Hammerless, Damascus Barrel, Light Engraving, Checkered Stock, Double Trigger, Curio....................	700	775	775
Model 1894 BE, Various Gauges, Hammerless, Damascus Barrel, Automatic Ejector, Light Engraving, Checkered Stock, Curio....................	775	875	875
Model 1894 BEO, Various Gauges, Hammerless, Steel Barrel, Automatic Ejector, Light Engraving, Checkered Stock, Curio....................	775	900	900
Model 1894 BO, Various Gauges, Hammerless, Steel Barrel, Light Engraving, Checkered Stock, Double Trigger, Curio....................	725	775	775
Model 1894 C, Various Gauges, Hammerless, Damascus Barrel, Engraved, Checkered Stock, Double Trigger, Curio....................	750	850	850
Model 1894 CE, Various Gauges, Hammerless, Damascus Barrel, Automatic Ejector, Engraved, Checkered Stock, Curio....................	850	950	950
Model 1894 CEO, Various Gauges, Hammerless, Steel Barrel, Automatic Ejector, Engraved, Checkered Stock, Curio....................	900	975	975
Model 1894 CO, Various Gauges, Hammerless, Steel Barrel, Engraved, Checkered Stock, Double Trigger, Curio....................	775	875	875
Model 1894 D, Various Gauges, Hammerless, Damascus Barrel, Fancy Engraving, Fancy Checkering, Fancy Wood, Curio....................	1,000	1,250	1,250
Model 1894 DE, Various Gauges, Hammerless, Damascus Barrel, Automatic Ejector, Fancy Engraving, Fancy Checkering, Curio...............	1,150	1,350	1,350
Model 1894 DEO, Various Gauges, Hammerless, Steel Barrel, Automatic Ejector, Fancy Engraving, Fancy Checkering, Curio...............	1,200	1,400	1,400
Model 1894 DO, Various Gauges, Hammerless, Steel Barrel, Fancy Engraving, Fancy Checkering, Fancy Wood, Curio....................	1,250	1,450	1,450
Model 1894 E, Various Gauges, Hammerless, Damascus Barrel, Fancy Engraving, Fancy Checkering, Fancy Wood, Curio....................	1,500	1,800	1,800
Model 1894 EE, Various Gauges, Hammerless, Damascus Barrel, Automatic Ejector, Fancy Engraving, Fancy Checkering, Curio...............	1,750	1,900	1,900
Model 1894 EEO, Various Gauges, Hammerless, Steel Barrel, Automatic Ejector, Fancy Engraving, Fancy Checkering, Curio...............	2,250	2,500	2,500
Model 1894 EO, Various Gauges, Hammerless, Steel Barrel, Fancy Engraving, Fancy Checkering, Fancy Wood, Curio....................	2,000	2,250	2,250
Model 1894 Special, Various Gauges, Hammerless, Steel Barrel, Automatic Ejector, Fancy Engraving, Fancy Checkering, Curio...............	6,000	7,000	7,000

	V.G.	Exc	Prior Edition
Model 1900 K ED , 12 and 16 Gauges, Hammerless, Damascus Barrel, Automatic Ejector, Palm Rest, Checkered Stock, Curio...............	$475	$50	$550
Model 1900 K, 12 and 16 Gauges, Hammerless, Steel Barrel, Plain, Checkered Stock, Curio.............	625	675	675
Model 1900 KD , 12 and 16 Gauges, Hammerless, Damascus Barrel, Plain, Checkered Stock, Curio..........	425	500	500
Model 1900 KE, 12 and 16 Gauges, Hammerless, Steel Barrel, Automatic Ejector, Plain, Checkered Stock, Curio.................	650	750	750
Model Parker AHE, 12 Ga., Double Trigger, Checkered Stock, Modern..........			

SHOTGUN, SEMI-AUTOMATIC

	V.G.	Exc	Prior Edition
Autoloading, 12 Ga., for Solid Rib, Add $35.00–$75.00			
Autoloading–0, 12 Ga., Takedown, Riot Gun, Plain, Modern................	400	450	250
Autoloading–1, 12 Ga., Takedown, Plain, Modern................	200	250	250
Autoloading–2, 12 Ga., Takedown, Checkered Stock, Modern.............	275	325	325
Autoloading–4, 12 Ga., Takedown, Fancy Checkering, Fancy Wood, Engraved, Modern...............	750	850	850
Autoloading–6, 12 Ga., Takedown, Fancy Checkering, Fancy Wood, Fancy Engraving, Modern...............	1,000	1,250	1,250
Model 11, for Vent Rib, Add $45.00–$100.00			
Model 11, Raised Solid Rib, Add $30.00–$50.00			
Model 11 Sportsman, Various Gauges, Skeet Grade, Vent Rib, Light Engraving, Checkered Stock, Modern............	225	275	275
Model 11-48A , Various Gauges, Plain Barrel, Modern............	200	250	250
Model 11-48B, Various Gauges, Vent Rib, Checkered Stock, Fancy Wood, Modern............	225	275	275
Model 11–48 D Tournament, Various Gauges, Vent Rib, Fancy Wood, Fancy Engraving, Fancy Checkering, Modern............	700	800	800
Model 11-48F Premier, Various Gauges, Vent Rib, Fancy Wood, fancy Engraving, Fancy Checkering, Modern............	1,200	1,450	1,450
Model 11–48 R, 12 Ga., Riot Gun, Plain Barrel, Modern............	500	550	225
Model 11–48 RSS, 12 Ga., Open Rear Sight, Slug, Checkered Stock, Modern............	225	275	275
Model 11–48 SA, Various Gauges, Skeet Grade, Vent Rib, Checkered Stock, Modern............	250	325	325
Model 11–48 Special, Various Gauges, Vent Rib, Checkered Stock, Modern............	375	425	275
Model 1100, 12 Ga. Lightweight, Add $25.00–$50.00			
Model 1100, 12 Ga., Bicentennial, Skeet Grade, Vent Rib, Checkered Stock, Modern............	350	325	400
Model 1100, for .28 Ga. or .410 Ga., Add $25.00–$50.00			
Model 1100, for Left Hand, Add $35.00–$75.00			
Model 1100, Various Gauges, Plain Barrel, Checkered Stock, Modern............	250	225	275
Model 1100, Various Gauges, Plain Barrel, Magnum, Checkered Stock, Modern............	300	275	350
Model 1100, Various Gauges, Skeet Grade, Vent Rib, Checkered Stock, Modern............	300	425	350
Model 1100, Various Gauges, Vent Rib, Checkered Stock, Modern............	275	275	325
Model 1100, Various Gauges, Vent Rib, Magnum, Checkered Stock, Modern............	350	300	400
Model 1100 Cutts, Various Gauges, Skeet Grade, Vent Rib, Checkered Stock, Modern............	450	450	375

	V.G.	Exc	Prior Edition
Model 1100 D Tournament, Various Gauges, Vent Rib, Fancy Checkering, Fancy Wood, Fancy Engraving, Modern	$1,500	$1,800	$1,800
Model 1100 Deer Gun, Various Gauges, Open Rear Sight, Checkered Stock, Modern	250	325	300
Model 1100 Premier, Various Gauges, Vent Rib, Fancy Checkering, Fancy Wood, Fancy Engraving, Modern	3,250	4,000	3,500
Model 1100 TA, 12 Ga., Bicentennial, Trap Grade, Vent Rib, Checkered Stock, Modern	275	325	325
Model 1100 TA, 12 Ga., Bicentennial, Trap Grade, Vent Rib, Monte Carlo Stock, Checkered Stock, Modern	300	350	350
Model 1100 TA, 12 Ga., Trap Grade, Vent Rib, Checkered Stock, Modern	250	300	300
Model 1100 TA, 12 Ga., Trap Grade, Vent Rib, Checkered Stock, Monte Carlo Stock, Modern	300	350	350
Model 11A, 12 Ga., Plain Barrel, Modern	175	250	225
Model 11A, 12 Ga., Plain Barrel, Fancy Wood, Checkered Stock, Modern	200	250	250
Model 11A Sportsman, 12 Ga., Plain Barrel, Fancy Wood, Light Engraving, Checkered Stock, Modern	225	275	275
Model 11A Sportsman, Various Gauges, Plain Barrel, Light Engraving, Modern	175	225	225
Model 11C, 12 Ga., Plain Barrel, Trap Grade, Fancy Checkering Fancy Wood, Modern	325	375	375
Model 11D, 12 Ga., Plain Barrel, Fancy Checkering, Fancy Wood, Fancy Engraving, Modern	575	650	650
Model 11D Sportsman, Various Gauges, Plain Barrel, Engraved, Fancy Checkering, Modern	550	625	625
Model 11E, 12 Ga., Plain Barrel, Fancy Checkering, Fancy Wood, Fancy Engraving, Modern	750	900	900
Model 11E Sportsman, Various Gauges, Plain Barrel, Fancy Checkering, Fancy Wood, Fancy Engraving, Modern	800	950	950
Model 11F, 12 Ga., Plain Barrel, Fancy Checkering, Fancy Wood, Fancy Engraving, Modern	1,000	1,150	1,150
Model 11F Sportsman, Various Gauges, Plain Barrel, Fancy Checkering, Fancy Wood, Fancy Engraving, Modern	1,000	1,125	1,125
Model 11R, 12 Ga., Riot Gun, Commercial, Modern	400	450	200
Model 11R, 12 Ga., Riot Gun, Military, Modern	650	750	250
Model 48–D Sportsman, Various Gauges, Vent Rib, Fancy Checkering, Fancy Wood, Fancy Engraving, Modern	700	775	775
Model 48–F Sportsman, Various Gauges, Vent Rib, Fancy Checkering, Fancy Wood, Fancy Engraving, Modern	1,600	1,800	1,800
Model 48–SA Sportsman, Various Gauges, Skeet Grade, Vent Rib, Rib, Checkered Stock, Modern	200	250	250
Model 48A Sportsman, Various Gauges, Plain Barrel, Modern	175	200	200
Model 48B Sportsman, Various Gauges, Vent Rib, Checkered Stock, Modern	225	275	275
Model 58 ADL, 12 and 20 Gauges, Vent Rib, Recoil Pad, Checkered Stock, Magnum, Modern	250	300	300
Model 58 ADL, Various Gauges, Plain Barrel, Checkered Stock, Modern	200	250	250
Model 58 ADL, Various Gauges, Vent Rib, Checkered Stock, Modern	250	300	300
Model 58 ADX, Various Gauges, Vent Rib, Checkered Stock, Fancy Wood, Modern	200	250	250

	V.G.	Exc	Prior Edition
Model 58 BDL, Various Gauges, Plain Barrel, Checkered Stock, Fancy Wood, Modern	$250	$300	$300
Model 58 BDL, Various Gauges, Vent Rib, Checkered Stock, Fancy Wood, Modern	300	350	350
Model 58 D Tournament, Various Gauges, Vent Rib, Fancy Checkering, Fancy Wood, Fancy Engraving, Modern	600	700	700
Model 58 F Premier, Various Gauges, Vent Rib, Fancy Checkering, Fancy Wood, Fancy Engraving, Modern	1,100	1,300	1,300
Model 58 RSS, 12 Ga. Slug, Open Rear Sight, Checkered Stock, Modern	200	250	250
Model 58 SA, Various Gauges, Skeet Grade, Vent Rib, Checkered Stock, Modern	275	325	325
Model 58 TB, 12 Ga., Trap Grade, Vent Rib, Checkered Stock, Modern	275	325	325
Model 878 A, 12 Ga., Plain Barrel, Modern	150	200	200
Model 878 A, 12 Ga., Vent Rib, Modern	175	225	225
Model 878 ADL, 12 Ga., Plain Barrel, Checkered Stock, Modern	175	225	225
Model 878 ADL, 12 Ga., Vent Rib, Checkered Stock, Modern	200	250	250
Model 878 D, 12 Ga., Vent Rib, Fancy Checkering, Fancy Wood, Fancy Engraving, Modern	575	650	650
Model 878 F, 12 Ga., Vent Rib, Fancy Checkering, Fancy Wood, Fancy Engraving, Modern	1,050	1,200	1,200
Model 878 SA, 12 Ga., Skeet Grade, Vent Rib, Checkered Stock, Modern	200	250	250

SHOTGUN, SINGLESHOT

	V.G.	Exc	Prior Edition
Model 3 (M1893), 12 Ga., 24 Ga., 28 Ga., Add $35.00			
Model 3 (M1893), Various Gauges, Takedown, Plain, Curio	125	150	150
Model 9 (M1902), Various Gauges, Automatic Ejector, Plain, Curio	100	150	150
Model Parker, 12 Ga., Trap Grade, Vent Rib, Automatic Ejector, Fancy Checkering, Modern	—		—
Model Parker, 12 Ga., Trap Grade, Vent Rib, Automatic Ejector, Fancy Checkering, Fancy Engraving, Modern	—		—

SHOTGUN, SLIDE ACTION

	V.G.	Exc	Prior Edition
Model 108, 12 Ga., Takedown, Checkered Stock, Fancy Wood, Modern	175	250	250
Model 10A, 12 Ga., Takedown, Plain, Modern	175	225	225
Model 10C, 12 Ga., Takedown, Fancy Wood, Checkered Stock, Modern	250	300	300
Model 10D, 12 Ga., Takedown, Fancy Checkering, Fancy Wood, Engraved, Modern	550	625	625
Model 10E, 12 Ga., Takedown, Fancy Checkering, Fancy Wood, Fancy Engraving, Modern	750	825	825
Model 10F, 12 Ga., Takedown, Fancy Checkering, Fancy Engraving, Fancy Wood, Modern	950	1,100	1,100
Model 10R, 12 Ga., Takedown, Riot Gun, Plain, Modern	125	175	175
Model 10S, 12 Ga., Takedown, Trap Grade, Checkered Stock, Modern	200	250	250
Model 17, 20 Ga., for Solid Rib, Add $25.00–$40.00			
Model 17A, 20 Ga., Takedown, Plain, Modern	175	225	225
Model 17B, 20 Ga., Takedown, Checkered Stock, Modern	225	275	275
Model 17C, 20 Ga., Takedown, Fancy Wood, Checkered Stock, Modern	300	350	350

	V.G.	Exc	Prior Edition
Model 17D, 20 Ga., Takedown, Fancy Wood, Fancy Checkering, Engraved, Modern..............	$525	$600	$600
Model 17E, 20 Ga., Takedown, Fancy Wood, Fancy Checkering, Fancy Engraving, Modern..............	750	850	850
Model 17F, 20 Ga., Takedown, Fancy Wood, Fancy Checkering, Fancy Engraving, Modern..............	950	1,075	1,075
Model 17R, 20 Ga., Takedown, Riot Gun, Plain, Modern..............	175	225	225
Model 1908–0, 12 Ga., Takedown, Riot Gun, Plain, Modern..............	175	225	225
Model 1908–1, 12 Ga., Takedown, Plain, Modern..............	175	225	225
Model 1908–3, 12 Ga., Takedown, Checkered Stock, Fancy Wood, Modern..............	225	275	275
Model 1908–4, 12 Ga., Takedown, Fancy Checkering, Fancy Wood, Engraved, Modern..............	525	600	600
Model 1908–6, 12 Ga., Takedown, Fancy Checkering, Fancy Wood, Fancy Engraving, Modern..............	950	1,075	1,075
Model 29, for Solid Rib, Add $25.00–$35.00			
Model 29, for Vent Rib, Add $35.00–$55.00			
Model 29A Sportsman, 12 Ga., Plain Barrel, Takedown, Modern..........	175	225	225
Model 29B, 12 Ga., Checkered Stock, Takedown, Modern..............	175	225	225
Model 29C, 12 Ga., Trap Grade, Takedown, Modern..............	225	275	275
Model 29R, 12 Ga., Riot Gun, Plain Barrel, Modern..............	150	200	200
Model 29S, 12 Ga., Trap Grade, Plain Barrel, Checkered Stock, Modern..............	200	250	250
Model 29TA, 12 Ga., Trap Grade, Vent Rib, Checkered Stock, Modern..............	275	325	325
Model 29TC, 12 Ga., Trap Grade, Vent Rib, Checkered Stock, Fancy Wood, Modern..............	300	375	375
Model 29TD, 12 Ga., Trap Grade, Vent Rib, Fancy Checkering, Fancy Wood, Engraved, Modern..............	475	575	575
Model 29TE, 12 Ga., Trap Grade, Vent Rib, Fancy Checkering, Fancy Wood, Fancy Engraving, Modern..............	700	775	775
Model 29TF, 12 Ga., Trap Grade, Vent Rib, Fancy Checkering, Fancy Wood, Fancy Engraving, Modern..............	950	1,050	1,050
Model 31, for Solid Rib, Add $15.00–$30.00			
Model 31, for Vent Rib, Add $45.00–$60.00			
Model 31, Various Gauges, Skeet Grade, Vent Rib, Checkered Stock, Fancy Wood, Modern..............	400	475	475
Model 31A, Various Gauges, Plain Barrel, Modern..............	375	325	325
Model 31B, Various Gauges, Plain Barrel, Checkered Stock, Fancy Wood, Modern..............	375	450	450
Model 31D Tournament, Various Gauges, Plain Barrel, Checkered Stock, Fancy Wood, Engraved, Modern..............	775	800	800
Model 31E Expert, Various Gauges, Plain Barrel, Fancy Checkering, Fancy Wood, Fancy Engraving, Modern..............	875	975	975
Model 31F Premier, Various Gauges, Plain Barrel, Fancy Checkering, Fancy Wood, Fancy Engraving, Modern..............	1,500	1,800	1,800
Model 31H Hunter, Various Gauges, Checkered Stock, Fancy Wood, Plain, Barrel, Modern..............	300	375	375
Model 31R, 12 Ga., Plain Barrel, Riot Gun, Modern..............	175	225	225
Model 31S, 12 Ga., Raised Matted Rib, Checkered Stock, Fancy Wood, Modern..............	425	500	500
Model 31TC, 12 Ga., Trap Grade, Vent Rib, Recoil Pad, Modern..........	450	525	525
Model 870 SC, Various Gauges, Skeet Grade, Vent Rib, Checkered Stock, Modern..............	250	300	300
Model 870, for .28 Ga. 0r .410 Ga., Add $20.00–$25.00			

	V.G.	Exc	Prior Edition
Model 870, for Left Hand, Add $10.00–$15.00			
Model 870, For Lightweight 20, Add $20.00–$25.00			
Model 870, Various Gauges, Plain Barrel, Checkered Stock, Modern	$175	$225	$225
Model 870, Various Gauges, Plain Barrel, Magnum, Checkered Stock, Modern	200	250	250
Model 870, Various Gauges, Vent Rib, Checkered Stock, Modern	225	275	275
Model 870, Various Gauges, Vent Rib, Magnum, Checkered Stock, Modern	225	300	300
Model 870 All American, 12 Ga., Trap Grade, Vent Rib, Fancy Checkering, Engraved, Modern	600	675	675
Model 870 Brushmaster, 12 and 20 Gauges, Open Rear Sight, Recoil Pad, Checkered Stock, Modern	225	275	275
Model 870 Competition, 12 Ga., Trap Grade, Vent Rib, Checkered Stock, Singleshot, Modern	325	400	400
Model 870 D Tournament, Various Gauges, Vent Rib, Fancy Checkering, Fancy Wood, Fancy Engraving, Modern	1,600	1,800	1,800
Model 870 Deergun, 12 Ga., Open Rear Sight, Checkered Stock, Modern	225	275	275
Model 870 F Premier, Various Gauges, Vent Rib, Fancy Checkering, Fancy Wood, Fancy Engraving, Modern	3,500	3,900	3,900
Model 870 Police, 12 Ga., Open Rear Sight, Modern	200	250	250
Model 870 Police, 12 Ga., Plain Barrel, Modern	175	225	225
Model 870SA Cutts, Various Gauges, Skeet Grade, Vent Rib, Checkered Stock, Modern	225	275	275
Model 870SA, 12 Ga., Bicentennial, Skeet Grade, Vent Rib, Checkered Stock, Modern	250	300	300
Model 870SA, Various Gauges, Skeet Grade, Vent Rib, Checkered Stock, Moden	250	300	300
Model 870TB, 12 Ga., Bicentennial, Trap Grade, Vent Rib, Checkered Stock, Modern	250	300	300
Model 870TB, 12 Ga., Bicentennial, Trap Grade, Vent Rib, Checkered Stock, Monte Carlo Stock, Modern	250	300	300
Model 870TB, 12 Ga., Trap Grade, Vent Rib, Checkered Stock, Modern	225	275	275
Model 870TB, 12 Ga., Trap Grade, Vent Rib, Checkered Stock, Monte Carlo Stock, Modern	250	300	300
Model 870TC, 12 Ga., Trap Grade, Vent Rib, Checkered Stock, Modern	325	375	375
Model 870TC, 12 Ga., Trap Grade, Vent Rib, Checkered Stock, Monte Carlo Stock, Modern	350	400	400

REPUBLIC Spain, unknown maker.

HANDGUN, SEMI-AUTOMATIC

	V.G.	Exc	Prior Edition
.32 ACP, Clip Fed, Long Grip, Modern	125	150	150

RETRIEVER Made by Thomas Ryan, Norwich, Conn. 1870–1876.

HANDGUN, REVOLVER

	V.G.	Exc	Prior Edition
.32 Short R.F., 5 Shot, Spur Trigger, Solid Frame, Single Action, Antique	150	175	175

	V.G.	Exc	Prior Edition

REV–O–NOC Made by Crescent for Hibbard–Spencer–Bartlett Co., Chicago.

SHOTGUN, DOUBLE BARREL, SIDE-BY-SIDE

	V.G.	Exc	Prior Edition
Various Gauges, Hammerless, Damascus Barrel, Modern.....................	$150	$175	$175
Various Gauges, Hammerless, Steel Barrel, Modern.............................	175	200	200
Various Gauges, Outside Hammers, Damascus Barrel, Modern.............	150	175	175
Various Gauges, Outside Hammers, Steel Barrel, Modern.....................	175	200	200

SHOTGUN, SINGLESHOT

Various Gauges, Hammer, Steel Barrel, Modern...................................	75	100	100

REVELATION Trade name used by Western Auto.

RIFLE, BOLT ACTION

Model 107, .22 WMR, Clip Fed, Modern..	50	75	75
Model 210B, 7mm Rem. Mag., Checkered Stock, Monte Carlo Stock, Modern...	150	175	175
Model 220A, .308 Win., Checkered Stock, Monte Carlo Stock, Modern...	150	175	175
Model 220AD, .308 Win., Checkered Stock, Monte Carlo Stock, Fancy Wood, Modern...	175	200	200
Model 220B, .243 Win., Checkered Stock, Monte Carlo Stock, Modern...	150	175	175
Model 220BD, .243 Win., Checkered Stock, Monte Carlo Stock, Fancy Wood, Modern...	150	200	200
Model 220C, .22-250, Checkered Stock, Monte Carlo Stock, Modern...	150	175	175
Model 220CD, .22-250, Checkered Stock, Monte Carlo Stock, Fancy Wood, Modern...	150	200	200

RIFLE, LEVER ACTION

Model 117, .22 L.R.R.F., Tube Feed, Modern...	50	75	75

RIFLE, SEMI-AUTOMATIC

Model 125, .22 L.R.R.F., Clip Fed, Modern..	25	50	50

RIFLE, SINGLESHOT

Model 100, .22 L.R.R.F, Modern..	25	50	50

SHOTGUN, BOLT ACTION

Model 312B, 12 Ga., Clip Fed, Modern..	25	50	50
Model 312BK, 12 Ga., Clip Fed, Adjustable Choke, Modern.................	50	75	75
Model 316B, 16 Ga., Clip Fed, Modern..	25	50	50
Model 316BK, 16 Ga., Clip Fed, Adjustable Choke, Modern.................	25	50	50
Model 325B, 20 Ga., Clip Fed, Modern..	25	50	50
Model 325BK, 20 Ga., Clip Fed, Adjustable Choke, Modern.................	25	50	50
Model 330, .410 Ga., Clip Fed, Modern..	25	50	50

SHOTGUN, SLIDE ACTION

Model 310, Various Gauges, Plain Barrel, Takedown, Modern...............	125	150	150
Model 31OR, Various Gauges, Vent Rib, Takedown, Modern...............	125	150	150

	V.G.	Exc	Prior Edition

REYNOLDS, PLANT & HOTCHKISS Also see Plant's
Mfg. Co.

HANDGUN, REVOLVER

.25 Short R.F., 5 Shot, Single Action, Spur Trigger, 3" Barrel,
Antique... $150 $200 $200

R.G. INDUSTRIES R.G. tradename belongs to Rohm GmbH,
Sontheim/Brenz, West Germany, and after 1968 also made in Miami, Fla.
for American consumption. Operations ceased in 1986.

HANDGUN, DOUBLE BARREL, OVER-UNDER

	V.G.	Exc	Prior Edition
RG–16, .22 WMR, 2 Shot, Derringer, Modern.................................	50	75	50
RG–17, .38 Special, 2 Shot, Derringer, Modern...........................	75	100	50

HANDGUN, REVOLVER

	V.G.	Exc	Prior Edition
Partner RG–40P, .38 Special, 6 Shot, Double Action, Swing–Out Cylinder, Modern..	75	100	100
RG–14, .22 L.R.R.F., 6 Shot, Double Action, Modern.............................	75	100	50
RG–23, .22 L.R.R.F., 6 Shot, Double Action, Modern.............................	50	75	50
RG–30, .22 L.R.R.F., 6 Shot, Double Action, Swing–Out Cylinder, Modern..	50	75	50
RG–30, .22 LR/.22 WMR Combo, 6 Shot, Double Action, Swing–Out Cylinder, Modern...	75	100	75
RG–30, .22 WMR, 6 Shot, Double Action, Swing–Out Cylinder, Modern..	50	75	50
RG–40, .38 Special, 6 Shot, Double Action, Swing–Out Cylinder, Modern..	75	100	125
RG–57, .357 Magnum, 6 Shot, Double Action, Swing–Out Cylinder, Modern..	100	125	100
RG–57, .44 Magnum, 6 Shot, Double Action, Swing–Out Cylinder, Modern..	125	150	150
RG–63, .22 L.R.R.F., 6 Shot, Double Action, Western Style, Modern..	25	50	50
RG–63, .22 LR/.22 WMR Combo, 6 Shot, Single Action, Western Style, Modern..	50	75	50
RG–66T, .22 LR/.22 WMR Combo, 6 Shot, Single Action, Western Style, Adjustable Sights, Modern.......................	50	75	75
RG–74, .22 L.R.R.F., 6 Shot, Double Action, Swing–Out Cylinder, Modern..	50	75	125
RG–88, .357 Magnum, 6 Shot, Double Action, Swing–Out Cylinder, Modern..	75	100	125

HANDGUN, SEMI-AUTOMATIC

	V.G.	Exc	Prior Edition
RG–25, .25 ACP, Modern..	50	75	50
RG–26, .25 ACP, Modern..	50	75	50

	V.G.	Exc	Prior Edition

RHEINMETALL Rheinsche Metallwaren u. Maschinenfabrik, Sommerada, Germany 1922–1927.

HANDGUN, SEMI-AUTOMATIC

7.65mm, Clip Fed, Blue, Curio..	$250	$300	$300

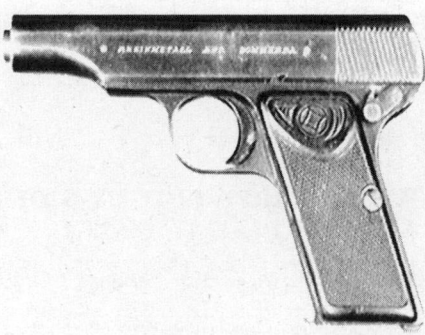

Rheinmetall

RICHARDS, JOHN London & Birmingham, England 1745–1810.

SHOTGUN, FLINTLOCK

Blunderbuss, Half–Octagon, Steel Barrel, Folding Bayonet, Antique..	775	1,000	1,000

RICHARDS, W. Belgium, c. 1900.

SHOTGUN, DOUBLE BARREL, SIDE-BY-SIDE

Various Gauges, Hammerless, Damascus Barrel, Modern......................	150	175	175
Various Gauges, Hammerless, Steel Barrel, Modern..............................	150	175	175
Various Gauges, Outside Hammers, Damascus Barrel, Modern.............	150	175	175
Various Gauges, Outside Hammers, Steel Barrel, Modern.....................	150	175	175

SHOTGUN, SINGLESHOT

Various Gauges, Hammer, Steel Barrel, Modern....................................	50	75	75

RICHARDSON INDUSTRIES New Haven, Conn.

SHOTGUN, SINGLESHOT

Model R–5, 12 Ga., 24" Barrel, Modern..	25	50	50

	V.G.	Exc	Prior Edition

RICHLAND ARMS CO. Importer. Bussfield, Mich.

RIFLE, PERCUSSION

	V.G.	Exc	Prior Edition
Wesson Rifle, .50, Set Triggers, Target Sights, Reproduction, Antique	$200	$250	$250

SHOTGUN, DOUBLE BARREL, OVER-UNDER

	V.G.	Exc	Prior Edition
Model 808, 12 Ga., Single Trigger, Checkered Stock, Vent Rib, Modern	375	425	425
Model 810, 10 Ga. 3½", Double Trigger, Checkered Stock, Vent Rib, Modern	450	525	525
Model 828, 28 Ga., Single Trigger, Checkered Stock, Modern	400	475	375
Model 844, 12 Ga., Single Trigger, Checkered Stock, Modern	275	350	350

SHOTGUN, DOUBLE BARREL, SIDE-BY-SIDE

	V.G.	Exc	Prior Edition
Model 200, Various Gauges, Double Trigger, Checkered Stock, Modern	275	300	325
Model 202, Various Gauges, Double Trigger, Extra Shotgun Barrel, Modern	250	275	300
Model 707 Deluxe, 12 and 20 Gauges, Double Trigger, Modern	275	300	350
Model 707 Deluxe, 12 and 20 Gauges, Double Trigger, Checkered Stock, Extra Shotgun Barrel, Modern	300	350	400
Model 711, 10 Ga. 3½", Double Trigger, Modern	275	325	325
Model 711, 12 Ga. Mag. 3", Double Trigger, Modern	300	350	350

RICHTER, CHARLES Made by Crescent for New York Sporting Goods Co. c. 1900.

SHOTGUN, DOUBLE BARREL, SIDE-BY-SIDE

	V.G.	Exc	Prior Edition
Various Gauges, Hammerless, Damascus Barrel, Modern	125	150	150
Various Gauges, Hammerless, Steel Barrel, Modern	150	175	175
Various Gauges, Outside Hammers, Damascus Barrel, Modern	125	150	150
Various Gauges, Outside Hammers, Steel Barrel, Modern	150	175	175

SHOTGUN, SINGLESHOT

	V.G.	Exc	Prior Edition
Various Gauges, Hammer, Steel Barrel, Modern	50	75	75

RICKARD ARMS Made by Crescent for J.A. Rickard Co. Schenectady, N.Y.

SHOTGUN, DOUBLE BARREL, SIDE-BY-SIDE

	V.G.	Exc	Prior Edition
Various Gauges, Hammerless, Damascus Barrel, Modern	150	175	175
Various Gauges, Hammerless, Steel Barrel, Modern	150	200	200
Various Gauges, Outside Hammers, Damascus Barrel, Modern	150	175	175
Various Gauges, Outside Hammers, Steel Barrel, Modern	150	200	200

SHOTGUN, SINGLESHOT

	V.G.	Exc	Prior Edition
Various Gauges, Hammer, Steel Barrel, Modern	75	100	100

	V.G.	Exc	Prior Edition

RIGARMI Industria Galesi, Brescia, Italy.

HANDGUN, SEMI-AUTOMATIC

	V.G.	Exc	Prior Edition
Militar, .22 L.R.R.F., Clip Fed, Hammer, Double Action, Modern..........	$150	$175	$175
Pocket, 7.65mm, Clip Fed, Hammer, Double Action, Modern................	125	150	150
RG–217, .22 Long R.F., Clip Fed, Modern...	75	100	100
RG–218, .22 L.R.R.F., Clip Fed, Modern...	100	125	125
RG–219, 6.35mm, Clip Fed, Modern..	75	100	100

RIGBY, JOHN & CO. Dublin, Ireland & London, England from 1867.

RIFLE, BOLT ACTION

	V.G.	Exc	Prior Edition
.275 Rigby, Sporting Rifle, Express Sights, Checkered Stock, Modern..	6,500	7,500	3,750
.275 Rigby, Sporting Rifle, Lightweight, Express Sights, Checkered Stock, Modern..	7,000	8,000	3,700
.350 Rigby, Sporting Rifle, Express Sights, Checkered Stock, Modern..	7,500	8,500	3,750
Big Game, .416 Rigby, Sporting Rifle, Express Sights, Checkered Stock, Modern..	8,500	9,500	3,950

RIFLE, DOUBLE BARREL, SIDE-BY-SIDE

	V.G.	Exc	Prior Edition
Best Grade, Various Calibers, Sidelock, Double Trigger, Express Sights, Fancy Engraving, Fancy Checkering, Modern...............................	40,000	45,000	45,000
Secon Grade, Various Calibers, Box Lock, Double Trigger, Express Sights, Fancy Engraving, Fancy Checkering, Modern.................	20,000	25,000	25,000
Third Grade, Various Calibers, Box Lock, Double Trigger, Express Sights, Engraved, Fancy Checkering, Modern............................	7,000	10,000	10,000

SHOTGUN, DOUBLE BARREL, SIDE-BY-SIDE

	V.G.	Exc	Prior Edition
Chatsworth, Various Gauges, Box Lock, Automatic Ejector, Double Trigger, Fancy Engraving, Fancy Checkering, Modern...............	3,000	3,500	3,500
Regal, Various Gauges, Sidelock, Automatic Ejector, Double Trigger, Fancy Engraving, Fancy Checkering, Modern...........................	10,000	12,000	12,000
Sackville, Various Gauges, Box Lock, Automatic Ejector, Double Trigger, Fancy Engraving, Fancy Checkering, Modern.........................	4,000	5,000	5,000
Sandringham, Various Gauges, Sidelock, Automatic Ejector, Double Trigger, Fancy Engraving, Fancy Checkering, Modern.................	7,500	8,500	8,000

RINO GALESI Industria Galesi, Brescia, Italy.

HANDGUN, SEMI-AUTOMATIC

	V.G.	Exc	Prior Edition
Model 9, 6.35mm, Clip Fed, Blue, Modern..	100	125	125

RIOT Made by Stevens Arms.

SHOTGUN, PUMP

	V.G.	Exc	Prior Edition
Model 520, 12 Ga., Takedown, Modern..	125	150	150
Model 620, Various Gauges, Takedown, Modern......................................	150	175	175

	V.G.	Exc	Prior Edition

RIPOLI
HANDGUN, MIQUELET-LOCK
Ball Butt, Brass Inlay, Light Ornamentation, Antique.............................. $2,250 $2,500 $2,500
Pair, Fluted Barrel, Pocket Pistol, Engraved, Silver Furniture,
Antique.. 7,000 7,500 7,500

RITTER, JACOB Phil., Pa. 1775–1783. See Kentucky Rifles and Pistols.

RIVERSIDE ARMS CO. Made by Stevens Arms & Tool Co.
SHOTGUN, DOUBLE BARREL, SIDE-BY-SIDE
Model 215, 12 and 16 Gauges, Outside Hammers, Steel Barrel,
Modern.. 150 175 175

ROB ROY Made by Hood Firearms Norwich, Conn., c. 1880.
HANDGUN, REVOLVER
.22 Short R.F., 7 Shot, Spur Trigger, Solid Frame, Single Action,
Antique.. 150 175 175

ROBBINS & LAWRENCE Robbins, Kendall & Lawrence, Windsor, Vt. 1844–1857. Became Robbins & Lawrence about 1846. Also see Sharps, U.S. Military.
HANDGUN, PERCUSSION
Pepperbox, Various Calibers, Ring Trigger, Antique.............................. 850 1,000 700

ROBIN HOOD Made by Hood Firearms Norwich, Conn., c. 1875.
HANDGUN, REVOLVER
.22 Short R.F., 7 Shot, Spur Trigger, Solid Frame, Single Action,
Antique.. 125 150 150
.32 Short R.F., 5 Shot, Spur Trigger, Solid Frame, Single Action,
Antique.. 150 175 175

ROESSER, PETER Lancaster, Pa. 1741–1782. See Kentucky Rifles and Pistols.

Prior
V.G.   Exc   Edition

ROGERS & SPENCER Willowvale, N.Y., c. 1862.
HANDGUN, PERCUSSION
.44 Army, Single Action, Antique.. $1,000 $1,250 $1,250

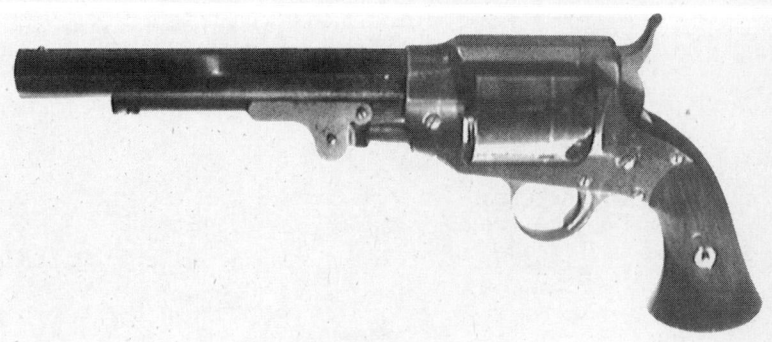

Rogers & Spencer

ROLAND Francisco Arizmendi, Eibar, Spain, c. 1922.
HANDGUN, SEMI-AUTOMATIC
6.35mm, Clip Fed, Blue, Curio..   100   125   125
7.65mm, Clip Fed, Blue, Curio..   125   150   150

ROME REVOLVER AND NOVELTY WORKS Rome, N.Y., c. 1880.
HANDGUN, REVOLVER
.32 Short R.F., 5 Shot, Spur Trigger, Solid Frame, Single Action,
Antique..   125   150   150

	V.G.	Exc	Prior Edition

ROMER Romerwerke AG, Suhl, Germany, 1924–1926.

HANDGUN, SEMI-AUTOMATIC

.22 L.R.R.F., Clip Fed, 2½" and 6½" Barrels, Blue, Curio...................... $600 $700 $900

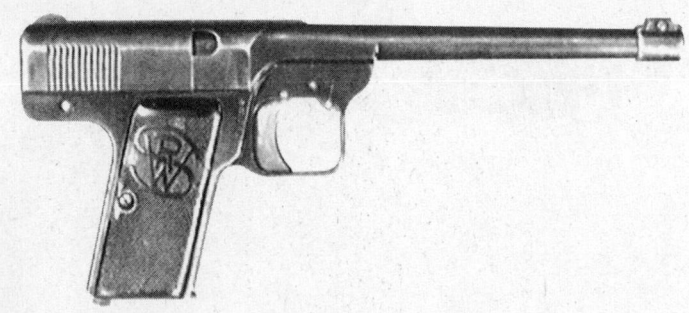

Romer

.22 L.R.R.F., Clip Fed, One Barrel, Blue, Curio.. 550 650 750

ROOP, JOHN Allentown, Pa., c. 1775. See Kentucky Rifles.

ROSS RIFLE CO. Quebec, Canada. Also see Canadian Military.
1896–1915.

RIFLE, BOLT ACTION

Canadian Issue, .303 British, Military, Modern.. 225 350 275
Model 1903 MK I, .303 British, Sporting Rifle, Open Rear Sight,
Modern... 250 275 300
Model 1905 MK II, Various Calibers, Open Rear Sight,
Modern... 250 300 300
Model 1910 MK III, Various Calibers, Open Rear Sight,
Checkered Stock, Modern... 275 325 325

ROSSI Amadeo Rossi S.A., Sao Leopoldo, Brazil. Also see Garrucha.

HANDGUN, REVOLVER

Model 31, .38 Special, Solid Frame, Swing–Out Cylinder, 5 Shot,
4" Barrel, Modern.. 75 100 125
Model 51, .22 L.R.R.F., Solid Frame, Swing–Out Cylinder,
Adjustable Sights, 5 Shot, 6" Barrel, Modern...................................... 75 100 100
Model 68, .38 Special, Solid Frame, Swing–Out Cylinder,
Adjustable Sights, 5 Shot, 3" Barrel, Modern...................................... 100 125 125

	V.G.	Exc	Prior Edition
Model 68/2, .38 Special, Solid Frame, Swing–Out Cylinder, Adjustable Sights, 5 Shot, 2" Barrel, Modern..	$125	$150	$175

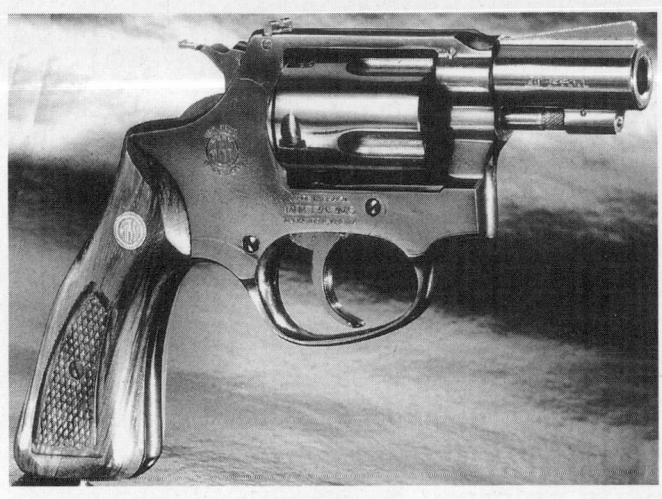

Rossi 68/2

Model 69, .32 S & W Long, Solid Frame, Swing–Out Cylinder, Adjustable Sights, 5 Shot, 3" Barrel, Modern...	75	100	100
Model 70, .22 Short R.F., Solid Frame, Swing–Out Cylinder, Adjustable Sights, 5 Shot, 3" Barrel, Modern...	75	100	100
Model 88, .38 Special, Solid Frame, Swing–Out Cylinder, Adjustable Sights, Stainless Steel, 5 Shot, 3" Barrel, Modern...................	125	150	175
Model 89, The Stainless Lady, .38 Special, Stainless, 3" Barrel, Modern..	150	175	200

	V.G.	Exc	Prior Edition
Model 94, .38 Special, Medium Frame, Shrouded Ejector Rod, Modern..	$100	$125	$100

Rossi 94

HANDGUN, SINGLESHOT

.22 Short R.F., Derringer, Modern...	25	50	50

RIFLE, SLIDE ACTION

Gallery, .22 L.R.R.F., Tube Feed, Takedown, Hammer, Modern............	100	125	175

Rossi Gallery Rifle

Gallery, .22 L.R.R.F., Tube Feed, Takedown, Hammer, Octagon Barrel, Modern..	125	150	175

	V.G.	Exc	Prior Edition
Saddle Ring, .357 Mag., Tube Feed, Hammer, Carbine, Modern............	$125	$175	$225

Rossi Saddle Ring Carbine Rifle

Saddle Ring, .357 Mag., Tube Feed, Hammer, Carbine, Nickel, Modern.................	150	200	250

SHOTGUN, DOUBLE BARREL, SIDE-BY-SIDE

12 Ga. Mag. 3", Checkered Stock, Hammerless, Double Trigger, Modern........	175	225	225
12 Ga. Mag. 3", Hammerless, Double Trigger, Modern.......................	200	200	200
Overland, 12 and 20 Gauges, Checkered Stock, Outside Hammers, Double Trigger, Modern..................	200	225	225
Overland, 12 and 20 Gauges, Outside Hammers, Double Trigger, Modern.................	200	225	225

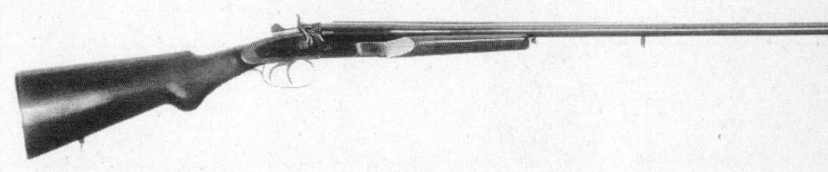

Rossi Overland Shotgun

Overland II, Various Gauges, Checkered Stock, Outside Hammers, Double Trigger, Modern................	225	250	250
Squire Model 14, Various Gauges, Hammerless, Double Trigger, Modern................	250	300	300

ROTTWEIL Germany, Imported by Eastern Sports Milford, N.H.

RIFLE, DOUBLE BARREL, OVER-UNDER

Standard Grade, Various Calibers, Engraved, Fancy Checkering, Open Rear Sight, Modern.................	2,000	2,150	2,150

SHOTGUN, DOUBLE BARREL, OVER-UNDER

American, 12 Ga., Trap Grade, Single Selective Trigger, Automatic Ejector, Vent Rib, Engraved, Modern....................	1,500	1,950	1,950
Montreal, 12 Ga., Trap Grade, Vent Rib, Single Selective Trigger, Checkered Stock, Modern.....:..............	1,350	1,600	1,600
Olympia, 12 Ga., Skeet Grade, Single Selective Trigger, Automatic Ejector, Vent Rib, Engraved, Modern....................	1,500	1,850	1,850
Olympia, 12 Ga., Trap Grade, Single Selective Trigger, Automatic Ejector, Vent Rib, Engraved, Modern....................	1,500	1,850	1,850

	V.G.	Exc	Prior Edition

Olympia 72, 12 Ga., Skeet Grade, Trap Grade, Single Selective
Trigger, Checkered Stock, Modern... $1,450 $1,650 $1,650
Supreme, 12 Ga., Field Grade, Single Selective Trigger,
Automatic Ejector, Vent Rib, Engraved, Modern..................................... 1,500   1,950   1,950
Supreme, 12 Ga., Vent Rib, Single Selective Trigger, Checkered
Stock, Modern... 1,200   1,550   1,550

ROVIRO, ANTONIO   Iqualada, Spain, c. 1790.

HANDGUN, MIQUELET-LOCK

Pair, Belt Pistol, Belt Hook, Engraved, Light Ornamentation,
Antique.. 4,500   5,500   5,500

ROYAL   M. Zulaika y Cia., Eibar, Spain.

HANDGUN, SEMI-AUTOMATIC

12 Shot, 7.65mm, Clip Fed, Long Grip, Modern....................................... 225   250   250

Royal 12 Shot

7.65mm, Clip Fed, Long Grip, Modern.. 175   200   200
Mauser M1896 Type, 7.63mm, Blue, Modern.. 325   375   375
Novelty, 6.35mm, Clip Fed, Blue, Curio.. 175   200   200

	V.G.	Exc	Prior Edition
Novelty, 7.65mm, Clip Fed, Blue, Curio..	$200	$225	$225

Royal Novelty .32

ROYAL Possibly Hopkins & Allen, c. 1880.

HANDGUN, REVOLVER

.22 Short R.F., 7 Shot, Spur Trigger, Solid Frame, Single Action, Antique...	150	175	175
.32 Short R.F., 5 Shot, Spur Trigger, Solid Frame, Single Action, Antique...	150	175	175

RUBY Gabilondo y Cia., Vitoria, Spain.

HANDGUN, REVOLVER

Ruby Extra, For Chrome Plating Add $35.00–$75.00
Ruby Extra, For Engraving Add $60.00–$100.00

Ruby Extra Model 12, .38 Spec., Double Action, Blue, Swing–Out Cylinder, Curio...	50	75	75
Ruby Extra Model 14, .22 L.R.R.F., Double Action, Blue, Swing–Out Cylinder, Curio...	50	75	75

	V.G.	Exc	Prior Edition
Ruby Extra Model 14, .32 S & W Long, Double Action, Blue, Swing–Out Cylinder, Curio..	$50	$75	$75

Ruby .32

HANDGUN, SEMI-AUTOMATIC

7.35mm, Clip Fed, Blue, Curio...	150	175	175

Ruby .45

RUMMEL Made by Crescent for A.J. Rummel Arms Co., Toledo, Ohio.

SHOTGUN, DOUBLE BARREL, SIDE-BY-SIDE

Various Gauges, Hammerless, Damascus Barrel, Modern....................	150	175	175
Various Gauges, Hammerless, Steel Barrel, Modern.............................	150	200	200
Various Gauges, Outside Hammers, Damascus Barrel, Modern.............	150	175	175
Various Gauges, Outside Hammers,Steel Barrel, Modern......................	150	175	175

	V.G.	Exc	Prior Edition

SHOTGUN, SINGLESHOT
Various Gauges, Hammer, Steel Barrel, Modern..................................... $50 · $75 · $75

RUPERTUS, JACOB Philadelphia, Pa., 1858–1899.

HANDGUN, DOUBLE BARREL, SIDE-BY-SIDE
.22 Short R.F., Derringer, Side–Swing Barrel, Iron Frame, Spur
Trigger, Antique.. 650 · 800 · 800

HANDGUN, REVOLVER
.22 Short R.F., 5 Shot, Spur Trigger, Solid Frame, Single Action,
Antique.. 275 · 300 · 225
.22 Short R.F., Pepperbox, 8 Shot, Iron Frame, Spur Trigger,
Antique.. 500 · 575 · 575
.25 Short R.F., 6 Shot, Spur Trigger, Solid Frame, Single Action,
Antique.. 3,000 · 3,500 · 3,250
.36 Patent Navy, Percussion, 6 Shot, Antique.. 5,500 · 7,000 · 7,000

Jacob Rupertus Patent Navy Six Shot, .36 Caliber

.44 Patent Army, 6 Shot, Solid Frame, Single Action,
Antique.. 4,000 · 4,500 · 4,250

HANDGUN, SINGLESHOT
.22 Short R.F., Derringer, Side–Swing Barrel, Iron Frame, Spur
Trigger, Antique... 250 · 300 · 300
.32 Short R.F., Derringer, Side–Swing Barrel, Iron Frame, Spur
Trigger, Antique... 200 · 250 · 250
.38 Short R.F., Derringer, Side–Swing Barrel, Iron Frame, Spur
Trigger, Antique... 225 · 275 · 275
.41 Short R.F., 5 Shot, Spur Trigger, Solid Frame, Single Action,
Antique.. 250 · 300 · 300

RUPP, HERMAN Pa. 1784. See Kentucky Rifles.

RUPP, JOHN Allentown, Pa. See U.S. Military, Kentucky Rifles and Pistols.

	V.G.	Exc	Prior Edition

RUPPERT, WILLIAM Lancaster. Pa., c. 1776. See U.S. Military, Kentucky Rifles and Pistols.

RUSH, JOHN Philadelphia, Pa. 1740–1750. See Kentucky Rifles and Pistols.

RUSSIAN MILITARY Czarist and Communist plants include: Tula, Izshevsky, and many others. Foreign manufacturers for Czarist Russia include: SIG Neuhasen, Switzerland; St. Etienne, France, and Remington Arms U.S.A. Foreign manufacturers for Moisin–Nagant only. Tokarev and SKS Communist Russia produced.

HANDGUN, FREE PISTOL

	V.G.	Exc	Prior Edition
MC, .22 L.R.R.F., Clip Fed, Modern	$200	$225	$225

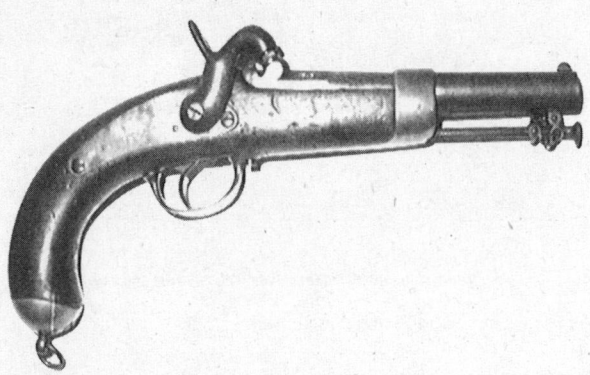

Russian Military Handgun Percussion

	V.G.	Exc	Prior Edition
MCU, .22 Short, Clip Fed, Modern	225	275	275
Vostok M–TOZ–35, .22 L.R.R.F., Modern	500	575	575
Vostok M–TOZ–35, .22 L.R.R.F., Cased with Accessories, Modern	775	875	875

	V.G.	Exc	Prior Edition

HANDGUN, REVOLVER

M1890, 7.62mm Nagant, Gas–Seal Cylinder, Communist, Curio............ $175 $200 $200

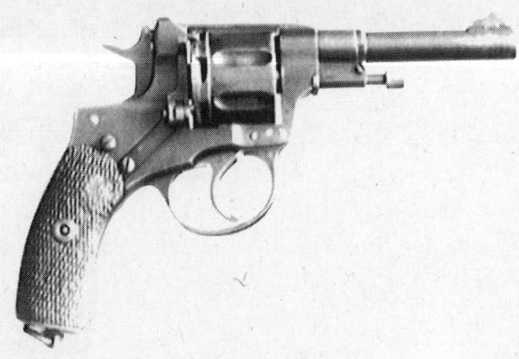

Russian Military M1890 Communist

M1890, 7.62mm Nagant, Gas–Seal Cylinder, Imperial, Curio................. 200 250 250
M1890, 7.62mm Nagant, Gas–Seal Cylinder, Police, Curio..................... 175 225 225

HANDGUN, SEMI-AUTOMATIC

Makarov, 9mm Makarov, Clip Fed, Double Action, Modern................. 750 900 900

Russian Military Makarov

	V.G.	Exc	Prior Edition
Tokarev TT–30, 7.62mm Tokarev, Clip Fed, Modern...........................	$250	$300	$300

Russian Military Tokarev

Tokarev TT–33 Early, 7.62mm Tokarev, Clip Fed, Modern.................	200	250	250

RIFLE, BOLT ACTION

1891 Moisin–Nagant, 7.62 Cal., 31–Inch Barrel, Bolt Action. (The rear sight of these early rifles are graduated not in meters but in arshins. An arshin is eqivalent to .78 yards. After the revolution, Russia adopted the metric system and the sights for the Model 1891/30 and later rifles and carbines are graduated in meters)	75	100	100
1891 Remington, Same as Russian Nagent, Except made in U.S.A., By Remington For Export To Czarist Russia. (Few were ever delivered. Much higher quality than Russian produced models)	125	150	150
1891/30 Sniper Rifle, Especially Selected For Accuracy, Bolt Handle Turned Down and Fitted with Either 4 X P.E. or 3.5 X P.U. Telescopic Sight, (Still in use in Russia.) Very Rare	575	650	650
1891/38 Carbine, 7.62.54 Cal., 20–Inch Barrel, Hooded Front Sight, Rear Sight Graduated From 100–1000 Meters, No Bayonet Mounting	100	125	125
1938 Russian Tokarev, Semi–Automatic Gas Operated Rifle, Two Piece Stock, 10 Shot Magazine, Fitted with Muzzlebreak, Cleaning Rod On Right Side Of Stock, First of Tokarev Series	275	350	350
1940 Tokarev Model , 24–Inch Barrel, Semi–Automatic Gas Operated Rifle, (Similar to Model 1938 but much more rugged, was very successful action similar to that of Belgian FN Rifle.)	250	300	300
KK M, CM 2 , .22 L.R.R.F., Match Rifle, Target Sights, Modern...........	300	375	375
M1919, 7.62 X 54R Russian, Military, Carbine, Modern.........................	200	250	250
Russian SKS, 7.62.39M43 Cal., 20–Inch Barrel, (A Russian attempt to develop a gas operated carbine) 10 Shot Magazine, Folding Bayonet, Very Well Made	200	250	250

	V.G.	Exc	Prior Edition

RWS Rheinische–Westfalische Sperengstoff, since 1931. Now Dynamit Nobele AG, Troisdorf–Oberlar, West Germany.

RIFLE, BOLT ACTION

Repeater, Various Calibers, Checkered Stock, Set Triggers, Open
Sights, Modern.. $400 $475 $475

RYAN, THOMAS Norwich, Conn., c. 1870.

HANDGUN, REVOLVER

.22 Short R.F., 7 Shot, Spur Trigger, Solid Frame, Single Action,
Antique... 150   175   175
.32 Short R.F., 5 Shot, Spur Trigger, Solid Frame, Single Action,
Antique... 150   175   175

S

S–M CORP. Sydney Manson, Alexandria, Va., c. 1953.

HANDGUN, SEMI-AUTOMATIC

	V.G.	Exc.	Prior Edition
Sporter, .22 L.R.R.F., Blowback, Modern..	$125	$150	$150

SABLE Belgium, Maker unknown.

HANDGUN, REVOLVER

Baby Hammerless, .22 Short R.F., Folding Trigger, Modern..................	100	125	125

SAKO O. Y. Sako AB, Riihmaki, Finland.

RIFLE, BOLT ACTION

Deluxe (Garcia), Various Calibers, Sporting Rifle, Monte Carlo Stock, Fancy Checkering, Long Action, Modern......................................	650	725	725
Deluxe (Garcia), Various Calibers, Sporting Rifle, Monte Carlo Stock, Fancy Checkering, Medium Action, Modern.................................	650	725	725
Deluxe (Garcia), Various Calibers, Sporting Rifle, Monte Carlo Stock, Fancy Checkering, Short Action, Modern....................................	650	725	725
Finnbear, Various Calibers, Sporting Rifle, Monte Carlo Stock, Checkered Stock, Long Action, Modern......................................	625	700	700
Finnbear Carbine, Various Calibers, Sporting Rifle, Monte Carlo Stock, Checkered Stock, Long Action, Full–Stocked, Modern.................	675	750	750
Forester, Various Calibers, Sporting Rifle, Monte Carlo Stock, Checkered Stock, Medium Action, Modern..............................	600	675	675
Forester, Various Calibers, Sporting Rifle, Monte Carlo Stock, Checkered Stock, Medium Action, Heavy barrel, Modern.......................	600	675	675
Forester Carbine, Various Calibers, Sporting Rifle, Monte Carlo Stock, Checkered Stock, Medium Action, Full–Stocked, Modern...........	650	725	725
Hi–Power Mauser (FN), Various Calibers, Sporting Rifle, Monte Carlo Stock, Checkered Stock, Modern.....................................	475	550	550
Magnum Mauser (FN), Various Calibers, Sporting Rifle, Monte Carlo Stock, Checkered Stock, Modern...........................	575	650	650
Model 74 (Garcia), Various Calibers, Sporting Rifle, Monte Carlo Stock, Checkered Stock, Long Action, Modern.......................	400	475	475
Model 74 (Garcia), Various Calibers, Sporting Rifle, Monte Carlo Stock, Checkered Stock, Medium Action, Modern....................	400	475	475
Model 74 (Garcia), Various Calibers, Sporting Rifle, Monte Carlo Stock, Checkered Stock, Short Action, Modern......................	400	475	475
Model 74 (Garcia), Various Calibers, Sporting Rifle, Monte Carlo Stock, Checkered Stock, Heavy Barrel, Medium Action, Modern...........	425	500	500

	V.G.	Exc	Prior Edition
Model 74 (Garcia), Various Calibers, Sporting Rifle, Monte Carlo Stock, Checkered Stock, Heavy Barrel, Short Action, Modern.................	$425	$500	$500
Model 78 (Stoeger), .22 Hornet, Sporting Rifle, Monte Carlo Stock, Checkered Stock, Modern......................	300	375	375
Model 78 (Stoeger), .22 L.R.R.F., Sporting Rifle, Monte Carlo Stock, Checkered Stock, Modern......................	250	325	325
Model 78 (Stoeger), .22 L.R.R.F., Sporting Rifle, Monte Carlo Stock, Checkered Stock, Heavy Barrel, Modern........................	400	475	475
Model 78 (Stoeger), .22 W.M.R., Sporting Rifle, Monte Carlo Stock, Checkered Stock, Modern......................	375	450	450
Vixen, Various Calibers, Sporting Rifle, Monte Carlo Stock, Checkered Stock, Short Action, Modern......................	650	750	750
Vixen, Various Calibers, Sporting Rifle, Monte Carlo Stock, Checkered Stock, Short Action, Heavy Barrel, Modern..........................	700	800	800
Vixen Carbine, Various Calibers, Sporting Rifle, Monte Carlo Stock, Checkered Stock, Short Action, Full–Stocked, Modern.................	750	850	850

RIFLE, LEVER ACTION

	V.G.	Exc	Prior Edition
Finnwolf, Various Calibers, Sporting Rifle, Monte Carlo Stock, Checkered Stock, Modern........	525	600	600

SAMPLES, BETHUEL Urbana, Ohio. See Kentucky Rifles and Pistols.

SANDERSON Portage, Wisc.

SHOTGUN, SINGLESHOT

	V.G.	Exc	Prior Edition
M200–S 1, Various Gauges, Checkered Stock, Automatic Ejectors, Engraved, Modern........................	350	425	425
Neumann, 10 Gauge Mag., Checkered Stock, Automatic Ejectors, Engraved, Modern........................	350	425	425
Neumann, Various Gauges, Checkered Stock, Automatic Ejectors, Engraved, Modern........................	225	275	275

SANTA BARBARA Santa Barbara of America, Inc. of Irving, Tx. on Mauser actions made in La Caruna, Spain.

RIFLE, BOLT ACTION

	V.G.	Exc	Prior Edition
Sporter, Various Calibers, Custom Made, High Quality, Modern............	150	200	200
Sporter, Various Calibers, Custom Made, Medium Quality, Modern........................	125	150	150

SARASQUETA, FELIX Eibar, Spain, imported by Sarasquetta of N.A., Coral Gables, Fla.

SHOTGUN, DOUBLE BARREL, OVER-UNDER 'MERKE'

	V.G.	Exc	Prior Edition
Model 500, 12 Gauge, Checkered Stock, Boxlock, Light Engraving, Double Triggers, Modern........................	175	275	275
Model 510, 20 Gauge, Checkered Stock, Boxlock with Sideplates, Light Engraving, Double Triggers, Modern.............................	150	225	225

	V.G.	Exc	Prior Edition

SARASQUETE, VICTOR Victor Sarasqueta, Eibar, Spain from 1934.

RIFLE, DOUBLE BARREL, SIDE-BY-SIDE

	V.G.	Exc	Prior Edition
Various Calibers, Sidelock, Automatic Ejector, Fancy Engraving, Fancy Checkering, Modern	$1,750	$2,500	$2,500

SHOTGUN, DOUBLE BARREL, SIDE-BY-SIDE

	V.G.	Exc	Prior Edition
#10E, Various Gauges, Sidelock, Fancy Checkering, Fancy Engraving, Modern	1,500	1,650	1,650
#11E, Various Gauges, Sidelock, Fancy Checkering, Fancy Engraving, Modern	1,600	1,750	1,750
#12E, Various Gauges, Sidelock, Fancy Checkering, Fancy Engraving, Modern	1,750	2,000	2,000
#3, Various Gauges, Double Trigger, Checkered Stock, Light Engraving, Modern	500	600	600
#4, Various Gauges, Sidelock, Checkered Stock, Light Engraving, Modern	475	525	525
#4E, Various Gauges, Sidelock, Checkered Stock, Light Engraving, Modern	500	575	575
#6E, Various Gauges, Sidelock, Fancy Checkering, Engraved, Modern	650	750	750
#7E, Various Gauges, Sidelock, Fancy Checkering, Engraved, Modern	700	800	800
203, Various Gauges, Sidelock, Fancy Checkering, Fancy Engraving, Modern	525	600	600
203E, Various Gauges, Sidelock, Fancy Checkering, Fancy Engraving, Modern	600	700	700

SATA Sabolti & Tantagiro Fabbrica o' Armi, Gardone Val Trompia, Italy.

HANDGUN, SEMI-AUTOMATIC

	V.G.	Exc	Prior Edition
.22 Short, Clip Fed, Blue, Modern	125	150	150
6.35mm, Clip Fed, Blue, Modern	150	175	175

SAUER, J. P. & SOHN 1855 to date, first in Suftt, now in Eckernforde, West Germany. Also see Hawes.

COMBINATION WEAPON, DRILLING

	V.G.	Exc	Prior Edition
Model 3000E, Various Calibers, Double Trigger, Engraved, Checkered Stock, Modern	2,600	2,800	2,800
Model 3000E Deluxe, Various Calibers, Double Trigger, Fancy Engraving, Fancy Checkering, Modern	3,000	3,250	3,250

	V.G.	Exc	Prior Edition

HANDGUN, MANUAL REPEATER

Bar Pistole, 7mm, Double Barrel, 4 Shot, Folding Trigger, Curio........... $325 $375 $375

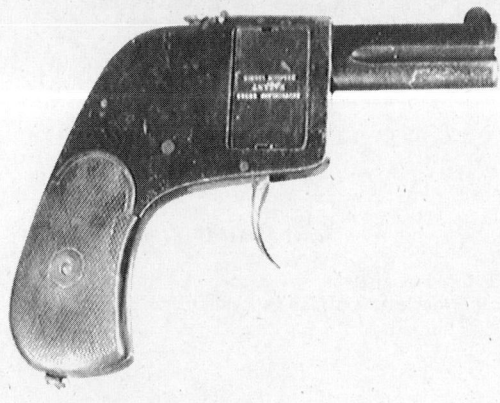

Sauer Bar Pistole

HANDGUN, SEMI-AUTOMATIC

	V.G.	Exc	Prior Edition
Behorden, .32 ACP, Clip Fed, Modern...	200	250	250
Behorden, .32 ACP, Clip Fed, Lightweight, Modern...............................	350	400	400
Behorden 4mm, .32 ACP, Clip Fed, Extra Barrel, Modern......................	700	800	800
Behorden Dutch Navy, .32 ACP, Clip Fed, Military, Modern.................	350	400	400
Model 1913, .25 ACP, Clip Fed, Modern...	225	275	275

Sauer Model 1913, .25

	V.G.	Exc	Prior Edition
Model 1913, .32 ACP, Clip Fed, Modern...	$225	$275	$275

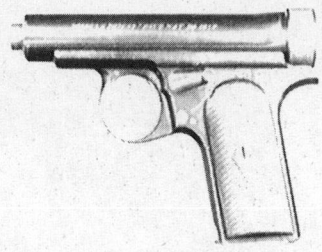

Sauer Model 1913, .32

	V.G.	Exc	Prior Edition
Model 28, .25 ACP, Clip Fed, Modern...	250	300	300
Model 38H, .22 L.R., Double Action, Clip Fed, Hammer, Curio...	1,500	2,000	1,750

Sauer Model 38H

	V.G.	Exc	Prior Edition
Model 38H, .380 ACP, Double Action, Clip Fed, Hammer, Modern..	750	1,000	1,000
Model 38H, .380 ACP, Double Action, Clip Fed, Hammer, Commercial, Modern...	225	275	275
Model 38H, .380 ACP, Double Action, Clip Fed, Hammer, Nazi–Proofed, Military, Modern...	225	325	325
Model 38H, .380 ACP, Double Action, Clip Fed, Hammer, Nazi–Proofed, No Safety, Military, Modern...	275	325	325
Model 38H, .380 ACP, Double Action, Clip Fed, Hammer, Lightweight, Modern..	475	550	550

	V.G.	Exc	Prior Edition
Roth–Sauer, 8mm, Clip Fed, Curio..	$900	$1,200	$1,200

Sauer Roth-Sauer

W.T.M. 1922, .25 ACP, Clip Fed, Modern...	300	350	300
W.T.M. 1928, .25 ACP, Clip Fed, Modern...	275	325	325
W.T.M. 1928/2, .25 ACP, Clip Fed, Modern..	225	275	275

RIFLE, BOLT ACTION

Mauser Custom, Various Calibers, Set Trigger, Checkered Stock, Octagon Barrel, Modern..	600	650	550

COMBINATION WEAPON, OVER-UNDER

BBF, Various Calibers, Double Trigger, Set Trigger, Engraved, Checkered Stock, Modern...	1,700	1,900	1,900
BBF Deluxe, Various Calibers, Double Trigger, Set Trigger, Fancy Engraving, Fancy Checkering, Modern......................................	1,900	2,100	2,100

SHOTGUN, DOUBLE BARREL, OVER-UNDER

Model 66 GR I, 12 Ga., Single Selective Trigger, Selective Ejector, Hammerless, Sidelock, Engraved, Modern...	1,650	1,800	1,800
Model 66 GR I, 12 Ga., Skeet Grade, Selective Ejector, Hammerless, Sidelock, Engraved, Modern...	1,450	1,600	1,600
Model 66 GR II, 12 Ga., Single Selective Trigger, Selective Ejector, Hammerless, Sidelock, Fancy Engraving, Modern......................	2,500	2,800	2,800
Model 66 GR II, 12 Ga., Skeet Grade, Selective Ejector, Hammerless, Sidelock, Fancy Engraving, Modern..................................	2,300	2,550	2,550
Model 66 GR II, 12 Ga., Trap Grade, Selective Ejector, Hammerless, Sidelock, Fancy Engraving, Modern..................................	2,350	2,600	2,600
Model 66 GR III, 12 Ga., Single Selective Trigger, Selective Ejector, Hammerless, Sidelock, Fancy Engraving, Modern......................	3,000	3,500	3,500
Model 66 GR III, 12 Ga., Skeet Grade, Selective Ejector, Hammerless, Sidelock, Fancy Engraving, Modern..................................	2,500	3,000	3,000
Model 66 GR III, 12 Ga., Trap Grade, Selective Ejector, Hammerless, Sidelock, Fancy Engraving, Modern..................................	2,500	3,000	3,000

SHOTGUN, DOUBLE BARREL, SIDE-BY-SIDE

.410 Gauge, Double Trigger, Light Engraving, Modern...........................	625	675	675

	V.G.	Exc	Prior Edition
Artemis I, 12 Ga., Single Selective Trigger, Engraved, Checkered Stock, Modern............	$3,500	$4,500	$4,500
Artemis II, 12 Ga., Single Selective Trigger, Fancy Engraving, Fancy Checkering, Modern............	4,500	5,500	5,500
Model Kim, Various Gauges, Double Triggers, Checkered Stock, Light Engraving, Modern............	250	300	300
Model VIII, Various Gauges, Double Triggers, Checkered Stock, Light Engraving, Modern............	250	300	300
Model VIII DES, Various Gauges, Single Selective Trigger, Selective Ejectors, Checkered Stock, Light Engraving, Modern............	250	300	300
Model VIII DES–01, Various Gauges, Single Selective Trigger, Selective Ejectors, Checkered Stock, Engraved, Modern............	325	375	375
Model VIII DES–05, Various Gauges, Single Selective Trigger, Selective Ejectors, Checkered Stock, Fancy Engraving, Sideplates, Modern............	700	800	800
Model VIII DES–07, Various Gauges, Single Selective Trigger, Selective Ejectors, Checkered Stock, Fancy Engraving, Modern............	425	500	500
Royal, 12 and 20 Gauges, Single Selective Trigger, Engraved, Checkered Stock, Modern............	1,000	1,250	1,600

SAVAGE ARMS CO. Utica, N.Y. 1893–1899, renamed Savage Arms Co. 1899. J. Stevens Arms Co. Springfield Arms Co. and A. H. Fox are all part of Savage. Also see U.S. Military. Also see Commemorative section.

HANDGUN, SEMI-AUTOMATIC

	V.G.	Exc	Prior Edition
Military Model, .45 ACP. Clip Fed, Original, Curio............	5,000	6,000	6,000
Military Model, .45 ACP. Clip Fed, Surplus, Reblue, Curio............	3,500	4,000	4,000
Model 1907 (1908), .32 ACP, Clip Fed, Burr Cocking Piece, (under #10,899), Curio............	300	350	350
Model 1907 (1909), .32 ACP, Clip Fed, Burr Cocking Piece, (#'s–10,900–70,499), Curio............	275	325	325
Model 1907 (1912), .32 ACP, Clip Fed, Burr Cocking Piece, (Higher # than 70500), Curio............	250	300	300
Model 1907 (1913), .380 ACP, Clip Fed, Burr Cocking Piece, Curio............	325	375	375
Model 1907 (1914), .32 ACP, Spur Cocking Piece, Curio............	250	300	300
Model 1907 (1914), .380 ACP, Spur Cocking Piece, Curio............	300	350	325
Model 1907 (1918), .308 ACP, Clip Fed, Burr Cocking Piece, (After #10000B), Curio............	325	375	375
Model 1907 (1918), .32 ACP, Clip Fed, no Cartridge Indicator, Burr Cocking Piece, Curio............	225	275	275
Model 1907 (1918), .380 ACP, Clip Fed, Spur Cocking Piece, (After # 195000), Curio............	250	300	300
Model 1907 Military, .32 ACP, Clip Fed, Burr Cocking Piece, Curio............	275	325	275
Model 1907 Military, .32 ACP, Clip Fed, Burr Cocking Piece, (Portuguese Contract), Curio............	375	425	425
Model 1907, Factory Nickel, Add $50.00–$95.00			
Model 1907, Grade A Engraving (Light), Add $100.00–$150.00			
Model 1907, Grade C Engraving (Light), Add $325.00–$450.00			
Model 1915, .32 ACP, Clip Fed, Hammerless, Grip Safety, Curio............	250	300	300
Model 1915, .380 ACP, Clip Fed, Hammerless, Grip Safety, Curio............	500	575	350

	V.G.	Exc	Prior Edition
Model 1917, .32 ACP, Clip Fed, Spur Cocking Piece, Flared Grip, Curio	$400	$450	$250
Model 1917, .380 ACP, Clip Fed, Spur Cocking Piece, Flared Grip, Curio	325	375	275

HANDGUN, SINGLESHOT

	V.G.	Exc	Prior Edition
Model 101, .22 L.R.R.F., Western Style, Single Action, Swing–Out Cylinder, Modern	125	150	150

RIFLE, BOLT ACTION

	V.G.	Exc	Prior Edition
Model 10, .22 L.R.R.F., Target Sights, (Anschutz), Modern	150	175	225
Model 110, Magnum Calibers, Add $35.00			
Model 110, Various Calibers, Open Rear Sight, Checkered Stock, Modern	175	200	200
Model 110–B, Various Calibers, Open Rear Sight, Modern	225	275	275
Model 110–BL, Various Calibers, Open Rear Sight, Left–Hand, Modern	250	300	300

Savage 110-BL

	V.G.	Exc	Prior Edition
Model 110–C, Various Calibers, Clip Fed, Open Rear Sight, Modern	200	250	250
Model 110–CL, Various Calibers, Clip Fed, Open Rear Sight, Left–Hand, Modern	225	275	275
Model 110–E, Various Calibers, Open Rear Sight, Modern	175	200	200
Model 110–EL, Various Calibers, Open Rear Sight, Left–Hand, Modern	175	225	225
Model 110–ES, Various Calibers, Internal Box Mag. Scope, Modern	250	300	300
Model 110–M, Various Calibers, Open Rear Sight, Monte Carlo Stock, Checkered Stock, Magnum Action, Modern	175	225	225
Model 110–MC, Various Calibers, Open Rear Sight, Monte Carlo Stock, Checkered Stock, Modern	150	175	175
Model 110–MCL, Various Calibers, Open Rear Sight, Monte Carlo Stock, Checkered Stock, Left–Hand, Modern	150	200	200
Model 110–ML, Various Calibers, Open Rear Sight, Monte Carlo Stock, Checkered Stock, Magnum Action, Left–Hand, Modern	175	225	225
Model 110–P, Various Calibers, Open Rear Sight, Fancy Wood, Monte Carlo Stock, Fancy Checkering, Sling Swivels, Modern	300	350	350
Model 110–PE, Various Calibers, Engraved, Fancy Checkering, Fancy Wood, Sling Swivels, Modern	550	600	600
Model 110–PEL, Various Calibers, Engraved, Fancy Checkering, Fancy Wood, Sling Swivels, Left–Hand, Modern	550	600	600
Model 110–PL, Various Calibers, Fancy Wood, Monte Carlo Stock, Fancy Checkering, Sling Swivels, Left–Hand, Modern	350	400	400
Model 110–S Silhouette Rifle, .308 Winchester and 7mm–08 Remington, Free Floating Barrel, Monte Carlo Stock, Modern	275	325	325

	V.G.	Exc	Prior Edition
Model 110–V Varmint, Various Calibers, 26" Heavy Barrel, Modern........................	$300	$350	$350
Model 111, Various Calibers, Clip Fed, Monte Carlo Stock, Checkered Stock, Modern........................	200	250	250
Model 112–V, Various Calibers, Singleshot, no Sights, Modern............	250	300	300
Model 1407, Sights Only, Add $150.00			
Model 1407 "I.S.U.," .22 L.R.R.F., Heavy Barrel, no Sights, (Anschutz), Modern........................	425	475	475

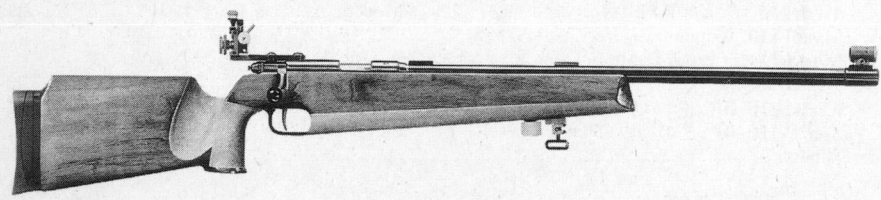

Savage Anschutz 1407

	V.G.	Exc	Prior Edition
Model 1407–L "I.S.U.," .22 L.R.R.F., Heavy Barrel, no Sights, Left–Hand, (Anschutz), Modern........................	450	500	500
Model 1408, .22 L.R.R.F., Heavy Barrel, no Sights, (Anschutz), Modern........................	350	400	400

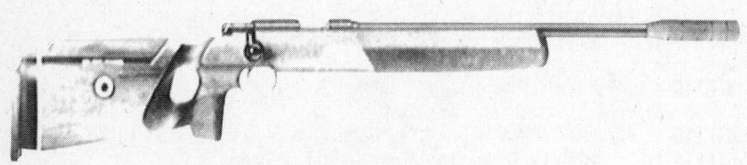

Savage Anschutz 1408

	V.G.	Exc	Prior Edition
Model 1408–ED, .22 L.R.R.F., Heavy Barrel, no Sights, (Anschutz), Modern........................	450	500	500

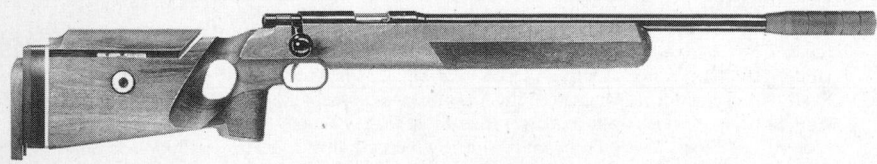

Savage Anschutz 1408-ED

	V.G.	Exc	Prior Edition
Model 1408–L, .22 L.R.R.F., Heavy Barrel, no Sights, Left–Hand, (Anschutz), Modern........................	325	375	375
Model 1411, Sights Only, Add $125.00			

	V.G.	Exc	Prior Edition

Model 1411 "Prone," .22 L.R.R.F., Heavy Barrel, no Sights, (Anschutz), Modern.. $425 $500 $500

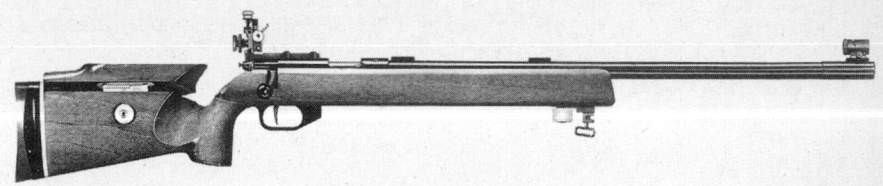

Savage Anschutz 1411

Model 1411–L "Prone," .22 L.R.R.F., Heavy Barrel, no Sights, Left–Hand, (Anschutz), Modern... 425 500 500

Model 1413, .22 L.R.R.F., Sights Only, Add $125.00

Model 1413 "Match," .22 L.R.R.F., Heavy Barrel, no Sights, (Anschutz), Modern.. 625 700 700

Model 1413–L "Match," .22 L.R.R.F., Heavy Barrel, No Sights, Left–Hand, (Anschutz), Modern... 675 750 750

Model 1418, .22 L.R.R.F., Clip Fed, Mannlicher, Fancy Checkering, (Anschulz), Modern.. 300 350 350

Model 1432, .22 Hornet, Sporting Rifle, Clip Fed, Fancy Checkering, (Anschulz), Modern.. 425 500 500

Model 1433, .22 Hornet, Mannlicher, Clip Fed, Fancy Checkering, (Anschutz), Modern.. 450 550 550

Model 1518, .22 WMR, Clip Fed, Mannlicher, Fancy Checkering, (Anschutz), Modern.. 300 375 375

Model 1533, .222 Rem., Mannlicher, Clip Fed, Fancy Checkering, (Anschutz), Modern.. 450 525 525

Model 164, .22 L.R.R.F., Sporting Rifle, Clip Fed, Checkered Stock, (Anschutz), Modern.. 225 275 275

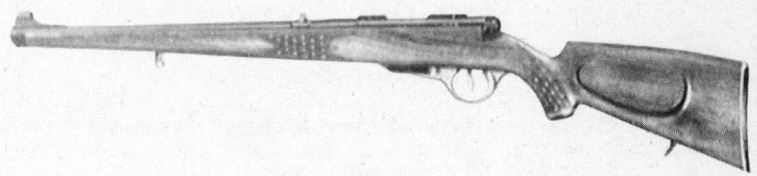

Savage Anschutz 164

	V.G.	Exc	Prior Edition
Model 164–M, .22 WMR, Sporting Rifle, Clip Fed, Checkered Stock, (Anschutz), Modern....................................	$225	$275	$275

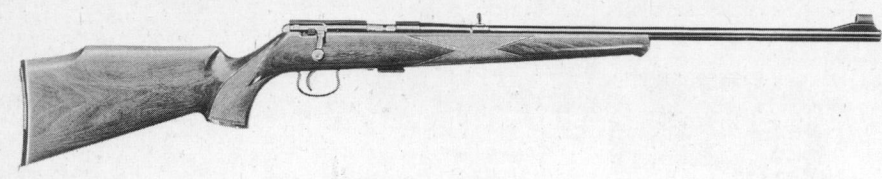

Savage Anschutz 164-M

	V.G.	Exc	Prior Edition
Model 19–H, .22 Hornet, 5 Shot Clip, Peep Sights, Modern..................	350	400	400
Model 19–L, .22 L.R.R.F., 5 Shot Clip, Lyman Sights, Modern.............	225	250	250
Model 19–M, .22 L.R.R.F., 5 Shot Clip, Heavy Barrel, Modern.............	225	275	275
Model 19–N.R.A., .22 L.R.R.F., 5 Shot Clip, Full–Stocked, Peep Sights, Modern..............	200	225	225
Model 19–Speed Lock, .22 L.R.R.F., 5 Shot Clip, Peep Sights, Modern..............	200	225	225
Model 1904, .22 L.R.R.F., Singleshot, Takedown, Modern..................	100	125	125
Model 1904–Special, .22 L.R.R.F., Singleshot, Takedown, Fancy Wood, Modern..............	125	150	150
Model 1905, .22 L.R.R.F., Target, Singleshot, Takedown, Swiss Buttplate, Modern..............	100	125	125
Model 1905–B, .22 L.R.R.F., Modern..............	125	150	150
Model 1905–Special, .22 L.R.R.F., Fancy Wood, Modern..................	150	175	175
Model 1911, .22 Short R.F., Target, Singleshot, Takedown, Modern..............	75	100	100
Model 20, Various Calibers, Open Rear Sight, Modern..................	250	300	300
Model 20, Various Calibers, Peep Sights, Modern..............	275	325	325
Model 23A, .22 L.R.R.F., 5 Shot Clip, Open Rear Sight, Modern..........	125	175	175
Model 23AA, .22 L.R.R.F., 5 Shot Clip, Open Rear Sight, Monte Carlo Stock, Modern..............	125	175	175
Model 23B, .25 WCF, 5 Shot Clip, Open Rear Sight, Monte Carlo Stock, Modern..............	150	200	200
Model 23C, .32–20 WCF, 5 Shot Clip, Open Rear Sight, Monte Carlo Stock, Modern..............	150	200	200
Model 23D, .22 Hornet, 5 Shot Clip, Open Rear Sight, Monte Carlo Stock, Modern..............	225	275	275
Model 3, .22 L.R.R.F., Singleshot, Takedown, Open Rear Sight, Modern..............	75	100	100
Model 3–S, .22 L.R.R.F., Singleshot, Takedown, Peep Sights, Modern..............	75	100	100
Model 3–ST, .22 L.R.R.F., Singleshot, Takedown, Peep Sights, Sling Swivels, Modern..............	75	100	100
Model 340, Various Calibers, Clip Fed, Modern..............	175	225	225
Model 340–C, Various Calibers, Clip Fed, Carbine, Modern..................	175	225	225
Model 340–S Deluxe, Various Calibers, Clip Fed, Peep Sights, Modern..............	225	275	275
Model 342, .22 Hornet, Clip Fed, Modern..............	200	250	250
Model 342–S, .22 Hornet, Clip Fed, Peep Sights, Modern..............	175	225	225
Model 35, .22 L.R.R.F., Clip Fed, Modern..............	75	100	100
Model 35–M, .22 W.M.R., Clip Fed, Modern..............	75	100	100
Model 36, .22 L.R.R.F., Singleshot, Modern..............	75	100	100

	V.G.	Exc	Prior Edition
Model 4, .22 L.R.R.F., 5 Shot Clip, Takedown, Modern	$100	$125	$125
Model 4–M, .22 WMR, 5 Shot Clip, Takedown, Modern	100	125	125
Model 4–S, .22 L.R.R.F., 5 Shot Clip, Takedown, Peep Sights, Modern	75	100	100
Model 40, Various Calibers, Open Rear Sights, Modern	275	325	325
Model 45 Super, Various Calibers, Peep Sights, Checkered Stock, Modern	300	375	375
Model 5, .22 L.R.R.F., Tube Feed, Takedown, Open Rear Sight, Modern	100	125	125
Model 5–S, .22 L.R.R.F., Tube Feed, Takedown, Peep Sights, Modern	100	125	125
Model 54, .22 L.R.R.F., Sporting Rifle, Clip Fed, Fancy Checkering, (Anschutz), Modern	350	400	400
Model 54–M, .22 WMR, Sporting Rifle, Clip Fed, Fancy Checkering, (Anschutz), Modern	375	425	425
Model 63, .22 L.R.R.F., Singleshot, Open Rear Sight, Modern	50	75	75
Model 63–K, .22 L.R.R.F., Singleshot, Open Rear Sight, Modern	50	75	75
Model 63–M, .22 WMR, Singleshot, Open Rear Sight, Modern	75	100	100
Model 64, .22 L.R.R.F., Sights Only, Add $30.00–$55.00			
Model 64, .22 L.R.R.F., Heavy Barrel, no Sights, (Anschutz), Modern	200	250	250
Model 64–CS, .22 L.R.R.F., Heavy Barrel, no Sights, Lightweight, (Anschutz), Modern	200	275	275
Model 64–CSL, .22 L.R.R.F., Heavy Barrel, no Sights, Left–Hand, Lightweight, (Anschutz), Modern	225	275	275
Model 64–L, .22 L.R.R.F., Heavy Barrel, no Sights, Left–Hand, (Anschutz), Modern	200	250	250
Model 64–S, .22 L.R.R.F., Heavy Barrel, no Sights, (Anschutz), Modern	225	275	275
Model 64–SL, .22 L.R.R.F., Heavy Barrel, no Sights, Left–Hand, (Anschutz), Modern	250	300	300
Model 65–M, .22 WMR, Clip Fed, Open Rear Sight, Modern	75	100	100
Model 73, .22 L.R.R.F., Singleshot, Modern	50	75	75
Model 73–Y Boys, .22 L.R.R.F., Singleshot, Modern	50	75	75

RIFLE, LEVER ACTION

	V.G.	Exc	Prior Edition
Model 1895, .303 Savage, Hammerless, Rotary Magazine, Open Rear Sight, Antique	1,050	1,350	1,350
Model 1899, .30–30 Win., Hammerless, Rotary Magazine, Full–Stocked Military, Modern	1,000	1,250	1,250
Model 1899, Various Calibers, Hammerless, Rotary Magazine, Open Rear Sight, Modern	450	600	600
Model 89, .22 L.R.R.F., Singleshot, Open Rear Sight, Modern	50	75	75
Model 99, for Extra Barrel, Add $110.00–$150.00			
Model 99 E, Various Calibers, Solid Frame, Carbine, Hammerless, Rotary Magazine, Modern	300	350	350
Model 99–1895 Anniversary, .308 Win., Octagon Barrel, Hammerless, Rotary Magazine, Modern	325	375	375
Model 99–358, .358 Win., Solid Frame, Hammerless, Rotary Magazine, Modern	350	400	400
Model 99–A, Various Calibers, Solid Frame, Hammerless, Rotary Magazine, Modern	425	500	500
Model 99–B, Various Calibers, Takedown, Hammerless, Rotary Magazine, Modern	675	750	750

	V.G.	Exc	Prior Edition
Model 99–C, Various Calibers, Clip Fed, Solid Frame, Featherweight, Hammerless, Modern..	$400	$475	$475

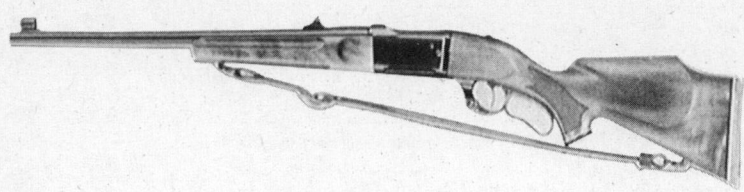

Savage Model 99-C

	V.G.	Exc	Prior Edition
Model 99–CD, Various Calibers, Hammerless, Clip Fed, Solid Frame, Monte Carlo Stock, Modern..	375	425	425
Model 99–D, Various Calibers, Solid Frame, Hammerless, Rotary Magazine, Modern...	275	325	325
Model 99–DE, Various Calibers, Solid Frame, Monte Carlo Stock, Light Engraving, Hammerless, Rotary Magazine, Modern......................	550	650	650
Model 99–DL, Various Calibers, Solid Frame, Monte Carlo Stock, Hammerless, Rotary Magazine, Modern............................	250	300	300
Model 99–EG, Various Calibers, Takedown, Checkered Stock, Hammerless, Rotary Magazine, Modern............................	375	425	425
Model 99–F, Various Calibers, Featherweight, Takedown, Hammerless, Rotary Magazine, Modern............................	275	325	325
Model 99–F, Various Calibers, Solid Frame, Featherweight, Hammerless, Rotary Magazine, Modern............................	250	300	300
Model 99–G, Various Calibers, Takedown, Checkered Stock, Hammerless, Rotary Magazine, Modern............................	475	525	525
Model 99–H, Various Calibers, Carbine, Solid Frame, Hammerless, Rotary Magazine, Modern............................	250	325	325
Model 99–K, Various Calibers, Takedown, Light Engraving, Checkered Stock, Hammerless, Rotary Magazine, Modern......................	1,500	1,700	1,700
Model 99–PE, Various Calibers, Solid Frame, Monte Carlo Stock, Engraved, Hammerless, Rotary Magazine, Modern...................................	750	900	900
Model 99–R, Various Calibers, Solid Frame, Checkered Stock, Pre–War, Hammerless, Rotary Magazine, Modern...	400	450	450
Model 99–R, Various Calibers, Solid Frame, Checkered Stock, Hammerless, Rotary Magazine, Modern............................	250	300	300
Model 99–RS, Various Calibers, Solid Frame, Peep Sights, Pre–War, Hammerless, Rotary Magazine, Modern..............................	475	525	525
Model 99–RS, Various Calibers, Solid Frame, Peep Sights, Hammerless, Rotary Magazine, Modern............................	275	325	325
Model 99–T, Various Calibers, Solid Frame, Featherweight, Hammerless, Rotary Magazine, Modern............................	275	325	325

	V.G.	Exc	Prior Edition

COMBINATION WEAPON, OVER-UNDER

Model 24, Various Calibers, Hammer, Modern... $100 $125 $125

Savage Model 24

	V.G.	Exc	Prior Edition
Model 24–C, .22/20 Ga., Hammer, Modern..	125	150	150
Model 24–D, Various Calibers, Hammer, Modern..............................	170	200	200
Model 24–V, Various Calibers, Checkered Stock, Hammer, Modern..........................	225	250	250
Model 389, Various Calibers, Checkered Stock, Hammer, Modern........................	450	550	550

RIFLE, SEMI-AUTOMATIC

	V.G.	Exc	Prior Edition
Model 6, .22 L.R.R.F., Takedown, Tube Feed, Open Rear Sight, Modern........................	75	100	100
Model 6–S, .22 L.R.R.F., Takedown, Tube Feed, Peep Sights, Modern........................	100	125	125
Model 60, .22 L.R.R.F., Monte Carlo Stock, Checkered Stock, Tube Feed, Modern........................	75	100	100
Model 7, .22 L.R.R.F., 5 Shot Clip, Takedown, Open Rear Sight, Modern........................	75	100	100
Model 7–S, .22 L.R.R.F., 5 Shot Clip, Takedown, Open Rear Sight, Modern........................	100	125	125
Model 80, .22 L.R.R.F., Tube Feed, Modern...	50	75	75
Model 88, .22 L.R.R.F., Tube Feed, Modern...	50	75	75
Model 90, .22 L.R.R.F., Carbine, Tube Feed, Modern............................	75	100	100
Model 987 Stevens Rimfire, .22 Autoloader, Tubular Mag. 15 Rounds, Walnut Stock, Modern........................	100	125	125
Model 987–T Stevens Rimfire, .22 Autoloader, Tubular Mag. 15 Rounds, 4 X Scope and Mount, Modern......................	100	125	125

RIFLE, SINGLESHOT

	V.G.	Exc	Prior Edition
Model 219, Various Calibers, Hammerless, Top Break, Open Rear Sight, Modern........................	100	125	100
Model 219L, Various Calibers, Hammerless, Top Break, Open Rear Sight, Side Lever, Modern........................	75	100	100
Model 221, .30–30 Win., Hammerless, Top Break, Extra Shotgun Barrel, Modern........................	75	100	100
Model 222, .30–30 Win., Hammerless, Top Break, Extra Shotgun Barrel, Modern........................	75	100	125
Model 223, .30–30 Win., Hammerless, Top Break, Extra Shotgun Barrel, Modern........................	75	100	125
Model 227, .30–30 Win., Hammerless, Top Break, Extra Shotgun Barrel, Modern........................	75	100	125
Model 228, .30–30 Win., Hammerless, Top Break, Extra Shotgun Barrel, Modern........................	75	100	125

	V.G.	Exc	Prior Edition
Model 229, .30–30 Win., Hammerless, Top Break, Extra Shotgun Barrel, Modern..	$75	$100	$125
Model 71 Stevens Favorite, .22 L.R.R.F., Lever Action, Falling Block, Favorite, Modern............................	125	150	150
Model 72, .22 L.R.R.F., Lever Action, Falling Block, Modern...............	75	100	100
Model 89 Stevens Rimfire, .22 L.R.R.F., Lever Action, 18" Barrel, Sporting Sights, Modern..............................	100	125	125

RIFLE, SLIDE ACTION

Model 170, Various Calibers, Open Rear Sight, Modern........................	150	175	175

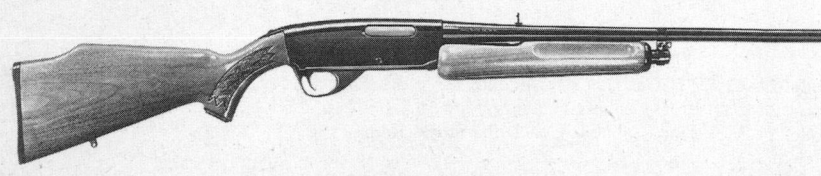

Savage 170

Model 170–C, .30–30 Win., Carbine, Open Rear Sight, Modern.............	125	150	150
Model 1903, .22 L.R.R.F., Hammerless, Clip Fed, Octagon Barrel, Modern..	175	200	200
Model 1903–EF, .22 L.R.R.F., Hammerless, Clip Fed, Octagon Barrel, Fancy Wood, Engraved, Modern.....................	450	525	525
Model 1903–Expert, .22 L.R.R.F., Hammerless, Clip Fed, Octagon Barrel, Checkered Stock, Light Engraving, Modern.........	250	275	275
Model 1909, .22 L.R.R.F., Half–Octagon Barrel, Takedown, Clip Fed, Modern..	125	150	150
Model 1914, .22 L.R.R.F., Half–Octagon Barrel, Takedown, Tube Feed, Modern..	175	225	225
Model 1914–E.F., .22 L.R.R.F., Half–Octagon Barrel, Takedown, Tube Feed, Fancy Engraving, Modern.....................	600	675	675
Model 1914–Expert, .22 L.R.R.F., Half–Octagon Barrel, Takedown, Tube Feed, Fancy Engraving, Modern.....................	425	475	475
Model 1914–Gold Medal, .22 L.R.R.F., Half–Octagon Barrel, Takedown, Tube Feed, Checkered Stock, Light Engraving, Modern........	250	300	300
Model 25, .22 L.R.R.F., Tube Feed, Octagon Barrel, Open Rear Sight, Monte Carlo Stock, Modern.....................	200	250	250
Model 29, .22 L.R.R.F., Tube Feed, Octagon Barrel, Open Rear Sight, Monte Carlo Stock, Modern.....................	175	225	225
Model 29, .22 L.R.R.F., Tube Feed, Round Barrel, Open Rear Sight, Modern..	150	175	175
Model 29–G, .22 Short R.F., Tube Feed, Modern....................................	150	175	175

SHOTGUN, BOLT ACTION

Model 58, .410 Ga., Singleshot, Modern...................................	50	75	75

SHOTGUN, DOUBLE BARREL, OVER-UNDER

Model 242, .410 Ga., Hammer, Single Trigger, Modern........................	200	275	150

	V.G.	Exc	Prior Edition
Model 330, 12 and 20 Gauges, Hammerless, Extra Shotgun Barrel, Cased, Modern...	$425	$475	$475

Savage Model 333

	V.G.	Exc	Prior Edition
Model 330, 12 and 20 Gauges, Hammerless, Single Selective Trigger, Modern..	350	400	400
Model 333, 12 and 20 Gauges, Hammerless, Vent Rib, Single Selective Trigger, Modern...	350	400	500
Model 333–T, 12 Ga., Hammerless, Vent Rib, Trap Grade, Single Selective Trigger, Modern...	400	450	475
Model 420, Various Gauges, Hammerless, Takedown, Double Trigger, Modern..	250	300	300
Model 420, Various Gauges, Hammerless, Takedown, Single Trigger, Modern..	300	350	350
Model 430, Various Gauges, Hammerless, Takedown, Checkered Stock, Recoil Pad, Double Trigger, Modern...	300	350	350
Model 430, Various Gauges, Hammerless, Takedown, Checkered Stock, Recoil Pad, Single Trigger, Modern...	375	425	425
Model 440, 12 Ga., Hammerless, Vent Rib, Single Selective Trigger, Checkered Stock, Modern...	375	425	350
Model 440–T, 12 Ga., Hammerless, Vent Rib, Checkered Stock, Modern...	400	450	400
Model 444, 12 Ga., Hammerless, Vent Rib, Single Selective Trigger, Checkered Stock, Selective Ejector, Modern...	425	475	425

RIFLE/SHOTGUN COMBINATION

	V.G.	Exc	Prior Edition
Model 2400 Field Combo, .22 L.R. Top Barrel, 4 10 Bore or 20 Gauge Bottom Barrel, Walnut Stock, Modern...	475	525	175
Model 2400–C Combo Gun Camper's Break Action, .22 L.R. Top Barrel, 20 Gauge Bottom Barrel, Modern...	500	550	200
Model 2400–CS Camper /Survival Combo Gun, Break Action, .22 L.R. Top Barrel, 20 Gauge Bottom Barrel, Pistol Grip, Satin Nickel, Modern...	550	600	225
Model 2400–D Combo Gun, .22 L.R., Top Barrel, 20 Gauge Bottom Barrel, Folding Rear Sight, Modern...	550	600	225
Model 2400–V Combo Gun, Break Action, .22 Hornet, Top Barrel, 20 Gauge Bottom Barrel, Monte Carlo Stock, Modern...	550	600	225
Model 2400–VS Camper/Survival Combo Gun, Break Action, .357 Magnum Top Barrel, 20 Gauge Bottom Barrel, Pistol Grip, Satin Nickel, Modern...	575	625	250

	V.G.	Exc	Prior Edition

SHOTGUN, DOUBLE BARREL, SIDE-BY-SIDE

Model B Fox, Various Gauges, Hammerless, Vent Rib, Double
Trigger, Modern.. $175 $225 $225

Savage Fox Model B

Model B–SE Fox, Various Gauges, Hammerless, Vent Rib,
Selective Ejector, Single Trigger, Modern............................... 225 275 275

SHOTGUN, SEMI-AUTOMATIC

Model 720, 12 Ga., Tube Feed, Checkered Stock, Plain Barrel,
Modern.. 125 175 175
Model 720–P, 12 Ga., Checkered Stock, Adjustable Choke,
Modern.. 125 175 175
Model 720–R, 12 Ga., Riot Gun, Modern............................. 300 350 150
Model 721, 12 Ga., Tube Feed, Checkered Stock, Raised Matted
Rib, Modern.. 150 200 200
Model 722, 12 Ga., Tube Feed, Checkered Stock, Vent Rib,
Modern.. 150 200 200
Model 723, 16 Ga., Tube Feed, Checkered Stock, Plain Barrel,
Modern.. 100 150 150
Model 724, 16 Ga., Tube Feed, Checkered Stock, Raised Matted
Rib, Modern.. 125 175 175
Model 725, 16 Ga., Tube Feed, Checkered Stock, Vent Rib,
Modern.. 125 175 175
Model 726, 12 and 16 Gauges, 3 Shot, Checkered Stock, Plain
Barrel, Modern.. 125 175 175
Model 727, 12 and 16 Gauges, 3 Shot, Checkered Stock, Raised
Matted Rib, Modern.. 125 175 175
Model 728, 12 and 16 Gauges, 3 Shot, Checkered Stock, Vent Rib,
Modern.. 125 175 175
Model 740–C, 12 and 16 Gauges, Skeet Grade, Modern............ 175 225 225
Model 745, 12 Ga., Lightweight, Modern............................... 150 200 200
Model 750, 12 Ga., Modern.. 175 225 225
Model 750–AC, 12 Ga., Adjustable Choke, Modern................ 175 225 225
Model 750–SC, 12 Ga., Adjustable Choke, Modern................ 175 225 225
Model 755, 12 and 16 Gauges, Modern................................. 125 175 175
Model 755–SC, 12 and 16 Gauges, Adjustable Choke, Modern.............. 150 200 200
Model 775, 12 and 16 Gauges, Lightweight, Modern............... 150 200 200
Model 775–SC, 12 and 16 Gauges, Adjustable Choke, Lightweight,
Modern.. 150 200 200

SHOTGUN, SINGLESHOT

Model 220, Various Gauges, Hammerless, Takedown, Modern.............. 75 100 75
Model 220–AC, Various Gauges, Hammerless, Takedown,
Adjustable Choke, Modern.. 50 75 75

	V.G.	Exc	Prior Edition
Model 220–P, Various Gauges, Hammerless, Takedown, Adjustable Choke, Modern	$50	$75	$75
Model 94, Various Gauges, Hammer, Takedown, Modern	100	125	125
Model 94–C, Various Gauges, Hammer, Takedown, Modern	75	100	100
Model 94–Y Youth, Various Gauges, Hammer, Takedown, Modern	50	75	75

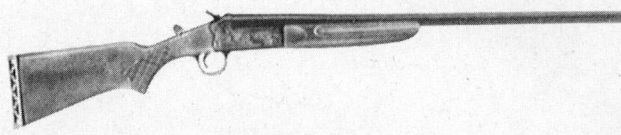

Savage Model 94-Y

	V.G.	Exc	Prior Edition
Model 9478, Various Gauges, Hammer, Auto Ejection, 42" to 52" Overall, Modern	100	125	125

SHOTGUN, SLIDE ACTION

	V.G.	Exc	Prior Edition
Model 21–A, 12 Ga., Hammerless, Takedown, Modern	125	175	175
Model 21–B, 12 Ga., Hammerless, Takedown, Raised Matted Rib, Modern	125	175	175
Model 21–C, 12 Ga., Hammerless, Takedown, Riot Gun, Modern	100	150	150
Model 21–D, 12 Ga., Hammerless, Takedown, Trap Grade, Modern	200	250	250
Model 21–E, 12 Ga., Hammerless, Takedown, Fancy Wood, Fancy Checkering, Vent Rib, Modern	250	300	300
Model 28–A, 12 Ga., Hammerless, Takedown, Modern	125	175	175
Model 28–B, 12 Ga., Hammerless, Takedown, Raised Matted Rib, Modern	125	175	175
Model 28–C, 12 Ga., Hammerless, Takedown, Riot Gun, Modern	100	150	150
Model 28–D, 12 Ga., Hammerless, Takedown, Trap Grade, Modern	200	250	250
Model 28–S, 12 Ga., Hammerless, Takedown, Fancy Checkering, Modern	200	250	250
Model 30, For Vent Rib, Add $15.00–$20.00			
Model 30, Various Gauges, Hammerless, Solid Frame, Modern	150	175	150

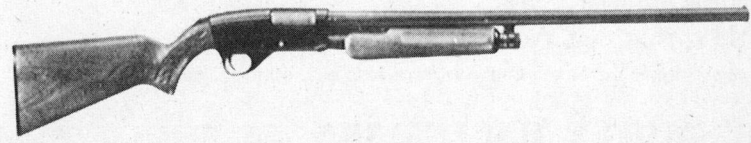

Savage Model 30

	V.G.	Exc	Prior Edition
Model 30–AC, Various Gauges, Hammerless, Solid Frame, Adjustable Choke, Modern	175	200	150
Model 30–ACL, Various Gauges, Hammerless, Solid Frame, Left–Hand, Adjustable Choke, Modern	175	200	150
Model 30–D, Various Gauges, Hammerless, Solid Frame, Light Engraving, Recoil Pad, Modern	125	175	175

	V.G.	Exc	Prior Edition
Model 30–L, Various Gauges, Hammerless, Solid Frame, Left–Hand, Modern	$150	$175	$150
Model 30–Slug, 12 Ga., Hammerless, Solid Frame, Modern	150	175	150

Savage Model 30-Slug

Model 30–T, 12 Ga., Hammerless, Solid Frame, Monte Carlo Stock, Recoil Pad, Vent Rib, Modern	125	175	175
Model 67, 12 or 20 Gauge, Tubular Mag, Hammerless, Walnut Stock, Modern	150	200	200
Model 67–T Stevens, 12 or 20 Gauge, Three Choke Tubes, 28" Barrel, Modern	175	225	225
Model 67–VR Stevens, 12 Gauge, 4 Shot Tubular, Vent Ribs, Modern	175	225	225
Model 69–N Guard Gun, 12 Gauge, 7 Shot Tubular Mag., 18¼" Cylinder Bore, Nickel, Modern	225	275	275
Model 69–R Guard Gun, 12 Gauge, 5 Shot Tubular Mag., 20" Cylinder Bore, Modern	175	225	225
Model 69–RXL Guard Gun, 12 Gauge, 7 Shot Tubular Mag., 18¼" Cylinder Bore, Modern	175	225	225

SCHALL & CO. Hartford, Conn.

HANDGUN, MANUAL REPEATER

.22 L.R.R.F., Target Pistol, Clip Fed, Curio	350	425	425

SCHEANER, WM. Reading, Pa. 1779–1790. See Kentucky Rifles.

SCHILLING, V. CHARLES Suhl, Germany. Also see Bergmann, German Military.

RIFLE, BOLT ACTION

Model 88 Sporter, Various Calibers, Checkered Stock, Curio	300	350	350

SCHMIDT & HABERMANN Suhl, Germany, 1920–1940.

COMBINATION WEAPON, OVER-UNDER

Various Calibers, Pre–WW2, Engraved, Checkered Stock, Curio	650	750	750

	V.G.	Exc	Prior Edition

SCHMIDT, ERNST Suhl, Germany.

RIFLE, SINGLESHOT

8mm Roth–Steyr, Schutzen Rifle, Engraved, Set Trigger,
Takedown, Octagon Barrel, Modern... $750 $850 $850

SCHMIDT, HERBERT Ostheim/Rhon, West Germany.

HANDGUN, REVOLVER

Liberty 11, .22 L.R.R.F., Double Action, Swing–Out Cylinder,
Blue, Modern... 50 75 75
Texas Scout, .22 L.R.R.F., Western Style, Blue, Modern........................ 50 75 75

SCHOUBOE Dansk Rekylriffel Syndikat, Copenhagen, Denmark 1902–1917.

HANDGUN, SEMI-AUTOMATIC

Model 1902/07, 11.35mm Sch., Curio....................................... 4,000 5,000 5,000
Model 1902/10, 11.35mm Sch., Curio....................................... 4,000 5,000 5,000
Model 1902/10, 11.35mm Sch., with Holster Stock, Curio..................... 5,500 6,500 6,500
Model 1903, 7.65mm, Clip Fed, Blue, Curio.. 3,250 4,000 4,000

SCHULTZ & LARSEN Otterup, Denmark.

HANDGUN, SINGLESHOT

Free Pistol, .22 L.R.R.F., Bolt Action, Target Trigger, Target
Sights, Modern.. 275 350 350

RIFLE, BOLT ACTION

Model 47, .22 L.R.R.F., Target Rifle, Thumbhole Stock,
Adjustable Trigger, Singleshot, Modern... 550 650 650
M54, Various Calibers, Modern.. 725 800 800
Model 61, .22 L.R.R.F., Target Rifle, Thumbhole Stock,
Adjustable Trigger, Singleshot, Modern... 650 750 750
Model 62, Various Calibers, Target Rifle, Thumbhole Stock,
Adjustable Trigger, Singleshot, Modern... 800 950 950
Model 65DL, Various Calibers, Sporting Rifle, Checkered Stock,
Adjustable Trigger, no Sights, Repeater, Modern.................................... 575 650 650
Model 68DL, .458 Win. Mag., Sporting Rifle, Checkered Stock,
Adjustable Trigger, no Sights, Repeater, Modern.................................... 650 750 750
Model 68DL, Various Calibers, Sporting Rifle, Checkered Stock,
Adjustable Trigger, no Sights, Repeater, Modern.................................... 575 650 650

SCHUTZEN RIFLE EXAMPLES

RIFLE, SINGLESHOT

Aydt System, Various Calibers, Dropping Block, Fancy Tyrol
Stock, Fancy Engraving, Target Sights, Modern...................................... 1,000 1,200 1,200
Aydt System, Various Calibers, Dropping Block, Plain Tyrol
Stock, Light Engraving, Target Sights, Modern....................................... 750 900 900

	V.G.	Exc	Prior Edition
Martini System, Various Calibers, Dropping Block, Fancy Tyrol Stock, Fancy Engraving, Target Sights, Modern..	$750	$1,000	$1,000

SCHWARZLOSE Andreas W. Schwarlose, Berlin, Germany 1911–1927.

HANDGUN, SEMI-AUTOMATIC

M 1908 Pocket, 7.65mm, Blow–Forward, Clip Fed, Grip Safety, Curio...	400	475	475
M 1908 W.A.C. Pocket, 7.65mm, Blow–Forward, Clip Fed, Grip Safety, Curio..	375	450	450

Schwarzlose M 1908 WAC

M96 Standardt, 7.65mm Mauser, Clip Fed, Blue, Curio.........................	3,000	3,500	3,000

SCOTT ARMS CO. Norwich Falls Pistol Co., c. 1880.

HANDGUN, REVOLVER

.32 Short R.F., 5 Shot, Spur Trigger, Solid Frame, Single Action, Antique...	150	175	175

SCOTT REVOLVER–RIFLE Hopkins & Allen, c. 1880.

HANDGUN, REVOLVER

24½" Brass Barrel, .38 Short R.F., 5 Shot, Spur Trigger, Solid Frame, Single Action, Antique..	225	275	275

SCOTT, D. Edinburgh, Scotland, 1727–1745.

HANDGUN, FLINTLOCK

Queen Anne Type, .59, Screw Barrel, Holster Pistol, Marked "Edinboro," Antique..	1,250	1,750	1,750

	V.G.	Exc	Prior Edition

SCOUT Made by Hood Firearms for Frankfurt Hardware of Milwaukee, Wisc., c. 1870.

HANDGUN, REVOLVER

.32 Short R.F., 5 Shot, Spur Trigger, Solid Frame, Single Action,
Antique.. $150 $175 $175

SCOUT Made by Stevens.

SHOTGUN, DOUBLE BARREL, SIDE-BY-SIDE

Model 311, Various Gauges, Hammerless, Steel Barrel, Modern............. 175 200 200

S.E.A.M. Fab. d' Armes de Soc. Espanola de Armas y Municiones, Eibar, Spain.

HANDGUN, SEMI-AUTOMATIC

Eibar Type, 6.35mm, 11 Slide Grooves, Good Quality, Clip Fed,
Blue, Modern.. 150 175 175
Eibar Type, 6.35mm, 13 Slide Grooves, Fair Quality, Clip Fed,
Blue, Modern.. 100 125 125
Walther Type, 6.35mm, Clip Fed, Blue, Modern.................................... 175 225 225

SEARS Sears, Roebuck & Co., Chicago, Ill. Also see Ted Williams.

RIFLE, BOLT ACTION

Semi–Sporterized Mauser, 8mm Mauser, Converted Military,
Modern... 100 125 125
Sporterized Mauser, 8mm Mauser, Converted Military, Recoil
Pad, Modern... 125 150 150

SHOTGUN, BOLT ACTION

.410 Gauge, Clip Fed, Blue, Plain, Modern... 25 50 50
.410 Gauge, Singleshot, Plain, Modern... 25 50 50
12 or 20 Gauges, Clip Fed, Adjustable Choke, Blue, Plain,
Modern... 50 75 75

Sears 12 Ga. Bolt Action

12 or 20 Gauges, Clip Fed, Blue, Plain, Modern...................................... 25 50 50

SHOTGUN, SINGLESHOT

Various Gauges, Top Break, Plain, Modern... 25 50 50

	V.G.	Exc	Prior Edition
Youth, 20 or .410 Gauges, Plain, Modern	$25	$50	$50

Sears Youth

SECRET SERVICE SPECIAL Made for Fred Biffar, Chicago by Iver–Johnson and Meriden.

HANDGUN, REVOLVER

.32 S & W, 5 Shot, Top Break, Hammerless, Double Action, Modern	125	150	150
.38 S & W, 5 Shot, Top Break, Hammerless, Double Action, Modern	125	150	150

SECURITY INDUSTRIES OF AMERICA Little Ferry, N.J.

HANDGUN, REVOLVER

Police Pocket, .357 Magnum, Stainless Steel, 2" Barrel, Swing–Out Cylinder, Double Action, Spurless Hammer, Modern	175	225	225
Security Undercover, .357 Magnum, Stainless Steel, 2" Barrel, Swing–Out Cylinder, Double Action, Modern	175	225	225

SEDGLEY, R.F., INC. Philadelphia, Pa. 1911–1938. Successor to Henry Kolb.

HANDGUN, REVOLVER

Baby Hammerless, .22 L.R.R.F., Double Action, Folding Trigger, Modern	125	150	150

RIFLE, BOLT ACTION

Springfield, Carbine, Various Calibers, Sporting Rifle, Lyman Sights, Checkered Stock, Full–Stocked, Modern	1,000	1,250	700
Springfield, Various Calibers, Sporting Rifle, Lyman Sights, Checkered Stock, Modern	800	950	600
Springfield, Various Calibers, Sporting Rifle, Lyman Sights, Checkered Stock, Left–Hand, Modern	800	950	650

SELECTA Echave y Arizmendi, Eibar, Spain.

HANDGUN, SEMI-AUTOMATIC

Model 1918, 6.35mm, Double Safety, Clip Fed, Modern	125	150	150

	V.G.	Exc	Prior Edition
Model 1918, 6.35mm, Triple Safety, Clip Fed, Modern	$150	$175	$175
Model 1919, 7.65mm, Double Safety, Clip Fed, Modern	150	175	175

Selecta Model 1919

Model 1919, 7.65mm, Triple Safety, Clip Fed, Modern	150	200	200

SEMMERLING Semmerling Corp., Newton, Mass. Currently manufactured by American Derringer Corp. Waco, Texas.

HANDGUN, MANUAL REPEATER

LM–4, .45 ACP, Double Action, Clip Fed, Modern	1,250	1,500	1,200

SHAKANOOSA ARMS MFG. CO. 1862–1864. See Confederate Military.

RIFLE, PERCUSSION

.58, Military, (C S A), Antique	1,250	1,500	1,500
.58, Military, Carbine, (C S A), Antique	1,750	2,000	2,000

SHARPE English, 1670–1680.

HANDGUN, FLINTLOCK

Pair, Pocket Pistol, Screw Barrel, Octagon, High Quality, Antique	3,250	3,500	3,500

			Prior
	V.G.	Exc	Edition

SHARPS, CHRISTIAN Mill Creek, Pa. 1848; moved to Hartford, Conn. in 1851 and became Sharps Rifle Mfg. Co., changing its name to Sharps Rifle Co. in 1874, continuing operations until 1881. In 1854 formed C. Sharps & Co. in Philadelphia, Pa., became Sharps & Hankins in 1862, C. Sharps & Co. again in 1866, and continued until 1880.

HANDGUN, PERCUSSION

	V.G.	Exc	Prior Edition
Bryce Revolver, .25, Tip–Up, 6 Shot, Blue, Spur Trigger, Single Action, Antique	$1,600	$1,850	$1,350
Revolver, .25, Tip–Up, 6 Shot, Blue, Spur Trigger, Single Action, Antique	1,500	1,750	1,150

HANDGUN, MULTI-BARREL

	V.G.	Exc	Prior Edition
.22 R.F., Model 1A, 4 Barreled Pistol, Antique	350	400	450
.22 R.F., Model 1B, 4 Barreled Pistol, Antique	400	450	425
.22 R.F., Model 1C, 4 Barreled Pistol, Antique	375	425	425
.22 R.F., Model 1D, 4 Barreled Pistol, Antique	650	750	525
.30 R.F., Model 1E, 4 Barreled Pistol, Antique	1,500	1,750	450
.30 R.F., Model 2, 4 Barreled Pistol, Antique	550	650	475
.32 R.F., Model 3, 4 Barreled Pistol, Antique	475	550	450
.32 R.F., Model 4, 4 Barreled Pistol, Mechanism on Hammer, Antique	750	850	425
.32 R.F. Bulldog, Model 4, 4 Barreled Pistol, Pin on Side of Frame, Antique	425	475	475
.32 R.F. Bulldog, Model 4, 4 Barreled Pistol, Screw Under Frame, Antique	400	450	450

HANDGUN, SINGLESHOT

	V.G.	Exc	Prior Edition
Medium Frame, Various Calibers, Single Action, Dropping Block, Hammer, Antique	2,250	2,750	2,750
Small Frame, Various Calibers, Single Action, Dropping Block, Hammer, Antique	2,000	2,250	2,250

Christian Sharps Patent Single Shot, .36 Caliber

RIFLE, PERCUSSION

	V.G.	Exc	Prior Edition
1851 Carbine, .52, Maynard Primer, Antique	4,000	4,500	4,500

	V.G.	Exc	Prior Edition
1852 Carbine, .52, Pellet Primer, Antique	$2,250	$2,500	$1,750
1853 Carbine, .52, Pellet Primer, Antique	2,000	2,250	1,500
1855 Carbine, .52, Maynard Primer, Antique	3,000	3,500	1,500
1855 Rifle, .52, Maynard Primer, Antique	2,000	2,500	2,500
1859 Carbine, .52, Pellet Primer, Antique	1,750	2,000	1,500
1863 Carbine, .52, Lawrence Cut–off, Antique	1,250	1,500	1,500
1863 Rifle, .52, Lawrence Cut–off, Antique	1,500	1,750	1,750

RIFLE, SINGLESHOT

	V.G.	Exc	Prior Edition
1874 Hunting Rifle, Various Calibers, Open Sights, Antique	2,500	3,000	3,000
1874 Sporting Rifle, Various Calibers, Set Trigger, Target Sights, Antique	3,000	3,500	3,500
Long Range Rifle, Various Calibers, Target Sights, Antique	8,500	10,000	6,000

SHARPSHOOTER Hijos de Calixto Arrizabalaga, Eibar, Spain, c. 1920.

HANDGUN, SEMI-AUTOMATIC

	V.G.	Exc	Prior Edition
"Sharp–Shooter," .380 ACP, Clip Fed, Hammer, Hinged Barrel, Blue, Curio	250	275	275
"Sharp–Shooter," 6.35mm, Clip Fed, Hammer, Hinged Barrel, Blue, Curio	175	200	200
"Sharp–Shooter," 7.65mm, Clip Fed, Hammer, Hinged Barrel, Blue, Curio	200	225	225

SHATTUCK, C.S. Hatfield, Mass. 1880–1890.

HANDGUN, REVOLVER

Lincoln/Garfield Grips, Hard Rubber, Add 20%–30%

	V.G.	Exc	Prior Edition
.22 R.F., Single Action, Spur Trigger, Swing–Out Cylinder, Antique	200	250	300
.32 R.F., Single Action, Spur Trigger, Swing–Out Cylinder, Antique	225	275	275
.38 R.F., Double Action, Spur Trigger, Swing–Out Cylinder, Antique	300	300	350
.41 R.F., Double Action, Spur Trigger, Swing–Out Cylinder, Antique	375	350	450

SHAW, JOHN London, England, c. 1688.

HANDGUN, FLINTLOCK

	V.G.	Exc	Prior Edition
Holster Pistol, Engraved, Steel Mounts, High Quality, Antique	2,000	2,500	2,500

SHELL, JOHN Leslie County, Ky. 1810–1880. See Kentucky Rifles.

SHERIDEN Racine, Wisc. 1953–1960.

HANDGUN, SINGLESHOT

	V.G.	Exc	Prior Edition
Knockabout, .22 L.R.R.F., Tip–Up Barrel, Single Action, Hammer, Blue, Modern	100	125	125

	V.G.	Exc	Prior Edition

SHILEN Ennis, Tex.

RIFLE, BOLT ACTION

DGA Benchrest, Various Calibers, Target Rifle, Modern......	$625	$700	$700
DGA Silhouette, Various Calibers, Target Rifle, Modern......	550	600	600
DGA Sporter, Various Calibers, Blind Magazine, Plain Stock, Modern......	550	600	600
DGA Varmint, Various Calibers, Heavy Barrel, Modern......	550	600	600

SHILOH RIFLE MANUFACTURING CO. Mfg. of Sharps Rifle Replicas, Big Timber, Mt.

RIFLE, PERCUSSION

Model 1859 New Model Cavalry Carbine, .54, Reproduction	325	400	350
Model 1862 Robinson Confederate Cavalry Carbine, .54, Reproduction	650	750	600
Model 1863 Cavalry Carbine, .54, Reproduction	500	600	500
Model 1863 New Model Military Rifle, .54, Reproduction	600	700	600
Model 1863 Sporting Rifle #2, .54, Reproduction	450	550	450
Model 1863 Sporting Rifle #3, .54, Reproduction	400	500	425

RIFLE, SINGLESHOT

Model 1874 Business Rifle, Various Calibers, Reproduction, Modern......	550	625	625
Model 1874 Hunter's Rifle, Various Calibers, Reproduction, Modern......	500	575	425
Model 1874 Military Carbine, Various Calibers, Reproduction, Modern......	575	650	650
Model 1874 Military Rifle, Various Calibers, Reproduction, Modern......	650	750	750
Model 1874 Sporting Rifle #2, Various Calibers, Reproduction, Modern......	450	500	500
Model 1874 Sporting Rifle #3, Various Calibers, Reproduction, Modern......	550	625	625

SHORER, ANDREW Northhampton, Pa. 1775–1776. See Kentucky Rifles.

SICKEL'S ARMS CO. Belgium for Robert Sickels & Preston Co., Davenport, Iowa.

SHOTGUN, DOUBLE BARREL, SIDE-BY-SIDE

Various Gauges, Hammerless, Damascus Barrel, Modern......	150	1,750	175
Various Gauges, Hammerless, Steel Barrel, Modern......	175	200	200
Various Gauges, Outside Hammers, Damascus Barrel, Modern......	150	175	175
Various Gauges, Outside Hammers, Steel Barrel, Modern......	175	200	200

SHOTGUN, SINGLESHOT

Various Gauges, Hammer, Steel Barrel, Modern......	75	100	100

S.I.G. Schweizerische Industrie Gesellschaft, Neuhausen, Switzerland since 1857.

HANDGUN, SEMI-AUTOMATIC

P210 Luxus, Various Calibers, Clip Fed, Fancy Engraving, Gold Inlay, High–Polish Blue Finish, Carved Wood Grips, Modern.................. $2,500 $3,500 $3,500

P210–1, .22 L.R.R.F., Clip Fed, Blue, High–Polish Finish, Wood Grips, Modern...................................'................................. 1,250   1,450   1,450

P210–1, .22 L.R.R.F., Conversion Unit Only, Modern............................. 500   550   550

P210–1, .30 Luger, Clip Fed, Blue, High–Polish Finish, Wood Grips, Modern.. 1,350   1,500   1,500

P210–1, .9mm Luger, Clip Fed, Blue, High–Polish Finish, Wood Grips, Modern.. 1,400   1,550   1,550

P210–1, Various Calibers, Clip Fed, Blue, High–Polish Finish, with 3 Caliber Conv. Units, Wood Grips, Modern..................... 2,000   2,500   2,500

P210–2, .30 Luger, Clip Fed, Blue, Plastic Stock, Modern..................... 950   1,200   1,200

P210–2, .9mm Luger, Clip Fed, Blue, Plastic Stock, Modern.................. 1,000   1,150   1,150

P210–5, .30 Luger, Clip Fed, Blue, Plastic Stock, Target Pistol, 6" Barrel, Modern.. 1,200   1,450   1,450

P210–5, .9mm Luger, Clip Fed, Blue, Plastic Stock, Target Pistol, 6" Barrel, Modern.. 1,250   1,400   1,400

P210–6, .30 Luger & 4mm, Clip Fed, Blue, Plastic Stock, Target Pistol, 4½" Barrel, Modern.. 1,050   1,250   1,250

S.I.G. P210-6

P210–7, .9mm Luger, Clip Fed, Blue, Plastic Stock, Target Pistol, Long Barrel, Modern.. 2,250   2,500   2,500

P 220 SIG–Sauer, Various Calibers, Clip Fed, Double Action, Blue, Modern... 550   650   550

P 225 SIG–Sauer, .9mm Luger, Clip Fed, Double Action, Blue, Modern...:............. 525   625   550

P 230 SIG–Sauer, Various Calibers, Clip Fed, Double Action, Modern.. 350   400   400

	V.G.	Exc	Prior Edition
P 2305L SIG–Sauer, Various Calibers, Clip Fed, Double Action, Stainless, Modern..................	$400	$450	$375
SP 47/8 (Pre–210), 9mm Luger, Clip Fed, German Border Patrol, Modern..................	1,750	2,000	2,000
SP 47/8 (Pre–210), 9mm Luger, Clip Fed, Swiss Military, Modern.........	2,500	3,000	3,000

RIFLE, SEMI-AUTOMATIC

	V.G.	Exc	Prior Edition
SIG AMT, .308 Win., Clip Fed, Bipod, Modern..................	1,750	2,000	2,000
SIG STG–57, 7.5 Swiss, Clip Fed, Bipod, Modern..................	2,500	2,750	1,700

SILE   Imported by Sile Distributers, N.Y.C., N.Y.

HANDGUN, SEMI-AUTOMATIC

	V.G.	Exc	Prior Edition
Seecamp, .25 ACP, Double Action, Clip Fed, Stainless Steel, Modern..................	250	300	300

SIMPLEX   Made in Belgium. 1901–1906. Also see Bergmann.

HANDGUN, SEMI-AUTOMATIC

	V.G.	Exc	Prior Edition
Simplex, 8mm Bergmann, Blue, Curio..................	1,000	1,250	750

SIMSON & CO.   Waffenfabrik Simson & Co., Suhl, Germany 1910–1939. Also see Luger.

HANDGUN, SEMI-AUTOMATIC

	V.G.	Exc	Prior Edition
M1927 Vest Pocket, .25 ACP, Clip Fed, Blue, Curio..................	450	500	500

RIFLE, BOLT ACTION

	V.G.	Exc	Prior Edition
Model 1933, .22 Extra Long, Singleshot, Checkered Stock, Target Sights, Curio..................	100	125	125
Precision Carbine, 6mm Shot, Singleshot, Plain, Curio..................	125	150	75
Precision Carbine, 9mm Shot, Singleshot, Plain, Curio..................	125	150	75
Sportrifle #7, .22 Extra Long, Singleshot, Checkered Stock, Target Sights, Curio..................	75	100	100

SHOTGUN, DOUBLE BARREL, OVER-UNDER

	V.G.	Exc	Prior Edition
Trap Grade, 12 Ga., Automatic Ejectors, Checkered Stock, Engraved, Cocking Indicators, Curio..................	1,500	1,750	1,750

SHOTGUN, DOUBLE BARREL, SIDE-BY-SIDE

	V.G.	Exc	Prior Edition
Astora, Various Calibers, Checkered Stock, Plain, Curio..................	300	350	350
Magnum, 12 Ga. 3", Checkered Stock, Engraved, Curio..................	700	750	750
Monte Carlo, 12 Ga., Checkered Stock, Fancy Engraving, Automatic Ejectors, Sidelock, Curio..................	1,500	1,650	1,650

SINGER   Arizmendi y Geonaga, Eibar, Spain.

HANDGUN, SEMI-AUTOMATIC

	V.G.	Exc	Prior Edition
6.35mm, Clip Fed, Blue, Modern..................	100	125	125
7.65mm, Clip Fed, Blue, Modern..................	125	150	150

	V.G.	Exc	Prior Edition

SINGER Frantisek Dusek, Opocno, Czechoslovakia.

HANDGUN, SEMI-AUTOMATIC

Duo, 6.35mm, Clip Fed, Blue, Modern... $100 $125 $125

SJOGREN Sweden.

SHOTGUN, SEMI-AUTOMATIC

12 Ga., 5 Shot, Checkered Stock, Recoil Operated, Curio........................ 400 450 450

SKB Tokyo, Japan.

SHOTGUN, DOUBLE BARREL, OVER-UNDER

	V.G.	Exc	Prior Edition
Model 500, 12 and 20 Gauges, Field Grade, Selective Ejector, Vent Rib, Modern	475	500	425
Model 500, 12 Ga. Mag. 3", Field Grade, Selective Ejector, Vent Rib, Modern	525	550	450
Model 600, .410 Gauges, Skeet Grade, Selective Ejector, Vent Rib, Modern	525	575	550
Model 600, 12 and 20 Gauges, Field Grade, Selective Ejector, Vent Rib, Modern	625	675	475
Model 600, 12 and 20 Gauges, Skeet Grade, Selective Ejector, Vent Rib, Modern	625	650	525
Model 600, 12 Ga., Trap Grade, Selective Ejector, Vent Rib, Modern	600	650	550
Model 600, 12 Ga., Trap Grade, Selective Ejector, Vent Rib, Monte Carlo Stock, Modern	575	625	525
Model 600 Combo Set, Various Gauges, Skeet Grade, Selective Ejector, Vent Rib, Cased, Modern	750	1,000	1,350
Model 680 English, 12 and 20 Gauges, Field Grade, Selective Ejector, Vent Rib, Modern	700	750	625
Model 700, 12 and 20 Gauges, Skeet Grade, Selective Ejector, Vent Rib, Modern	825	875	750
Model 700, 12 Ga., Trap Grade, Selective Ejector, Vent Rib, Modern	850	800	725
Model 700, 12 Ga., Trap Grade, Selective Ejector, Vent Rib, Monte Carlo Stock, Modern	800	850	750
Model 700 Combo Set, Various Gauges, Skeet Grade, Selective Ejector, Vent Rib, Cased, Modern	1,500	1,750	1,650

SHOTGUN, SEMI-AUTOMATIC

	V.G.	Exc	Prior Edition
XL 900, 12 and 20 Gauges, Skeet Grade, Modern	250	325	300
XL 900, 12 Ga., Trap Grade, Monte Carlo Stock, Modern	250	325	300
XL 900 MR, 12 and 20 Gauges, Vent Rib, Modern	225	275	2,755
XL 900 Slug, 12 and 20 Gauges, Open Rear Sight, Modern	250	300	300

SLOANS Importers, N.Y.C. Also see Charles Daly.

SHOTGUN, DOUBLE BARREL, SIDE-BY-SIDE

POS, .410 Ga., Checkered Stock, Hammerless, Double Trigger, Modern.. 150 175 175

	V.G.	Exc	Prior Edition
POS, 10 Ga., 3½", Checkered Stock, Hammerless, Double Trigger, Modern.	$150	$200	$200
POS, 12 and 20 Gauges, Checkered Stock, Hammerless, Double Trigger, Modern.	150	175	175
POS Coach Gun, 12 and 20 Gauges, Checkered Stock, Outside Hammers, Double Trigger, Modern.	150	175	175

SMITH & WESSON   Started in Norwich, Conn. in 1855 as Volcanic Repeating Arms Co. Reorganized at Springfield, Mass. as Smith & Wesson in 1857 (Volcanic Repeating Arms moved to New Haven, Conn. in 1856 and was purchased in 1857 by Winchester Repeating Arms Co.). Smith & Wesson at Springfield, Mass. to date. Also see U.S. Military and the Commemorative section.

HANDGUN, REVOLVER

.32 Double Action, .32 S & W, 1st Model, Top Break, 5 Shot, Straight–Cut Sideplate, Rocker Cylinder Stop, Antique	3,500	4,000	4,000
.32 Double Action, .32 S & W, 2nd Model, Top Break, 5 Shot, Irregularly–Cut Sideplate, Rocker Cylinder Stop, Antique	425	475	300
.32 Double Action, .32 S & W, 3rd Model, Top Break, 5 Shot, Irregularly–Cut Sideplate, Antique	425	475	275
.32 Double Action, .32 S & W, 4th Model, Round–Back Trigger Guard, Top Break, 5 Shot, Irregularly–Cut Sideplate, Curio	275	300	350
.32 Double Action, .32 S & W, 5th Model, Round–Back Trigger Guard, Top Break, 5 Shot, Irregularly–Cut Sideplate, Front Sight Forged on Barrel, Curio	300	325	300
.32 Hand Ejector 1903, .32 S & W Long, Solid Frame, Swing–Out Cylinder, 6 Shot, Double Action, Curio	550	600	550
.32 Hand Ejector, (Bekeart), .32 S & W Long, Solid Frame, Swing–Out Cylinder, 6 Shot, Target Sights, Double Action, Curio	1,000	1,250	1,500

S & W .32 Hand Ejector

.32 Hand Ejector, .32 S & W Long, 1st Model, Solid Frame, Swing–Out Cylinder, Hammer Actuated Cylinder Stop, 6 Shot, Curio	775	825	825

	V.G.	Exc	Prior Edition
.32 Regulation Police, .32 S & W Long, Solid Frame, Swing–Out Cylinder, 6 Shot, Double Action, Curio......	$225	$250	$225
.32 Safety Hammerless, .32 S & W Long, 1st Model, Double Action, Top Break, 5 Shot, Push–Button Latch, Curio......	600	650	325
.32 Safety Hammerless, .32 S & W Long, 2nd Model, Double Action, Top Break, 5 Shot, T Latch, Curio......	425	450	225
.32 Safety Hammerless, .32 S & W, 3rd Model, Double Action, Top Break, 5 Shot, Over #170,000, Curio......	325	350	250
.32 Single Action, .32 S & W, 10" Barrel, Add 75%–100%			
.32 Single Action, .32 S & W, 6" or 8" Barrel, Add 50%–75%			
.32 Single Action, .32 S & W, Top Break, Spur Trigger, 5 Shot, Antique......	325	350	450
.38 D A Perfected, .38 S & W, made without Side Latch, Hand–Ejector Action, Top Break, Double Action, Curio......	500	750	550
.38 D A Perfected, .38 S & W, Solid Trigger Guard, Thumbpiece Hand–Ejector Action, Top Break, Double Action, Curio......	325	450	375
.38 Double Action, .38 S & W, 1st Model, Straight–Cut Sideplate, Rocker Cylinder Stop, Double Action, Top Break, 5 Shot, Antique......	700	775	775

S & W .38 Double Action

	V.G.	Exc	Prior Edition
.38 Double Action, .38 S & W, 2nd Model, Irregularly–Cut Sideplate, Rocker Cylinder Stop, Double Action, Top Break, 5 Shot, Antique......	200	250	250
.38 Double Action, .38 S & W, 3rd Model, Irregularly–Cut Sideplate, Double Action, Top Break, 5 Shot, Antique......	200	250	250
.38 Double Action, .38 S & W, 4th Model, #'s 32,701–539,000, Double Action, Top Break, 5 Shot, Curio......	225	250	225
.38 Double Action, .38 S & W, 5th Model, #'s 539,001–554,077, Double Action, Top Break, 5 Shot, Curio......	425	450	200
.38 Hand Ejector 1902, .38 Special, Military and Police, Solid Frame, Swing–Out Cylinder, Double Action, Curio......	375	325	225
.38 Hand Ejector 1902, .38 Special, Military and Police, Solid Frame, Swing–Out Cylinder, Double Action, Adjustable Sights, Curio......	450	500	500
.38 Hand Ejector 1905, .38 Special, Military and Police, Solid Frame, Swing–Out Cylinder, Double Action, Curio......	575	625	300
.38 Hand Ejector 1905, .38 Special, Military and Police, Solid Frame, Swing–Out Cylinder, Double Action, Adjustable Sights, Curio......	500	550	500

	V.G.	Exc	Prior Edition
.38 Hand Ejector, .38 Long Colt, 1st Model, Solid Frame, Swing–Out Cylinder, no Cylinder–Pin Front–Lock, U.S. Army Model, Curio.....	$425	$775	$775

S & W .38 Hand Ejector 1st Model

	V.G.	Exc	Prior Edition
.38 Hand Ejector, .38 Long Colt, 1st Model, Solid Frame, Swing–Out Cylinder, no Cylinder–Pin Front–Lock, U.S. Navy Model, Curio.....	700	750	750
.38 Hand Ejector, .38 Special, 1st Model, Solid Frame, Swing–Out Cylinder, no Cylinder–Pin Front–Lock, Adjustable Sights, Curio............	625	675	675
.38 Hand Ejector, .38 Special, 2nd Model, Solid Frame, Swing–Out Cylinder, Curio...................	400	450	375
.38 Hand Ejector, .38 Special, 2nd Model, Solid Frame, Swing–Out Cylinder, Adjustable Sights, Curio.......................	575	625	625
.38 Safety Hammerless, .38 S & W, 1st Model–Button Latch, Release on Left Topstrap, Top Break, Double Action, Antique................	500	550	425
.38 Safety Hammerless, .38 S & W, 2nd Model–Button Latch, Release on Top of Frame, Top Break, Double Action, Antique................	375	400	325
.38 Safety Hammerless, .38 S & W, 3rd Model–Button Latch, Release on Rear Topstrap, Top Break, Double Action, Antique...............	350	375	275
.38 Safety Hammerless, .38 S & W, 4th Model T-Shaped Latch, Top Break, Double Action, Curio.................	275	300	275
.38 Safety Hammerless, .38 S & W, 5th Model T-Shaped Latch, Top Break, Double Action, Front Sight Forged on Barrel, Curio.............	225	275	225

	V.G.	Exc	Prior Edition
.38 Single Action, .38 S & W, 1st Model, Baby Russian, Top Break, Spur Trigger, Antique....................	$425	$450	$425

S & W .38 Single Action

	V.G.	Exc	Prior Edition
.38 Single Action, .38 S & W, 2nd Model, Top Break, Spur Trigger, Short Ejector Housing, Antique.....................	375	400	300
.38 Single Action, .38 S & W, 3rd Model, Top Break, with Trigger Guard, Curio....................	600	675	675
.38 Single Action, .38 S & W, 3rd Model, Top Break, with Trigger Guard, with Extra Single–Shot Barrel, Curio....................	950	1,050	1,050
.38 Single Action, .38 S & W, Mexican Model, Top Break, Spur Trigger, 5 Shot, Curio....................	1,650	1,750	1,950
.38 Win. Double Action, .38–40 WCF, Top Break, Curio....................	1,100	1,250	1,250
.44 Double Action Frontier, for Target Sights, Add 20%–30%			
.44 Double Action, .44 Russian, 1st Model, Top Break, 6 Shot, Antique....................	525	950	600
.44 Double Action, for Target Sights, Add 20%–30%			
.44 Double Action, Wesson Favorite, 6 Shot, Lightweight, Top Break, Antique....................	1,700	2,500	1,850
.44 Hand Ejector, 1st Model, for Target Sights, Add 20%–30%			
.44 Hand Ejector, 2nd Model, for Target Sights, Add 20%–30%			
.44 Hand Ejector, 3rd Model, for Target Sights, Add 20%–30%			
.44 Hand Ejector, Calibers other than .44 Spec., Add 15%–25%			
.44 Hand Ejector, Calibers other than .44 Spec., Add 15%–25%			
.44 Hand Ejector, .44 Special, 1st Model, Triple–Lock, Solid Frame, Swing–Out Cylinder, New Century, Curio....................	725	800	800
.44 Hand Ejector, .44 Special, 2nd Model, Un–Shrouded Ejector Rod, Solid Frame, Swing–Out Cylinder, Curio....................	500	550	550
.44 Hand Ejector, .44 Special, 3rd Model, Shrouded Ejector Rod, Solid Frame, Swing–Out Cylinder, Curio....................	450	550	500
.44 New Model #3 Frontier, .44–40 WCF, Top Break, 6 Shot, Antique....................	700	1,500	850
.455 MK II Hand Ejector, Solid Frame, Swing–Out Cylinder, Double Action, Military, Curio....................	500	600	500
22/32 Bekeart Model, .22 L.R.R.F., #'s 138,220–139,275, Target Pistol, Double Action, Adjustable Sights, 6" Barrel, Curio....................	700	800	625
22/32 Kit Gun, .22 L.R.R.F., Early Model, Double Action Adjustable Sights, 4" Barrel, Curio....................	600	650	325
32/20 Hand Ejector 1902, .32–20 WCF, 2nd Model, Solid Frame, Swing–Out Cylinder, 6 Shot, Curio....................	450	500	375

	V.G.	Exc	Prior Edition
32/20 Hand Ejector 1902, .32–20 WCF, 2nd Model, Solid Frame, Swing–Out Cylinder, 6 Shot, Adjustable Sights, Curio	$500	$550	$550
32/20 Hand Ejector 1905, .32–20 WCF, Solid Frame, Swing–Out Cylinder, 6 Shot, Adjustable Sights, Curio	450	500	500
32/20 Hand Ejector 1905, .32–20 WCF, Solid Frame, Swing–Out Cylinder, 6 Shot, Curio	450	500	350
32/20 Hand Ejector, .32–20 WCF, 1st Model, Solid Frame, Swing–Out Cylinder, 6 Shot, no Cylinder–Pin Front–Lock, Curio	475	525	475
38/200 British (Model 11), .38 S & W, Military & Police, Solid Frame Swing–Out Cylinder, Double Action, Military, Curio	300	350	250
First Model Schofield, .45 S & W, Top Break, Single Action, Military, Antique	4,000	4,500	2,500
First Model Schofield, .45 S & W, Top Break, Single Action, Commercial, Antique	4,500	5,000	3,500
First Model Schofield, .45 S & W, Wells Fargo, Top Break, Single Action, Antique	2,500	3,000	3,000
K–22 Masterpiece, .22 L.R.R.F., 2nd Model, K–22 Hand Ejector, Speed Lock Action, Double Action, Adjustable Sights, 6" Barrel, Modern	875	950	525
K–22 Outdoorsman, .22 L.R.R.F., 1st Model, Double Action, Adjustable Sights, 6" Barrel, Modern	425	475	350
K–32 Masterpiece, .32 S & W Long, 1st Model, Pre–War, 6 Shot Adjustable Sights, Target Pistol, Modern	1,500	1,750	675
K–32 Masterpiece, .32 S & W Long, 2nd Model, Post–War, 6 Shot, Adjustable Sights, Target Pistol, Modern	850	950	325
Model "13," .357 Magnum, Double Action, Swing–Out Cylinder, Modern	500	575	575
Model #1, .22 Short R.F., 1st Issue, Tip–Up, Spur Trigger, 7 Shot, Antique	4,250	4,500	3,500
Model #1, .22 Short R.F., 2nd Issue, Tip–Up, Spur Trigger, 7 Shot, Antique	2,500	2,750	2,250
Model #1, .22 Short R.F., 3rd Issue, Tip–Up, Spur Trigger, 7 Shot, Antique	2,250	2,500	1,225
Model #1½, .32 Short R.F., 1st Issue, Tip–Up, Spur Trigger, 5 Shot, Non–Fluted Cylinder, Antique	400	450	450
Model #1½, .32 Short R.F., 2nd Issue, Tip–Up, Spur Trigger, 5 Shot, Fluted Cylinder, Antique	700	750	425
Model #2 Old Army, .22 Short R.F., Tip–Up, Spur Trigger, 6 Shot, Antique	750	850	550
Model #3 American, .44 Henry, 1st Model, Single Action, Top Break, 6 Shot, Antique	3,250	3,500	1,975
Model #3 American, .44 Henry, 2nd Model, #'s 8,000–32,800, Single Action, Top Break, 6 Shot, Antique	270	3,000	1,750
Model #3 American, .44 S & W, 1st Model, Single Action, Top Break, 6 Shot, Antique	2,250	2,500	1,275
Model #3 American, .44 S & W, 2nd Model, #'s 8,000–32,800, Single Action, Top Break, 6 Shot, Antique	2,000	2,250	1,050
Model #3 Fronter, .44–40 WCF, Single Action, Top Break, 6 Shot, Antique	1,500	1,750	1,500

Model #3 New Model, Calibers other than .44 Russian, Add 40%–60%
Model #3 New Model, .44 Russian, Argentine Model, Add 25%–35%
Model #3 New Model, .44 Russian, Japanese Navy Issue, Add 30%–45%
Model #3 New Model, .44 Russian, Australian Police with Shoulder Stock, Add 200%–225%

	V.G.	Exc	Prior Edition
Model #3 New Model, .44 S & W, Turkish Model, Add 15%–25%			
Model #3 New Model, Various Calibers, Calibers other than .44 Russian, Add 40%–60%			
Model #3 New Model, .44 Russian, Single Action, Top Break, 6 Shot, Antique	$1,750	$2,000	$950
Model #3 Russian, .44 Russian, 1st Model, Single Action, Top Break, 6 Shot, Military, Antique	2,250	2,500	1,050
Model #3 Russian, .44 Russian, 2nd Model, Finger–Rest Trigger Guard, Single Action, Top Break, 6 Shot, Antique	2,000	2,250	925
Model #3 Russian, .44 Russian, 2nd Model, Finger–Rest Trigger Guard, Single Action, Top Break, with Shoulder Stock, Antique	2,500	2,750	1,575
Model #3 Russian, .44 Russian, 3rd Model, Front Sight Forged on Barrel, Single Action, Top Break, 6 Shot, Antique	2,000	2,250	1,050
Model #3 Target, .32–44 S & W, 38–44 S & W, New Model #3, Single Action, Top Break, Curio	1,750	2,000	925
Target Models, For Target Hammer, Target Trigger, Target Stocks, Add $40.00–$75.00			
Target Models, For Target Hammer, Target Trigger, Target Stocks, Stocks, Add $45.00–$75.00			
Model 10, .38 Special, Double Action, Blue, Various Barrel Lengths, Swing–Out Cylinder, Modern	250	300	250
Model 10, .38 Special, Double Action, Swing–Out Cylinder, 4" Barrel, Heavy Barrel, Blue, Modern	300	350	275
Model 10, .38 Special, Double Action, Swing–Out Cylinder, 4" Barrel, Heavy Barrel, Nickel Plated, Modern	300	375	300
Model 10, .38 Special, Double Action, Swing–Out Cylinder, Various Barrel Lengths, Nickel Plated, Modern	275	325	275
Model 11 (.30/200), .38 S & W, Double Action, Swing–Out Cylinder, Modern	225	250	450
Model 12 (U.S.A.F. Model 13), .38 Special, Double Action, Swing–Out Cylinder, Lightweight, Modern	650	750	475
Model 12, .38 Special, Double Action, Swing–Out Cylinder, Various Barrel Lengths, Blue, Modern	225	250	350
Model 12, .38 Special, Double Action, Swing–Out Cylinder, Various Barrel Lengths, Nickel Plated, Modern	250	275	325
Model 14 SA, .38 Special, Single Action, Swing–Out Cylinder, 6" Barrel, Blue, Adjustable Sights, Modern	275	325	325
Model 14 SA, .38 Special, Single Action, Swing–Out Cylinder, 8 3/8" Barrel, Blue, Adjustable Sights, Modern	300	350	325
Model 14, .38 Special, Double Action, Swing–Out Cylinder, 6" Barrel, Blue, Adjustable Sights, Modern	225	275	275
Model 14, .38 Special, Double Action, Swing–Out Cylinder, 8 3/8" Barrel, Blue, Adjustable Sights, Modern	250	300	300

	V.G.	Exc	Prior Edition
Model 15, .38 Special, Double Action, Swing–Out Cylinder, Various Barrel Lengths, Blue, Adjustable Sights, Modern........................	$275	$300	$275

S & W Model 15

	V.G.	Exc	Prior Edition
Model 15, .38 Special, Double Action, Swing–Out Cylinder, Various Barrel Lengths, Nickel Plated, Adjustable Sights, Modern..........	250	325	300
Model 16, .32 S & W Long, Double Action, Swing–Out Cylinder, Adjustable Sights, Target Pistol, Modern..	650	750	425
Model 17, .22 L.R.R.F., Double Action, Swing–Out Cylinder, 6" Barrel, Adjustable Sights, Blue, Modern...	250	300	325
Model 17, .22 L.R.R.F., Double Action, Swing–Out Cylinder, 8 3/8" Barrel, Adjustable Sights, Blue, Modern...	275	325	325
Model 18, .22 L.R.R.F., Double Action, Swing–Out Cylinder, 4" Barrel, Adjustable Sights, Blue, Modern..	250	300	300
Model 19, .357 Magnum, Double Action, Swing–Out Cylinder, Various Barrel Lengths, Adjustable Sights, Blue, Modern.........................	300	350	350
Model 19, .357 Magnum, Double Action, Swing–Out Cylinder, Various Barrel Lengths, Adjustable Sights, Nickel Plated, Modern..	275	325	325
Model 1917, .45 Auto–Rim, Double Action, Swing–Out Cylinder, Brazilian Contract, Curio..	350	400	550
Model 1917, .45 Auto–Rim, Double Action, Swing–Out Cylinder, Military, Moden..	500	550	425
Model 20, .38 Special, Double Action, Swing–Out Cylinder, Modern...	400	450	450
Model 21 "1950 Military," .44 Special, Double Action, Swing–Out Cylinder, Various Barrel Lengths, Moddern...	100	1,250	575
Model 22 "1950 . 45 Military," .45 Auto–Rim, Double Action, Swing–Out Cylinder, Modern...	600	650	450
Model 23, .38 Special, Double Action, Swing–Out Cylinder, Adjustable Sights, Target Pistol, Modern...	475	525	525

	V.G.	Exc	Prior Edition
Model 24, .44 Special, Double Action, Swing–Out Cylinder, Various Barrel Lengths, Adjustable Sights, Modern.................................	$475	$525	$525
Model 25, .45 Auto–Rim, Double Action, Swing–Out Cylinder, Target Pistol, Blue, 125th Anniversary, Cased with Accessories, Modern........................	400	450	425
Model 25, .45 Auto–Rim, Double Action, Swing–Out Cylinder, Target Pistol, Blue, Modern........................	325	375	375
Model 26, .45 Auto–Rim, Double Action, Swing–Out Cylinder, Modern........................	600	700	550
Model 27 with Registration, .357 Magnum, Double Action, Swing–Out Cylinder, Pre–War, Adjustable Sights, Curio........................	1,500	1,750	1,250
Model 27, .357 Magnum, Double Action, 8 3/8" Barrel, Adjustable Sights, Cased with Accessories, Nickel Plated, Modern........................	400	475	400
Model 27, .357 Magnum, Double Action, 8 3/8" Barrel, Adjustable Sights, Cased with Accessories, Blue, Modern........................	400	450	400
Model 27, .357 Magnum, Double Action, Swing–Out Cylinder, Pre–War, Adjustable Sights, Curio........................	575	750	625
Model 27, .357 Magnum, Double Action, Swing–Out Cylinder, Various Barrel Lengths, Adjustable Sights, Blue, Modern........................	325	375	375
Model 27, .357 Magnum, Double Action, Swing–Out Cylinder, Nickel Plated, Modern........................	325	375	375
Model 27, .357 Magnum, Double Action, Swing Out Cylinder, 8 3/8" Barrel, Blue, Modern........................	375	400	375
Model 27, .357 Magnum, Double Action, Swing–Out Cylinder, 8 3/8" Barrel, Nickel Plated, Modern........................	375	450	375
Model 27, .357 Magnum, Double Action, Various Barrel Lengths, Adjustable Sights, Cased with Accessories, Blue, Modern........................	400	425	400
Model 27, .357 Magnum, Double Action, Various Barrel Lengths, Adjustable Sights, Cased with Accessories, Nickel Plated, Modern........................	350	425	400
Model 28, .357 Magnum, Double Action, Various Barrel Lengths, Adjustable Sights, Blue, Modern........................	250	300	300

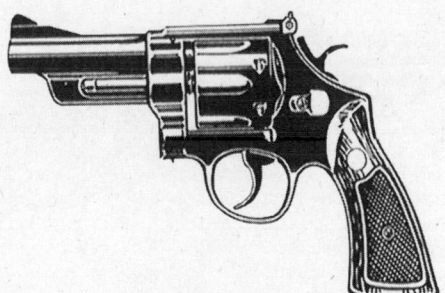

S & W Model 28

	V.G.	Exc	Prior Edition
Model 28, .357 Magnum, Double Action, Various Barrel Lengths, Target Grips, Adjustable Sights, Blue, Modern........................	250	300	300
Model 29, .44 Magnum, Double Action, 8 3/8" Barrel, Adjustable Sights, Swing–Out Cylinder, Blue, Modern........................	400	450	475
Model 29, .44 Magnum, Double Action, 8 3/8" Barrel, Adjustable Sights, Swing–Out Cylinder, Nickel Plated, Modern........................	400	475	450

	V.G.	Exc	Prior Edition
Model 29, .44 Magnum, Double Action, 8 3/8" Barrel, Adjustable Adjustable Sights, Cased with Accessories, Blue, Modern.......................	$425	$475	$475
Model 29, .44 Magnum, Double Action, 8 3/8" Barrel, Adjustable Adjustable Sights, Cased with Accessories, Nickel Plated, Modern.........	425	500	450
Model 29, .44 Magnum, Double Action, Various Barrel Lengths, Adjustable Sights, Swing–Out Cylinder, Blue, Modern...........................	375	425	425
Model 29, .44 Magnum, Double Action, Various Barrel Lengths, Adjustable Sights, Swing–Out Cylinder, Nickel Plated, Modern..............	375	425	425
Model 29, .44 Magnum, Double Action, Various Barrel Lengths, Adjustable Sights, Cased with Accessories, Blue, Modern.......................	400	450	450
Model 29, .44 Magnum, Double Action, Various Barrel Lengths, Adjustable Sights, Cased with Accessories, Nickel Plated, Modern..	400	475	450
Model 30, .32 S & W Long, Double Action, Swing–Out Cylinder, Modern..	300	350	350
Model 31, .32 S & W Long, Double Action, Swing–Out Cylinder, Various Barrel Lengths, Nickel Plated, Modern.......................................	250	300	375
Model 31, .32 S & W Long, Double Action, Swing–Out Cylinder, Various Barrel Lengths, Blue, Modern..	225	275	275
Model 32, .32 S & W, Double Action, Swing–Out Cylinder, 2" Barrel, Modern..	275	325	325
Model 33, .32 S & W, Double Action, Swing–Out Cylinder, Modern..	300	350	375
Model 34 "Kit Gun," .22 L.R.R.F., Double Action, Swing–Out Cylinder, Various Barrel Lengths, Adjustable Sights, Blue, Modern.......	275	325	325
Model 34 "Kit Gun," .22 L.R.R.F., Double Action, Swing–Out Cylinder, Various Barrel Lengths, Adjustable Sights, Nickel Plated, Modern...	300	350	275
Model 35, .22 L.R.R.F., Double Action, Swing–Out Cylinder, Target Pistol, Adjustable Sights, Modern...	325	375	375
Model 36, .38 Special, Double Action, Swing–Out Cylinder, Various Barrel Lengths, Blue, Modern..	225	275	275

S & W Model 36

Model 36, .38 Special, Double Action, Swing–Out Cylinder, Various Barrel Lengths, Nickel Plated, Modern.......................................	250	300	300

	V.G.	Exc	Prior Edition
Model 36, .38 Special, Double Action, Swing–Out Cylinder, 3" Barrel, Heavy Barrel, Blue, Modern......	$225	$275	$275
Model 36, .38 Special, Double Action, Swing–Out Cylinder, 3" Barrel, Heavy Barrel, Nickel Plated, Modern......	250	300	275
Model 37, .38 Special, Double Action, Swing–Out Cylinder, Various Barrel Lengths, Lightweight, Blue, Modern......	300	350	275
Model 37, .38 Special, Double Action, Swing–Out Cylinder, Various Barrel Lengths, Lightweight, Nickel Plated, Modern......	325	375	275
Model 38, .38 Special, Double Action, Swing–Out Cylinder, 2" Barrel, Hammer Shroud, Blue, Modern......	300	350	350

S & W Model 38

	V.G.	Exc	Prior Edition
Model 38, .38 Special, Swing–Out Cylinder, 2" Barrel, Hammer Shroud, Nickel Plated, Double Action, Modern......	275	325	325
Model 40, .38 Special, Double Action, Swing–Out Cylinder, Hammerless, Modern......	400	450	425
Model 42, .38 Special, Double Action, Swing–Out Cylinder, Hammerless, Lightweight, Modern......	275	300	550
Model 43, .22 L.R.R.F., Double Action, Swing–Out Cylinder, Adjustable Sights, Lightweight, Modern......	350	375	450
Model 45 USPO, .22 L.R.R.F., Double Action, Swing–Out Cylinder, Modern......	550	600	650
Model 45, .22 L.R.R.F., Double Action, Swing–Out Cylinder, Commercial, Modern......	450	500	850
Model 48, .22 WMR, Double Action, Swing–Out Cylinder, Various Barrel Lengths, Blue, Adjustable Sights, Modern......	325	350	250
Model 48, .22 WMR, Double Action, Swing–Out Cylinder, 8 3/8" Barrel, Blue, Adjustable Sights, Modern......	350	375	275
Model 49, .38 Special, Double Action, Swing–Out Cylinder, 2" Barrel, Hammer Shroud, Nickel Plated, Modern......	275	325	250
Model 49, .38 Special, Double Action, Swing–Out Cylinder, 2" Barrel, Hammer Shroud, Blue, Modern......	275	300	225

	V.G.	Exc	Prior Edition
Model 50, .38 Special, Double Action, Swing–Out Cylinder, Adjustable Sights, Modern...	$700	$775	$775
Model 51, .22 WMR Combo, Double Action, Swing–Out Cylinder Adjustable Sights, Modern..	300	350	475
Model 51, .22LR/.22 WMR Combo, Double Action, Swing–Out Cylinder, Adjustable Sights, Modern...	325	375	525
Model 53, .22 Rem. Jet, Double Action, Swing–Out Cylinder Adjustable Sights, Modern..	700	750	675
Model 53, .22 Rem. Jet, Double Action, Swing–Out Cylinder Adjustable Sights, Extra Cylnder, Modern...	750	800	725
Model 547, 9mm Luger, Double Action, Swing–Out Cylinder, Blue, Modern..	200	250	250

S & W Model 547

	V.G.	Exc	Prior Edition
Model 56, .38 Special, Double Action, Swing–Out Cylinder 2" Barrel, Adjustable Sights, Modern...	700	750	925
Model 57, .41 Magnum, Double Action, Swing–Out Cylinder Various Barrel Lengths, Blue, Adjustable Sights, Modern.........................	275	325	325
Model 57, .41 Magnum, Double Action, Swing–Out Cylinder Various Barrel Lengths, Nickel Plated, Adjustable Sights, Modern...	300	350	350
Model 57, .41 Magnum, Double Action, Swing–Out Cylinder 8 3/8" Barrel, Blue, Adjustable Sights, Modern......................................	300	350	350
Model 57, .41 Magnum, Double Action, Swing–Out Cylinder 8 3/8" Barrel, Nickel Plated, Adjustable Sights, Modern.........................	325	375	375
Model 57, .41 Magnum, Double Action, Swing–Out Cylinder Various Barrel Lengths, Blue, Cased with Accessories, Modern..............	300	350	350
Model 57, .41 Magnum, Double Action, Swing–Out Cylinder Various Barrel Lengths, Nickel Plated, Cased with Accessories, Modern...	325	375	375
Model 57, .41 Magnum, Double Action, Swing–Out Cylinder 8 3/8" Barrel, Blue, Cased with Accessories, Modern............................	325	375	375

	V.G.	Exc	Prior Edition
Model 57, .41 Magnum, Double Action, Swing–Out Cylinder 8 3/8" Barrel, Blue, Cased with Accessories, Modern..............................	$325	$375	$375
Model 58, .41 Magnum, Double Action, Swing–Out Cylinder 4" Barrel, Blue, Modern..........	250	300	300
Model 58, .41 Magnum, Double Action, Swing–Out Cylinder 4" Barrel, Nickel Plated, Modern........	275	325	325
Model 581, .357 Magnum, Double Action, Swing–Out Cylinder Blue, Modern........	175	200	225
Model 581, .357 Magnum, Double Action, Swing–Out Cylinder Nickel, Modern........	175	225	225
Model 586, .357 Magnum, Double Action, Swing–Out Cylinder Blue, Adjustable Sights, Modern........	275	325	275

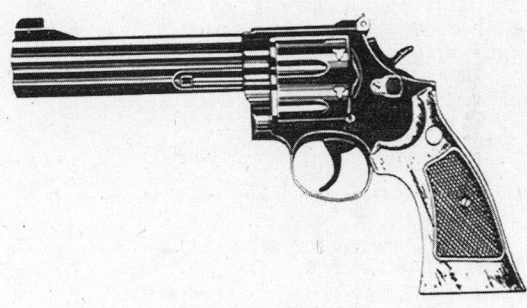

S & W Model 586

Model 586, .357 Magnum, Double Action, Swing–Out Cylinder Nickel, Adjustable Sights, Modern........	300	350	275

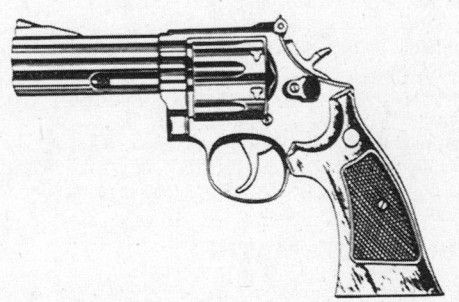

S & W Model 586 Stainless

Model 60, .38 Special, Double Action, Swing–Out Cylinder Stainless Steel, Adjustable Sights, Modern........	450	500	950
Model 60, .38 Special, Double Action, Swing–Out Cylinder Stainless Steel, 2" Barrel, Modern........	200	250	300
Model 60, .38 Special, Double Action, Swing–Out Cylinder High Polish Stainless Steel, 2" Barrel, Modern........	225	300	375

	V.G.	Exc	Prior Edition
Model 629, .44 Magnum, Double Action, Swing–Out Cylinder Stainless Steel, Adjustable Sights, Modern...	$375	$425	$475
Model 629, .44 Magnum, Double Action, Swing–Out Cylinder 8 3/8" Barrel, Stainless Steel, Adjustable Sights, Modern.........................	400	450	475
Model 63, .22 L.R.R.F., Double Action, Swing–Out Cylinder, Stainless Steel, 4" Barrel, Adjustable Sights, Modern..............................	250	300	300
Model 64, .38 Special, Double Action, Swing–Out Cylinder Stainless Steel, Various Barrel Lengths, Modern......................................	225	275	275
Model 649 Bodyguard, .38 Special, J Frame, 5 Shot, Stainless Steel, Modern..	300	325	375
Model 65, .357 Magnum, Double Action, Swing–Out Cylinder Stainless Steel, 4" Barrel, Heavy Barrel, Modern..............................	225	275	275
Model 650, .22 W.M.R., Double Action, Swing–Out Cylinder, Stainless Steel, Modern...	200	225	250
Model 651, .22 W.M.R., Double Action, Swing–Out Cylinder, Stainless Steel, Adjustable Sights, Modern...	200	250	325
Model 66, .357 Magnum, Double Action, Swing–Out Cylinder Stainless Steel, 2½"" Barrel, Modern..	300	350	350
Model 66, .357 Magnum, Double Action, Swing–Out Cylinder Stainless Steel, Various Barrel Lengths, Modern..................................	275	300	350
Model 67, .38 Special, Double Action, Swing–Out Cylinder Stainless Steel, 4" Barrel, Modern...	250	275	325
Model 681, .357 Magnum, Double Action, Swing–Out Cylinder Stainless Steel, Modern...	200	250	250
Model 686, .357 Magnum, Double Action, Swing–Out Cylinder Stainless Steel, Adjustable Sights, Modern...	225	275	275
Model M Head Ejector, .22 Long R.F., 1st Model Ladysmith, Solid Frame, Swing–Out Cylinder, Double Action, Curio......................	1,250	1,500	875
Model M Head Ejector, .22 Long R.F., 2nd Model Ladysmith, Solid Frame, Swing–Out Cylinder, Double Action, Curio......................	1,000	1,250	750
Model M Head Ejector, .22 Long R.F., 3rd Model Ladysmith, Solid Frame, Swing–Out Cylinder, Double Action, Curio......................	750	1,000	725
Model M Head Ejector, .22 Long R.F., 3rd Model Ladysmith, Solid Frame, Swing–Out Cylinder, Double Action, 2 ¼" & 6" Barrel, Curio...	1,250	1,500	975
Second Model Schofield, .45 S & W, Knurled Latch, Top Break, Single Action, Military, Antique..	4,000	4,500	4,000
Second Model Schofield, .45 S & W, Knurled Latch, Top Break, Single Action, Commercial, Antique..	4,250	4,750	1,850
Second Model Schofield, .45 S & W, Wells Fargo, Knurled Latch, Top Break, Single Action, Antique..	3,000	3,250	1,375
Victory, .38 Special Military & Police, Solid Frame, Swing–Out Cylinder, Double Action, Military, Modern..	200	250	250

HANDGUN, SEMI-AUTOMATIC

	V.G.	Exc	Prior Edition
.32 ACP, Blue, Curio...	2,500	2,750	2,750

	V.G.	Exc	Prior Edition
.35 S & W Automatic, Blue, Curio..	$525	$600	$600

S & W .35 Automatic

.35 S & W Automatic, Early Model, Curio..	550	700	700
Model 39, 9mm Luger, Double Action, Blue, Modern..............................	275	325	325

S & W Model 39

Model 39, 9mm Luger, Double Action, Nickel Plated, Curio...................	275	350	375
Model 39, 9mm Luger, Double Action, Steel Frame, Curio.....................	850	950	950
Model 41, .22 L.R.R.F., Various Barrel Lengths, Modern........................	550	600	550
Model 41–1, .22 Short R.F., Various Barrel Lengths, Modern.................	525	575	750
Model 44, 9mm Luger, Single Action, Modern..			
Model 46, .22 L.R.R.F., Various Barrel Lengths, Modern.......................	425	500	500

	V.G.	Exc	Prior Edition
Model 52A, .38 Special, Blue, Modern..	$2,250	$2,500	$2,250

S & W Model 52

Model 59, 9mm Luger, Double Action, Blue, Modern..............................	325	375	375
Model 59, 9mm Luger, Double Action, Nickel Plated, Modern...............	325	425	425
Model 61 Escort, .22 L.R.R.F., Clip Fed, Blue, Modern..........................	225	275	275

S & W Model 61

Model 61 Escort, .22 L.R.R.F., Clip Fed, Nickel Plated, Modern............	250	300	300
Model 439, 9mm Luger, Double Action, Blue, Modern...........................	300	325	350
Model 439, 9mm Luger, Double Action, Nickel Plated, Modern.............	300	350	375
Model 459, 9mm Luger, Double Action, Blue, Modern...........................	325	375	375
Model 459, 9mm Luger, Double Action, Nickel Plated, Modern.............	350	400	400
Model 469, (12 Shot), 9mm Luger, Double Action, Blue, Modern.........	300	350	375
Model 539, 9mm Luger, Double Action, Blue, Modern...........................	325	375	375
Model 539, 9mm Luger, Double Action, Nickel Plated, Modern.............	350	400	400
Model 639, 9mm Luger, Double Action, Stainless, Modern....................	300	350	425

	V.G.	Exc	Prior Edition
Model 659, (12 Shot), 9mm Luger, Double Action, Stainless Steel, Modern	$300	$350	$425
Model 659, 9mm Luger, Double Action, Stainless, Modern	325	375	450

HANDGUN, SINGLESHOT

	V.G.	Exc	Prior Edition
Model 1891, .22 L.R.R.F., Target Pistol, Single Action, 1st Model, Various Barrel Lenghts, Antique	600	650	425
Model 1891, .22 L.R.R.F., Target Pistol, Single Action, 2nd Model, no Hand or Cylinder Stop, Curio	550	600	400
Model 1891 Set, Various Calibers, Extra Cylinder, Extra Barrel, Target Pistol, Single Action, 1st Model, Antique	825	900	825
Perfected, .22 L.R.R.F., Double Action, Top Break, Target Pistol, Modern	375	425	425
Perfected Olympic, .22 L.R.R.F., Double Action, Top Break, Tight Bore and Chamber, Target Pistol, Modern	700	750	750
Straight Line, .22 L.R.R.F., Cased, Curio	1,250	1,500	1,250

S & W Straight Line

RIFLE, BOLT ACTION

	V.G.	Exc	Prior Edition
Model 1500, Various Calibers, Monte Carlo Stock, Checkered Stock, Modern	200	250	250
Model 1500 Deluxe, Various Calibers, Monte Carlo Stock, Checkered Stock, Modern	225	275	275
Model 1500 Magnum, Various Calibers, Monte Carlo Stock, Checkered Stock, Modern	200	250	250
Model 1500 Varmint, Various Calibers, Monte Carlo Stock, Checkered Stock, Heavy Barrel, Modern	225	275	275
Model 1700 Classic, Various Calibers, Monte Carlo Stock, Checkered Stock, Clip Fed, Modern	275	325	325
Model A, Various Calibers, Monte Carlo Stock, Checkered Stock, Modern	275	325	325
Model B, Various Calibers, Monte Carlo Stock, Checkered Stock, Modern	225	275	275
Model C, Various Calibers, Sporting Rifle, Checkered Stock, Modern	225	275	275
Model D, Various Calibers, Mannlicher, Checkered Stock, Modern	325	375	375

	V.G.	Exc	Prior Edition
Model E, Various Calibers, Monte Carlo Stock, Mannlicher, Modern...........	$325	$375	$375

RIFLE, REVOLVER

Model 320, .320 S & W Rifle, Single Action, Top Break, 6 Shot, Adjustable Sights, Cased with Accessories, Antique....................	6,000	6,500	6,000

RIFLE, SEMI-AUTOMATIC

Light Rifle, MK I, 9mm Luger, Clip Fed, Carbine, Curio........	1,250	1,500	1,500
Light Rifle, MK II, 9mm Luger, Clip Fed, Carbine, Curio.....	1,500	2,000	2,000

SHOTGUN, SEMI-AUTOMATIC

Model 1000 Field, 12 Ga., Vent Rib, Modern..................	250	300	300

S & W Model 1000

Model 1000 Skeet, 12 Ga., Vent Rib, Modern................	300	350	350
Model 1000 Super 12, 12 Ga., Vent Rib, Modern..............	375	425	325
Model 1000 Trap, 12 Ga., Open Sights, Modern.............	450	500	325

SHOTGUN, SLIDE ACTION

Model 916 Eastfield, Various Gauges, Plain Barrel, Modern........	125	150	150
Model 916T Eastfield, Various Gauges, Plain Barrel, Modern........	150	175	125
Model 3000 Field, 12 Ga. 3", Vent Rib, Modern..............	250	275	275
Model 3000 Police, 12 Ga., Open Sights, Modern.............	225	250	250
Model 3000 Police, 12 Ga., Open Sights, Folding Stock, Modern..........	250	300	300
Model 3000 Slug, 12 Ga. 3", Open Sights, Modern............	250	300	275

SMITH, ANTHONY Northampton, Pa. 1770–1779. See Kentucky Rifles and Pistols.

SMITH, L. C. GUN CO. Syracuse, N.Y., 1877–1890. Manufactured after 1890 by Hunter Arms, and in 1948 became a division of Marlin.

SHOTGUN, DOUBLE BARREL, SIDE-BY-SIDE

Crown Grade, 12 Ga., Double Trigger, Checkered Stock, Curio...........	4,000	4,500	4,250
Crown Grade, Various Calibers, Sidelock, Double Trigger, Automatic Ejector, Fancy Engraving, Fancy Checkering, Curio..............	4,750	5,250	5,850
Crown Grade, Various Calibers, Sidelock, Single Selective Trigger, Automatic Ejector, Fancy Engraving, Fancy Checkering, Curio.........	5,000	5,500	6,250
Eagle Grade, 12 Ga., Double Trigger, Checkered Stock, Vent Rib, Curio..........	3,500	4,000	3,750

	V.G.	Exc	Prior Edition
Field Grade, Various Calibers, Sidelock, Double Trigger, Checkered Stock, Light Engraving, Curio..................................	$750	$900	$1,275

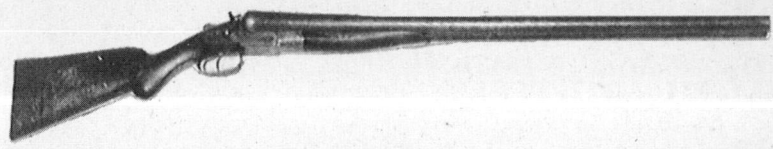

L.C. Smith Field Grade

	V.G.	Exc	Prior Edition
Field Grade, Various Calibers, Sidelock, Double Trigger, Automatic Ejector, Checkered Stock, Light Engraving, Curio..................	900	1,200	1,200
Field Grade, Various Calibers, Sidelock, Single Trigger, Checkered Stock, Light Engraving, Curio...	950	1,100	1,250
Field Grade, Various Calibers, Sidelock, Single Trigger, Automatic Ejector, Checkered Stock, Light Engraving, Curio..................	1,200	1,350	1,200
Ideal Grade, Various Calibers, Sidelock, Double Trigger, Checkered Stock, Engraved, Curio..	850	1,000	1,200
Ideal Grade, Various Calibers, Sidelock, Double Trigger, Automatic Ejector, Checkered Stock, Engraved, Curio...........................	1,150	1,300	1,400
Ideal Grade, Various Calibers, Sidelock, Single Selective Trigger, Checkered Stock, Engraved, Curio......................................	1,050	1,200	1,500
Ideal Grade, Various Calibers, Sidelock, Single Selective Trigger, Automatic Ejector, Engraved, Checkered Stock, Curio...............	1,300	1,450	1,550
Monogram Grade, Various Calibers, Sidelock, Single Selective Trigger, Automatic Ejector, Engraved, Checkered Stock, Curio.............	7,500	8,500	8,500
Skeet Grade, Various Calibers, Sidelock, Single Selective Trigger, Automatic Ejector, Engraved, Checkered Stock, Curio...........................	2,500	2,750	2,500
Skeet Grade, Various Calibers, Sidelock, Single Trigger, Automatic Ejector, Engraved, Checkered Stock, Curio...........................	2,750	3,000	1,750
Specialty Grade, Various Calibers, Sidelock, Double Trigger, Engraved, Checkered Stock, Curio...	2,250	2,500	2,500
Specialty Grade, Various Calibers, Sidelock, Single Selective Trigger, Automatic Ejector, Engraved, Checkered Stock, Curio...............	2,500	2,750	2,750
Trap Grade, 12 Ga., Sidelock, Single Selective Trigger, Automatic Ejector, Engraved, Checkered Stock, Curio............................	1,250	1,500	1,500

SHOTGUN, SINGLESHOT

	V.G.	Exc	Prior Edition
Crown Grade, 12 Ga., Trap Grade, Vent Rib, Automatic Ejector, Fancy Engraving, Fancy Checkering, Curio...	2,500	3,000	3,000
Olympic Grade, 12 Ga., Trap Grade, Vent Rib, Automatic Ejector, Engraved, Fancy Checkering, Curio...	1,250	1,500	1,500
Specialty Grade, 12 Ga., Trap Grade, Vent Rib, Automatic Ejector, Engraved, Fancy Checkering, Curio..	1,500	1,750	1,800

SMITH, OTIS A. Middlefield & Rockfall, Conn. 1873–1890.

HANDGUN, REVOLVER

	V.G.	Exc	Prior Edition
.22 Short R.F., 7 Shot, Spur Trigger, Solid Frame, Single Action, Antique..	200	250	250
.32 S & W, 5 Shot, Single Action, Top Break, Spur Trigger, Antique..	175	225	225

	V.G.	Exc	Prior Edition
.32 Short R.F., 5 Shot, Spur Trigger, Solid Frame, Single Action, Antique	$200	$250	$250
.38 Short R.F., 5 Shot, Spur Trigger, Solid Frame, Single Action, Antique	200	250	250
.41 Short R.F., 5 Shot, Spur Trigger, Solid Frame, Single Action, Antique	225	275	275

SMITH, STOEFFEL Pa. 1790–1800. See Kentucky Rifles and Pistols.

SMITH, THOMAS London, England, c. 1850.

RIFLE, PERCUSSION

16 Ga., Smoothbore, Anson–Deeley Lock, Octagon Barrel, Fancy Wood, Cased with Accessories, Antique	2,500	3,250	3,250

SMITH, WM. England.

HANDGUN, SEMI-AUTOMATIC

Pocket, 6.35mm, Clip Fed, 1906 Browning Type, Modern	375	450	450

SMOKER Made by Johnson Bye & Co. 1875–1884.

HANDGUN, REVOLVER

#1, .22 Short R.F., 7 Shot, Spur Trigger, Solid Frame, Single Action, Antique	150	175	175
#2, .32 Short R.F., 5 Shot, Spur Trigger, Solid Frame, Single Action, Antique	150	175	175
#3, .38 Short R.F., 5 Shot, Spur Trigger, Solid Frame, Single Action, Antique	150	175	175
#4, .41 Short R.F., 5 Shot, Spur Trigger, Solid Frame, Single Action, Antique	150	200	200

SNAPHAUNCE, EXAMPLE

HANDGUN, SNAPHAUNCE

.45 Italian Early 1700's, Holster Pistol, Half–Octagon Barrel, Engraved, Carved, High Quality, Furniture, Antique	2,000	2,500	2,500
Early 1800's Small, Plain, Antique	750	1,000	1,000
English Late 1500's, Ovoid Pommel, Engraved, Gold, Damascened, High Quality, Antique	15,000	20,000	20,000
Italian 1700's, High Quality, Belt Pistol, Light Ornamentation, Antique	2,500	3,000	3,000
Italian Early 1700's, Medium Quality, Brass Furniture, Plain, Antique	750	1,000	1,000

RIFLE, SNAPHAUNCE

Arabian, .59, Ornate, Inlaid with Silver, Ivory Buttstock Inlays, Antique	450	600	600
Italian Mid–1600's, Half–Octagon Barrel, Carved, Engraved, Silver Inlay, Steel Furniture, Ornate, Antique	7,500	10,000	10,000

	V.G.	Exc	Prior Edition

SODIA, FRANZ Ferlach, Austria

COMINATION WEAPON, MULTI-BARREL

Bochdrilling, Various Calibers, Fancy Wood, Fancy Checkering,
Fancy Engraving, Antique... $5,500 $6,500 $6,500
Doppelbuchse, Various Calibers, Fancy Wood, Fancy Checkering,
Fancy Engraving, Antique... 3,750 4,500 4,500
Over–Under Rifle, Various Calibers, Fancy Wood, Fancy
Checkering, Fancy Engraving, Antique...................................... 3,250 4,000 4,000

SOLER Ripoll, Spain, c. 1625.

HANDGUN, WHEEL-LOCK

Enclosed Mid–1600's, Ball Pommel, Ornate, Antique............................ 10,000 12,500 12,500

SOUTHERN ARMS CO. Made by Crescent for H. & D. Folsom, N.Y.C.

SHOTGUN, DOUBLE BARREL, SIDE-BY-SIDE

Various Gauges, Hammerless, Damascus Barrel, Modern...................... 150 175 175
Various Gauges, Hammerless, Steel Barrel, Modern.............................. 150 200 200
Various Gauges, Outside Hammers, Damascus Barrel, Modern............. 150 175 175
Various Gauges, Outside Hammers, Steel Barrel, Modern...................... 175 200 200

SHOTGUN, SINGLESHOT

Various Gauges, Hammer, Steel Barrel, Modern.................................... 75 100 100

SPAARMAN, ANDREAS Berlin, Germany, c. 1680.

RIFLE, FLINTLOCK

.72, Jaeger, Octagon Barrel, Swamped, Rifled, Iron Mounts,
Ornate, Set Trigger, Antique.. 3,500 4,000 4,000

SPANISH MILITARY Also see Astra, Star.

HANDGUN, SEMI-AUTOMATIC

Jo–Lo–Ar, 9mm Bergmann, Clip Fed, Military, Hammer, Curio............ 550 650 175

	V.G.	Exc	Prior Edition
M1913–16 Campo–Giro, 9mm Bergmann, Clip Fed, Military, Curio..	$425	$500	$175

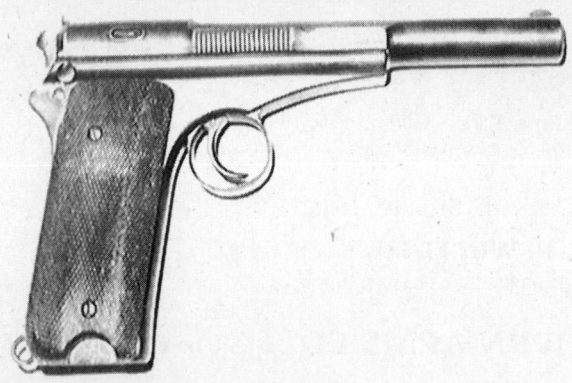

Spanish Military M1913–16

RIFLE, BOLT ACTION

Destroyer, 9mm Bayard Long, Clip Fed, Carbine, Modern.....................	150	175	100
M98 La Caruna, 8mm Mauser, Military, Curio..	150	175	75

RIFLE, SEMI-AUTOMATIC

CETME Sport, .308 Win., Clip Fed, Modern..	1,250	1,500	1,000

SPENCER ARMS CO. Windsor, Conn. 1886–1888.

SHOTGUN, SLIDE ACTION

Spencer, Roper, 12 Ga., Tube Feed, Antique..	350	400	400

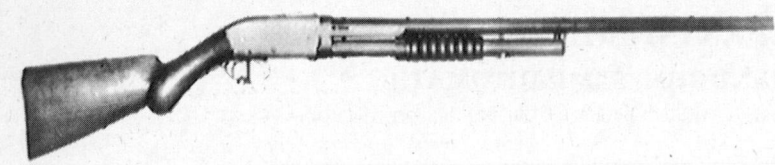

Spencer Roper

SPENCER GUN CO. Made by Crescent for Hibbard & Spencer Bartlett, c. 1900.

SHOTGUN, DOUBLE BARREL, SIDE-BY-SIDE

Various Gauges, Hammerless, Damascus Barrel, Modern......................	150	175	175
Various Gauges, Hammerless, Steel Barrel, Modern...............................	175	200	200
Various Gauges, Outside Hammers, Damascus Barrel, Modern.............	150	175	175

	V.G.	Exc	Prior Edition
Various Gauges, Outside Hammers, Steel Barrel, Modern......................	$175	$200	$200
SHOTGUN, SINGLESHOT			
Various Gauges, Hammer, Steel Barrel, Modern....................................	75	100	100

SPENCER SAFETY HAMMERLESS Made by Columbia Armory, Tenn., c. 1892.

HANDGUN, REVOLVER

.38 S & W, 5 Shot, Top Break, Hammerless, Double Action, Antique..	100	125	125

SPORTSMAN Made by Crescent for W. Bingham Co. Cleveland, Ohio, c. 1900.

SHOTGUN, DOUBLE BARREL, SIDE-BY-SIDE

Various Gauges, Hammerless, Damascus Barrel, Modern......................	125	150	150
Various Gauges, Hammerless, Steel Barrel, Modern..............................	150	175	175
Various Gauges, Outside Hammers, Damascus Barrel, Modern.............	125	150	150
Various Gauges, Outside Hammers, Steel Barrel, Modern......................	150	175	175

SHOTGUN, SINGLESHOT

Various Gauges, Hammer, Steel Barrel, Modern....................................	50	75	75

SPORTSMAN Made by Steven Arms.

SHOTGUN, DOUBLE BARREL, SIDE-BY-SIDE

M 315, Various Gauges, Hammerless, Steel Barrel, Antique....................	150	175	175

SHOTGUN, SINGLESHOT

Model 90, Various Gauges, Takedown, Automatic Ejector, Plain, Hammer, Antique...	50	75	75

SPRINGFIELD ARMORY Manufactured by Springfield, Inc. Genesco, Ill.

RIFLE, SEMI-AUTOMATIC

M1A Match, .308 Win., Clip Fed, Version of M–14, Modern.................	1,050	1,250	1,250
M1A Standard, .308 Win., Clip Fed, Version of M–14, Modern............	850	1,000	1,000
M1A Standard, .308 Win., Clip Fed, Version of M–14, Folding Stock, Modern..	950	1,100	1,100
M1A Super Match, .308 Win., Clip Fed, Version of M–14, Heavy Barrel, Modern..	1,250	1,500	1,450

SPRINGFIELD ARMS Made by Crescent, c. 1900.

SHOTGUN, DOUBLE BARREL, SIDE-BY-SIDE

Various Gauges, Hammerless, Damascus Barrel, Modern......................	150	175	175
Various Gauges, Hammerless, Steel Barrel, Modern..............................	175	200	200
Various Gauges, Outside Hammers, Damascus Barrel, Modern.............	150	175	175

	V.G.	Exc	Prior Edition
Various Gauges, Outside Hammers, Steel Barrel, Modern......................	$175	$200	$200

SHOTGUN, SINGLESHOT

Various Gauges, Hammer, Steel Barrel, Modern....................................	75	100	100

SPY Made by Norwich Falls Pistol Co., c. 1880.

HANDGUN, REVOLVER

.22 Short R.F., 7 Shot, Spur Trigger, Solid Frame, Single Action, Antique..	150	175	175

SQUARE DEAL Made by Crescent for Stratton–Warren Hdw. Co., Memphis, Tenn.

SHOTGUN, DOUBLE BARREL, SIDE-BY-SIDE

Various Gauges, Hammerless, Damascus Barrel, Curio..........................	150	175	175
Various Gauges, Hammerless, Steel Barrel, Curio....................................	175	200	200
Various Gauges, Outside Hammers, Damascus Barrel, Curio.................	150	175	175
Various Gauges, Outside Hammers, Steel Barrel, Curio..........................	175	200	200

SHOTGUN, SINGLESHOT

Various Gauges, Hammer, Steel Barrel, Curio..	75	100	100

SQUIBMAN Made by Squires, Bingham, Makati, Phillipines.

HANDGUN, REVOLVER

Model 100 D, .38 Spec., Double Action, Blue, Swing–Out Cylinder, Vent Rib, Modern..	100	125	125
Model 100 DC, .38 Spec., Double Action, Blue, Swing–Out Cylinder, Modern...	100	125	125
Thunder Chief, .38 Spec., Double Action, Blue, Swing–Out Cylinder, Vent Rib, Heavy Barrel, Modern.....................................	125	150	150

RIFLE, BOLT ACTION

M 14D, .22 L.R.R.F., Clip Fed, Checkered Stock, Modern....................	25	50	50
M 15, .22 WMR, Clip Fed, Checkered Stock, Modern.............................	50	75	75

RIFLE, SEMI-AUTOMATIC

M–16, .22 L.R.R.F., Clip Fed, Flash Hider, Modern..............................	50	75	75
M20D, .22 L.R.R.F., Clip Fed, Checkered Stock, Modern......................	50	75	75

SHOTGUN, SLIDE ACTION

M 30/28, 12 Ga., Plain, Modern..	75	100	100

ST. LOUIS ARMS CO. Belgium for Shapleigh Hardware Co., c. 1900.

SHOTGUN, DOUBLE BARREL, SIDE-BY-SIDE

Various Gauges, Hammerless, Damascus Barrel, Modern......................	150	175	175
Various Gauges, Hammerless, Steel Barrel, Modern...............................	150	200	200
Various Gauges, Outside Hammers, Damascus Barrel, Modern.............	150	175	175
Various Gauges, Outside Hammers, Steel Barrel, Modern......................	125	175	175

	V.G.	Exc	Prior Edition

SHOTGUN, SINGLESHOT

Various Gauges, Hammer, Steel Barrel, Modern...................................... $50 $75 $75

STAGGS–BILT Staggs Enterprises, Phoenix, Ariz., c. 1970.

COMBINATION WEAPON, OVER-UNDER

20 Ga./.30–30, Top Break, Hammerless, Double Triggers, Top
Break, Modern.. 100 125 125

STANDARD ARMS CO. Wilmington, Del., 1909–1911.

RIFLE, SEMI-AUTOMATIC

Model G, Various Calibers, Takedown, Tube Feed, Hammerless,
Curio... 400 450 450

RIFLE, SLIDE ACTION

Model M, Various Calibers, Takedown, Tube Feed, Hammerless,
Curio... 275 325 325

STANLEY Belgium, c. 1900.

SHOTGUN, DOUBLE BARREL, SIDE-BY-SIDE

Various Gauges, Hammerless, Damascus Barrel, Curio......................... 150 175 175
Various Gauges, Hammerless, Steel Barrel, Curio.................................. 175 200 200
Various Gauges, Outside Hammers, Damascus Barrel, Curio................ 150 175 175
Various Gauges, Outside Hammers, Steel Barrel, Curio......................... 175 200 200

SHOTGUN, SINGLESHOT

Various Gauges, Hammer, Steel Barrel, Curio.. 75 100 100

STANTON London, England, c. 1778.

HANDGUN, FLINTLOCK

.55 Officers, Belt Pistol, Screw Barrel, Box Lock, Brass,
Antique... 1,750 2,000 2,000

STAR Made by Bonifacio Echeverria, Eibar, Spain 1911 to date.

HANDGUN, SEMI-AUTOMATIC

Model A, .45 ACP, Clip Fed, Early Model, Adjustable Sights,
Various Barrel Lengths, Curio.. 275 300 275

	V.G.	Exc	Prior Edition
Model A, 7.63mm, Clip Fed, Curio..................	$250	$275	$250

Star Model A

	V.G.	Exc	Prior Edition
Model A, 9mm Bergmann, Clip Fed, Early Model, Adjustable Sights, Various Barrel Lengths, Curio.....................	175	225	225
Model A, 9mm, Clip Fed, Curio...................	250	275	250
Model A, Carbine, 7.63 Mauser, Clip Fed, Early Model, Adjustable Sights, Various Barrel Lengths, Stock Lug, Curio.	1,250	1,500	1,500
Model A, Various Calibers, Holster Stock, Add $250.00–$500.00			
Model AS, .38 Super, Clip Fed, Curio.............	200	250	250
Model B, 9mm Luger, Clip Fed, Curio.............	200	250	250
Model B, 9mm Luger, Clip Fed, German Military Marked, Modern...............	650	750	700
Model BKM, 9mm Luger, Clip Fed, Lightweight, Curio.............	225	275	275
Model BKS–Starlight, 9mm Luger, Clip Fed, Lightweight, Curio...............	225	250	300
Model BM, 9mm Luger, Clip Fed, Steel Frame, Curio.............	200	225	275
Model C, 9mm Browning Long, Clip Fed, 8 Shot, Curio.............	175	225	225
Model C O, 6.35mm, Clip Fed, Curio.............	150	200	200
Model C U, 6.35mm, Clip Fed, Lightweight, Curio.............	125	175	175
Model D, .380 ACP, Clip Fed, 15 Shot Clip, Curio.............	175	225	225
Model D, .380 ACP, Clip Fed, 6 Shot, Curio.............	150	200	200
Model DK, .380 ACP, Clip Fed, Lightweight, Curio.............	275	300	200
Model E Vest Pocket, .25 ACP, Clip Fed, Curio.............	150	200	200
Model F, .22 L.R.R.F., Clip Fed, Curio.............	125	175	175
Model F R S, .22 L.R.R.F., Clip Fed, Target Pistol, Adjustable Sights, Curio.............	175	200	225
Model F T B, .22 L.R.R.F., Clip Fed, Target Pistol, Curio.............	150	200	200
Model F–Olympic, .22 Short R.F., Clip Fed, Target Pistol, Curio.............	200	250	250
Model F–Sport, .22 L.R.R.F., Clip Fed, 6" Barrel, Curio.............	150	200	200
Model FR, .22 L.R.R.F., Clip Fed, Curio.............	125	175	175
Model H, 7.65mm, Clip Fed, 7 Shot, Curio.............	125	175	175
Model HF, .22 L.R.R.F., Clip Fed, Curio.............	150	200	200
Model HK Lancer, .22 L.R.R.F., Clip Fed, Lightweight, Curio.............	150	175	150
Model HN, .380 ACP, Clip Fed, Curio.............	150	175	175

	V.G.	Exc	Prior Edition
Model I, 7.65mm, Clip Fed, 9 Shot, Curio...	$200	$225	$150

Star Model 1 .32

Model IN, .380 ACP, Clip Fed, Curio..	225	275	275
Model M, .38 ACP, Clip Fed, Curio..	125	175	175
Model Military, 9mm, Clip Fed, Modern..	225	275	275
Model MMS, 7.63 Mauser, Clip Fed, Stock Lug, Curio........................	750	850	1,000
Model NZ, 6.35mm, Clip Fed, Curio...	375	450	450
Model P, .45 ACP, Clip Fed, Modern..	250	300	300
Model PD, .45 ACP, Clip Fed, Modern...	250	300	300
Model S, .380 ACP, Clip Fed, Modern..	175	200	250
Model S I, Modern...	200	225	250
Model SM, .380 ACP, Clip Fed, Modern...	200	250	250
Model Starfire, .380 ACP, Clip Fed, Lightweight, Modern..................	325	375	375
Model Starlet, 6.35mm, Clip Fed, Lightweight, Modern........................	225	250	275
Model Super A, .38 ACP, Clip Fed, Modern..	225	250	300
Model Super B, 9mm Luger, Clip Fed, Modern.....................................	200	225	300
Model Super P, .45 ACP, Clip Fed, Modern..	275	325	325
Model 28, 9mm Luger, Clip Fed, Modern..	300	350	350

RIFLE, SINGLESHOT

Rolling Block, Various Calibers, Carbine, Modern..................................	125	175	175

STAR GAUGE Spain, Imported by Interarms.

SHOTGUN, DOUBLE BARREL, SIDE-BY-SIDE

12 and 20 Gauges, Checkered Stock, Adjustable Choke, Double Trigger, Modern..	175	225	225

STARR ARMS CO. Yonkers and Binghamton, N.Y. 1860–1868.

HANDGUN, PERCUSSION

1858 Army, .44 Revolver, 6 Shot, 6" Barrel, Double Action, Antique...	550	650	650

	V.G.	Exc	Prior Edition
1858 Navy, .36 Revolver, 6 Shot, 6" Barrel, Double Action, Antique	$650	$750	$750
1862 Army, .44 Revolver, 6 Shot, 6" Barrel, Double Action, Antique	550	650	650

RIFLE, PERCUSSION

Carbine, .54, Underlever, Antique	700	850	850

RIFLE, SINGLESHOT

Carbine, .52 R.F., Underlever, Antique	800	950	950

STATE ARMS CO. Made by Crescent for J.H. Lau & Co., c. 1900.

SHOTGUN, DOUBLE BARREL, SIDE-BY-SIDE

Various Gauges, Hammerless, Damascus Barrel, Modern	125	175	175
Various Gauges, Hammerless, Steel Barrel, Modern	150	200	200
Various Gauges, Outside Hammers, Damascus Barrel, Modern	150	175	175
Various Gauges, Outside Hammers, Steel Barrel, Modern	150	200	200

SHOTGUN, SINGLESHOT

Various Gauges, Hammer, Steel Barrel, Modern	75	100	100

STEIGLEDER, ERNST Suhl & Berlin, Germany 1921–1935.

RIFLE, DOUBLE BARREL, SIDE-BY-SIDE

Various Calibers, Box Lock, Engraved, Checkered Stock, Color Case Hardened Frame, Modern	2,250	2,750	2,750

STENDA Stenda Werke Waffenfabrik, Suhl, Germany, c. 1920.

HANDGUN, SEMI-AUTOMATIC

7.65mm, Blue, Clip Fed, Curio	175	225	225

STERLING ARMS CO. Gasport and Lockport, N.Y.

HANDGUN, SEMI-AUTOMATIC

#283 Target 300, .22 L.R.R.F., Hammer, Adjustable Sights, Various Barrel Lengths, Modern	125	150	150
#284 Target 300, .22 L.R.R.F., Hammer, Adjustable Sights, Tapered Barrel, Modern	125	150	150
#285 Huskey, .22 L.R.R.F., Hammer, Heavy Barrel, Modern	100	125	125
#286 Trapper, .22 L.R.R.F., Hammer, Tapered Barrel, Modern	100	125	125
Model 300, .25 ACP, Blue, Modern	75	100	100
Model 300N, .25 ACP, Nickel Plated, Modern	75	100	100
Model 300S, .25 ACP, Stainless Steel, Modern	75	100	100
Model 302, .22 L.R.R.F., Blue, Modern	75	100	100
Model 302N, .22 L.R.R.F., Nickel Plated, Modern	75	100	100
Model 302S, .22 L.R.R.F., Stainless Steel, Modern	75	100	100
Model 400, .380 ACP, Blue, Clip Fed, Modern	200	225	150
Model 400N, .380 ACP, Nickel Plated, Clip Fed, Modern	225	250	150
Model 400S, .380 ACP, Stainless Steel, Clip Fed, Modern	250	275	175
Model 402, .22 L.R.R.F., Blue, Clip Fed, Modern	100	125	125
Model 402, .22 L.R.R.F., Nickel Plated, Clip Fed, Modern	100	125	125

	V.G.	Exc	Prior Edition
Model 402 MkII, .32 ACP, Blue, Clip Fed, Modern...............................	$125	$150	$150
Model 402 MkIIS, .32 ACP, Stainless Steel, Clip Fed, Modern.............	150	175	175
Model 450, .45 ACP, Clip Fed, Double Action, Adjustable Sights, Blue, Modern..	275	300	275
Model PPL, .380 ACP, Short Barrel, Clip Fed, Modern.........................	250	275	150

Sterling PPL

RIFLE, SINGLESHOT

Backpacker, .22 L.R.R.F., Takedown, Modern...	50	75	50

STERLING ARMS CORP. Made by Crescent for H. & D.
Folsom, c. 1900.

SHOTGUN, DOUBLE BARREL, SIDE-BY-SIDE

Various Gauges, Hammerless, Damascus Barrel, Modern.......................	150	175	175
Various Gauges, Hammerless, Steel Barrel, Modern..............................	175	200	200
Various Gauges, Outside Hammers, Damascus Barrel, Modern.............	150	175	175
Various Gauges, Outside Hammers, Steel Barrel, Modern.....................	175	200	200

SHOTGUN, SINGLESHOT

Various Gauges, Hammer, Steel Barrel, Modern.....................................	75	100	100

STERLING REVOLVERS c. 1880.

HANDGUN, REVOLVER

.22 Short R.F., 7 Shot, Spur Trigger, Solid Frame, Single Action, Antique...	150	175	175
.32 Short R.F., 5 Shot, Spur Trigger, Solid Frame, Single Action, Antique...	150	175	175

	Prior
V.G. Exc	Edition

STEVENS, J. ARMS & TOOL CO. Chicopee Falls, Mass.

1864–1886. Became J. Stevens Arms & Tool Co. in 1886, absorbed
Page–LewisArms Co., Davis–Warner Arms Co., and Crescent Firearms Co.
in 1926. Became a subsidiary of Savage in 1920. Also see the
Commemorative Section.

HANDGUN, SINGLESHOT

	V.G.	Exc	Prior Edition
1888 #1, Various Calibers, Tip–Up, Octagon Barrel, Open Rear Sight, Antique	$150	$175	$175
1888 #2 "Gallery," .22 L.R.R.F., Tip–Up, Octagon Barrel, Open Rear Sight, Antique	150	175	175
1888 #3 "Combined Sight," Various Calibers, Tip–Up, Octagon Barrel, Antique	150	175	175
1888 #4 "Combined Sight," .22 L.R.R.F., Tip–Up, Octagon Barrel, Antique	150	175	175
1888 #5 "Expert," Various Calibers, Tip–Up, Half Octagon Barrel, Antique	150	175	175
1894 "New Ideal," Various Calibers, Level Action, Falling Block, Vernier Sights, Antique	275	325	325
Model 10, .22 L.R.R.F., Tip–Up, Target, Various Barrel Lengths, Modern	150	175	175
Model 23 "Sure–Shot," .22 L.R.R.F., Side–Swing Barrel, Hammer, Antique	100	125	125
Model 34 "Hunters Pet," Various Rimfires, Tip–Up, Half–Octagon Barrel, with Shoulder Stock, Vernier Sights, Curio	450	500	500
Model 34 "Hunters Pet," Various Rimfires, Tip–Up, Octagon Barrel, with Shoulder Stock, Curio	400	450	450
Model 35 Target, .22 L.R.R.F., Tip–Up, Target, Ivory Grips, Various Barrel Lengths, Modern	325	350	400
Model 35 Target, .22 L.R.R.F., Tip–Up, Target, Various Barrel Lengths, Modern	275	300	350
Model 37 "Gould," Various Calibers, Tip–Up, Modern	250	300	300
Model 38 "Conlin," .22 L.R.R.F., Tip–Up, Modern	325	375	375
Model 40 New Model Pocket Rifle, Various Calibers, Tip–Up, with Shoulder Stock, Curio	400	450	450
Model 41, .22 L.R.R.F., Tip–Up, Pocket Pistol, Modern	275	300	175
Model 42 Reliable Pocket Rifle, .22 L.R.R.F., Tip–Up, with Shoulder Stock, Curio	250	300	300
Model 43 "Diamond," .22 L.R.R.F., Tip–Up, Spur Trigger, 6" Barrel, Octagon Barrel, Modern	175	200	200
Model 43 "Diamond," .22 L.R.R.F., Tip–Up, Spur Trigger, 10" Barrel, Octagon Barrel, Modern	200	225	225
Model 43 "Diamond," .22 L.R.R.F., Tip–Up, Spur Trigger, 6" Barrel, Globe Sights, Modern	200	225	225
Model 43 "Diamond," .22 L.R.R.F., Tip–Up, Spur Trigger, 10" Barrel, Globe Sights, Modern	225	275	275

RIFLE, BOLT ACTION

	V.G.	Exc	Prior Edition
Model 053 Buckhorn, Various Rimfires, Singleshot, Peep Sights, Modern	50	75	75
Model 056 Buckhorn, .22 L.R.R.F., 5 Shot Clip, Peep Sights, Modern	75	100	100

	V.G.	Exc	Prior Edition
Model 066 Buckhorn, .22 L.R.R.F., Tube Feed, Peep Sights, Modern	$75	$100	$100
Model 083, .22 L.R.R.F., Singleshot, Peep Sights, Takedown, Modern	50	75	75
Model 084, .22 L.R.R.F., 5 Shot Clip, Peep Sights, Takedown, Modern	50	75	75
Model 086, .22 L.R.R.F., Tube Feed, Takedown, Peep Sights, Modern	75	100	100
Model 15, .22 L.R.R.F., Singleshot, (Springfield), Modern	50	75	75
Model 15Y, .22 L.R.R.F., Singleshot, Modern	50	75	75
Model 322, .22 Hornet, Clip Fed, Carbine, Open Rear Sight, Modern	125	150	150
Model 322–S, .22 Hornet, Clip Fed, Carbine, Peep Sights, Modern	125	150	150
Model 325, .30–30 Win., Clip Fed, Carbine, Open Rear Sight, Modern	125	150	150
Model 325–S, .30–30 Win., Clip Fed, Carbine, Peep Sights, Modern	125	150	150
Model 416, .22 L.R.R.F., 5 Shot Clip, Peep Sights, Target Stock, Modern	200	225	225
Model 419, .22 L.R.R.F., Singleshot, Peep Sights, Modern	75	100	100
Model 48, .22 L.R.R.F., Singleshot, Takedown, Modern	50	75	75
Model 49, .22 L.R.R.F., Singleshot, Takedown, Modern	50	75	75
Model 50, .22 L.R.R.F., Singleshot, Takedown, Modern	50	75	75
Model 51, .22 L.R.R.F., Singleshot, Takedown, Modern	50	75	75
Model 52, .22 L.R.R.F., Singleshot, Takedown, Modern	50	75	75
Model 53, .22 L.R.R.F., Singleshot, Takedown, Modern	50	75	75
Model 56 Buckhorn, .22 L.R.R.F., 5 Shot Clip, Open Rear Sight, Modern	50	75	75
Model 65 "Little Krag," .22 L.R.R.F., Singleshot, Takedown, Modern	150	175	175
Model 66 Buckhorn, .22 L.R.R.F., Tube Feed, Open Rear Sight, Modern	50	75	75
Model 82, .22 L.R.R.F., Singleshot, Peep Sights, (Springfield), Modern	50	75	75
Model 83, .22 L.R.R.F., Singleshot, Open Rear Sight, Takedown, Modern	25	50	50
Model 84, .22 L.R.R.F., 5 Shot Clip, Open Rear Sight, Takedown, Modern	50	75	75
Model 86, .22 L.R.R.F., Tube Feed, Takedown, Open Rear Sight, Modern	50	75	75

RIFLE, LEVER ACTION

	V.G.	Exc	Prior Edition
Model 425, Various Calibers, Hammer, Curio	225	250	250
Model 430, Various Calibers, Hammer, Checkered Stock, Curio	250	300	300
Model 435, Various Calibers, Hammer, Light Engraving, Fancy Checkering, Curio	375	425	425
Model 440, Various Calibers, Hammer, Fancy Checkering, Fancy Engraving, Fancy Wood, Curio	800	950	950

COMBINATION WEAPON, OVER-UNDER

	V.G.	Exc	Prior Edition
Model 22–410, .22–.410 Ga., Hammer, Plastic Stock, Modern	75	100	100
Model 22–410, .22–.410 Ga., Hammer, Wood Stock, Modern	100	125	125

	V.G.	Exc	Prior Edition

RIFLE, SEMI-AUTOMATIC

	V.G.	Exc	Prior Edition
Model 057 Buckhorn, .22 L.R.R.F., 5 Shot Clip, Open Rear Sight, Modern	$75	$100	$100
Model 057 Buckhorn, .22 L.R.R.F., 5 Shot Clip, Peep Sights, Modern	75	100	100
Model 076 Buckhorn, .22 L.R.R.F., Peep Sights, Tube Feed, Modern	75	100	100
Model 085 Springfield, .22 L.R.R.F., 5 Shot Clip, Peep Sights, Modern	75	100	100
Model 76 Buckhorn, .22 L.R.R.F., Open Rear Sight, Tube Feed, Modern	75	100	100
Model 85 Springfield, .22 L.R.R.F., 5 Shot Clip, Open Rear Sight, Modern	75	100	100
Model 87, .22 L.R.R.F., Tube Feed, Open Rear Sight, Modern	75	100	100
Model 87-S, .22 L.R.R.F., Peep Sights, Tube Feed, Modern	75	100	100
Model 87K Scout, .22 L.R.R.F., Tube Feed, Open Rear Sight, Carbine, Modern	75	100	100

RIFLE, SINGLESHOT

	V.G.	Exc	Prior Edition
1888 #10 "Range," Various Calibers, Tip-Up, Half-Octagon Barrel, Fancy Wood, Vernier Sights, Antique	250	275	275
1888 #12 "Ladies," Various Calibers, Tip-Up, Half-Octagon Barrel, Open Rear Sight, Fancy Wood, Antique	375	325	325
1888 #13 "Ladies," Various Calibers, Tip-Up, Half-Octagon Barrel, Vernier Sights, Antique	225	275	275
1888 #14 "Ladies," Various Calibers, Tip-Up, Half-Octagon Barrel, Vernier Sights, Fancy Wood, Antique	275	325	325
1888 #15 "Crack Shot," Various Calibers, Tip-Up, Half-Octagon Barrel, Peep Sights, Antique	225	250	250
1888 #16 "Crack Shot," Various Calibers, Tip-Up, Half-Octagon Barrel, Peep Sights, Fancy Wood, Antique	250	275	275
1888 #22 "Ladies," Various Calibers, Tip-Up, Half-Octagon Barrel, Open Rear Sight, Antique	200	225	225
1888 #6 "Expert," Various Calibers, Tip-Up, Half-Octagon Barrel, Fancy Wood, Antique	200	225	225
1888 #7 "Premier," Various Calibers, Tip-Up, Half-Octagon Barrel, Globe Sights, Antique	175	225	225
1888 #8 "Premier," Various Calibers, Tip-Up, Half-Octagon Barrel, Fancy Wood, Globe Sights, Antique	225	275	275
1888 #9 "Range," Various Calibers, Tip-Up, Half-Octagon Barrel, Vernier Sights, Antique	175	225	225
Model 101 Featherweight, .44-40 WCF, Lever Action, Tip-Up, Smoothbore, Takedown, Half-Octagon Barrel, Modern	150	175	175
Model 101, with Extra 22 Barrel, 44-40 WCF, Lever Action, Tip-Up, Smoothbore, Takedown, Half-Octagon Barrel, Modern	225	250	250
Model 11 "Ladies," Various Rimfires, Tip-Up, Open Rear Sight, Modern	175	200	200
Model 12 "Marksman," Various Rimfires, Hammer, Lever Action, Tip-Up, Modern	150	175	175
Model 13 "Ladies," Various Rimfires, Tip-Up, Vernier Sights, Modern	175	200	200
Model 14 "Little Scout," .22 L.R.R.F., Hammer, Rolling Block, Curio	175	200	200
Model 14½ "Little Scout," .22 L.R.R.F., Hammer, Rolling Block, Modern	150	175	175

	V.G.	Exc	Prior Edition
Model 15 "Maynard Jr.," .22 L.R.R.F., Lever Action, Tip–Up, Modern	$125	$150	$150
Model 15½ "Maynard Jr.," .22 L.R.R.F., Lever Action, Tip–Up, Modern	125	150	150
Model 17, Various Rimfires, Lever Action, Takedown, Favorite, Open Rear Sight, Modern	150	175	175
Model 18, Various Rimfires, Lever Action, Takedown, Favorite, Vernier Sights, Modern	175	200	200
Model 19, Various Rimfires, Lever Action, Takedown, Favorite, Lyman Sights, Modern	150	175	175
Model 2, Various Rimfires, Tip–Up, Open Rear Sight, Modern	250	275	275
Model 20, Various Rimfires, Lever Action, Takedown, Favorite, Smoothbore, Curio	150	175	175
Model 26, Various Rimfires, Lever Action, Takedown, Open Rear Sight, Curio	150	175	175
Model 26½, Various Rimfires, Lever Action, Takedown, Smoothbore, Curio	150	175	175
Model 27, Various Rimfires, Lever Action, Takedown, Favorite, Octagon Barrel, Open Rear Sight, Modern	175	200	200
Model 28, Various Rimfires, Lever Action, Takedown, Favorite, Octagon Barrel, Vernier Sights, Modern	175	200	200
Model 29, Various Rimfires, Lever Action, Takedown, Favorite, Octagon Barrel, Lyman Sights, Modern	175	200	200
Model 404, .22 L.R.R.F., Hammer, Falling Block, Target Sights, Full–Stocked, Modern	475	525	525
Model 414 "Armory," .22 L.R.R.F., Lever Action, Lyman Sights, Modern	325	350	350
Model 417–0, Various Calibers, Lever Action, Walnut Hill, Modern	400	450	450
Model 417–1, Various Calibers, Lever Action, Lyman Sights, Walnut Hill, Modern	400	450	450
Model 417–2, Various Calibers, Lever Action, Vernier Sights, Walnut Hill, Modern	450	500	500
Model 417–3, Various Calibers, Lever Action, no Sights, Walnut Hill, Modern	425	475	475
Model 417½, Various Calibers, Lever Action, Walnut Hill, Modern	400	450	450
Model 418, .22 L.R.R.F., Lever Action, Takedown, Walnut Hill, Modern	300	325	325
Model 418½, Various Rimfires, Lever Action, Takedown, Walnut Hill, Modern	275	300	300
Model 44 "Ideal," Various Calibers, Lever Action, Rolling Block, Modern	325	350	350
Model 44½ "Ideal," Various Calibers, Lever Action, Falling Block, Modern	375	425	425
Model 49 "Ideal," Various Calibers, Walnut Hill, Lever Action, Falling Block, Engraved, Fancy Checkering, Modern	825	900	900
Model 5, Various Rimfires, Tip–Up, Vernier Sights, Modern	225	250	250
Model 51 "Pope," Various Calibers, Schutzen Rifle, Lever Action, Falling Block, Engraved, Fancy Checkering, Modern	775	825	825
Model 52 "Pope Jr," Various Calibers, Schutzen Rifle, Lever Action, Falling Block, Engraved, Fancy Checkering, Modern	750	825	825
Model 54 "Pope," Various Calibers, Schutzen Rifle, Lever Action, Falling Block, Fancy Engraving, Fancy Checkering, Modern	850	950	950

	V.G.	Exc	Prior Edition
Model 56 "Pope Ladies," Various Calibers, Schutzen Rifle, Lever Action, Falling Block, Fancy Checkering, Modern...................................	$425	$450	·$450
Model 7 "Swiss Butt," Various Rimfires, Tip–Up, Vernier Sights, Modern..	250	275	275

RIFLE, SLIDE ACTION

	V.G.	Exc	Prior Edition
Model 70, .22 L.R.R.F., Hammer, Solid Frame, Modern.........................	175	200	200
Model 71, .22 L.R.R.F., Hammer, Solid Frame, Modern.........................	200	225	225
Model 75, .22 L.R.R.F., Tube Feed, Hammerless, Modern......................	200	225	225
Model 80, Various Rimfires, Tube Feed, Takedown, Modern..................	150	175	175

SHOTGUN, BOLT ACTION

	V.G.	Exc	Prior Edition
Model 237, 20 Ga., Takedown, Singleshot, (Springfield), Modern..	25	50	50
Model 258, 20 Ga., Takedown, Clip Fed, Modern.............................	50	75	75
Model 37, 410 Ga., Takedown, Singleshot, (Springfield), Modern..........	50	75	75
Model 38, 410 Ga., Takedown, Clip Fed, (Springfield), Modern.............	50	75	75
Model 39, 410 Ga., Takedown, Tube Feed, (Springfield), Modern..........	50	75	75
Model 58, 410 Ga., Takedown, Clip Fed, Modern..................................	50	75	75
Model 59, 410 Ga., Takedown, Tube Feed, Modern..............................	50	75	75

SHOTGUN, DOUBLE BARREL, OVER-UNDER

	V.G.	Exc	Prior Edition
Model 240, .410 Ga., Hammer, Plastic Stock, Modern...........................	175	200	200
Model 240, .410 Ga., Hammer, Wood Stock, Modern............................	200	225	225

SHOTGUN, DOUBLE BARREL, SIDE-BY-SIDE

	V.G.	Exc	Prior Edition
M 315, Various Gauges, Hammerless, Steel Barrel, Modern....................	175	200	200
Model 215, 12 and 16 Gauges, Outside Hammers, Steel Barrel, Modern..	175	200	200
Model 235, Various Gauges, Outside Hammers, Checkered Stock, Steel Barrel, Modern..	150	175	175
Model 250, Various Gauges, Outside Hammers, Checkered Stock, Steel Barrel, Modern..	150	175	175
Model 255, 12 and 16 Gauges, Outside Hammers, Checkered Stock, Steel Barrel, Modern..	150	175	175
Model 260 "Twist," Various Gauges, Outside Hammers, Checkered Stock, Damascus Barrel, Modern..	150	175	175
Model 265 "Krupp," 12 and 16 Gauges, Outside Hammers, Checkered Stock, Steel Barrel, Modern...	175	200	200
Model 270 "Nitro," Various Gauges, Outside Hammers, Checkered Stock, Damascus Barrel, Modern..	175	200	200
Model 311, Various Gauges, Hammerless, Steel Barrel, Modern............	200	225	225
Model 311–R Guard Gun, 12 or 20 Gauge, Double Trigger, 18½" Bore, Solid Rib, Modern...	250	300	300
Model 311 ST, Various Gauges, Hammerless, Steel Barrel, Single Trigger, Modern...	200	225	225
Model 3151, Various Gauges, Hammerless, Recoil Pad, Front and Rear Bead Sights, Modern...	200	225	225
Model 330, Various Gauges, Hammerless, Checkered Stock, Modern..	175	200	200
Model 335, 12 and 16 Gauges, Hammerless, Steel Barrel, Checkered Stock, Double Trigger, Modern..	175	200	200
Model 345, 20 Ga., Hammerless, Checkered Stock, Steel Barrel, Double Trigger, MOdern...	175	200	200
Model 355, 12 and 16 Gauges, Hammerless, Steel Barrel, Checkered Stock, Double Trigger, Modern..	175	200	200

	V.G.	Exc	Prior Edition
Model 365 "Krupp," 12 and 16 Gauges, Hammerless, Checkered Stock, Steel Barrel, Double Trigger, Modern	$175	$200	$200
Model 375 "Krupp," 12 and 16 Gauges, Hammerless, Light Engraving, Fancy Checkering, Double Trigger, Steel Barrel, Modern	200	225	225
Model 385 "Krupp," 12 and 16 Gauges, Hammerless, Fancy Engraving, Fancy Checkering, Double Trigger, Steel Barrel, Modern	225	250	250
Model 515, Various Gauges, Hammerless, Modern	150	175	175
Model 5151, Various Gauges, Hammerless, Steel Barrel, Modern	175	200	200
Model 530, Various Gauges, Hammerless, Steel Barrel, Double Trigger, Modern	175	200	200
Model 530 ST, Various Gauges, Hammerless, Steel Barrel, Single Trigger, Modern	200	225	225
Model 530M, Various Gauges, Hammerless, Plastic Stock, Modern	150	175	175

SHOTGUN, PUMP

	V.G.	Exc	Prior Edition
Model 520, 12 Ga., Takedown, Modern	150	175	175
Model 620, Various Gauges, Takedown, Modern	150	175	175

SHOTGUN, SEMI-AUTOMATIC

	V.G.	Exc	Prior Edition
Model 124, 12 Ga., Plastic Stock, Modern	125	150	150

SHOTGUN, SINGLESHOT

	V.G.	Exc	Prior Edition
Various Gauges, Hammer, Automatic Ejector, Modern	50	75	75
Various Gauges, Hammer, Automatic Ejector, Raised Matted Rib, Modern	75	100	100
1888 "New Style," Various Gauges, Tip–Up, Hammer, Damascus Barrel, Antique	200	275	275
Model 100, Various Gauges, Selective Ejector, Hammer, Modern	50	75	75
Model 102, .410 Ga., Hammer, Featherweight, Modern	50	75	75
Model 102, 24, 28 and 32 Gauges, Hammer, Featherweight, Modern	50	75	75
Model 104, .410 Ga., Hammer, Featherweight, Automatic Ejector, Modern	50	75	75
Model 104, 24, 28 and 32 Gauges, Hammer, Automatic Ejector, Featherweight, Modern	50	75	75
Model 105, 20 Ga., Hammer, Modern	50	75	75
Model 105, 28 Ga., Hammer, Modern	50	75	75
Model 106, .32 Ga., Hammer, Modern	50	75	75
Model 106, .410 Ga. 2½", Hammer, Modern	50	75	75
Model 106, .44–40 WCF., Hammer, Smoothbore, Modern	50	75	75
Model 107, Various Gauges, Hammer, Automatic Ejector, Modern	50	75	75
Model 108, .32 Ga., Hammer, Automatic Ejector, Modern	50	75	75
Model 108, .410 Ga. 2½", Hammer, Automatic Ejector, Modern	50	75	75
Model 108, .44–40 WCF., Hammer, Automatic Ejector, Smoothbore, Modern	50	75	75
Model 110, Various Gauges, Selective Ejector, Checkered Stock, Hammer, Modern	50	75	75
Model 120, Various Gauges, Selective Ejector, Fancy Checkering, Hammer, Modern	50	75	75

	V.G.	Exc	Prior Edition
Model 125 Ladies, .20 Ga., Automatic Ejector, Hammer, Modern..............	$50	$75	$75
Model 125 Ladies, .28 Ga., Automatic Ejector, Hammer, Modern..............	50	75	75
Model 140, Various Gauges, Selective Ejector, Hammerless, Checkered Stock, Modern..............	50	75	75
Model 160, Various Gauges, Hammer, Modern..............	50	75	75
Model 165, Various Gauges, Automatic Ejector, Hammer, Modern..............	50	75	75
Model 170, Various Gauges, Automatic Ejector, Hammer, Checkered Stock, Modern..............	50	75	75
Model 180, Various Gauges, Hammerless, Automatic Ejector, Checkered Stock, Round Barrel, Modern..............	75	100	100
Model 182, 12 Ga., Hammerless, Automatic Ejector, Light Engraving, Checkered Stock, Trap Grade, Modern..............	125	150	150
Model 185, 12 Ga., Hammerless, Automatic Ejector, Checkered Stock, Half–Octagon Barrel, Modern..............	125	150	150
Model 185, For 16 or 20 Gauge, Add 20%			
Model 185, For Damascus Barrel, Deduct 25%			
Model 190, 12 Ga., Hammerless, Automatic Ejector, Fancy Checkering, Light Engraving, Half–Octagon Barrel, Modern..............	175	200	200
Model 190, For 16 or 20 Gauge, Add 20%			
Model 190, For Damascus Barrel, Deduct 25%			
Model 195, 12 Ga., Hammerless, Automatic Ejector, Fancy Checkering, Fancy Engraving, Half–Octagon Barrel, Modern..............	300	325	325
Model 195, For 16 or 20 Gauge, Add 20%			
Model 195, For Damascus Barrel, Deduct 25%			
Model 89 Dreadnaught, Various Gauges, Hammer, Modern..............	50	75	75
Model 90, Various Gauges, Takedown, Automatic Ejector Plain, Hammer, Modern..............	50	75	75
Model 93, 12 and 16 Gauges, Hammer, Modern..............	50	75	75
Model 94, Various Gauges, Takedown, Automatic Ejector Plain, Hammer, Modern..............	50	75	75
Model 944, .410 Ga., Hammer, Automatic Ejector, (Springfield), Modern..............	50	75	75
Model 94A, Various Gauges, Hammer, Automatic Ejector, Modern..............	50	75	75
Model 94C, Various Gauges, Hammer, Automatic Ejector, Modern, Modern..............	50	75	75
Model 95, 12 and 16 Gauges, Modern..............	50	75	75
Model 958, .410 Ga., Automatic Ejector, Hammer, Modern..............	50	75	75
Model 958, 38 Ga., Automatic Ejector, Hammer, Modern..............	50	75	75
Model 97, 12 and 16 Gauges, Hammer, Automatic Ejector, Modern..............	25	50	50
Model 970, 12 Gauge, Hammer, Automatic Ejector, Checkered Stock, Half–Octagon Barrel, Modern..............	50	75	75

SHOTGUN, SLIDE ACTION

	V.G.	Exc	Prior Edition
Model 520, 12 Ga., Takedown, Modern..............	150	175	175
Model 522, 12 Ga., Trap Grade, Takedown, Raised Matted Rib, Modern..............	150	175	175
Model 620, Various Gauges, Takedown, Modern..............	250	275	175
Model 621, Various Gauges, Hammerless, Checkered Stock, Raised Mtted Rib, Takedown, Modern..............	150	175	175

	V.G.	Exc	Prior Edition
Model 67, Various Gauges, Hammerless, Solid Frame, (Springfield), Modern..............	$150	$175	$150
Model 67–VR, Various Gauges, Hammerless, Solid Frame, Vent Rib, (Springfield), Modern........	175	200	150
Model 77, 12 and 16 Gauges, Hammerless, Solid Frame, Modern...........	150	175	175
Model 77, For Vent Rib, Add $10.00–$15.00			
Model 77, Various Gauges, Hammerless, Solid Frame, Modern.............	150	175	150
Mode 77 S C, 12 and 16 Gauges, Hammerless, Solid Frame, Recoil Pad, Adjustable Choke, Modern........	150	175	175
Model 77–AC , Various Gauges, Hammerless, Solid Frame, Adjustable Choke, Modern.........	125	150	150
Model 77–M, 12 Ga., Hammerless, Solid Frame, Adjustable Choke, Modern........	125	150	150
Model 820, 12 Ga., Hammerless, Solid Frame, Modern..........	125	150	150

STEVENS, JAMES

SHOTGUN, PERCUSSION

	V.G.	Exc	Prior Edition
14 Ga., Double Barrel, Side by Side, Engraved, Light Ornamentation, Antique........	450	550	550

STEYR Since 1863 in Steyr, Austria as Werndl Co.; in 1869 became Oesterreichische Waffenfabrik Gesellschaft; after WW I became Steyr Werke; in 1934 became Steyr–Daimler–Puch. Also see German Military, Austrian Military, Mannlicher–Schoenauer.

HANDGUN, SEMI-AUTOMATIC

	V.G.	Exc	Prior Edition
Model 1901 Mannlicher, 7.63mm Mannlicher, Commercial, Curio........	700	750	750
Model 1905 Mannlicher, 7.63mm Mannlicher, Military, Curio.............	375	425	425
Model 1908, 7.65mm, Clip Fed, Tip–Up, Modern............	225	250	250
Model 1909, 6.35mm, Clip Fed, Tip–Up, Modern............	225	275	275
Model 1909, 7.65mm, Clip Fed, Tip–Up, Modern............	250	300	300
Model 1911, 9mm Steyr, Commercial, Curio........	350	400	400
Model 1912, 9mm Luger, Nazi–Proofed, Military, Curio.........	400	450	450
Model 1912, 9mm Steyr, Military, Curio.......	200	225	225
Model 1912 Roumanian, 9mm Steyr, Military, Curio...........	250	275	275
Model GB, 9mm Luger, Clip Fed, Double Action, Modern..........	400	450	450
Model SP, .32 ACP, Clip Fed, Double Action, Modern..........	525	575	350
Solohurn, .32 ACP, Clip Fed, Modern.......	200	225	225

	V.G.	Exc	Prior Edition

STOCK, FRANZ Franz Stock Maschinen u. Werkbaufabrik, Berlin Germany 1920–1940.

HANDGUN, SEMI-AUTOMATIC

6.35mm, Clip Fed, Modern.. $300 $325 $325

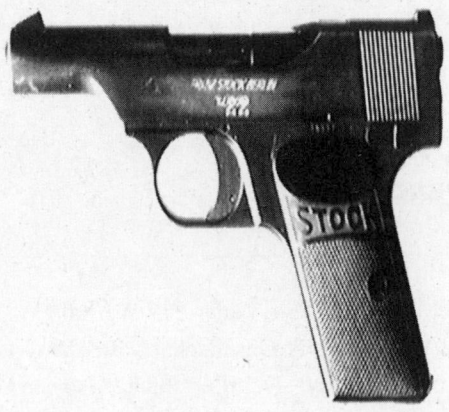

Franz Stock .22

7.65mm, Clip Fed, Modern.. 275 300 300

Franz Stock .25

	Prior
V.G. Exc	Edition

STOCKMAN, HANS Dresden, Germany 1590–1621.

HANDGUN, WHEEL-LOCK

Pair, Holster Pistol, Pear Pommel, Horn Inlays, Light
Ornamentation, Antique..$12,500 $15,000 $15,000

STOEGER, A.F. Stoeger Arms Corp., N.Y.C., now in South Hackensack, N.J. Also see Luger.

COMBINATION WEAPON, DRILLING

	V.G.	Exc	Prior Edition
Model 259, 3 Calibers, Side Barrel, Box Lock, Double Triggers, Checkered Stock, Modern	1,500	1,750	1,750
Model 297, Various Calibers, 2 Rifle Barrels, Box Lock, Double Triggers, Engraved, Checkered Stock, Modern	1,500	1,750	1,750
Model 300, Vierling, 4 Barrels, Box Lock, Double Triggers, Checkered Stock, Modern	1,500	2,000	2,000

COMBINATION WEAPON, OVER-UNDER

	V.G.	Exc	Prior Edition
Model 290, Various Calibers, Blitz System, Box Lock, Double Triggers, Engraved, Checkered Stock, Modern	1,250	1,500	1,500

SHOTGUN, DOUBLE BARREL, SIDE-BY-SIDE

	V.G.	Exc	Prior Edition
Victor Special, 12 Ga., Checkered Stock, Double Triggers, Modern	175	200	200

SHOTGUN, SINGLESHOT

	V.G.	Exc	Prior Edition
Model 27 Trap, 12 Ga., Engraved, Vent Rib, Checkered Stock, Recoil Pad, Modern	700	750	750

STOSEL Retolaza Hermanos, Eibar, Spain.

HANDGUN, SEMI-AUTOMATIC

	V.G.	Exc	Prior Edition
Model 1913, 6.35mm, Clip Fed, Modern	125	150	150

STUART, JOHAN Edinburgh, Scotland 1701–1750.

HANDGUN, SNAPHAUNCE

	V.G.	Exc	Prior Edition
All Steel Highland, Engraved, Scroll Butt, Ball Trigger, Antique	7,500	10,000	10,000

	V.G.	Exc	Prior Edition

STURM, RUGER & CO Southport, Conn. 1946–Date. Also see
Commemorative section.

HANDGUN, PERCUSSION

Old Army, .44, Single Action, Blue, Adjustable Sights,
Reproduction, Antique.. $250 $300 $175

Ruger Old Army

Old Army, .44, Single Action, Stainless, Adjustable Sights,
Reproduction, Antique.. 325 375 250

HANDGUN, REVOLVER

Brass GripFrame, Add $20.00–$30.00
.22 L.R.R.F., Western Style, Single Action, Blue, Lightweight,
Early Model, Modern.. 275 325 325
Bearcat, .22 L.R.R.F., Western Style, Single Action, Blue, Brass
Gripframe, Modern... 200 250 250
Bearcat, .22 L.R.R.F., Western Style, Single Action, Blue,
Aluminum Gripframe, Early Model, Modern................................. 225 275 275
Bisley Single Six, Modern... 250 275 275
Bisley Single Six, .22 L.R., Modern.. 200 225 275
Blackhawk, .30 Carbine, Western Style, Single Action, Blue, New
Model, Modern... 250 300 300
Blackhawk, .30 Carbine, Western Style, Single Action, Blue,
Modern.. 275 325 325
Blackhawk, .357 Magnum, Modern... 225 250 250
Blackhawk, .357 Magnum, Western Style, Single Action, Blue,
New Model, Modern.. 200 250 300
Blackhawk, .357 Magnum, Western Style, Single Action, Blue,
Modern.. 275 325 325
Blackhawk, .357 Magnum, Western Style, Single Action, Blue,
Flat–Top Frame, Early Model, Modern.. 325 375 350
Blackhawk, .357 Magnum, Western Style, Single Action, Blue,
10" Barrel, Modern... 425 475 400
Blackhawk, .357 Magnum, Western Style, Single Action, Blue,
New Model, Modern.. 300 325 350
Blackhawk, .357 Magnum, Western Style, Single Action,
Stainless Steel, New Model, Modern.. 325 375 325

	V.G.	Exc	Prior Edition
Blackhawk, .357 Magnum/9mm Combo, Western Style, Single Action, Blue, New Model, Modern..	$275	$325	$325
Blackhawk, .357 Magnum/9mm Combo, Western Style, Single Action, Blue, Modern...	275	325	325
Blackhawk, .41 Magnum, Modern..	225	250	250
Blackhawk, .41 Magnum, Western Style, Single Action, Blue, New Model, Modern..	250	300	300
Blackhawk, .41 Magnum, Western Style, Single Action, Blue, Modern..	275	325	325
Blackhawk, .44 Magnum, Modern..	225	250	250
Blackhawk, .45 Colt, Modern..	225	250	250
Blackhawk, .45 Colt, Western Style, Single Action, Blue, Modern..	325	375	375
Blackhawk, .45 Colt, Western Style, Single Action, Blue, New Model, Modern...	275	325	325
Blackhawk, .45 Colt/.45 ACP Combo, Western Style, Single Action, New Model, Blue, Modern.....................................	300	350	350
Blackhawk, .45 Colt/.45 ACP Combo, Western Style, Single Action, Blue, Modern..	300	350	350
BP–7 Old Army Cap and Ball Revolver, .44 Black Powder, Blue Walnut Grip, Reproduction, Antique...................................	200	300	225
KBP–7Old Army Cap and Ball Revolver, .44 Black Powder, Stainless, Walnut Grip, Reproduction, Antique......................	225	375	275
KRH–35 Redhawk Double Action Revolver, .357 Magnum, Stainless, 7½" Barrel, Modern...	300	350	350
KRH–355 Redhawk Double Action Revolver, .357 Magnum, Stainless, 5½" Barrel, Modern...	300	350	350
KRH–41 Redhawk Double Action Revolver, .41 Magnum, Stainless, 7½" Barrel, Modern...	300	350	350
KRH–415 Redhawk Double Action Revolver, .41 Magnum, Stainless, 5½" Barrel, Modern...	300	350	350
Redhawk, .44 Magnum, Double Actin, Stainless, Interchangeable Sights, Swing–Out Cylinder, Modern..............................	275	325	325

Ruger Redhawk

Security–Six, .357 Magnum, Double Action, Swing–Out Cylinder, Stainless Steel, Adjustable Sights, Modern.............................	200	250	250
Security–Six, .357 Magnum, Double Action, Swing–Out Cylinder, Blue, Adjustable Sights, Modern..	175	225	225

	V.G.	Exc	Prior Edition
Service–Six, .357 Magnum, Double Action, Swing–Out Cylinder, Blue, Modern	$175	$200	$200
Service–Six, .357 Magnum, Double Action, Swing–Out Cylinder, Stainless Steel, Modern	200	225	225
Service–Six, .38 Spec., Double Action, Swing–Out Cylinder, Blue, Modern	175	200	200
Service–Six, .38 Spec., Double Action, Swing–Out Cylinder, Stainless Steel, Modern	175	225	225
Service–Six, 9mm Luger, Double Action, Swing–Out Cylinder, Blue, Modern	175	200	200
Service–Six, 9mm Luger, Double Action, Swing–Out Cylinder, Stainless Steel, Modern	200	225	225
Single–Six, .22 L.R.R.F., Western Style, Single Action, Blue, Engraved, Cased, Modern	2,500	3,500	3,500
Single–Six, .22 L.R.R.F., Western Style, Single Action, Blue, Flat Loading Gate, Early Model, Modern	300	350	350
Speed–Six, .357 Magnum, Double Action, Swing–Out Cylinder, Blue, Modern	175	200	200
Speed–Six, .357 Magnum, Double Action, Swing–Out Cylinder, Stainless Steel, Modern	200	250	250
Speed–Six, .38 Spec., Double Action, Swing–Out Cylinder, Blue, Modern	200	225	225
Speed–Six, .38 Spec., Double Action, Swing–Out Cylinder, Blue, Stainless Steel, Modern	225	250	250
Speed–Six, 9mm Luger, Double Action, Swing–Out Cylinder, Blue, Blue, Modern	175	200	200
Super Blackhawk, .44 Magnum, Western Style, Single Action, Blue, New Model, 10½" Barrel, Modern	275	325	325
Super Blackhawk, .44 Magnum, Western Style, Single Action, Blue, New Model, Modern	275	325	325
Super Blackhawk, .44 Magnum, Western Style, Single Action, Stainless, New Model, Modern	325	375	375
Super Blackhawk, .44 Magnum, Western Style, Single Action, Stainless, New Model, 10½" Bull Barrel, Modern	350	400	400
Super Blackhawk, .44 Magnum, Western Style, Single Action, Stainless, 10½" Barrel, New Model, Modern	350	400	400
Super Blackhawk, .44 Magnum, Western Style, Single Action, Blue, Modern	300	350	350
Super Blackhawk, .44 Magnum, Western Style, Single Action, Blue, Flat–Top Frame, Early Model, Modern	600	650	650
Super Blackhawk, .44 Magnum, Western Style, Single Action, Blue, 10" Barrel, Modern	625	675	675
Super Single Six, .22 LR/.22 WMR Combo, Western Style, Single Action, Blue, New Model, Modern	150	200	200
Super Single Six, .22 LR/.22 WMR Combo, Western Style, Single Action, Blue, New Model, 9½" Barrel, Modern	150	200	200
Super Single Six, .22 LR/.22 WMR Combo, Western Style, Single Action, Blue, Modern	175	225	225
Super Single Six, .22 LR/.22 WMR Combo, Western Style, Single Action, Blue, 9½" Barrel, Modern	200	250	250
Super Single Six, .22 LR/.22 WMR Combo, Western Style, Single Action, Stainless Steel, New Model, Modern	175	225	225

	V.G.	Exc	Prior Edition

HANDGUN, SEMI-AUTOMATIC

MK I, .22 L.R.R.F., Clip Fed, Adjustable Sights, Target Pistol,
Modern... $125 $175 $175

MK I, .22 L.R.R.F., Clip Fed, Adjustable Sights, Target Pistol,
Wood Grips, Modern.. 150 175 175

MK II, .22 L.R.R.F., Clip Fed, Adjustable Sights, Stainless,
Modern... 200 250 250

MK II, .22 L.R.R.F., Clip Fed, Adjustable Sights, Target Pistol,
Modern... 125 175 175

MK II, .22 L.R.R.F., Clip Fed, Adjustable Sights, Target Pistol,
Bull Barrel, Modern... 175 225 225

Ruger MK II Bull Barrel

MK II, .22 L.R.R.F., Clip Fed, Adjustable Sights, Target Pistol,
Bull Barrel, Stainless, Modern.. 225 275 275

Ruger MK II

MK II Standard, .22 L.R.R.F., Clip Fed, Fixed Sights, Stainless,
Modern... 200 250 250

	V.G.	Exc	Prior Edition
Standard, .22 L.R.R.F., Clip Fed, Modern...............................	$125	$150	$150
Standard (Under #25600), .22 L.R.R.F., Clip Fed, Early Model, Blue, Modern..	250	500	500
Standard MK II, .22 L.R.R.F., Clip Fed, Modern...................................	125	150	150

HANDGUN, SINGLESHOT

Hawkeye, .256 Win. Mag., Western Style, Single Action, Blue, Modern.............................	950	1,200	1,200

RIFLE, BOLT ACTION

M–77, for .338 Win. Mag., Add $15.00–$35.00
M–77, for .488 Win. Mag., Add $50.00–$75.00

M–77R, Various Calibers, Checkered Stock, Scope Mounts, no Sights, Modern........................	275	325	325
M–77RL, Various Calibers, Checkered Stock, Scope Mounts, Ultra Light, no Sights, Modern........................	275	325	325
M–77RS, Various Calibers, Checkered Stock, Open Rear Sight, Scope Mounts, Modern........................	300	350	350
M–77RS Tropical, .458 Win. Mag., Checkered Stock, Open Rear Sight, Scope Mounts, Modern........................	375	450	450
M-77RSI, Various Calibers, Checkered Stock, Open Rear Sight, Mannlicher Stock, Scope Mounts, Modern........................	325	375	375
M–77ST, Various Calibers, Checkered Stock, Open Rear Sight, Modern........................	275	325	325
M–77V, Various Calibers, Heavy Barrel, Varmint, no Sights, Scope Mounts, Checkered Stock, Modern........................	275	325	325

Ruger Model 77V

M–77/22R, .22 Caliber Rimfire, Detachable Ten Shot Magazine, Blue, Modern.............................	300	350	350

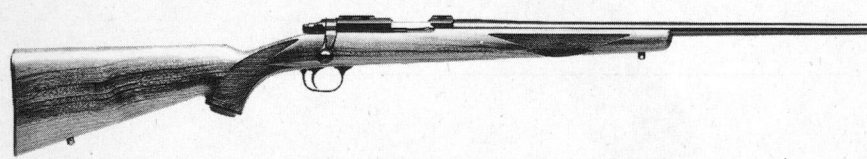

Ruger .22 Rimfire

M–77/22S, .22 Caliber Rimfire, Detachable Ten Shot Magazine, Blue, Modern.............................	300	350	350

	V.G.	Exc	Prior Edition

RIFLE, SEMI-AUTOMATIC

	V.G.	Exc	Prior Edition
10/22, .22 L.R.R.F., Clip Fed, Plain, Modern..	$100	$125	$125
10/22 Deluxe, .22 L.R.R.F., Clip Fed, Checkered Stock, Modern............	150	175	175
10/22 International, .22 L.R.R.F., Clip Fed, Full–Stocked, Modern..	325	375	375
10/22 Sporter I, .22 L.R.R.F., Clip Fed, Monte Carlo Stock, Modern..	125	150	150
10/22 Sporter II, .22 L.R.R.F., Clip Fed, Checkered Stock, Modern..	125	150	150
K Mini–14/20 GB, .223 Rem., Clip Fed, Carbine, with Flash Hider and Bayonet Stud, Folding Stock, Modern..	400	450	450
K Mini–14/20 GB–F, .223 Rem., Clip Fed, Carbine, Stainless, with Flash Hider and Bayonet Stud, Folding Stock, Modern............................	425	475	475
Mini–14, .223 Rem., Clip Fed, Carbine, Modern.......................................	300	350	350
Mini–14, .223 Rem., Clip Fed, Carbine, Stainless, Modern......................	325	375	375
Mini–14/20 GB, .223 Rem., Clip Fed, Carbine, with Flash Hider and Bayonet Stud, Modern...	300	350	350
Mini–14/20 GB–F, .223 Rem., Clip Fed, Carbine, Stainless, with Flash Hider and Bayonet Stud, Modern..	325	375	375
Model 44 Deluxe, .44 Magnum, Tube Feed, Plain, Peep Sights, Sling Swivels, Modern...	350	400	400
Model 44 International, .44 Magnum, Tube Feed, Full–Stocked, Modern..	500	550	550
Model 44 Sporter, .44 Magnum, Tube Feed, Monte Carlo Stock, Modern..	300	350	350
Model 44 Standard, .44 Magnum, Tube Feed, Plain, Open Rear Sight, Modern..	275	325	325

Ruger 44 Magnum Rifle

XGI, .308, Modern..	—	RARE	—

	V.G.	Exc	Prior Edition

RIFLE, SINGLESHOT

#1 International, Various Calibers, Open Rear Sight, Checkered
Mannlicher Stock, Modern... $425 $475 $475

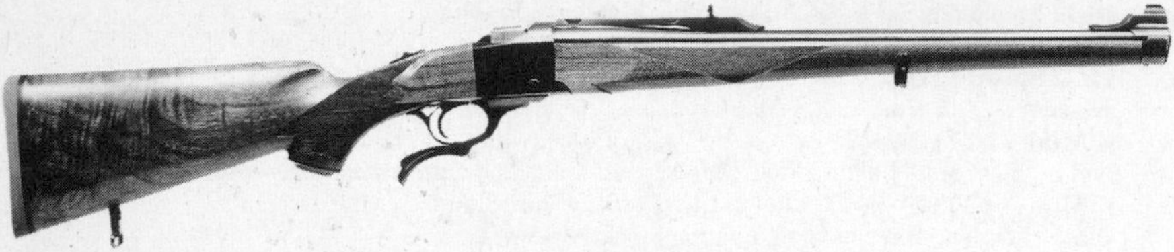

Ruger #1 International

#1 Light Sporter, Various Caliber, Open Rear Sight, Checkered
Stock, Modern.. 375 425 425
#1 Medium Sporter, Various Caliber, Open Rear Sight,
Checkered Stock, Modern.. 300 350 350
#1 Standard Sport, Various Calibers, no Sights, Scope
Mounts, Checkered Stock, Modern.. 300 350 350

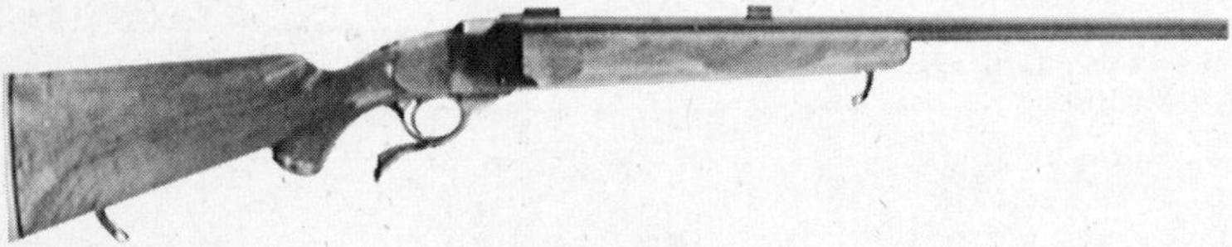

Ruger #1 Sporter

#1 Tropical, Various Calibers, Open Rear Sight, Checkered,
Modern.. 350 400 400

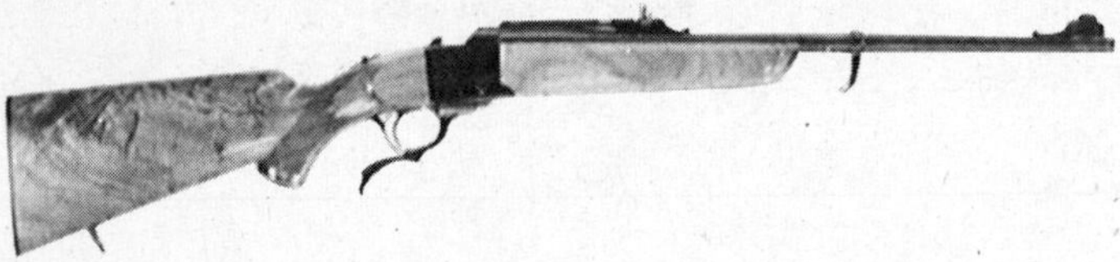

Ruger #1 Tropical

#1 Varminter, Various Calibers, Heavy Barrel, no Sights,
Checkered Stock, Modern.. 325 375 375

	V.G.	Exc	Prior Edition
#3 Carbine, Various Calibers, Open Rear Sight, Modern........................	$175	$200	$200

Ruger #3 Carbine

SHOTGUN, DOUBLE BARREL, OVER-UNDER

Red Label, 12 or 20 Gauges, Checkered Stock, Single Trigger, Modern...	600	675	675

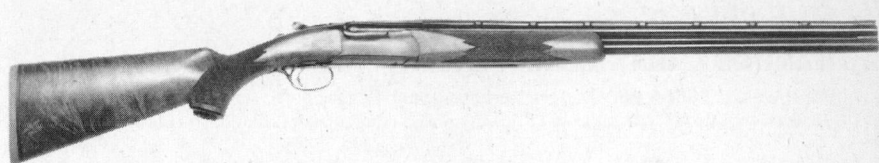

Ruger Red Label

SULLIVAN ARMS CO. Made by Crescent for Sullivan Hardware, Anderson, S.C., c. 1900.

SHOTGUN, DOUBLE BARREL, SIDE-BY-SIDE

Various Gauges, Hammerless, Damascus Barrel, Modern......................	150	175	175
Various Gauges, Hammerless, Steel Barrel, Modern..............................	175	200	200
Various Gauges, Outside Hammers, Damascus Barrel, Modern.............	150	175	175
Various Gauges, Outside Hammers, Steel Barrel, Modern......................	175	200	200

SHOTGUN, SINGLESHOT

Various Gauges, Hammer, Steel Barrel, Modern.....................................	75	100	100

SUPER DREADNAUGHT Made by Stevens Arms.

SHOTGUN, SINGLESHOT

Model 89 Dreadnaught, Various Gauges, Hammer, Modern..................	50	75	75

SUPER RANGE GOOSE Made by Stevens Arms.

RIFLE, SEMI-AUTOMATIC

Model 85 Springfield, .22 L.R.R.F., 5 Shot Clip, Open Rear Sight, Modern...	50	75	75

	V.G.	Exc	Prior Edition

SUTHERLAND, JAMES Edinburgh, Scotland, c. 1790.

HANDGUN, FLINTLOCK

.50, All Steel, Engraved, Ram's Horn Butt, Antique.................................. $2,500 $2,750 $2,750

SUTHERLAND, RAMSEY London and Birmingham, England, 1790–1827.

HANDGUN, FLINTLOCK

.67, George III, Calvary Pistol, Military, Tapered Round Barrel, Brass Furniture, Antique... 1,000 1,200 1,200

RIFLE, FLINTLOCK

.75, 3rd Model Brown Bess, Musket, Military, Antique............................ 1,250 1,500 1,500

SVENDSEN E. Svendsen, Itasca, Ill., c. 1965.

HANDGUN, MANUAL REPEATER

Four Aces, .22 Short, Four Barrels, Derringer, Spur Trigger, Modern.. 100 125 75

SWAMP ANGEL Made by Forehand & Wadsworth, Worcester, Mass., c. 1871.

HANDGUN, REVOLVER

.41 Short, 5 Shot, Spur Trigger, Solid Frame, Single Action, Antique.. 175 200 200

SWEDISH MILITARY

HANDGUN, REVOLVER

M1887 Husqvarna, 7.5mm, Double Action, Blue, Antique..................... 250 275 250

RIFLE, BOLT ACTION

M1896 Mauser, 6.5 X 55mm, Gustav, Curio.. 200 225 225

RIFLE, SINGLESHOT

M1867/89 Remington, 11.7mm, Full Stock, Antique.............................. 350 400 350

SWEITZER, DANIEL & CO. Lancaster, Pa. 1808–1814. See Kentucky Rifles.

SWIFT Made by Iver Johnson, Fitchburg, Mass. 1890–1900.

HANDGUN, REVOLVER

.38 S & W, 5 Shot, Double Action, Top Break, Curio................................ 75 100 100
.38 S & W, 5 Shot, Top Break, Hammerless, Double Action, Curio.. 75 100 100

	V.G.	Exc	Prior Edition

SWISS MILITARY

HANDGUN, REVOLVER

	V.G.	Exc	Prior Edition
M1872 Swiss Ordnance, 10.4mm R.F., Double Action, Blue, Military, Antique	$800	$850	$850
M1872/78 Swiss Ordnance, 10.4mm C.F., Double Action, Blue, Military, Antique	400	475	475
M1882 Swiss Ordnance, 7.5mm, Double Action, Blue, Military, Antique	150	200	200
M1882 Swiss Ordnance, 7.5mm, Double Action, Blue, Military, with Holster Stock and All Leather, Antique	1,250	1,500	1,500

RIFLE, BOLT ACTION

	V.G.	Exc	Prior Edition
Vetterli, Bern 1878, .41 Swiss R.F., Tube Feed, Military, Antique	200	225	175
Vetterli, Bern 1878/81, .41 Swiss R.F., Tube Feed, Military, Antique	175	200	200
Vetterli, Carbine, .41 Swiss R.F., Tube Feed, Military, Antique	575	650	450
M1893, 7.5 X 55 Swiss, Military, Curio	400	450	450
M 1889/1900, 7.5 X 55 Swiss, Short Rifle, Curio	400	450	450
M1889, 7.5 X 55 Swiss, Military, Modern	175	200	200
M1911 Schmidt Rubin, 7.5 X 55 Swiss, Clip Fed, Carbine, Military, Curio	125	150	150
M1911 Schmidt Rubin, 7.5 X 55 Swiss, Clip Fed, Military, Curio	100	125	125

RIFLE, PERCUSSION

	V.G.	Exc	Prior Edition
Federal Rifle, .41 Caliber, Full Stocked, Antique	750	850	850

T

	V.G.	Exc.	Prior Edition

T.A.C. Trocaola, Aranzabal y Cia., Eibar, Spain.

HANDGUN, REVOLVER

	V.G.	Exc.	Prior Edition
Modelo Militar, .44 Spec., S & W Triple Lock Copy, Double Action, Blue, Moden	$175	$225	$225
OP No.2 Mk I, .455 Eley, British, Double Action, Top Break, Curio	150	175	175
S & W Frontier Copy, .44 American, Double Action, Top Break, Blue, Modern	125	150	150
S & W M&P Copy,38 Spec., Double Action, Blue, Modern	75	100	100

TALLARES Tallares Armas Livianas Argentinas, Punta Alta, Argentina.

HANDGUN, SEMI-AUTOMATIC

	V.G.	Exc.	Prior Edition
T.A.L.A., .22 L.R.R.F., Clip Fed, Modern	125	150	150

TANARMI Made in Italy, Imported by Excam.

HANDGUN, REVOLVER

	V.G.	Exc.	Prior Edition
E-15, For Chrome, Add $5.00			
E-15, .22 L.R.R.F, Single Action, Western Style, Modern	25	50	50
E-15, .22LR/.22 WMR Combo, Single Action, Western Style, Modern	25	50	50
TA-22, For Chrome, Add $5.00			
TA-22, .22 L.R.R.F, Single Action, Western Style, Brass Grip Frame, Modern	25	50	50
TA-22, .22LR/.22 WMR Combo, Single Action, Western Style, Brass Grip Frame, Modern	50	75	75
TA-76, For Chrome, Add $5.00			
TA-76, .22 L.R.R.F, Single Action, Western Style, Modern	25	50	50
TA-76, .22LR/.22 WMR Combo, Single Action, Western Style, Modern	25	50	50

TANKE

HANDGUN, SEMI-AUTOMATIC

	V.G.	Exc.	Prior Edition
.25 ACP, Clip Fed, Modern	75	100	150

	V.G.	Exc	Prior Edition

TANNER Andrae Tanner, Werkstatte fur Praszisionswaffen, Fulenbach, Switzerland.

RIFLE, BOLT ACTION

300m Match, .308 Win., Offhand Target Rifle, Target Stock, Palm
Rest, Modern.. $3,500 $3,750 $4,000
50m Match, .22 L.R.R.F., Offhand Target Rifle, Target Stock,
Palm Rest, Modern.. 3,250 3,500 2,500
Hunting Match, Various Calibers, Checkered monte Carlo Stock,
Singleshot, Modern.. 2,500 2,750 2,750
Standard UIT, .308 Win., Repeater, Target Rifle, Monte Carlo
Target Stock, Modern... 3,250 3,500 3,500
Standard UIT, .308 Win., Singleshot, Target Rifle, Monte Carlo
Target Stock, Modern... 3,250 3,500 3,900

TANQUE Ojanguran y Vidosa, Eibar, Spain, c. 1930.

HANDGUN, SEMI-AUTOMATIC

6.35mm, Clip Fed, Modern.. 150 175 175

TARGA Guiseppi Tanfoglio, Gardone Val Trompia, Italy, imported by Excam.

HANDGUN, SEMI-AUTOMATIC

Chrome Plating, For All Models, Add $5.00
GT22B, .22 L.R.R.F., Clip Fed, Blue , Modern... 75 100 100
GT27, .25 ACP, Clip Fed, Blue , Modern... 25 50 50
GT32C, .22 L.R.R.F., Clip Fed, Blue , Modern... 75 100 100
GT32XBE, .32 ACP, Clip Fed, Modern... 125 150 150
GT380B, .380 ACP, Clip Fed, Blue , Modern... 100 125 125
GT380BE, .380 ACP, Clip Fed, Engraved, Blue , Modern....................... 125 150 150
GT380XE, .380 ACP, Clip Fed, Modern... 125 150 150

T.A.R.N. Swift Rifle Co., London, England, c. 1943.

HANDGUN, SEMI-AUTOMATIC

Polish Air Force, 9mm Luger, Clip Fed, Blue, Curio.............................. 3,500 4,000 4,000

TAURUS Forjas Taurus S.A., Porto Alegre, Brazil.

HANDGUN, REVOLVER

Model 65, .38 Special, Solid Frame, Swing–Out Cylinder, Double
Action, Modern... 175 225 225
Model 66, .38 Special, Solid Frame, Swing–Out Cylinder, Double
Action, Adjustable Sights, Modern.. 200 250 250
Model 73, .32 S & W Long, Solid Frame, Swing–Out Cylinder,
Double Action, Nickel Finish, Modern.. 150 200 200
Model 74, .32 S & W Long, Solid Frame, Swing–Out Cylinder,
Double Action, Adjustable Sights, Modern.. 125 175 175

	V.G.	Exc	Prior Edition
Model 80, .38 Special, Solid Frame, Swing–Out Cylinder, Double Action, Modern................	$125	$175	$175
Model 82, .38 Special, Solid Frame, Swing–Out Cylinder, Double Action, Heavy Barrel, Modern................	150	175	175
Model 83, .38 Special, Solid Frame, Swing–Out Cylinder, Double Action, Adjustable Sights, Modern................	150	175	175
Model 85, .38 Special, Solid Frame, Swing–Out Cylinder, Double Action, 3" Barrel, Modern................	175	200	200
Model 86, .38 Special, Solid Frame, Swing–Out Cylinder, Double Action, Adjustable Sights, 6" Barrel, Modern................	200	225	225
Model 94, .22 L.R.R.F., Solid Frame, Swing–Out Cylinder, Double Action, Adjustable Sights, Modern................	150	175	175

HANDGUN, SEMI-AUTOMATIC

PT–92, 9mm Luger, Clip Fed, Blue, Double Action,, Modern................	350	400	400
PT–99, 9mm Luger, Clip Fed, Blue, Double Action,, Modern................	375	425	425

T.D.E. El Monte, Calif. Also see Auto–Mag.

HANDGUN, SEMI-AUTOMATIC

Backup, .380 ACP. Stainless Steel, Modern................	225	250	250

TED WILLIAMS Trade name of Sears Roebuck, also see Sears.

RIFLE, BOLT ACTION

Model 52703, .22 L.R.R.F., Singleshot, Plain, Modern................	25	50	50
Model 52774, .22 L.R.R.F., Clip Fed, Plain, Modern................	50	75	75
Model 53, Various Calibers, Checkered Stock, Modern................	150	175	175

RIFLE, LEVER ACTION

Model 120, .30/30 Win.,Carbine, Modern................	75	100	100

RIFLE, SEMI-AUTOMATIC

Model 34, .22 L.R.R.F., Modern................	50	75	75
Model 34, .22 L.R.R.F., Carbine, Modern................	50	75	75
Model 3T, .22 L.R.R.F., Checkered Stock, Modern................	75	100	100
Model 52811, .22 L.R.R.F., Plain, Tube Feed, Takedown, Modern................	50	75	75
Model 52814, .22 L.R.R.F., Checkered Stock, Clip Fed, Takedown, Modern................	100	125	125

SHOTGUN, BOLT ACTION

Model 51106, 12 or 20 Gauges, Clip Fed, Adjustable Choke, Modern................	50	75	75
Model 51142, .410 Gauge, Clip Fed, Modern................	25	50	50

SHOTGUN, DOUBLE BARREL, OVER-UNDER

Model Laurona, 12 Ga., Checkered Stock, Light Engraving, Double Trigger, Vent Rib, Modern................	325	350	350
Model Zoli, 12 and 20 Gauges, Checkered Stock, Light Engraving, Double Trigger, Vent Rib, Modern................	275	300	300
Model Zoli, 12 Ga., Checkered Stock, Light Engraving, Double Trigger, Vent Rib, Automatic Ejector, Modern................	275	300	300

	V.G.	Exc	Prior Edition

SHOTGUN, DOUBLE BARREL, SIDE-BY-SIDE

Model 51226, 12 and 20 Gauges, Plain, Double Trigger, Modern...........	$125	$150	$150
Model Laurona, 12 and 20 Gauges, Checkered Stock, Light Engraving, Hammerless, Modern.................	150	175	175

SHOTGUN, SEMI-AUTOMATIC

Model 300, 12 and 20 Gauges, Checkered Stock, Vent Rib, Adjustable Choke, Modern........................	175	200	200
Model 300, 12 and 20 Gauges, Checkered Stock, Vent Rib, Modern............	175	200	200
Model 300, 12 Ga., Plain, Modern.................	150	175	175

SHOTGUN, SINGLESHOT

Model 5108, Various Gauges, Plain, Modern.............................	25	50	50

SHOTGUN, SLIDE ACTION

Model 200, 12 and 20 Gauges, Checkered Stock, Plain Barrel, Modern.............	125	150	150
Model 200, 12 and 20 Gauges, Checkered Stock, Vent Rib, Adjustable Choke, Modern.............	150	175	175
Model 200, 12 and 20 Gauges, Checkered Stock, Vent Rib, Modern.............	125	150	150
Model 200, 12 and 20 Gauges, Plain, Modern.............................	100	125	125
Model 51454, .410 Ga., Plain, Modern.................	100	125	125

TEN STAR Belgium, c. 1900.

SHOTGUN, DOUBLE BARREL, SIDE-BY-SIDE

Various Gauges, Hammerless, Damascus Barrel, Modern.......................	150	175	175
Various Gauges, Hammerless, Steel Barrel, Modern...............................	175	200	200
Various Gauges, Outside Hammers, Damascus Barrel, Modern............	150	175	175
Various Gauges, Outside Hammers, Steel Barrel, Modern......................	175	200	200

SHOTGUN, SINGLESHOT

Various Gauges, Hammer, Steel Barrel, Modern....................................	75	100	100

TERRIBLE Hijos de Calixto Arrizabalaga, Eibar, Spain, c. 1930.

HANDGUN, SEMI-AUTOMATIC

.25 ACP, Clip Fed, Blue, Modern.........................	125	150	150

TERRIER Made by J. Rupertus, Philadelphia, Pa. Sold by Tryon Bros., c. 1880.

HANDGUN, REVOLVER

.22 Short R.F., 7 Shot, Spur Trigger, Solid Frame, Single Action, Antique..............	150	175	175
.32 Short R.F., 5 Shot, Spur Trigger, Solid Frame, Single Action, Antique..............	150	175	175
.38 Short R.F., 5 Shot, Spur Trigger, Solid Frame, Single Action, Antique..............	150	175	175

	V.G.	Exc	Prior Edition
.41 Short R.F., 5 Shot, Spur Trigger, Solid Frame, Single Action, Antique	$175	$200	$200

TERROR Made by Forehand & Wadsworth, c. 1870.

HANDGUN, REVOLVER

.32 Short R.F., 5 or 6 Shot, Spur Trigger, Solid Frame, Single Action, Antique	150	175	175

TEUF–TEUF Arizmendi y Goenaga, Eibar, Spain, c. 1912.

HANDGUN, SEMI-AUTOMATIC

.25 ACP, Clip Fed, Blue, Curio	125	150	150

TEUF–TEUF Belgian maker, c. 1907.

HANDGUN, SEMI-AUTOMATIC

.25 ACP, Clip Fed, Blue Curio	150	175	175

TEXAS RANGER Made by Stevens Arms.

SHOTGUN, SINGLESHOT

Model 95, 12 and 16 Gauges, Modern	25	50	50

THAMES ARMS CO Norwich, Conn., c. 1907.

HANDGUN, REVOLVER

.22 L.R.R.F., 7 Shot, Double Action, Top Break, Curio	150	175	125
.32 S & W, 5 Shot, Double Action, Top Break, Curio	100	125	100
.38 S & W, 5 Shot, Double Action, Top Break, Curio	125	150	100

THAYER, ROBERTSON & CARY Norwich, Conn., c. 1907.

HANDGUN, REVOLVER

.32 S & W, 5 Shot, Double Action, Top Break, Curio	75	100	100
.38 S & W, 5 Shot, Double Action, Top Break, Curio	75	100	100

THOMPSON Developed by Auto–Ordnance, invented by Gen. John T. Thompson, made by various companies. Also see Numrich Arms.

HANDGUN, SEMI-AUTOMATIC PISTOL/CARBINE

Model 27A5, .45 ACP, Clip Fed, Finned Barrel, Adjustable Sights, with Compensator, (Numrich), Modern	450	500	325

RIFLE, SEMI-AUTOMATIC

Model 27 A 1, .45 ACP, Clip Fed, without Compensator, (Numrich), Modern	550	600	375
Model 27 A 1, .45 ACP, Clip Fed, without Compensator,Cased with Accessories, (Numrich), Modern	500	550	350

	V.G.	Exc	Prior Edition
Model 27 A 1 Deluxe, .45 ACP, Clip Fed, Finned Barrel, Adjustable Sights, with Compensator, (Numrich), Modern	$675	$750	$350
Model 27 A 3, .22 L.R.R.F., Clip Fed, Finned Barrel, Adjustable Sights, with Compensator, (Numrich), Modern	300	350	375

THOMPSON, SAMUEL Columbus, Ohio 1820–1822. See Kentucky Rifles.

THOMPSON/CENTER ARMS Rochester, N.H.

HANDGUN, PERCUSSION

	V.G.	Exc	Prior Edition
.45 Patriot, Set Trigger, Octagon Barrel, Reproduction, Antique	200	250	250
.45 Patriot, Set Trigger, Octagon Barrel, with Accessories, Reproduction, Antique	225	275	275

HANDGUN, SINGLESHOT

	V.G.	Exc	Prior Edition
Contender, Various Calibers, Adjustable Sights, Modern	325	350	275
Contender, Various Calibers, Adjustable Sights, Heavy Barrel, Modern	225	275	275
Contender, Various Calibers, Adjustable Sights, Super 14" Barrel, Modern	275	325	325
Contender, Various Calibers, Adjustable Sights, Vent Rib, Modern	350	375	300
Contender, Various Calibers, Heavy Barrel, no Sights, Modern	225	275	275

RIFLE, FLINTLOCK

	V.G.	Exc	Prior Edition
.45 Hawken, Set Trigger, Octagon Barrel, Reproduction, Antique	275	325	325
.45 Hawken, Set Trigger, Octagon Barrel, with Accessories, Reproduction, Antique	300	350	350
.50 Hawken, Set Trigger, Octagon Barrel, Reproduction, Antique	275	325	325
.50 Hawken, Set Trigger, Octagon Barrel, with Accessories, Reproduction, Antique	300	350	350
Hawken Cougar, .45 and .50 Caliber Caplock, Stainless Furniture, Reproduction, Antique	375	425	425

RIFLE, PERCUSSION

	V.G.	Exc	Prior Edition
Cherokee, .32 or .45 Caliber, Brass Furniture, 24" Barrel, Modern	300	350	350

Thompson/Center Cherokee

	V.G.	Exc	Prior Edition
.36 Seneca, Set Trigger, Octagon Barrel, Reproduction, Antique	250	300	300
.36 Seneca, Set Trigger, Octagon Barrel, with Accessories, Reproduction, Antique	275	325	325

	V.G.	Exc	Prior Edition
.45 Hawken, Set Trigger, Octagon Barrel, Reproduction, Antique..........	$250	$300	$300
.45 Hawken, Set Trigger, Octagon Barrel, with Accessories, Reproduction, Antique.....................	275	325	325
.45 Seneca, Set Trigger, Octagon Barrel, Reproduction, Antique.............	250	300	300
.45 Seneca, Set Trigger, Octagon Barrel, with Accessories, Reproduction, Antique....................	275	325	325
.50 Hawken, Set Trigger, Octagon Barrel, Reproduction, Antique..........	250	300	300
.50 Hawken, Set Trigger, Octagon Barrel, with Accessories, Reproduction, Antique....................	275	325	325
.54 Renegade, Set Trigger, Octagon Barrel, Reproduction, Antique........	225	275	225
.54 Renegade, Set Trigger, Octagon Barrel, with Accessories, Reproduction, Antique....................	250	300	250

RIFLE, SINGLESHOT

TCR83 Sports Rifle, Various Calibers, Interchangeable Barrels, Adjustable Double Set Triggers, Modern....................	500	550	550

THREE–BARREL GUN CO. Moundsville, W. Va., 1906–1908, also at Wheeling, W. Va. as Royal Gun Co. and as Hollenbeck Gun Co.

COMBINATION WEAPON, DRILLING

Various Calibers, Damascus barrel, Antique.........................	950	1,200	1,200

THUNDER Martin Bascaran, Eibar, Spain, made for Alberdi, Teleria y Cia. 1912–1919.

HANDGUN, SEMI-AUTOMATIC

M1919, .25 ACP, Clip Fed, Curio...........................	100	125	125

TIGER c. 1880.

HANDGUN, REVOLVER

#2, .32 Short R.F., 5 Shot, Spur Trigger, Solid Frame, Single Action, Antique...........................	150	175	175

TIGER Made by Crescent for J.H. Hill Co. Nashville, Tenn., c. 1900.

SHOTGUN, DOUBLE BARREL, SIDE-BY-SIDE

Various Gauges, Outside Hammers, Damascus Barrel, Modern.............	150	175	175
Various Gauges, Outside Hammers, Steel Barrel,			

SHOTGUN, SINGLESHOT

Various Gauges, Hammer, Steel Barrel, Modern.....................	75	100	100

TIKKA Oy Tikkakoski AB, Tikkakoski, Finland.

RIFLE, BOLT ACTION

Model 55 Deluxe, Various Calibers, Clip Fed, Checkered Stock, Modern..............	475	550	550
Model 55 Sporter, Various Calibers, Clip Fed, Checkered Stock, Heavy Barrel, Modern...........................	475	550	550

	V.G.	Exc	Prior Edition
Model 55 Standard, Various Calibers, Clip Fed, Checkered Stock, Modern...........	$450	$525	$525
Model 65 Deluxe, Various Calibers, Clip Fed, Checkered Stock, Modern.............	475	550	550
Model 65 Sporter, Various Calibers, Clip Fed, Checkered Stock, Target Rifle, Heavy Barrel, Modern...........	550	650	650
Model 65 Standard, Various Calibers, Clip Fed, Checkered Stock, Modern............	450	525	525

TINDALL & DUTTON   London, England 1790–1820.

HANDGUN, FLINTLOCK

Pocket Pistol, Various Calibers, Boxlock, Antique............	350	450	450

TINGLE MFG. CO.   Shelbyville, Ind.

HANDGUN, PERCUSSION

Model 1960 Target, Octagon Barrel, Rifled, Reproduction, Antique............	125	150	150

RIFLE, PERCUSSION

Model 1962 Target, Octagon Barrel, Brass Furniture, Rifled, Reproduction, Antique............	175	200	200

SHOTGUN, PERCUSSION

Model 1960, 10 or 12 gauges, Vent Rib, Double Barrel, Over–Under, Reproduction, Antique............	200	225	225

TIPPING & LAWDEN   Birmingham, England, c. 1875.

HANDGUN, MANUAL REPEATER

Sharps Derringer, Various Calibers, 4 Barrels, Spur Trigger, Cased with Accessories, Antique............	625	700	700

HANDGUN, REVOLVER

Thomas Patent, .450, Solid Frame, Double Action, Antique............	500	575	575

TITAN   Guiseppi Tanfoglio, Gardone Val Trompia, Italy. Also see F.I.E.

HANDGUN, SEMI-AUTOMATIC

Ppocket, .25 ACP, Clip Fed, Hammer, Modern............	50	75	75

TITAN   Retolaza Hermanos, Eibar, Spain, c. 1900.

HANDGUN, SEMI-AUTOMATIC

M 1913, 6.35mm, Clip Fed, Curio............	100	125	125

TITANIC   Retoloza Hermanos, Eibar, Spain, c. 1900.

HANDGUN, SEMI-AUTOMATIC

M 1913, 6.35mm, Clip Fed, Curio............	100	125	125

	V.G.	Exc	Prior Edition
M 1914, 7.65mm, Clip Fed, Curio...	$125	$150	$150

TOMPKINS Varsity Mfg. Co., Springfield, Mass., c. 1947.
HANDGUN, SINGLESHOT
Target, .22 L.R.R.F., Full Stock, Modern................................. 200 225 225

TOWER'S POLICE SAFETY Made by Hopkins & Allen, Nor–wich, Conn. c. 1875.
HANDGUN, REVOLVER
.38 Short R.F., 5 Shot, Spur Trigger, Solid Frame, Single Action,
Antique.. 150 175 175

TRADEWINDS Tacoma, Wash., Also see HVA.
RIFLE, BOLT ACTION
Husky (Early), Various Calibers, Checkered Stock, Monte Carlo
Stock, Modern.. 225 375 450
Husky M–5000, Various Calibers, Checkered Stock, Clip Fed,
Modern... 275 325 350
Husqvarna, Various Calibers, Checkered Stock, Monte Carlo
Stock, Lightweight, Modern............................... 525 575 575
Husqvarna, Various Calibers, Checkered Stock, Monte Carlo
Stock, Lightweight, Full–Stocked, Modern.................... 525 600 600
Husqvarna Crown Grade, Various Calibers, Checkered Stock,
Monte Carlo Stock, Modern................................ 575 625 625
Husqvarna Imperial, Various Calibers, Checkered Stock, Monte
Carlo Stock, Lightweight, Modern....................... 500 550 550
Husqvarna Imperial Custom, Various Calibers, Checkered Stock,
Monte Carlo Stock, Modern............................... 475 525 525
Husqvarna Presentation, Various Calibers, Checkered Stock,
Monte Carlo Stock, Modern.. 700 750 750
Model 1998, .222 Rem., no Sights, Heavy Barrel, Target Stock,
Modern.. 475 525 525
Model 600K, Various Calibers, Clip Fed, no Sights, Heavy Barrel,
Set Trigger, Modern... 300 350 350
Model 600S, Various Calibers, Clip Fed, Heavy Barrel, Octagon
Barrel, Modern.. 475 525 525

RIFLE, SEMI-AUTOMATIC
Model 260A, .22 L.R.R.F., 5 Shot Clip, Checkered Stock,
Modern.. 150 200 140

SHOTGUN, DOUBLE BARREL, OVER-UNDER
Gold Shadow Indy, 12 Ga., Field Grade, Engraved, Fancy
Checkering, Automatic Ejector, Vent Rib, Modern.......... 1,200 1,550 1,550
Gold Shadow Indy, 12 Ga., Skeet Grade, Engraved, Fancy,
Checkering, Automatic Ejector, Vent Rib, Modern.............. 1,250 1,500 1,500
Gold Shadow Indy, 12 Ga., Trap Grade, Engraved, Fancy,
Checkering, Automatic Ejector, Vent Rib, Modern................ 1,450 1,600 1,600
Shadow Indy, 12 Ga., Field Grade, Automatic Ejector, Vent Rib,
Checkered Stock, Modern... 475 525 525

	V.G.	Exc	Prior Edition
Shadow Indy, 12 Ga., Skeet Grade, Automatic Ejector, Vent Rib, Checkered Stock, Modern......................	$500	$550	$550
Shadow Indy, 12 Ga., Trap Grade, Automatic Ejector, Vent Rib, Checkered Stock, Modern.......................	525	575	575
Shadow–7, 12 Ga., Field Grade, Automatic Ejector, Vent Rib, Modern.....................	325	350	350
Shadow–7, 12 Ga., Skeet Grade, Automatic Ejector, Vent Rib, Modern.....................	350	375	375
Shadow–7, 12 Ga., Trap Grade, Automatic Ejector, Vent Rib, Modern.....................	375	400	400

SHOTGUN, DOUBLE BARREL, SIDE-BY-SIDE

	V.G.	Exc	Prior Edition
Model G–1032, 10 Ga. 3½", Checkered Stock, Modern..........................	225	250	250
Model G–1228, 12 Ga. Mag. 3", Checkered Stock, Modern..................	250	275	275
Model G–2028, 20 Ga. Mag., Checkered Stock, Modern........................	250	275	275

SHOTGUN, SEMI-AUTOMATIC

	V.G.	Exc	Prior Edition
Model D–200, 12 Ga., Field Grade, Vent Rib, Engraved, Modern...........	250	300	300
Model H–150, 12 Ga., Field Grade, Modern............................	200	225	225
Model H–170, 12 Ga., Field Grade, Vent Rib, Modern..........................	225	275	300
Model T–220, 12 Ga., Trap Grade, Vent Rib, Engraved, Modern............	250	300	300

SHOTGUN, SINGLESHOT

	V.G.	Exc	Prior Edition
Model M50, 10 Ga., 3½" Barrel, Checkered Stock, Modern...................	125	175	175

TRAMPS TERROR Made by Hoods Firearms Co. Norwich, Conn., c. 1870.

HANDGUN, REVOLVER

	V.G.	Exc	Prior Edition
.22 Short R.F., 7 Shot, Spur Trigger, Solid Frame, Single Action, Antique............................	150	175	175

TRIOMPH Apaolozo Hermanos, Eibar, Spain.

HANDGUN, SEMI-AUTOMATIC

	V.G.	Exc	Prior Edition
6.35mm, Clip Fed, Blue, Modern............................	100	125	125

TRIUMPH Made by Stevens Arms.

SHOTGUN, DOUBLE BARREL, SIDE-BY-SIDE

	V.G.	Exc	Prior Edition
Model 311, Various Gauges, Hammerless, Steel Barrel, Modern.............	150	175	175

TRUE BLUE Made by Norwich Falls Pistols Co., c. 1880.

HANDGUN, REVOLVER

	V.G.	Exc	Prior Edition
.32 Short R.F., 5 Shot, Spur Trigger, Solid Frame, Single Action, Antique............................	125	175	175

	V.G.	Exc	Prior Edition

TRUST Fab. d' Armes de Guerre de Grande Precision, Eibar, Spain.

HANDGUN, SEMI-AUTOMATIC

	V.G.	Exc	Prior Edition
6.36mm, Clip Fed, Blue, Modern	$100	$125	$125
7.65mm, Clip Fed, Blue, Modern	125	150	150

TRUST SUPRA Fab. d' Armes de Guerre de Grande Precision, Eibar, Spain.

HANDGUN, SEMI-AUTOMATIC

	V.G.	Exc	Prior Edition
6.35mm, Clip Fed, Blue, Modern	100	125	125

TUE–TUE C. F. Galand, Liege, Belgium and Paris, France.

HANDGUN, REVOLVER

	V.G.	Exc	Prior Edition
Velo Dog, Various Calibers, Double Action, Hammerless, Curio	125	150	150

TURBIAUX J. E. Turbiaux, Paris, France, c. 1885.

HANDGUN, MANUAL REPEATER

	V.G.	Exc	Prior Edition
Le Protector, Various Calibers, Palm Pistol, Antique	550	650	750

TURNER Dublin, c. 1820.

HANDGUN, FLINTLOCK

	V.G.	Exc	Prior Edition
.62, Double Barrel, Pocket Pistol, Platinum Furniture, Plain, Antique	1,000	1,500	1,500

TURNER & ROSS Made by Hood Firearms, Norwich, Conn., c. 1875.

HANDGUN, REVOLVER

	V.G.	Exc	Prior Edition
.22 Short R.F., 7 Shot, Spur Trigger, Solid Frame, Single Action, Antique	150	175	175

TWIGG London, England 1760–1813.

HANDGUN, FLINTLOCK

	V.G.	Exc	Prior Edition
.58 , Pair, Belt Pistol, Flared, Octagon Barrel, Cased with Accessories, Plain, Antique	3,000	3,500	3,500

TYCOON Made by Johnson–Bye, Worcester, Mass. 1873–1887.

HANDGUN, REVOLVER

	V.G.	Exc	Prior Edition
#1, .22 Short R.F., 7 Shot, Spur Trigger, Solid Frame, Single Action, Antique	150	175	175
#2, .32 Short R.F., 5 Shot, Spur Trigger, Solid Frame, Single Action, Antique	150	200	200

	V.G.	Exc	Prior Edition
#3, .38 Short R.F., 5 Shot, Spur Trigger, Solid Frame, Single Action, Antique	$150	$175	$175
#4, .41 Short R.F., 5 Shot, Spur Trigger, Solid Frame, Single Action, Antique	125	150	150
#5, Short R.F., 5 Shot, Spur Trigger, Solid Frame, Single Action, Antique	200	250	250

TYROL   Made in Belgium for Tyrol Sport Arms, Englewood, Colo., c. 1963.

RIFLE, BOLT ACTION

	V.G.	Exc	Prior Edition
Model DC, Various Calibers, Mannlicher Style, Checkered Stock, Modern	275	200	200
Model DCM, Various Calibers, Mannlicher Style, Checkered Stock, Recoil Pad, Modern	225	250	250
Model DM, Various Calibers, Checkered Stock, Modern	150	175	175

U

UHLINGER, W. L. & CO. Philadelphia, Pa., c. 1880.

HANDGUN, REVOLVER

.22 R.F., 7 Shot, Spur Trigger, Solid Frame, Single Action,
Antique.. $225 $275 $225
.32 Short R.F., 6 Shot, Spur Trigger, Solid Frame, Single Action,
Antique.. 325 375 275

U.M.C. ARMS CO. Probably Norwich Arms Co., c. 1880.

HANDGUN, REVOLVER

.32 Short R.F., 5 Shot, Spur Trigger, Solid Frame, Single Action,
Antique.. 95 175 175

UNION Fab. Francaise.

HANDGUN, SEMI-AUTOMATIC

7.65mm, Ruby Style, Clip Fed, Modern................................. 225 275 200
7.65mm, Ruby Style, With Horseshoe Magazine, Modern...... 650 750 750

UNION France, M. Seytres.

HANDGUN, SEMI-AUTOMATIC

.25 ACP, Clip Fed, Long Grip, Modern................................. 100 125 125
.32 ACP, Clip Fed, Long Grip, Modern................................. 125 150 150

UNION Unceta y Cia., Guernica, Spain 1924–1931.

HANDGUN, SEMI-AUTOMATIC

Model I, 6.35mm, Clip Fed, Modern..................................... 100 150 150
Model II, 6.35mm, Clip Fed, Modern.................................... 125 150 150
Model III, 7.65mm, Clip Fed, Modern.................................. 150 175 175
Model IV, 7.65mm, Clip Fed, Modern................................... 150 175 175

UNION FIREARMS CO. Toledo, Ohio, 1903–1913.

HANDGUN, SEMI-AUTOMATIC

Lefever Patent Revolver, .32 Caliber, 6 Shot, Top Break, Curio............ 1,200 1,450 875
Reifgraber Patent Pistol, .32 S & W, 8 Shot, Curio................ 1,400 1,650 950

	V.G.	Exc	Prior Edition

UNION JACK Made by Hood Firearms Norwich, Conn., c. 1880.

HANDGUN, REVOLVER

.22 Short R.F., 7 Shot, Spur Trigger, Solid Frame, Single Action,
Antique... $125 $150 $150
.32 Short R.F., 5 Shot, Spur Trigger, Solid Frame, Single Action,
Antique... 150 175 175

UNION REVOLVER Maker unknown, c. 1880.

HANDGUN, REVOLVER

.22 Short R.F., 7 Shot, Spur Trigger, Solid Frame, Single Action,
Antique... 125 150 150
.32 Short R.F., 5 Shot, Spur Trigger, Solid Frame, Single Action,
Antique... 150 175 175

UNIQUE Made by C.S. Shattuck, 1880–1915.

HANDGUN, REPEATER

Shattuck Palm Pistol, Various Calibers, 4 Shot, Curio........................... 575 1,250 650

HANDGUN, REVOLVER

.32 Short R.F., 5 Shot, Spur Trigger, Solid Frame, Single Action,
Antique... 150 200 200
.38 Short R.F., 5 Shot, Spur Trigger, Solid Frame, Single Action,
Antique... 150 200 200

UNIQUE Mre. d' Armes de Pyrenees, Hendaye, France, 1923 to date.

HANDGUN, SEMI-AUTOMATIC

Kreigsmodell, 7.65mm, Clip Fed, Magazine Disconnect, 9 Shot,
Nazi–Proofed, Hammer, Curio... 250 275 300
Model 10, 6.35mm, Clip Fed, Magazine Disconnect, Modern................. 150 200 200
Model 11, 6.35mm, Clip Fed, Magazine Disconnect, Safety,
Cartridge Indicator, Modern... 200 250 250
Model 12, 6.35mm, Clip Fed, Magazine Disconnect, Grip Safety,
Modern.. 200 225 225
Model 13, 6.35mm, Clip Fed, Magazine Disconnect, Grip Safety,
7 Shot, Modern.. 200 225 225
Model 14, 6.35mm, Clip Fed, Magazine Disconnect, Grip Safety,
9 Shot, Modern.. 175 225 225
Model 15, 7.65mm, Clip Fed, Magazine Disconnect, 6 Shot,
Modern.. 200 250 250
Model 16, 7.65mm, Clip Fed, Magazine Disconnect, 7 Shot,
Modern.. 200 250 250
Model 17, 7.65mm, Clip Fed, Magazine Disconnect, 9 Shot, Nazi–
Proofed, Curio... 300 350 350
Model 17, 7.65mm, Clip Fed, Magazine Disconnect, 9 Shot,
Modern.. 225 275 275
Model 18, 7.65mm, Clip Fed, Magazine Disconnect, 6 Shot,
Modern.. 200 250 250

	V.G.	Exc	Prior Edition
Model 19, 7.65mm, Clip Fed, Magazine Disconnect, 7 Shot, Modern..	$200	$250	$250
Model 20, 7.65mm, Clip Fed, Magazine Disconnect, 9 Shot, Modern..	225	275	275
Model 21, .380 ACP, Clip Fed, Magazine Disconnect, 6 Shot, Modern..	225	275	275
Model 51, .380 ACP, Clip Fed, Magazine Disconnect, 6 Shot, Modern..	200	250	250
Model 51, 7.65mm, Clip Fed, Magazine Disconnect, 9 Shot, Modern..	200	250	250
Model 52, .22 L.R.R.F., Clip Fed, Hammer, Various Barrel Lengths, Modern...........................	175	225	225
Model 540, 7.65mm, Clip Fed, Magazine Disconnect, 9 Shot, Modern..	200	250	250
Model 550, .380 ACP, Clip Fed, Magazine Disconnect, 6 Shot, Modern..	200	250	250
Model C, 7.65mm, Clip Fed, 9 Shot, Hammer, Modern.........................	200	250	250
Model D–1, .22 L.R.R.F., Clip Fed, Hammer, 3" Barrel, Modern............	200	250	250
Model D–2, .22 L.R.R.F., Clip Fed, Hammer, Adjustable Sights, 4" Barrel, Modern...................	225	275	275
Model D–3, .22 L.R.R.F., Clip Fed, Hammer, Adjustable Sights, 8" Barrel, Modern...................	200	250	250
Model D–4, .22 L.R.R.F., Clip Fed, Hammer, Muzzle Brake, Adjustable Sights, 9½" Barrel, Modern...................	225	275	275
Model D–6, .22 L.R.R.F., Clip Fed, Hammer, Adjustable Sights, 6" Barrel, Modern...................	225	275	275
Model DES/69, .22 L.R.R.F., Clip Fed, Target Pistol, Modern................	300	350	550
Model DES/VO 79, .22 L.R.R.F., Clip Fed, Rapid FireTarget Pistol, Gas Ports, Modern...................	650	750	750
Model DES/VO, .22 L.R.R.F., Clip Fed, Rapid FireTarget Pistol, Modern..	525	600	600
Model E–1, .22 Short R.F., Clip Fed, Hammer, 3" Barrel, Modern.........	100	125	125
Model E–2, .22 Short R.F., Clip Fed, Hammer, Adjustable Sights, 4" Barrel, Modern...................	125	150	150
Model E–3, .22 Short R.F., Clip Fed, Hammer, Adjustable Sights, 8" Barrel, Modern...................	125	150	150
Model E–4, .22 Short R.F., Clip Fed, Hammer, Muzzle Brake, Adjustable Sights, 9½" Barrel, Modern...................	150	200	200
Model F, .380 ACP, Clip Fed, 8 Shot, Hammer, Modern........................	225	275	275
Model L (Corsair), .22 L.R.R.F., Clip Fed, Hammer, Modern..............	175	225	225
Model L (Corsair), .22 L.R.R.F., Clip Fed, Hammer, Lightweight, Modern..	175	225	225
Model L (Corsair), .32 ACP, Clip Fed, Hammer, Modern.....................	125	150	150
Model L (Corsair), .32 ACP, Clip Fed, Hammer, Lightweight, Modern..	125	150	150
Model L (Corsair), .380 ACP, Clip Fed, Hammer, Modern...................	150	175	175
Model L (Corsair), .380 ACP, Clip Fed, Hammer, Lightweight, Modern..	125	150	150
Model Mikros, .25 ACP, Clip Fed, Magazine Disconnect, 6 Shot, Modern..	150	175	175
Model RD (Ranger), .22 L.R.R.F., Clip Fed, Hammer, Modern............	75	100	100
Model RD (Ranger), .22 L.R.R.F., Clip Fed, Muzzle Brake, Hammer, Modern................................	100	125	125

	V.G.	Exc	Prior Edition

RIFLE, BOLT ACTION

Audax, .22 L.R.R.F., Checkered Stock, Open Sights, Modern................. $150 · $175 · $175

Dioptra 3121, .22 L.R.R.F., Checkered Stock, Open Sights, Modern...... 450 · 500 · 500

Dioptra 3121, .22 L.R.R.F., Checkered Stock, Target Sights, Modern...... 575 · 650 · 650

Dioptra 4131, .22 WMR., Checkered Stock, Open Sights, Modern...... 575 · 650 · 650

Model T–66, .22 L.R.R.F., Target Stock, Target Sights, Singleshot, Modern...... 375 · 425 · 425

UNITED STATES ARMS Riverhead, N.Y., distributed by Mossberg.

HANDGUN, REVOLVER

Abilene, .44 Magnum, Single Action, Western Style, Adjustable Sights, Modern...... 300 · 350 · 350

Abilene, .44 Magnum, Stainless Steel, Single Action, Western Style, Adjustable Sights, Modern...... 325 · 375 · 375

Abilene, .44 Magnum, Stainless Steel, Single Action, Western Style, 10" Barrel, Adjustable Sights, Modern...... 350 · 400 · 400

Abilene, Various Calibers, Single Action, Western Style, Adjustable Sights, Modern...... 300 · 350 · 350

Abilene, Various Calibers, Single Action, Western Style, Adjustable Sights, Stainless Steel, Modern...... 325 · 375 · 375

UNIVERSAL Hialeah, Fla., Now owned by Iver Johnson, Inc. Currently manufactured in Jacksonville, Ar.

HANDGUN, SEMI-AUTOMATIC

Model 3000 Enforcer, .30 Carbine, Clip Fed, Blued, Modern...... 175 · 200 · 250

Model 3000 Enforcer, .30 Carbine, Clip Fed, Nickel Plated, Modern...... 225 · 250 · 275

Model 3000 Enforcer, .30 Carbine, Clip Fed, Stainless, Modern...... 225 · 275 · 275

RIFLE, SEMI-AUTOMATIC

Model 1001, .30 Carbine, Carbine, Clip Fed, Modern...... 150 · 200 · 200

Model 1002, .30 Carbine, Carbine, Clip Fed, Bayonet Lug, Modern...... 200 · 250 · 250

Model 1003, .30 Carbine, Carbine, Clip Fed, Walnut Stock, Modern...... 125 · 175 · 175

Model 1004, .30 Carbine, Carbine, Clip Fed, Scope Mounted, Modern...... 200 · 250 · 250

Model 1010, .30 Carbine, Carbine, Clip Fed, Nickel Plated, Modern...... 225 · 275 · 275

Model 1011 Deluxe, .30 Carbine, Carbine, Clip Fed, Nickel Plated, Monte Carlo Stock, Modern...... 250 · 300 · 300

Model 1015, .30 Carbine, Carbine, Clip Fed, Gold Plated, Modern...... 250 · 300 · 300

Model 1016 Deluxe, .30 Carbine, Carbine, Clip Fed, Gold Plated, Monte Carlo Stock, Modern...... 300 · 350 · 350

	V.G.	Exc	Prior Edition
Model 1025 Ferret, .256 Win. Mag., Carbine, Clip Fed, Sporting Rifle, Modern............	$175	$225	$225
Model 1025 Ferret, .30 Carbine, Carbine, Clip Fed, Sporting Rifle, Modern............	175	225	225
Model 1941 Field Commander, .30 Carbine, Carbine, Clip Fed, Fancy Wood, Modern............	175	225	225

RIFLE, SLIDE ACTION

	V.G.	Exc	Prior Edition
Vulcan 440, .44 Magnum, Clip Fed, Sporting Rifle, Open Rear Sight, Modern............	150	200	200

SHOTGUN, DOUBLE BARREL, OVER-UNDER

	V.G.	Exc	Prior Edition
Baikal 1J–27, 12 Ga., Double Trigger, Vent Rib, Engraved, Checkered Stock, Modern............	200	250	250
Baikal 1J–27, 12 Ga., Double Trigger, Vent Rib, Engraved, Checkered Stock, Automatic Ejector, Modern............	225	275	275

SHOTGUN, SINGLESHOT

	V.G.	Exc	Prior Edition
Model 1J18, 12 Ga., Hammerless, Modern............	50	75	75
Model 7212, 12 Ga., Trap Grade, Vent Rib, Engraved, Checkered Stock, Monte Carlo Stock, Modern............	850	950	950

UNIVERSAL Made by Hopkins & Allen, Norwich, Conn., c. 1880.

HANDGUN, REVOLVER

	V.G.	Exc	Prior Edition
.32 S & W, 5 Shot, Double Action, Solid Frame, Curio............	75	100	100

UNWIN & ROGERS Yorkshire, England, c. 1850.

HANDGUN, PERCUSSION

	V.G.	Exc	Prior Edition
Knife Pistol, with Ramrod and Mould, Cased with Accessories, Antique............	1,000	1,250	1,250

U.S. ARMS CO. Brooklyn, N.Y. 1874–1878.

HANDGUN, REVOLVER

	V.G.	Exc	Prior Edition
.22 Short R.F., 7 Shot, Spur Trigger, Solid Frame, Single Action, Antique............	125	175	175
.32 Short R.F., 5 Shot, Spur Trigger, Solid Frame, Single Action, Antique............	150	175	175
.38 Short R.F., 5 Shot, Spur Trigger, Solid Frame, Single Action, Antique............	150	175	175

	V.G.	Exc	Prior Edition
.41 Short R.F., 5 Shot, Spur Trigger, Solid Frame, Single Action, Antique	$150	$200	$200

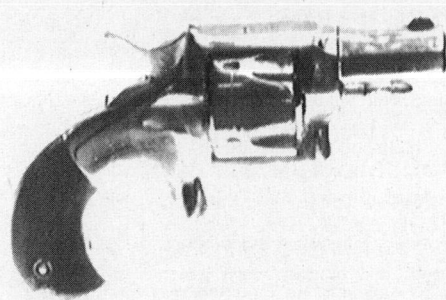

U.S. Arms Co. .41

U.S. ARMS CO. Made by Crescent for H. & D. Folsom, c. 1900.

SHOTGUN, DOUBLE BARREL, SIDE-BY-SIDE

Various Gauges, Hammerless, Damascus Barrel, Modern	150	200	200
Various Gauges, Hammerless, Steel Barrel, Modern	150	200	200
Various Gauges, Outside Hammers, Damascus Barrel, Modern	150	175	175
Various Gauges, Outside Hammers, Steel Barrel, Modern	150	200	200

SHOTGUN, SINGLESHOT

Various Gauges, Hammer, Steel Barrel, Modern	75	100	100

U.S. MILITARY

HANDGUN, FLINTLOCK

.54 M1805 (06), Singleshot, Smoothbore, Brass Mounts, Dated 1806, Antique	10,000	12,500	10,500
.54 M1805 (06), Singleshot, Smoothbore, Brass Mounts, Dated 1807, Antique	5,000	6,500	5,500
.54 M1805 (06), Singleshot, Smoothbore, Brass Mounts, Dated 1808, Antique	6,000	7,500	6,500
.54 M1807–8, Singleshot, Smoothbore, Brass Mounts, Various Contractors, Antique	6,500	7,500	7,500
.54 M1816, Singleshot, Smoothbore, S North Army, Brass Furniture, Antique	1,500	1,750	1,500
.54 M1819, Singleshot, Smoothbore, S North Army, Iron Mounts, Antique	1,500	1,750	1,750
.54 M1826, Singleshot, Smoothbore, S North Army, Iron Mounts, Antique	5,250	5,000	3,500
.54 M1836, Singleshot, Smoothbore, R Johnson Army, Iron Mounts, Antique	1,250	1,500	1,200
.64 M1808, Singleshot, Smoothbore, S North Army, Brass Furniture, Antique	7,000	8,500	6,500
.69 M1799, Singleshot, North & Cheney, Brass Furniture, Brass Frame, Antique	25,000	30,000	30,000

	V.G.	Exc	Prior Edition
.69 M1811, Singleshot, Smoothbore, S North Army, Brass Furniture, Antique	$4,500	$5,500	$4,500
.69 M1817 (18), Singleshot, Smoothbore, Springfield, Iron Mounts, Antique	8,000	9,500	7,500

HANDGUN, PERCUSSION

	V.G.	Exc	Prior Edition
.54 M1836, Singleshot, Smoothbore, U.S. Navy Conversion from Flintlock, Iron Mounts, Antique	1,250	1,500	1,500
.54 M1842 Aston, Singleshot, Smoothbore, Brass Mounts, Antique	1,000	1,250	950
.54 M1842 Johnson, Singleshot, Smoothbore, Brass Mounts, Antique	1,250	1,500	900
.54 M1843 Deringer Army, Singleshot, Rifled, Brass Mounts, Antique	2,250	2,500	1,750
.54 M1843 Deringer Army, Singleshot, Smoothbore, Brass Mounts, Antique	1,250	1,500	1,200
.54 M1843 Deringer Navy, Singleshot, Smoothbore, Brass Mounts, Antique	1,500	1,750	1,500

HANDGUN, SINGLESHOT

	V.G.	Exc	Prior Edition
Liberator, .45 ACP, Military, Curio	500	550	600

RIFLE, BOLT ACTION

	V.G.	Exc	Prior Edition
M1871 Ward–Burton, .50 C.F., Iron Mountings, Carbine, Antique	2,000	2,500	2,500
M1871 Ward–Burton, .50 C.F., Iron Mountings, Rifle, Antique	1,750	2,000	2,000
M1882 Chaffee–Reese, 45–70, Rifle, Antique	2,000	2,500	1,500
M1892/6 Krag, .30–40 Krag, Rifle, Antique	550	600	550
M1895 Lee Straight Pull, 6mm Lee Navy, Musket, Antique	1,000	1,250	1,200
M1896 Krag, .30–40 Krag, Cadet, Antique	20,000	25,000	15,000
M1896 Krag, .30–40 Krag, Carbine, Antique	1,000	1,250	1,000
M1896 Krag, .30–40 Krag, Rifle, Antique	650	750	650
M1898 Krag, .30–40 Krag, Carbine, Curio	1,250	1,500	450
M1898 Krag, .30–40 Krag, Rifle, Curio	650	750	450
M1899 Krag, .30–40 Krag, Carbine, Curio	850	1,000	700
M1903 MKI Pedersen, .30–06 Springfield, Curio	15,000	17,500	16,500
M1903 National Match, .30–06 Springfield, Target Rifle, Curio	2,500	2,750	2,500
M1903 Sniper, .30–06 Springfield, Scope Mounts, Curio	3,000	3,500	3,500
M1903, .30–06 Springfield, Machined Parts, Modern	12,500	15,000	12,500
M1903/5, .30–03 Springfield, Curio	6,000	7,500	6,000
M1903/5, .30–06 Springfield, Curio	2,250	2,500	2,000
M1903/7, .30–06 Springfield, Early Receivers, Curio	1,750	2,000	1,500
M1903/Postwar, .30–06 Springfield, Curio	1,250	1,500	1,250
M1903/WWI, .30–06 Springfield, Curio	2,000	2,250	1,000
M1903A1 National Match, .30–06 Springfield, Target Rifle, Curio	2,250	2,500	2,000
M1903A1, .30–06 Springfield, Parkerized, Checkered Butt, Machined Parts, Curio	1,000	1,250	1,500
M1917 Eddystone, .30–06 Springfield, Curio	500	650	550
M1917 Remington, .30–06 Springfield, Curio	525	700	575
M1917 Winchester, .30–06 Springfield, Curo	550	750	600
M1922 Trainer, .22 L.R.R.F., Target Rifle, Curio	2,250	2,500	2,500
M1922M2 Trainer, .22 L.R.R.F., Target Rifle, Curio	1,000	1,250	1,000

	V.G.	Exc	Prior Edition

RIFLE, FLINTLOCK

.52, M1819 Hall Whitney, Rifled, Breech Loader, 32½" Barrel, 3 Bands, Antique	$3,000	$5,000	$4,000
.52, M1819 Hall, Rifled, Breech Loader, 32½" Barrel, 3 Bands, Antique	3,000	5,000	5,000
.54, M1807 Springfield, "Indian Carbine," 27¾" Barrel, Antique	15,000	22,500	12,000
.54, M1814, Rifled, 36" Barrel, Antique	3,500	5,000	3,500

RIFLE, PERCUSSION

.45–70, M1873 U.S., "Trapdoor," Carbine, 22" Barrel, Single Band, Antique	850	1,500	1,250
.45–70, M1873 U.S., "Trapdoor," Rifle, 32-5/8" Barrel, 2 Bands, Antique	750	1,200	1,000
.45–70, M1888 U.S., "Trapdoor," Rifle, 32-5/8" Barrel, 2 Bands, Ramrod–Bayonet, Antique	500	1,000	1,000
.57, M1841 U.S. Cadet Musket, 40" Barrel, 2 Bands, Antique	4,500	10,000	90,000
.57, M1851 U.S. Cadet Musket, Rifled, 40" Barrel, 2 Bands, Antique	750	1,500	1,200
.57, M1851 U.S. Cadet Musket, Smoothbore, 40" Barrel, 2 Bands, Antique	750	1,500	1,100
.58 Lindner, Breech Loader, Carbine, Rising Block, Antique	2,500	3,750	1,750
.58, M1841 Contract, Rifled, 33" Barrel, 2 Bands, (Mississippi Rifle), Antique	2,000	2,500	2,500
.58, M1855 U.S., Carbine, Rifled, 22" Barrel, 1 Band, with Tape Priming System, Antique	7,000	12,500	7,500
.58, M1855 U.S., Rifled, 40" Barrel, 3 Bands, with Tape Priming System, Antique	2,500	4,000	3,000
.58, M1861 U.S., Rifled, 40" Round Barrel, 3 Bands, Antique	1,000	2,000	2,000
.58, M1863 U.S., Rifled, 40" Round Barrel, 3 Bands, Antique	1,000	2,000	2,000
.64, M1836 Hall-North, Rifled, Breech Loader, Carbine, 26 1/8" Barrel, 2 Bands, Antique	2,500	3,000	3,000
.69, M1842 U.S., Musket, 42" Barrel, 3 Bands, Antique	2,250	2,500	1,500
.69, M1842 U.S., Rifled, Musket, 42" Barrel, 3 Bands, Antique	2,250	2,500	1,250
.69, M1847 Artillery, Musketoon, 26" Barrel, 2 Bands, Steel Furniture, Antique	3,000	3,250	3,000
.69, M1847 Cavalry, Musketoon, 26" Barrel, 2 Bands, Brass Furniture, Antique	2,500	2,750	2,500
.69, M1847 Sappers, Musketoon, 26" Barrel, 2 Bands, Bayonet Stud on Right Side, Antique	3,500	4,000	3,500
M1864 Training Rifle, Military, Wood Barrel, Antique	200	250	250

RIFLE, SEMI-AUTOMATIC

M–1 Carbine IBM, .30 Carbine, Clip Fed, Curio	625	700	700
M–1 Carbine Inland, .30 Carbine, Clip Fed, Curio	525	600	600
M–1 Carbine Irwin–Pedersen, .30 Carbine, Clip Fed, Curio	1,000	1,200	1,200
M–1 Carbine Nat. Postal Meter, .30 Carbine, Clip Fed, Curio	600	650	650
M–1 Carbine Quality Hdw., .30 Carbine, Clip Fed, Curio	550	600	600
M–1 Carbine Rockola, .30 Carbine, Clip Fed, Curio	750	850	850
M–1 Carbine Underwood, .30 Carbine, Clip Fed, Curio	550	600	600
M–1 Carbine Winchester, .30 Carbine, Clip Fed, Curio	800	850	850
M–1 Garand National Match, .30–06 Springfield, Military, Target Sights, Target Trigger, Target Barrel, Curio	1,000	1,200	1,200
M–1 Garand Winchester, .30–06 Springfield, Pre WWII, Curio	1,000	1,250	1,250
M–1 Garand, .30–06 Springfield, Military, Curio	725	800	800
M–1A1 Carbine, .30 Carbine, Clip Fed, Folding Stock, Modern	750	850	650

	V.G.	Exc	Prior Edition
M1941 Johnson, 30–06 Springfield, Military, Curio...............................	$775	$850	$850

U.S. REVOLVER CO.

MADE BY IVER JOHNSON

	V.G.	Exc	Prior Edition
.32 S & W, 5 Shot, Double Action, Solid Frame, Modern.........................	75	100	100
.32 S & W, 5 Shot, Top Break, Double Action, Modern...........................	75	100	100
.32 S & W, 5 Shot, Top Break, Hammerless, Double Action, Modern..	75	100	100
.32 Short R.F., 5 Shot, Spur Trigger, Solid Frame, Single Action, Antique..	150	175	175
.38 S & W, 5 Shot, Double Action, Top Break, Modern..........................	75	100	100
.38 S & W, 5 Shot, Double Action, Solid Frame, Modern........................	50	75	75
.38 S & W, 5 Shot, Top Break, Hammerless, Double Action, Modern..	75	100	100

V

VALIANT   Made by Stevens Arms for Spear & Co., Pittsburgh, Pa.

RIFLE, BOLT ACTION

	V.G.	Exc.	Prior Edition
Model 51, .22 L.R.R.F., Singleshot, Takedown, Modern.........................	$25	$50	$50

VALMET   Valmet Oy, Tourula Works, Jyvaskyla, Finland.

RIFLE, SEMI-AUTOMATIC

	V.G.	Exc.	Prior Edition
M–62S, 7.62 X 39 Russian, Clip Fed, AK–47 Type, Sporting Version of Military Rifle, Modern..	1,000	1,250	850
M–71S, .223 Rem., Clip Fed, AK–47 Type, Sporting Version of Military Rifle, Modern..	750	1,000	750
M78 HV, .223 Rem., Clp Fed, Bipod, Modern..	1,000	1,200	1,200
M78 Standard, .308 Win., Clip Fed, Bipod, Modern.............................	1,000	1,200	1,200

VALOR ARMS   Importers Miami, Fla.

HANDGUN, REVOLVER

	V.G.	Exc.	Prior Edition
.22 L.R.R.F., Double Action, Lightweight, Modern................................	25	50	50
.32 S & W, Double Action, Lightweight, Modern....................................	25	50	50

VANDERFRIFT, ISSAC AND JEREMIAH   Philadelphia, Pa. 1809–1815. See Kentucky Rifles and Pistols.

VEGA   Sacramento, Calif.

HANDGUN, SEMI-AUTOMATIC

	V.G.	Exc.	Prior Edition
Vega 1911A1, .45 ACP, Stainless Steel, Clip Fed, Modern.....................	300	350	350

VELO DOG   Various makers, c. 1900.

HANDGUN, REVOLVER

	V.G.	Exc.	Prior Edition
5mm Velo Dog, Hammerless, Folding Trigger, Curio..............................	100	125	125
5mm Velo Dog, Hammerless, Folding Trigger, Curio.............................	75	100	100
5mm Velo Dog, Hammerless, Trigger Guard, Curio...............................	75	100	100
.25 ACP, Hammer, Folding Trigger, Curio...	100	125	125
.25 ACP, Hammerless, Folding Trigger, Curio..	100	125	125

	V.G.	Exc	Prior Edition

VENCEDOR San Martin y Cia., Eibar, Spain.
HANDGUN, SEMI-AUTOMATIC

	V.G.	Exc	Prior Edition
.25 ACP, Clip Fed, Blue, Modern.	$100	$125	$125
.35 ACP, Clip Fed, Blue, Modern.	125	150	150

VENTURA IMPORTS (CONTENDO) Seal Beach, Calif.
Also see Bertuzzi and Piotti.

SHOTGUN, DOUBLE BARREL, OVER-UNDER

	V.G.	Exc	Prior Edition
MK–1 Contento, 12 Ga., Field Grade, Automatic Ejector, Single Selective Trigger, Engraved, Checkered Stock, Modern.	850	1,000	1,000
MK–2 Contento, 12 Ga., Field Grade, Automatic Ejector, Single Selective Trigger, Engraved, Checkered Stock, Modern.	1,100	1,300	1,300
MK–2 Contento, 12 Ga., Trap Grade, With Extra Single Trap Barrel, Engraved, Checkered Stock, Modern.	1,400	1,600	1,600
MK–2 Luxe Contento, 12 Ga., Field Grade, Automatic Ejector, Single Selective Trigger, Engraved, Checkered Stock, Modern.	1,000	1,200	1,200
MK–2 Luxe Contento, 12 Ga., Trap Grade, With Extra Single Trap Barrel, Engraved, Checkered Stock, Modern.	1,500	1,800	1,800
MK–3 Contento, 12 Ga., Field Grade, Automatic Ejector, Single Selective Trigger, Engraved, Checkered Stock, Modern.	1,250	1,500	1,500
MK–3 Contento, 12 Ga., Trap Grade, With Extra Single Trap Barrel, Engraved, Checkered Stock, Modern.	2,000	2,500	2,500
MK–3 Luxe Contento, 12 Ga., Field Grade, Automatic Ejector, Single Selective Trigger, Engraved, Checkered Stock, Modern.	1,500	1,800	1,800
MK–3 Luxe Contento, 12 Ga., Trap Grade, With Extra Single Trap Barrel, Engraved, Checkered Stock, Modern.	2,500	3,000	3,000
Nettuno Contento, 12 Ga., Field Grade, Automatic Ejector, Single Selective Trigger, Engraved, Checkered Stock, Modern.	400	450	450

SHOTGUN, DOUBLE BARREL, SIDE-BY-SIDE

	V.G.	Exc	Prior Edition
Ventura Model 51, 12 and 20 Gauges, Boxlock, Checkered Stock, Modern.	350	400	400
Ventura Model 62 Standard, 12 and 20 Gauges, Sidelock, Checkered Stock, Engraved, Modern.	800	900	900
Ventura Model 64 Standard, 12 and 20 Gauges, Sidelock, Checkered Stock, Engraved, Modern.	775	850	850

VENUS Tomas de Urizar y Cia., Eibar, Spain.
HANDGUN, SEMI-AUTOMATIC

	V.G.	Exc	Prior Edition
7.65mm, Clip Fed, Modern.	100	150	150

VENUS Venus Waffenwerk Oskar Will, Zella Mehils, Germany, c. 1912.
HANDGUN, SEMI-AUTOMATIC

	V.G.	Exc	Prior Edition
7.65mm, Target Pistol, Hammerless, Blue, Curio.	500	600	600

	V.G.	Exc	Prior Edition

VERNEY–CARRON St. Etienne, France.

HANDGUN, SEMI-AUTOMATIC

6.35mm, Clip Fed, Blue, Modern... $150 $175 $175

SHOTGUN, DOUBLE BARREL, OVER-UNDER

Field Grade, 12 Ga., Automatic Ejectors, Checkered Stock,
Engraved, Modern... 800 950 950

VESTA Hijos de A. Echevera, Eibar, Spain.

HANDGUN, SEMI-AUTOMATIC

Pocket, 7.65mm, Clip Fed, Long Grip, Modern....................................... 125 150 150
Vest Pocket, 6.35mm, Clip Fed, Modern.. 100 125 125

Vesta

VETERAN Made by Norwich Falls Pistol Co., c. 1880.

HANDGUN, REVOLVER

.32 Short R.F., 5 Shot, Spur Trigger, Solid Frame, Single Action,
Antique.. 125 175 175

VETO c. 1880.

HANDGUN, REVOLVER

.32 Short R.F., 5 Shot, Spur Trigger, Solid Frame, Single Action,
Antique.. 150 175 175

	V.G.	Exc	Prior Edition

VICI Belgian.
HANDGUN, SEMI-AUTOMATIC
7.65mm, Clip Fed, Modern.. $100 $125 $125

Vici

VICTOR Francisco Arizmendi, Eibar, Spain, c. 1916.
HANDGUN, SEMI-AUTOMATIC
6.35mm, Clip Fed, Blue, Curio.. 100 125 125
7.65mm, Clip Fed, Blue, Curio.. 125 150 150

VICTOR Made by Crescent, c. 1900.
SHOTGUN, DOUBLE BARREL, SIDE-BY-SIDE
Various Gauges, Hammerless, Damascus Barrel, Modern....................... 150 175 175
Various Gauges, Hammerless, Steel Barrel, Modern.............................. 175 200 200
Various Gauges, Outside Hammers, Damascus Barrel, Modern............. 150 175 175
Various Gauges, Outside Hammers,Steel Barrel, Modern....................... 150 200 200
SHOTGUN, SINGLESHOT
Various Guages, Hammer, Steel Barrel, Modern..................................... 75 100 100

VICTOR # 1 Made by Harrington & Richardson, c. 1876.
HANDGUN, REVOLVER
#1, .22 Short R.F., 7 Shot, Spur Trigger, Solid Frame, Single
Action, Antique... 150 175 175
#2, .32 Short R.F., 5 Shot, Spur Trigger, Solid Frame, Single
Action, Antique... 150 175 175
.32 S & W, 5 Shot, Single Action, Solid Frame, Antique.......................... 75 100 100

	V.G.	Exc	Prior Edition

VICTOR SPECIAL Made by Crescent for Hibbard–Spencer–Bartlett Co., c. 1900.

SHOTGUN, DOUBLE BARREL, SIDE-BY-SIDE

	V.G.	Exc	Prior Edition
Various Gauges, Hammerless, Damascus Barrel, Modern......	$150	$175	$175
Various Gauges, Outside Hammers, Steel Barrel, Modern......	150	200	200

SHOTGUN, SINGLESHOT

Various Gauges, Hammer, Steel Barrel, Modern..........	75	100	100

VICTORIA Made by Hood Firearms, c. 1875.

HANDGUN, REVOLVER

.32 Short R.F., 5 Shot, Spur Trigger, Solid Frame, Single Action, Antique..........	150	175	175

VICTORIA Spain, Esperanza y Unceta, c. 1900.

HANDGUN, SEMI-AUTOMATIC

6.35mm, Clip Fed, Modern..........	100	125	125

Victoria

M1911, .32 ACP, Clip Fed, Modern..........	125	150	150

VICTORY M. Zulaica y Cia., Eibar, Spain.

HANDGUN, SEMI-AUTOMATIC

6.35mm, Clip Fed, Modern..........	100	150	150

	V.G.	Exc	Prior Edition

VILAR Spain, 1920–1938.

HANDGUN, SEMI-AUTOMATIC

	V.G.	Exc	Prior Edition
Pocket, 7.65mm, Clip Fed, Long Grip, Modern..	$100	$125	$125

VINCITOR M. Zulaica y Cia., Eibar, Spain.

HANDGUN, SEMI-AUTOMATIC

Model 14 No. 2, 7.65mm, Clip Fed, Blue, Curio......................................	150	175	175
Model 1914, 6.35mm, Clip Fed, Blue, Curio..	125	150	150

VINDEX Mre. d' Armes des Pyrenees, Hendaye, France.

HANDGUN, SEMI-AUTOMATIC

7.65mm, Clip Fed, Blue, Modern...	100	125	125

VIRGINIA ARMS CO. Made by Crescent for Virginia–Caroline Co., c. 1900.

SHOTGUN, DOUBLE BARREL, SIDE-BY-SIDE

Various Gauges, Hammerless, Damascus Barrel Modern.......................	150	175	175
Various Gauges, Hammerless, Steel Barrel Modern...............................	175	200	200
Various Gauges, Outsde Hammers, Steel Barrel, Modern.......................	175	200	200
Various Gauges, Outside Hammers, Damascus Barrel Modern.............	150	175	175

SHOTGUN, SINGLESHOT

Various Gauges, Hammer, Steel Barrel, Modern....................................	75	100	100

VIRGINIAN Imported and manufactured (1976–1984) by Interarms, Alexandria, Va.

HANDGUN, REVOLVER

Dragoon, Buntline , Various Calibers, Single Action, Western Style, Target Sights, Blue, Modern......................	200	250	250
Dragoon, Deputy, Various Calibers, Single Action, Western Style, Fixed Sights, Blue, Modern........................	175	200	225
Dragoon, Deputy, Various Calibers, Single Action, Western Style, Fixed Sights, Stainless Steel, Modern....................	175	225	225
Dragoon, Engraved, Various Calibers, Single Action, Western Style, Target Sights, Blue, Modern......................	375	450	425
Dragoon, Engraved, Various Calibers, Single Action, Western Style, Target Sights, Presentation Case, Modern....................	400	525	450
Dragoon, Silhouette, .44 Magnum, Single Action, Western Style, Target Sights, Stainless Steel, Modern....................	225	275	275
Dragoon, Standard, Various Calibers, Single Action, Western Style, Target Sights, Blue, Modern......................	200	225	250
Dragoon, Standard, Various Calibers, Single Action, Western tyle, Target Sights, Stainless Steel, Modern....................	200	250	250

	V.G.	Exc	Prior Edition

VITE Echave y Arizmendi, Eibar, Spain, c. 1913.

HANDGUN, SEMI-AUTOMATIC

	V.G.	Exc	Prior Edition
Model 1912, 6.35mm, Clip Fed, Blue, Curio..	$100	$125	$125
Model 1915, 7.65mm, Clip Fed, Blue, Curio..	125	150	150

VOERE Voere GmbH, Vohrenbach, West Germany. Owned by Mauser since 1987.

RIFLE, BOLT ACTION

	V.G.	Exc	Prior Edition
Model 2145, .308 Win., Match Rifle, Target Stock, Modern....................	700	800	800
Model 3145 DJV, .223 Rem., Match Rifle, Target Stock, Modern..	500	550	550
Premier Mauser, Various Calibers, Sporting Rifle, Checkered Stock, Recoil Pad, Open Rear Sight, Modern..	300	350	350
Shikar, Various Calibers, Sporting Rifle, Fancy Checkering, Fancy Wood, Recoil Pad, no Sights, Modern..	450	500	500
Titan–Menor, Various Calibers, Sporting Rifle, Checkered Stock, Recoil Pad, Open Rear Sight, Modern...	350	400	400

VOERE Voere Tiroler Jagd u. Sportwaffenfabrik, Kufstein, Austria.

RIFLE, BOLT ACTION

	V.G.	Exc	Prior Edition
Model 2155, Various Calibers, Sporting Rifle, Checkered Stock, Open Rear Sight, Modern...	325	375	375
Model 2165/1, Various Calibers, Sporting Rifle, Checkered Stock, Recoil Pad, Open Rear Sight, Modern...	475	525	525

VOLUNTEER Made by Stevens Arms for Belknap Hardware Co., Louisville, Ky.

SHOTGUN, SINGLESHOT

	V.G.	Exc	Prior Edition
Model 94, Various Gauges, Takedown, Automatic Ejector, Plain, Hammer, Modern..	50	75	75

VULCAN ARMS CO. Made by Crescent, c. 1900.

SHOTGUN, DOUBLE BARREL, SIDE-BY-SIDE

	V.G.	Exc	Prior Edition
Various Gauges, Hammerless, Damascus barrel, Modern......................	150	175	175
Various Gauges, Hammerless, Steel Barrel, Modern...............................	175	200	200
Various Gauges, Outside Hammers, Damascus Barrel, Modern.............	150	175	175
Various Gauges, Outside Hammers, Steel Barrel, Modern......................	175	200	200

SHOTGUN, SINGLESHOT

	V.G.	Exc	Prior Edition
Various Gauges, Hammer, Steel Barrel, Modern....................................	75	100	100

W

	V.G.	Exc.	Prior Edition

WAFFENFABRIK BERN Eidgenosssische Waffenfabrik, Bern, Switzerland. Also see Swiss Military.

RIFLE, BOLT ACTION

	V.G.	Exc.	Prior Edition
Model 31, 7.5mm Swiss, Military Style, Modern	$575	$650	$650
Model 31 Target, 7.5mm Swiss, Military Style, Match Rifle, Target Sights, Modern	775	850	850

WALDMAN Arizmendi Y Goenaga, Eibar, Spain.

HANDGUN, SEMI-AUTOMATIC

	V.G.	Exc.	Prior Edition
6.35mm, Clip Fed, Curio	100	125	125
7.65mm, Clip Fed, Curio	125	150	150

WALMAN F. Arizmendi Y Goenaga, Eibar, Spain.

HANDGUN, SEMI-AUTOMATIC

	V.G.	Exc.	Prior Edition
.380 ACP, Clip Fed, Curio	175	225	225
6.35mm, Clip Fed, Curio	100	125	125
7.65mm, Clip Fed, Curio	125	150	150

WALSH FIREARMS CO. N.Y.C., c. 1860.

HANDGUN, PERCUSSION

	V.G.	Exc.	Prior Edition
Navy, .36, Revolver, 12 Shot, Double–Charge Cylinder, Antique	3,000	3,500	3,500

	V.G.	Exc	Prior Edition
Pocket, .31, Revolver, 12 Shot, Double–Charge Cylinder, Antique.........	$1,500	$1,750	$1,250

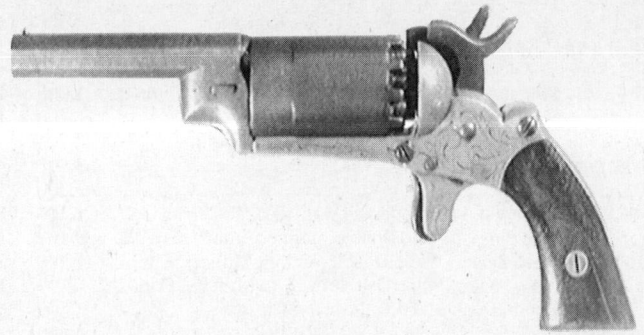

Walsh Pocket .31

WALSH, JAMES Philadelphia, Pa. 1775–1779. See Kentucky Rifles and Pistols and U.S. Military.

WALTHER First started in 1886 by Carl Walther in Zella Mehlis, Germany. After his death in 1915 the firm was operated by his sons Fritz, George, and Erich. Post WWII production in Ulm/Donau, West Germany. Also see German Military and Manurhin.

AIRGUNS

Model CP–2 C02, .177 Caliber, Single Shot, Blue	500	600	600
Model LGR Match, .177 Caliber, Singleshot, Blue	1,250	1,500	1,750
Model LGR Running Boar, .177 Caliber, Singleshot, Blue	1,000	1,250	1,000
Model LGR, .177 Caliber, Singleshot, Blue	800	1,000	1,000
Model LP–3, .177 Caliber, Single Shot, Blue	375	475	475

TARGET PISTOLS

Model GSP C, .22 Short, 5 Shot Clip, Target Pistol, Modern..................	1,050	1,300	1,200
Model GSP C, .22 Short, 5 Shot Clip, Target Pistol, with .22 L.R. Conversion Kit	750	1,000	900
Model GSP, .22 L.R.R.F., 5 Shot Clip, Target Pistol, Modern.................	950	1,200	1,100
Model OSP, .22 Short, Blue, Five Rounds Capacity, Modern.................	850	1,100	1,000
Olympia Rapid Fire, .22 L.R.R.F., Target Pistol, Modern......................	750	900	750
Olympia Sport, .22 L.R.R.F., Target Pistol, Modern.............................	600	850	850

HANDGUN, SEMI-AUTOMATIC - PRE 1945

Model 1, .25 ACP, Blue, Curio..	400	450	450
Model 2, .25 ACP, Pop–Up Rear Sight, Blue, Curio...............................	950	1,350	425
Model 3, .32 ACP, Blue, Curio..	1,250	1,500	1,500
Model 4, .32 ACP, Blue, Curio..	350	400	400
Model 5, .25 ACP, Solid Rib, Blue, Curio...	300	350	350
Model 6, 9mm Luger, Blue, Curio..	4,500	5,500	5,000

	V.G.	Exc	Prior Edition
Model 7, .25 ACP, Blue, Curio	$450	$625	$500
Model 8, .25 ACP, Blue, Curio	375	500	400
Model 9, .25 ACP, Blue, Curio	400	500	425
Model HP, .30 Luger, Single Action, Curio	4,000	5,000	5,000
Model HP, .30 Luger, Single Action, Wood Grips, Curio	4,500	5,500	5,500
Model HP, 9mm, H Prefix Serial Number, Curio	1,200	1,500	1,200
Model HP, 9mm, Hi–Gloss Blue, Curio	1,000	1,200	1,000
Model HP, 9mm, Military, Blue with Eagle/359 on right slide, Curio	1,000	1,200	1,200
Model HP, 9mm, Military, Blue, Curio	800	1,000	1,000
Model HP, Commercial Finish, 9mm Luger, Double Action, Lightweight, Curio	3,500	4,000	3,650
Model P38, 9mm, Curio	1,200	1,500	1,500
P–38, "480," 9mm, Double Action, Military, Curio	1,300	2,000	1,650
P–38, 1st, Model Zero Series, 9mm, Double Action, Curio	3,500	4,500	3,400
P–38, 2nd, Model Zero Series, 9mm, Double Action, Military, Curio	2,200	3,500	2,950
P–38, 3rd, Model Zero Series, 9mm, Double Action, Military, Curio	800	1,200	650
P–38, ac No Date, 9mm, Double Action, Military, Curio	3,500	6,000	5,775
ac40 (40 added), 9mm, Double Action, Curio	900	1,500	500
P–38, ac–40, 9mm, Double Action, Military, Curio	900	1,200	1,500
P–38, ac–41 Military Finish, 9mm, Double Action, Military, Curio	500	650	360
P–38, ac–41, 9mm, Double Action, Military, Curio	700	1,000	480
P–38, ac–42, 9mm, Double Action, Military, Curio	450	650	495
P–38, ac–43 Double Line, 9mm, Double Action, Military, Curio	400	500	425
P–38, ac–43 Police, 9mm, Double Action, Military, Curio	2,000	3,000	2,100
P–38, ac–43 WaA 135, 9mm, Double Action, Military, Curio	900	1,200	1,310
P–38, ac–43, Single Line, 9mm, Double Action, Military, Curio	450	700	300
P–38, ac–44 WaA140 Frame, 9mm, Double Action, Military, Curio	425	500	385
P–38, ac–44 Police, 9mm, Double Action, Military, Curio	2,000	3,000	2,800
P–38, ac–44, 9mm, Double Action, Military, Curio	325	400	290
P–38, ac–45 Mismatch, 9mm, Double Action, Military, Curio	300	375	375
P–38, ac–45, 9mm, Double Action, Military, Curio	350	400	305
P–38 ac–45 Zero Series, 9mm, Double Action, Military, Curio	700	1,000	1,000
P–38, byf–42, 9mm, Double Action, Military, Curio	650	500	320
P–38, byf–43 Police, 9mm, Double Action, Military, Curio	1,000	1,500	1,775
P–38, byf–43, 9mm, Double Action, Military, Curio	400	500	320
P–38, byf–44 police F Dual T, 9mm, Double Action, Military, Curio	1,000	1,500	1,500
P–38, byf–44 Police L Dual T, 9mm, Double Action, Military, Curio	1,800	2,500	1,850
P–38, byf–44 Police L, 9mm, Double Action, Military, Curio	1,000	1,500	1,000
P–38, byf–44, 9mm, Double Action, Military, Curio	400	500	350
P–38, crq Zero Series, 9mm, Double Action, Military, Curio	600	750	375
P–38, crq, 9mm, A or B Prefix, Curio	450	600	600
P–38, crq, 9mm, Double Action, Military, Curio	325	375	325
P–38, svw–45 French, 9mm, Double Action, Military, Curio	350	350	625
P–38, svw–45 Police, 9mm, Double Action, Military, Curio	2,000	3,000	2,300
P–38, svw–45, 9mm, Double Action, Military, Curio	550	800	300
P–38, svw–46 French, 9mm, Double Action, Military, Curio	400	500	750
PP "A.F. Stoeger, Inc., New York," .32 ACP, Double Action, Pre–War, High–Polish Finish, Curio	1,250	1,500	1,500
PP "Chas A. Heyer & Co., Nairobi," .32 ACP, Double Action, Pre–War, High–Polish Finish, Curio	—	RARE	—
PP (Early) 90 Degree Safety, .32 ACP, Double Action, Pre–War, Commercial, High–Polish Finish, Curio	700	775	775
PP (Early) Bottom Magazine, .380 ACP, Double Action, Pre–War, Commercial, High–Polish Finish, Curio	800	900	850

	V.G.	Exc	Prior Edition
PP AC Police F, .32 ACP, Double Action, Pre–War, Nazi–Proofed, Curio	$700	$775	$775
PP AC Waffenamt, .32 ACP, Double Action, Pre–War, Nazi–Proofed, Curio	350	400	350
PP AC, .32 ACP, Double Action, Nazi–Proofed, Curio	275	300	300
PP Bottom Magazine Release, .32 ACP, Double Action, Pre–War, Commercial, High–Polish Finish, Curio	850	1,000	850
PP Bottom Magazine Release, .32 ACP, Double Action, Pre–War, Commercial, High–Polish Finish, Lightweight, Curio	—	RARE	—
PP Czech, .32 ACP, Double Action, Pre–War, Commercial, High–Polish Finish, Curio	800	900	900
PP NSKK, .32 ACP, Double Action, Pre–War, High–Polish Finish, Nazi–Proofed, Curio	2,000	2,500	2,000
PP PDM, .32 ACP, Double Action, Pre–War, High–Polish Finish, Curio	750	900	800
PP Persian, .380 ACP, Double Action, Pre–War, Commercial, High–Polish Finish, Curio	1,800	2,000	1,750
PP Police C, .32 ACP, Double Action, Pre–War, High–Polish Finish, Nazi–Proofed, Curio	900	1,150	900
PP Police C, .32 ACP, Double Action, Pre–War, Nazi–Proofed, Curio	725	800	800
PP Police F, .32 ACP, Double Action, Pre–War, Nazi–Proofed, Curio	600	650	650
PP RFV, .32 ACP, Double Action, Pre–War, High–Polish, Curio	600	650	650
PP RJ, .32 ACP, Double Action, Pre–War, High–Polish Finish, Curio	650	700	700
PP SA, .32 ACP, Double Action, Pre–War, High–Polish Finish, Curio	1,250	1,500	1,500
PP Verchromt, .32 ACP, Double Action, Pre–War, Commercial, Curio	1,250	1,500	1,500
PP Verchromt, .380 ACP, Double Action, Pre–War, Commercial, Curio	1,800	2,250	2,000
PP Waffenamt, .32 ACP, Double Action, Pre–War, High–Polish Finish, Nazi–Proofed, Curio	450	500	500
PP Waffenamt, .32 ACP, Double Action, Pre–War, Nazi–Proofed, Curio	400	450	450
PP Waffenamt, .380 ACP, Double Action, Pre–War, High–Polish Finish, Nazi–Proofed, Curio	850	1,000	750
PP with Lanyard Loop, .32 ACP, Double Action, Pre–War, Commercial, High–Polish Finish, Nazi–Proofed, Modern	450	500	500
PP, .22 L.R.R.F., Double Action, Pre–War, Commercial, Nickel Plated, Curio	—	RARE	—
PP, .22 L.R.R.F., Double Action, Pre–War, Commercial, Nickel Plated, Nazi–Proofed, Curio	—	RARE	—
PP, .22 L.R.R.F., Double Action, Pre–War, Commercial, High–Polish Finish, Curio	750	900	850
PP, .22 L.R.R.F., Double Action, Pre–War, Commercial, High–Polish Finish, Nazi–Proofed, Curio	750	900	800
PP, .25 ACP, Double Action, Pre–War, Commercial, High–Polish Finish, Curio	3,000	3,250	3,250
PP, .32 ACP, Double Action, Pre–War, Commercial, High–Polished Finish, Curio	400	450	400
PP, .32 ACP, Double Action, Pre–War, Commercial, High–Polished Finish, Nazi–Proofed, Curio	400	450	400
PP, .32 ACP, Double Action, Pre–War, Commercial, Lightweight, High–Polish Finish, Curio	600	675	550
PP, .32 ACP, Double Action, Pre–War, Commercial, Nazi–Proofed, Curio	325	375	375

	V.G.	Exc	Prior Edition
PP, .32 ACP, Double Action, Pre–War, Commercial, Nickel Plated, Nazi–Proofed, Curio.............	—	RARE	—
PP, .32 ACP, Double Action, Pre–War, Commercial, Nickel Plated, Curio.............	—	RARE	—
PP, .32 ACP, Double Action, Pre–War, Nazi–Proofed, Lightweight, High–Polish Finish, Curio.............	$600	$675	$525
PP, .32 ACP, Double Action, Pre–War, Nazi–Proofed, Lightweight Curio.............	400	450	450
PP, .380 ACP, Double Action, Pre–War, Commercial, High–Polish Finish, Curio.............	800	900	850
PP, .380 ACP, Double Action, Pre–War, Commercial, High–Polish Finish, Nazi–Proofed, Curio.............	800	900	875
PP, .380 ACP, Double Action, Pre–War, Commercial, Nickel Plated, Curio.............	—	RARE	—
PP, .380 ACP, Double Action, Pre–War, Commercial, Nickel Plated, Nazi–Proofed, Curio.............	—	RARE	—
PPK "Cas A. Heyer & Co., Nairobi,".32 ACP, Double Action, Pre–War, High–Polish Finish, Curio.............	—	RARE	—
PPK "Stoeger," .32 ACP, Double Action, Pre–War, High–Polish Finish, Curio.............	—	RARE	—
PPK (Early) 90 Degree Safety, .32 ACP, Double Action, Pre–War, Commercial, High–Polish Finish, Curio.............	550	600	600
PPK Czech, .32 ACP, Double Action, Pre–War, Commercial, High–Polish Finish, Curio.............	850	1,000	900
PPK DRP, .32 ACP, Double Action, Pre–War, High–Polish Finish, Curio.............	850	900	800
PPK Party Leader, .32 ACP, Double Action, Pre–War, High–Polish Finish, Curio.............	2,250	2,500	2,250
PPK PDM, .32 ACP, Double Action, Pre–War, High–Polish Finish, Lightweight, Curio.............	1,350	1,500	950
PPK Police C, .32 ACP, Double Action, Pre–War, High–Polish Finish, Nazi–Proofed, Curio.............	675	750	750
PPK Police C, .32 ACP, Double Action, Pre–War, Nazi–Proofed, Curio.............	550	600	600
PPK Police F, .32 ACP, Double Action, Pre–War, Nazi–Proofed, Curio.............	800	900	750
PPK RFV, .32 ACP, Double Action, Pre–War, High–Polish Finish, Curio.............	850	950	950
PPK RZM, .32 ACP, Double Action, Pre–War, High–Polish Finish, Curio.............	850	900	850
PPK Verchromt, .32 ACP, Double Action, Pre–War, Commercial, Curio.............	1,800	2,000	1,800
PPK Verchromt, .380 ACP, Double Action, Pre–War, High–Polish Finish, Curio.............	2,000	2,250	2,250
PPK Waffenamt, .32 ACP, Double Action, Pre–War, High–Polish Finish, Nazi–Proofed, Curio.............	875	1,000	800
PPK Waffenamt, .32 ACP, Double Action, Pre–War, Nazi–Proofed, Curio.............	750	800	750
PPK, .22 L.R.R.F., Double Action, Pre–War, Commercial, High–Polish Finish, Curio.............	1,000	1,200	1,000
PPK, .22 L.R.R.F., Double Action, Pre–War, Commercial, High–Polish Finish, Nazi–Proofed, Curio.............	1,000	1,200	1,050
PPK, .25 ACP, Double Action, Pre–War, Commercial, High–Polish Finish, Curio.............	4,500	5,500	5,500

	V.G.	Exc	Prior Edition
PPK, .32 ACP, Double Action, Pre–War, Commercial, High–Polish Finish, Curio	$475	$525	$525
PPK, .32 ACP, Double Action, Pre–War, Commercial, High–Polish Finish, Nazi–Proofed, Curio	475	525	525
PPK, .32 ACP, Double Action, Pre–War, Commercial, Lightweight, High–Polish Finish, Curio	650	700	600
PPK, .32 ACP, Double Action, Pre–War, Commercial, Nazi–Proofed, Curio	450	500	500
PPK, .32 ACP, Double Action, Pre–War, Nazi–Proofed, Lightweight, High–Polish Finish, Curio	650	700	550
PPK, .32 ACP, Double Action, Pre–War, Nazi–Proofed, Lightweight, Curio	550	600	600
PPK, .380 ACP, Double Action, Pre–War, Commercial, High–Polish Finish, Curio	1,800	2,000	1,800
PPK, .380 ACP, Double Action, Pre–War, Commercial, High–Polish Finish, Nazi–Proofed, Curio	1,800	2,000	1,000
PPK, .380 ACP, Double Action, Pre–War, Commercial, Nickel Plated, Curio	—	RARE	—
PPK, .380 ACP, Double Action, Pre–War, Commercial, Nickel Plated, Nazi–Proofed, Curio	—	RARE	—

HANDGUN, SEMI-AUTOMATIC - POSTWAR

P–1, 9mm, Double Action, Alloy Frame, Modern	350	450	525
P–38, .22 L.R.R.F., Double Action, Modern	600	850	850
P–38, .30 Luger, Double Action, Blue, Modern	700	850	850
P–38, 9mm, Double Action, Modern	400	600	750
P–38–IV (P–4), 9mm, Double Action, Modern	350	500	500
P–38k, 9mm, Double Action, Short Barrel, Modern	600	800	800
P–5, 9mm, Interarms, Double Action, Blue, Modern	550	700	700
PP Super, 9 x 18mm, Clip Fed, Blue, Modern	400	650	650
PP, .22 L.R.R.F., Double Action, Modern	500	650	475
PP, .32 ACP, Double Action, Blue, Modern	450	600	425
PP, .380 ACP, Double Action, Blue, Modern	500	650	450
PPK, .22 L.R.R.F., Double Action, Lightweight, Post–War, Modern	600	700	475
PPK, .22 L.R.R.F., Double Action, Post–War, Modern	650	750	700
PPK, .32 ACP, Double Action, Lightweight, Post–War, Modern	425	500	400
PPK, .32 ACP, Double Action, Post–War, Modern	450	525	450
PPK, .380 ACP, Double Action, Modern	600	700	600
PPK/S, .22 L.R.R.F., Double Action, Modern	575	650	600
PPK/S, .32 ACP, Double Action, Blue, Modern	425	475	475
PPK/S, .380 ACP, Double Action, Blue, Modern	525	600	550
PPK/S, .380 ACP, Double Action, Blue, Seven Rounds Capacity, Modern	400	500	450
PPK/S, .380 ACP, Double Action, Stainless Steel, Seven Rounds Capacity, Modern	400	500	450
TPH, .22 L.R.R.F., Double Action, Clip–Fed, Modern	500	650	650
TPH, .22 L.R.R.F., Double Action, Clip–Fed, German Manuf., Modern	400	575	650
TPH, .25 ACP, Double Action, Clip–Fed, Modern	350	450	450
TPH, .25 ACP, Double Action, Clip–Fed, German Manuf., Modern	375	600	700

HANDGUN, SEMI-AUTOMATIC - WALTHER MARK II

PP Mark II "Manurhin," .22 L.R.R.F., Double Action, High–Polish Finish, Blue, Curio	350	425	425
PP Mark II "Manurhin," .32 ACP, Double Action, High–Polish Finish, Blue, Curio	300	375	375

	V.G.	Exc	Prior Edition
PP Mark II "Manurhin," .380 ACP, Double Action, High–Polish Finish, Blue, Curio....................	$300	$400	$400
PPK Mark II "Manurhin," .22 L.R.R.F., Double Action, High– Polish Finish, Blue, Curio....................	500	550	500
PPK Mark II "Manurhin," .22 L.R.R.F., Double Action, High– Polish Finish, Blue, Lightweight, Curio....................	500	550	550
PPK Mark II "Manurhin," .32 ACP, Double Action, High–Polish Finish, Blue, Curio....................	375	450	400
PPK Mark II "Manurhin," .32 ACP, Double Action, High–Polish Finish, Blue, Lightweight, Curio....................	450	500	450
PPK Mark II "Manurhin," .380 ACP, Double Action, High–Polish Finish, Blue, Curio....................	500	550	450

RIFLE, BOLT ACTION

	V.G.	Exc	Prior Edition
KKJ, .22 Hornet, 5 Shot Clip, Open Rear Sight, Checkered Stock, Modern....................	500	700	700
KKJ, .22 Hornet, 5 Shot Clip, Open Rear Sight, Checkered Stock, Set Trigger, Modern....................	650	850	750
KKJ, .22 L.R.R.F., 5 Shot Clip, Open Rear Sight, Checkered Stock, Modern....................	400	500	500
KKJ, .22 L.R.R.F., 5 Shot Clip, Open Rear Sight, Checkered Stock, Set Trigger, Modern....................	450	600	650
KKJ, .22 WMR, 5 Shot Clip, Open Rear Sight, Checkered Stock, Modern....................	500	700	700
KKJ, .22 WMR, 5 Shot Clip, Open Rear Sight, Checkered Stock, Set Trigger, Modern....................	650	850	850
KKM International Match, .22 L.R.R.F., Singleshot, Target Stock, with Accessories, Modern....................	600	800	750
KKM–S Silhouette, .22 L.R., Singleshot, Blue, Modern....................	650	850	850
Model B, Various Caliber, Checkered Stock, Mauser Action, Set Triggers, Modern....................	350	425	425
Model GX–1, .22 L.R., Singleshot, Blue, Modern....................	1,200	1,500	1,500
Model KKW, .22 L.R.R.F., Pre–WW2, Singleshot, Tangent Sights, Military Style Stock, Modern....................	350	500	450
Model V "Meisterbushe," Singleshot, Pistol–Grip Stock, Target Sights, Modern....................	350	450	450
Model V, Singleshot, Sporting Rifle, Open Rear Sight, Modern....................	300	375	375
Moving Target, .22 L.R.R.F., Singleshot, Target Stock, with Accessories, Modern....................	550	700	750
Olympic, .22 L.R.R.F., Singleshot, Target Stock, with Accessories, Modern....................	750	950	950
Prone "400," .22 L.R.R.F., Singleshot, Target Stock, with Accessories, Modern....................	550	650	650
Running Boar, .22 L.R., Singleshot, Blue, Modern....................	650	900	900
U.I.T.–E. Universal Match, .22 L.R., Singleshot, Blue, Modern....................	950	1,200	1,200
UIT Match, .22 L.R.R.F., Singleshot, Target Stock, with Accessories, Modern....................	750	1,000	1,000
UIT Special, .22 L.R.R.F., Singleshot, Target Stock, with Accessories, Modern....................	900	1,200	1,200

RIFLE, SEMI-AUTOMATIC

	V.G.	Exc	Prior Edition
Model 1, Clip Fed, Carbine, Modern....................	300	375	375
Model 2, .22 L.R.R.F., Clip Fed, Modern....................	375	475	475

	V.G.	Exc	Prior Edition

SHOTGUN, DOUBLE BARREL, SIDE-BY-SIDE

	V.G.	Exc	Prior Edition
Model S.F., 12 or 16 Gauges, Checkered Stock, Cheekpiece, Double Triggers, Sling Swivels, Modern	$375	$475	$475
Model S.F.D., 12 or 16 Gauges, Checkered Stock, Cheekpiece, Double Triggers, Sling Swivels, Modern	500	600	600

WAMO Wamo Mfg. Co., San Gabriel, Calif.

HANDGUN, SINGLESHOT

Powermaster, .22 L.R.R.F., Target Pistol, Modern	100	125	125

WARNANT L. & J. Warnant Freres, Hognee, Belgium.

HANDGUN, REVOLVER

.32 S & W, Double Action, Folding Trigger, Break Top, Curio	75	100	100
.38 S & W, Double Action, Folding Trigger, Break Top, Curio	100	125	100

HANDGUN, SEMI-AUTOMATIC

6.35mm, Clip Fed, Blue, Curio	175	225	225

HANDGUN, SINGLESHOT

Traff, 6mm R.F., Spur Trigger, Parlor Pistol, Curio	100	125	75
Traff, 9mm R.F., Spur Trigger, Parlor Pistol, Curio	100	125	75

RIFLE, SINGLESHOT

Amelung, Various Rimfires, Checkered Stock, Set Triggers, Parlor Rifle, Curio	75	100	100
Amelung, Various Rimfires, Plain, Parlor Rifle, Curio	50	75	75

WARNER Warner Arms Corp., Brooklyn, N.Y., formed about 1912, moved to Norwich, Conn. in 1913, and in 1917 merged and became Davis–Warner Arms Corp., Assonet, Mass., out of business about 1919. See also Schwarzlose.

SEMI-AUTOMATIC

Infallable, .32 ACP, Clip Fed, Modern	275	325	325
Revolver, .32 CAL., 5–Shot, Modern	125	150	150

WARREN ARMS CORP. Belgium, c. 1900.

SHOTGUN, DOUBLE BARREL, SIDE-BY-SIDE

Various Gauges, Hammerelss, Damascus Barrel, Modern	150	175	175
Various Gauges, Hammerless, Steel Barrel, Modern	175	200	200
Various Gauges, Outside Hammers, Damascus Barrel, Modern	150	175	175
Various Gauges, Outside Hammers, Steel Barrel, Modern	175	200	200

SHOTGUN, SINGLESHOT

Various Gauges, Hammer, Steel Barrel, Modern	75	100	100

	V.G.	Exc	Prior Edition

WATSON BROS. London, England 1885–1931.

RIFLE, BOLT ACTION

.303 British, Express Sights, Sporting Rifle, Checkered Stock, Modern.. $625 $700 $700

RIFLE, DOUBLE BARREL, SIDE-BY-SIDE

.450/.400 N.E. 3", Double Trigger, Recoil Pad, Plain, Cased, Modern.. 3,500 4,000 4,000

WATTERS, JOHN Carlisle, Pa. 1778–1785. See Kentucky Rifles.

WEATHERBY South Gate, Calif. 1945 to date.

HANDGUN, SINGLESHOT

Mk. V. Slihouette, Various Calibers, Thumbhole Target Stock, Target Sights, Modern.. 1,750 2,000 1,000

RIFLE, BOLT ACTION

For German Manufacture, Add 30%–50%
Deluxe, .378 Wby. Mag., Magnum, Checkered Stock, Modern............... 850 950 400
Deluxe, Various Calibers, Checkered Stock, Modern............................. 800 900 900
Deluxe, Various Calibers, Magnum, Checkered Stock, Modern............... 825 925 925
Mark V, .378 Wby. Mag., Checkered Stock, Modern............................ 900 1,100 1,100
Mark V, .460 Wby. Mag., Checkered Stock, Modern............................ 1,000 1,250 1,250
Mark V, Various Calibers, Checkered Stock, Modern............................ 650 750 850

Weatherby Mark V

Mark V, Various Calibers, Varmint, Checkered Stock, Modern............. 850 950 950
Mark V Crown Custom, Various Calibers, 24" or 26" Barrel, Right Hand Only, Modern.. 3,000 3,500 3,500
Mark V Fibermark, Various Calibers, Fiberglass, Right Hand Only, Modern.. 750 850 1,000
Mark V Lazermark, Various Calibers, Carved Stock (Carved With Laser Beam), Modern.. 850 1,100 1,100
Vanguard, Various Calibers, Checkered Stock, Modern........................ 400 450 500

RIFLE, SEMI-AUTOMATIC

Mark XXII, .22 L.R.R.F., Clip Fed, Checkered Stock, Modern............... 300 325 325
Mark XXII, .22 L.R.R.F., Tube Feed, Checkered Stock, Modern........... 325 350 350
Model M–82, Various Gauges, Gas Operated, Various Barrel Lengths, Modern.. 400 450 450

	V.G.	Exc	Prior Edition

SHOTGUN, DOUBLE BARREL, OVER-UNDER

Athena Skeet Grade, 12 Gauge, Single Selective Trigger,
26" Barrels, Modern... $1,250 $1,500 $1,250

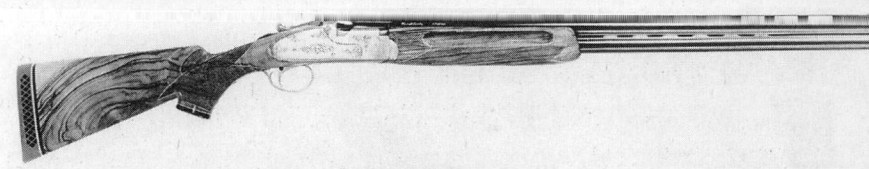

Weatherby Athena

	V.G.	Exc	Prior Edition
Athena Trap Grade, 12 Gauge, Single Selective Trigger, 30" Barrels, Modern..........	1,000	1,250	1,250
Orion 20 Field Grade, 20 Gauge, Single Selective Trigger, 26" or 28" Barrel, Modern..........	775	850	850
Orion Field Grade, 12 Gauge, Single Selective Trigger, 26" or 28" Barrel, Modern..........	775	800	800
Orion Skeet Grade, 12 Gauge, Single Selective Trigger, 26" Barrels, Modern..........	750	825	875
Orion Trap Grade, 12 Gauge, Single Selective Trigger, 30" or 32" Barrel, Modern..........	750	825	875
Regency, 12 Gauge, Trap Grade, Vent Rib, Checkered Stock, Engraved, Single Selective Trigger, Modern..........	675	750	800
Regency, Field Grade, 12 and 20 Gauges, Vent Rib, Checkered Stock, Engraved, Single Selective Trigger, Modern..........	725	775	775

SHOTGUN, SEMI-AUTOMATIC

	V.G.	Exc	Prior Edition
Centurion, 12 Gauge, Field Grade, Vent Rib, Checkered Stock, Modern..........	225	275	275
Centurion, 12 Gauge, Trap Grade, Checkered Stock, Vent Rib, Modern..........	200	250	300
Centurion Deluxe, 12 Gauge, Checkered Stock, Vent Rib, Light Engraving, Fancy Wood, Modern..........	250	300	375

SHOTGUN, SLIDE ACTION

	V.G.	Exc	Prior Edition
Model M-92, 12 Gauge, Vent Rib, Three Sheel Mag., Modern..........	225	275	275
Patrician, 12 Gauge, Field Grade, Checkered Stock, Vent Rib, Modern..........	200	225	225
Patrician, 12 Gauge, Trap Grade, Checkered Stock, Vent Rib, Modern..........	225	250	250
Patrician, Deluxe, 12 Gauge, Checkered Stock, Light Engraving, Fancy Wood, Vent Rib, Modern..........	225	275	275

WEAVER, CRYPRET Pa., c. 1818. See Kentucky Rifles.

	V.G.	Exc	Prior Edition

WEBLEY & SCOTT LTD. Located in Birmingham, England
operating as P. Webley & Son, 1860–1897; Webley & Scott Revolver &
Arms Co., 1898–1906; Webley & Scott 1906–1979.

HANDGUN, REVOLVER

	V.G.	Exc	Prior Edition
#1, .577 Eley, Solid Frame, Double Action, Blue, Curio	$150	$200	$200
British Bulldog, Various Calibers, Solid Frame, Double Action, Curio	300	350	350
Tower Bulldog, Various Calibers, Solid Frame, Double Action, Curio	275	325	325
Webley Kaufman, .45 Colt, Top Break, Square–Butt, Commercial, Antique	400	475	475
Webley MK 1, .455 Revolver Mk 1, Top Break, Round–Butt, Military, Antique	225	250	250
Webley MK 1*, .455 Revolver Mk 1, Top Break, Round–Butt, Military, Antique	200	225	225
Webley MK 1** Navy, .455 Revolver Mk 1, Top Break, Round Butt, Military, Modern	200	225	225
Webley MK 2, .455 Revolver Mk 1, Top Break, Round Butt, Military, Antique	225	250	250
Webley MK 2*, .455 Revolver Mk 1, Top Break, Round Butt, Military, Curio	225	250	250
Webley MK 2**, .455 Revolver Mk 1, Top Break, Round Butt, Military, Curio	225	250	250
Webley MK 3, .455 Revolver Mk 1, Top Break, Round Butt, Military, Curio	250	275	275
Webley MK 4, .455 Revolver Mk 1, Top Break, Round Butt, Military, Curio	200	250	250
Webley MK 5, .455 Revolver Mk 1, Top Break, Round Butt, Military, Curio	225	275	275
Webley MK 6, .455 Revolver Mk 1, Top Break, Square– Butt, Military, Curio	300	350	350
Webley MK 6, Detachable Buttstock Only,	300	350	350
Webley Mk III M & P, .38 S & W, Top Break, Square–Butt, Commercial, Modern	250	300	300
Webley Mk IV, .38 S & W, Top Break, Square–Butt, Military, Curio	225	275	200
Webley Mk VI, .22 L.R.R.F., Top Break, Square–Butt, Commercial, Modern	400	475	475
Webley R I C, .455 Revolver Mk 1, Solid Frame, Square–Butt, Commercial, Antique	225	250	250
Webley–Green, .455 Revolver Mk 1, Top Break, Square–Butt, Commercial, Target Pistol, Antique	425	475	475
Webley–Green, .476 Enfield Mk 3, Top Break, Square–Butt, Commercial, Target Pistol, Antique	425	475	475

HANDGUN, SEMI-AUTOMATIC

	V.G.	Exc	Prior Edition
Model 1904, .455 Webley Auto., Clip Fed, Grip Safety, Hammer, Curio	650	750	750
Model 1906, .25 ACP, Clip Fed, Hammer, Modern	225	250	250
Model 1909 M & P, 9mm Browning Long, Clip Fed, Hammer, Curio	400	450	450

	V.G.	Exc	Prior Edition
Model 1909 M & P, 9mm Browning Long, South African Police, Clip Fed, Hammer, Curio	$500	$550	$550
Model 1909, .25 ACP, Clip Fed, Hammerless, Modern	225	250	250
Model 1909, 9mm, Clip Fed, Hammerless, Modern	400	450	200
Model 1911 Metro Police, .32 ACP, Clip Fed, Hammer, Modern	625	700	700
Model 1911 Metro Police, .380 ACP, Clip Fed, Hammer, Modern	700	800	800
Model 1912, .455 Caliber, Clip Fed, Hammerless, Curio	400	450	450
Model 1913 Mk 1 #2, .455 Webley Auto., Clip Fed, Grip Safety, Adjustable Sights, Hammer, Curio	950	1,200	1,200
Model 1913 Mk 1, .455 Webley Auto., Clip Fed, Grip Safety, Military, Hammer, Curio	2,000	2,250	2,250
Model 1913, .38 ACP, Clip Fed, Hammerless, Curio	1,000	1,250	1,250

SHOTGUN, DOUBLE BARREL, SIDE-BY-SIDE

	V.G.	Exc	Prior Edition
Model 700, 12 and 20 Gauges, Box Lock, Hammerless, Checkered Stock, Light Engraving, Single Trigger, Modern	1,450	1,600	1,600
Model 701, 12 and 20 Gauges, Box Lock, Hammerless, Checkered Stock, Fancy Engraving, Double Trigger, Modern	2,000	2,500	2,500
Model 701, 12 and 20 Gauges, Box Lock, Hammerless, Checkered Stock, Fancy Engraving, Single Trigger, Modern	2,200	2,600	2,600
Model 702, 12 and 20 Gauges, Box Lock, Hammerless, Checkered Stock, Engraved, Double Trigger, Modern	1,750	2,200	2,200
Model 702, 12 and 20 Gauges, Box Lock, Hammerless, Checkered Stock, Engraved, Single Trigger, Modern	1,800	2,250	2,250

WELSHANTZ, DAVID   York, Pa. 1780–1783. See Kentucky Rifles, U.S. Military.

WELSHANTZ, JACOB   York, Pa. 1777–1792. See Kentucky Rifles, U.S. Military.

WELSHANTZ, JOSEPH   York, Pa. 1779–1983. See Kentucky Rifles, U.S. Military.

WESSON & HARRINGTON   Worcester, Mass. 1871–1874.

Succeeded by Harrington and Richardson.

HANDGUN, REVOLVER

	V.G.	Exc	Prior Edition
.22 Short R.F., 7 Shot, Spur Trigger, Solid Frame, Single Action, Antique	150	175	175
.32 Short R.F., 5 Shot, Spur Trigger, Solid Frame, Single Action, Antique	150	175	175
.38 Short R.F., 5 Shot, Spur Trigger, Solid Frame, Single Action, Antique	175	200	200

WESSON, FRANK Worcester, Mass. 1854 to 1865. 1865–1875 at Springfield, Mass. Also see U.S. Military, Wesson & Harrington, Harrington & Richardson.

HANDGUN, DOUBLE BARREL, OVER-UNDER

	V.G.	Exc	Prior Edition
Vest Pocket, .22 Short, Twist Barrel, Spur Trigger, Antique	$700	$1,000	$800
Vest Pocket, .32 Short, Twist Barrel, Spur Trigger, Antique	500	550	550
Vest Pocket, .41 Short, Twist Barrel, Spur Trigger, with Knife, Antique	1,000	1,250	850

HANDGUN, SINGLESHOT

	V.G.	Exc	Prior Edition
Model 1859, .22 Short, Tip–Up Barrel, Spur Trigger, Antique	400	450	650
Model 1859, .32 R.F., Tip–Up Barrel, Spur Trigger, Antique	450	500	500
Model 1859, .39 R.F., Tip–Up Barrel, Spur Trigger, Antique	450	500	500
Model 1862, .22 Short, Tip–Up Barrel, Spur Trigger, Antique	300	350	550
Model 1862, .30 R.F., Tip–Up Barrel, Spur Trigger, Antique	450	500	500
Model 1862, .32 R.F., Tip–Up Barrel, Spur Trigger, Antique	450	500	500
Model 1862 Pocket Rifle, Various Calibers, Medium Frame, Spur Trigger, Target Sights, Detachable Stock, Antique	500	550	550
Model 1870 Pocket Rifle, .22 Short, Small Frame, Spur Triffer, Target Sights, Detachable Stock, Antique	400	450	450
Model 1870 Pocket Rifle, Various Calibers, Large Frame, Spur Trigger, Target Sights, Detachable Stock, Antique	725	775	775
Model 1870 Pocket Rifle, Various Calibers, Medium Frame, Spur Trigger, Target Sights, Detachable Stock, Antique	350	400	400

RIFLE, SINGLESHOT

	V.G.	Exc	Prior Edition
.32 Long R.F., Two–Trigger, Tip–Up, Antique	500	550	550

WESTERN ARMS CO.

HANDGUN, REVOLVER

	V.G.	Exc	Prior Edition
.32 Long .F., 5 Shot, Folding Trigger, Double Action, Antique	75	100	100

WESTERN FIELD Trade name for Montgomery Ward.

RIFLE, BOLT ACTION

	V.G.	Exc	Prior Edition
Model 56 Buckhorn, .22 L.R.R.F., 5 Shot Clip, Open Rear Sight, Modern	50	75	75
Model 724, .30–06 Springfield, Checkered Stock, Full–Stocked, Modern	125	175	175
Model 732, .30–06 Springfield, Checkered Stock, Recoil Pad, Modern	125	175	175
Model 734, 7mm Rem. Mag., Checkered Stock, Recoil Pad, Modern	125	175	175
Model 765, .30–06 Springfield, Checkered Stock, Modern	100	150	150
Model 770, Various Calibers, Checkered Stock, Sling Swivels, Modern	125	175	175
Model 78, Various Calibers, Checkered Stock, Sling Swivels, Modern	125	175	175

	V.G.	Exc	Prior Edition
Model 780, Various Calibers, Checkered Stock, Sling Swivels, Modern	$150	$175	$175
Model 815, .22 L.R.R.F., Singleshot, Modern	25	50	50
Model 822, .22 WMR, Clip Fed, Modern	25	50	50
Model 83, .22 L.R.R.F., Singleshot, Open Rear Sight, Takedown, Modern	25	50	50
Model 830, .22 L.R.R.F., Clip Fed, Modern	25	50	50
Model 832, .22 L.R.R.F., Clip Fed, Checkered Stock, Modern	25	50	50
Model 84, .22 L.R.R.F., 5 Shot Clip, Open Rear Sight, Takedown, Modern	25	50	50
Model 840, .22 WMR, Clip Fed, Modern	50	75	75
Model 852 , .22 L.R.R.F., Clip Fed, Modern	25	50	50
Model 86, .22 L.R.R.F., Tube Feed, Takedown, Open Rear Sight, Modern	25	50	50
Modl 842, .22 L.R.R.F., Tube Feed, Modern	25	50	50

RIFLE, LEVER ACTION

	V.G.	Exc	Prior Edition
Model 72, .30–30 Win., Pistol Grip Stock, Plain, Tube Feed, Modern	100	125	125
Model 72C, .30–30 Win., Straight Grip, Plain, Tube Feed, Modern	100	125	125
Model 79, .30–30 Win., Pistol Grip Stock, Plain, Tube Feed, Modern	100	125	125
Model 865, .22 L.R.R.F., Tube Feed, Sling Swivels, Modern	50	75	75
Model 895, .22 L.R.R.F., Tube Feed, Carbine, Modern	50	75	75

RIFLE, SEMI-AUTOMATIC

	V.G.	Exc	Prior Edition
Model 808, .22 L.R.R.F., Tube Feed, Modern	25	50	50
Model 828, .22 L.R.R.F., Clip Fed, Checkered Stock, Modern	50	75	75
Model 836, .22 L.R.R.F., Tube Feed, Modern	50	75	75
Model 846, .22 L.R.R.F., Tube Feed, Modern	50	75	75
Model 850, .22 L.R.R.F., Clip Fed, Modern	50	75	75
Model 880, .22 L.R.R.F., Tube Feed, Moden	50	50	50
Model M–1, .30 Carbine, Clip Fed, Modern	125	150	150

SHOTGUN, BOLT ACTION

	V.G.	Exc	Prior Edition
Model 150, .410 Ga., Clip Fed, Modern	25	50	50
Model 172–5, 12 and 20 Gauges, Magnum, Clip Fed, Adjustable Choke, Modern	50	75	75

SHOTGUN, DOUBLE BARREL, SIDE-BY-SIDE

	V.G.	Exc	Prior Edition
12 and 20 Gauges, Single Trigger, Hammerless, Checkered Stock, Modern	125	150	150
Long–Range, Various Gauges, Double Trigger, Hammerless, Modern	150	175	175
Long–Range, Various Gauges, Single Trigger, Hammerless, Modern	175	200	200
Model 330, Various Gauges, Hammerless, Checkered Stock, Modern	125	150	150
Model 5151, Various Gauges, Hammerless, Steel Barrel, Modern	125	150	150
Various Gauges, Hammerless, Plain, Modern	100	125	125

SHOTGUN, SEMI-AUTOMATIC

	V.G.	Exc	Prior Edition
Model 60, 12 Ga., Takedown, Plain Barrel, Checkered Stock, Modern	125	150	150

	V.G.	Exc	Prior Edition
Model 600, 12 Ga., Takedown, Vent Rib, Checkered Stock, Modern..	$125	$150	$150

SHOTGUN, SINGLESHOT

Model 100, Various Gauges, Hammerless, Adjustable Choke, Modern..	25	50	50
Trap, 12 Ga., Hammer, Solid Rib, Checkered Stock, Modern.................	75	100	100

SHOTGUN, SLIDE ACTION

Model 500, .410 Ga., Plain, Takedown, Modern......................................	100	125	125
Model 502, .410 Ga., Checkered Stock, Light Engraving, Takedown, Vent Rib, Modern..	100	125	125
Model 520, 12 Ga., Takedown, Modern..	100	125	125
Model 550, 12 and 20 Gauges, Checkered Stock, Light Engraving, Vent Rib, Takedown, Modern..	100	125	125
Model 550, 12 and 20 Gauges, Checkered Stock, Light Engraving, Vent Rib, Takedown, Adjustable Choke, Modern....................................	125	150	150
Model 550, 12 and 20 Gauges, Plain, Takedown, Modern.......................	100	125	125
Model 620, Various Gauges, Takedown, Modern....................................	125	150	150

WESTLEY RICHARDS Birmingham, England, Since 1812.

RIFLE, BOLT ACTION

Stalker, Various Calibers, Express Sights, Fancy Wood, Fancy Checkering, Repeater, Modern...	8,000	9,000	8,500

RIFLE, DOUBLE BARREL, SIDE-BY-SIDE

Best Quality, Various Calibers, Sidelock, Double Trigger, Fancy Engraving, Fancy Checkering, Express Sights, Modern............................	30,000	35,000	35,000

SHOTGUN, DOUBLE BARREL, OVER-UNDER

Owundo, 12 Ga., Sidelock, Single Selective Trigger, Selective Ejector, Fancy Engraving, Fancy Checkering, Modern...............................	10,000	12,500	17,500

SHOTGUN, DOUBLE BARREL, SIDE-BY-SIDE

10 Ga. Pinfire, Engraved, Carbine, Antique...	850	950	950
Best, Pigeon, 12 Ga. Mag. 3", Sidelock, Hammerless, Fancy Engraving, Fancy Checkering, Double Trigger, Modern..........................	17,500	20,000	20,000
Best, Pigeon, 12 Ga. Mag. 3", Sidelock, Hammerless, Fancy Engraving, Fancy Checkering, Single Selective Trigger, Modern............	18,500	21,000	21,000
Best Quality, Various Gauges, Box Lock, Hammerless, Fancy Engraving, Fancy Checkering, Single Selective Trigger, Modern............	11,000	13,000	13,000
Best Quality, Various Gauges, Sidelock, Hammerless, Fancy Engraving, Fancy Checkering, Double Trigger, Modern..........................	17,500	20,000	20,000
Best Quality, Various Gauges, Sidelock, Hammerless, Fancy Engraving, Fancy Checkering, Single Selective Trigger, Modern............	20,000	22,500	22,500
Best Quality, Various Gauges, Sidelock, Hammerless, Fancy Engraving, Fancy Checkering, Double Trigger, Modern..........................	10,000	12,000	12,000
Deluxe Quality, Various Gauges, Box Lock, Hammerless, Fancy Engraving, Fancy Checkering, Double Trigger, Modern..........................	9,000	10,500	10,500
Deluxe Quality, Various Gauges, Box Lock, Hammerless, Fancy Engraving, Fancy Checkering, Single Selective Trigger, Modern............	9,500	11,500	11,500
Deluxe Quality, Various Gauges, Sidelock, Hammerless, Fancy Engraving, Fancy Checkering, Double Trigger, Modern..........................	12,500	15,000	15,000

	V.G.	Exc	Prior Edition
Deluxe Quality, Various Gauges, Sidelock, Hammerless, Fancy Engraving, Fancy Checkering, Single Selective Trigger, Modern............	$13,500	$16,000	$16,000
Model E, Various Gauges, Box Lock, Hammerless, Engraved, Double Trigger, Selective Ejector, Modern....................................	5,000	5,500	5,500
Model E, Various Gauges, Box Lock, Hammerless, Engraved, Double Trigger, Modern........................	4,000	4,250	4,250
Model E Pigeon, 12 Ga. Mag. 3", Box Lock, Hammerless, Engraved, Double Trigger, Selective Ejector, Modern.............................	6,000	6,000	6,000
Model E Pigeon, 12 Ga. Mag. 3", Box Lock, Hammerless, Engraved, Double Trigger, Modern.......................................	4,250	4,750	4,750

SHOTGUN, SINGLESHOT

12 Ga., Trap Grade, Vent Rib, Fancy Engraving, Fancy Checkering, Hammerless, Modern...	7,500	8,500	8,500
12 Ga., Vent Rib, Plain, Monte Carlo Stock, Trap Grade, Modern..	2,500	3,000	3,000

WESTON, EDWARD Sussex, England 1800–1835.

HANDGUN, FLINTLOCK

.67, Pair, Duelling Pistols, Octagon Barrel, Silver Furniture, Plain, Antique..	4,000	4,500	2,750

WHEEL-LOCK EXAMPLES

COMBINATION WEAPON, PISTOL

German, 1500's War–Hammer, All Metal, Antique.................................	9,000	15,000	15,000

HANDGUN, WHEEL-LOCK

Augsburg, Late 1500's, Ball Pommel, Engraved, Ornate, Antique..........	14,000	20,000	20,000
Brescian, Mid–1600's, Military, Fish–Tail Butt, Plain, Antique...............	1,500	2,600	2,600
Embellished Original, Ornate, Antique......................................	2,500	3,550	3,550
Enclosed Lock German, Mid 1600's, Engraved, Holster Pistol, Antique...	3,000	3,800	3,800
Enclosed Lock, Late 1600's, Military, Plain, Antique.............................	1,500	2,500	2,500
English, Mid 1600's, Military, Holster Pistol, Plain, Antique..................	1,500	2,500	2,500
English, Mid 1600's, Ornate, Antique..	14,000	20,000	20,000
Franch, Early 1600's, Military, Silver Inlays, Antique.............................	2,500	3,600	3,600
German Puffer, Late 1500's, Horn Inlays, Ball Pommel, Antique..........	6,000	10,000	10,000
German Style, Reproduction, Engraved, Inlays, High Quality, Antique...	1,400	2,000	2,000
German, 1600, Dagger–Handle Butt, Military, Plain, Antique................	2,000	2,800	2,800
German, Late 1500's, Carved, Horn Inlays, Ball Pommel, Flattened, Antique..	12,500	18,000	18,000
German, Mid–1500's, Horn Inlays, Dagger–Handle Butt, Gold and Silver Damascened, Ornate, Antique.......................................	35,000	55,000	55,000
German, Mid–1600's, Military, Fish–Tail Butt, Plain, Antique...............	1,250	2,000	2,000
Italian, 1500's, Dagger–Handle, External Mechanism, Antique..............	9,000	16,500	16,500
Late 1500's Odd Butt, all Metal, Engraved, Ornate, Antique................	7,000	10,000	10,000
Old Reproduction, High Quality, Antique...	1,200	1,800	1,800
Pair Brescian, Mid–1600's, Inlays, Engraved, Ornate, Fish–Tail Butt, Antique..	18,000	25,000	25,000
Pair Dutch, Mid–1600's, Holster Pistol, Gold Damascened, Inlays, Ornate, Antique..	18,000	25,000	25,000

	V.G.	Exc	Prior Edition
Pair Saxon, Late 1500's, Ball Pommel, Inlays, Engraved, Antique	$24,000	$30,000	$30,000
Pair Saxon, Late 1500's, Ball Pommel, Light Ornamentation, Antique	9,000	15,000	15,000
Pair Saxon, Late 1500's, Ball Pommel, Medium Ornamentation, Antique	14,000	20,000	20,000
Saxon, Dated 1579, Horn Inlays, Engraved, Ball Pommel, Antique	6,000	10,000	10,000
Saxon, Double Barrel, Over–Under, Inlays, Ornate, Ball Pommel, Antique	24,000	30,000	30,000
Saxon, Late 1500's, Ball Pommel, Checkered Stock, Military, Plain, Antique	4,000	6,000	6,000

RIFLE, WHEEL-LOCK

	V.G.	Exc	Prior Edition
Brandenburg 1620, Cavalry Rifle, Military, Antique	5,500	8,000	8,000

WHIPPET Made by Stevens Arms.

SHOTGUN, SINGLESHOT

	V.G.	Exc	Prior Edition
Model 94A, Various Gauges, Hammer, Automatic Ejector, Modern	50	75	75

WHITE POWDER WONDER Made by Stevens Arms.

SHOTGUN, SINGLESHOT

	V.G.	Exc	Prior Edition
Model 90, Various Gauges, Takedown, Automatic Ejector, Plain, Hammer, Modern	50	75	75

WHITE STAR c. 1880.

HANDGUN, REVOLVER

	V.G.	Exc	Prior Edition
.32 Short R.F., 5 Shot, Spur Trigger, Solid Frame, Single Action, Antique	150	175	175

WHITE, ROLLIN ARMS CO. Hartford, Conn. 1849–1858; Lowell, Mass. 1864–1892.

HANDGUN, REVOLVER

	V.G.	Exc	Prior Edition
.22 Short R.F., 7 Shot, Spur Trigger, Tip–Up, Antique	425	500	500

	V.G.	Exc	Prior Edition

HANDGUN, SINGLESHOT

SS Pocket, .32 Cal., no Trigger Guard, Antique... $500 $650 $650

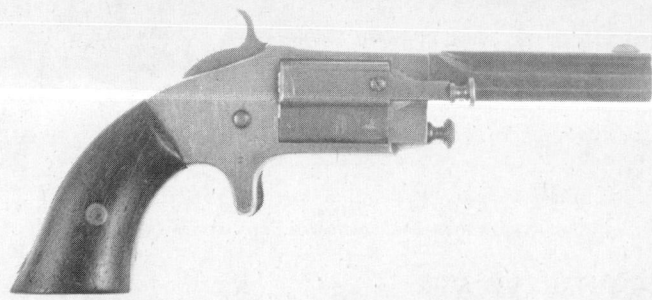

Rollin White Single Shot Pocket Pistol, .32 Caliber

WHITENEYVILLE ARMORY See Whitney Arms Co.

WHITNEY ARMS CO. New Haven, Conn. 1866–1876, also see U.S. Military.

HANDGUN, PERCUSSION

	V.G.	Exc	Prior Edition
Eagle Navy, .36, 6 Shot, Colt 1851 Type, Antique....................................	1,500	1,750	1,000
Hooded Cylinder, .28, 6 Shot, Hammer, Antique....................................	2,000	2,250	2,000
New Pocket Model, .28, 6 Shot, Single Action, Antique.........................	625	700	700
Pocket Model, .31, 5 Shot, Single Action, Antique..................................	675	750	750
Whitney Navy, .36, 6 Shot, Antique..	750	1,000	1,650
Whitney–Beals Walking Beam Pocket Revolver, .31 6 Shot, Antique..	1,000	1,200	1,800

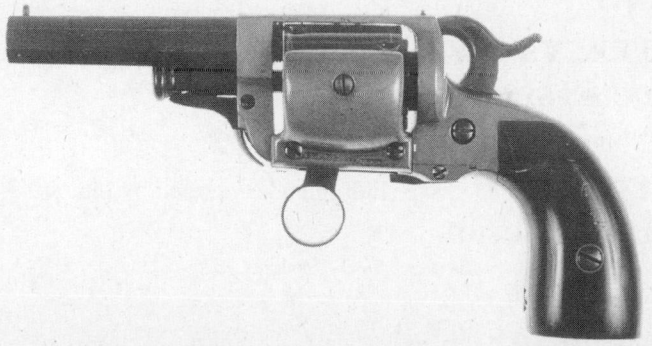

Whitney–Beals Walking Beam Pocket Revolver, .31 Caliber

	V.G.	Exc	Prior Edition
Whitney–Beals, .31, Ring Trigger, 7 Shot, Antique	$2,500	$3,500	$3,250

Whitney–Beals Standard Revolver, .31 Caliber

HANDGUN, REVOLVER

.22 Short R.F., 7 Shot, Spur Trigger, Solid Frame, Single Action, Antique	275	325	325
.32 Short R.F., 5 or 6 Shots, Spur Trigger, Solid Frame, Single Action, Antique	225	275	350
.38 Short R.F., 5 Shot, Spur Trigger, Solid Frame, Single Action, Antique	275	325	325

RIFLE, LEVER ACTION

Kennedy, Various Calibers, Tube Feed, Plain, Antique	1,250	1,500	1,500
Model 1886, Various Calibers, Tube Feed, Plain, Antique	1,750	2,000	1,750

RIFLE, SINGLESHOT

Phoenix, Various Calibers, Carbine, Hammer, Antique	1,750	2,000	2,000
Phoenix, Various Calibers, Rifle, Hammer, Antique	2,000	2,250	1,250
Rolling Block, Various Calibers, Carbine, Antique	750	1,000	1,250
Rolling Block, Various Calibers, Rifle, Antique	650	750	1,000
Whitney–Howard, .44 R.F., Carbine, Lever Action, Antique	1,000	1,250	1,500
Whitney–Howard, .44 R.F., Rifle, Lever Action, Antique	750	1,000	1,250

SHOTGUN, DOUBLE BARREL, SIDE-BY-SIDE

12 Ga., Damascus Barrel, Outside Hammers, Antique	550	650	750

WHITNEY FIREARMS CO. Hartford, Conn. 1955–1962.

HANDGUN, SINGLESHOT

Wolverine, .22 L.R.R.F., Blue, Modern	400	475	475

WHITWORTH Made in England, imported by Interarms.

RIFLE, BOLT ACTION

Express, Various Calibers, Checkered Stock, Modern	550	650	750

	V.G.	Exc	Prior Edition

WICHITA ARMS CO. (ENGINEERING & SUPPLY) Wichita, Kans.

HANDGUN, SINGLESHOT

	V.G.	Exc	Prior Edition
Classic, Various Calibers, Singleshot, Target, Modern	$2,000	$2,250	$2,750
Silhouette Pistol, Various Calibers, Bolt Action, Modern	750	850	1,000

RIFLE, BOLT ACTION

Classic Magnum, Various Calibers, Repeater, Modern	1,000	1,250	2,750
Classic Silhouette, Various Calibers, Singleshot, Target, Modern	1,250	1,500	2,500
Classic Varmint, Various Calibers, Repeater, Target, Modern	1,250	1,500	1,800

WICKLIFFE Triple–S Development, Wickliffe, Ohio. (Discontinued)

RIFLE, SINGLESHOT

'76 Deluxe, Various Calibers, Falling Block, Modern	350	400	450
'76 Standard, Various Calibers, Falling Block, Modern	300	350	400
Stinger Deluxe, Various Calibers, Falling Block, Modern	350	400	475
Stinger Standard, Various Calibers, Falling Block, Modern	300	350	400
Traditional 1st, Various Calibers, Falling Block, Modern	300	350	400

WIDE AWAKE Made by Hood Fire Arms, Norwich, Conn., c. 1875.

HANDGUN, REVOLVER

.32 Short R.F., 5 Shot, Spur Trigger, Solid Frame, Single Action, Antique	150	175	175

WILKINSON ARMS Parma, Idaho.

HANDGUN, SEMI-AUTOMATIC

Linda, 9mm Luger, Clip Fed, Blue, Modern	250	300	325

WILKINSON ARMS South El Monte, Calif., c. 1976.

HANDGUN, SEMI-AUTOMATIC

Diane, .25 ACP, Clip Fed, Blue, Modern	100	125	150

WILKINSON ARMS CO. Made in Belgium for Richmond Hard–ware Co. Richmond, Va., c. 1900.

SHOTGUN, DOUBLE BARREL, SIDE-BY-SIDE

Various Gauges, Hammerless, Damascus Barrel, Modern	150	175	175
Various Gauges, Outside Hammers, Steel Barrel, Modern	175	200	200
Various Gauges, Hammerless, Steel Barrel, Modern	175	200	200
Various Gauges, Outside Hammers, Damascus Barrel, Modern	150	175	175

SHOTGUN, SINGLESHOT

Various Gauges, Hammer, Steel Barrel, Modern	75	100	100

	V.G.	Exc	Prior Edition

WILLIAMS, FREDERICK Birmingham, England 1893–1929.
SHOTGUN, DOUBLE BARREL, SIDE-BY-SIDE
Gga., Damascus Barrel, Outside Hammers, Checkered Stock,
Engraved, Antique.. $400 $450 $450

WILLIAMSON, DAVID Brooklyn, N.Y. and Greenville, N.J. 1864–1874. Also see Moore's Patent Firearms. Co.
HANDGUN, SINGLESHOT
.41 Short R.F., Derringer, Nickel Plated, Antique.................................... 400 450 325

WILLIS, RICHARD Lancaster, Pa., c. 1776. See Kentucky Rifles and Pistols.

WILMONT ARMS CO. Belgium, c. 1900.
SHOTGUN, DOUBLE BARREL, SIDE-BY-SIDE
Various Gauges, Hammerless, Damascus Barrel, Modern.................... 150 175 175
Various Gauges, Outside Hammer, Steel Barrel, Modern...................... 175 200 200
Various Gauges, Hammeless, Steel Barrel, Modern............................... 175 200 200
Various Gauges, Outside Hammer, Damascus Barrel, Modern.............. 150 175 175
SHOTGUN, SINGLESHOT
Various Gauges, Hammer, Steel Barrel, Modern.................................... 75 100 100

WILSON, R. London, England 1720–1750.
SHOTGUN, FLINTLOCK
Fowling, 9 Ga., Queen Anne Style, Half–Stock, Antique........................ 1,250 1,500 1,500

WILTSHIRE ARMS CO. Belgium, c. 1900.
SHOTGUN, DOUBLE BARREL, SIDE-BY-SIDE
Various Gauges, Hammerless, Damascus barrel, Modern..................... 150 175 175
Various Gauges, Outside Hammers, Steel Barrel, Modern................... 175 200 200
Various Gauges, Hammerless, Steel Barrel, Modern............................. 175 200 200
Various Gauges, Outside Hammers, Damascus Barrel, Modern............ 150 175 175
SHOTGUN, SINGLESHOT
Various Gauges, Hammer, Steel Barrel, Modern.................................... 75 100 100

	V.G.	Exc	Prior Edition

WINCHESTER REPEATING ARMS CO. New Haven,

Conn. 1866 to date. In 1857 Oliver Winchester reorganized the Volcanic Repeating Arms Co. into the New Haven Arms Co., and it became Winchester Repeating Arms Co. in 1866. In 1869 Winchester absorbed Fogerty Repeating Rifle Co., and the American Rifle Co. In 1870 it acquired The Spencer Repeating Arms Co. and Adirondack Arms Co. in 1874. In 1981 was purchased by U.S. Repeating Arms Co. Also see U.S. Military and the Commemorative section.

RIFLE, BOLT ACTION

	V.G.	Exc	Prior Edition
Hotchkiss 1st Model Fancy, .45–70 Gov't, Sporting Rifle, Antique.......	$800	$1,000	$750
Hotchkiss 1st Model, .40–65 Win., Sporting Rifle, Antique....................	750	850	1,000
Hotchkiss 1st Model, .45–70 Government, Carbine, Antique..	750	850	700
Hotchkiss 1st Model, .45–70 Government, Military, Carbine, Antique..	750	1,000	1,000
Hotchkiss 1st Model, .45–70 Government, Military, Rifle, Antique.......	2,250	2,500	2,500
Hotchkiss 2nd Model, .45–70 Government, Military, Rifle, Antique..	700	800	900
Hotchkiss 2nd Model, .45–70 Government, Navy Rifle, Antique..........	750	950	900
Hotchkiss 2nd Model, .45–70 Government, Sporting Rifle, Antique..	800	1,000	700
Hotchkiss 3rd Model, .45–70 Government, Military, Carbine, Antique..	700	900	900
Hotchkiss 3rd Model, .45–70 Government, Military, Rifle, Antique..	800	1,000	850
Lee Straight–Pull, 6mm Lee Navy, Musket, Antique....................	485	850	850
Lee Straight–Pull, 6mm Lee Navy, Sporting Rifle,, Antique..................	825	900	900
M121 Deluxe, .22 L.R.R.F., Singleshot, Modern....................................	100	150	75
M121, .22 L.R.R.F., Singleshot, Modern..	100	125	75
M121–Y, .22 L.R.R.F., Singleshot, Modern...	100	125	75
M131, .22 L.R.R.F., Clip Fed, Open Rear Sight, Modern........................	100	150	125
M135, .22 WMR, Clip Fed, Modern...	100	125	125
M141, .22 WMR, Tube Feed, Modern...	125	150	150
M145, .22 WMR, Tube Feed, Modern...	125	150	150
M1900, .22 Long R.F., Singleshot, Modern...	300	350	350
M1902, Various Rimfires, Singleshot, Curio..	200	250	175
M1904, Various Rimfires, Singleshot, Curio..	175	200	200
M43 Special Grade, Various Calibers, Modern.....................................	525	600	600
M43, Various Calibers, Sporting Rifle, Modern.....................................	475	550	550
M47, .22 L.R.R.F., Singleshot, Modern..	200	250	300
M52 International Prone, .22 L.R.R.F., Modern....................................	600	650	650
M52 International, .22 L.R.R.F., Modern..	625	700	700
M52 Slow–Lock, .22 L.R.R.F., Modern..	450	400	350
M52 Speed–Lock, .22 L.R.R.F., Modern..	400	450	450
M52 Sporting, .22 L.R.R.F., Rifle, Modern...	1,500	1,800	1,800
M52, .22 L.R.R.F., Heavy Barrel, Modern..	525	575	400
M52–B, .22 L.R.R.F., Modern..	450	525	1,600
M52–B, .22 L.R.R.F., Bull Gun, Modern..	575	625	625
M52–B, .22 L.R.R.F., Heavy Barrel, Modern.......................................	550	600	600

	V.G.	Exc	Prior Edition
M52–B, .22 L.R.R.F., Sporting Rifle, Modern	$1,350	$1,600	$1,600
M52–C, .22 L.R.R.F., Modern	550	600	600
M52–C, .22 L.R.R.F., Bull Gun, Modern	575	650	650
M52–C, .22 L.R.R.F., Standard Target, Modern	550	600	525
M52–D, .22 L.R.R.F., Modern	475	525	525
M54 , Various Calibers, Sporting Rifle, Modern	500	575	575
M54 Match, Various Calibers, Sniper Rifle, Modern	675	750	750
M54 National Match, Various Calibers, Modern	750	850	850
M54 Super Grade, Various Calibers, Modern	725	825	825
M54 Target, Various Calibers, Modern	550	600	600
M54, .270 Win., Carbine, Curio	600	650	650
M54, .30–06 Springfield, Sniper Rifle, Modern	750	850	850
M54, Various Calibers, Carbine, Modern	575	650	650
M56, .22 L.R.R.F., Sporting Rifle, Modern	450	500	500
M57, Various Rimfires, Target, Modern	450	500	500
M58, .22 L.R.R.F., Singleshot, Modern	250	275	275
M59, .22 L.R.R.F., Singleshot, Modern	375	425	425
M60, .22 L.R.R.F., Singleshot, Modern	200	250	350
M60–A, .22 L.R.R.F., Target, Singleshot, Modern	325	375	475
M67 Boy's Rifle, Various Rimfires, Singleshot, Modern	150	175	125
M67, Various Rimfires, Singleshot, Modern	100	125	125
M68, Various Rimfires, Singleshot, Modern	125	150	150
M69 Match, .22 L.R.R.F., Clip Fed, Modern	150	200	200
M69 Target, .22 L.R.R.F., Clip Fed, Modern	125	175	175
M69, .22 L.R.R.F., Clip Fed, Modern	150	175	175
M70 Action Only, Various Calibers, Pre '64, Modern	300	350	350
M70 African, .458 Win. Mag., Pre '64, Modern	1,400	1,600	1,600
M70 Alaskan, Various Calibers, Pre '64, Checkered Stock, Modern	1,500	1,700	1,700
M70 Barreled Action Only, Various Calibers, Pre '64, Checkered Stock, Modern	475	550	550
M70 Bull Gun, Various Calibers, Pre '64, Checkered Stock, Modern	1,250	1,500	1,500
M70 Carbine, Various Calibers, Pre '64, Checkered Stock, Modern	1,250	1,500	1,500
M70 Featherweight Sporter Grade, Various Calibers, Pre '64, Checkered Stock, Modern	1,500	1,750	1,750
M70 Featherweight, Various Calibers, Pre '64, Checkered Stock, Modern	775	850	850
M70 National Match, .30–06 Springfield, Pre '64, Modern	100	1,200	1,200
M70 Target, Various Calibers, Pre '64, Checkered Stock, Modern	750	1,000	1,000
M70 Varmint, Various Calibers, Pre '64, Checkered Stock, Modern	650	800	800
M70 Westerner, Various Calibers, Pre '64, Checkered Stock, Modern	650	800	800
M70, For Mint Unfired, Pre '64, Add 50%–100%			
M70, for Pre–War, Add 25%–50%			
M72, .22 L.R.R.F., Tube Feed, Modern	225	275	150
M75 Target, .22 L.R.R.F., Clip Fed, Modern	450	500	500
M75, .22 L.R.R.F., Sporting Rifle, Clip Fed, Modern	625	700	700
M99 Thumb Trigger, Various Rimfires, Singleshot, Modern	1,000	1,250	375
Model 52 I.M. Kenyon, .22 L.R.R.F., Post '64, Heavy Barrel, Target Stock, Modern	450	500	500

	V.G.	Exc	Prior Edition
Model 52 I.M., .22 L.R.R.F., Post '64, Heavy Barrel, Target Stock, Modern	$425	$475	$475
Model 52 I.M.I.S.U., .22 L.R.R.F., Post '64, Heavy Barrel, Target Stock, Modern	525	575	575
Model 52 International Prone, .22 L.R.R.F., Post '64, Heavy Barrel, Target Stock, Modern	425	475	475
Model 52D, .22 L.R.R.F., Post '64, Heavy Barrel, Target Stock, Modern	500	550	425
Model 677, Various Calibers, Post '64, Scope Mounted, Modern	1,000	1,250	1,000
Model 70 African, .458 Win. Mag., Post '64, Checkered Stock, Open Rear Sight, Magnum Action, Modern	600	675	675
Model 70 International Match, .308 Win., Post '64, Checkered Stock, Target Stock, Modern	575	650	650
Model 70 Standard, Various Calibers, Post '64, Checkered Stock, Open Rear Sight, Modern	275	325	325
Model 70 Target, Various Calibers, Post '64, Checkered Stock, Target Stock, Modern	475	525	525
Model 70 Varmint, Various Calibers, Post '64, Checkered Stock, Heavy Barrel, Modern	300	350	350
Model 70, Various Calibers, Pre '64, Checkered Stock, Open Rear Sight, Magnum Action, Modern	250	300	300
Model 70A Police, Various Calibers, Post '64, Modern	250	300	300
Model 70A Standard, Various Calibers, Post '64, Modern	225	275	275
Model 70A, Various Calibers, Post '64, Magnum Action, Modern	300	350	350
Model 70XTR Featherweight, Various Calibers, No Sights, Modern	350	400	400
Model 70XTR Featherweight, Various Calibers, With Sights, Modern	400	450	450
Model 70XTR Super Express Magnum, .375 H&H, Modern	500	575	575
Model 70XTR Super Express Magnum, .458 Win., Modern	525	600	600
Model XTR Ranger, Various Calibers, No Scope, Modern	275	325	325
Model XTR Sporter, Various Calibers, Modern	325	375	375
Model XTR Varmint, Various Calibers, Modern	325	375	375
Thumb Trigger, .22 L.R.R.F., Singleshot, Curio	450	500	275

RIFLE, LEVER ACTION

	V.G.	Exc	Prior Edition
Henry, .44 Henry, Brass Frame, Military, Rifle, Antique	20,000	25,000	20,000
Henry, .44 Henry, Brass Frame, Rifle, Antique	10,000	15,000	15,000
Henry, .44 Henry, Iron Frame, Rifle, Antique	35,000	40,000	25,000
M1866, .44 Henry, Carbine, Antique	7,500	10,000	10,000
M1866, .44 Henry, Rifle, Antique	17,500	20,000	12,000

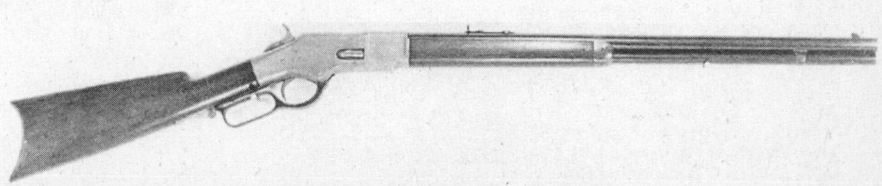

Winchester M1866

	V.G.	Exc	Prior Edition
M1866 Improved Henry, .44 Henry, Carbine, Antique	7,500	9,000	9,000
M1866 Improved Henry, .44 Henry, Rifle, Antique	5,500	7,000	7,000

	V.G.	Exc	Prior Edition
M1873, Various Calibers, Carbine, Curio...	$2,000	$2,500	$2,500
M1873, Various Calibers, Musket, Curio...	1,500	1,800	1,800
M1873, Various Calibers, Rifle, Curio...	1,750	2,000	2,000

Winchester M1873

	V.G.	Exc	Prior Edition
M1873 1 of 1,000, Various Calibers, Rifle, Antique.................................	50,000	75,000	75,000
M1873, For Deluxe, Add $500.00–$750.00			
M1873, For Extra Fancy Deluxe, Add $5000.00–$7500.00			
M1873, under #525,299, Various Calibers, Carbine, Antique..................	2,500	2,750	2,750
M1873, under #525,299, Various Calibers, Musket, Antique..................	1,750	2,000	2,000
M1873, under #525,299, Various Calibers, Rifle, Antique......................	2,000	2,200	2,200
M1876, For Deluxe, Add $550.00–$750.00			
M1876, For Extra Fancy Deluxe, Add $2000.00–$5000.00			
M1876, Various Calibers, Carbine, Antique...	3,000	3,500	2,250
M1876, Various Calibers, Musket, Antique..	4,250	5,000	5,000
M1876, Various Calibers, Octagon Barrel, Rifle, Antique........................	1,750	2,000	1,600
M1876, Various Calibers, Round Barrel, Rifle, Antique...........................	2,000	2,250	1,400
M1876 RCMP, Various Calibers, Carbine, Antique.................................	4,000	4,500	3,500
M1886, For Deluxe, Add $400.00–$750.00			
M1886, For Extra Fancy Deluxe, Add $3500.00–$5000.00			
M1886, under #118,433, Various Calibers, Carbine, Antique..................	5,500	6,000	6,000
M1886, under #118,433, Various Calibers, Musket, Antique..................	8,500	9,500	8,000
M1886, under #118,433, Various Calibers, Rifle, Antique......................	3,000	3,500	4,000
M1886, Various Calibers, Carbine, Curio..	4,500	5,000	5,000
M1886, Various Calibers, Musket, Curio...	6,000	7,000	7,000
M1886, Various calibers, Rifle, Curio..	2,250	2,500	3,500
M150, .22 L.R.R.F., Tube Feed, Modern..	75	100	125
M250, .22 L.R.R.F., Tube Feed, Modern..	75	100	125
M250 Deluxe, .22 L.R.R.F., Tube Feed, Modern....................................	100	125	150
M255, .22 WMR, Tube Feed, Modern..	100	125	150
M255 Deluxe, .22 WMR, Tube Feed, Modern...	125	150	175
M53, Various Calibers, Modern..	2,000	2,500	1,250
M55, Various Calibers, Modern..	1,000	1,250	750
M64, .219 Zipper, Pre '64 Modern..	1,750	2,000	650
M64, .30-30 Win., Late Model, Modern...	300	350	250
M64, Various Calibers, Pre '64, Modern...	1,500	1,750	550
M64 Deer Rifle, Various Calibers, Pre '64, Modern...............................	1,750	2,000	750
M65, .218 Bee, Modern...	3,000	3,500	2,500
M65, Various Calibers, Modern..	2,500	3,000	2,000
M71, .348 Win., Tube Feed, Modern...	725	800	800
M71 Special, .348 Win., Tube Feed, Modern...	750	950	950
M92, under #103316, Various Calibers, Carbine, Antique......................	1,750	2,000	2,000
M92, under #103316, Various Calibers, Musket, Antique......................	8,500	9,500	5,000
M92, under #103316, Various Calibers, Rifle, Antique..........................	1,500	1,750	1,750
M92, For Takedown, Add $150.00–$275.00			

	V.G.	Exc	Prior Edition
M92, Various Calibers, Carbine, Curio	$1,250	$1,500	$1,500
M92, Various Calibers, Musket, Curio	7,500	8,500	1,750
M92, Various Calibers, Rifle, Curio	1,000	1,250	1,250
M94, .30–30 Win., Carbine, Late Model, Modern	200	250	250
M94, .44 Magnum, Carbine, Modern	225	275	275
M94, Various Calibers, Carbine, Pre '64, Modern	1,250	1,500	450
M94, Various Calibers, Carbine, Pre–War, Curio	1,500	1,750	850
M94, Various Calibers, Rifle, Pre–War, Curio	1,750	2,000	750
M94, Various Calibers, Rifle, Takedown, Pre–War , Curio	2,000	2,250	900
M94, under #50,000 Various Calibers, Carbine, Antique	1,750	2,000	2,000
M94, under #50,000 Various Calibers, Rifle, Antique	2,000	2,500	1,500
M94 Standard, .30–30 Win., Modern	175	250	250
M94 Trapper, .30–30 Win., Pre '64, Curio	200	2,500	275
M94XTR Big Bore, .375 Win., Modern	200	275	275

Winchester M94XTR Big Bore

M94XTR, .30–30 Win., Modern	175	250	250
M95, Various Calibers, Carbine, Curio	1,250	1,500	1,500
M95, Various Calibers, Musket, Curio	1,000	1,250	1,250
M95, Various Calibers, Rifle, Curio	1,500	2,000	2,000
M95, For Takedown, Add $100.00–$200.00			
M95, under #19,477, Various Calibers, Carbine, Antique	1,500	2,000	2,000
M95, under #19,477, Various Calibers, Rifle, Antique	2,000	2,500	2,500
Model 9422, .22 L.R.R.F., Tube Feed, Modern	200	250	250
Model 9422M, .22 WMR, Tube Feed, Modern	250	275	275
Model 9422MXTR, .22 WMR, Tube Feed, Modern	300	325	325
Model 9422XTR, .22 L.R.R.F., Tube Feed, Modern	275	300	300

RIFLE, SEMI-AUTOMATIC

M100, Various Calibers, Clip Fed, Modern	400	450	325
M100, Various Calibers, Clip Fed, Carbine, Modern	500	550	375
M190, .22 L.R.R.F., Tube Feed, Modern	100	125	125
M1903, .22 Win. Auto R.F., Tube Feed, Curio	275	325	375
M1905, Various Calibers, Clip Fed, Curio	500	550	400
M1907 Police, .351 Win. Self–Loading, Clip Fed, Curio	400	450	525
M1907, .351 Win. Self–Loading, Clip Fed, Curio	350	400	600
M1910, .401 Win. Self–Loading, Clip Fed, Curio	475	550	50
M290 Deluxe, .22 L.R.R.F., Tube Feed, Modern	125	150	150
M490 Deluxe, .22 L.R.R.F., Clip Fed, Monte Carlo Stock, Modern	200	225	225
M55 Automatic, .22 L.R.R.F., Modern	125	150	175
M63, .22 L.R.R.F., Tube Feed, Modern	400	475	475
M74, .22 L.R.R.F., Clip Fed, Modern	150	175	175
M77, .22 L.R.R.F., Clip Fed, Modern	125	150	150
M77, .22 L.R.R.F., Tube Feed, Modern	150	175	175

	V.G.	Exc	Prior Edition

RIFLE, SINGLESHOT

	V.G.	Exc	Prior Edition
High–Wall, Various Calibers, Musket, Curio..	$1,250	$1,500	$1,750
High–Wall, Various Calibers, Schutzen Rifle, Curio...............................	4,500	5,500	4,500
High–Wall, Various Calibers, Schutzen Style Rifle, Curio......................	3,500	4,000	4,000
High–Wall, Various Calibers, Sporting Rifle, Curio...............................	1,500	1,750	1,500
Low–Wall, .22 Long R.F., Carbine, Curio..	4,500	5,000	4,500
Low–Wall, Various Calibers, Sporting Rifle, Curio................................	775	850	650
Model 310, .22 L.R.R.F., Bolt Action, Modern...................................	150	175	100
Winder, .22 Long R.F., Musket, Curio..	700	800	700

RIFLE, SLIDE ACTION

	V.G.	Exc	Prior Edition
M1890, under #64,521, Various Rimfires, Case Hardened, Antique........	4,000	4,500	4,250
M1890, Various Rimfires, Curio...	700	750	625
M1906, .22 L.R.R.F., Tube Feed, Hammer, Modern..............................	600	650	650
M270, .22 L.R.R.F., Tube Feed, Modern...	75	100	100
M270 Deluxe, .22 L.R.R.F., Tube Feed, Modern.................................	100	125	125
M275, .22 WMR, Tube Feed, Modern..	100	125	125
M275 Deluxe, .22 WMR, Tube Feed, Modern.....................................	125	150	150
M61, .22 L.R.R.F., Tube Feed, Modern...	425	475	475
M61, Various Rimfires, Tube Feed, Octagon Barrel, Modern..................	850	1,000	1,000
M61 Magnum, .22 WMR, Tube Feed, Modern.....................................	550	600	600
M62, .22 L.R.R.F., Tube Feed, Hammer, Modern................................	400	450	400
M62 Gallery, .22 Short R.F., Tube Feed, Hammer, Modern...................	750	900	425

SHOTGUN, BOLT ACTION

	V.G.	Exc	Prior Edition
Model 36, 9mm Shotshell, Takedown, Singleshot, Curio.......................	425	475	600
Model 41, .410 Ga., Takedown, Singleshot, Modern.............................	300	350	475
Model 41, .410 Ga., Takedown, Singleshot, Checkered Stock, Modern..	325	375	500

SHOTGUN, DOUBLE BARREL, OVER-UNDER

	V.G.	Exc	Prior Edition
Model 101 Pigeon 3 Barrel Set, Various Gauges, Skeet Grade, Single Trigger, Automatic Ejector, Checkered Stock, Engraved, Modern..........	2,500	3,000	3,000
Model 101 Magnum, 12 Ga. 3", Single Trigger, Automatic Ejector, Engraved, Modern..	700	800	800
Model 101 Pigeon, 12 and 20 Gauges, Skeet Grade, Checkered Stock, Single Trigger, Automatic Ejector, Engraved, Modern...................	1,000	1,200	1,200
Model 101 Pigeon, 12 Ga., Trap Grade, Monte Carlo Stock, Single Trigger, Automatic Ejector, Engraved, Modern.............................	1,350	1,600	1,250
Model 101 Pigeon, 12 Ga., Trap Grade, Single Trigger, Automatic Ejector, Engraved, Modern..	1,250	1,500	1,200
Model 101, 12 Ga. Mag. 3", Trap Grade, Single Trigger, Automatic Ejector, Checkered Stock, Engraved, Modern...............................	675	750	750
Model 101, 12 Ga., Field Grade, Single Trigger, Automatic Ejector, Engraved, Modern..	800	900	725
Model 101, 12 Ga., Trap Grade, Monte Carlo Stock, Single Trigger, Automatic Ejector, Engraved, Modern...............................	850	1,000	1,200
Model 101, 12 Ga., Trap Grade, Single Trigger, Automatic Ejector, Checkered Stock, Engraved, Modern...............................	800	950	1,200
Model 101, Various Gauges, Featherweight, Single Trigger, Automatic Ejector, Checkered Stock, Engraved, Modern......................	850	950	950
Model 101, Various Gauges, Skeet Grade, Single Trigger, Automatic Ejector, Checkered Stock, Engraved, Modern......................	700	800	975
Model 96, 12 and 20 Gauges, Field Grade, Checkered Stock, Vent Rib, Modern...	575	625	625

	V.G.	Exc	Prior Edition
Model 96, 12 and 20 Gauges, Skeet Grade, Checkered Stock, Vent Rib, Modern....................	$600	$650	$650
Model 96, 12 Ga., Trap Grade, Checkered Stock, Vent Rib, Modern....................	500	550	650
Model 96, 12 Ga., Trap Grade, Monte Carlo Stock, Vent Rib, Modern....................	550	600	650

SHOTGUN, DOUBLE BARREL, SIDE-BY-SIDE

	V.G.	Exc	Prior Edition
Model 21, For Extra Barrels, Add 25%–30%			
Model 21, For Vent Rib, Add $400.00–$600.00			
Model 21, 12 and 16 Gauges, Field Grade, Double Trigger, Automatic Ejector, Hammerless, Modern....................	2,500	3,000	3,500
Model 21, 12 and 16 Gauges, Field Grade, Double Trigger, Automatic Ejector, Hammerless, Modern....................	2,750	3,000	3,600
Model 21, 12 and 16 Gauges, Field Grade, Single Selective Trigger, Automatic Ejector, Hammerless, Modern....................	3,250	3,500	3,800
Model 21, 12 and 16 Gauges, Field Grade, Single Selective Trigger, Selective Ejector, Hammerless, Modern....................	3,000	3,250	3,850
Model 21, 12 and 16 Gauges, Skeet Grade, Hammerless, Single Selective Trigger, Selective Ejector, Vent Rib, Modern....................	3,000	3,500	3,000
Model 21, 12 Ga., Trap Grade, Hammerless, Single Selective Trigger, Selective Ejector, Vent Rib, Modern....................	3,500	3,750	3,750
Model 21, 12 Ga., Trap Grade, Hammerless, Single Selective Trigger, Selective Ejector, Raised Matted Rib, Modern....................	3,000	3,250	3,250
Model 21, 20 Ga., Field Grade, Double Trigger, Automatic Ejector, Hammerless, Modern....................	2,250	2,500	3,750
Model 21, 20 Ga., Field Grade, Double Trigger, Selective Ejector, Hammerless, Modern....................	3,250	3,500	4,000
Model 21, 20 Ga., Field Grade, Single Selective Trigger, Automatic Ejector, Hammerless, Modern....................	3,750	4,250	4,250
Model 21, 20 Ga., Field Grade, Single Selective Trigger, Selective Ejector, Hammerless, Modern....................	4,000	4,500	4,500
Model 21, 20 Ga., Skeet Grade, Hammerless, Single Selective Trigger, Selective Ejector, Vent Rib Modern....................	4,500	4,750	5,000
Model 21, 20 Ga., Skeet Grade, Hammerless, Single Selective Trigger, Selective Ejector, Raised Matted Rib, Modern....................	4,250	4,500	4,750
Model 21, 410 Ga., Checkered Stock, Fancy Wood, Modern....................	20,000	25,000	25,000
Model 21 Custom, 12 Ga., Hammerless, Single Selective Trigger, Selective Ejector, Fancy Engraving, Fancy Checkering, Modern....................	6,750	7,500	7,500
Model 21 Custom, 20 Ga., Hammerless, Single Selective Trigger, Selective Ejector, Fancy Checkering, Fancy Engraving, Modern....................	7,500	8,500	8,500
Model 21 Duck, 12 Ga. Mag. 3", Hammerless, Single Selective Trigger, Selective Ejector, Raised Matted Rib, Modern....................	3,250	3,750	3,750
Model 21 Duck, 12 Ga. Mag. 3", Hammerless, Single Selective Trigger, Selective Ejector, Vent Rib, Modern....................	3,750	4,250	4,250

	V.G.	Exc	Prior Edition
Model 21 Grand American, 12 Ga., Hammerless, Single Selective Trigger, Selective Ejector, Fancy Engraving, Fancy Checkering, Modern..........	$10,500	$12,500	$12,500

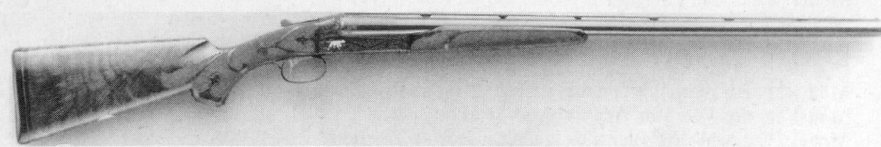

Winchester Model 21 Grand American

	V.G.	Exc	Prior Edition
Model 21 Grand American, 20 Ga., Hammerless, Single Selective Trigger, Selective Ejector, Fancy Checkering, Fancy Engraving, Modern.......................	12,500	15,000	15,000
Model 21 Pigeon, 12 Ga., Hammerless, Single Selective Trigger, Selective Ejector, Fancy Engraving, Fancy Checkering, Modern.............	7,500	10,000	10,000
Model 21 Pigeon, 20 Ga., Hammerless, Single Selective Trigger, Selective Ejector, Fancy Engraving, Fancy Checkering, Modern.............	15,000	17,500	17,500
Model 23 English, 12 or 20 Gauges, Hammerless, Single Trigger, Selective Ejector, Fancy Checkering, Engraved, Modern.........................	850	1,000	1,000
Model 23 Grand European, 12 Ga., Hammerless, Single Selective Trigger, Selective Ejector, Fancy Engraving, Fancy Checkering, Modern........................	1,250	1,450	1,450
Model 23 Pigeon, 12 or 20 Gauges, Hammerless, Single Trigger, Selective Ejector, Engraved, Fancy Checkering, Modern........................	900	1,050	1,050

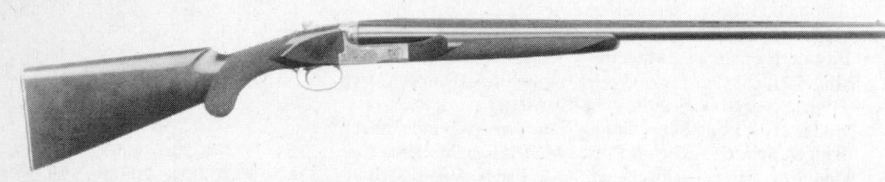

Winchester Model 23 Pigeon

	V.G.	Exc	Prior Edition
Model 24, Various Gauges, Double Trigger, Automatic Ejector, Modern..........................	450	500	500

SHOTGUN, LEVER ACTION

	V.G.	Exc	Prior Edition
1901, 10 Ga., 2 1/8, Tube Feed, Plain, Curio..	1,000	1,250	1,250
M 1887, 10 Ga., 2 1/8, Tube Feed, Plain, Curio..	1,650	1,850	1,850
M 1887, Deluxe Grade, 10 Ga., 2 7/8, Tube Feed, Checkered Stock, Damascus barrel, Curio...............	2,500	2,750	2,750
M 1887, Deluxe Grade, Various Gauges, Antique.....................................	2,250	2,500	2,500
M 1887, Various Gauges, Antique...	1,500	1,750	1,750

SHOTGUN, SEMI-AUTOMATIC

	V.G.	Exc	Prior Edition
Model 1400 Deer, 12 Ga.,Open Sights, Slug Gun, Modern....................	225	250	250
Model 1400 Field, 12 and 20 Gauges, Winchoke, Modern....................	225	275	325

	V.G.	Exc	Prior Edition
Model 1400 Field, 12 and 20 Gauges, Winchoke, Vent Rib, Modern..	$250	$300	$350

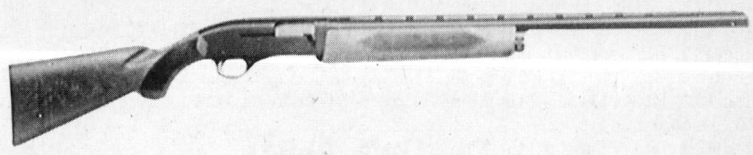

Winchester Model 1400

Model 1400 Skeet, 12 and 20 Gauges, Vent Rib, Modern......................	300	350	350
Model 1400 Trap, 12 Ga., Monte Carlo Stock, Vent Rib, Modern..........	325	375	375
Model 1400 Trap, 12 Ga., Vent Rib, Modern...............................	300	350	350
Model 1400 Trap, 12 Ga., Vent Rib, Recoil Reducer, Modern...............	375	425	425
Model 1500, 12 or 20 Gauges, Field Grade, Plain, Modern....................	225	275	275
Model 1500, 12 or 20 Gauges, Field Grade, Vent Rib, Modern...............	250	300	300
Model 1911, 12 Ga., Takedown, Checkered Stock, Modern..................	375	425	425
Model 1911, 12 Ga., Takedown, Plain, Modern...........................	350	400	400
Model 40, 12 Ga., Takedown, Field Grade, Modern............................	375	425	425
Model 40, 12 Ga., Takedown, Skeet Grade, Adjustable Choke, Modern..	425	475	475
Model 50, 12 and 20 Gauges, Field Grade, Plain Barrel, Checkered Stock, Modern...	300	350	350
Model 50, 12 and 20 Gauges, Field Grade, Vent Rib, Checkered Stock, Modern...	350	400	400
Model 50, 12 and 20 Gauges, Skeet Grade, Vent Rib, Checkered Stock, Modern...	375	425	400
Model 50, 12 Ga., Trap Grade, Vent Rib, Monte Carlo Stock, Modern..	350	400	400

SHOTGUN, SINGLESHOT

Model 101, 12 Ga., Trap Grade, Vent Rib, Modern..........................	850	1,000	650
Model 20, .410 Ga., 21/8", Takedown, Hammer, Checkered Stock, Modern..	325	375	275
Model 37A, For Red Letter, Add 25%–40%			
Model 37A, .410 Ga., Takedown, Automatic Ejector, Plain Barrel, Modern..	175	200	175
Model 37A, 12 Ga., Takedown, Automatic Ejector, Plain Barrel, Modern..	125	150	150
Model 37A, 16 Ga., Takedown, Automatic Ejector, Plain Barrel, Modern..	125	150	150
Model 37A, 20 Ga., Takedown, Automatic Ejector, Plain Barrel, Modern..	125	150	150
Model 37A, 28 Ga., Takedown, Automatic Ejector, Plain Barrel, Modern..	150	175	500

SHOTGUN, SLIDE ACTION

Model 12, 12 Ga., Post '64, Trap Grade, Checkered Stock, Modern..	550	600	600
Model 12, 12 Ga., Post '64, Trap Gun, Monte Carlo Stock, Modern..	575	625	625
Model 12, 12 Ga., Pre '64, Takedown, Trap Grade, Raised Matted Rib, Modern...	675	750	750

	V.G.	Exc	Prior Edition
Model 12, 12 Ga., Pre '64, Takedown, Trap Grade, Vent Rib, Modern	$725	$800	$800
Model 12, 12 Ga., Pre '64, Takedown, Trap Grade, Vent Rib, Monte Carlo Stock, Modern	775	850	850
Model 12, 12 Ga., Pre–War, Takedown, Riot Gun, Curio	750	800	700
Model 12, 12 Ga., Pre–War, Takedown, Vent Rib, Curio	650	700	650
Model 12, Featherweight, Various Gauges, Pre '64, Takedown, Modern	400	450	550
Model 12, Heavy Duck, 12 Ga. Mag. 3", Pre '64, Takedown, Vent Rib, Modern	450	550	650
Model 12, Heavy Duck, 12 Ga. Mag. 3", Pre '64, Takedown, Raised Matted Rib, Modern	475	525	625
Model 12, Pigeon Grade, 12 Ga., Pre '64, Takedown, Trap Grade, Vent Rib, Modern	1,500	1,750	1,800
Model 12, Pigeon Grade, 12 Ga., Pre '64, Takedown, Trap Grade, Raised Matted Rib, Modern	1,450	1,650	1,650
Model 12, Pigeon Grade, 12 Ga., Various Gauges, Pre '64, Takedown, Skeet Choke, Raised Matted Rib, Modern	1,400	1,550	1,550
Model 12, Pigeon Grade, Various Gauges, Pre '64, Takedown, Skeet Choke, Vent Rib, Modern	1,400	1,600	1,600
Model 12, Pigeon Grade, Various Gauges, Pre '64, Takedown, Skeet Choke, Plain Barrel, Adjustable Choke, Modern	1,000	1,250	900
Model 12, Pigeon Grade, Various Gauges, Pre '64, Takedown, Plain Barrel, Modern	1,600	1,850	1,500
Model 12, Pigeon Grade, Various Gauges, Pre '64, Takedown, Vent Rib, Modern	1,550	1,900	1,750
Model 12, Standard, Various Gauges, Pre '64, Takedown, Modern	600	700	600
Model 12, Super Pigeon, 12 Ga., Post '64, Takedown, Vent Rib, Engraved, Checkered Stock, Modern	2,000	2,500	2,500
Model 12, Various Gauges, Pre '64, Takedown, Raised Matted Rib, Modern	450	650	600
Model 12, Various Gauges, Pre '64, Takedown, Skeet Grade, Raised Matted Rib, Modern	700	775	650
Model 12, Various Gauges, Pre '64, Takedown, Skeet Grade, Vent Rib, Modern	750	825	700
Model 12, Various Gauges, Pre '64, Takedown, Skeet Grade, Plain Barrel, Modern	675	750	625
Model 12, Various Gauges, Pre '64, Takedown, Skeet Grade, Plain Barrel, Adjustable Choke, Modern	700	775	650
Model 1200, For Recoil Reducer, Add $50.00–$75.00			
Model 1200 Deer, 12 Ga., Open Sights, Modern	150	200	200
Model 1200 Defender, 12 Ga., Modern	125	250	250
Model 1200 Field, 12 and 20 Gauges, Modern	150	200	200
Model 1200 Field, 12 and 20 Gauges, Adjustable Choke, Modern	200	250	250
Model 1200 Field, 12 and 20 Gauges, Adjustable Choke, Vent Rib, Modern	225	275	275
Model 1200 Field, 12 and 20 Gauges, Vent Rib, Modern	175	225	225
Model 1200 Field, 12 Ga. Mag. 3", Modern	175	200	200
Model 1200 Field, 12 Ga. Mag. 3", Vent Rib, Modern	175	225	225
Model 1200 Police Stainless, 12 Ga., Modern	200	250	250
Model 1300, 12 or 20 Gauges, Plain Barrel, Modern	250	300	300
Model 1300, 12 or 20 Gauges, Plain Barrel, Winchoke, Modern	300	350	350
Model 1300, 12 or 20 Gauges, Vent Rib, Modern	275	325	325

	V.G.	Exc	Prior Edition
Model 1300, 12 or 20 Gauges, Vent Rib, Winchoke, Modern..................	$325	$375	$375
Model 1300 Deer, 12 Ga., Open Sights, Modern..................................	275	325	325
Model 25, 12 Ga., Solid Frame, Plain Barrel, Modern..............................	300	350	350
Model 42, .410 Ga., Field Grade, Takedown, Modern............................	750	850	850
Model 42, .410 Ga., Field Grade, Takedown, Raised Matted Rib, Modern..	750	1,000	1,000
Model 42, .420 Ga., Skeet Grade, Takedown, Raised Matted Rib, Modern..	1,500	1,750	1,550
Model 42 Deluxe, .410 Ga., Takedown, Vent Rib, Fancy Checkering, Fancy Wood, Modern..	1,750	2,000	1,750
Model 97, 12 Ga., Solid Frame, Plain, Modern..................................	500	550	550
Model 97, 12 Ga., Solid Frame, Riot Gun, Modern..............................	650	750	475
Model 97, 12 Ga., Takedown, Plain, Modern....................................	550	600	600
Model 97, 12 Ga., Takedown, Riot Gun, Modern................................	700	800	425
Model 97, 16 Ga., Solid Frame, Plain, Modern..................................	550	600	500
Model 97, 16 Ga., Takedown, Plain, Modern....................................	600	650	550
Model 97 Pigeon, 12 Ga., Takedown, Checkered, Modern......................	2,000	2,500	2,500
Model 97 Tournament, 12 Ga., Takedown, Checkered Stock, Modern..	800	900	900
Model 97 Trap, 12 Ga., Takedown, Checkered Stock, Modern..............	750	850	850
Model 97 Trench, 12 Ga., Solid Frame, Riot Gun, Military, Curio..	1,500	1,750	750
Model 97 Trench, 12 Ga., Solid Frame, Riot Gun, Military, with Bayonet, Curio..	1,600	1,850	800

WINFIELD ARMS CO. Made by Crescent, c. 1900.

SHOTGUN, DOUBLE BARREL, SIDE-BY-SIDE

Various Gauges, Hammerless, Damascus Barrel, Modern......................	150	175	175
Various Gauges, Hammerless, Steel Barrel, Modern.............................	175	200	200
Various Gauges, Outside Hammers, Damascus Barrel, Modern.............	150	175	175
Various Gauges, Outside Hammers, Steel Barrel, Modern......................	175	200	200

SHOTGUN, SINGLESHOT

Various Gauges, Hammer, Steel Barrel, Modern....................................	75	100	100

WINFIELD ARMS CO. Made by Norwich Falls Pistol Co., c. 1880.

HANDGUN, REVOLVER

.32 Short R.F., 5 Shot, Spur Trigger, Solid Frame, Single Action, Antique...	150	175	175

WINGERT, RICHARD Lancaster, Pa. 1775–1777. See Kentucky Rifles, U.S. Military.

WINOCA ARMS CO. Made by Crescent for Jacobi Hardware Co., Philadelphia, Pa.

SHOTGUN, DOUBLE BARREL, SIDE-BY-SIDE

Various Gauges, Hammerless, Damascus Barrel, Modern......................	150	175	175
Various Gauges, Hammerless, Steel Barrel, Modern.............................	175	200	200

	V.G.	Exc	Prior Edition
Various Gauges, Outside Hammers, Damascus Barrel, Modern.............	$150	$175	$175
Various Gauges, Outside Hammers, Steel Barrel, Modern.....................	175	200	200

SHOTGUN, SINGLESHOT

Various Gauges, Hammer, Steel Barrel, Modern....................................	75	100	100

WINSLOW ARMS CO. Established in Venice, Fla. in 1962, moved to Osprey, Fla. in 1976, and is now in Camden, S.C.

RIFLE, BOLT ACTION

For Left–Hand Act, Add $70.00–$100.00

Commander, Various Calibers, Fancy Checkering, Inlays, Modern...	500	550	500
Crown, Various Gauges, Carved, Fancy Wood, Inlays, Modern.............	1,250	1,500	1,250
Emperor, Various Gauges, Carved, Fancy Engraving, Ornate, Fancy Wood, Inlays, Modern..	7,500	6,500	5,500
Imperial, Various Gauges, Carved, Engraved, Fancy Wood, Inlays, Modern...	3,500	3,750	3,250
Regal, Various Calibers, Fancy Checkering, Inlays, Modern...................	600	650	600
Regent, Various Calibers, Inlays, Carved, Fancy Wood, Modern............	725	775	725
Regimental, Various Calibers, Carved, Inlays, Modern...........................	850	1,000	900
Royal, Various Calibers, Carved, Fancy Wood, Inlays, Modern..............	1,500	1,750	1,500

WITHERS, MICHAEL Lancaster, Pa. 1774–1805. See Kentucky Rifles, U.S. Military.

WITTES HDW. CO. Made by Stevens Arms.

SHOTGUN, DOUBLE BARREL, SIDE-BY-SIDE

Model 311, Various Gauges, Hammerless, Steel Barrel, Modern.............	150	175	175

SHOTGUN, SINGLESHOT

Model 90, Various Gauges, Takedown, Automatic Ejector, Plain, Hammer, Modern...	50	75	75
Model 94, Various Gauges, Takedown, Automatic Ejector, Plain, Hammer, Modern...	50	75	75

WOGDON London, England & Dublin, Ireland 1760–1797.

HANDGUN, FLINTLOCK

.56, Officers, Holster Pistol, Flared, Octagon Barrel, Steel Furniture, Engraved, High Quality, Antique...	2,500	3,000	3,000

WOLF Spain, c. 1900.

HANDGUN, SEMI-AUTOMATIC

7.65mm, Clip Fed, Modern..	125	150	150

	V.G.	Exc	Prior Edition

WOLF, A. W. Suhl, Germany, c. 1930.

SHOTGUN, DOUBLE BARREL, SIDE-BY-SIDE

	V.G.	Exc	Prior Edition
12 Ga., Engraved, Platinium Inlays, Ivory Inlays, Ornate, Cased, Modern...	$6,000	$7,000	$7,000

WOLFHEIMER, PHILIP Lancaster, Pa., c. 1774. See Kentucky Rifles.

WOLVERINE ARMS CO. Made by Crescent for Fletcher Hard–ware Co., c. 1900.

SHOTGUN, DOUBLE BARREL, SIDE-BY-SIDE

	V.G.	Exc	Prior Edition
Various Gauges, Hammerless, Damascus Barrel, Modern......................	150	175	175
Various Gauges, Hammerless, Steel Barrel, Modern...............................	175	200	200
Various Gauges, Outside Hammers, Damascus Barrel, Modern.............	150	175	175
Various Gauges, Outside Hammers, Steel Barrel, Modern......................	175	200	200

SHOTGUN, SINGLESHOT

	V.G.	Exc	Prior Edition
Various Gauges, Hammer, Steel Barrel, Modern....................................	75	100	100

WOODWARD, JAMES & SONS London, England.

SHOTGUN, DOUBLE BARREL, OVER-UNDER

	V.G.	Exc	Prior Edition
Best Quality, Various Gauges, Sidelock, Automatic Ejector, Double Trigger, Fancy Engraving, Fancy Checkering, Modern...............	20,000	25,000	25,000
Best Quality, Various Gauges, Sidelock, Automatic Ejector, Single Trigger, Fancy Engraving, Fancy Checkering, Modern.................	22,000	27,000	27,000

SHOTGUN, DOUBLE BARREL, SIDE-BY-SIDE

	V.G.	Exc	Prior Edition
Best Quality, Various Gauges, Sidelock, Automatic Ejector, Double Trigger, Fancy Engraving, Fancy Checkering, Modern...............	15,000	20,000	20,000
Best Quality, Various Gauges, Sidelock, Automatic Ejector, Single Trigger, Fancy Engraving, Fancy Checkering, Modern.................	17,000	22,000	22,000

SHOTGUN, SINGLESHOT

	V.G.	Exc	Prior Edition
12 Ga., Trap Grade, Vent Rib, Hammerless, Fancy Engraving, Fancy Checkering, Modern..	7,000	9,500	9,500

WORTHINGTON ARMS Made by Stevens Arms.

SHOTGUN, DOUBLE BARREL, SIDE-BY-SIDE

	V.G.	Exc	Prior Edition
M 315, Various Gauges, Hammerless, Steel Barrel, Modern...................	150	175	175
Model 215, 12 and 16 Gauges, Outside Hammers, Steel Barrel, Modern...	150	175	175

	V.G.	Exc	Prior Edition

WORTHINGTON ARMS CO. Made by Crescent for Geo.
Worthington Co., Cleveland, Ohio.

SHOTGUN, DOUBLE BARREL, SIDE-BY-SIDE

	V.G.	Exc	Prior Edition
Various Gauges, Hammerless, Damascus Barrel, Modern......................	$150	$175	$175
Various Gauges, Hammerless, Steel Barrel, Modern................................	175	200	200
Various Gauges, Outside Hammers, Damascus Barrel, Modern.............	150	175	175
Various Gauges, Outside Hammers, Steel Barrel, Modern......................	175	200	200

SHOTGUN, SINGLESHOT

Various Gauges, Hammer, Steel Barrel, Modern....................................	75	100	100

WORTHINGTON, GEORGE Made by Stevens Arms.

SHOTGUN, DOUBLE BARREL, SIDE-BY-SIDE

M 315, Various Gauges, Hammerless, Steel Barrel, Modern....................	150	175	175
Model 215, 12 and 16 Gauges, Outside Hammers, Steel Barrel, Modern...	125	150	150
Model 311, Various Gauges, Hammerless, Steel Barrel, Modern.............	150	175	175

WUETHRICH W. Wuethrich, Werkzeugbau, Lutzelfluh, Switzerland.

RIFLE, SINGLESHOT

Falling Block, Various Calibers, Engraved, Fancy Wood, Scope Mounted, Modern...	1,000	1,250	1,250

Y

YATO Hamada Arsenal, Japan

HANDGUN, SEMI-AUTOMATIC

	V.G.	Exc.	Prior Edition
Yato, .32 ACP, Clip Fed, Military, Curio..	$2,000	$2,200	$2,200
Yato, .32 ACP, Clip Fed, Pre–War, Curio..	2,500	3,000	3,000

YDEAL Made by Francisco Arizmendi, Eibar, Spain.

HANDGUN, SEMI-AUTOMATIC

	V.G.	Exc.	Prior Edition
6.35mm, Clip Fed, Blue, Curio..	100	125	125
7.65mm, Clip Fed, Blue, Curio..	125	150	150

YOU BET Made by Hopkins & Allen, c. 1880.

HANDGUN, REVOLVER

	V.G.	Exc.	Prior Edition
.22 Short R.F., 7 Shot, Spur Trigger, Solid Frame, Single Action, Antique..	150	175	175

YOUNG AMERICA See Harrington & Richardson Arms Co.

YOUNG, HENRY Easton, Pa. 1774–1780. See Kentucky Rifles.

YOUNG, JOHN Easton, Pa. 1775–1788. See Kentucky Rifles, U.S. Military.

Z

Z Ceska Zbrojovka, Prague, Czechoslovakia.

HANDGUN, SEMI-AUTOMATIC

Vest Pocket, 6.35mm, Clip Fed, Modern.. $100 $125 $125

ZABALA Zabala Hermanos, Eibar, Spain.

SHOTGUN, DOUBLE BARREL, SIDE-BY-SIDE

12 Ga., Boxlock, Checkered Stock, Double Triggers, Modern................. 150 175 175

ZANOTTI Brescia, Italy. 1625–Date.

HANDGUN, FLINTLOCK

Brescia Style, .50, Carved Stock, Engraved, Reproduction,
Antique... 125 150 150

ZARAGOZA Zaragoza, Mexico.

HANDGUN, SEMI-AUTOMATIC

Corla, Type 1, .22 L.R.R.F., Colt System, Clip Fed, Blue,
Modern... 575 650 650
Corla Type 2, .22 L.R.R.F., Colt System, Blue, Modern........................ 400 450 450

ZASTAVA ARMS Zavodi Crvena Zastava, Kragujevac, Yugoslavia.
Also see Mark X.

HANDGUN, SEMI-AUTOMATIC

Model 65, 9mm Luger, Clip Fed, Blue, Modern..................................... 325 375 250
Model 67, .32 ACP, Clip Fed, Blue, Modern... 225 275 150

ZEHNA Made by E. Zehner Waffenfabik, Suhl, Germany 1919–1928.

HANDGUN, SEMI-AUTOMATIC

Vest Pocket, 6.35mm, Clip Fed, Blue, Curio.. 300 350 350
Vest Pocket, 6.35mm, Under #5,000, Clip Fed, Blue, Curio.................... 250 300 300

	V.G.	Exc	Prior Edition

ZEPHYR Tradename of A. F. Stoeger.

SHOTGUN, DOUBLE BARREL, SIDE-BY-SIDE

	V.G.	Exc	Prior Edition
Sterlingworth II, Various Gauges, Checkered Stock, Sidelock, Double Triggers, Light Engraving, Modern	$575	$650	$650
Woodlander II, Various Gauges, Checkered Stock, Boxlock, Double Triggers, Light Engraving, Modern	425	475	475

ZOLI, ANGELO Brescia, Italy.

RIFLE, PERCUSSION

.50 Hawkin, Brass Furniture, Reproduction, Antique	150	175	175

SHOTGUN, DOUBLE BARREL, OVER-UNDER

Angel, 12 and 20 Gauges, Field Grade, Single Selective Trigger, Engraved, Checkered Stock, Modern	675	750	750
Angel, 12 Ga., Trap Grade, Single Selective Trigger, Engraved, Checkered Stock, Modern	700	775	775
Condor, 12 and 20 Gauges, Single Selective Trigger, Field Grade, Checkered Stock, Engraved, Modern	600	675	675
Condor, 12 Ga., Trap Grade, Single Selective Trigger, Engraved, Checkered Stock, Modern	625	700	700
Monte Carlo, 12 and 20 Gauges, Field Grade, Single Selective Trigger, Engraved, Checkered Stock, Modern	750	850	850
Monte Carlo, 12 Ga., Trap Grade, Single Selective Trigger, Engraved, Checkered Stock, Modern	775	875	875

ZOLI, ANTONIO Gardone, V.T., Italy.

SHOTGUN, DOUBLE BARREL, OVER-UNDER

Golden Snipe, 12 and 20 Gauges, Skeet Grade, Single Trigger, Automatic Ejector, Engraved, Checkered Stock, Modern	450	550	600
Golden Snipe, 12 and 20 Gauges, Vent Rib, Single Trigger, Automatic Ejector, Engraved, Checkered Stock, Modern	350	450	550
Golden Snipe, 12 Ga., Trap Grade, Single Trigger, Automatic Ejector, Engraved, Checkered Stock, Modern	450	550	500
Silver Snipe, 12 and 20 Gauges, Skeet Grade, Single Trigger, Vent Rib, Engraved, Checkered Stock, Modern	450	500	500
Silver Snipe, 12 and 20 Gauges, Vent Rib, Single Trigger, Engraved, Checkered Stock, Modern	425	475	475
Silver Snipe, 12 Ga., Trap Grade, Single Trigger, Vent Rib, Engraved, Checkered Stock, Modern	450	500	500

SHOTGUN, DOUBLE BARREL, SIDE-BY-SIDE

Silver Hawk, 12 and 20 Gauges, Double Trigger, Engraved, Checkered Stock, Modern	400	450	450

ZONDA Hispano Argentina Fab. de Automiviles, Buenos Aires, Argentina.

HANDGUN, SINGLESHOT

.22 L.R.R.F., Blue, Modern	225	275	275

	V.G.	Exc	Prior Edition

ZULAICA M. Zulaica y Cia., Eibar, Spain.

HANDGUN, SEMI-AUTOMATIC

Royal , .32 ACP, Clip Fed, Blue, Military, Curio.....................................	$150	$175	$175

AUTOMATIC, REVOLVER

.22 L.R.R.F., Zig–Zag Cylinder, Blue, Curio..	650	750	750

Cartridge Prices

	V.G.	Exc.	Prior Edition
.22 Short R.F., Copper Case Raised "H," Antique	$2.00	$3.35	$3.35
.145 Alton Jones, Modern	4.50	6.00	6.00
.17 Rem, Jacketed Bullet, Modern	0.75	1.15	1.15
.17Alton Jones, Modern	2.50	3.25	3.25
.218 Bee, Various Makers, Modern	0.75	1.15	1.15
.219 Zipper, Various Makers, Modern	0.95	1.60	1.60
.22 15–60 Stevens, Lead Bullet, Curio	3.00	5.00	5.00
.22 BB Cap R.F., Lead Bullet, Antique	0.20	.30	.30
.22 CB Cap R.F., Lead Bullet, Antique	0.20	.30	.30
.22 CB Cap R.F., Two Piece Case, Antique	0.25	.45	.45
.22 Extra Long R.F., Various Makers, Curio	1.25	1.65	1.65
.22 Hi–Power, Various Makers, Modern	1.15	1.75	1.75
.22 Hornet, Various Makers, Modern	0.75	1.05	1.05
.22 L.R.R.F., Brass Case Austrian, Antique	0.35	.55	.55
.22 L.R.R.F., Brass Case Russian, Antique	0.45	.60	.60
.22 L.R.R.F., British Raised K, Antique	2.50	3.75	3.75
.22 L.R.R.F., Devastator, Modern	0.20	.30	.30
.22 L.R.R.F., Shotshell, Various Makers, Modern	0.15	.20	.20
.22 L.R.R.F., Tracer, Gevelot, Modern	0.25	.40	.40
.22 L.R.R.F., Tracer, U.M.C., Modern	0.75	1.15	1.15
.22 L.R.R.F., U.M.C., "S & W Long," Modern	3.50	5.55	5.55
.22 L.R.R.F., Various Makers, Modern	0.10	.15	.15
.22 L.R.R.F., Wadcutter, Modern	0.35	.60	.60
.22 Long R.F., Lead Bullet, Antique	0.20	.30	.30
.22 Long R.F., Various Makers, Modern	0.09	.11	.11
.22 Maynard Extra Long, Various Makers, Curio	1.75	2.25	2.25
.22 Newton, Soft Point Bullet, Modern	12.00	17.00	17.00
.22 Rem. Auto. R.F., Various Makres, Modern	0.35	.50	.50
.22 Rem. Jet, Jacketed Bullet, Modern	0.65	.95	.95
.22 Short R.F., Blank, Various Makers, Modern	0.10	.15	.15
.22 Short R.F., Copper Case Raised "U," Antique	2.25	3.85	3.85
.22 Short R.F., Lead Bullet, Antique	0.20	.30	.30
.22 Short R.F., Various Makers, Modern	0.06	.10	.10
.22 WCF, Various Makers, Modern	0.65	.80	.80
.22 Win. Auto. R.F., Various Makers, Modern	0.25	.40	.40
.22 WMR, Shotshell, Various Makers, Modern	0.20	3.53	.35
.22 WMR, Various Makers, Modern	0.15	.25	.25
.22 WRF, Various Makers, Modern	0.15	.20	.20
.22–250, Various Makers, Modern	0.50	.90	.90
.22–3000 G and H, Soft Point Bullet, Modern	1.50	3.05	3.05
.220 Swift, Various Makers, Modern	0.85	1.70	1.70
.221 Rem. Fireball, Various Makers, Modern	0.45	.85	.85
.222 Rem. Mag., Various Makers, Modern	0.40	.65	.65
.222 Rem., Various Makers, Modern	0.45	.85	.85
.223 Armalite, Experimental, Modern	4.00	6.25	6.25
.223 Rem., Military, Various Makers, Modern	0.55	.70	.70

	V.G.	Exc	Prior Edition
.223 Rem., Various Makers, Modern	$0.65	$0.80	$0.80
.224 Wby, Varmintmaster, Modern	1.00	1.75	1.75
.224 Win., E2 Ball WCC 58, Modern	5.00	6.75	6.75
.224 Win., Experimental, Modern	3.75	5.50	5.50
.225 Win, Various Makers, Modern	0.50	.85	.85
.230 Long, Various Makers, Modern	1.25	1.95	1.95
.230 Short, Various Makers, Modern	0.75	1.20	1.20
.236 U.S. Navy Rimless, Modern	7.50	10.00	10.00
.236 U.S. Navy Rimmed, Modern	4.00	6.50	6.50
.240 Belted N.E., Jacketed Bullet, Modern	1.50	2.00	2.00
.240 Flanged N.E., Various Makers, Modern	2.00	3.50	3.50
.240 Wby Mag., Modern	1.00	1.65	1.65
.242 Rimless N.E., Various Makers, Modern	4.00	5.50	5.50
.243 Win., Various Makers, Modern	0.65	.95	.95
.244 H and H Mag., Jacketed Bullet, Modern	4.00	5.40	5.40
.244 Halger Mag., Various Makers, Modern	20.00	31.00	31.00
.244 Rem., Various Makers, Modern	1.10	1.40	1.40
.246 Purdy, Soft Point Bullet, Modern	3.00	4.50	4.50
.247 Wby Mag., Modern	1.10	1.75	1.75
.25 ACP, Various Makers, Modern	0.35	.45	.45
.25 L.F., Various Makers, #50 Allen, Curio	3.50	5.25	5.25
.25 Rem., Various Makers, Modern	0.80	1.45	1.45
.25 Short R.F. , Lead Bullet, Antique	0.25	.55	.55
.25 Stevens Long R.F., Various Makers, Modern	0.40	.50	.50
.25 Stevens R.F., Wood Shotshell Bullet, Modern	1.25	1.75	1.75
.25 Stevens Short R.F., Various Makers, Modern	0.25	.55	.55
.25–06 Rem., Various Makers, Modern	0.75	.95	.95
.25–20 WCF, Jacketed Bullet, Various Makers, Modern	0.45	.60	.60
.25–20 WCF, Lead Bullet, Various Makers, Modern	0.40	.55	.55
.25–21, Jacketed Bullet, Curio	3.25	4.75	4.75
.25–25, Various Makers, Modern	3.00	4.50	4.50
.25–35 WCF, Various Makers, Modern	0.60	1.05	1.05
.25–36, Jacketed Bullet, Curio	1.90	2.85	2.85
.250 Savage, Various Makers, Modern	0.65	1.00	1.00
.255 Rook, Various Makers, Curio	0.90	1.65	1.65
.256 Gibbs Mag., Various Makers, Modern	4.25	5.50	5.50
.256 Newton, Soft Point Bullet, Modern	1.75	2.75	2.75
.256 Win. Mag., Various Makers, Modern	0.60	.85	.85
.257 Roberts, Various Makers, Modern	0.75	.95	.95
.257 Wby. Mag., Modern	1.00	1.60	1.60
.26 BSA, Soft Point Bullet, Modern	3.25	4.75	4.75
.264 Win. Mag., Various Makers, Modern	0.65	1.00	1.00
.267 Rem. R.F., Experimental, Curio	8.50	11.25	11.25
.270 Wby. Mag., Modern	1.10	1.50	1.50
.270 Win., Flare Cartridge, Various Makers, Modern	1.85	2.70	2.70
.270 Win., Various Makers, Modern	0.80	1.00	1.00
.275 Flanged Mag., Various Makers, Modern	1.85	2.75	2.75
.275 H and H Mag., Various Makers, Modern	3.50	4.75	4.75
.275 Rigby, Various Makers, Modern	3.00	4.25	4.25
.276 Enfield, Various Makers, Military, Modern	6.50	8.75	8.75
.276 Garand, Military, Experimental, Curio	3.00	3.75	3.75
.276 Pederson, Various Makers, Military, Curio	3.00	3.75	3.75
.28 Cup Primed Cartridge, Various Makers, Curio	9.50	11.25	11.25
.28–30–120 Stevens, Lead Bullet, Curio	4.25	5.00	5.00
.280 Flanged N.E., Various Makers, Modern	4.00	4.75	4.75

	V.G.	Exc	Prior Edition
.280 Halgar Mag., Various Makers, Modern	$4.10	$4.95	$4.95
.280 Jeffery, Various Makers, Modern	4.75	6.50	6.50
.280 Rem., Various Makers, Modern	0.75	1.05	1.05
.280 Ross, Various Makers, Modern	3.25	3.95	3.95
.280/30 Experimental, Various Makers, Military, Modern	8.75	10.50	10.50
.284 Win., Various Makers, Modern	0.75	1.05	1.05
.295 Rook, Various Makers, Modern	1.10	1.55	1.55
.295/.250 Rook, Various Makers, Modern	1.10	1.55	1.55
.297 R.F. Revolver, Various Makers, Modern	4.00	4.75	4.75
.297/.230 Morris Short, Various Makers, Modern	1.00	1.20	1.20
.297/.230 Morris, Various Makers, Modern	1.05	1.40	1.40
.30 Carbine, Various Makers, Modern	0.50	.75	.75
.30 Carbine, Various Makers, Military, Modern	0.55	.65	.65
.30 Cup Primed Cartridge, Various Makers, Curio	1.55	2.25	2.25
.30 H and H Super Mag. Flanged, Various Makers, Modern	2.75	4.25	4.25
.30 Long R.F., Merwin Cone base, Antique	25.00	32.00	32.00
.30 Long R.F., Various Makers, Antique	1.90	2.75	2.75
.30 Luger, Various Makers, Modern	0.50	.75	.75
.30 Newton, Soft Point Bullet, Modern	2.75	3.50	3.50
.30 Pederson, Various Makers, Military, Modern	3.00	3.75	3.75
.30 Rem, Various Makers, Modern	0.65	.95	.95
.30 Short R.F., Various Makers, Curio	3.25	4.95	4.95
.30–03 Springfield, Various Makers, Curio	1.50	2.75	2.75
.30–06 Springfield, Accelerator, Modern	0.75	1.20	1.20
.30–06 Springfield, Flare Cartridge, Various Makers, Modern	2.25	2.75	2.75
.30–06 Springfield, Various Makers, Modern	0.75	1.10	1.10
.30–06 Springfield, Various Makers, Military, Modern	0.45	.65	.65
.30–30 Wesson, Lead Bullet, Curio	26.00	29.75	29.75
.30–30 Win., Bicentennial, Various Makers, Modern	0.75	.95	.95
.30–30 Win., Flare Cartridge, Various Makers, Modern	2.25	3.00	3.00
.30–30 Win., Various Makers, Modern	0.75	.95	.95
.30–40 Krag, Various Makers, Modern	0.80	1.10	1.10
.300 AMU Mag., Various Makers, Military, Modern	2.75	3.50	3.50
.300 H and H Mag., Various Makers, Modern	0.85	1.40	1.40
.300 Hoffman Mag., Soft Point Bullet, Modern	3.50	4.25	4.25
.300 Rook, Various Makers, Modern	1.35	1.65	1.65
.300 Savage, Various Makers, Modern	0.90	1.10	1.10
.300 Sherwood, Various Makers, Modern	2.75	3.50	3.50
.300 Wby. Mag., Modern	1.25	1.80	1.80
.300 Win. Mag., Various Makers, Modern	1.10	1.50	1.50
.303 British, Various Makers, Modern	0.90	1.10	1.10
.303 Lewis Rimless, Various Makers, Military, Modern	3.90	4.40	4.40
.303 Mag., Various Makers, Modern	4.25	4.75	4.75
.303 Savage, Various Makers, Modern	0.90	1.10	1.10
.303/.22, Soft Point Bullet, Modern	7.50	10.00	10.00
.305 Rook, Various Makers, Modern	2.00	2.50	2.50
.308 Norma Mag., Various Makers, Modern	1.65	1.85	1.85
.308 Win., Flare Cartridge, Various Makers, Modern	2.25	2.75	2.75
.308 Win., Various Makers, Modern	0.90	1.10	1.10
.308 Win., Various Makers, Military, Modern	0.55	.70	.70
.31 Crispin, Patent Ignition, Antique	165.00	195.00	195.00
.31 Eley R.F., Lead Bullet, Dished Base, Modern	12.00	17.00	17.00
.31 Milbank, Patent Ignition, Antique	57.50	62.50	62.50
.31 Theur, Patent Ignition, Antique	15.00	16.90	16.90
.31 Volcanic, Patent Ignition, Antique	17.50	19.50	19.50

	V.G.	Exc	Prior Edition
.310 Cadet, Various Makers, Modern	$1.75	$2.25	$2.25
.318 Rimless N.E., Various Makers, Modern	2.00	2.35	2.35
.32 ACP, Various Makers, Modern	0.45	.65	.65
.32 Ballard Extra Long, Lead Bullet, Curio	1.60	1.80	1.80
.32 Colt New Police, Various Makers, Modern	0.50	.65	.65
.32 Extra Long R.F., Various Makers, Curio	6.00	8.00	8.00
.32 Extra Short R.F., Lead Bullet, Antique	1.20	1.40	1.40
.32 Ideal, Lead Bullet, Curio	1.65	2.00	2.00
.32 L.F., Various Makers, #52 Allen, Curio	7.90	8.55	8.55
.32 Long Colt, Various Makers, Modern	0.45	.60	.60
.32 Long R.F., Shotshell, Curio	0.65	.75	.75
.32 Long R.F., Various Makers, Modern	7.25	9.00	9.00
.32 Long Rifle, Lead Bullet, Antique	4.50	5.25	5.25
.32 Rem. Rimless, Various Makers, Modern	1.05	1.20	1.20
.32 Rem., Various Makers, Modern	0.90	1.10	1.10
.32 S and W Long, Various Makers, Modern	0.35	.45	.45
.32 S and W, Blank Cartridge Various Makers, Modern	0.25	.30	.30
.32 S and W, Shotshell, Various Makers, Modern	0.45	.55	.55
.32 S and W, Various Makers, Modern	0.35	.45	.45
.32 Short Colt, Various Makers, Modern	0.45	.45	.45
.32 Short R.F., Various Makers, Modern	0.40	.50	.50
.32 Teat–Fire Cartridge, Various Makers, Curio	3.80	4.25	4.25
.32 Win. Self–Loading, Various Makers, Modern	0.90	1.10	1.10
.32 Win. Special, Various Makers, Modern	0.90	1.10	1.10
.32–20 Rem., Lead Bullet, Curio	4.75	5.35	5.35
.32–20 WCF, Jacketed Bullet, Various Makers, Modern	1.65	1.70	1.70
.32–20 WCF, Lead Bullet, Various Makers, Moden	0.90	1.10	1.10
.32–35 Stevens and Maynard, Lead Bullet, Curio	4.25	4.75	4.75
.32–40 Bullard, Lead Bullet, Curio	3.00	3.50	3.50
.32–40 Rem., Lead Bullet, Curio	3.25	3.70	3.70
.32–40 WCF, Various Makers, Modern	0.90	1.05	1.05
.320 Extra Long Rifle, Various Makers, Modern	2.75	3.25	3.25
.320 Rook, Various Makers, Modern	1.05	1.40	1.40
.322 Swift, Various Makers, Modern	6.25	7.00	7.00
.33 BSA, Soft Point Bullet, Modern	3.75	4.50	4.50
.33 Win., Soft Point Bullet, Modern	1.95	2.15	2.15
.333 Flanged N.E., Various Makers, Modern	4.75	5.40	5.40
.333 Rimless N.E., Various Makers, Modern	5.25	5.70	5.70
.338 Win. Mag., Various Makers, Modern	1.35	1.60	1.60
.340 R.F. Revolver, Various Makers, Modern	2.75	3.25	3.25
.340 Wby. Mag., Modern	1.50	1.75	1.75
.348 Win, Various Makers, Modern	1.50	1.80	1.80
.35 Allen R.F., Lead Bullet, Curio	14.50	17.00	17.00
.35 Newton, Soft Point Bullet, Modern	4.25	4.75	4.75
.35 Rem., Various Makers, Modern	0.80	1.10	1.10
.35 S and W Auto., Jacketed Bullet, Curio	1.35	1.60	1.60
.35 Win. Self–Loading, Various Makers, Modern	0.85	1.10	1.10
.35 Win., Various Makers, Modern	3.25	3.75	3.75
.35–30 Maynard, Lead Bullet, with Riveted Head, Curio	12.50	15.00	15.00
.35–30 Maynard, Lead Bullet, without Riveted Head, Curio	7.25	8.00	8.00
.35–40 Maynard, Various Makers, Curio	15.00	16.50	16.50
.350 Rem. Mag., Various Makers, Modern	1.45	1.70	1.70
.350 Rigby, Various makers, Modern	3.75	4.50	4.50
.351 Win. Self–Loading, Various Makers, Modern	2.35	2.70	2.70
.357 Magnum, Jacketed Bullet, Various Makers, Modern	0.55	.70	.70

	V.G.	Exc	Prior Edition
.357 Magnum, Lead Bullet, Various Makers, Modern	$0.55	$0.70	$0.70
.358 Norma Mag., Various Makers, Modern	1.40	1.70	1.70
.358 Win., Various Makers, Modern	1.35	1.65	1.65
.36 Crispin, Patent Ignition, Antique	190.00	210.00	210.00
.36 L.F., #56 Allen, Various Makers, Curio	6.00	8.50	8.50
.36 Theur Navy, Patent Ignition, Antique	14.50	16.50	15.50
.360 #5 Rook, Various Makers, Modern	14.50	16.50	16.50
.360 N.E. #2, Various Makers, Curio	3.00	3.50	3.50
.360 N.E., Various Makers, Modern	2.25	2.50	2.50
.369 Purdey, Soft Point Bullet, Curio	6.75	7.50	7.50
.370 Flanged, Various Makers, Modern	2.10	2.30	2.30
.375 Flanged Mag. N.E., Various Makers, Modern	3.00	3.50	3.50
.375 Flanged N.E., Various Makers, Modern	4.25	4.45	4.45
.375 H and H Mag., Various Makers, Modern	1.75	2.00	2.00
.375 Rimless N.E. 2¼", Various makers, Curio	1.50	1.70	1.70
.375/.303 Axite, Various Makers, Curio	3.25	3.55	3.55
.378 Wby. Mag., Modern	3.35	3.75	3.75
.38 ACP, Various Makers, Modern	0.25	.50	.50
.38 AMU, Various Makers, Military, Modern	0.80	1.00	1.00
.38 Ballard Extra Long, Lead Bullet, Curio	2.15	2.50	2.50
.38 Extra Long R.F., Lead Bullet, Curio	6.00	6.50	6.50
.38 Long C.F., Lead Bullet, Curio	0.95	1.10	1.10
.38 Long Colt, Various Makers, Modern	0.50	.70	.70
.38 Long R.F., Various Makers, Curio	4.75	5.25	5.25
.38 S and W, Blank Cartridge, Various Makers, Modern	0.35	.50	.50
.38 S and W, Various Makers, Modern	0.45	.65	.65
.38 Short Colt, Various Makers, Modern	0.35	.50	.50
.38 Short R.F., Shotshell, Curio	0.65	.80	.80
.38 Short R.F., Various Makers, Modern	3.75	4.25	4.25
.38 Special, Blank Cartridge, Various Makers, Modern	0.25	.30	.30
.38 Special, Flare Cartridge, Various Makers, Modern	2.25	2.75	2.75
.38 Special, Lead Bullet, Various Makers, Modern	0.35	.50	.50
.38 Special, Shotshell, Various Makers, Modern	0.35	.50	.50
.38 Special, Sub–Velocity Ammo, Various Makers, Modern	0.35	.50	.50
.38 Special, Tracer, Military, Modern	0.50	.75	.75
.38 Super, Various Makers, Modern	0.45	.65	.65
.38–40 Rem. Hepburn, Various Makers, Curio	3.70	4.40	4.40
.38–40 WCF, Various Makers, Modern	0.80	.95	.95
.38–44, Various Makers, Modern	0.50	.65	.65
.38–45 Bullard, Lead Bullets, Curio	6.00	6.75	6.75
.38–50 Ballard, Lead Bullet, Curio	5.75	6.40	6.40
.38–50 Maynard, Various Makers, Curio	14.50	16.50	16.50
.38–50 Rem. Hepburn, Lead Bullet, Curio	4.00	4.45	4.45
.38–55 Win. and Ballard, Various Makers, Modern	1.65	2.00	2.00
.38–56 Win, Lead Bullet, Curio	2.75	3.50	3.50
.38–72 Win., Lead Bullet, Curio	4.75	5.10	5.10
.38–90 Win. Express, Lead Bullet, Curio	6.75	7.75	7.75
.380 ACP, Various Makers, Modern	0.45	.65	.65
.380 Revolver, Shotshel, Modern	1.25	1.55	1.55
.380 Revolver, Various Makers, Military, Modern	0.50	.80	.80
.40–90 Peabody "What Cheer," Lead Bullet, Curio	57.00	62.00	62.00
.40/.350 Rigby Flanged, Various Makers, Modern	4.50	5.25	5.25
.40–110 Win., Lead Bullet, Curio	27.00	32.00	32.00
.40–40 Maynard, Lead Bullet, Curio	12.50	16.00	16.00
.40–50 Sharps (Necked), Lead Bullet, Curio	6.50	7.25	7.25

	V.G.	Exc	Prior Edition
.40–50 Sharps (Straight), Lead Bullet, Curo	$5.50	$6.05	$6.05
.40–60 Marlin, Various Makers, Curio	15.00	18.00	18.00
.40–60 Maynard, Lead Bullet, Curio	17.00	23.00	23.00
.40–60 Win., Various Makers, Modern	4.75	5.00	5.00
.40–63 Ballard, Lead Bullet, Antique	8.50	9.50	9.50
.40–65 Win., Lead Bullet, Curio	4.75	5.40	5.40
.40–70 Ballard, Lead Bullet, Curio	6.10	6.95	6.95
.40–70 Maynard, Lead Bullet, Curio	20.00	25.50	25.50
.40–70 Peabody "What Cheer," Lead Bullet, Curio	37.00	41.00	41.00
.40–70 Rem., Lead Bullet, Curio	5.25	6.00	6.00
.40–70 Sharps (Necked), Various Makers, Curio	6.25	7.00	7.00
.40–70 Sharps (Straight), Various Makers, Curio	5.75	6.50	6.50
.40–70 Win., Lead Bullet, Antique	4.75	5.50	5.50
.40–72 Win., Various Makers, Modern	4.80	5.55	5.55
.40–75 Bullard, Lead Bullet, Curio	7.25	8.00	8.00
.40–82 Win., Shotshell, Various Makers, Modern	5.25	6.00	6.00
.40–82 Win., Vaious Makers, Modern	3.75	4.25	4.25
.40–85 Ballard, Lead Bullet, Curio	6.50	7.25	7.25
.40–90 Ballard, Lead Bullet, Curio	7.50	10.00	10.00
.40–90 Sharps (Necked), Various Makers, Curio	7.50	8.25	8.25
.40–90 Sharps (Straight), Lead Bullet, Curio	14.50	16.00	16.00
.400 Nitro #", Various Makers, Modern	7.50	8.25	8.25
.400/.360 Purdey Flanged, Various Makers, Curio	4.50	5.25	5.25
.400/.375 H and H, Various Makers, Modern	4.50	5.25	5.25
.401 Herter Mag., Various Makers, Modern	1.25	1.70	1.70
.401 Win. Self–Loading, Various Makers, Modern	1.50	1.90	1.90
.404 N.E., Various Makers, Modern	4.50	5.00	5.00
.405 Win., Jacketed Bullet, Modern	1.75	2.25	2.25
.41 Long Colt, Various Makers, Modern	1.05	1.20	1.20
.41 Long Colt, Wood Shotshell Bullet, Modern	2.00	2.30	2.30
.41 Long R.F., Various Makers, Curio	5.00	6.00	6.00
.41 Magnum, Jacketed Bullet, Various Makers, Modern	0.50	.65	.65
.41 Magnum, Lead Bullet, Various Makers, Modern	0.50	.70	.70
.41 Short C.F., Lead Bullet, Modern	0.70	.85	.85
.41 Short R.F., Various Makers, Modern	3.75	4.20	4.20
.41 Swiss R.F., Kynoch with Raised "C," Antique	5.50	6.00	6.00
.41 Swiss R.F., Various Makers, Modern	2.75	3.45	3.45
.41 Volcanic, Patent Ignition, Antique	22.50	25.00	25.00
.42 Allen R.F., Lead Bullet, Antique	4.75	5.25	5.25
.42 Cup Primed Cartridge, Various Makers, Curio	9.75	10.75	10.75
.425 Westley Richards Mag., Various Makers, Modern	4.75	5.45	5.45
.44 AMP, Various Makers, Modern	1.25	1.60	1.60
.44 Bulldog, Lead Bullet, Antique	0.95	1.20	1.20
.44 Colt, Various Makers, Modern	1.25	1.60	1.60
.44 Crispin, Patent Ignition, Antique	150.00	180.00	180.00
.44 Evans Short, Various makers, Curio	6.75	7.50	7.50
.44 Extra Long Ballard, Lead Bullet, Curio	10.00	12.50	12.50
.44 Henry R.F., Blank Cartridge, Curio	5.00	6.00	6.00
.44 Henry R.F., Lead Bullet, Curio	3.75	4.25	4.25
.44 L.F., #58 Allen, Various Makers, Curio	22.00	24.00	24.00
.44 Long R.F., Various Makers, Curio	5.50	7.00	7.00
.44 Magnum, Shotshell, Various Makers, Modern	0.75	.95	.95
.44 Magnum, Various Makers, Modern	0.80	1.05	1.05
.44 Russian, Various Makers, Curio	1.25	1.60	1.60
.44 S and W, Sub–Velocity Ammo, Various Makers, Modern	0.30	.40	.40

	V.G.	Exc	Prior Edition
.44 S and W, Various Makers, Modern	$0.50	$0.65	$0.65
.44 Short R.F., Blank Cartridge, Antique	0.60	.85	.85
.44 Short R.F., Lead Bullet, Curio	1.75	2.25	2.25
.44 Theur, Patent Ignition, Antique	25.00	28.00	28.00
.44 Webley, Blank Cartridge, Curio	0.90	1.10	1.10
.44-90 Sharps, Various Makers, Curio	10.00	12.00	12.00
.44-100 Ballard, Lead Bullet, Curio	15.00	18.50	18.50
.44-100 Wesson, Lead Bullet, Curio	4.50	5.00	5.00
.44-40 WCF, Shotshell, Various Makers, Modern	1.10	1.40	1.40
.44-40 WCF, Various Makers, Modern	0.95	1.10	1.10
.44-60 Sharps, Lead Bullet, Curio	5.75	6.25	6.25
.44-60 Win., Lead Bullet, Curio	4.05	4.45	4.45
.44-70 Maynard, Lead Bullet, Curio	45.00	48.00	48.00
.44-75 Ballard Everlasting, Lead Bullet, Curio	5.50	6.25	6.25
.44-77 Sharps and Rem. Lead Bullet, Curio	5.50	6.25	6.25
.44-90 Rem. Special, Various Makers, Curio	25.00	27.50	27.50
.44-90 Rem., Lead Bullet, Curio	12.00	13.75	13.75
.44-95 Peabody "What Cheer," Lead Bullet, Curio	37.50	42.50	42.50
.440 Eley R.F., Lead Bullet, no Headstamp, Modern	0.55	1.20	1.20
.442 Eley R.F., Lead Bullet, no Headstamp, Modern	1.50	1.65	1.65
.444 Marlin, Various Makers, Modern	1.05	1.30	1.30
.45 ACP, Military, Tracer, Modern	1.10	1.30	1.30
.45 ACP, Various Makers, Modern	0.55	.70	.70
.45 Auto-Rim, Various Makers, Modern	0.55	.70	.70
.45 Colt, Various Makers, Modern	0.55	.70	.70
.45 Colt, Wood Shotshell Bullet, Modern	2.25	2.75	2.75
.45 Danish R.F., Lead Bullet, no Headstamp, Modern	22.50	25.00	25.00
.45 S and W, Various Makers, Modern	3.75	4.50	4.50
.45 Teat-Fire Cartridge, Various Makers, Curio	57.50	62.50	62.50
.45 Webley, Lead Bullet, Modern	1.50	1.70	1.70
.45-90 Win., Jacketed Bullet, Curio	4.75	5.15	5.15
.45-90 Win., Lead Bullet, Curio	4.00	4.45	4.45
.45-100 Ballard, Various Makers, Curio	15.00	17.00	17.00
.45-100 Sharps, Lead Bullet, Curio	24.50	26.00	26.00
.45-125 Win., Lead Bullet, Curio	27.50	31.50	31.50
.45-50 Peabody, Lead Bullet, Curio	22.00	24.50	24.50
.45-60 Win., Lead Bullet, Curio	4.00	4.50	4.50
.45-70 Government, Various Makers, Modern	0.85	1.10	1.10
.45-70 Marlin, Various Makers, Modern	5.50	6.50	6.50
.45-70 Van Choate, Lead Bullet, Curio	31.00	36.50	36.50
.45-75 Sharps, Lead Bullet, Curio	10.00	12.00	12.00
.45-75 Sharps, Lead Bullet, (Rigby), Curio	15.00	18.00	18.00
.45-75 Win., Various Makers, Modern	3.25	3.70	3.70
.45-80 Sharpshooter, Various Makers, Curio	3.50	4.00	4.00
.45-85 Marlin, Various Makers, Modern	6.25	7.00	7.00
.45-85 Win., Lead Bullet, Curio	5.75	6.50	6.50
.450 #1 Carbine, Various Makers, Modern	5.50	6.05	6.05
.450 #2 N.E. 3½", Various Makers, Modern	10.75	12.25	12.25
.450 Gatling, Various Makers, Modern	6.50	7.00	7.00
.450 Long Revolver, Various Makers, Curio	2.75	3.25	3.25
.450 N.E. 3¼", Various Makers, Curio	6.00	6.50	6.50
.450 N.E. 3¼", Various Makers, New Make, Modern	5.50	6.00	6.00
.450 Revolver, Various Makers, Curio	1.50	1.75	1.75
.450 Rigby Match 2.4", Soft Point Bullet, Modern	5.00	5.50	5.50
.450/.400 BPE, Various Makers, Modern	4.75	5.25	5.25

	V.G.	Exc	Prior Edition
.450/.400 Mag. N.E. 3¼", Various Makers, Modern	$6.25	$6.70	$6.70
.450/.400 N.E. 3", Various Makers, Modern	5.50	6.00	6.00
.454 Casull Mag., Various Makers, Modern	1.20	1.40	1.40
.455 Revolver Mk 1, Jacketed Bullet, Military, Modern	0.95	1.10	1.10
.455 Webley Mk 2, Various Makers, Modern	1.25	1.60	1.60
.458 Win. Mag., Soft Point Bullet, Various Makers, Modern	1.50	1.80	1.80
.458 Win. Mag., Various Makers, Full Jacketed Bullet, Modern	2.25	2.75	2.75
.46 Extra Long R.F., Various Makers, Curio	22.50	26.00	26.00
.46 Extra Short R.F., Lead Bullet, Curio	27.50	32.50	32.50
.46 Long R.F., Lead Bullet, Antique	4.25	4.70	4.70
.46 Remington and Ballard, Lead Bullet, Curio	7.50	8.25	8.25
.46 Short R.F., Various Makers, Curio	7.25	8.00	8.00
.460 Wby. Mag., Modern	2.75	3.45	3.45
.470 N.E., Various Makers, Modern	5.75	6.50	6.50
.475 #2 N.E., Various Makers, Modern	8.25	9.00	9.00
.475 N.E., Various Makers, Modern	8.00	9.25	9.25
.476 N.E., Soft Point Bullet, Modern	8.50	9.25	9.25
.50 BMG, Various Makers, Military, Modern	2.10	2.40	2.40
.50 Rem. Navy R.F., Various Makers, Curio	30.00	34.00	34.00
.50 Rem., Various Makers, Curio	4.15	4.55	4.55
.50 U.S. Carbine, Various Makers, Curio	5.50	6.25	6.25
.50–100 Win., Lead Bullet, Curio	5.00	5.75	5.75
.50–100 Win., Various Makers, Curio	7.50	8.50	8.50
.50–115 Bullard, Lead Bullet, Curio	7.00	7.75	7.75
.50–140 Sharps, Lead Bullet, Curio	47.50	53.50	53.50
.50–140 Win. Express, Lead Bullet, Curio	115.00	135.00	135.00
.50–50 Maynard, Lead Bullet, Curio	7.50	8.25	8.25
.50–70 Government R.F., Various Makers, Curio	35.00	44.00	44.00
.50–70 Musket, New Make, Various Makers, Modern	2.75	3.25	3.25
.50–70 Musket, Shotshell, Various Makers, Modern	6.00	8.50	8.50
.50–70 Musket, Various Makers, Curio	16.50	19.00	19.00
.50–90 Sharps, Lead Bullet, Curio	22.00	27.50	27.50
.50–90 Win., Various Makers, Curio	3.25	4.00	4.00
.500 #2 Express, Soft Pint Bkue, Modern	5.50	7.00	7.00
.500 Irish Constabulary Revolver, Various Makers, Modern	25.00	29.50	29.50
.500 Jeffery, Various Makers, Modern	20.00	24.00	24.00
.500 N.E. 3", Various Makers, Modern	5.50	6.25	6.25
.500 Nitro BPE, Various Makers, Curio	8.75	10.75	10.75
.500/.450 #1 Express, Various Makers, Modern	5.75	6.50	6.50
.500/.450 #2 Musket, Various makers, Modern	4.00	4.75	4.75
.500/.450 Mag. N.E. 3¼", Various Makers, Modern	7.75	9.25	9.25
.500/.465 N.E., Various Makers, Modern	6.25	7.00	7.00
.505 Gibbs, Lead Bullet, Modern	8.25	9.50	9.50
.52–70 Sharps R.F., Lead Bullet, Curio	38.00	44.00	44.00
.54 Ballard R.F., Lead Bullet, Curio	52.50	55.50	55.50
.55–100 Maynard, Lead Bullet, Curio	45.00	51.00	51.00
.56–46 Spencer R.F., Various Makers, Curio	30.00	35.00	35.00
.56–50 Spencer R.F., WRA, Commercial, Antique	3.50	4.00	4.00
.56–52 Spencer R.F., Shotshell, Various Makers, Curio	20.00	22.25	22.25
.56–52 Spencer R.F., Various makers, Curio	4.50	5.35	5.35
.56–56 Spencer R.F., Various makers, Antique	7.50	8.25	8.25
.577 N.E. 2¾", Various Makers, Modern	8.75	10.25	10.25
.577 N.E. 3", Various makers, Modern	10.50	11.25	11.25
.577 Snyder, Shotshell, Various Makers, Modern	7.50	8.25	8.25
.577 Snyder, Various Makers, Modern	5.25	6.50	6.50

	V.G.	Exc	Prior Edition
.577/.450 Martini–Henry, Various Makers, Modern	$6.25	$7.00	$7.00
.577/.500 31/8", Various Makers, Modern	7.50	8.00	8.00
.58 Berdan, Various makers, Curio	6.50	7.70	7.70
.58 Gatling R.F., Lead Bullet, Curio	30.00	35.00	35.00
.58 Joslyn Carbine R.F., Various Makers, Curio	37.50	42.50	42.50
.58 Mont Storm R.F., Various Makers, Curio	45.00	51.00	51.00
.58 U.S. Musket, Lead Bullet, Curio	20.00	24.00	24.00
.600 N.E., Lead Bullet, Curio	32.00	37.00	37.00
.70–150 Win., Cartridge Board Dummy, Curio	145.00	170.00	170.00
10.15 X 61R Jarmann, Paper–Patched, Lead Bullet, Curio	5.50	6.40	6.40
10.3 X 65R Baenziger, Soft Point Bullet, Modern	4.75	5.50	5.50
10.4 Italian Revolver, Military, Modern	1.75	2.60	2.60
10.4 X 47R Italian Vetterli, Jacketed Bullet, Modern	1.25	1.70	1.70
10.4mm Swiss Ordnance Rev., Various Makers, Modern	3.75	4.50	4.50
10.6mm Schulhof, Various Makers, Modern	2.25	2.80	2.80
10.6mm Spanish Ordnance Rev., Various Makers, Modern	2.00	2.50	2.50
10.75 X 58R Berdan, Military, Various Makers, Curio	2.00	2.50	2.50
10.75 X 68 Mauser, Various Makers, Modern	2.25	2.75	2.75
10.75 X 73, Various Makers, Modern	2.50	2.85	2.85
10mm Hirst Auto Pistol, Various Makers, Modern	25.00	29.00	29.00
10mm Soerabaja, Lead Bullet, Antique	4.00	4.75	4.75
11 X 59R Gras., Jacketed Bullet, Curio	1.75	2.25	2.25
11 X 59R Gras., Lead Bullet, Curio	2.25	2.70	2.70
11.15 X 58R Werndl, Lead Bullet, Modern	5.75	6.50	6.50
11.15 X 60R Mauser, Lead Bullet, Modern	5.00	5.75	5.75
11.15 X 65R , Lead Bullet, Modern	3.75	4.25	4.25
11.2mm Gasser, Various Makers, Modern	7.50	10.00	10.00
11.43 X 50R Egyptian, Various Makers, Modern	2.75	3.50	3.50
11.43 X 50R Egyptian, Wood Shotshell Bullet, Modern	3.75	4.50	4.50
11.5 X 57R Spanish, Various Makers, Modern	3.75	4.50	4.50
11.5mm Montenegrin–Gasser, Various Makers, Modern	8.75	10.25	10.25
11.5mm Werder, Various Makers, Modern	7.25	8.75	8.75
11mm Chassepot, Patent Ignition, Antique	6.00	6.75	6.75
11mm Danish Ordnance Rev., Various Makers, Modern	35.00	39.00	39.00
11mm Devisme, Patent Ignition, Antique	15.00	18.00	18.00
11mm French Ordnance, Various Makers, Curio	1.25	1.55	1.55
11mm German Service, Various Makers, Curio	1.75	2.40	2.40
11mm Loran, Patent Ignition, Antique	3.50	4.25	4.25
11mm Mannlicher, Military, Paper–Patched Lead Bullet, Curio	0.55	.75	.75
11mm Rapnael, Patent Ignition, Inside Primed, Antique	42.00	47.00	47.00
11mm Rapnael, Patent Ignition, Outside Primed, Antique	35.00	40.00	40.00
12.7 Russian M.G., Various Makers, Military, Modern	1.25	1.50	1.50
15mm French Rev., Various Makers, Modern	17.00	20.50	20.50
19.8mm Montenegrin Rev., Various Makers, Modern	17.50	23.50	23.50
2.8mm Kolibri, Jacketed Bullet, Curio	16.50	19.50	19.50
2mm Rimfire, Blank Cartridge, Modern	0.25	.30	.30
2mm Rimfire, Lead Bullet, Modern	0.40	.55	.55
3mm Kolibri, Various Makers, Modern	18.00	23.50	23.50
4 Ga., Various Makers, Paper Case, Shotshell, Modern	3.50	4.75	4.75
4.25mm Liliput, Jacketed Bullet, Curio	6.50	8.00	8.00
416 Rigby, Soft Point Bullet, Modern	5.50	6.25	6.25
4mm R.F., Lead Bullet, Antique	0.25	.35	.35
5.5mm Soemmerda, Various Makers, Modern	3.75	5.00	5.00
5.5mm Velo Dog, Lead Bullet, Curio	0.90	1.10	1.10
5.6 X 33 Rook, Various Makers, Modern	1.75	2.15	2.15

	V.G.	Exc	Prior Edition
5.6 X 35R Vierling, Various Makers, Modern	$1.60	$1.70	$1.70
5.6 X 50 Mag., Various Makers, Modern	1.25	1.75	1.75
5.6 X 50R Mag., Various Makers, Modern	1.50	2.05	2.05
5.6 X 52R, Various Makers, Modern	1.00	1.40	1.40
5.6 X 57, Various Makers, Modern	1.25	1.75	1.75
5.6 X 57R, Various Makers, Modern	1.25	1.85	1.85
5.6 X 61 Vom Hofe Express, Soft Point Bullet, Modern	4.75	5.50	5.50
5.6 X 61R Vom Hofe Express, Various Makers, Modern	5.25	6.00	6.00
5.75mm Vel–Dog Short, Various Makers, Modern	3.00	3.85	3.85
5.75mm Velo Dog, Various Makers, Modern	1.25	2.00	2.00
5.7mm Target Pistol, Various Makers, Modern	4.75	5.45	5.45
5–in-One, Blank Cartridge, Various Makers, Modern	0.70	.90	.90
5mm Bergmann, Grooved, Various Makers, Curio	7.50	8.00	8.00
5mm Bergmann, Various Makers, Curio	8.25	10.50	10.50
5mm Brun, Various Makers, Modern	20.00	24.00	24.00
5mm Clement, Soft Point Bullet, Curio	4.25	5.25	5.25
5mm French Revolver, Various Makers, Modern	1.15	1.40	1.40
5mm Pickert, Various Makers, Modern	18.00	23.00	23.00
5mm Rem. RFM, Jacketed Bullet, Modern	0.20	.30	.30
6 X 58 Forster, Various Makers, Curio	8.75	9.50	9.50
6 X 58R Forster, Various Makers, Curio	4.25	4.95	4.95
6.35mm Forster, Various Makers, Modern	5.50	6.25	6.25
6.5 X 48R Sauer, Various Makers, Curio	2.75	3.50	3.50
6.5 X 52 Mannlicher–Carcano, Various Makers, Modern	0.90	1.10	1.10
6.5 X 54 Mauser, Soft Point Bullet, Modern	2.75	3.50	3.50
6.5 X 54 MS, Various Makers, Modern	1.50	2.15	2.15
6.5 X 55 Swedish, Various Makers, Modern	1.05	1.40	1.40
6.5 X 57, Various Makers, Modern	1.20	1.80	1.80
6.5 X 57R, Various Makers, Modern	1.20	1.80	1.80
6.5 X 58 Vergueiro, Various Makers, Military, Modern	5.00	6.25	6.25
6.5 X 58R Sauer, Jacketed Bullet, Modern	2.35	3.50	3.50
6.5 X 68 Schuler, Various Makers, Modern	1.50	2.30	2.30
6.5 X 68R, Various Makers, Modern	2.25	3.00	3.00
6.50mm Mannlicher, Various Makers, Modern	6.50	7.25	7.25
6.5mm Bergmann Grooved, Various Makers, Curio	7.50	9.05	9.05
6.5mm Bergmann, Various Makers, Curio	11.75	14.00	14.00
6.5mm Dutch, Various Makers, Military, Modern	0.20	.35	.35
6.5mm Jap, Various Makers, Modern	0.75	1.25	1.25
6.5mm Reg,. Mag., Various Makers, Modern	1.20	1.60	1.60
6.8mm Gasser, Various Makers, Modern	5.75	6.50	6.50
6.8mm Schulhof, Various Makers, Modern	3.50	4.35	4.35
6mm Flobert, 2 Piece Case, Antique	0.70	1.00	1.00
6mm Lee Navy, Various Makers, Military, Modern	3.25	3.75	3.75
6mm Loron, Patent Ignition, Antique	4.25	4.75	4.75
6mm Merveilleux, Various Makers, Modern	2.50	3.25	3.25
6mm Protector, Various Makers, Modern	1.85	2.40	2.40
6mm Rem., Various Makers, Modern	0.85	1.10	1.10
7 X 57R, Various Makers, Modern	1.25	1.65	1.65
7 X 61 Norma, Various Makers, Modern	1.30	1.70	1.70
7 X 64 Brenneke, Various Makers, Modern	1.40	1.90	1.90
7 X 64, Various Makers, Modern	1.50	2.00	2.00
7 X 65R, Vaious Makers, Modern	1.75	2.05	2.05
7 X 72R, Dummy Cartridge Curio	3.25	4.00	4.00
7 X 72R, Various Makers, Modern	3.50	.42	4.25
7 X 73 Vom Hofe, Soft Point Bullet, Modern	9.50	11.75	11.75

	V.G.	Exc	Prior Edition
7.25mm Adler, Various Makers, Modern	$85.00	$105.00	$105.00
7.35mm Carcano, Various Makers, Military, Modern	0.25	.35	.35
7.5 X 54 MAS, Various Makers, Military, Modern	0.25	.30	.30
7.5 X 55 Swiss, Military, Modern	1.00	1.20	1.20
7.5mm Swedish Nagent, Various Makers, Modern	1.05	1.30	1,30
7.5mm Swiss Nagent, Modern	1.20	1.55	1.55
7.62 X 39 Russian, Various Makers, Modern	1.10	1.35	1.35
7.62 X 39 Russian, Various Makers, Military, Modern	0.75	.90	.90
7.62 X 54R Russian, Various Makers, Modern	0.90	1.25	1.25
7.62mm Nagent, Various Makers, Military, Modern	2.25	2.85	2.85
7.62mm Takarev, Various Makers, Military, Modern	0.95	1.20	1.20
7.63 Mannlicher, Various Makers, Military, Modern	0.25	.30	.30
7.63 Mauser, Various makers, Modern	0.30	.45	.45
7.65 Argentine Navy Match, Military, Curio	37.50	42.00	42.00
7.65 Argentine, Various Makers, Modern	0.95	1.25	1.25
7.65 Borchardt, Various Makers, Modern	3.25	3.75	3.75
7.65 Pickert, Various Makers, Modern	4.50	5.25	5.25
7.65 Roth–Sauer, Various Makers, Curio	3.50	4.00	4.00
7.65 X 53 Mauser, Military, Modern	0.90	1.20	1.20
7.65mm Francotte, Various Makers, Modern	28.00	32.50	32.50
7.65mm Glisenti, Various Makers, Modern	95.00	110.00	110.00
7.66mm Mauser Revolver, Various Makers, Modern	7.50	10.00	10.00
7.7mm Bittner, Various Makers, Modern	35.00	39.00	39.00
7.7mm Jap, Various Makers, Modern	1.05	1.25	1.25
7.8mm Bergmann #5, Various Makers, Modern	7.50	8.40	8.40
7.92 x 33 Kurz, Various Makers, Military, Modern	1.25	1.70	1.70
7mm Baer, Various Makers, Modern	2.50	3.25	3.25
7mm Charola, Various Makers, Modern	6.50	7.25	7.25
7mm Flobert, Lead Bullet, Antique	0.70	.95	.95
7mm French Revolve, Various Makers, Modern	1.75	2.10	2.10
7mm H and H, Soft Point Bullet, Modern	2.50	3.25	3.25
7mm Mauser, Various Makers, Modern	0.85	1.20	1.20
7mm Mauser, Various Makers, Military, Modern	0.30	.50	.50
7mm Nambu, Various Makers, Curio	8.35	9.55	9.55
7mm Rem. Mag., Various Makers, Modern	0.95	1.30	1.30
7mm Rem. Mag., Various Makers, Flare Cartridge, Modern	2.20	2.70	2.70
7mm Rigby Mag., Soft Point Bullet, Modern	3.10	3.75	3.75
7mm Target Pistol, Various Makers, Modern	2.25	2.95	2.95
7mm Vom Hofe S.F., Various Makers, Modern	7.50	9.25	9.25
7mm Wby. Mag., Modern	1.25	1.80	1.80
8 Ga., Various Makers, Paper Case, Shotshell, Modern	3.25	4.50	4.50
8 X 48R Sauer, Various Makers, Curio	4.50	5.25	5.25
8 X 50R Lebel, Various Makers, Military, Modern	0.30	.50	.50
8 X 50R Mannlicher, Various Makers, Modern	2.25	2.95	2.95
8 x 51 Mauser, Various Makers, Curio	1.25	1.95	1.95
8 x 51R Mauser, Various Makers, Curio	6.50	7.40	7.40
8 x 56R Kropatschek, Various Makers, Military, Curio	0.55	.70	.70
8 x 56R Mannlicher, Various Makers, Military, Modern	4.95	6.75	6.75
8 x 57 Jrs, Various Makers, Modern	1.25	1.70	1.70
8 X 57S, Various Makers, Modern	0.95	1.15	1.15
8 X 58R Krag, Jacketed Bullet, Military, Modern	3.50	4.15	4.15
8 X 58R Saver, Various Makers, Curio	3.75	4.75	4.75
8 X 60 Mauser, Various Makers, Modern	2.75	3.25	3.25
8 X 60S, Various Makers, Modern	1.75	2.30	2.30
8 X 64 Brenneke, Various Makers, Modern	2.25	2.75	2.75

	V.G.	Exc	Prior Edition
8 X 68S, Various Makers, Modern	$1.65	$2.15	$2.15
8 X 75, Various Makers, Curio	4.50	5.00	5.00
8 X 75R, Various Makers, Curio	3.75	4.50	4.50
8.1 X 72R, Lead Bullet, Modern	3.85	4.40	4.40
8.15 X 46R, Lead Bullet, Modern	1.25	1.65	1.65
8.15 X 46R, Soft Point Bullet, Modern	2.50	2.75	2.75
8mm Bergmann #4, Various Makers, Modern	17.50	20.00	20.00
8mm Bergmann–Simplex, Various Makers, Modern	2.50	3.25	3.25
8mm Dormus, Various Makers, Modern	27.50	32.50	32.50
8mm Gaulois, Various Makers, Curio	1.25	1.75	1.75
8mm Kromar, Vaious Makers, Modern	44.75	49.50	49.50
8mm Lebel Revolver, Various Makers, Modern	1.65	2.10	2.10
8mm Lebel Revolver, Various Makers, Military, Modern	0.85	1.20	1.20
8mm Mauser, Various Makers, Modern	0.95	1.20	1.20
8mm Mitrailleuse, Various Makers, Modern	1.55	1.95	1.95
8mm Nambu, Various Makers, Military, Modern	3.75	4.40	4.40
8mm Pieper Revolver, Lead Bullet, Modern	1.75	2.10	2.10
8mm Protector, Various Makers, Modern	1.45	1.70	1.70
8mm Rast–Gasser, Various Makers, Modern	1.75	2.10	2.10
8mm Roth–Steyr, Various Makers, Modern	1.75	2.10	2.10
8mm Schulhof, Various Makers, Modern	6.50	7.20	7.20
8mm Steyr Revolver, Various Makers, Modern	58.00	65.00	65.00
9 X 5.6 M.S., Soft Point Bullet, Modern	1.35	1.65	1.65
9 X 63, Various Makers, Modern	3.50	4.25	4.25
9.3 X 53R Swiss, Lead Bullet, Curio	1.25	1.70	1.70
9.3 X 57, Various Makers, Modern	1.30	1.75	1.75
9.3 X 57R, Various Makers, Modern	4.50	5.25	5.25
9.3 X 62 Mauser, Various Makers, Modern	1.75	2.10	2.10
9.3 X 64 Brenneke, Various Makers, Modern	2.25	2.75	2.75
9.3 X 72R, Various Makers, Modern	2.25	2.75	2.75
9.3 X 74R, Various Makers, Modern	2.40	2.85	2.85
9.3 X 82R, Lead Bullet, Modern	2.75	3.50	3.50
9.3 X 82R, Soft Point Bullet, Modern	3.50	3.85	3.85
9.4mm Dutch Rev., Various Makers, Modern	3.75	4.25	4.25
9.5 X 57 M.S., Various Makers, Modern	2.25	2.75	2.75
9.5 X 60R Turkish, Lead Bullet, Modern	28.50	34.00	34.00
9mm Bayard Long, Various Makers, Military, Modern	0.55	.70	.70
9mm Bergmann, Jacketed Bullet, Military, Modern	0.30	.55	.55
9mm Borchardt, Various Makers, Modern	72.50	80.00	80.00
9mm Browning Long, Various Makers, Modern	1.25	1.95	1.95
9mm Campo Giro, Various Makers, Modern	17.00	20.00	20.00
9mm Danish Ronge, Lead Bullet, Modern	0.95	1.20	1.20
9mm Devisme, Modern	2.50	2.85	2.85
9mm Devisme, Patent Ignition, Antique	15.00	18.00	18.00
9mm Flobert, Lead Bullet, Antique	0.45	.60	.60
9mm Gasser–Kropatschek Rev., Various Makers, Modern	4.50	5.25	5.25
9mm Glisenti, Various Makers, Modern	1.25	1.95	1.95
9mm Luger, Various Makers, Modern	0.55	.70	.70
9mm Luger, Various Makers, Military, Modern	0.35	.50	.50
9mm Makarov, Jacketed Bullet, Military, Modern	15.00	19.50	19.50
9mm Mauser, Various Makers, Modern	1.25	1.65	1.65
9mm Nagent, Various Makers, Modern	2.25	2.85	2.85
9mm Salvo Squeze Bore, Various Makers, Curio	22.50	26.00	26.00
9mm Steyr, Various Makers, Military, Modern	1.05	1.30	1.30
9mm, Lead Bullet, Modern	5.25	5.95	5.95

GLOSSARY

ACP. Abbreviation for Automatic Colt Pistol, applied to ammunition designed originally or adopted by Colt.

ACTION. That part of a firearm made up of the breech and the parts designed to fire and cycle cartridges.

ADJUSTABLE CHOKE. Device attached to the muzzle of a shotgun enabling a change of choke by a rotational adjustment or by changing tubes.

ANTIQUE. A legal classification that in the United States is applied to weapons manufactured in or before 1898, and replicas that don't fire fixed ammunition.

ARSENAL. Military installation that stores and usually upgrades and modifies military weapons, and sometimes also applies to governmental weapon manufacturing facilities.

AUTOMATIC. Action type that ejects a spent cartridge and brings a fresh cartridge into firing position without manual intervention and has the capability of firing more than one shot with each pull of the trigger.

AUTOMATIC EJECTOR. Cases are ejected from the firearm when the action is opened without any manual intervention.

AUTOMATIC REVOLVER. Firearm action which resembles a conventional revolver except that on firing the cylinder is rotated and the hammer recocked by the recoil energy of the firing cartridge.

AUTOMATIC SAFETY. A block that prevents firing which is applied by the gun every time the action is cycled.

AYDT ACTION. A singleshot action utilizing a curved breechblock and a hinged section below the forward part of the chamber. The breechblock moves downward in an arc when pressure is applied to the finger lever.

BACK LOCK. Self-contained hammer, sear, and spring mounted on a single plate with the exposed hammer on the forward part of the plate, set into the side of a gun.

BACKSTRAP. Rearmost part of the grip portion of a handgun frame.

BARREL. Tube through which the bullet or shot passes on firing.

BARREL BAND. Metal band that secures the barrel to the forend.

BARREL LINER. Thin steel tube usually permanently inserted into the barrel to either change the caliber, restore the gun, or to make the gun more functional when the barrel is formed from softer material.

BARRELED ACTION. The assembled barrel and complete action.

BAYONET. A knife or spike designed to be attached to a firearm.

BAYONET LUG. Metal projection at the end of the barrel for attaching a bayonet.

BEAD SIGHT. Usually a round bead on the forward top of the barrel to aid in aiming (pointing) without the aid of a rear sight.

BEAVERTAIL FOREND. A wide, hand-filling forestock on long guns.

BENCHREST RIFLE. A heavy rifle designed for accurate shooting supported on a bench.

BIPOD. A two-legged support attached to the forend of a rifle.

BLOW-BACK ACTION. Automatic and semiautomatic action in which the breechblock is held forward only by spring pressure and cycles from the rearward gas thrust of the fired cartridge.

BLOW-FORWARD ACTION. Automatic and semi-automatic action which has a fixed breechblock and in which spring pressure secures a barrel that reciprocates and cycles the action from the pressure of expanding gasses when a cartridge is fired.

BLUE. An artificial oxidation process that yields some rust protection and leaves steel surfaces with a blue-black color.

BLUNDERBUSS. A smoothbore weapon with a very flared muzzle.

BOLT ACTION. A manual action cycled by moving a reciprocating breechbolt.

BORE. The inside of a barrel; the diameter of a barrel.

BOX LOCK. Generally a break top action which contains the hammer, sear, springs, and trigger in an integral unit directly behind the breech.

BREAK TOP. Action which exposes the breech by unlocking and the barrel(s) tipping downward, rotating on a point just forward of the breech.

BREECH. Rear end of the barrel; that part of the action that contacts the rear of the cartridge.

BREECHBOLT. The part of the action that secures the cartridge in the chamber.

BULL BARREL. A heavy barrel, usually with no taper.

BUTT. The rearmost portion of a stock.

BUTT PLATE. A plate fastened to the rear of the butt.

CALIBER. Bore diameter usually measured land to land in decimals of an inch or in millimeters.

CARBINE. A short, lightweight rifle.

CARTRIDGE. A self-contained unit of ammunition.

CASE HARDENED. A surface hardening; usually done so as to leave a broad spectrum of colors on the metal.

CENTER FIRE. Cartridge that contains a primer in the center of the base of the case.

CHAMBER. Portion of the gun in which the cartridge is placed.

CHECKERING. Geometric carving in the shape of parallel lines that cross to form diamonds, and used for both beauty and to provide a better handgrip.

CHEEKPIECE. A raised portion of the stock where the shooter's cheek touches the butt.

CHOKE. A muzzle constriction on shotguns which is used to control the pattern of shot.

CLIP. A detachable box that holds and feeds ammunition into the gun by spring pressure.

COMBINATION GUN. A multibarreled weapon that has a rifle barrel and a shotgun barrel.

CONDITION. The state of newness or wear of a gun. See the chapter on Factors That Determine Value for a complete description.

CONVERSION. The rebuilding of a military arm into a sporting arm; converting the arm to use a different cartridge; changing the general configuration of a gun.

CURIO. Curios and relics are a legal subclassification of modern arms. See the complete definition in the chapter titled Historic Relics.

CUT-OFF. A device that can stop the flow of ammunition from the magazine.

CYLINDER. The rotating container with cartridge chambers in a revolver.

DAMASCENE. An overlay of metal, usually gold leaf, sometimes combined with light engraving and used for decoration.

DAMASCENING. Also called Engine Turning or Jeweling, this is an ornamental polishing consisting of repeated and overlapping circles.

DAMASCUS. A metal formed usually by twisting strands of iron and steel and repeatedly hammer-welding them.

DERINGER. A small percussion pistol developed by Henry Deringer.

DERRINGER. A copy of the Deringer, now meaning any very small manually operated pistol.

DOUBLE ACTION. The ability to both cock and fire a gun by the single pull of a trigger.

DOUBLE-BARREL. A gun having two barrels.

DOUBLE TRIGGER. A gun having two triggers, each usually firing a different trigger.

DRILLING. A three-barreled gun usually consisting of two shotgun barrels and one rifle barrel.

DUMMY SIDEPLATES. Metal plates usually used for decorative purposes and on the sides of box lock actions to simulate sidelocks.

DUST COVER. Usually a sliding or turning piece of sheet metal used to keep foreign matter out of the action.

EJECTOR. Metal stud or rod that forcibly knocks cases out of the chamber.

ENGRAVING. Metal carving for decoration.

EXPRESS SIGHTS. The rear open rifle sight that has folding leafs for different elevations.

EXTRACTOR. The metal part that lifts the case out of the chamber.

FALLING BLOCK. Singleshot action type in which the breechblock moves vertically, propelled by a finger lever.

FIELD GRADE. Usually the standard grade of gun with little or no embellishment.

FINGER GROOVE. A groove cut into the forend of a long gun to aid in gripping.

FINISH. Materials used to coat the wood or the treatment of the metal parts.

FIXED SIGHTS. Nonadjustable sights.

FLASH HIDER. A device that reduces the amount of muzzle flash.

FLINTLOCK. Muzzle-loading action type that utilizes a hammer holding a flint that strikes a spring-loaded frizzen/pan cover to produce ignition.

FLOBERT. Singleshot action for low-power cartridges employing a hammer and rotating breechblock.

FLUTED BARREL. A barrel with longitudinal grooves cut into it for decoration and for strength.

FOLDING GUN. Usually a break top shotgun that pivots until folded in half.

FOREND. The forward part of a long gun's stock forward of the breech and under the barrel.

FRAME. The metal part of the gun that contains the action.

FREE PISTOL. A handgun designed for certain types of target shooting.

FREE RIFLE. A rifle designed for certain types of target shooting.

FRIZZEN. The part of the flintlock or snaphaunce lock that is hit by the flint to produce sparks.

FURNITURE. Metal parts except for the action and barrel.

GALLERY GUN. A gun designed to fire .22 Shorts for use in shooting galleries.

GAS OPERATED. Automatic or semiautomatic action type using vented gasses from the fired cartridge to cycle the action.

GAUGE. A unit of shotgun bore measurement derived from the number of lead balls of that diameter to a pound.

GERMAN SILVER. Also known as nickel silver, consisting of copper, nickel, and zinc, used for gun decorations.

GRIP. The portion of the gun to the rear of the trigger that is held by the firing hand.

GRIPFRAME. On handguns, that portion of the frame that is held by the hand.

GRIP SAFETY. A mechanical block that is released when the gun is held by hand in the firing position.

GRIPS. On handguns, the stocks.

GRIPSTRAP. The exposed metal portion of the gripframe to the front or rear of the grips.

HAMMER. The part of the mechanism that hits and imparts thrust to the firing pin.

HAMMER SHROUD. A device that covers the sides of a hammer while leaving the top exposed.

HAMMERLESS. A term applied to both striker-actuated guns and guns with hammers hidden within the action.

HANDGUARD. On rifles, the forestock above the barrel and forward of the breech.

HANDGUN. A firearm designed to be held and fired with one hand.

HEAT CARVING. Decorative patterns in wood formed either by heat or the combination of heat and pressure.

HOLSTER STOCK. A holster usually made of wood, or wood and leather, that attaches to a handgun for use as a shoulderstock.

HOODED SIGHT. A front sight with a protective cover over it.

INLAY. Decoration made by inlaying patterns on metal or wood.

IRON SIGHTS. Open sights, usually with a rear sight adjustable for elevation and a front sight adjustable for windage by drifting it.

KENTUCKY RIFLE. A style of gun developed around 1770 in Pennsylvania and produced first in flintlock and later in percussion varieties.

KNURLING. Checkering on metal.

LANYARD RING. A ring used to secure the gun by a lanyard to the shooter so it won't be lost if dropped.

LEVER ACTION. Usually a repeating type of action with a reciprocating breechblock powered by a finger lever.

LIP-FIRE. An early type of rimfire cartridge.

LOCK. The part of the action that carries the firing mechanism.

LONG GUN. A term used to describe rifles and shotguns.

MAGAZINE. In repeating arms, a storage device that feeds cartridges into the breech.

MAGNUM. Usually refers to arms or cartridges that are more powerful than normal, or of higher pressure.

MANNLICHER. In common usage does not refer to the man or his guns but to a type of rifle stock in which the forestock extends to the end of the muzzle.

MANUAL SAFETY. A block which prevents discharge that must be engaged and disengaged manually.

MARTINI ACTION. A singleshot action that utilizes a rear pivoting breechblock with a striker operated by finger lever.

MATCH RIFLE. A rifle specifically designed for target shooting.

MATCHLOCK. A muzzle loading arm that uses "Slow Match" to ignite a priming charge.

MATTE FINISH. A dull finish that does not reflect light.

MAUSER ACTION. A type of reciprocating turn-bolt action.

MIQUELET LOCK. A flintlock action that has an exposed sear on the outside of the lockplate.

MODERN. A legal term applied to cartridge firearms manufactured after 1898. Also see "Condition" in Factors That Determine Value.

MONTE CARLO. A raised portion on the top of the buttstock that elevates the cheek over the level of the buttplate.

MUSKET. A long military-style gun with a long forend.

MUZZLE. The most forward end of the barrel.

MUZZLE BRAKE. A device to capture powder gasses at the end of the muzzle to reduce recoil and barrel climb.

MUZZLE LOADER. A black powder arm that is loaded through the muzzle.

NIPPLE. The hollow projection that the percussion cap is fitted to.

OCTAGON BARREL. A barrel with the outside ground into an octagonal shape.

OFF-HAND RIFLE. A target rifle designed to be held, not rested.

OPEN SIGHTS. Iron sights.

OVER-UNDER. Barrel mounting on double-barreled guns with the barrels superposed over one another.

PALM REST. Hand support on the forend of an off-hand match rifle.

PAN. The place on flintlock and earlier arms in which the priming powder is placed.

PARKERIZED. A matte, phosphated finish that is highly rust resistant and usually placed on military arms.

PATCH BOX. A container inletted into the butt of a muzzle-loading long gun.

PEEP SIGHT. A circular rear sight with a small hole in the center to aim through.

PEPPERBOX. A revolving pistol with multiple rotating barrels.

PERCUSSION ARM. A muzzle loader that uses a percussion cap placed over a nipple to ignite the powder charge.

PERCUSSION CAP. A small disc that contains a fulminating chemical to ignite a powder charge.

PINFIRE. A type of cartridge with an exposed side pin that detonates the primer when struck.

PISTOL. A nonrevolving handgun.

PISTOL GRIP. The grip on a pistol.

PLAINS RIFLE. Percussion rifle design of the mid-1800s developed in St. Louis.

POCKET REVOLVER. A small revolver.

PORT. An opening into the action for ejected cases to pass through; an opening for gasses to flow through.

PROOF. The testing of a gun to see if it stands the stress of firing.

PUMP ACTION. Slide action.

RAMP SIGHT. A front sight mounted on a ramp.

RAMROD. A rod used to push the charge down the barrel of a muzzle loader.

RECEIVER. The part of the frame that houses the bolt or breechblock.

RECOIL. The rearward push of the gun when fired.

RECOIL OPERATED. An automatic or semiautomatic action that is cycled by the recoil from the fired cartridge.

RECOIL PAD. A rubber pad at the end of the butt to absorb recoil.

REPEATER. Capable of firing more than one round of ammunition; having a magazine.

REVOLVER. A firearm with a revolving cylinder containing multiple chambers.

RIFLE. A long gun with a rifled barrel.

RIFLING. Grooves cut into the bore to impart a spin to a bullet.

RIMFIRE. Cartridges containing the priming compound in the rim.

ROLLING BLOCK. Action with a pivoting breechblock that rotates ahead of the hammer, and which is locked by the hammer.

SADDLE RING. A ring on the side of rifles to attach a lanyard to.

SAFETY. A mechanical block that prevents the gun from firing.

SAWED-OFF SHOTGUN. A legal term describing a shotgun with barrels shorter than 16″; a Class III weapon.

SCHNABEL FOREND. A downcurving projection at the end of a forestock.

SCHUETZEN RIFLE. A type of fancy singleshot target rifle used for off-hand matches.

SCOPE. Telescopic sights.

SCOPE BASES. The mounts that attach scopes to guns.

SEAR. That part of the action that engages the striker, or hammer, and allows them to fall when released by the trigger.

SEMIAUTOMATIC. Action type that ejects the spent case and cycles a new round into the chamber with the energy of the fired round, and only fires one shot with each pull of the trigger.

SET TRIGGER. A trigger that can be "cocked" so that the final pull is very light.

SHOTGUN. A smoothbore gun designed to fire small shot pellets.

SIDE-BY-SIDE. A double-barreled gun with the barrels mounted next to each other.

SIDEHAMMER. A gun having the hammer mounted on the side rather than in the center.

SIDE LEVER. A gun with the action operating lever on the side of the action.

SIDELOCK. An action that is contained on the inside of a plate mounted directly behind the breech.

SIDEPLATE. A plate that covers the action, or that the action is mounted on.

SIGHT. A device that allows precise aim.

SIGHT COVER. Protective covering placed around a sight to prevent damage from jarring.

SIGHT RADIUS. The distance between the front and rear sight.

SILENCER. A device that reduces the noise of firing.

SINGLE ACTION. An action type that requires manual cocking for each shot.

SINGLESHOT. A gun capable of firing only one shot; having no magazine.

SKELETON BUTTPLATE. A buttplate with the center section removed to let the wood show through.

SKELETON STOCK. A buttstock, generally of wood or plastic, with the center removed to lighten the weight.

SLEEVE. Either a barrel liner or a tube placed on the outside of target barrel to stiffen it.

SLIDE. The reciprocating part of a semiautomatic pistol containing the breechblock.

SLIDE ACTION. A repeating action with a reciprocating forestock connected to the breechbolt.

SLING. A carrying strap on a long gun.

SLUG GUN. A shotgun designed to shoot lead slugs rather than pellets.

SNAPHAUNCE. An early form of flintlock with a manual frizzen.

SOLID FRAME. A nontakedown gun; a revolver that does not have a hinged frame.

SOLID RIB. A raised sighting plane on a barrel.

SPLINTER FOREND. A small wood forend under the barrel.

SPORTERIZED. A conversion of military arms to sporting type.

SPUR TRIGGER. A trigger with no guard, but protected by a sheath.

STIPPLING. An area roughened by center-punching for improved grip.

STOCK. The nonmetal portion of the gun which is actually held.

STRIKER. A spring-activated firing pin held in place by a sear which when released has enough energy to fire a primer.

SWIVELS. The metal loop that the sling is attached to.

TAKEDOWN. Capable of coming apart easily.

TARGET. Designed for target shooting.

TARGET STOCK. A stock designed for target shooting.

THUMB REST. A ledge on the side of target grips for the thumb to rest on.

THUMBHOLE STOCK. A stock with a hole for the thumb to wrap around in the pistol grip.

TIP-UP. A revolver with a frame hinged at the upper rear portion; a single shot pistol that has a break-top action.

TOE. The area on the bottom of the buttplate and the bottom rear of the stock.

TOGGLE ACTION. A semiautomatic action with a toggle joint that locks the breech-block.

TOP BREAK. Another term for tip-up, meaning that the barrel assembly swivels down on a hinge pin to expose the action.

TOP LEVER. An action actuated or opened with a lever on top.

TOP STRAP. The portion of a revolver above the cylinder.

TOUCH HOLE. The hole into the chamber area on muzzle loaders through which the priming flash ignites the charge.

TRIGGER. The exterior sear release.

TRIGGER, DOUBLE PULL. Two-stage trigger in which the slack must be taken up before the sear can be released.

TRIGGER GUARD. A band usually of metal that encircles the trigger preventing accidental discharge.

TRIGGER PULL. The amount of force required to release the sear.

TRIGGER SHOE. An accessory fitted to the trigger to provide a wide gripping surface.

TRIGGER STOP. A device to prevent trigger overtravel.

TRY-GUN. A long gun with a completely adjustable stock for measuring the proper fit of a custom gun.

TUBE FEED. A magazine with cartridges loaded behind one another instead of stacked.

TWIST BARREL. A gun with superposed barrels that are manually turned to bring a fresh charge into play; damascus steel barrel.

UNDER LEVER. An action actuated or opened by a lever underneath the action.

UNDERHAMMER. An action with the hammer on the bottom of the frame.

VARMINT RIFLE. A heavy barreled small caliber hunting rifle designed for accuracy.

VENT RIB. A raised sighting plane on barrels with air vents between it and the barrel.

VIERLING. A combination weapon with four barrels.

WATER TABLE. The flat part of the action forward of the standing breech on break open actions.

WHEEL-LOCK. A muzzle-loading action that uses a spring-operated spinning wheel to ignite sparks.

WITNESS MARK. A line placed on assembled parts to show proper line-up between the two.

WILDCAT. A nonstandard cartridge.

ZWILLING. A double-barrel long gun with one smoothbore barrel and one rifled barrel.

INDEX

ABOUT THE AUTHOR

Robert H. Balderson holds a BA in economics with a minor in history, and a Master of Business Administration. Both degrees are with honors, an award of academic distinction, and he also received the Wall Street Journal Student Achievement Award. He teaches classes at California State University encompassing economics, investments, marketing, and appraisal.

For twenty years Robert Balderson has been involved in the area of antiques and collectibles as a collector, dealer, appraiser, writer, and bookseller. His comprehension of varying prices, based on regional preferences, is derived from traveling nationally as a full-time dealer for ten years, and having resided and maintained business operations on both coasts. Numerous widely known collections have been appraised, purchased, and cataloged by Mr. Balderson. Frequently he is called upon to act in an advisory capacity and as agent for both buyers and sellers, to aid in searches for rare and hard-to-find pieces, and to oversee the settlement of estates.

Originally from Baltimore, Mr. Balderson served in the United States Air Force as a flight engineer and is a Vietnam veteran. He has successfully managed businesses ranging from small to multinational corporations.

Respected sources, including the Smithsonian Institution and *Maloney's Antiques and Collectibles Resource Directory*, list Mr. Balderson as an authority in several areas of the antiques and collectibles field. Robert H. Balderson may be contacted as a consultant or appraiser at P.O. Box 254886, Sacramento, CA 95865. For appraisals, he requests that as much information (description, photographs, etc.) as possible be included with the first correspondence.

LOAD UP WITH *THE OFFICIAL*® *GUIDE TO GUNMARKS*, THE *BEST* IDENTIFICATION GUIDE ON THE MARKET !

- Over 1,500 gunmarks illustrated and indexed for easy reference
- Proof and inspection marks from the late nineteenth century to date, indicating country of origin, date of manufacture, and the test performed to qualify the gun
- Includes Military Acceptance marks
- Alphabetical listing of tradenames and codes for guns without trademarks
- Special section on the *Waffenamt* numerical system used by the Germans during World War II

HOUSE OF COLLECTIBLES

SERVING COLLECTORS FOR MORE THAN THIRTY-FIVE YEARS